Educational Communications and Technology: Issues and Innovations

More information about this series at http://www.springer.com/series/11824

Peter J. Rich • Charles B. Hodges
Editors

Emerging Research, Practice, and Policy on Computational Thinking

Springer

Editors
Peter J. Rich
150K MCKB
Brigham Young University
Provo, UT, USA

Charles B. Hodges
Georgia Southern University
Statesboro, GA, USA

Educational Communications and Technology: Issues and Innovations
ISBN 978-3-319-52690-4 ISBN 978-3-319-52691-1 (eBook)
DOI 10.1007/978-3-319-52691-1

Library of Congress Control Number: 2017935613

Printed on acid-free paper

This Springer imprint is published by Springer Nature
The registered company is Springer International Publishing AG
The registered company address is: Gewerbestrasse 11, 6330 Cham, Switzerland

Preface

Emerging Research, Practice, and Policy on Computational Thinking

Computational thinking is quickly becoming an essential literacy for modern learners (Wright, Rich, & Leatham, 2012). The International Society for Technology in Education recently defined computational thinking as students "develop[ing] and employ[ing] strategies for understanding and solving problems in ways that leverage the power of technological methods to develop and test solutions" (http://www.iste.org/standards/standards/for-students-2016). The US Bureau of Labor Statistics projects that the need for computer programmers will be three times greater than the current number of computer science graduates. Perhaps more importantly, many contend that people in a diversity of fields will need to demonstrate the ability to think computationally and to manipulate technology to advance our abilities in different fields (Wing, 2009). Thus, computing is no longer a topic of study just for programmers, but for all pupils.

At the time of this writing, computing has become a compulsory topic in school in over a half dozen different countries, with over a dozen more committing to make it so by 2020 (Balanskat & Englehardt, 2015), including a handful that ask students to learn computing from the earliest levels. With this increasing attention to the need to teach computing at earlier ages comes the responsibility to study and understand effective teaching and learning practices in computing education, especially for non-computer science students. Up to this point, most attention has focused on changing policies and practices. This volume is an attempt to bring together emerging research around computational thinking, from primary education to high school and on through higher education.

We issued a call for chapters and received dozens of submissions, demonstrating that there are many who are studying the emerging practices of teaching computing to new groups. The chosen 25 chapters represent authors from nearly a dozen different countries. Each chapter was first reviewed editorially and then peer-reviewed by other authors. The resulting volume is divided into six different sections: (a) K-12 education, (b) higher education, (c) teacher development, (d) assessment practices in computational thinking, (e) computational thinking tools, and (f) computational thinking policies.

Chapters in *K-12 education* represent the ways in which computing has been implemented in a public school context during the formative years. D'Alba and Huett share the result of working with middle and high school students in an after-school context in which parents played a collaborative role in learning to code. Seneviratne presents the successes and challenges of working specifically with high school girls, a typically underrepresented group in computer science education. Jones-Harris and Chamblee describe the results of working with African-American students in a precalculus course. Delcker and Ifenthaler describe how one German state is implementing a new required computer science course in their upper secondary schools. Finally, Tatar, Harrison, Stewart, Frisina, and Musaeus explore the type of thinking that must first occur in order to prepare middle school students to begin to think computationally and its associated challenges.

Higher education chapters present a look at the ways in which computational thinking is being integrated with university courses to improve instruction across a diverse range of subjects. Musaeus, Tatar, and Rosen explore what computational thinking would look like in medical education and how this might improve students' analytical abilities. Rambally demonstrates how computational thinking can improve students' abilities to understand discrete mathematical structures. Quaye and Dasuki propose a method for teaching computational thinking in an introductory programming course in Nigeria using a virtual world context. Kaya and Cagiltay show how focusing on computational thinking in an introductory computing course for non-CS majors can successfully lead to increased understanding of core concepts. Liu, Perera, and Klein report on efforts to teach computational thinking while promoting collaboration, problem-solving, and the sharing of educational resources.

The *teacher development* section focuses on the preparation of teachers who formerly had received no training in computing and how they might successfully teach it to their pupils. The chapters by Hester-Croff and Buss and Gamboa both report on efforts to train teachers to foster and recognize computational thinking patterns in middle and high school students. Both Yadav, Gretter, Good, and Mclean and Sadik, Ottenbreit-Leftwich, and Nadiruzzaman focus on how to prepare preservice teachers during their formative teacher education to teach computational thinking. Toikkanen and Leinonen report on the design and executing of a MOOC with over 1000 teachers as they prepare for the mandatory integration of computing in primary education in Finland.

The section on *assessment practices in computational thinking* attempts to better understand what and how to measure as students engage with computational thinking practices. Mueller, Becket, Hennessey, and Shodiev analyzed Canada core competencies for alignment with computational thinking practices. In so doing, they found several areas where computational thinking might already be assessed in related topics and discuss areas for improvement and integration. Grover proposes a system of assessments that go beyond measuring just cognitive outcomes. She then demonstrates how this is being applied in a middle school course on foundations of computational thinking.

The *tools* section shares resources for teaching, assessing, and implementing computational thinking. Repenning, Basawapatna, and Escherle present a framework for different tools that scaffold learners through three important stages of computational thinking: problem formation, solution expression, and execution/evaluation. Lawanto, Close, Ames, and Brasiel demonstrate how the Dr. Scratch tool can be used to measure students' computational thinking skills. Similarly, Brasiel et al. outline the development, use, and research of the FUN! Tool, a Python-based framework for measuring minute-by-minute interactions in the Scratch environment.

Policy chapters demonstrate the changing landscape and efforts of different governments and groups as they attempt to implement computational thinking. Pan describes the restructuring of CS0, a required introductory computing course for all non-CS majors in the People's Republic of China, to include computational thinking principles and practices. Similarly, in response to the Korean government's designation to include software education as part of its core curriculum by 2018, Lee presents an exposition of representative projects created from a group of 72 pilot schools nationwide that showcase how computational thinking might be integrated into the curriculum. Ruberg and Owens describe a district-wide approach to implementing computing from kindergarten all the way through grade 12, including both in-school and after-school efforts to integrate computing across the curriculum. Finally, Kafai and Burke, two of the early promoters of computational thinking, end the book with a reconceptualization of computational thinking to the broader notion of computational participation, an idea that promotes the integration of computing into communities of practice that extend beyond simply problem-solving and creating to also including individual and group expression and everyday solutions to life.

Together, these chapters paint a picture of the emerging research and practice surrounding efforts to include the teaching and learning computational thinking in an increasingly computational world. While they are by no means a comprehensive report of all that is occurring, it is our hope that they are representative of the challenges and successes that students, teachers, and policy makers face as computing becomes an essential and required subject of study.

Provo, UT, USA — Peter J. Rich
Statesboro, GA, USA — Charles B. Hodges

References

Balanskat, A., & Englehardt, K. (2015). *Computing our future. Computing programming and coding. Priorities, school curricula and initiatives across europe*. European Schoolnet.

Wing, J. M. (2009). Computational thinking. *Journal of Computing Sciences in Colleges*, *24*(6), 6–7.

Wright, G. A., Rich, P., & Leatham, K. R. (2012). How programming fits with technology education curriculum. *Technology and Engineering Teacher*, *71*(7), 3.

Contents

About the Editors and Contributors

About the Editors

Peter J. Rich is an associate professor of instructional psychology and technology at Brigham Young University in Provo, Utah, USA. His research focuses primarily on the theory of convergent cognition, which proposes that there is a synergistic effect of learning two complementary subjects. For example, learning a second language affects one's first language and vice versa. Likewise, learning computer programming affects one's mathematical thinking. Peter trains local schools and teachers to integrate computing and engineering into elementary education. He has been responsible for establishing several coding, robotics, and engineering clubs for children.

Charles B. Hodges is an associate professor of instructional technology at Georgia Southern University in Statesboro, Georgia, USA. Charles earned degrees in mathematics (B.S., Fairmont State University; M.S., West Virginia University) before earning a Ph.D. from the Learning Sciences and Technologies program in the School of Education at Virginia Tech. He worked for several years as a university mathematics instructor at Concord University and Virginia Tech. Charles conducts research usually involving self-efficacy of learners or teachers in technology-rich or online learning environments. He has published his research in peer-reviewed journals such as *The International Review of Research in Open and Distributed Learning*, *Journal of Computers in Mathematics and Science Teaching*, *The Internet and Higher Education*, *Instructional Science*, and *TechTrends*. He is the editor in chief of the journal *TechTrends*.

About the Contributors

Clarence Ames is a master's student in the Instructional Technology and Learning Sciences program at Utah State University. He has a bachelor's degree in public relations from Central Washington University. He is passionate about helping people become independent and self-sufficient through education. His life goal is to empower students and teachers and create a system of education in which the only limitations on breadth or depth of learning are one's own desire, passion, motivation, and assiduousness. He is currently completing his master's thesis on teachers' perceptions of factors influencing technology integration in K-12 schools.

Ashok R. Basawapatna is an assistant professor in the Mathematics, Computer and Information Science Department at the State University of New York College at Old Westbury (SUNY Old Westbury) and has been part of the Scalable Game Design project at the University of Colorado Boulder since 2009. His research focuses on enabling computational thinking in the classroom through the development of innovative tools, mechanisms allowing formative and summative assessment of CT skills, and coding workshops aimed at motivating students through creative projects. Prior to arriving at SUNY Old Westbury, Dr. Basawapatna worked at the Indian Institute of Technology (IIT) Bombay as a visiting assistant professor in the Educational Technology program and worked as a researcher at the University of Applied Sciences and Arts Northwestern Switzerland (FHNW).

Danielle Beckett is a final-stage Ph.D. candidate in the Joint Ph.D. in Educational Studies program at Brock University. Her dissertation study was conducted to investigate exemplary teachers' understandings and implementation of classroom assessment in a twenty-first-century context. Her current research has expanded into the assessment of problem-solving and computational thinking skills across disciplines, which is supported by an SSHRC Insight Development Grant. Danielle is a certified elementary teacher and has extensive teaching experience at the postsecondary level. Courses taught include classroom assessment and evaluation, educational psychology, academic writing, and new literacies in the twenty-first century. She also spent 2 years of her doctoral program as the president of the Canadian Committee for Graduate Students in Education. In addition, Danielle founded a company whose flagship product is an interactive electronic children's book series that evaluates children's reading performance using voice recognition. She received an Applied Research and Commercialization Grant to develop the prototype software. Danielle actively presents her research at local and international conferences and has published in academic and professional venues (e.g., *Canadian Journal of Education* and *Education Canada*).

Sarah Brasiel is an education research scientist at the Institute of Education Sciences (IES). Dr. Brasiel received a Ph.D. in mathematics education from the University of Texas at Austin. Dr. Sarah Brasiel has over 20 years of experience in the education sector. Dr. Brasiel's prior experience includes 15 years of teaching grades 5–12 reading, mathematics, and science (regular and special education). Her research interests have focused on improving teacher pedagogical content knowledge and student achievement in mathematics and science. More recently she has been involved in research projects measuring outcomes from interdisciplinary STEM (science, technology, engineering, and math) activities, including activities to engage students in grades 4 to 12 in engineering, design, and computer programming.

Quinn Burke is an assistant professor at the College of Charleston (SC) Department of Teacher Education. Focusing on integrating computer science into middle and high school math and ELA classrooms, Quinn examines the particular affordances of different activities (e.g., digital storytelling, video game making) and different introductory programming languages (e.g., Blockly, Scratch, Python) in successfully integrating computer science into core curriculum classrooms. Quinn sits on the advisory board of the statewide Exploring Computing Education Pathways program as well as the advisory board of Charleston's Chamber of Commerce Computer Science Outreach program. He has authored several articles involving integrating computer science at the middle and high school levels. His new book (with Yasmin B. Kafai) entitled *Connected Gaming: What Making Video Games Can Teach Us About Learning and Literacy* will be published by MIT Press in the fall of 2016.

Alan Buss is an associate professor in elementary and early childhood education at the University of Wyoming. He conducts research on meaningful integration of educational technologies to enhance students' understanding of science and mathematics. The technologies include geographic information systems (GIS), Global Positioning System (GPS), dynamic geometry software, Vernier Probeware, LEGO robotics, computer gaming, and 3D visualization in immersive virtual reality environments. Dr. Buss recently completed curricular materials and a 3D simulation for use in large-scale visualization facilities to better help middle school students and preservice elementary school teachers understand the concept of density. Initial results from this work are scheduled to be published in *TechTrends*, in "A Framework for Aligning Instructional Design Strategies with Affordances of CAVE Immersive Virtual Reality Systems" (Ritz & Buss).

Kursat Cagiltay is professor of the Department of Computer Education and Instructional Technology at Middle East Technical University (METU), Ankara, Turkey. He holds a double Ph.D. in cognitive science and instructional systems technology from Indiana University, Bloomington, USA. He is the founder of three research groups at METU: Simulations and Games in Education (SIMGE, simge.metu.edu.tr), HCI research group (hci.metu.edu.tr), and Educational Neuroscience/Neurotechnology (http://ed-neuro.ceit.metu.edu.tr/en/). His research focuses on human-computer interaction, instructional technology, social and cognitive issues of electronic games, sociocultural aspects of technology, technology-enhanced learning, human performance technologies, and educational neuroscience/neurotechnology. He is the director of METU's Audio/Visual Research Center.

Gregory Chamblee is a professor in the Department of Teaching in the College of Education at Georgia Southern University. Dr. Chamblee teaches undergraduate and graduate middle grades and secondary mathematics education courses and a graduate course on technology in the K-12 mathematics classroom. Dr. Chamblee is a former high school mathematics and computer science teacher. Dr. Chamblee has published in *Computers and Schools*, *Journal of Technology and Teacher Education*,

Journal of Computer in Mathematics and Science Teaching, and Society for Information Technology and Teacher Education (SITE) conference proceedings. Dr. Chamblee has made many presentations to various audiences on K-12 mathematics education topics and the integration of technology into K-12 mathematics classrooms. Dr. Chamblee has received numerous federal grants to work with K-12 mathematics teachers and is a recipient of the Georgia Council of Teachers of Mathematics John Neff Award.

Kevin Close is a student in the Instructional Technology and Learning Sciences M.Ed. program at Utah State University (USU). He earned a B.A. in religion from Carleton College in Minnesota. Before attending USU, Kevin spent 5 years teaching around the world. Specifically, Kevin taught English and SAT mathematics at Wuhan Foreign Languages School in Wuhan, China; developmental mathematics at Salt Lake Community College in Taylorsville, Utah; and Chinese language at Kearns-St. Ann Catholic Elementary School in Salt Lake City, Utah. Kevin enjoys traveling the world and speaks Mandarin Chinese and a little Mongolian. When not traveling, he enjoys anything in the outdoors, specifically playing ultimate frisbee and backpacking. Kevin's research interests include educator dashboards, alternative assessment methods, and learning analytics.

Carla Hester-Croff worked in the information technology industry for over 18 years in the areas of computer software, computer hardware installation, computer user support, computer user training, soft skill training, training documentation, network programs, web development, and programming for such companies as Unisys; US Sprint; the Department of State, Office of Foreign Missions; and the Department of Justice US Attorney's Office. For the past 14 years, she has taught college courses in computer science and web development at Western Wyoming Community College. She has received various awards including Outstanding Faculty and the Master Distance Educator of the Year. Currently, she is working on an NSF ITEST Grant entitled Visualization Basics: uGame-iCompute with the University of Wyoming, on the Scalable Game Design (SGD) initiative with the University of Colorado Boulder, and with Google on implementing AP principles in computer science in high schools.

Adriana D'Alba is an assistant professor at the University of West Georgia in the College of Education where she teaches graduate courses in the Department of Educational Technology and Foundations. She holds a Ph.D. in educational computing and an M.Phil. in 2D/3D motion graphics. Her research interests include multimedia applications and technology integration in the classroom; design, development, and assessment of three-dimensional online environments for learning; game-based learning; and integration of emerging technologies in STEM curriculum. In 2015, Adriana received the Outstanding Research Award from the University of West Georgia's College of Education for her work in virtual environments for learning. She is a member of the American Educational Research Association (AERA), the Society for Information Technology and Teacher Education, the International Society of Teacher Education, and the Association for Educational Communications and Technology (AECT).

Salihu Ibrahim Dasuki teaches at the School of Information Technology and Computing at the American University of Nigeria (AUN), Yola. He obtained a bachelor of science degree in information technology from Eastern Mediterranean University, North Cyprus; a master of science degree in information systems management from Brunel University, UK; and the doctor of philosophy degree in information systems from Brunel University. His research interests include the social, political, and economic implication of implementing information systems in developing countries.

Jan Delcker is a research assistant of the chair of learning, design, and technology at the University of Mannheim, Germany. His research interest focuses on educators' professionalization in digital media, educational technology, and game-based learning.

Nora A. Escherle earned a Ph.D. in English literature in 2013. She joined the team of Prof. Alexander Repenning, chair of computer science education at the University of Applied Sciences and Arts Northwestern Switzerland, in November 2014. Since then, she has familiarized herself with the field of computer science education and has contributed in conducting research and coauthored several papers and other publications.

Chris Frisina received his M.S. in computer science in 2016 from Virginia Tech.

Ruben Gamboa is a professor in the Department of Computer Science at the University of Wyoming. His research interests are in the formalization of mathematics via programs that can produce formal proofs. He is passionate about fostering computational thinking throughout K-16 education, and he has been a member of numerous outreach efforts that introduce computing via games, robots, science, and art.

Jon Good is a doctoral candidate in the Educational Psychology and Educational Technology program at Michigan State University. His research interests include computational thinking, computer science education, teacher education, and creativity. He previously worked in pre-K through grade 12 schools in the areas of faculty development, technology management, curriculum development, and teaching multiple courses related to computing. He has published in *Education and Information Technologies* and *TechTrends*. His awards include the College of Education Dean's Scholar Fellowship, the Frank B. Martin CUMREC Fellowship (2013–2014), and the German Federal Ministry of Education and Research/ Humboldt University of Berlin.

Sarah Gretter is a doctoral candidate in educational psychology and educational technology at Michigan State University. Her research focuses on digital literacies. Specifically, she is interested in the competencies that educators should acquire to successfully help students understand and create digital media. Previous work includes an Ed.M. in mind, brain, and education from Harvard University, where she researched the cognitive implications of digital literacies for teaching and learning. Her dissertation project focuses on integrating digital literacies in teacher education programs, as well as understanding the factors that play a role in the integration of these skills in K-12 education.

Shuchi Grover is a senior research scientist at SRI International's Center for Technology in Learning. Her work in computer science (CS) education since 2001 has spanned several informal and formal settings. Over the last decade, her research has been a quest to help children develop computational thinking skills. Her current research centers on studying computational thinking (CT) and CS education mainly in K-12 settings. Her doctoral work at Stanford in K-12 CS education resulted in the highly cited paper coauthored with her advisor Dr. Roy Pea – "Computational Thinking in K-12: A Review of the State of the Field." Her dissertation research resulted in *Foundations for Advancing Computational Thinking*, a first-of-its-kind middle school introductory CS curriculum designed for blended in-class learning. She has received funding from the National Science Foundation (STEM+Computing and Cyberlearning programs) to design and study middle school CS curricula and examine programming process using computational learning analytics techniques for evidence of CT practices in log data captured from block-based programming environments. Other ongoing research involves using novel multimodal analytics techniques to examine collaborative problem-solving in pair programming. She is a member of the CSTA Task Force on Computational Thinking and an advisor to the K-12 CS Education Framework effort. She has master's degrees in computer science (CWRU) and in technology, innovation, and education (Harvard University) and a Ph.D. in learning sciences and technology design (Stanford University).

Steve Harrison is an associate professor in the Department of Computer Science and the School of Visual Arts at Virginia Tech. He directs the Human-Centered Design program.

Eden Hennessey is a Ph.D. candidate in social psychology at Wilfrid Laurier University. Eden's research interests include (1) perceptions of excellence and diversity in the context of hiring, (2) responses to perceived gender discrimination among women from diverse cultural backgrounds, (3) methods to increase and retain women in STEM (i.e., science, technology, engineering, and math) postsecondary programs and careers, and (4) assessing computational thinking in education. While these lines of research are distinct, they are connected by an overarching theme of diversity promotion and discrimination reduction. Eden was the 2014/2015 Laurier Graduate Researcher of the Year and creator of the photo-research exhibition #DistractinglySexist: Confronting Sexism in Canada's Tech Triangle. Her work has been funded by the Social Sciences and Humanities Research Council of Canada (SSHRC), the Ontario Graduate Scholarship (OGS), and the Society for the Psychological Study of Social Issues (SPSSI), and she is the student research coordinator of the Laurier Centre for Women in Science (WinS).

Kim C. Huett is an assistant professor in the Department of Educational Technology and Foundations at the University of West Georgia, where she has taught for 8 years. Prior to teaching in higher education, Kim taught English and Spanish at the secondary level for 6 years in Texas and Georgia public schools. Currently, she is actively involved in bringing computer science education to young people through uCode@UWG and through K-12 school-based outreach programs. Her research interests include the design of K-12 student-centered learning environments and K-12 computer science education. In 2015, Kim published a qualitative study exploring the use of multimedia case studies in introductory engineering courses in the *Journal of STEM Education: Innovations and Research.* Kim has received several teaching awards, including the 2014 University System of Georgia Regents' Online Teaching Excellence Award and Outstanding Distance Learning Faculty and Distinguished Educator awards from the Instructional Technology Council (2012).

Dirk Ifenthaler is chair and professor for learning, design, and technology at the University of Mannheim, Germany; adjunct professor at Deakin University, Australia; and affiliate research scholar at the University of Oklahoma, USA. His previous roles include professor and director, Centre for Research in Digital Learning at Deakin University, Australia; manager of applied research and learning analytics at Open Universities, Australia; and professor for applied teaching and learning research at the University of Potsdam, Germany. He was a 2012 Fulbright Scholar-in-Residence at the Jeannine Rainbolt College of Education at the University of Oklahoma, USA. Dirk Ifenthaler's research focuses on the intersection of cognitive psychology, educational technology, learning science, data analytics, and computer science. His research outcomes include numerous coauthored books, book series, book chapters, journal articles, and international conference papers, as well as successful grant funding in Australia, Germany, and the USA – see Dirk's website for a full list of scholarly outcomes at www.ifenthaler.info. He is editor in chief of the Springer journal *Technology, Knowledge and Learning* (www.springer.com/10758).

Phil Janisiewicz is a data scientist consultant who works with Dr. Sarah Brasiel in the Department of Instructional Technology and Learning Sciences at Utah State University conducting research in data management and data modeling. Phil supports research projects by investigating and implementing new models and techniques for predicting student learning and behavior and inferring the relevance and impact of recommendations and personalized content, using a rich corpus of student data. This is a strategic role where he is responsible for identifying new analysis methods and pursuing the execution of projects with a high level of autonomy. For more than 5 years, Phil has been involved in designing and developing databases, web-based applications, analysis methods, and data visualization techniques. He has also worked to develop and implement data management plans that ensure the confidentiality and protection of data and participant information. The research projects he has participated include projects funded by the US Department of Education, the National Science Foundation, and the Bill and Melinda Gates Foundation. He has designed and implemented security and quality assurance measures to meet the highest regulations for data management.

Soojeong Jeong is a Ph.D. student in the Department of Instructional Technology and Learning Sciences at Utah State University. She earned an M.A. in education, with an emphasis in educational technology, from Korea University in Seoul, South Korea. She also holds a B.A. in education and a B.S. in mathematics education, both of which she obtained at the same university. While studying for her master's degree, Soo participated in many projects related to the use of technology to improve human learning. She also studied how using laptop computers influences college students during class for her master's thesis. In addition, she worked as a math instructor and a private tutor for middle and high school students for about 10 years. Currently, Soo is studying how new technologies promote math achievement for elementary and middle school students. Her main research interests include cognitive load theory, mathematics education, metacognition, and meta-analysis.

Cristal Jones-Harris is a 2015–2016 recipient of the Albert Einstein Distinguished Educator Fellowship sponsored by the US Department of Energy and Oak Ridge Institute of Science and Education (ORISE). Her fellowship is located at the National Aeronautics and Space Administration (NASA) at Goddard Space Flight Center in Greenbelt, MD, and NASA Headquarters in Washington, DC. Dr. Jones-Harris is a Georgia Southern University 2010 alumna (Ed.D., curriculum studies) from the College of Education. She has taught computer science, robotics, and information technology to middle and high school students and teachers to promote interdisciplinary approaches to STEM teaching and learning. Dr. Jones-Harris has conducted numerous presentations, facilitated teacher workshops, and worked with state and federal agencies to broaden participation in STEM education.

Kadir Yucel Kaya is a research assistant and Ph.D. candidate at the Department of Computer Education and Instructional Technology, at the Middle East Technical University (METU), Ankara, Turkey. He received his B.S. from the same department in Dokuz Eylul University in 2009. His research interests include computer programming education, visual programming, computational thinking, and game-based learning. His dissertation is about developing a visual programming course for novice programmers. In addition to research, he works also as a teaching assistant for several courses including multimedia design and development, instructional design operating systems, and visual programming for Android OS. He currently lives in Ankara, Turkey.

Yasmin B. Kafai is professor of learning sciences at the University of Pennsylvania. She is a researcher and developer of tools, communities, and materials to promote computational participation, crafting, and creativity across K-16. Her recent books include *Connected Code: Why Children Need to Learn Programming* and the forthcoming *Connected Gaming: What Making Video Games Can Teach Us About Learning and Literacy* (both with Quinn Burke), *Connected Play: Tweens in a Virtual Worlds* (with Deborah Fields), and editions such as *Textile Messages: Dispatches from the World of E-Textiles and Education* and *Beyond Barbie and Mortal Kombat: New Perspectives on Gender and Gaming*. Kafai earned a doctorate in education from Harvard University while working with Seymour Papert at the MIT Media Lab. She is an elected fellow of the American Educational Research Association and past president of the International Society for the Learning Sciences.

Jerry W. Klein has broad experience in learning and instruction in both the public and private sectors including 20 years at Bell Laboratories creating technical training programs for software design engineers. Dr. Klein's experience includes teaching math in an inner-city middle school, implementing individualized math and reading programs for the K-8 Hopi Indian schools, and directing a project to deliver graduate-level teacher education programs in rural areas of West Virginia. As a freelance instructional designer, Jerry directed the development of an interactive multimedia instructional program for the Air Force on data fusion and developed a manufacturing technician certification program for the *Virginia Council on Advanced Technology Skills*. Recent projects include working with the faculty at Embry-Riddle Aeronautical University to develop courses in mathematical modeling and developing standardized courses for Embry-Riddle Aeronautical University's high school dual enrollment program. Jerry also is an adjunct professor in the Department of Instructional Design, Development and Evaluation at Syracuse University. He received a Ph.D. in instructional systems design and an M.S. in educational research and testing from Florida State University and a B.A. in mathematics, physics, and secondary education from Adams State University of Colorado.

Kevin Lawanto is a master's student in the Department of Instructional Technology and Learning Sciences (ITLS) at Utah State University. He holds a bachelor of science degree in psychology. Kevin's research interest includes neuroscience, cognition and metacognition, and game-based learning. During his studies, he has coauthored several research papers and posters for journals and conferences across the USA. During his study, he also had the experience working as a research technician in the brain and behavior laboratory at the Utah Science Technology and Research (USTAR) facility where he was involved in conducting rodents' behavior analysis, perfusion, brain sectioning, and staining. Currently, he is working as a research assistant in the Active Learning Lab in the Department of ITLS. His master's thesis focuses on understanding the development of computational thinking as students learn to program in Scratch, an application developed by MIT and used by students all over the world.

Miran Lee is a principal research program manager of the Microsoft Research Outreach Group at Microsoft Research where she is responsible for academic collaboration in Korea and Asia-Pacific regions. Lee joined Microsoft Research Asia in 2005 as university relations manager to build long-term and mutually beneficial relations with academia. She is based in Korea, where she engages with leading research universities, research institutes, and relevant government agencies. She establishes strategies and directions, identifies business opportunities, designs various programs and projects, and manages the budget. She works with students, researchers, faculty members, and university administrators to build strong partnerships and works closely with the research groups at Microsoft Research, focusing on research collaboration, curriculum development, talent fostering, and academic exchanges. She has successfully ran a number of global and regional programs such as Gaming & Graphics, Web-Scale NLP, Machine Translation, eHealth, SORA (Software Radio), Kinect, and Microsoft Azure for Research.

Teemu Leinonen is an associate professor of new media design and learning at Aalto University School of Arts, Design and Architecture in Helsinki, Finland. Teemu holds over two decades of experience in the field of research and development of web-based learning. Teemu conducts research, designs, and publishes in different forums. He has published two books, over ten peer-reviewed or invited book chapters, over 20 peer-reviewed scientific articles in journals and conferences, and more than 15 software prototypes. Furthermore, Teemu has served as a member of the program committee, reviewer, or jury member in over 20 international conferences and festivals. Teemu is a well-known advocate of open-source/free software in education, free knowledge, and open education.

Hong P. Liu was awarded a Ph.D. in mathematics and M.S. in computer science at the University of Arkansas Fayetteville in 2000. He currently serves as a professor in mathematics and computing at Embry-Riddle Aeronautical University, Daytona Beach, Florida. He taught a wide variety of mathematics courses ranging from lower-division undergraduate mathematics to graduate courses, including statistics, computer sciences, and software engineering courses. He published 30 articles and book chapters in partial differential equations, software engineering, data mining, and computational science education. He also serves as the advisor of the SIAM student chapter at Embry-Riddle and mentors a team of student researchers in SIAM chapter to build a fleet of autonomous underwater vehicle called Eco-Dolphins. Hong Liu served as the PI and co-PI of 12 funded projects in software development, robotics, and undergraduate STEM education.

Taylor Martin is principal learning scientist at O'Reilly Media. Her research has involved examining how people learn from doing or active participation, both physical and social. She has examined how mobile and social learning environments provided online and in person influence content learning in mathematics, engineering, and computational thinking using learning analytics methods to understand learning processes at a fine-grained level.

Tamika McLean is a doctoral student in the Educational Psychology and Educational Technology program at Michigan State University. She did her undergraduate studies at the University of Notre Dame where she received a B.S. in computer engineering and B.A. in psychology. Her research interest is STEM education focusing on students' thinking and learning. Her research is examining how students' understanding and conceptualization of STEM concepts are represented or developed in both formal and informal learning environments. Some of her projects involved working in an after-school program called 2020 Girls to increase the access of technology education to girls in grades 4–8 through the Information Technology Empowerment Center (ITEC) in Lansing, Michigan.

Julie Mueller is an associate professor with the Faculty of Education at Laurier teaching in the areas of educational psychology and physical education. She is the current president of the Canadian Association for Teacher Education. Dr. Mueller's research in the area of integration of technology for teaching and learning has been supported by both internal and external grants including a 3-year SSHRC Standard

Research Grant. She is currently working under an SSHRC Insight Development Grant to address emerging questions related to computational thinking and assessment across disciplines at all levels of education from kindergarten to postsecondary. Dr. Mueller has mobilized knowledge from her research in a variety of ways stretching from traditional book chapters and empirical journals in both education and psychology (e.g., *Computers and Education*, *Journal of Educational Psychology*), through national and international conference presentations and invited talks, to practitioner-directed publications (e.g., Put Their Learning in Their Hands: A Guide to iPad Implementation in the Classroom) and multiple media outlets including CBC Radio, TVOntario, Twitter, and podcasts.

Peter Musaeus is an associate professor, educational scientist, and faculty developer, who researches transformational learning and medical curriculum. Since 2011, Peter has been a tenure-track associate professor in health sciences education at Aarhus University. He has been a visiting professor/scholar at the University of Central Florida, UC-Berkeley, University of Sussex, and Virginia Tech.

Hamid Nadiruzzaman is a doctoral student in instructional systems technology at Indiana University. He is also serving as an associate instructor in the School of Education. Prior to this, he had taught middle and high school math in a public school in Kansas. His research interests are problem-based learning, design problem-solving, teacher education, technology integration in K-12, and computer-supported collaborative learning. He has been a member of AECT and AERA and actively presents at their conferences.

Anne-Ottenbreit Leftwich is an associate professor of instructional systems technology at Indiana University, Bloomington. Dr. Ottenbreit-Leftwich's expertise lies in the areas of the design of digital curriculum resources, the use of technology to support preservice teacher training, and the development/implementation of professional development for teachers and teacher educators. Dr. Ottenbreit-Leftwich has experience working on large-scale funded projects, including projects supported by the US Department of Education. Her current research focuses on teachers' value beliefs related to technology and how those beliefs influence teachers' technology uses and integration. She is currently working on a project associated with K-12 teachers' uses of technology, particularly iPads and computer science education.

Aileen Owens is the director of technology and innovation for South Fayette Township School District. Aileen has an extensive 15-year history and diverse experiences building and leading innovative teaching and learning opportunities in K-12 and higher education. Since joining the South Fayette team in 2010, Aileen has focused on building a vertically aligned computational thinking initiative K-12. Challenged and supported by The Grable Foundation to make innovation happen in Western Pennsylvania, Aileen has been developing and leading outreach initiatives in computational thinking to schools in the region through the STEAM Innovation Summer Institute. She is the recipient of the Consortium for School Networking (CoSN) Frank Withrow Outstanding CTO Award 2016; Digital Innovation in Learning, Administrator Trailblazer Award 2014; the Digital Innovation in Learning,

Administrators Winners Choice Award 2014; and PAECT Chief Technology Officer of the Year 2015. She shares and collaborates with educators nationally, recently presenting at ISTE 2015, World Maker Faire NYC 2015, Scratch@MIT 2014, and the Digital Media and Learning Conference 2014. Aileen is actively involved in the Pittsburgh Remake Learning Network. For more information, please see http://www.aileenowens.net and http://www.steaminnovation.net/.

Tien-Yo (Tim) Pan is university relations director of Microsoft Research Asia, responsible for the lab's academic collaboration in the Asia-Pacific region. Tim Pan leads a regional team with members based in China, Japan, and Korea engaging universities, research institutes, and certain relevant government agencies. He establishes strategies and directions, identifies business opportunities, and designs various programs and projects that strengthen partnership between Microsoft Research and academia. Tim Pan earned his Ph.D. in electrical engineering from Washington University in St. Louis. He had 20 years of experience in the computer industry and cofounded two technology companies. Tim has great passion for talent fostering. He served as a board member of St. John's University (Taiwan) for 10 years, offered college-level courses, and wrote a textbook in information security.

Sirani M. Perera has received a B.Sc. special degree in mathematics with first-class honors from the University of Sri Jayewardenepura, Sri Lanka, in 2004; a master's degree of advanced study in mathematics with honors from the University of Cambridge, UK, in 2006; and a Ph.D. in mathematics from the University of Connecticut, USA, in 2012. She works as an assistant professor in the Mathematics Department at Embry-Riddle Aeronautical University while working in the field of numerical linear algebra. Her research focus is to derive fast algorithms and use those in signal processing, image processing, solving systems of questions, theories of interpolations, approximations, orthogonal polynomials, and eigenvalue problems. As an early career woman in mathematics, she has received fellowships and scholarships including Advanced Doctoral Fellowship (2012), Doctoral Dissertation Fellowship (2012), and Predoctoral Fellowship (2010) by the University of Connecticut, USA; Industrial Research Scholarship (2008) by City, University London, UK; and Shell Centenary Scholarship by the Cambridge Commonwealth Trust (2005–2006), University of Cambridge, UK.

Ago MacGranaky Quaye was educated in Ghana, Canada, and the USA. He also worked as a programmer analyst and was a member of the programming team who helped in the implementation of the Social Security and National Insurance Trust System in Ghana. In January 2006, Ago moved from Virginia State University to join the AUN. He is the department head of the information systems and information technology program. He loves to teach, mentor, and interact with his colleagues and students. Dr. Quaye has published many articles in peer-reviewed, scholarly journals.

Gerard Rambally is a professor of computer science in the Department of Mathematics and Information Sciences at the University of North Texas at Dallas. He earned his bachelor's degree in mathematics from the University of Saskatchewan,

Canada; his master's degree in mathematics from the University of Waterloo in Ontario, Canada; and his doctoral degree in computer science from the University of Oregon, USA. Dr. Rambally has served as an academic dean for 13 years. He teaches both computer science and mathematics courses at UNT Dallas and has published research papers in the areas of computational thinking, computers in education, algorithms, bioinformatics, and artificial intelligence.

Alexander Repenning is the Hasler professor and chair of computer science education at the PH FHNW (School of Teacher Education at the University of Applied Sciences and Arts Northwestern Switzerland), a computer science professor at the University of Colorado, and a founder of AgentSheets Inc. He is directing the Scalable Game Design initiative at the University of Colorado. Repenning's research interests include education, end-user programmable agents, and artificial intelligence. He has worked in research and development at Asea Brown Boveri, Xerox PARC, Apple Computer, and Hewlett-Packard. Repenning is the creator of the AgentSheets and AgentCubes simulation and game computational thinking tools. He has offered game design workshops in the USA, Mexico, South America, Europe, and Japan. His work has received numerous awards including the Gold Medal from the mayor of Paris for "most innovative application in education of the World Wide Web," as well as "best of the best innovators" by ACM, and has been featured in *WIRED* magazine. Repenning has been a Telluride Tech Festival honoree for contributions to computer science. Repenning is an advisor to the National Academy of Sciences, the European Commission, the National Science Foundation, the Japanese Ministry of Education, and the Organisation for Economic Co-operation and Development (OECD).

Michael Rosen is an associate professor of anesthesiology and critical care medicine at the Johns Hopkins University School of Medicine. He is a human factors psychologist with research interests in the areas of teamwork and patient safety as well as simulation-based training, performance measurement, naturalistic decision making, and quality and safety improvement. In 2009, he was a co-recipient of the M. Scott Myers Award for Applied Research in the Workplace from the Society for Industrial and Organizational Psychology. This award was given in recognition of his work in developing innovative team decision-making training for explosive ordnance disposal teams, including a simulation-based curriculum and performance measurement tools.

Laurie F. Ruberg received her Ph.D. in curriculum and instruction at Virginia Tech. She served as a visiting assistant professor in the College of Education and Human Services at West Virginia University while writing this chapter. She currently heads up a small business called PLANTS (plant lessons and engaging technology systems), which provides innovative e-learning curriculum for K-12 schools and community audiences. Previously, she served as senior instructional designer and associate director for the NASA Classroom of the Future at Wheeling Jesuit University for 19 years. Her instructional design, development, and evaluation projects have been funded by the National Science Foundation (NSF), National

Aeronautics and Space Administration (NASA), Department of Labor, Mine Safety and Health Administration, TechConnect West Virginia, and regional foundations. Her research interests include instructional design, program evaluation, and online learning, where she has received awards for multimedia high school biology curriculum design (1999), NASA Explorer Schools evaluation (2007), and a nomination for outstanding teaching in the WVU Online Instructional Design and Technology master's degree program (2016).

Olgun Sadik is a doctoral student in the Instructional Systems Technology program at Indiana University. He worked 3 years as a computer science teacher and taught programming at a high school before he moved to academia. As a doctoral student, he taught programming and multimedia applications to preservice teachers in a computer educator licensure program and worked on redesigning the certification program courses based on the current CS education standards. His current research interests include computer science education, teacher education and professional development, and teacher technology integration in K-12. He had experience working in National Science Foundation projects and published studies on technology integration and CS education.

Oshani Seneviratne obtained her Ph.D. in computer science from the Massachusetts Institute of Technology (MIT) in 2015 under the guidance of Prof. Sir Tim Berners-Lee. She earned a master's degree (2009) in computer science from MIT and a bachelor of science (Hons) degree (2007) in computer science and engineering from the University of Moratuwa, Sri Lanka. Oshani's primary research focus has been content reuse on the web. For her doctoral work, she has developed a web protocol called HTTPA (Hypertext Transfer Protocol with Accountability) and reference Transparent Web Systems. She was the computer science instructor for MIT Women's Technology program in 2010 and has also taught mathematics for computer science and linked data ventures courses at MIT. Additionally, she was the lead technical instructor for MIT Accelerating Information Technology program (now called Global Startup Labs) in Kenya and the Philippines where she taught university undergraduate and master's level students to build socially impactful mobile phone applications.

Hasan Shodiev is an adjunct professor of physics and computer science, specializing in the development and study of new technologies for computational thinking and visualization in science education. His work on computational thinking resulted in a publication and presentations in a number of regional and international conferences on education. He is coauthor of an SSHRC Insight Development Grant on computational thinking and assessment across disciplines at all levels of education from kindergarten to postsecondary.

Michael Stewart is a Ph.D. candidate in computer science at Virginia Tech.

Deborah Tatar is professor of computer science and, by courtesy, psychology at Virginia Tech, where she is also a member of the Center for Human-Computer Interaction and the program for Women and Gender Studies; a fellow of the Institute for Creativity, Arts, and Technology; and a fellow of the Institute of Gerontology. She holds a doctorate in psychology from Stanford and a bachelor's degree in English and American literature and language from Harvard. She spent 16 years working in industry and industrial research. Established accomplishments in computer science and related fields include her 1986 LISP textbook and her early CSCW (computer-supported collaborative work) projects, including her analysis of the Xerox PARC Colab project. Much of her work focuses on the design of multiuser face-to-face systems, especially those designed to fit into and improve classroom interactions. This interest dovetails with an interest in the design of technologies as background, the notion of zensign (that what is left out can be as important as what is put into a user interface), phenomena of sharing, and human attention. She cares about how people's images of themselves are shaped by their interactions with technology.

Tarmo Toikkanen is a researcher of educational psychology and designer of learning environments at Aalto University School of Arts, Design and Architecture in Helsinki, Finland. His design work has influenced thousands of classrooms and teachers across Europe. Tarmo is a seasoned teacher trainer and disseminator of academic findings to wider audiences. He works with many nonprofit organizations in Finland and internationally, e.g., Creative Commons, EFF, Wikimedia Foundation, EU Code Week, and several technology and teacher associations. He's lately joined LifeLearn Platform as their chief science officer, working to create a global channel where learners and learning opportunities meet.

Aman Yadav is an associate professor in educational psychology and educational technology at Michigan State University. Dr. Yadav's research focuses on computational thinking, computer science education, and problem-based learning. His work has been published in a number of leading journals, including the *ACM Transactions on Computing Education*, *Journal of Research in Science Teaching*, *Journal of Engineering Education*, and *Communications of the ACM*. Dr. Yadav teaches courses on computational thinking, educational research methodology, learning theories, cognition, and computing technologies at the undergraduate and graduate level. He serves as an associate editor for the *ACM Transactions on Computing Education*, a journal that publishes research on computing education. He is the teacher education representative on the CSTA board and chairs the CSTA Assessment Task Force.

Part I
K-12 Education

Learning Computational Skills in uCode@ UWG: Challenges and Recommendations

Adriana D'Alba and Kim C. Huett

Abstract In order to compete in a global economy, higher education institutions, K-12 schools, government officials, school districts, teachers, and afterschool programs must provide students with opportunities to acquire computational thinking and twenty-first century skills. In the United States, thousands of new jobs in areas such as computer science, database administration, software development, and information research open each year; yet, there are not enough American students graduating with those degrees, thus having to fill computing positions with international workers. In addition, other professional fields such as healthcare, education, financial services, and administration are becoming more technology dependent, requiring their employees to acquire computational skills. Recognizing this need, and the often-disheartening lack of opportunities outside the classroom for students to be inspired and to acquire computational skills, the College of Education at the University of West Georgia opened a coding club for kids 7–17 in the spring of 2014 named uCode@ UWG. This chapter presents those efforts, and the current status of the program.

Keywords Computational thinking • Social interaction • Afterschool programs • Parental involvement • Advanced placement courses

Introduction

In January of 2016, the White House launched an initiative named "Computer science for all" (Smith, 2016), which aims to provide American students with the computer science (CS) skills needed to be globally competitive. Speaking at the State of the Union, President Obama proposed that every student from kindergarten through high school should have access to computer science and mathematics courses, in order to be equipped with the computational thinking skills to become not only consumers but creators of technology. In his plan, President Obama called for a $4.1 billion budget distributed in 3 years to provide professional development for

A. D'Alba (✉) • K.C. Huett
Department of Educational Technology and Foundations, University of West Georgia, Carrollton, GA 30118, USA
e-mail: adalba@westga.edu; khuett@westga.edu

P.J. Rich, C.B. Hodges (eds.), *Emerging Research, Practice, and Policy on Computational Thinking*, Educational Communications and Technology: Issues and Innovations, DOI 10.1007/978-3-319-52691-1_1

teachers and expand access to high-quality instructional materials. In addition, renewing funding for current and previous supported programs for CS such as National Science Foundation (NSF) and the Corporation for National and Community Service (CNCS) were noted priorities. The president requested the involvement from governors, mayors, and educational leaders to expand their support for CS in schools. As read in the Office of the Press Secretary (2016) press release of January 30, 2016, "by some estimates, just one quarter of all the K-12 schools in the United States offer CS with programming and coding, and only 28 states allow CS courses to count towards high-school graduation, even as other advanced economies are making CS available for all of their students" (para. 2). Other nations are further along in making CS central to curricula. In 2014, CS became part of England's primary school curriculum. Israel, New Zealand, and some states in Germany have updated their CS high-school syllabus, and Australia and Denmark are doing the same (A is for Algorithm, 2014).

In the United States, the situation is different. According to The College Board (2015), during the 2014–2015 academic year, from all the 21,594 schools across the country offering Advanced Placement (AP) courses to one or more students, only 4310 schools offered the AP Computer Science A course, and the number of males who enrolled in those was overwhelmingly larger than their female counterparts (38,216 vs. 10,778).

In the State of Georgia (USA), only 1658 students took the AP Computer Science A test in 2015. Of those, 817 were White (49%), 174 were Black (10%), 491 were Asian (29%), and 97 students (5%) identified themselves as Hispanic. Considering that in the same period, 108,301 students in Georgia public schools were enrolled in AP courses, and 82,936 students in Georgia public high schools completed AP exams, this indicates that approximately 1% of Georgia AP students took the AP Computer Science A test. Across the 2015 Georgia high-school population of 501,252, the percentage of students taking the high-school AP Computer Science A test is only slightly greater than zero (Georgia Department of Education, 2015).

In an effort to make computer science more accessible and engaging, the National Science Foundation aided the College Board to develop the AP Computer Science Principles (National Science Foundation, 2014). Schools will begin offering it in the fall of 2016, and the first test will be administered in the summer of 2017. The course content was specifically designed to appeal to a wider group of students, by teaching the creative aspects of computing and computational thinking, and helping students to be creators, and not only consumers of technology. Students will apply creative processes to develop artifacts, which will solve computational problems.

Why Computational Thinking Is Important

Wing (2006) defines computational thinking (CT) as a skill that everyone, not only computer scientists, should acquire in order to design systems, solve problems, and understand human behavior, by drawing on the concepts fundamental to computer science. Computational thinking requires people to understand what humans can do better than computers, what computers can do better than humans, and how answering those questions can solve problems by designing efficient systems. Some characteristics of CT include:

- Formulating problems and using computers and other applications to solve them
- Logically organizing and analyzing data
- Deciding which details in a problem need to be highlighted and which ones can be ignored, also known as the abstraction process
- Representing data with models and simulations
- Automating solutions through a series of steps, known as algorithmic thinking
- Identifying, analyzing, and implementing possible solutions by using the most efficient and effective combination of steps and resources
- Generalizing and transferring this problem-solving process to a wide variety of problems (Wing, 2008)

According to the Bureau of Labor Statistics (2015), from the years 2014 to 2024, national employment in computer and information technology will grow 12%, and 488,500 jobs will be added. In addition, more industries and jobs of the future will require that employees possess training in CS and demonstrate computational thinking. The White House indicates that by 2018, 51% of all the Science, Technology, Engineering, and Mathematics (STEM) jobs will be in CS-related fields, and a growing number of industries, including healthcare, education, financial services, and transportation, will require employees trained in CS (Office of the Press Secretary, 2016, January 30). The data indicate a clear need to acquire computational thinking and computer science skills, especially among younger generations who will fill the jobs of the future, which is one of the rationales for the creation of uCode@UWG, a computer club for kids hosted at the University of West Georgia.

The idea of introducing computational thinking for all as coined by Wing (2006) is not new, especially in K-12 settings. In the decade of the 1980s, Seymour Papert, Cynthia Solomon, Wally Feurzeig, and others introduced the programming language Logo in local schools near the Massachusetts Institute of Technology (MIT). The language, developed at MIT, was used to train children to think logically and solve problems (Papert, 1980, 1996). Among other activities, students were able to program a turtle robot and produce line graphics on the floor or on tables.

This exercise was adapted at uCode@UWG, for an activity (Fig. 1) that consisted of using the language Scratch, developed by the Logo Foundation at the Massachusetts Institute of Technology—http://el.media.mit.edu/logo-foundation/index.html—to program finch robots, designed at the Carnegie Mellon's CREATE lab (http://www.cmucreatelab.org/).

Learning Environments to Teach Computational Thinking and Computer Science

Despite the importance of introducing CT and CS concepts to students to fill the jobs of the future, there is a lack of CS programs and courses available for students enrolled in the American educational system. Fortunately, initiatives, such as Code

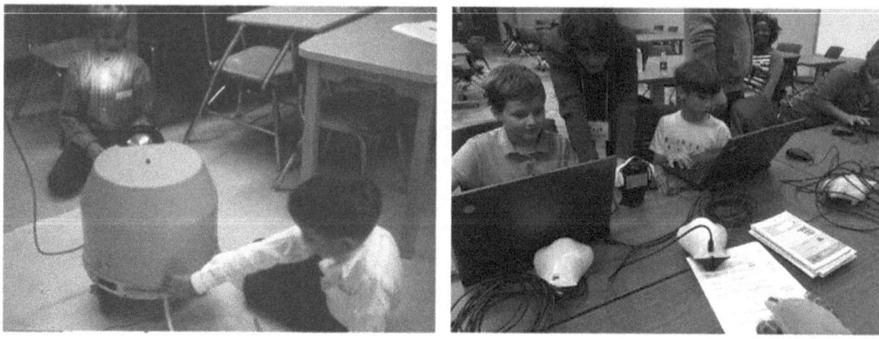

Fig. 1 *Left*, fifth graders using the first turtle robot (Image used with permission of Cynthia Solomon). *Right*, participants at uCode@UWG using Scratch and Finch robots

Academy, https://www.codecademy.com/; Google Code School, https://www.code-school.com/google; CoderDojo, https://coderdojo.com/; Girls who Code, http://girlswhocode.com/; and many others, are allowing American students to access collaborative sessions with mentors and volunteers in safe learning environments. In 2013 Google partnered with Facebook, Apple, Microsoft, Khan Academy, and Yahoo!, among other institutions, to create the nonprofit Hour of Code—http://hourofcode.com—which aims to expand participation in computer science education by making it available in more schools and to change policies in all 50 US states to categorize CS as part of the math/science core curriculum.

Another Google initiative, named *CS First*—https://www.cs-first.com/—for kids ages 9–14, was offered as an afterschool and summer activity. As of 2015 it had over 1400 afterschool programs across America. A report from the Afterschool Alliance (2011) suggests that afterschool programs are having a positive impact in academic achievement, through the improvement of students' education and behavior. For example, 60% of students enrolled in afterschool and summer programs in Chicago are pursuing degrees in STEM-related fields, and 95% of those who participated in Chicago afterschool programs have graduated high school. Participants of STEM afterschool programs are becoming familiar with the engineering design process, computer coding, web development, robotics, and other such technologies (Krishnamurthi, Ballard, & Noam, 2014).

In a 2010 employee survey, Google (2010) discovered that 98% of its Computer Science majors had had CS exposure prior to college. That exposure varied from reading about CS, afterschool programs or camps, or middle and high-school CS classes. In 2011 the organization launched the now defunct Computing and Programming Experience (CAPE), which aimed to expose early secondary school students to computer science.

Other informal educational initiatives similar to afterschool programs started to surge to fill the need for CS in schools. In 2011, James Whelton and Bill Liao opened the first CoderDojo in Dublin, Ireland (CoderDojo, 2013). As of January 2016, there are over 875 dojos in 63 countries. CoderDojo is a nonprofit organization focused on teaching children from 7 to 17 how to make the shift from consumers of computer programming to producers of technology by learning to program and use Scratch, HTML, CSS, JavaScript, Python, and Ruby, among other languages. During the sessions, children have the opportunity to develop computational thinking skills related to problem solving, creativity, abstraction, and collaboration. Students show progress by earning different belts, in a fashion similar to martial arts. CoderDojo is volunteer-based and requires the involvement of mentors, parents, community stakeholders, and children.

uCode@UWG: Teaching Computer Science to Children and Parents

Faculty and staff in the Department of Educational Technology and Foundations (ETF) and in the Department of Computer Science at the University of West Georgia understand the importance of teaching computational thinking and CS concepts to K-12 students, not only to awaken their interest in programming but to provide them with the foundational learning required in a wide variety of careers. In the spring of 2014, a faculty group began the planning phase to create an informal learning environment for coding inspired by the CoderDojo model (D'Alba, Huett, Remshagen, & Rolka, 2015).

In August 2014, uCode@UWG, a free computer-programming club aimed at kids 7–17 offered its first session. The mission of uCode@UWG is to provide an environment where kids can access computer programming—conceptually and culturally—in a fun, informal environment, supported by experts and caring volunteers in the local community of Carrollton, Georgia. Kid participants, mentors, and volunteers come from within and beyond the county.

uCode@UWG is a coding club sponsored by the College of Education (COE) and the College of Science and Mathematics (COSM), and receives support from the Office of Research and Sponsored Projects, and Information Technology Services. In addition to providing free of charge coding sessions for kids from 7 to 17 years and their parents and guardians, the monthly club offers research and educational experiences for undergraduate students enrolled in the College of Education, and faculty involved in the project are receiving credit toward promotion and/or tenure. In addition, the club provides opportunities for community outreach and contributes to build a positive public image of the University of West Georgia. uCode@UWG involves a group of faculty and professional experts in different areas such as education, computer science, administration, and mathematics, who are committed to give back to the community by providing free access to the rich human and infrastructural resources at the university.

The majority of volunteers in the program were experts in computer science. Each session had a "lead mentor" who was responsible for conceiving of and directing the session, and one or more "support mentors" who wandered among students during instruction to assist in a one-on-one format. Three mentors were recruited from the university computer science department, three from the educational technology, one from facilities, and three from the university technical support unit.

In addition, ten mentors came from private industry and included several professional web developers, software engineers, app developers, and the owner of a technology services consulting firm. Five mentors were computer science students at the undergraduate and graduate levels. At the university, mentor recruitment happened through the university "daily report" announcement mechanism, emails to the university community, and through a booth set up at an undergraduate fair for recruiting students to service opportunities. Outside of the university, recruitment happened primarily through involvement with a regional technology organization. uCode representatives explained the project and invited tech workers to participate. This two-prong approach produced a large enough body of mentors to create the mentor-to-learner ratios needed. Often, mentors invited other mentors, and this also helped to grow the group. A lead mentor might spend between one and 10 h preparing educational materials and posting them to the uCode@UWG wiki page for their learners or to another site like GitHub.

In addition to volunteers who mentored in computer science, uCode@UWG made use of a small number of volunteers—between one and four per session—to aid in logistical and hosting functions such as putting out parking signs or signing in participants upon arrival. Those were recruited from within the College of Education or were parents of students attending uCode.

The Logic Model of uCode@UWG

In the autumn of 2013, the authors of this chapter began conversations about opening a free, informal computer-programming club housed at the university, along the lines of the CoderDojo model. Though the concept of developing a computer-programming club seemed fairly straightforward, further examination revealed the necessity and value of systematic program planning to crystalize personally held assumptions and goals, to clarify programmatic purpose, and to serve as a guide for ongoing conversations related to systematic improvements of the program.

Through logic modeling, the organizers identified necessary *resources* and stakeholders at the university and within the community, outlined *activities* involved in running the program and related strategies (see Tables 1 and 2), and set *goals* for intended results (W. K. Kellogg Foundation, 2004).

Intended results were broken down into three levels of impact: short-term *outputs* would refer to immediately observable deliverables related to administering sessions (e.g., number of flyers disseminated, number of females served in a given session, number of coding sessions offered on a given Saturday); longer-term *outcomes* related to changes expected to occur at an individual level within 1–6 years (e.g., participant changes in knowledge and skill, growth in CS mentor self-efficacy); and still longer-term *impacts* occurring at the organizational and community level (e.g., increased enrollments in CS in local K-12 schools, increased local teacher capacity for supporting CS learning in K-12).

Table 1 Logic model: planned work—resources and activities

Resources/inputs →	Activities →
Mentors to lead kids through CS Volunteers to assist with events UWG faculty/staff to run program, conduct evaluation, and research Support of COE, COSM, & ITS; public safety & ORSP Community input (e.g., schools, businesses, public library) Marketing Learning space in COE with parking and storage Technology hardware and support Data collection forms	12 Dojo events (@ 3 h) • Exploring coding and other CS domain knowledge and skills through fun projects • Mentors spurring interest • Volunteers facilitating • Setup and breakdown Recruit mentors and volunteers Training for mentors and volunteers Curriculum development Visit other dojos; interface with community Promote the dojo and maintain an RSVP list Submit IRB for data collection Conduct formative evaluation activities

Table 2 Logic model: intended results by outputs, outcomes, and impact

Outputs →	Outcomes →	Impact
12 3-h Saturday sessions from August 2014–July 2015 B: 15–30 kids served per session B: A 2:1 kid/mentor ratio B: At least 3 volunteers per session B: Capture kid CS artifacts B: Document and capture each session's "plan" B: Distribute 100–200 flyers B: Attract at least 25% females and at least 25% disadvantaged B: Attract at least 1 K-12 teacher per session (as parent, volunteer, or mentor) B: Attract repeat visitors	Change in attitudes regarding CS domain with increases in interest, awareness, willingness to test/play/fail/persevere, and development of mentor identity and reduced fear/anxiety Changes in knowledge and skills in CS domain with increased abilities in computational thinking and problem-solving with technology Changes in knowledge and skills in practice fields/project-based learning with collaboration, reflection, and ownership of learning Changes in mentor knowledge/skills in designing project-based environments	G: Strengthen internal university relationships G: Strengthen university-community relationships G: Increase no. of students pursuing CS-related coursework/specialization in HS or postsecondary G: Reduce the barriers for minorities and females into the CS field G: Increase local teacher capacity and willingness to support CS domain interests among students

Note. *B* benchmark, *G* goal

Multiple drafts of the logic model were developed from January through July 2014 as organizers met with stakeholders involved in the process. Through meetings with COE and COSM faculty, leaders in the Information Systems Technology department, and leaders in the Office of Research and Sponsored projects, the organizers expressed the logic model through a presentation followed by constructive exchange of ideas. In this way, the model was continually refined over a 6-month process leading up to the first event. The logic model has been a useful tool for expressing "who we are, what we do, how we do it, and to what effect" and guiding constructive conversations among organizers, mentors, and parents. It continues to be refined at the end of each year during the summative organizer meeting (Fig. 2).

Fig. 2 The Idea Space, where kids provided suggestions and thoughts for upcoming sessions

At uCode@UWG, students take ownership of their learning and engage in a self-paced, challenging, and collaborative environment. Often, parents are working along with their children not only helping them to finish the tasks but also learning the concepts presented at the sessions. Using a project-based learning approach (Barrows, 1992; Blumenfeld, Krajcik, Marx, & Soloway, 1994; Solomon, 2003; Tretten & Zachariou, 1995; Thomas, 2000), students are constructing knowledge in a highly engaging technology environment (Bell, 2010). At the beginning of each session, the students start developing a small task, which then builds upon itself, with mentors and volunteers guiding and advising them continuously. To mention an example, in the September–November 2015 period, the younger group of students (7–12 years old) was asked to animate a turtle using the programming language Python, by coding color paths that turned into geometrical shapes (Fig. 3). Once the mentor showed them how to code a color and draw a square path, volunteers challenged them to change it to a different color and to try other shapes. Often, kids were seen incorporating new lines to the code without any guidance or intervention and offering advice to other children. Through the deliberate toolset choice of Python and GitHub (for housing coding starting points), the mentors sparked kids' and parents' interest in coding by connecting them to tools and practices used in the everyday workplace, such as automated systems for security, data and IT management, smart machines, simulators of phenomena, robotics, and virtual collaboration, among others.

The Sessions

As of April 2016, the team has offered 14 monthly sessions with two different tracks or topics. Each session has lasted between 3 and 3½ h, and the number of volunteers and mentors has varied; however, each session counted with at least two lead mentors (one per track) and five to seven volunteers distributed between the two tracks. The topics for the sessions have varied from teaching HTML and Scratch to programming in Java and Python and using the website codeacademy.com. The sessions covered basic principles of the programming languages, and students were able to develop their own websites, games in Scratch, or animations in Python, which they could take home after the session ended. The first period, or *Year1*, had a total of eight sessions and ran from August 2014 to April 2015. The average number of students attending each of the sessions was 25, with the largest number of students occurring in August 2014 (n = 44) and the smallest number in September 2014 (n = 7). During *Year2*, a total of six sessions occurred from September to December 2015, resumed in February and ended in April 2016. The average age of children who attended uCode in both *Year1* and *Year2* was 10.7 years. A table with the numbers of mentors, volunteers, topics covered, ages of attendees, sex of participants, and average numbers can be consulted in the Appendix.

One of the requirements at uCode@UWG is that kids 12 years or younger must be accompanied by a parent or guardian during the sessions. Parents of older students can drop them off and pick them up once the session has ended.

Previous to launching the first session of uCode, the team met several times to talk about logistics and marketing. The College of Education (COE) offered two classrooms, and its media library, the TecHUB, provided a cart with 15 PC laptops. Forty-four children attended the first session in August 2014, and the two tracks offered were HTML and Scratch. Previous to the session, parents registered their children by phone or through Meetup (http://www.meetup.com/). Organizers provided instructions for parking, and participants were encouraged to bring their own laptops.

Seeking Feedback from Session Participants

The team placed two boards in the back of the classrooms, named "The Idea Space" (Fig. 2), where kids noted their level of knowledge about coding and provided feedback and suggestions for next sessions. The idea for the boards was adapted from a visit to a CoderDojo in Atlanta (https://www.versionone.com/). The board included four introductory messages (i.e., *I have not coded before, I have a project, I would like to help starting a project,* and *I would like to show something I did*), and three

Fig. 3 Kids and parents learning to program in Python and creating shapes with a digital turtle

feedback notes (*What do I want to learn next session, What can you help us with,* and *How can we improve?*), where kids and their parents could post their ideas. The team met briefly after each of the sessions to review the feedback, talk about what went right and what could be improved, and to start suggesting ideas for the next session.

This informal feedback system was used during the first sessions of *Year1*, until the team decided to migrate uCode to the COE computer classrooms in January 2015. This allowed the team to ease the administrative load for uCode and focus on the content of the sessions, as there was no longer a need to work on logistics to setup the classrooms, previous to the sessions. Feedback started to get collected with an end-of-session form.

In addition to having eight monthly sessions at the University of West Georgia in *Year1*, the team offered Scratch programming to 150 third grade students at a local Title 1 elementary school from January–April 2015 and to 40 gifted students at a local middle school in May 2015.

Transitioning to Year 2 of Coding Program

At the end of *Year1*, the team, mentors, and volunteers met to conduct an informal summative evaluation of uCode. At this meeting, it was decided to continue offering uCode for a second year, as the team recognized its impact in the local community and the importance of the program for the COE as a source for educational research, service, outreach, and public presence. However, the number of sessions was cut, from one each month to three sessions in fall 2015 and three sessions in spring 2016, to allow the members of the team to focus on other academic responsibilities. It was also decided to offer dynamic project-based content that builds throughout 3-month blocks, rather than having individual-content monthly sessions.

The first meeting of *Year2* occurred in September 2015 with the attendance of 41 students. After the winter break, the February 2016 session registered an attendance of 51 children. This session offered three tracks: Scratch, HTML, and Minecraft Modding with Java. The team eliminated the use of Meetup and started using Facebook for announcements, communications, and session reservations. All the documentation and supportive materials are kept in a university-supported Google Drive folder, and the team maintains constant email communication and receives input from mentors and volunteers when planning the sessions. The team continued collecting feedback from attendees using exit questionnaires and conducting informal interviews with parents and children.

Parental Involvement in Learning at uCode@UWG

Although learning is a layered process that involves different stakeholders such as administrators, teachers, parents, students, and their peers, this section takes a closer look at the role of parental involvement in learning, as parents play an essential role in their children's experience at uCode@UWG.

Parents enjoy being involved in their children's school life (Christenson, 2003; Jeynes, 2007) and worry that responsibilities such as work, lack of time, and demands from other children prevent them from becoming more involved (Williams, Williams, & Ullman, 2002). Studies report that parental involvement in student homework seems to be related to student achievement (Hoover-Dempsey et al., 2001; Parker, Boak, Griffin, Ripple, & Peay, 1999), and parents believe their involvement will make a positive difference (Hoover-Dempsey & Sandler, 1997; Jeynes, 2007; Lee & Bowen, 2006).

Seven parents who attended uCode@UWG with their children were interviewed in the spring of 2015. Four of them had brought their kids to every session, one of them was a first-time visitor, and two had attended one or two sessions. Five of them were female. All of them had two or more children, and one parent was homeschooling their kids. The uCode team wanted to understand their motivation to bring their children to the sessions, their parental involvement in school, their participation in afterschool activities and their children's homework and wanted to know how interested and motivated their children were in pursuing computer science careers.

All the seven parents were said to be very involved with their children's homework, but not all of them were involved in school activities; four cited lack of time or having to work. When asked why they were bringing their kids to uCode, some of the individual responses were "to learn something new and useful," "his friend came last month and he wanted to learn computers too," and "jobs are going to be towards programming and making games so I want her to learn that." Their responses suggest parents want their kids to be prepared for the future and learn useful skills. Researchers also asked parents why they thought their kids were interested in computer science. Individual responses varied from having someone at home who works on computer science (parent or relative) who inspires them, showing interest in computer games and wanting to learn how to make them (three parents responded something similar regarding their kids playing computer games), wanting to learn to use the computer since they were very young (2–3 years old), and using computers at school and wanting to learn more about them. These responses seem to be related to the accessibility to computers at home/school and wanting to learn how they work.

These responses corroborate the literature on parent involvement cited earlier in this section. As the Office of the Press Secretary (2016) notes:

- More than nine out of ten parents... say they want CS taught at their child's school. They understand that today's elementary, middle and high school students are tomorrow's engineers, entrepreneurs, and leaders who must be equipped with strong computational thinking skills and the ability to solve complex problems. (The Need for CS for All, Sect. 1, para. 2)

As mentioned earlier in the chapter, parents are welcome to stay at uCode. Those who do, almost always, are actively engaged with their children in the event (see Fig. 4), and some of them have expressed further interest in learning to code. They often are seen using the lab computers to participate in the lessons, helping the kids, or asking the mentors where to get more information about the programs used in the session. According to Hoover-Dempsey and Sandler (1995), there are three mechanisms of parental influence on children's educational outcomes: modeling, reinforcement, and direct instruction (p. 319). When parents participate in activities related to schooling, such as reviewing homework, engaging with teachers and mentors, or attending school events, children are more likely to emulate this behavior. Parents often give praise and rewards related to school success, thus reinforcing a good performance and propelling positive educational outcomes. In addition, parents who practice direct instruction in the form of commands, requests for correct answers, working with their children to solve a problem, or asking for other ideas on how to solve homework issues have a positive effect on children's learning. Researchers have observed nearly all the parents consistently displaying these three behaviors at uCode sessions (see Fig. 4).

Child Interactions at uCode@UWG

The uCode team wanted to observe the social interactions (see Fig. 5) occurring in the sessions, to better understand the collective dynamics happening in uCode, particularly regarding collaboration, leadership, and decision-making, which are

Fig. 4 Parents participating actively in the sessions

Fig. 5 Engagement and group collaboration at uCode

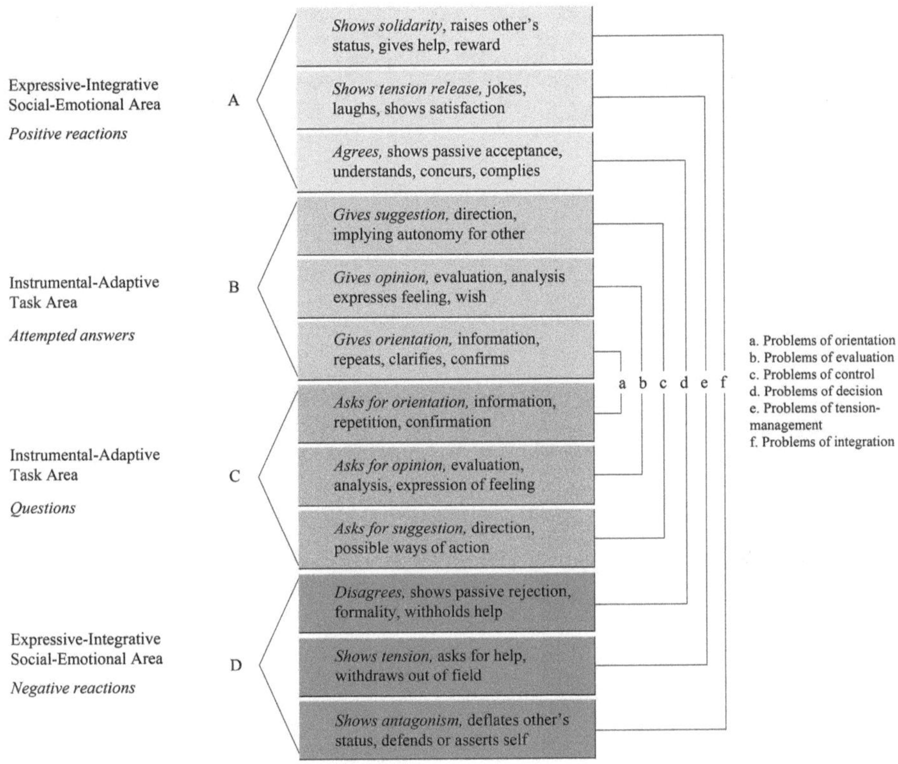

Fig. 6 Bales Social Interaction System showing the four behavioral areas and the 12 categories

essential twenty-first century skills. The literature about social interaction is extensive, and it often focuses on one or many of its features (Fahy, 2006; Synder & Swann, 1978).

The team selected Bales (1950) to categorize the behaviors occurring at uCode, as his work is considered to be seminal in the analysis and classification of social group interaction (Burke, 2006; Keyton, 2003).

Bales proposed 12 categories of interaction (see Fig. 6), while acknowledging that there are three broad variables that can affect the occurrences in a certain social interaction: (1) personalities of the individual members, (2) characteristics that those members have in common, and (3) the organization of the group. However, as he argued, there is a series of conditions arising from the nature of the social exercise, which change as the group interaction moves through time.

The team selected the September and October 2015 sessions to conduct unobtrusive observations solely with children, as they are considered to be the primary participants at uCode@UWG. The analysis and coding of the observations offered an effective classification of the verbal and nonverbal behaviors presented by the students.

Seventeen participants were chosen randomly (seven in September, ten in October), and the team conducted individual unobtrusive observations for a period of time between 5 and 10 min per person. Every time the participant expressed

	Sep-15							Oct-15										
Participant Code	F11	M9	M12	M12	M7	M12	F12	M15	F11	F9	F12	M13	F8	M14	M13	M10	F10	Number of Occurrences
1 Shows Solidarity			1	2	2	2	1		1	2	1		3	1	1		1	18
2 Shows Tension Release	4	2	2	2	1	2	3		2	3	1	2	1	2	1	2	1	31
3 Agrees	6	3	3	1	1	2	1		1	1		4	2		2		2	29
4 Gives Suggestion	1			2			2		1			1	2	2				11
5 Gives Opinion		2		3	1		2		1			1		1	1	2		14
6 Gives Orientation	2		1			1				2							2	8
7 Asks for Orientation	1	2						1			2			1				7
8 Asks for Opinion								1										1
9 Asks for Suggestion			1													1		2
10 Disagrees								1										1
11 Shows Tension																		0
12 Shows Antagonism																		0

Fig. 7 Occurrences presented in participants selected for unobtrusive observations

certain behavior that fell into Bales' categories (verbal or nonverbal), it was annotated on a table. Figure 7 shows the students observed during each month and the list of Bales categories. The participant code refers to the sex (M for male, F for female), and age of the student.

Categories 2, "*Shows tension release, jokes, laughs, shows satisfaction*," and 3, "*Agrees, shows passive acceptance, understands, concurs, complies*" presented the majority of occurrences. This can be interpreted as students having fun, releasing tension, and showing enthusiasm, pleasure, and joy during the sessions (Category 2) and expressing confirmation, conviction, and concurrence about what they are learning (Category 3). In addition, students showed 14 occurrences in Category 5 "*Gives opinion, evaluation, analysis, expresses feeling, wish*." This, according to Bales, is the most frequently used category in many observation situations, and it includes problem-solving decisions and expressions of understanding or insight. Another category where students showed a higher number of occurrences (n = 18) was Category 1, "*Shows solidarity, raises other's status, gives help, reward.*" This includes any act showing sympathy or similarity of feeling, expressing desire for cooperation, showing a nurturing attitude, complimenting, or congratulating others.

Another category that was noteworthy is 4, "*Gives suggestion, direction, implying autonomy for other*" with students, showing 11 occurrences. Bales included in this category any act that takes the lead in the activity, such as attempting to guide, to persuade, and to inspire people to perform some actions.

Results of the data analysis suggest students are presenting collaborative, leadership, and decision-making skills when attending the sessions at uCode. Children are creating partnerships with others, are providing suggestions, and are becoming leaders by offering guidance to their peers. It is not clear from the investigation if these skills are a result of their participation at uCode, as the team is still conducting follow-up interviews to corroborate findings; however, the interactions show uCode@UWG provides a positive and nurturing environment for learners.

The *occurrences* or behaviors presented at uCode@UWG are tied to what Brennan and Resnick (2012) listed as the three computational thinking perspectives, included in their computational thinking framework: kids are *expressing* themselves through the development and creation of coding projects, they are *connecting* and creating partnerships with others during the sessions, and they are *questioning* how technology works and how they can use it to make sense of the world.

Next Steps and the Future of uCode@UWG

The team remains committed to the project and is exploring opportunities for its expansion. Recruitment of expert mentors and volunteers is a priority, as they are the vital force driving uCode. There are several inquiries being explored to conduct qualitative research, including parents' perceptions of learning in uCode, mentors' experiences, student' attitudes toward computer science after attending uCode, and parental engagement, among others. In addition, researchers will attempt to conduct in-depth individual interviews with parents and kids to corroborate findings regarding social interaction and to investigate new lines of research that emerged from the parents' individual interviews, such as peer motivation to attend uCode and self-motivation to learn computer science.

There are some challenges at uCode that need to be addressed: The team needs to design a better way for student placement in the different session tracks, not only by age but by the amount of experience they already have regarding the topics. Some kids already know what is being taught at the sessions, and although they seem to take a leadership role by helping their peers, some become disengaged. A possible solution worth exploring is to ask parents beforehand their children's baseline knowledge and subdivide the tracks in *beginners* and *experts* using names that are appealing to the kids and are related to UWG, e.g., using the University mascot—a wolf—and naming the groups *Scratch pups* and *Scratch alphas*. The team is receiving continuous feedback and advice from mentors and volunteers and engaging in conversations with expert scholars to address these issues. A second area that needs further analysis is a better understanding of the reasons behind parents halting their children's attendance after one or more sessions. Is it because of their kids' experience at uCode, or are there other factors preventing them from attending more frequently? The team needs to do a better job gathering summative feedback from children and adult attendees.

Originally, uCode@UWG was a one-year project that started with a conversation between two colleagues from the Department of Educational Technology and Foundations at the University of West Georgia. Today, 2 years later, the program has grown and continues to present valuable learning opportunities for kids, parents, faculty, administrators, and the local community. The team remains dedicated to the project and hopes to inspire other higher education institutions to open their doors and share their human resources and facilities, to provoke the minds of the younger generation, and to prepare them for the challenges of an increasingly competitive world.

Acknowledgments The authors would like to acknowledge the following University of West Georgia units for support of uCode@UWG operations during the first 2 years: the College of Education, the College of Science and Mathematics, Information Technology Services, the Office of Research and Sponsored Projects, and UWG Online. In addition, the authors appreciate the tireless dedication of uCode@UWG mentors and volunteers, without whom there would be no program.

Overview of Sessions from August 2014 Through April 2016

Month and year	No. of sessions	Sessions offered	No. of mentors	No. of volunteers	No. of coders	Median age	Sex
August 2014	2	Scratch; HTML	4	3	44	11	19 fem. 25 male
September 2014	2	Java; HTML and CSS	5	5	7	11	4 fem. 3 male
October 2014	2	Java; HTML and CSS	5	3	42	12	22 fem. 20 male
November 2014	3	Java; Scratch; Snap + Finch Robots	4	3	20	11	7 fem. 13 male
December 2014	4	Java; Scratch; Snap + Finch Robots; Hour of Code	3	3	23	10	12 fem. 11 male
January 2015	4	Java; Scratch; Snap + Finch Robots; Code Academy	5	5	20	11	9 fem. 11 male
March 2015	3	Java; Scratch; Snap + Finch Robots	3	4	22	11	10 fem. 12 male
April 2015	1	Minecraft Modding with JavaScript	3	8	24	13	9 fem. 15 male
Average numbers for *Year1*			4	4.2	25.2		
September 2015	2	Python: Shapes and Turtles; Python: Puzzles and Games	7	2	41	11	18 fem. 23 male
October 2015	2	Python: Shapes and Turtles; Python: Puzzles and Games	8	2	30	11	13 fem. 17 male
November 2015	2	Python: Shapes and Turtles; Python: Puzzles and Games	7	2	22	11	8 fem. 14 male
February 2016	3	Web Design; Scratch; Java Programming in Minecraft	10	2	51	12	22 fem. 29 male

(continued)

Month and year	No. of sessions	Sessions offered	No. of mentors	No. of volunteers	No. of coders	Median age	Sex
March 2016	3	Web Design; Scratch; LittleBits	11	2	29	11	12 fem. 17 male
April 2016	2	Web Design; Scratch	7	2	19	12	8 fem. 11 male
Average numbers for *Year2*			8.3	2	32		

References

A is for Algorithm (2014). *The economist.* Retrieved from http://www.economist.com/news/international/21601250-global-push-more-computer-science-classrooms-starting-bear-fruit.

Afterschool Alliance (2011). Evaluations backgrounder: A summary of formal evaluations of afterschool programs' impact on academics, behavior, safety and family life. Retrieved from http://www.afterschoolalliance.org/documents/EvaluationsBackgrounder2011.pdf.

Bales, R. (1950). *Interaction process analysis: A method for the study of small groups.* Cambridge, MA: Addison-Wesley.

Barrows, H. S. (1992). *The tutorial process.* Springfield, IL: Southern Illinois University School of Medicine.

Bell, S. (2010). Project-based learning for the 21st century: Skills for the future. *The Clearing House, 83*, 39–43.

Blumenfeld, P. C., Krajcik, J. S., Marx, R. W., & Soloway, E. (1994). Lessons learned: How collaboration helped middle grade science teachers learn project-based instruction. *The Elementary School Journal, 94*(5), 539–551.

Brennan, K., & Resnick, M. (2012). New frameworks for studying and assessing the development of computational thinking. In *Annual American Educational Research Association Meeting.* British Columbia: Vancouver.

Bureau of Labor Statistics (2015). U.S. Department of Labor, Occupational Outlook Handbook, 2016–17 Edition, Computer and Information Research Scientists. Retrieved from http://www.bls.gov/ooh/computer-and-information-technology/computer-and-information-research-scientists.htm.

Burke, P. J. (2006). Interaction in small groups. In J. DeLamater (Ed.), *Handbook of social psychology* (pp. 363–387). New York, NY: Kluwer Academic/Plenum.

Christenson, S. L. (2003). The family-school partnership: An opportunity to promote the learning competence of all students. *School Psychology Quarterly, 18*, 454–482.

CoderDojo (2013). About Coder Dojo. Retrieved from http://coderdojo.com.

D'Alba, A., Huett, K., Remshagen, A., & Rolka, C. (2015). uCode@UWG: Building kids' interest in STEM-C. In D. Slykhuis & G. Marks (Eds.), *Proceedings of society for information technology and teacher education international conference* (pp. 96–99). Chesapeake, VA: Association for the Advancement of Computing in Education (AACE).

Dumas, J., & Albin, J. (1986). Parent training outcome: does active parental involvement matter? *Behaviour Research and Therapy, 24*(2), 227–230.

Fahy, P. J. (2006). Online and face-to-face group interaction processes compared using Bales' interaction process analysis (IPA). *European Journal of Open, Distance and E-Learning.* Retrieved from http://www.eurodl.org/materials/contrib/2006/Patrick_J_Fahy.htm.

Georgia Department of Education (2015). Quick facts about Georgia public education. Retrieved from https://www.gadoe.org/.

Google (2010). Google in education: A new and open world for learning. Retrieved from: http://static.googleusercontent.com/media/www.google.com/en/us/edu/pdf/Google_EDU_Report_FULL.pdf.

Hoover-Dempsey, K., & Sandler, H. (1995). Parental involvement in children's education: Why does it make a difference? *Teachers College Record, 95*, 310–331.

Hoover-Dempsey, K., & Sandler, H. (1997). Why do parents become involved in their children's education? *Review of Educational Research, 67*(1), 3–42.
Hoover-Dempsey, K. V., Battiato, A. C., Walker, J. M. T., Reed, R. P., DeJong, J. M., & Jones, K. P. (2001). Parental involvement in homework. *Educational Psychologist, 36*, 195–209.
Jeynes, W. (2007). The relationship between parental involvement and urban secondary school student academic achievement: A meta-analysis. *Urban Education, 42*, 82–110.
Keyton, J. (2003). Observing group interaction. In R. Y. Hitokawa, R. S. Cathcart, L. A. Samovar, & L. D. Henman (Eds.), *Small group communication: Theory and practice* (pp. 256–266). Los Angeles, CA: Roxbury Publishing.
Krishnamurthi, A., Ottinger, R., & Topol, T. (2013). STEM learning in afterschool and summer programming: An essential strategy for STEM education reform. In T. Peterson (Ed.), *Expanding minds and opportunities: Leveraging the power of afterschool and summer learning for student success*. Collaborative Communications Group. Retrieved from http://www.expandinglearning.org/expandingminds.
Krishnamurthi, A., Ballard, M., Noam, G. (2014). Examining the impact of afterschool STEM programs. Paper commissioned by the Noyce Foundation. Retrieved from http://files.eric.ed.gov/fulltext/ED546628.pdf.
Lee, J. S., & Bowen, N. K. (2006). Parent involvement, cultural capital, and the achievement gap among elementary school children. *American Education Research Journal, 43*(2), 193–218.
National Science Foundation (2014). College Board launches new AP Computer Science Principles course. Retrieved from http://www.nsf.gov/news/news_summ.jsp?cntn_id=133571.
Office of the Press Secretary (2016). FACT SHEET: President Obama announces computer science for all initiative. Retrieved from https://www.whitehouse.gov/the-press-office/2016/01/30/fact-sheet-president-obama-announces-computer-science-all-initiative-0.
Papert, S. (1980). *Mindstorms: Children, computers, and powerful ideas*. New York, NY: Basic Books.
Papert, S. (1996). An exploration in the space of mathematics educations. *International Journal of Computers for Mathematical Learning, 1*(1), 95–123.
Parker, F., Boak, A., Griffin, K., Ripple, C., & Peay, L. (1999). Parent-child relationship, home learning environment, and school readiness. *School Psychology Review, 28*(3), 413–425.
Smith, M. (2016). Computer science for all. In *The White House*. Retrieved from https://www.whitehouse.gov/blog/2016/01/30/computer-science-all.
Solomon, G. (2003). Project-base learning: A primer. *Technology and Learning, 23*(6), 20–26.
Synder, M., & Swann, W. (1978). Behavioral confirmation in social interaction: From social perception to social reality. *Journal of Experimental Social Psychology, 14*, 148–162.
The College Board (2015). National Summary Report. Retrieved from http://research.collegeboard.org/programs/ap/data/participation/ap-2015.
Thomas, J. W. (2000). *A review of research on project-based learning*. San Rafael, CA: Autodesk Foundation.
Tretten, R., & Zachariou, P. (1995). *Learning about project-based learning: Self-assessment preliminary report of results*. San Rafael, CA: The Autodesk Foundation.
W. K. Kellogg Foundation (2004). W. K. Kellogg Foundation logic model development guide. Retrieved from: https://www.wkkf.org/resource-directory/resource/2006/02/wk-kellogg-foundation-logic-model-development-guide.
Williams, B., Williams, J., & Ullman, A. (2002). *Parental involvement in education*. London: Department for Education and Skills.
Wing, J. (2006). Computational thinking. *Communications of the ACM, 49*(3), 33–35.
Wing, J. M. (2008). Computational thinking and thinking about computing. *Philosophical Transactions of the Royal Society, 366*, 3717–3725.

Making Computer Science Attractive to High School Girls with Computational Thinking Approaches: A Case Study

Oshani Seneviratne

Abstract Computational thinking is a fundamental skill that extends beyond computer science. Conceptually it involves logic, algorithms, patterns, abstraction, and evaluation. The approach for developing a computational mind-set may involve experimenting, creating, debugging, and collaborating. Due to certain implicit biases and societal and cultural factors, girls may not be exposed to these computational thinking concepts and approaches. This has resulted in a decrease in the number of women in computer science since the 1980s. This chapter summarizes some of the challenges faced when teaching introductory computer science to high school girls and the approaches taken to overcome those challenges.

Keywords Gender issues • Computational thinking techniques

Introduction

Gender gap in computer science is a much-studied topic in the recent years (Margolis & Fisher, 2003). According to a report titled "Why So Few?" (Hill, Corbett, & Rose, 2010), only a very small percentage of girls, around 0.4 %, entering college intend to major in computer science, and women only made up 14 % of all computer science graduates, down from 36 % in 1984. In a 2009 poll of young people aged 8–17, only 5 % of girls had said they were interested in an engineering career. Another recent poll found that while 74 % of college-bound boys aged 13–17 said that computer science or computing would be a good college major for them, only a 32 % of their female peers said the same (Association for Computing Machinery; WGBH Educational Foundation, 2009). It has also been shown that, from early adolescence, girls express less interest in math or science careers than boys do (Lapan, Adams, Turner, & Hinkelman, 2000; Turner, 2008). Even girls and women who excel in mathematics often do not want to pursue computer science or any

O. Seneviratne (✉)
Massachusetts Institute of Technology, Cambridge, MA 02139, USA
e-mail: oshani@csail.mit.edu

P.J. Rich, C.B. Hodges (eds.), *Emerging Research, Practice, and Policy on Computational Thinking*, Educational Communications and Technology: Issues and Innovations, DOI 10.1007/978-3-319-52691-1_2

other STEM fields. Given these disparities, there are many academic programs at various institutions that are trying to address the problem head on and break the glass ceilings in which women may be discouraged in pursuing a career in computer science.

The MIT Women's Technology Program (WTP)[1] is a program that has been running since 2002 with the goal of attracting more high school girls to engineering and computer science. WTP facilitates a rigorous residential summer program for high achieving college bound girls who are either high school juniors or seniors from all over the USA who did not have any prior exposure to computer science. The hallmark of the program is that, it introduces the concepts in a hands-on team-based format with a focus on problem solving. The program has daily lectures, labs with fun team-based projects, and several hours of homework. There are no grades for WTP because the program encourages students to go outside their comfort zones and not worry about a perfect score or making mistakes. During my doctoral studies at MIT, I was very fortunate to teach computer science through WTP to high school girls. The teaching staff included myself who was the main instructor responsible for preparing and delivering all the material, and tutors who help the students during the labs and their homework. The tutors are typically advanced undergraduate students who are majoring in computer science.

Before the summer program began, it was my responsibility, as the instructor, to prepare the curriculum for basics of computer science with comprehensive examples, mini quizzes, and projects the students can try out. Learning in WTP is supposed to be incremental, where the lessons would build up from the previous day. The curriculum covered basic syntax for programming in Python, control structures, functions, object-oriented programming, data structures, algorithms, and recursion. Students were expected to complete challenging conceptual exercises, daily programming assignments, and a final project.

Despite all the preparations we took, when the program started, the teaching staff realized that the students' perception towards computer science needs to be changed to instill a computational thinking mind-set before going ahead with the lessons. The high school girls were previously exposed to concepts such as patterns and abstraction through high school level math and science courses. However, we noticed that some of the students had difficulty in applying such skills they already had to learning basics of computer science theory.

The reasons were twofold: (1) gender-based stereotypes and (2) learning subject matter they were not exposed to before. Although the first issue is only applicable to girls, the second issue is equally applicable to both genders. The following sections illustrate the above-mentioned issues in depth along with the approaches we took to overcome those challenges.

---

[1] http://wtp.mit.edu/.

Overcoming the Gender Stereotypes

Overcoming Implicit Gender Bias

As the teaching staff, it was our duty to encourage a supportive community spirit of learning together (Johnson & Johnson, 1987), so that the learning process will not be overwhelming to the students during the fast-paced short summer course. So, in this spirit of learning together, we facilitated a classroom discussion on what computer science meant to the students at the beginning of the course. We asked few open-ended questions like: "Who has met a computer scientist/programmer?", "What do you think computer scientists do?", etc. Based on some of the answers, it was clear that some of the students had certain implicit gender stereotypes. A family member, an older friend, or a friend of a friend was "into computers," but many of them were male, and it seemed as if the students would most certainly equate these people they knew to asocial geeks who keep to themselves typing all day in dark basements and do not see the light of day. As for what they think the computer scientists do, most of the students (rightfully) had the impression that computer science meant coming up with code, but they didn't equate that to solving problems.

As explained in the "Blindspot" (Banaji & Greenwald, 2013) even among individuals who actively reject gender stereotypes, implicit bias can be common. This bias not only affects individuals' attitudes toward others but may also influence their own interest in math and science topics. This indirectly hinders a girl's computational thinking skills. Not only would a girl more likely to associate computer science with men than with women, but she may also encounter negative opinions for women in such "masculine" positions. It was shown that as early as elementary school, children are aware of these stereotypes and can express stereotypical beliefs about which science courses are suitable for females and males (Joyce & Farenga, 2000). Furthermore, girls and young women have been found to be aware of, and negatively affected by, the stereotypical image of a scientist as a man (Luce et al., 2008). Even looking at my own (the author's) career path as a computer scientist and of my very few female peers, I can see that women face a particular set of difficulties when they are in a male-majority field. The presence of female role models can be hard to come by when you're one of the only girls in your computer science class.

No Need for Self-Inflicted High Standards

Studies have shown that girls hold themselves to a higher standard in subjects like math (Correll, 2004). Because of this, girls are less likely to believe that they will succeed in a STEM field such as computer science, and therefore, are less likely to express interest in a career in computer science. In a study done in 2005, it was found that gender differences in self-confidence in STEM subjects begin in middle school and increase in high school and college, with girls reporting less confidence than boys do in their math and science ability (Pajares, 2005). In part, boys develop greater confidence in STEM through experience developing relevant skills, and girls may lose the opportunity to develop such skills due to their vulnerability in losing confidence in STEM areas.

However, WTP was a level playing field, because all the students were girls. Plus, WTP did not emphasize on grades, but rather on learning in a collaborative environment. So, since none of the girls had the pressure to hold themselves to high standards, we encouraged them to be very confident about their abilities, ask questions, and learn from each other.

Female Role Models

As mentioned above, computer science has a bad image among girls, or they were not confident in the skills they already had. Thus, it was clear that we had to address the stereotypes the students associated with computer science. A study reported an increase in girls' interest in computer science and engineering after the girls were exposed to a 20-min narrative delivered by a computer-generated female agent describing the lives of female engineers and the benefits of computer science and engineering careers (Plant, Baylor, Doerr, & Rosenberg-Kima, 2009). Therefore, getting to know female computer scientists who can potentially be the girls' role models can be a huge boost to the girls' self-confidence and increase their interest in the field.

Thus, we decided to get the girls exposed to as many female role models as possible during the program. Unlike in their high school environments, during the summer long program, the students already had lot of access to female role models. The staff members of WTP including the tutors were all female, and the girls felt especially connected to the tutors since they were only few years senior to them. We made sure that the students felt comfortable talking to anybody in the staff during the classroom sessions, during programming labs, and during after-hours in which they completed their homework. Problem solving is an iterative process (Wing, 2006), and acquiring the skills needed to solve or debug a solution to a problem can take a long time or maybe even impossible if the proper support structures are not present, and the students may be discouraged early on and do not develop an interest. This is especially important since the students really need to come out of their comfort zones and experiment with the unknown in order to fix an error in their program. For a novice this can be very intimidating, and thus having access to people who can help them can be very beneficial. The students should not be in a position to give up the entire field if they were not able to correctly write their first program, or debug their code, or do not understand something that can be useful in figuring out the underlying basic CS concepts.

Interacting with women who use computer science in their professional lives gives them an idea of something to go after besides an endless string of code. Therefore, we organized a lunch series throughout the duration of the program and invited successful female computer scientists, professors, engineers from the industry, and female CS Ph.D. students at MIT, to talk to the high school girls informally about how they first got into computer science and what they are passionate about other than computer science. Most of the speakers were working to solve some very interesting challenges such as finding cures for diseases like cancer, tackling global warming, developing renewable energy sources, developing robots to help the elderly, working on speech synthesis, and understanding the origins of the universe, to name a few. In fact few of the guests did not even identify themselves as computer scientists as their day-to-day work was in some other field such as physics or chemistry. However, they all were influenced by computer science at some point in their lives. Many of the guests had very interesting hobbies, including playing musical instruments, hosting shows on the local radio station, running marathons, and even performing in dance and music festivals! They all had very interesting stories to share about how they got interested in the field and how computer science has helped in their day-to-day lives. After hearing these stories, the girls had several role models to look up to, and most of them later indicated in their WTP exit surveys that this experience positively changed their attitudes toward computer science.

Emphasizing the Importance of Female Presence in Science and Technology Innovation

We also wanted to make it clear to the students that computer science is now a discipline that is playing a key role in invention and creation across all sorts of disciplines from biological science to film and animation. This expansion of the field of computer science and how critical it is across all disciplines increasingly makes it more meaningful to study computer science and related technologies. As computers have become integrated into other disciplines like digital media, including music and film, the geek image has shifted from that of a socially isolated person to include a chic geek image where it can be cool to know about computers. So, the students' perception towards computer science as just "coding" is no longer applicable. Thus, the "geek" image is improving. Movements such as the "#ILookLikeAnEngineer" and "#ILookLikeAProgrammer" hashtag on social media introduce women who contribute to the society in meaningful ways as computer scientists and engineers (Guynn, 2015).

In the classroom, we discussed some examples of the dangers of not having enough female participation in technical roles. For example, some early voice-recognition systems were calibrated to typical male voices. As a result, women's voices were literally unheard. Many of the computer games were designed to cater to young males, and it would be difficult to find games that are equally amenable to both genders. Similar cases are found in many other industries. For instance, a predominantly male group of engineers tailored the first generation of automotive airbags to adult male bodies, resulting in avoidable deaths for women and children

(Margolis & Fisher, 2003). Discussing such imbalances in gender in fields that are near and dear to our lives can be detrimental to our society, and the students seem to understand the broader implications. With a more diverse workforce that includes equal participation from women, scientific and technological products, services, and solutions are likely to be better designed.

Effective Teaching Methodologies

Show and Tell

We wanted to teach the students that programming isn't just about using a particular language. The 1972 Turing award winner Edsger Dijkstra had once said "teaching code to programmers is like teaching how to use telescopes to astronomers" (Haines, 1993). The syntax is vitally important but utterly trivial. Therefore, to help the students understand that computer science is not about typing at the computer all day, or learning some esoteric programming language, we utilized several props in the classroom to convey the message that a computer language is merely a tool. We brought in things like a canvas and a paintbrush to the classroom. Just as these are tools for an artist to paint an imagery that was conceptualized in her mind, the computer is a tool to either express an idea or solve a problem that will be difficult without the tool (i.e., the computer). This kind of "show and tell" approach was very effective throughout the program, as it was very exciting to have physical objects that would not normally belong in a computer science lecture room.

Classroom Discussions

Since many of the concepts in computer science cannot be easily demonstrated using the above-mentioned show and tell approach, we thought of filling in the gap with the day-to-day activities the students engage in using computers. For example, for the very first lesson where algorithms were introduced, we asked the students to get into groups and discuss what things they do in their day-to-day activities that use a computer, what kind of things are easy for a computer to do but hard for a human to do, and vice versa. The students came up with examples such as "web search," "email," and "Facebook." Going by their interest areas, we tried to explain how computer scientists have made those services work. Search engines such as Google use algorithms to put a set of search results into order, so that more often than not the result we're looking for is at the top of the front page. Likewise, the Facebook news feed is derived from our friends' status updates and other activity, but it only shows that activity which the algorithm thinks we will be most interested in seeing. The recommendations we get from Amazon, Netflix, and eBay are algorithmically generated, based in part on what other people are interested in. Given the extent to which so much of our lives are affected by algorithms, we iterated the importance of learning algorithms, so that they can also create a novel algorithm that can help solve a problem.

Based on some of the initial answers we got, we realized that the students thought computers are only those devices that have screens, keyboards, and mice in addition to the microprocessor, memory, etc. They did not know other household devices that they had access to, such as calculators, smartphones, cars, and Roombas as "computers". Therefore, we wanted to illustrate the ubiquity of computer science. The calculator app on our smartphones is able to perform complex calculations that would take a normal human a considerable amount of time to compute, the GPS in our cars is able to tell us directions, and there are other such examples where the computing capabilities that are already readily available to the students are easily overlooked: Computers in our cars help us with cruise control and to display information based on the inputs to its sensors; Roombas in our houses clean the floor in an autonomous manner without any human intervention whatsoever; gaming consoles are able to load the programs and respond to the inputs from the joysticks or even use our body movements in the case of innovations like Kinect.

Discussion on these everyday-computing devices proved to be a very good exercise and a good entry point to explain what computer programs are capable of. All such devices that have a computer inside need to be programmed using an algorithm. Even a simple application such as the calculator needs the user to understand and interpret the problem before the calculator can help out with the arithmetic.

Examples First, Theory Later

Some research studies have found that men outscore women by a medium to large margin in the area of spatial skills, specifically on measures of mental rotation (Linn & Petersen, 1985) (Voyer, Voyer, & Bryden, 1995). Well-developed three-dimensional spatial visualization skills are a must for subfields of computer science such as robotics and computer graphics. However, studies have found that spatial skills are not innate but developed (Sorby & Baartmans, 2000). Lego Mindstorms where students can take things apart and put them back together again and do visual block programming can greatly help develop these essential spatial skills. In our experience, many computer science programs often focus on technical aspects of programming early in the curriculum with a strong focus on theory and without much focus on the applications of the concepts. This can be a deterrent to students, who may be interested in broader, multidisciplinary applications. Thus, during the course of WTP, we always made it a point to talk about the applications; no matter how trivial they might be related to the topic, the students are learning.

Teaching Algorithms

When delivering the lessons beyond these introductory concepts, we always made it a point to start the lecture with a fun activity related to the lesson. For example, to illustrate what an algorithm is like and how they can get started to conceptualize algorithms, we asked a volunteer to explain how to write a program to make a peanut butter and jelly sandwich. We brought the ingredients necessary to make the sandwich to the class; and a staff member was acting as the computer, and the volunteer was the programmer. The student volunteer had to give the staff member the exact steps as to how to make the sandwich. The end goal was the delicious sandwich.

The instructions have to be "programmed" in a certain order, and if it is not in the desired order, the computer (i.e., the staff member) will not perform the actions. For example, if the student said, "spread jelly on bread," and at that time the jelly jar was not open, the staff member will not perform any activity since the jelly was not reachable. Instead, the staff member will make a funny face to indicate the error. Once the student realized the mistake and mentioned "open jelly jar" before "spread jelly on bread," the staff member would perform the activities, and the volunteer got the peanut butter and jelly sandwich as reward. Even though this was a very simple example, students enjoyed this exercise very much, and they really got the idea that writing a program is like writing a recipe and can be very relatable to the activities we perform in our day-to-day lives.

Teaching Loops and Conditionals

Another such activity involved marching as a preamble to loops and conditionals, where a student had to follow a path through the classroom to reach a certain destination based on the instructions given. Then the class was asked to come up with the pseudocode to illustrate what the student volunteer performed. This resulted in a very engaging atmosphere, where students were able to conceptualize the program, and also were able to discuss their code in a collective manner.

Teaching Functions

We had the most interesting set of challenges when teaching functions. Some of the popular mistakes that students made were confusing the "return" statement with "print" (in python), not understanding that a function remembers where it came from and goes back there when it is done, and that a function can be used to encapsulate blocks of code. Many of these concepts were a bit abstract for many of the students. With an example involving dessert recipes, we were able to illustrate that; for example, a chef can delegate different parts of a dessert (say, tiramisu()) to other worker chefs. These worker chefs can act as routines that create subparts of the dessert like ladyfingers() and cream(). If the chef wants to make another dessert such as ice cream() or parfait(), she can call the same cream() function that was used in tiramisu(). Although it was tempting to introduce things like stacks when teaching functions, we thought that it may be a bit too overwhelming for these beginner level students at WTP. It should be introduced only at an advanced level or if a student questions about the inner workings of function calls.

Teaching Sorting

For the lesson on sorting, going with the same approach of a fun activity before class, we asked several students to line up and asked the rest of the class to come up with a way to order them according to their height. To our surprise, the students came up with bubble and selection sort algorithms by themselves! We also utilized online videos available on different sort techniques before diving into the nuts and bolts of implementing the algorithms. Visuals are powerful tools in the classroom, and there is no better way to teach such abstract concepts.

Live Examples

In order to complete the homework assignments, the students had to use Linux machines. But many of them were not familiar with the operating system. Therefore, the teaching staff decided to do a live demonstration of the system. The staff member would perform something, and the students were expected to follow. We also did a live debugging session during class, highlighting the instructor's thought process that went in to fixing the problem and also showing how to use the tools that are at the disposal to them.

Let's Build a Game!

While many parents often worry about recreational "screen time", some educators now believe that gaming could be a way to get girls interested in coding and even to increase the numbers of girls in computer science. Therefore, we decided to have the students implement a Tetris game for the final project. Even though the task of implementing a game seems daunting, most of the components that were already required were completed in previous lab sessions. However, since the project may seem overly ambitious especially given all the difficulties some of the students were having during the previous lab sessions, we told them to work in pairs for the project. All the groups had a working game in the end and had time to play with it in class. Pretty much all of them were excited to have the working product in the end.

Results

Through several classroom activities, we managed to teach some of the core principles of computational thinking that many of the girls already knew by intuition: Logic is essential for predicting and analyzing things we want to be computed, algorithms to make steps and rules about executing an idea, decomposition to breaking down a problem to manageable chunks, patterns for spotting and using similarities, abstraction for removing unnecessary details from a given problem and generalizing to fit a broader class of problems, and, finally, evaluation to verify whether the solution worked for a given problem or not (Wing, 2006).

Since the start of MIT WTP in 2002, over 500 students have participated in the program so far. According to the WTP Director and WTP-EECS Track Coordinator, Cynthia Skier, of the 431 students who have participated in WTP over the years, over 64 % are in a field of engineering or computer science, while another 21 % are in math or science fields. Furthermore, the numbers from the 2015 cohort show increased enthusiasm in computer science toward the end of the program. The students were asked about their perception toward computer science and STEM in general, both before and after the commencement of WTP. The percentage of students definitely planning to take college classes in computer science moved from 38 % before starting WTP to 80 % after completing WTP. 60 % listed CS as a probable college major in the exit surveys, which was a 50 % increase over the numbers in the entrance surveys. Some of the answers to qualitative questions in the exit survey indicated that the students got a better understanding and a better outlook on CS after the program. Many students liked the lunch series where we brought in female role models to talk to the students, the activities conducted before the lessons, and the final project where the students had to build a functioning computer game.

This upward trend in girls' interest in computer science is evident at the national level as well. In 2013 girls only made up 18.5 % of A.P. computer science test takers nationwide[2]. In three states, no girls took the test at all. During the recent years, these numbers have been growing steadily. In 2014 25 % of the A.P. computer science test takers were female[3], and in 2015 that number increased to 27%[4]. While these numbers are not representative of the population, many efforts by educators and nonprofit organizations seem to have made positive impact in making computer science attractive to girls. Over the years, WTP has produced many shining stars who were equipped with the necessary computational thinking skills. One of the best examples is Tamara Broderick, who in 2002 completed WTP as a high school student and in 2015 returned to MIT as an assistant professor[5].

---

[2] http://research.collegeboard.org/programs/ap/data/participation/ap-2015.

[3] http://research.collegeboard.org/programs/ap/data/archived/ap-2014.

[4] http://research.collegeboard.org/programs/ap/data/participation/ap-2015.

[5] https://www.eecs.mit.edu/news-events/media/tamara-broderick-woman-technology.

Conclusion

Utilizing computational thinking approaches coupled with strong role models can especially be useful for getting young girls interested in computer science. It is our belief that girls are easily discouraged from computer science due to many reasons that are not related to their personal capabilities. Even though the girls have many computational thinking skills, they are either not aware of them or hold themselves to very high standards.

From our experience with WTP, the approaches to instill computational thinking in high school girls who have not been exposed to computer science previously are numerous: First, the students should be guided in an encouraging manner with mentorship, fun activities, and ample computer science related exercises. Second, they should be encouraged to tinker with a solution by iterating and playing around with multiple solutions ready to throw away any solution if needed. Third, the debugging process should be mastered, where the focus is to find and fix the errors introduced from the creation and tinkering processes, without getting frustrated or losing sight of the end goal. Thus, a collaborative and supportive environment with plenty of guidance can help gain the necessary skills to think like a computer scientist and achieve one's full potential.

References

Association for Computing Machinery; WGBH Educational Foundation (2009). *New Image for Computing Report.*

Banaji, M. R., & Greenwald, A. G. (2013). *Blindspot: Hidden biases of good people.* New York: Delacorte Press.

Correll, S. J. (2004). Constraints into preferences: Gender, status, and emerging career aspirations. *American Sociological Review, 69*, 93.

Guynn, J. (2015). *#ILookLikeAnEngineer challenges stereotypes. USA TODAY* Published: August 4, 2015, http://www.usatoday.com/story/tech/2015/08/03/isis-wenger-tech-sexism-stereotypes-ilooklikeanenginer/31088413/.

Haines, M. D. (1993). Distributed runtime support for task and data management. Ph.D. Dissertation, Colorado State University.

Hill, C., Corbett, C., & Rose, A. S. (2010). *Why so few? Women in science, technology, engineering, and mathematics.* Washington, DC: AAUW.

Johnson, D. W., & Johnson, R. T. (1987). *Learning together and alone: Cooperative, competitive, and individualistic learning.* Englewood Cliffs, NJ: Prentice-Hall.

Joyce, B. A., & Farenga, S. J. (2000). Young girls in science: Academic ability, perceptions and future participation in science. *Roeper Review, 22*, 261.

Lapan, R. T., Adams, A., Turner, S., & Hinkelman, J. M. (2000). Seventh graders' vocational interest and efficacy expectation patterns. *Journal of Career Development, 26*, 215.

Linn, M. C., & Petersen, A. C. (1985). Emergence and characterization of sex differences in spatial ability: A meta-analysis. *Child Development, 56*, 1479.

Luce, S. A., Servon, C., Sherbin, L. J., Shiller, L., Sosnovich, P., & Sumberg, E. (2008). The athena factor: Reversing the brain drain in science, engineering and technology. *Harvard Business Review Research Report.*

Margolis, J., & Fisher, A. (2003). *Unlocking the clubhouse*. Cambridge, MA: MIT.
Pajares, F. (2005). Gender differences in mathematics self-efficacy beliefs. In *Gender differences in mathematics: An integrative psychological approach*. New York: Cambridge University Press.
Plant, E. A., Baylor, A. L., Doerr, C. E., & Rosenberg-Kima, R. B. (2009). Changing middleschool students' attitudes and performance regarding engineering with computerbased social models. *Computers and Education, 53*, 209.
Sorby, S. A., & Baartmans, B. J. (2000). The development and assessment of a course for enhancing the 3-D spatial visualization skills of first year engineering students. *Journal of Engineering Education, 89*, 301.
Turner, S. L. (2008). Gender differences in Holland vocational personality types: Implications for school counselors. *Professional School Counseling, 11*, 317.
Voyer, D., Voyer, S., & Bryden, M. P. (1995). Magnitude of sex differences in spatial abilities: A meta-analysis and consideration of critical variables. *Psychological Bulletin, 117*, 250.
Wing, J. M. (2006). Computational thinking. *Communications of the ACM, 49*, 33–35.

Understanding African-American Students' Problem-Solving Ability in the Precalculus and Advanced Placement Computer Science Classroom

Cristal Jones-Harris and Gregory Chamblee

Abstract This study was conducted to assess African-American student's problem-solving strategies and solutions between similar mathematics and computer science tasks. Six African-American participants comprised of five high school students and one high school graduate who had taken or jointly enrolled in precalculus and AP computer science courses participated in the study. Data collected were precalculus and computer science problem solutions, think-aloud and retrospective interviews, problem-solving strategies used to solve problems, and analytic scoring rubric scale scores. Student problem-solving strategies when engaged in solving precalculus and computer science problems were coded by the researcher and co-rater to determine inter-rater agreement. Student precalculus and computer science solutions were graded using an analytic scoring rubric scale to determine levels of problem-solving ability. Results found that students did not exhibit the same problem-solving strategies in both contexts. Implications of this finding between mathematical and computer science problem-solving are presented.

Keywords Computer programming • Computer science • Computational thinking • Problem-solving

C. Jones-Harris (✉)
Evaluation Manager (Paragon TEC, Inc.), NASA Glenn Research Center, Office of Education, 3740 Carnegie Avenue, Cleveland, OH 44114, USA
e-mail: charris@paragon-tec.com; cristal.harris@nasa.gov

G. Chamblee
Georgia Southern University, Statesboro, GA 30458, USA
e-mail: gchamblee@georgiasouthern.edu

P.J. Rich, C.B. Hodges (eds.), *Emerging Research, Practice, and Policy on Computational Thinking*, Educational Communications and Technology: Issues and Innovations, DOI 10.1007/978-3-319-52691-1_3

Introduction

Problem-solving ability is essential in gaining mathematical understanding (Seeley, 2005). Exposure to mathematical problem-solving tasks increases students' metacognitive ability or knowledge about their own thinking coupled with making effective strategy choices. Metacognitive processes in precalculus and an alternative curriculum, computer science, were identified to see if a relationship exists in developing mathematical problem-solving ability. When students are engaged in the active process of why certain problem-solving strategies are appropriate or inappropriate [metacognition], they are analyzing mathematical problem-solving techniques (Siegler, 2003). "Analytical thinking is among the central goals of mathematics education, in part because it is an inherently constructive process" (Siegler, 2003, p. 299). Computational thinking have a relationship to mathematical thinking as it uses analytical thinking processes to solve a problem (Wing, 2008).

The core element of computational thinking is to develop or gain abstract knowledge. "Abstractions are the mental tools of computing" (Wing, 2008, p. 3718). Through this analytical thinking process of building abstract intelligence or abstraction, computational thinking is defining the right abstraction: what learning has emphasis (foreground) and what tools or mediums are used to deliver the learning or content (background). Abstraction is defined as layers: the "layer of interest and the layer below" (Wing, 2008, p. 3718). Once the right abstraction is gained through the process of mental math, computational thinking and mathematical understanding are developed.

Mathematical understanding, known as "mental math," develops conceptual ability (Seeley, 2005). Conceptual ability is a metacognitive process where concept attainment and concept formation meet. Conceptual ability occurs when students use metacognitive thinking processes in a problem-solving task. Metacognition is intelligent thinking that occurs during planning and monitoring of a person's actions. "Metacognitive thought is thought that can be directed by the thinker that is conscious, intentional, intelligent, logically or empirically falsifiable and verbally communicable" (Fox & Riconscente, 2008, p. 378).

Computing concepts, such as computer science, are used to interpret those deeper abstractions that allows communication capabilities such as representing and processing data through use of a computer (Wing, 2008) and is part of our metacognitive ability. Learning computer science using an object-oriented programming language, such as Java, also is a process of creating increasingly more complex conceptual structures (conceptual ability) to solve a problem (Blume & Schoen, 1988). Zahorik (1997) posits "problem-solving tasks are critical to the growth of student [programming] constructions" (p. 32). Students learn new programming constructs with embedded domain-specific content, and based on the ability to create executable programs, students learn the problem-solving strategies as accommodating new knowledge and as the process of developing mathematics problem-solving ability. This construction is through a process of concept attainment. Concept attainment occurs through classifying and categorizing objects.

Students make connections with prior domain knowledge and classify which object-oriented programming constructs are needed to create a program. Prior knowledge is categorized with programming knowledge to develop programming instructions, which forms an executable program application or software. Concept formation is the programming instructions (classified domain knowledge categorized with programming constructs) needed to create an executable program. Studies in mathematics problem-solving and computer programming have identified similar problem-solving strategies when students are engaged in a mathematics or computer science task. Studies involving African-American students have found metacognitive and problem-solving ability is best developed through analytical thinking processes (Berry, 2003; Malloy, 1994; Siegler, 2003). Therefore, to increase African-Americans' problem-solving ability is to promote their analytical ability. The research questions for this study were:

1. What problem-solving strategies do African-American students who have taken or are jointly enrolled in precalculus and AP computer science course demonstrate when solving precalculus problems?
2. What problem-solving strategies do African-American students who have taken or are jointly enrolled in precalculus and AP computer science courses demonstrate when solving computer science problems?
3. Are there relationships between the problem-solving strategies African-American students who have taken or are jointly enrolled in precalculus and AP computer science use to solve precalculus and computer science problems?

Literature Review

The National Council of Teachers of Mathematics (NCTM) (1980) *Agenda for Action* publication posited that the mathematics curriculum be organized around problem-solving. The National Council of Teachers of Mathematics (2000) *Principles and Standards for School Mathematics* [PSSM] noted problem-solving as one of the five overarching process standards for all school mathematics (National Council of Mathematics, 2000, p. 30). PSSM defined problem-solving as:

> [E]ngaging in a task for which the solution method is not known in advance. In order to find a solution, students must draw on their knowledge, and through this process, they will often develop new mathematical understandings. Solving problems is not only a goal of learning mathematics but also a major means of doing so. (p. 52)

Problem-solving is the course of action of finding an unknown and using problem-solving behavior in developing an answer. Problem-solving is a form of human intelligence using procedures, or a "scheme of well-related operations" (Polya, 1962, p. 122) as a series of organized thoughts and processes. Polya (1957) posits solving a problem is a four-stage process: understanding the problem, devising a plan, carrying out the plan, and looking back (Polya, 1957). Understanding the problem is obtaining mathematical knowledge or facts. However, devising a plan is fundamental to determining which method or strategies are appropriate in obtaining a solution (Polya, 1957). Planning is fundamental to the problem-solving process. Without knowing what methods or strategies to use to solve a problem, an individual lacks the planning stage of problem-solving and may be unable to produce an accurate solution (Rudder, 2006).

Bruner, Goodnow, and Austin (1962) define problem-solving behavior as the processes of thinking. Thinking is carried out through classification or categorizing knowledge construction known as conceptual thinking. To think conceptually begins with a process of classifying objects by placing objects into a category or finding connections of these objects having relational attributes. Classifying an object with another object is finding criteria or defining attributes that groups the object into a category. Classifying is the process of categorization. Devising strategies is the nature of the process as well as strategic cues. These facets describe problem-solving or decision-making behavior. The process of categorization defines all cognitive ability (Bruner, Goodnow, & Austin, 1962).

Metacognition is intelligent thinking that occurs during planning and monitoring of a person's actions. Garofalo and Lester (1985) defined two aspects of metacognition: (1) knowledge of cognition and (2) regulation of cognition. Knowledge of cognition is a person's knowledge about the cognitive abilities, processes, and resources relating to the performance of specific cognitive tasks. Knowledge of cognition is redefined as a set of beliefs and derived from facts or nonfacts. These beliefs are known as subjective knowledge. Knowledge of cognition is categorized based on the influence of person, task, or strategy factors on performance. The person category is the belief about oneself and others as cognitive beings. The task category deals with requirements, scope, and conditions of tasks' and their difficulty level. Strategies include "having knowledge of general and specific cognitive strategies along with an awareness of potential usefulness for approaching and executing certain tasks" (Garofalo & Lester, 1985, pp. 164–165). Using rote and procedural strategies does involve cognition but not metacognition.

Research on African-American students and problem-solving has produced several findings. Malloy (1994) found a majority of the problem-solving behaviors (strategies) eighth-grade African-Americans exhibited were the backward strategy, list or chart, and pattern strategy, drawing a picture or making a list or chart, disregard unnecessary data, and logical deduction. Few strategies student exhibited were guess and check, forward strategy, and the algebraic method.

Berry (2003) found African-American students' learning preference is relational understanding. The relational style of learning is synonymous to African-Americans' cultural style, such as the "freedom of movement, variety, creativity, divergent thinking, inductive reasoning and focus on people" (Berry, 2003, p. 246). Siegler (2003) found African-American students' mathematical problem-solving ability can be improved by increasing their "metacognitive or knowledge about their own thinking" (p. 294).

There have been several studies linking computer programming with mathematical problem-solving processes or strategies. Wells (1981) sought to identify similar processes and strategies in programming [BASIC (Beginners All-purpose Symbolic Instruction Code)] and mathematical problem-solving by observing the participants' behaviors. Wells found strategies such as trial and error or guess and check, recall-related problems, and looking back strategies were prevalent in computer programming. Blume and Schoen (1988) researched the problem-solving processes of eighth-grade programmers [BASIC (Beginners All-purpose Symbolic Instruction Code)] and nonprogrammers. Blume and Schoen found programmers and nonprogrammers did not have statistically significant differences in the planning process and frequent or effectiveness in utilizing variables and equations in obtaining a correct solution. Willis (1999) conducted a quantitative studies to investigate whether object-oriented programming had a higher influence of problem-solving ability than structured languages. Willis found increased problem-solving ability is linked to object-oriented programming (OOP). Stockwell (2002) conducted a quantitative study to see if undergraduate college students who learn computer programming using an object-oriented programming software, C+, had gains in mathematics skills. Stockwell found a strong relationship between learning C programming and developing mathematics skills.

Participants

The participants in the study were five African-American high school students and one high school graduate, totaling six students, enrolled in an urban school in a suburban area in Georgia. The school has a diverse student body, with an 89 % African-American student population. The first author was the instructor of the AP computer science class and the researcher for this study. There were a total of 11 students in the AP computer science course. Students were selected if they were jointly enrolled in an AP computer science and an advanced mathematics course (precalculus) to assess levels of problem-solving ability. The students' ages ranged from 16 to 19 years old. Participants [all names have been changed] are further described in Table 1:

Table 1 Participant information

Name	Description
Jay	Male senior jointly enrolled in precalculus and AP computer science
Diane	Female senior jointly enrolled in precalculus and AP computer science
John	Male senior jointly enrolled in precalculus and AP computer science
Nancy	Female senior jointly enrolled in precalculus and AP computer science
Donald	Former male student. During the previous year, Donald was a senior and took precalculus and AP computer science courses concurrently. Currently majoring in computer engineering
Belinda	Female senior jointly enrolled in precalculus and AP computer science

Methods

This study used a mixed-methods research design. Precalculus problem-solving activities were obtained from the text, *Advanced mathematical concepts: Precalculus with applications* (Holliday, Cuevas, McClure, Carter & Marks, 2001), used to teach the course. The computer science problems were obtained from the texts, *Java software solutions for AP computer science* Lewis, Loftus, & Cocking, 2007) and *A guide to programming in Java* (Brown, 2007), used to teach the course. Students solved two comparable precalculus mathematics problems and two computer science problems regarding quadratic equations and trigonometric ratios shown in Appendix 1. Two certified mathematics teachers and two university professors reviewed the precalculus problems, and two computer science experts assessed the computer science problems to determine relevance to course objectives and correlation between task expectations. A problem-solving strategy classification list based on Wells (1981), Blume and Schoen (1988), Malloy (1994), Rudder (2006), and Sarver's (2006) problem-solving frameworks was developed to code students' problem-solving strategies when solving mathematics or computer science (Appendix 2). An analytic problem-solving scoring scale was adapted from the books *How to Evaluate Progress in Problem-Solving* by Charles, Lester, and O'Daffer (1987) and *Mathematics Assessment: A Practical Handbook for Grades 9–12* by the National Council of Teachers of Mathematics (1999). The analytic scoring scales from the texts were blended and reorganized based on Polya's four-step process by using the understanding a problem, devising a plan (planning a solution), carrying out a plan (implementing a strategy), and looking back (getting an answer) categories (Appendix 3). A retrospective interview protocol was developed based on Malloy's (1994) protocol (Appendix 4).

Problem-solving sessions were conducted in a private office. A digital video camera with audio capabilities was positioned in the office to provide full, body-length view of the student. A desktop computer was setup for students to complete computer science problems. Math problems were documented using a pencil and paper format. Students were informed of the presence of a video camera and were asked to pay no attention to the equipment. The problem-solving activity comprised of two sessions. Session One consisted of a think-aloud protocol session solving precalculus problems followed by a retrospective interview. Session Two consisted of a think-aloud protocol session solving computer science problems using Java followed by a retrospective interview. The first author and a co-rater viewed the videotapes of each session separately to identify students' behaviors to map their problem-solving processes using the problem-solving strategies from the strategy list. Retrospective interviews were used to code additional strategies or thought processes that may not have been verbalized by the student during the think-aloud sessions. The frequency of problem-solving strategies within each phase was calculated. To determine inter-rater agreement of problem-solving strategies, the researcher and co-rater used the videotape transcriptions to code strategies. Differences in coding were discussed and resolved between the first author and co-rater for coding precision. For instance, during the think-aloud session, if a student was reading aloud or went back to the problem sheet to reread the problem statement, the code of "A1" (reading the problem silent or aloud) was mapped as a strategy. Mathematics and computer science teachers graded student participants' precalculus and computer science solutions using the researchers' analytic scoring scale, respectively.

Results

Jay utilized a high frequency of problem-solving strategies and high phase score in the understanding the problem, planning a process, and implementing the plan phases when solving precalculus and computer science problems. For precalculus problem #1, Jay utilized the understanding the problem (orientation process) and planning the process (organization process) phases and had a high problem-solving ability. For precalculus problem #2, Jay utilized the understanding the problem phase (orientation process) and had a low problem-solving ability. For computer science problem #1, Jay utilized the implementing the plan phases (execution process) and had low problem-solving ability.

For computer science problem #2, Jay utilized the implementing the plan phase (execution process) and had average problem-solving ability.

Belinda had a high frequency of problem-solving strategies and high phase score in the understanding the problem, planning a process, implementing the plan, and looking back phases when solving precalculus and computer science problems. For precalculus problem #1, Belinda utilized the understanding the problem (orientation process), planning the process (organization process), and looking back phases (verification process) and had average problem-solving ability. For precalculus problem #2, Belinda utilized the understanding the problem (orientation process), planning the process (organization process), and looking back phases (verification process) and had average problem-solving ability. For computer science problem #1, Belinda utilized the implementing the plan phase (execution process) and had high problem-solving ability. For computer science problem #2, Belinda utilized the implementing the plan phase (execution process) and had average problem-solving ability.

Donald had a high frequency of problem-solving strategies and high phase score in the planning a process and implementing the plan phases when solving precalculus and computer science problems. For precalculus problem #1, Donald had no frequency of problem-solving strategies and had low problem-solving ability. For precalculus problem #2, Donald utilized the planning the process phase (organization process) and had low problem-solving ability. For computer science problem #1, Donald utilized implementing the plan phase (execution process) and had average problem-solving ability. For computer science problem #2, Donald had implementing the plan phase (execution process) and had low problem-solving ability.

Diane had a high frequency of problem-solving strategies and high phase score in the understanding the problem and implementing the plan phases when solving precalculus and computer science problems. For precalculus problem #1, Diane utilized the understanding the problem phase (orientation process) and had low problem-solving ability. For precalculus problem #2, Diane utilized the implementing the plan phase (execution process) and had average problem-solving ability. For computer science problem #1, Diane utilized the implementing the plan phase (execution process) and had low problem-solving ability. For computer science problem #2, Diane utilized the implementing the plan phase (execution process) and had low problem-solving ability.

Nancy had a high frequency of problem-solving strategies and high phase score in the understanding the problem, planning a process, implementing the plan, and looking back phases when solving precalculus and computer science problems. For precalculus problem #1, Nancy utilized the planning the process phase (organization process) and had high problem-solving ability. For precalculus problem #2, Nancy utilized the planning the process phase (organization process) and had high problem-solving ability. For computer science problem #1, Nancy utilized the understanding the problem (orientation process) and implementing the plan phase (execution process) and had low problem-solving ability. For computer science problem #2, Nancy utilized the understanding the problem (orientation process), planning the process (organization process), and looking back phases (verification process) and had high problem-solving ability.

John had a high frequency of problem-solving strategies and high phase score in the understanding the problem, planning a process, implementing the plan, and looking back phases when solving precalculus and computer science problems. For precalculus problem #1, John utilized the understanding the problem phase (orientation process) and had low problem-solving ability. For precalculus problem #2, John utilized the understanding the problem (orientation process) and planning the process phases (organization process) and had high problem-solving ability. For computer science problem #1, John utilized the looking back phase (verification process) and had high problem-solving ability. For computer science problem #2, John utilized the implementing the plan phase (execution process) and had average problem-solving ability.

Results confirmed that students who utilized all four problem-solving phases or episodes in sequence had average to high problem-solving ability. Students who utilized the first phase of problem-solving and understanding the problem had low problem-solving ability. Students who utilized the second problem-solving phase, planning the process or fourth phase, and verifying the outcomes of the plan had high problem-solving ability. Students who utilized the problem-solving phase out of sequence or had a missing problem-solving phase within a mathematics or computer science problem-solving task had low or average problem-solving ability. Students who utilized the organization episode or planning the process phase within the sequence of problem-solving phases or as a sole phase during the mathematics or computer science tasks obtained high levels of problem-solving ability. Devising a plan, which is fundamental to continuing the problem-solving task, involves the utilization of metacognitive abilities such as developing understanding and setting up alternatives or possibilities.

Results found that computer science problems allowed students to engage and maximize mathematical problem-solving activity. Students engaged in solving computer science problems took long periods of time to obtain a solution. Computer science problems ranged from 30 to 90 min to solve. Computer science problems were open ended by deciding which mathematics content knowledge and which Java programming construct to use to obtain a correct solution. Students' computer science solutions were varied in procedure or method used in solving the problem. Students utilized the highest frequency of problem-solving strategies in all four problem-solving phases, particularly in the implementing the plan phase or execution phase. Students are engaged in high levels of mathematical problem-solving activity using a cognitive process, execution, which is regulation of behavior to conform to plans. Execution strategies are identified in the implementing the plan phase and were utilized most by students in this study when solving computer science problems.

Students reached average or high problem-solving ability in the "C" quadrant or implementing the plan phase. This is equivalent to Polya's carrying out the plan problem-solving phase or broad category of execution on the metacognitive framework. Implementation is a cognitive skill that allows one to execute a strategy based on his or her understanding, analysis, and planning. Students must have proficiency in the "A" and "B" quadrants to move forward to execution process or implementing the plan phase. Table 2 shows the level of problem-solving ability based on Polya's four steps of problem-solving aligned with the problem-solving process when solving two precalculus (P1, P2) and two computer science problems (CS1, CS2).

Conclusions

Since the progressive movement in the 1960s, education reforms involved "a 'thinking' curriculum aimed at deep understanding" (Darling-Hammond, 1996, p. 8). Dewey ideals in the twentieth century are similar to the computer era of the twenty-first century (Darling Hammond, 1996). Problem-solving ability is a constructivist activity involving metacognition, which is individualized learning and self-regulated behavior of one's control of their thoughts and actions. Metacognition is intelligent thinking that occurs during planning and monitoring of a person's actions. Students solved precalculus and computer science problems and were engaged in varying levels of metacognitive ability. The National Council of Teachers of Mathematics stated that "Conceptual understanding is an essential component of the knowledge needed to deal with novel problems and solutions" (National Council of Teachers of Mathematics, 2000, p. 20). Similarly, computational thinking "complements and combines mathematical [and engineering] thinking" (Wing, 2006, p. 35). When engaged in computer science, it inherits mathematical thinking concepts usually found in all sciences where the foundations rely on mathematics (Wing, 2006). Computer science and mathematics complement one another. Data indicate that (1)

Table 2 Level and range of problem-solving ability, cognitive ability, and metacognitive ability when solving precalculus and computer science problems

Student levels of problem-solving ability	Orientation Episode 1: Reading and understanding the problem (Cognitive)	Organization Episode 2: Planning of behavior and choice of actions (Metacognitive)	Execution Episode 3: Implementing (cognitive)	Verification Episode 4: Verifying (metacognitive)	No frequency or did not solve problem
Polya's four steps of problem-solving	Understanding the problem	Devising a plan	Carrying out the plan	Looking back	
Low	Jay(P2) Diane(P1) John(P1) Nancy(CS1)	Jay(P2) Donald(P2)	Jay(P2, CS1) Donald(CS1) Diane(CS1, CS2) Nancy(CS1)	John(CS1)	Donald(P1)
Average	Belinda(P1, P2)	Belinda(P1, P2)	Belinda(P1, P2) Diane(P2) Jay(CS1) Belinda(CS2) Donald(CS1) John(CS2)	Belinda(P1, P2)	
High	Jay(P1) John(P1) Nancy(CS2)	Jay(P1) Nancy(P1, P2) John(P1) Nancy(CS2)	Belinda(CS1)	Nancy(CS2)	

computer science develops conceptual ability through knowledge construction of object-oriented programming concepts taught in AP computer science; (2) solving precalculus problems utilizes regulation of cognition or making effective decision-making strategies to obtain a correct solution; and (3) computer science and precalculus complement one another by developing similar metacognition strategies needed to solve both mathematics and computer science tasks. These findings are similar to Wells (1981), Willis (1999), and Malloy (1994) findings. In general, precalculus concepts enable students to have a knowledge base of mathematics formulas and choose an appropriate and effective strategy with objectives, known as the planning stage or devising a plan during the problem-solving task. Precalculus mathematics concepts allow effective strategy choices and decision-making known as regulation of cognition, which is the second aspect of metacognition. Recommendations based on this study are:

- Encouraging African-American students to enroll in computer science courses has the potential to enhance problem-solving skills in mathematics courses.
- School administrators can utilize the computer science curriculum as an alternative to mathematics support or mathematics laboratory courses to engage students in problem-solving tasks.
- Mathematics lab assignments infused with computer science curriculum have the potential to promote mathematics problem-solving strategies.
- African-American students' problem-solving ability can be improved by increasing their metacognitive ability through problem-solving and knowledge about their own thinking (Siegler, 2003) via computer science classes.

These recommendations are systemic reform approaches to "the advancement of teaching" (Darling-Hammond, 1996, p. 7), to look beyond how students learn according to the standards or how we assess and evaluate based on rote learning. We need to offer approaches based on students' needs and foster personalized learning to develop intellectual knowledge aimed at strategies inclusive of diverse learners (Darling-Hammond, 1996). Thinking or intellectual curriculum can be accomplished through computational thinking, where metacognitive skills are practiced, cognitive thinking is developed, and mathematics problem-solving activity is actualized.

Appendix 1

Precalculus problems	Computer science problems
1. State the number of complex roots of the equation $18x^2 + 3x - 1 = 0$. Then find the roots (Holliday et al., 2001, p. 207)	1. *Create a Quadratic Equation application that gives the solution to any quadratic equation.* The application should prompt the user for values for a, b, and c ($ax^2 + bx + c = 0$) and then display the roots, if any. Use the quadratic equation. The application output should look similar to: Enter value for a: Enter value for b: Enter value for c: The roots are: (Brown, 2007, p. 126)
2. The sine of an acute <R of a right triangle is 3/7. Find the values of the reciprocal trigonometric ratios for this angle (Holliday et al., 2001, p. 289)	2. *Create a TrigFunctions application that displays trigonometric and reciprocal ratios given the following conditions:* The sine of an acute <R of a right triangle is 3/7. Find the values of the reciprocal trigonometric ratios for this angle. The application should display output similar to: The angle in degrees: Sine: Cosine: Tangent: The values in radians are: The Math library (Java) provides methods for performing trigonometric functions Class Math (java.lang.Math) Methods sin (double angle)—returns the sine of angle, where angle is in radians cos (double angle)—returns the cos of angle, where angle is in radians tan (double angle)—returns the tan of angle, where angle is in radians. to Radians (double deg) converts degrees to radians (Brown, 2007, p. 128)

Appendix 2

Episode 1 strategies/indicators (A) [reading and understanding phase]	Episode 2 strategies/indicators (B) [planning the process]
1. Reading the problem silent or aloud 2. Restating the problem in his or her own words/reminding himself or herself of the requirements of the problem 3. *Asking for clarification of the meaning of the problem* 4. *Stating or asking whether he or she has done a similar problem in the past/ knowledge of a similar problem* 5. *Representing the problem by drawing a picture, writing key facts, or making a table, diagram, or list* 6. Representing the problem by assigning variables or using symbolic notation 7. *Says that he/she doesn't understand problem* 8. Other	1. Describing an approach that he or she intends to use to solve the problem (steps to be taken or a general strategy to be used) 2. Using deductive or inductive reasoning 3. Synthesizing (creating) 4. *Stating operative proposition (theorem, pattern search, equation, algorithm,* etc. *such as Pythagorean theorem, Gauss theorem, system of equations, percentage formula, pattern recognition, factoring, summation formula, ratios, computation, probability knowledge, algebra, counting)* 5. Using a calculator 6. *Stating that he/she has forgotten procedure stating that he/she has forgotten how to solve* 7. *Stating that he/she will try random trial and error* 8. Other

Episode 1 strategies/indicators (A) [reading and understanding phase]	Episode 2 strategies/indicators (B) [planning the process]
Episode 3 strategies/indicators (C) [implementing the plan]	Episode 4 strategies/indicators (D) [verifying the outcomes of the plan]
1. Using successive approximations (using trial and error) 2. Engaged in an orderly, coherent, and well-structured series of calculations/ uses algorithm 3. Stop working to see what has been done and where it is leading 4. Reviews solution 5. Checks that all hypothesis have been used or checks solution 6. Corrects any errors 7. *Says he/she cannot remember formula, algorithm,* etc. 8. Other	Obtaining an intermediate correct or incorrect solution by: 1. Checking the solution by substitution, retracing steps, or if the solution makes sense 2. Checking that the solution satisfies conditions Obtaining a final correct or incorrect solution by: 3. *Questioning uniqueness of solution* 4. *Expresses liking for problem* 5. Solving problem by alternate method 6. Attempting to simplify solution Reaching an impasse by: 7. *Expressing uncertainty about solution shows concerns for performance and admits confusion* 8. Other

NOTE: Non-verbal strategies are shown in plain text. Verbal strategies are shown in italics text. Verbal strategies will be coded for the retrospective interview. Non-verbal strategies are coded for the think-aloud protocol sessions

Appendix 3

Understanding the problem phase [Episode 1] 2: Complete understanding of the problem is illustrated by choice of models or diagrams to reframe problem 1: Part of the problem misunderstood—weak choice of way to represent the problem 0: Little evidence of understanding
Planning a solution (choosing a strategy) phase [Episode 2] 2: Chooses a correct strategy that could lead to a correct solution 1: Chooses a strategy that could possibly lead to a solution, but route has many pitfalls or is inefficient 0: Inappropriate strategy chosen
Execution of the solution (carrying out the plan) phase [Episode 3] 2: Implements a correct strategy with minor errors or no errors 1: Implements a partially correct strategy, or chooses a correct strategy but implements it poorly 0: Poor strategy with poor implementation, or correct strategy with no implementation
Looking back phase [Episode 4] 2: Checks solution for accuracy. Solution is correct and has correct label for the answer 1: Checks solution for accuracy, but there is a computational error or partial answer for a problem with multiple answers 0: Student does not utilize heuristics of checking for accuracy. There is no answer or wrong answer based on an inappropriate plan

Appendix 4

Retrospective Interview Questions *adapted from* Malloy (1994).

1. What were you thinking when you first read the problem?
2. Explain the precalculus (or computer-programming problem) in your own words.
3. Was there anything that you did not understand about the problem?
4. Did you understand the problem right away?
5. Have you ever solved the other problems like this before?
6. If you drew a picture or diagram, ask: Can you show me your diagram or picture and tell me about it?
7. Tell me about your thoughts as you solved the problem. What steps or algorithm do you have to solve the problem?
8. How did you feel about solving the problem?
9. Could you have found the answer to the problem another way?
10. How did you decide to solve the problem the way you did?
11. For computer science: Did you program compile and execute at the first attempt? If not, what did you do to see if the program generated the correct output?

References

Berry III, R. (2003). Mathematics standards, cultural styles, and learning preferences: The plight and promise of African-American students. *The Clearing House: A Journal of Educational Strategies, Issues and Ideas, 76*(5), 244–249.

Blume, G. W., & Schoen, H. L. (1988). Mathematical problem solving performance of eighth-grade programmers and nonprogrammers. *Journal for Research in Mathematics Education, 19*(2), 142–156.

Brown, B. (2007). *A guide to programming in Java*. Upper Saddle River, NJ: Lawrenceville Press.

Bruner, J., Goodnow, J., & Austin, G. (1962). *A study of thinking*. New York, NY: Science Editions.

Charles, R., Lester, F., & O'Daffer, P. (1987). *How to evaluate progress in problem solving*. Reston, VA: National Council of Teachers of Mathematics.

Darling-Hammond, L. (1996). *The right to learn and the advancement of teaching: Research, policy and practice for democratic education.* Education Researcher. American Educational Research Association. Retrieved from: http://www.jstor.org/stable/1176043.

Fox, E., & Riconscente, M. (2008). Metacognition and self-regulation in James, Piaget, and Vygotsky. *Educational Psychology Review, 20*, 373–389.

Garofalo, J., & Lester Jr., F. (1985). Metacognition, cognitive monitoring, and mathematical performance. *Journal of Research in Mathematics Education, 16*(3), 163–176.

Holliday, B., Cuevas, G., McClure, M., Carter, J., & Marks, D. (2001). *Advanced mathematical concepts: Pre-calculus with applications*. New York, NY: McGraw-Hill.

Horstmann, C. (2003). *Computing concepts with java essentials* (3rd ed.). New York, NY: Wiley.

Lewis, J., Loftus, W., & Cocking, C. (2007). *Java software solutions* (2nd ed.). Boston, MA: Pearson Education.

Malloy, C. (1994). African-American eighth grade students' mathematics problem solving characteristics, strategies, and success. *Dissertation Abstracts International, 56*(07), 2597. (UMI No. 9538448).

National Council of Teachers of Mathematics. (1980). *An agenda for action*. Reston, VA: National of Council of Teachers of Mathematics.
National Council of Teachers of Mathematics. (1999). In W. S. Bush & A. S. Greer (Eds.), *Mathematics assessment: A practical handbook for grades 9–12*. Reston, VA: National of Council of Teachers of Mathematics.
National Council of Teachers of Mathematics. (2000). *Principles and standards for school mathematics*. Reston, VA: National of Council of Teachers of Mathematics.
Polya, G. (1957). *How to solve it: A new aspect of mathematical method*. New York, NY: Doubleday.
Polya, G. (1962). *Mathematical discovery on understanding, learning and teaching problem-solving* (Vol. I). New York, NY: Wiley.
Rudder, C. (2006). Problem solving: Case studies investigating the strategies used by American and Singaporean students. *Dissertation Abstracts* (UMI No. 3232443).
Sarver, M. (2006). Metacognition and mathematical problem solving: Case studies of six seventh-grade students. *Dissertation Abstracts International* (UMI No. 1095440231).
Seeley, C. (2005). President's message: Do the math in your head! *NCTM News Bulletin, 42*(3), 3.
Siegler, R. (2003). Implications of cognitive science research for mathematics education. In J. Kilpatrick, W. G. Martin, & D. Schifter (Eds.), *A research companion to principles and standards for school mathematics* (p. 291). Reston, VA: National Council of Teachers of Mathematics.
Stockwell, W. F. (2002). The effects of learning "C" programming on college students' mathematics skill. *Dissertation Abstracts International, 63*(10), 885. UMI No. 3045840.
Wells, G. (1981). The relationship between the processes involved in problem solving and the processes involved in computer programming (Doctoral dissertation, University of Cincinnati, 1981). *Dissertation Abstracts International, 42*(5), 2009.
Willis, J. M. (1999). Using computer programming to teach problem solving and logic skills: The impact of object-oriented languages. Unpublished Master's Thesis, University of Houston, Clear Lake, Texas.
Wing, J. M. (2006). Viewpoint: computational thinking. *Communications of the ACM, 49*(3), 33–35. Retrieved June 8, 2016 from https://www.cs.cmu.edu/~15110-s13/Wing06-ct.pdf.
Wing, J. M. (2008). Computational thinking and thinking about computing. *Philosophical Transactions of the Royal Society, 366*, 3717–3725. Retrieved June 4, 2016 from https://www.cs.cmu.edu/~CompThink/papers/Wing08a.pdf.
Zahorik, J. (1997). Encouraging and challenging students' understandings. *Educational Leadership*. Retrieved January 15, 2016 from Academic Search Premier Database.

Computational Thinking as an Interdisciplinary Approach to Computer Science School Curricula: A German Perspective

Jan Delcker and Dirk Ifenthaler

Abstract The German school system is very complex and inconsistent, due to the policy of states being responsible for the state curricula. One of the most heterogeneous fields is the teaching of computer science (CS). Although the topic is becoming more and more important for students growing up in a digital media society, stakeholders are not able to find common ground on the matter of whether and how computer science should be taught at German schools. With the beginning of the 2016–2017 school year, the State of Baden-Württemberg is planning to introduce a new state curriculum. In this curriculum, named Educational Plan 16, computer science is integrated into the higher secondary track schools as an interdisciplinary task. This chapter introduces computational thinking as a thinking method that (1) enables stakeholders in Germany to integrate computer science into their classes and (2) close the gap between different classes to support an interdisciplinary approach to computer science teaching. Reaching these targets involves meeting specific personal, institutional, and systemic conditions and overcoming existing limitations. This chapter also describes the possibility of strengthening an approach to an international computer science education by developing and distributing computational thinking projects across national borders.

Keywords Interdisciplinary computer science education • Computational thinking in Germany • Educational Plan 2016 • Integrated computer science education

J. Delcker
University of Mannheim, 68131 Mannheim, BW, Germany
e-mail: jdelcker@mail.uni-mannheim.de

D. Ifenthaler (✉)
University of Mannheim, 68131 Mannheim, BW, Germany

Curtin University, Bentley, WA 6102, Australia
e-mail: dirk@ifenthaler.info

P.J. Rich, C.B. Hodges (eds.), *Emerging Research, Practice, and Policy on Computational Thinking*, Educational Communications and Technology: Issues and Innovations, DOI 10.1007/978-3-319-52691-1_4

Introduction

The school system in Germany is highly influenced by the federalist structure of the German state, leading to a vast variety of curricula. While some subjects are taught equally throughout the country, there are great differences with regard to computer science (CS) teaching and the usage of technology, ranging from computers and smartphones to interactive whiteboards as well as personalized learning platforms. In recent years, approaches for coping with the increasing presence of technology in student life have seemed hastily developed and often inconsistent, leading to situations in which computer science became mandatory in 1 year just to be canceled the following year. From summer 2016 on, the State of Baden-Württemberg is introducing a new state curriculum focusing on media literacy as an integral part of students' skills (Bildungsplan 2016, Educational Plan 2016). To reach this goal, the state is integrating media literacy into a variety of courses. The following text will give an overview of the newly developed state curriculum, with a focus on the integration of media literacy and the linking of computer science with other courses in Baden-Württemberg's higher track secondary school.

German Education: International Context

Due to the great international differences between educational systems, it is first necessary to provide a short introduction to the German school system to be able to compare the presented ideas with programs from other countries. As mentioned above, the school system is not standardized, even within Germany itself. The statements made in this text apply only to the State of Baden-Württemberg, where children attend primary school for 4 years, from the age of 6–7 to 10–11. In the 5th grade, students are split up between lower (ending at 9th grade), middle (at 10th grade), and higher track secondary schools (at 12th grade), primarily according to their performance in primary school. This text focuses on the higher track secondary schools, the so-called Gymnasiums, which are comparable to grammar schools (GB) or sixth form colleges and preparatory high schools (US). The Gymnasium is classified at ISCED level 3 (OECD, 2015). In 2014–2015, approximately 313,000 students were enrolled at Baden-Württemberg's 459 Gymnasiums (Bundesamt, 2015). Classes taught in the Gymnasiums are aiming at providing the students with an extensive knowledge, therefore distributing lessons evenly on the different fields, namely, German, mathematics, foreign languages (e.g., English, French, Spanish), as well as natural and human science. As students get older, they can specialize in a specific track. Those tracks are (1) the natural science track, focusing on biology, chemistry, and physics; (2) the human science track, approaching history and social studies; and (3) the linguistic track, adding an additional language to a student's curriculum. Although a specialization is possible, students still have to take mandatory classes in German, mathematics, and at least one foreign language.

Computer Science in German Higher Track Secondary Schools

The lack of consistency between the school systems of the German states is reflected in the diversity of computer science (CS) courses implemented into the states' curricula. In five states (out of 16), CS is a mandatory course every higher track secondary school student has to take, while in five other states, CS is not offered at all. There are a variety of different models, ranging from mandatory courses to no courses: In the State of Schleswig-Holstein, the schools themselves decide whether to offer CS as a mandatory or elective course, while in Brandenburg they can decide whether to provide any CS courses at all. In Berlin, CS is mandatory in grades 7 and 8 and becomes an elective course in grades 9 and 10. Hessen's approach is to offer CS for the first 4 years of school but without a strict educational plan, which is only introduced in higher grades. The state curricula are subject to often radical and quick changes, for example, in the State of Hamburg, where CS was mandatory until 2013. As early as October 2014, attempts were made to change the voluntary courses back to mandatory again. Furthermore, the content of the different CS courses and CS teaching models described above shows great diversity.

Differences in CS implementation into higher track secondary schools can only partially be put down to the federalist character of the German school system. A second, more complex cause is the lack of a unified definition for CS. Compared to other classes, the extent of CS seems too great for stakeholders to be able to find common ground on where CS teaching should start and which topics should be left out of the curriculum. Stakeholders' opinions about which CS content should be taught in schools range from basic computer skills (e.g., using office software) to programming knowledge and a discussion of media society.

By not trying to limit CS teaching to specific topics, Baden-Württemberg's 2016 state curriculum circumvents the need for a closed definition. The following section will present the understanding of CS and the interdisciplinary teaching approach of this new curriculum.

Computer Science in the Baden-Württemberg's 2016 State Curriculum

The Educational Plan 2016 (EP16 for short) is the successor of the Educational Plan 2004, which was the outcome of an educational reform inside the Baden-Württemberg school system. Developed over 10 years, EP04 was built around a competency approach, marking a paradigm shift in the Baden-Württemberg school system, because it switched the focus to student competencies (output) and away from learning material and courses (input) (von Hentig, 2004). The competency-oriented approach remains one of the main characteristics of the newer EP16. Additionally, it formulates a unified curriculum for the lower and middle track schools for the first time (Schulentwicklung, 2015a). Another core development is the introduction of six key objectives, each representing a set of skills and knowledge that is to be taught in an interdisciplinary context (Schulentwicklung, 2015b):

- Sustainable development literacy
- Diversity literacy
- Health promotion and prevention
- Labor market orientation
- Media literacy
- Consumer literacy

Media literacy (ML) will be the main key objective discussed in this text, because it is the main source for CT potential and potential CT ideas in the EP16. ML is characterized as an important part of general education due to the evolving media society and the role it plays in students' everyday life.

The understanding of media literacy in the EP16 is very similar to a framework proposed by Lin, Li, Deng, and Lee (2013), where, in addition to four types of literacy (functional consuming, critical consuming, functional presuming, critical presuming), a set of ten indicators is introduced (consuming skill, understanding, analysis, synthesis, evaluation, presuming skill, production, distribution, participation, and creation). These indicators have equivalent counterparts in the media literacy section of the EP16.

To specify the key objective of ML, the authors of the EP16 subsume eight items under the term "media literacy" (Schulentwicklung, 2015c): (1) media society, (2) media analysis, (3) information and knowledge, (4) communication and cooperation, (5) production and presentation, (6) youth media law, (7) informational self-determination and data privacy, and (8) information technology basics.

The items are not distinct but rather overlap partially. Furthermore, they include sets of skills and knowledge that are traditionally taught in multiple classes. The EP16 acknowledges the widespread presence of ML in more than one class by labeling it an interdisciplinary task, and as a direct result, ML topics have to be comprehensively implemented into every class. For example, "media society" could be a relevant topic in a social studies class, whereas the item "information technology basics" is more closely related to a technology or mathematics class.

The plan of strengthening the role of ML aspects involves wide-ranging objectives. The main goals are to empower students to "consciously face the challenges of media society" and to teach the ability to "include media in everyday life in a meaningful, thoughtful, and responsible way" (Schulentwicklung, 2015c).

Computer science is an important part of the key objective of ML, although it is not explicitly stated as "computer science." The creators of the EP16 seem to avoid the established terms to underline the ideas of integrated CS teaching introduced by the new curriculum and also to avoid the public debate that is causing the multiple models of CS teaching in German schools. In Germany, the word *Informatik* is commonly used as an expression for topics related to CS and finds its expression in the item "information technology basics" in the EP16. Apart from the semantics of the items, another way to locate CS aspects in the EP16 is to compare the definition of CS teaching in K–12 (Tucker et al. 2003) with the description of school subjects:

In the EP16, a table is created for each subject that shows the planned contributions to the key objectives. An analysis of these subjects exposes the existence of certain criteria included in the definition mentioned above. The following section describes the contributions of the subjects "natural science and technology" and "mathematics" as examples for existing CS principles in the EP16.

Natural Science and Technology: ML Contribution

Important aspects of CS are taught in this class. It highlights the topic of information processing against the backdrop of the relation between nature and technology. Principles of analog and digital (en)coding as well as basic controlling and regulation systems are key elements for younger students. As the students' knowledge increases, fundamental principles of algorithms become part of the curriculum. Not only do the students learn how algorithms work in theory, but they are also taught to develop their own algorithms, including the coding of decisions and logical operators. Additional topics are the opportunities and risks of information technology (Schulentwicklung, 2015d).

Mathematics: ML Contribution

In mathematics, the CS focus lies on the extraction, examination, validation, and critical reflection of statistical data. Students conduct their own survey using technical tools, such as computers, tablets, smartphones, and adequate software. In using software for spreadsheets or to display geometric figures, students enhance their understanding of mathematics and learn how the software works. Another objective is the use of media to strengthen the students' skills in presenting their own thoughts and solutions. The contribution of mathematics to CS education overlaps with those of physics, chemistry, and every other class in which data can be collected and analyzed.

The counterparts of these contributions in the definition include programming, hardware design, databases, information retrieval, software design, and logic. CS is tightly integrated into the key objective of ML and therefore also into the EP16. The examples used above also show how media (CS) can be integrated "into everyday life in a meaningful, thoughtful, and responsible way" (Schulentwicklung, 2015c), one of the key objectives of ML. Computers, software, or, in more general terms, CS skills are used to solve problems or find explanations that occur in different subjects or topics. Instead of learning how to write an algorithm with the goal of "learning how to program," students learn how to write an algorithm to find a solution they come across in mathematics. For example, instead of using a made-up table provided by the teacher, students collect their own data from an experiment to discover coherencies with computer software they use or build themselves.

For some students (and teachers), this is not something new, because CS is already integrated into their curricula in one way or another. This could be due to a special science class that focuses on the use of computers or because the teacher likes to use and teach CS as part of his or her teaching methods. The presence of CS in schools is not groundbreaking in general, but the way the EP16 integrates CS into different topics offers great opportunities for students at higher track schools in Baden-Württemberg to develop and improve their CS skills, because it exposes students to CS not by chance (e.g., because a teacher uses technology) but as a requirement.

Teachers and students alike have to meet essential conditions to profit from the new EP16 and especially from the interdisciplinary approach to CS teaching. Computational thinking can help to prepare and support stakeholders with the successful transition to this new principle.

Using Computational Thinking for Interdisciplinary Computer Science Teaching

The following short summary illustrates the capability of computational thinking for an interdisciplinary approach to teaching CS at schools. In 2006, Jeanette Wing reintroduced the term computational thinking to describe the process of "drawing on the concepts fundamental to computer science" to solve problems, design systems, and understand human behavior (Wing, 2006, p. 33). To do so, well-known concepts are used, including problem decomposition, data representation, and modeling, as well as less familiar ideas, such as binary search, recursion, and parallelization (Barr, Harrison, & Conery, 2011). Stephenson and Barr formulate a more tangible definition, calling CT an approach to "solving problems in a way that can be implemented with a computer…, a problem solving methodology that can be automated and transferred and applied across subjects" (p. 51). A set of characteristics that can further enhance the understanding of CT, especially in a K–12 environment, was compiled in the computational thinking teachers' resources (Barr & Stephenson, 2011):

1. CT is not only the way to formulate problems so they can be solved using a computer.
2. It is also the logical organization and analysis of data.
3. Models and simulations are introduced to represent data through abstraction.
4. By thinking in algorithms, students can create automated solutions.
5. One of the goals is to achieve the most efficient and effective combination of steps and resources by identifying, analyzing, and implementing a variety of possible solutions.
6. The whole process of solving one particular problem can be generalized and transferred to a variety of problems.

In addition, "dispositions and attitudes [which] are an essential dimension of CT" are listed. CT helps to give students confidence in their skills for dealing with complex, difficult, or open-ended problems. They also develop a tolerance for ambiguity as well as the ability to work as a team to achieve a common goal or solution (Barr & Stephenson, 2011).

The reason why computational thinking is a useful principle for teaching CS in an interdisciplinary context can be summarized as the idea of "common language" or "common principle."

Common language is the term for a cluster of words and expressions that is used by everyone working with CT. We have already encountered some of these words, such as "data collection," "abstraction," "algorithm," or "simulation," which are often used in different senses depending on the context. For a biologist, data collection can mean counting the cells in a petri dish, while data collection for a sociologist could be conducting an interview. A physician interprets reading the value shown on a thermometer as data collection. All of this is data collection and could be interpreted as "gathering information that can be used in the problem solving process."

The important thing about common language is the generalized usability of words in more than one context: If a biology teacher is talking about data collection and teaches students how to collect biological data, students will be able to transfer their data collection skills to other subjects, under the premise that both teachers are using the same expression, namely, data collection. If the biology teacher is talking about "counting cells" and the physics teacher is talking about "reading the thermometers," a transfer of knowledge is less likely to happen. The principles of CT allow various subject-specific words to be subsumed under a common expression, a common language, which could also be referred to as common knowledge of CT concepts and capabilities.

This common language not only supports a students' transfer of knowledge between subjects; it also helps them to communicate with each other using words like "sequences, inputs, outputs, saved value, how complex the solution is" (Barr & Stephenson, 2011, p. 51). The common language also helps teachers to prepare projects or classes, especially when cooperating with a teacher from another subject. The idea of a common language is closely related to the idea of common principles present in computational thinking.

Common principle refers to the utilization of the same steps and concepts throughout different projects. Teachers and students engaged in computational thinking do not only possess a common knowledge for a process but also share a strategy for bringing together different processes in a distinct order or making the same references between different steps of a project with the goal of finding a solution to a problem which can be supported with a computer. As with common language, the common principle can be used to transfer knowledge from one subject to another. Especially in an interdisciplinary approach to CS education, transferring ideas and concepts between the different subjects is a key concept.

Through common language and principles, computational thinking builds up a platform on which students and teachers can share ideas and thoughts between different subjects. Additionally, computational thinking also offers a way to solve real-life problems. The fact that real-life problems are often similar between different subjects is a reason to use computational thinking as a link between those subjects. One way to link two problems is to use a principle of CS to function as an abstraction of the original problem. During this interdisciplinary process, students gain knowledge about a multitude of aspects. They learn to find similarities between problems and tasks and are enabled to transfer and alter solutions between and for those problems. CS skills and methods used for this process become learning tools and learning content at the same time.

The ideas behind computational thinking are hard to grasp, and it seems impossible to explain the concept without using examples (Computational thinking—Teacher resources second edition). To show the way computational thinking can be utilized in a CS teaching process, we present an example from a German CS teaching project in the following section.

Practice Example: "Kids in Command"

The following example from a project by Alexandra Quiring-Tegeder shows what an interdisciplinary CS project might look like, which basic CT characteristics can be found in it, and how it could be implemented in the EP16. The project "Kids in Command" aims at introducing students to the world of computers, especially programming language and algorithms, and can be seen as a modified version of the MarchingOrdersactivitybyComputerScienceUnplugged(ComputerScienceUnplugged, 2005; Quiring-Teder, 2016).

Setting and Task

A path that leads through the room is created in the school's gym, including different obstacles. The task is to lead a robot (played by a student) along the path by using special commands, which are given by the other students.

Theoretical Background

Machines follow strict instructions, which are given by humans. These instructions are also called the programs or programming of machines. Which aspects are important if a human wants to program a machine? What happens if a machine only follows strict instructions?

By leading each other through the obstacle course, the students learn how important it is to give precise instructions and what happens if the instructions are unclear or can be understood in multiple ways. Most likely, students will run into obstacles or simply stop when a command is wrong and therefore learn through personal experience which commands are useful. Additionally, they will understand the principle of programming language, where a word or an expression means only one thing (e.g., "move," "stop"). These expressions have to be understood by humans and machines alike and can be further refined through additional information ("turn 90° to the left," "move five steps forward").

Adding Complexity

Students can literally program each other by using audio records of their instructions. They create a chain of commands for a specific path, which can be interpreted as an algorithm. Afterward, a robot student can listen to the audio record and follow the algorithm. Students can get feedback directly from their partners when instructions are unclear or in the wrong order by simply watching them walk through the gym.

A more complex execution that gets even closer to real-life programming is the use of a simplified program language that shortens the original commands (e.g., "t 90 l," "m 5 f") or combines complex tasks to form a single command. Another idea is to let multiple robots walk through the course from different directions, adding timing components to the task.

Use for Interdisciplinary CS Teaching

The project combines aspects of the subjects technology, sports, and language and can be conducted for students of different ages, depending on the complexity that is chosen. While younger students can be taught through the initial voice-command structure, more experienced and skilled students could even write a program that shows the instructions on a smartphone or similar device. Teachers can also vary the focus on the different subjects by implementing movements (e.g., "do a squat") or by only allowing expressions in a foreign language.

The students' understanding of programming basics can be fostered through the connection between abstract expressions and real-life actions. When the teacher tells the students to "program" their robots, "implementing" their "commands" in the form of "algorithms," the students learn to use adequate vocabulary. Transporting the learning content in a playful way can change students' perception of CS as a topic that deals with rigid constructs.

The Role of CT

Many CT concepts can be found in the "Kids in Command" project. Before students can start to program their robots, they need to have a close look at the task, especially the structure and complexity of the obstacle course. They have to gather the information that is needed and check constantly to ensure that they do not miss a step: They are *collecting and analyzing data*. The next step is the *representation* of the data using words or symbols to visualize the path the robot will follow. The general task has to be broken up into smaller sections: Which phrases are good instructions? When is the right time to give an instruction? Which measurements of distance are reliable? Using *abstractions* and *algorithms*, students can create a program that allows the robot to complete the obstacle course. The guided movements of the robots can be interpreted as a simulation of the students' plans and thoughts on mastering the task (ComputerScienceUnplugged, 2005).

The knowledge gained through the process of generating a program for the robot can be transferred to other subjects as well as to other situations in the students' lives. Students can learn the importance of adequate instructions and expressions, for example, when they are giving a presentation. If they want their listeners to comprehend a topic, they have to "speak the same language." Presenters cannot use terms that are unknown, or if they do, they have to explain them first. The presentation has to follow a basic structure to prevent important information from being excluded. The instructions given to the robot can be compared to instructions given when a person is asking for directions. The two situations are very similar regarding the need for accuracy of expressions or shared concepts for measuring distances.

"Kids in Command" in the EP16: Basic Course in Media Education

The basic course in media education was created for 5th grade students under the assumption that children's skills and knowledge concerning media differ a lot at this time in their lives. The main goal of the basic course is to compensate for these differences in skills and knowledge and to enable students to participate together in further media education involving teaching on CS foundations. The "Kids in Command" project seems to be a good way to start CS teaching in schools, because it does not require any CS knowledge in its most basic form. Additionally, it can be used to start the teaching and utilization of basic ideas and concepts of computational thinking, enabling the students to increase their knowledge on CS and CT through further projects.

Limitations and Difficulties

Modeling the secondary track high school education in regard to CS aspects involves a multitude of conditions, which can be categorized as personal, systemic, and institutional. Although the conditions overlap in part, we will present them separately to allow a closer look at the different aspects.

Personal Conditions

Interdisciplinary integration of CS elements with the help of CT is a big challenge for teachers at higher track secondary schools. To be able to successfully teach CS, teachers must possess CS as well as CT knowledge themselves. The preparation of teachers is key for the success of CS teaching, as is CT implementation into this process. According to a report by Initiative D12, teacher education in Germany does not place sufficient emphasis on media competency (including CS competency). The teaching of CS skills is often not a (mandatory) part of teacher education at universities, which are seldom equipped with enough technical and personal (media) infrastructures. Continuing education for teachers often concentrates solely on the handling of technical devices (e.g., interactive whiteboards) instead of teaching methods and CS skills. In addition, teachers who lack certain skills are less likely to attend continuing education programs (Wetter, Martin, & Rave, 2014).

Well-trained teachers are the key to a successful realization of CT-based CS teaching, and the responsible authorities have to create and support effective and efficient ways to enhance teacher education. In addition, teachers and trainee teachers have to open themselves up to using CT and CS in their classes. Their beliefs can function as a barrier for further development (Ertmer, 2005). Changes in curricula almost always mean a greater workload on teachers, especially when they have to add new material to their existing knowledge base. In the case of CS and CT, a web-based, state-wide network could help teachers to exchange thoughts, ideas, and projects, strengthening the position of CS through the use of CT. The contact with teachers who already have CT experience can help those who do not to learn more about CT techniques they might already be using without knowing it and show them where CT can be fitted into existing methods (Wetter, Martin, & Rave, 2014).

Institutional Conditions

The second group of conditions can be categorized as institutional. The inadequate equipment available at universities has already been mentioned above, but it is a common situation at German schools as well. Many schools are not properly connected to the World Wide Web, lacking a sufficient broadband connection or school-wide wireless connectivity. Existing and future equipment (both software and hardware) is often maintained by teachers, who are rarely fully trained for this special task. Additionally, schools often do not provide access to digital material, or the material does not meet legal requirements.

The main reason the conditions are not met or are only partially met is insufficient funding. Strengthening CS teaching at schools means first providing the educational system with enough money to be able to equip schools with adequate devices and software as well as personnel and infrastructure. Ideas for compensating for some of the deficits and reducing costs for the schools are implementing bring-your-own-device projects or reducing administrative costs by hiring technical staff responsible for more than one school.

Institutions have to supply teachers with additional time and workspace to encourage continuing education, especially as it applies to CS. Additionally, teachers must be granted access to cooperative projects to create synergies between teachers with different levels of knowledge and experience in CS education.

Systemic Conditions

The current CS teaching situation in Germany is highly fragmented. There is no institution that could lead a nationwide approach to a homogenous CS curriculum. Bringing together the different state stakeholders is a complicated task, even within the states themselves (Wetter, Martin, & Rave, 2014). Resources invested in programs with the potential to improve the implementation of CS in schools are often used in ineffective and inefficient ways, because they are seldom realized over an extended period of time or in a large area. Statements about the sustainability and success of such programs are therefore difficult to verify.

The lack of interdisciplinary cooperation between teachers can also be seen as a systemic condition that limits the employment of CT methods. The current system is not designed to bring different stakeholders together due to the competitive situation regarding financial and human resources. Improving the situation for a field (e.g., CS) almost always places other subjects in danger of losing resources, leading to a defensive attitude toward changes in curricula.

International Context

Although the present chapter embeds the idea of interdisciplinary CS education using CT principles in the context of the new EP16 in Baden-Württemberg, Germany, the basic ideas are in no way limited or restricted to a particular country. The interdisciplinary CS–CT teaching and learning approach is flexible enough to build up a CS curriculum or extend and improve existing curricula in all European school systems, regardless of whether they require (1) no CS education, (2) partial/voluntary CS education, (3) interdisciplinary CS education, or (4) consistent mandatory CS education. It is not restricted to the higher secondary track schools envisaged in the presented text, to a certain form of school, or to students with a particular state of knowledge or of a certain age.

Although the problems described in this chapter are a representation of the current situation in Germany, the limitations can be transferred to other national settings, as can the theoretical benefits. Most likely, systems already supporting the cooperation of subjects and teachers are using some of the techniques already. Furthermore, the approach or parts of the approach will be more easily realized in countries with an existing CS curriculum, assuming that those countries are less restricted regarding the limitations presented in this article.

The effects of teachers cooperating outside of their subjects within a nation through the use of common CT language and CT principles could foster an international exchange of educational experiences, ideas, and projects. The project "Kids in Command" provides an example of how globalized teaching methods can overcome national borders in this way.

Conclusions and Perspective

The interdisciplinary approach to CS education integrated into the EP16 is not based on the principle of computational thinking. In fact, the creators of the EP16 do not provide any guidelines on how CS should be integrated in practice. Even so, the CT principles can function as a method to close the gap between the theoretical foundation of the EP16 and the situations at schools. Forcing schools to integrate CS into all subjects demands methods and principles based on the transfer of knowledge and sufficient flexibility for more than one subject. Apart from the limitations owing to institutional restrictions, the keystones of the concept on which CT is based are the personal effort of teachers to cooperate with their colleagues and the students' ability to transfer knowledge between subjects. These fundamentals are massively influenced by the teachers' eagerness to improve the CS education of their students. Support by education system authorities and stakeholders is not yet sufficiently focused yet will be crucial for the upcoming challenges of CS integration.

Curricular reforms are one of the most widely discussed processes in Germany and Baden-Württemberg. In the past years, discussions and stakeholders have focused on different schooling modes, such as the conversion from a 13- to a 12-year higher secondary school track or the changes to the system of mandatory courses in upper-level classes, following the EP04. The EP16 redirects public interest to content-related aspects or more specifically to the philosophy and anthropology on which the curriculum is based. Critics of the EP16 interpret the key objective of achieving diversity literacy as interfering with students' and parents' right to sex education. In light of this situation, the changes and ideas made to improve the state of CS education are in danger of being left by the wayside. Education researchers are thus called on to make an effort to introduce teachers to CS and CT principles in training and practice, creating an environment in which CS education can be fostered. Existing CS education projects have to be further developed and analyzed to reduce the danger of wasted resources, and evidence for the practicality of the CT method is required to improve acceptance and the integration of CT into curricula. The introduction of the EP16 marks an ideal point in time to provide guidance to stakeholders and initiate research projects on the introduction of CS education. By investing in thoughtfully planned, widespread, long-term studies, educational researchers can help to design projects, methods, and environments that enable teachers to improve their CS teaching. As a result, the CS knowledge of students can be improved, equipping them with the necessary tools and capabilities for media society.

If the interdisciplinary approach to CS education and the use of CT principles prove to be helpful for students and teachers in Baden-Württemberg, other states might integrate it into their own curricula, leading to a higher CS education standard throughout Germany. Through exchange and cooperation, teachers from all over Europe could profit from the experience made and the knowledge gained from the EP16.

References

Barr, V., & Stephenson, C. (2011). Bringing computational thinking to K-12: What is Involved and what is the role of the computer science education community? *ACM Inroads, 2*(1), 48–54. doi:10.1145/1929887.1929905.

Barr, D., Harrison, J., & Conery, L. (2011). Computational thinking: A digital age skill for everyone. *Learning and Leading with Technology, 6*(38), 20–33.

Bundesamt, S. (2015). *Bildung und Kultur–Allgemeinbildende Schulen Schuljahr 2014/2015*. Retrieved from Wiesbaden: https://www.destatis.de/DE/Publikationen/Thematisch/BildungForschungKultur/Schulen/AllgemeinbildendeSchulen2110100157004.pdf?__blob=publicationFile.

Computational Thinking—Teacher Resources second edition. (2017) Retrieved from https://csta.acm.org/Curriculum/sub/CurrFiles/472.11CTTeacherResources_2ed-SP-vF.pdf.

ComputerScienceUnplugged (2005). Marching orders–programming languages. Retrieved from http://csunplugged.org/wp-content/uploads/2014/12/unplugged-12-programming_languages.pdf.

Ertmer, P. A. (2005). Teacher pedagogical beliefs: The final frontier in our quest for technology integration? *Educational Technology Research and Development, 53*(4), 25–39. doi:10.1007/bf02504683.

Lin, T.-B., Li, J.-Y., Deng, F., & Lee, L. (2013). Understanding new media literacy: An explorative theoretical framework. *Journal of Educational Technology and Society, 16*(4), 160–170.

OECD. (2015). *ISCED 2011 operational manual: guidelines for classifying national education programmes and related qualifications*. Paris: OECD Publishing.

Quiring-Teder, A. (2016). Kinder gegen Kommandos. Retrieved from https://kinder-geben-kommandos.de/kinder-geben-kommandos/.

Schulentwicklung, L. F. (2015a). Bildungsp006Cäne 2016–Einführungstext. Retrieved from http://www.bildungsplaene-bw.de/,Lde/Startseite/Informationen/Einf%C3%BChrungstext.

Schulentwicklung, L. F. (2015b). Bildungspläne 2016–Verweisstruktur der Leitperspektiven. Retrieved from http://www.bildungsplaene-bw.de/,Lde/Startseite/Informationen/Leitperspektiven.

Schulentwicklung, L. F. (2015c). Leitperspektiven Medienbildung. Retrieved from http://www.bildungsplaene-bw.de/,Lde/Startseite/Informationen/de_MB.

Schulentwicklung, L. F. (2015d). NwT 3.2.4.3 Informationsverarbeitung. Retrieved from http://www.bildungsplaene-bw.de/,Lde/Startseite/de_a/a_gym_NWT_ik_8-10_04_03.

Tucker, A., Deek, F., Jones, J., McCowan, D., Chris, S., & Verno, A. (2003). A model curriculum for K-12 computer science: Final report of the ACM K-12 task force curriculum committee. Retrieved from New York: https://csta.acm.org/Curriculum/sub/CurrFiles/K-12ModelCurr2ndEd.pdf.

von Hentig, H. (2004). Einführung in den Bildungsplan 2004. Retrieved from http://www.bildung-staerkt-menschen.de/service/downloads/Sonstiges/Einfuehrung_BP.pdf.

Wetter, F. B., Martin; Rave, M. (2014). Medienbildung an deutschen Schulen. Retrieved from http://www.initiatived21.de/wp-content/uploads/2014/11/141106_Medienbildung_Onlinefassung_komprimiert.pdf.

Wing, J. M. (2006). Computational thinking. *Communications of the ACM, 49*(3), 33. doi:10.1145/1118178.1118215.

Proto-computational Thinking: The Uncomfortable Underpinnings

Deborah Tatar, Steve Harrison, Michael Stewart, Chris Frisina, and Peter Musaeus

Abstract The idea of computational thinking (CT) has resulted in widespread action at all levels of the American educational system. Some action focuses on programming, some on cognition, and some on physical action that is seen as embodying computational thinking concepts. In a K–12 educational context, the observation that computing is usually about some *non*-computational thing can lead to an approach that integrates computational thinking instruction with existing core curricular classes. A social justice argument can be made for this approach, because all students take courses in the core curriculum.

Utilizing university students in co-development activities with teachers, the current study located and implemented opportunities for integrated computational thinking in middle school in a large, suburban, mixed-socioeconomic standing (SES), mixed-race district. The co-development strategy resulted in plausible theories of change and a number of different educational projects suitable for classroom instruction. However, a major outcome of the study was to advance the importance of *proto*-computational thinking (PCT). We argue that, in the absence of preexisting use of representational tools for thinking, *proto*-computational thinking may lead to enhanced facility in computational thinking per se. At the same time, the absence of opportunities for *proto*-computational thinking may leave students less open to acquiring sophisticated approaches to computational thinking itself. An approach that values proto-computational thinking may be uncomfortable because it calls attention to implicit ceilings in instruction, especially in low-SES circumstances. We argue for addressing those ceilings through proto-computational thinking.

Keywords Integrated computational thinking • Proto-computational thinking • Middle School • Sound of Fractions • Critisearch • SES • Socio-economic-status

---

D. Tatar (✉) • S. Harrison • M. Stewart • C. Frisina
Department of Computer Science, Virginia Tech, Blacksburg, VA 24060, USA
e-mail: tatar@cs.vt.edu; srh@cs.vt.edu; tgm@cs.vt.edu; frisina@cs.vt.edu

P. Musaeus
Centre for Health Sciences Education, Aarhus University, Aarhus, Denmark
e-mail: peter@cesu.au.dk

P.J. Rich, C.B. Hodges (eds.), *Emerging Research, Practice, and Policy on Computational Thinking*, Educational Communications and Technology: Issues and Innovations, DOI 10.1007/978-3-319-52691-1_5

Introduction

Computational thinking (CT) has been considered important, necessary (Wing, 2006), *and also* controversial (Computer Science and Telecommunications Board, 2010). While teaching children something about computing is widely accepted as important, it is not always clear who needs to learn what and why? Is programming the essential thing? If CT is something more than programming, what is it? How do we know whether CT has been achieved in teaching and learning?

Although Wing's article crystallized the need for educators to take action, it entered into an intellectual arena that was already rife with history. Universities had long been teaching programming and computer science more generally. Educational research had long sought to teach a wide variety of topics, including programming, in K–12 education settings utilizing the affordances of technology. The notion of CT brought these two communities together. It stands to reason that many efforts to increase CT in K–12 education do so directly, by implementing programming. The direct approach leads to institutional foci (such as the revamping and creation of the CS Advanced Placement exam), the creation of frameworks and standards, and new curricula (Computer Science Principles (https://code.org/educate/csp), Exploring Computer Science (http://www.exploringcs.org/), Beauty and Joy of Computing (http://bjc.berkeley.edu/), and Computer Science Fundamentals (https://code.org/educate/k5)). The direct approach may incorporate elements not on the computer at all (CS Unplugged (http://csunplugged.org/)) (Kafura & Tatar, 2011). And this approach may utilize tools and curricula that bear explicit connection to the rich philosophical and empirical basis of the learning sciences (National Research Council, 1999), such as Scratch (http://scratch.mit.edu/) (Resnick et al. 2009; Maloney et al. 2004; Wolz, Stone, Pullmood, & Pearson, 2010), NetLogo (https://ccl.northwestern.edu/netlogo/) (Resnick & Wilensky, 1998; Wilensky & Stroup, 2000; Wilensky & Stroup, 1999; Wilensky, 2002), and AgentSheets/AgentCubes (Repenning, Webb, & Ioannidou, 2010).

The direct approach to teaching computer science has many advantages, including that it harnesses directed effort and experiences from universities and keeps a focus on the goal of training more people in computer science. However, it also has risks and limitations. The most fundamental of these is how CT interacts with issues of equity. For the foreseeable future, the direct approach to CT is likely to be at best optional for most middle and high school students. More affluent students are more likely to both attend schools that offer sophisticated computing and to take advantage of the opportunity, contributing to the more general association between parental socioeconomic standing (SES, a measure that combines wealth and education) and student achievement. In the United States, students who come from the lowest 10th percentile of parental income are more likely on the average to be 3–4 years behind students from the 90th percentile of parental income in middle and high school (Reardon, 2011).

In this chapter, we report research that started from another approach, *integrated* computational thinking (ICT). This approach complements direct instruction but utilizes existing teachers in core curricular classes that every pupil takes. This approach is relatively widespread in elementary school (http://stelar.edc.org/

authors/joyce-malyn-smith), where teachers are well positioned to enact an integrated approach and in informal learning contexts (the PBS program "Peg and Cat" whose narratives concern structured problem-solving involving pattern-recognizing, representation, and logic). The integrated approach is less common in older grades, although the CT-STEM project in the Center for Connected Learning and Computer-Based Modeling at Northwestern (http://ct-stem.northwestern.edu/) builds on a long history (Resnick & Wilensky, 1998) to create embedded activities at the high school level (Weintrop et al. 2016). A number of initiatives at the University of Delaware have targeted students at middle and high school as well as elementary levels (Mouza, Marzocchi, Pan, & Pollock, 2016a, 2016b; Burns, Pollock, & Harvey, 2012; Pollock & Harvey, 2011; Pollock, McCoy, Carberry, Hundigopal, & You, 2004). In particular, the Teams4Youth project (https://sites.google.com/site/computeteams4youth/) engages undergraduates in computer science through the mechanism of a university class in work with teachers to develop CT activities for in-class use. Compute Teams4Youth focuses on game design for education, using XO Laptops and working with a local, high-needs charter school.

Like the Teams4Youth project, the project reported here piloted a method of developing integrated computational tasks that depended on university teams, here composed of graduate students in human–computer interaction and undergraduate Capstone students in software engineering. The teams were to identify possible locations for ICT tasks, engage in participatory design with the teachers in a partner district, and implement the integrated tasks in the classrooms. The co-design mechanism featured (a) asking teachers to identify subject matter that was difficult for students to learn and (b) identifying joint CT opportunities/content-area opportunities through iterative team-based efforts with guidance from Virginia Tech ("VT") faculty. A constraint of the undergraduate capstone class was that initial testing of a prototype had to be completed by the end of the semester.

The mechanism of producing integrated tasks was quite successful. Over the course of two class offerings, the project produced six projects that were implemented at least once in the classroom. Each of these mini-projects was founded around a *theory of change* that articulated how using the technology in a certain way was likely to lead to enhanced student learning.

The purpose of this chapter is to consider a complex outcome: in our study, the result of student classroom observations, interviews with teachers, and participatory engagement rarely led to activities that fit the prototype of CT if CT means using elements easily recognizable to computer scientists as computer science, that is, creating algorithms and meta-level descriptions of code, coding, engaging in explicit acts of structure creation, structured top-down problem-solving, and so forth. Instead, we found important opportunities to address *proto*-computational thinking (PCT). PCT consists of aspects of thought that may not put all the elements of CT together in a way that clearly distinguishes them from other human intellectual activity. PCT activities may draw out the use of a representation, stimulate thought about the utility of different representations, partially instantiate abstractions, or increase focus on a systems' level analysis. They might emphasize systematicity in problem-solving but not emphasize problem-solving in ways that are enactable on a computer. We argue that a focus on PCT is uncomfortable because it may call out deficits in prior instruction in low-SES circumstances. However, these students require a response that acknowledges deficits while building on existing strengths and interests.

Background: The Integrated Computational Thinking Project

The integrated computational thinking (ICT) project generated novel classroom activities with the dual aims of (1) increasing CT in 6–12 grade (6–12 G) classrooms and (2) improving instruction in core content areas: mathematics, science, social sciences, and language arts.

The long-term aim was to significantly impact CT by providing 4–6 activities for each core curricular area for every year from 6 to 12 G. Every activity had to address the immediate needs of teacher and student in core curricular areas, but no single activity had to embody CT in its entirety. Instead, the aim was to build a program of that focuses on aspects of CT, each of which contributes to overall learning progressions.

The method that the ICT project used to generate the individual activities constituted novel and ongoing research whereby VT students were grouped in class and paired with classroom teachers in a participatory design context. The university student–classroom teams constituted an *engine* for idea generation, exploration, and implementation. This engine or laboratory of ideas resulted in preliminary, usable classroom activities that embody a facet of CT as well as a facet of thinking about focused classroom content. The preliminary idea generated by the team would then be iteratively refined, made ready for more widespread use, and integrated into a larger program of presenting facets of CT.

Project Settings

Virginia Tech worked with a large, mixed-SES, mixed-race district in central Virginia that was committed to the use of technology in everyday teaching practice. A district-wide laptop program provided every student from 6th to 12th G with 24/7 access to a district-owned laptop, and every school with staff not only for technical support but also for support for the development and use of laptops in the classroom.

The ICT project meant piloting not only the VT class itself but multiple forms of coordination with the district, including teacher recruitment, technical coordination (about firewalls, servers, student software, and so forth), and coordination with the teachers by both project personnel and university students. Although not discussed in this paper, we also gathered demographic and attitudinal information about teachers and students, conducted before and after in-depth (1–1/2 h) semi-structured interviews with the project teachers, and conducted 30+ semi-structured interviews with teachers, principals, and technical support personnel across the district before the beginning of the VT classes. These interviews helped us understand the local context of the school and its participants including teacher backgrounds, political concerns including teaching conditions in a mixed-school district, relationship with the department and the school, and prior experiences with technology and teaching. In the interviews, we investigated teachers' perceptions about their students' difficulties. We saw teachers as change agents and wanted to elicit their views on how technology could fit into their classrooms in a more active way to solve problems relating to students' difficulties with subject matter.

Methodology

The investigative methodology combined research through design (Zimmerman, Forlizzi, & Evenson, 2007), design-based research (Cobb, Confrey, Lehrer, & Schauble, 2003), and participatory design (Ehn, 1989; Kensing & Blomberg, 1998) supplemented by ethnographically informed qualitative methods. The focus in these methods is on uncovering important components of fit to the socio-technical system that must be addressed by the design and that may be overlooked by other methods.

The VT Classes and the Teachers

During spring and fall 2012, 8 graduate and 16 undergraduate students formed six project groups working with six 8th grade teachers, one 7th grade, and one 6th grade teacher. Undergraduates were in a senior capstone class in software engineering; graduate students were in an upper-level seminar on human–computer interaction. The two 16-week classes met at the same time in the same place. They were conducted on a studio model, with one 3-h meeting a week. After teams were formed, some members of each team were able to travel to the schools to observe classes and meet teachers. Subsequently, the team conducted semi-structured interviews over Skype of the teachers about the class, teaching condition, and their use of representations in teaching. They met with the teachers once a week via Skype or Flashmeeting as well as communicating through the VT scholar website, email, phone, and Google docs. Some members of each VT team were able to travel to the classrooms on 2–3 more occasions, with the professors spending two supplementary days on-site. University students took notes and recorded video that was available for analysis by the entire team, using two cameras per classroom observation. Teams developed projects using the technological infrastructure (mostly Java) that was most expedient for them. Middle school students and teachers accessed programs to be downloaded via websites.

Teachers were recruited by and through the school district. In spring 2012, they consisted of 8th grade teachers with considerable classroom experience (more than 5 years), a history of proactive engagement as teacher leaders, and previous participation in the district digital initiative. All teachers taught with technology in the sense of using technological products in the classroom, but none had a stake in what constitutes CT. Two teachers were drawn from earth sciences, three from English, and one from mathematics. All taught in high- to mixed-SES schools within the district but half had prior experience in low-SES environments. In fall 2012, we continued to work with one 8th grade earth science teacher and one 8th grade English teacher and added a 6th grade mathematics and a 7th grade social studies teacher, both from high-poverty schools (nearly all students eligible for free and reduced price lunch), one of which was designated as "failing" and the other of which was close to such designation. Failing was an assessment based on student performance on high-stakes standardized tests. The schools were, respectively, 96% and 91% African-American.

The six activities were in the areas of English (two projects), mathematics (algebra, fractions), earth science, and social studies. Based on teacher interest and availability, the second VT class continued the development of the earth science and one of the English projects to conduct a second iteration implementation and design and initiated two new projects: one in mathematics (fractions) and one in social studies. Each project was brought successfully to the stage of preliminary classroom use, in regular classroom teaching, by the teams and the co-participating teachers. Given the challenge of going from initial ideation to classroom implementation in one semester and the number of skills that the university students had to master, we did not attempt to create measures of student learning gains. The goal was proof-of-concept for the approach.

During the VT classes, the researchers operated as active participant observers (Spradley, 1980; Kensing & Blomberg, 1998). The participant observers had access to all participants, sites, documents, and technological artifacts. Here we focus on the relationship between middle school teachers, the affordance of the classroom materials including technologies and middle school students, as illustrated in Fig. 1.

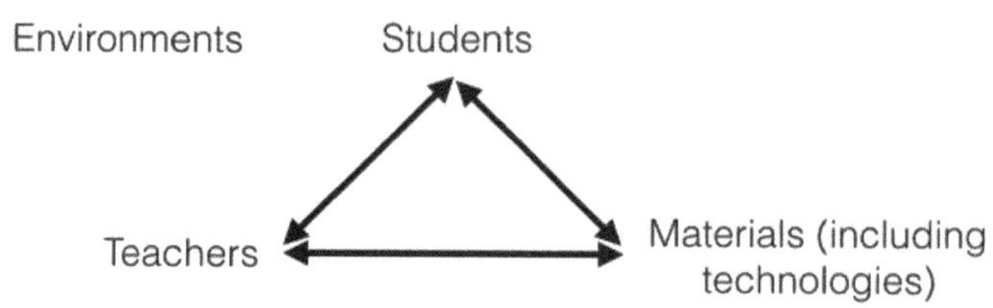

Fig. 1 Instruction as interaction (Cohen, Raudenbush, & Ball, 2003)

Initial Observations and the Move to PCT

There are many different concepts of CT (Computer Science and Telecommunications Board, 2010), and these have been evolving quickly over the past few years (Grover & Pea, 2013). We started with open-ended descriptive approach that included two facets: (a) the representation and manipulation of information that a computer scientist might regard as constituting a model and (b) the representation and manipulation of processes. The idea was to cast a wide and opportunistic net. The strategy would be to call out existing CT components more explicitly.

Initial Findings

Teacher Reports

Teachers were asked what was difficult for their students to learn. A wide range of problems were articulated including that students did not pay enough attention to the details of language morphology, that is, how words work to form phrases, phrases work to form sentences, sentences work to form paragraphs, and paragraphs work to form stories (English); that they did not understand what they were reading in document-based research (social studies); that they did not understand scale in earth science; and that they did not understand coefficients: "what a, b and c do in the equation $y = ax^2 + bx + c$" in algebra. Two comments that we focus on in this paper were that "students 'got lost' doing web searches" (in English class) and that students would "add 1/2 and 1/3 by adding the top and adding the bottom to get 2/5." The teacher who reported this difficulty with fractions was a 6th grade teacher charged with teaching fractions to students who had failed the 5th grade high-stakes mathematics test that focused on fractions. He also reported a series of what we might characterize as systems-level problems with place value and borrowing, in which students somehow missed the crucial meaning of notations and numerals, meaning that is given by the place that those notations and numerals have in the larger system. Students struggled with negative numbers, whether "−6" was bigger or smaller than, say, "1". These kinds of problems are well documented in the literature on mathematics education (Empson & Levi, 2011; Empson, 1999; Steffe, 2010; Norton & Wilkens, 2013) (which might possibly be why the teacher picked these students and cases to report to us).

Illustrations and Instructions Versus Representations

In general, students interacted with handouts made by the teacher, with resources made available online by special school content providers or, rarely, with textbooks. Teacher handouts generally involved a paragraph setting up the activity followed an ordered list of steps that walked the students through a process (without making process an object of reflection).

Teacher handouts and online resources were frequently decorated with illustrations. Across the range of classes, visual stimuli consisted pictures of people (a famous scientist), everyday situations (coal burning in a power plant), or readily observable phenomena (lightning to illustrate atmospheric weather). The pictures often illustrated narratives about the topic studied. Across all classes, there were very few uses of tables, graphs, schematic processes, or visual explanations (such as timelines).

Confirmation of Confusion: English

Our observation of students in one of the English classes included some of the 2 weeks of instruction that they received by the librarian on conducting web-based research and subsequent classes in which the students conducted web-based research for projects. We confirmed that, as the teacher had reported, students, indeed, appeared to be lost and confused doing web searches, often sitting and staring at the screen without moving for long periods of time and sometimes making bad choices about what to click through on (e.g., choosing sites that offered papers for sale rather than providing information useful for completing the assignment). Their confusion caused us to begin to reflect on how and what search engines represent for students. Search engines, quite naturally, prioritize the presentation of search results, as if the user has no trouble remembering the question that led to the choice of terms that led to those particular results. Yet the results of a search may distract students from their original question or how that question was translated into search terms. If they click through on a hit, they then return to the same confusing page.

Inactivity in the Math Classroom

In the 6th grade mathematics classroom, we observed the teacher using two kinds of representations to teach. He drew long rectangles on his Smart Board (an electronic whiteboard) and divided them into portions to illustrate wholes and parts of fractions. He also used number lines centered on zero to scaffold questions about the addition of negative and positive numbers. With his help, students in whole class discussion could walk through exercises based on these representations and arrive at correct calculations. But by the second week of school, they were almost uniformly slumped over and disengaged. The instruction that we witnessed was quite focused on the operations of adding negative numbers rather than, for example, an integration of the representational affordances of the number line with motivation for executing the desired operations.

Few Opportunities for CT

In general, we did not perceive the kinds of openings to CT that we had anticipated. The middle school students did not seem to be engaging with content in a way that was complex enough to admit of the kind of intervention we had initially imagined. In particular, there was very little use of data. Data provides opportunities for CT because the structuring of data for purposes of analysis creates information. Some opportunities did present themselves to create interventions that would have tied curriculum together with central CT processes and patterns. But the elements that appeared most like CT turned out to support learning that the teachers considered unproblematic or trivial. Second, the little ideas that we had for CT seemed unimportant when compared to the more general lack of representation and systems thinking.

Proto-computational Thinking

While many definitions of CT are aspirational or normative, that is, they describe the behavior and practices that researchers and educators would like to see as an outcome of their interventions, our approach had been developmental from the start. We found that classroom activities did not appear to be using sufficiently rich and complex material to afford the full form that would allow a computer scientist to immediately identify the augmentations as CT. However, we found that we were able to look for opportunities to promote *proto*-computational thinking by promoting some aspect of systematicity or even the *need* for systematicity.

The provisional strategy we develop was to perceive PCT opportunities where:

1. Students might not perceive that a system exists.
2. Systems thinking could be an outcome rather than a prerequisite for student action.
3. Problem-solving could be developed into a more important and explicit activity, something that could itself be subject to reflection, scrutiny, and analysis.
4. Students could engage in representation, structure creation, or sequencing, especially through creating, contrasting, and analyzing alternative representations, even when an entire system of representation tied to action was not possible.
5. The abstract and formal could be made concrete and manipulable.

Sometimes the interventions turned out to be quite simple. Sometimes they entailed the development of an entirely new approach to pedagogy in the area. We offer one example of each.

Two Examples

Two examples illustrate the identification of possible areas and the design of support for integrated PCT through a combination of technology and curriculum. The first example was quite simple. The second was only realized well enough in the semester to suggest that the direction was promising and that it required quite complex technology and curricular adjustments.

CritiSearch

CritiSearch starts from one English teacher's observation that her students "get lost doing research." In the K–12 context, the word "research" is usually used to mean online searching for information, so "getting lost doing research" means that students became overwhelmed and distracted when conducting online searches. This observation suggested a strategy of putting the students in charge of making judgments about search results.

This teacher taught 8th grade in a largely white, mixed-SES school, with less than 30% of students eligible for free and reduced price lunch. Her classes were usually 20–25 students. She felt free to engage students with many creative and personalized tasks, and her walls were adorned with student drawings. Students received 2 weeks of instruction on research from the school librarian at the beginning of the school year.

The tool we developed (Fig. 2) sits in (or on) the browser and gives the user the ability to demote or promote search results without reformulating the search. It can be conceptualized as a kind of brutally simple markup language for search results, leading to the re-representation of the material. In an example shown in Fig. 2a, the student "researches" a typical 8th grade book, John Hersey's *Hiroshima*. The results of this search remind us that search engines can produce confusing results. Even excluding sales sites, the student is faced mostly with non-scholarly options. Without CritiSearch, he/she must distinguish between useful and non-useful hits and make a choice about which hit to follow first. After following a hit and returning to the search page, he/she must repeat the task of distinguishing between useful and non-useful hits before being able to make a second selection. Attempting to refine the search terms might be a better choice, but it also constitutes a distraction. It means thinking not about the task at hand, but what constitutes a better search term *for a search engine*. This means conceptualizing different ways that the search engine might confuse the task at hand with other, similar tasks. In all cases, the student is distracted, rather than reinforced, from the accomplishment of the initial goal.

With CritiSearch, the students leave marks to record the work that they have already done to distinguish which hits are useful. Students receive the initial list of hits (Fig. 2a). They mark some as important by rolling the cursor over them and hitting the "thumbs-up" icon. This turns each hit they select in this way green (Fig. 2b). They may also hit the "x" icon to cross hits out (see also Fig. 2b). The CritiSORT button allows them to move the green (selected as important) hits to the top and the x'd out (selected as unimportant) to the bottom (as in Fig. 2c). Any categorization can be changed at any time.

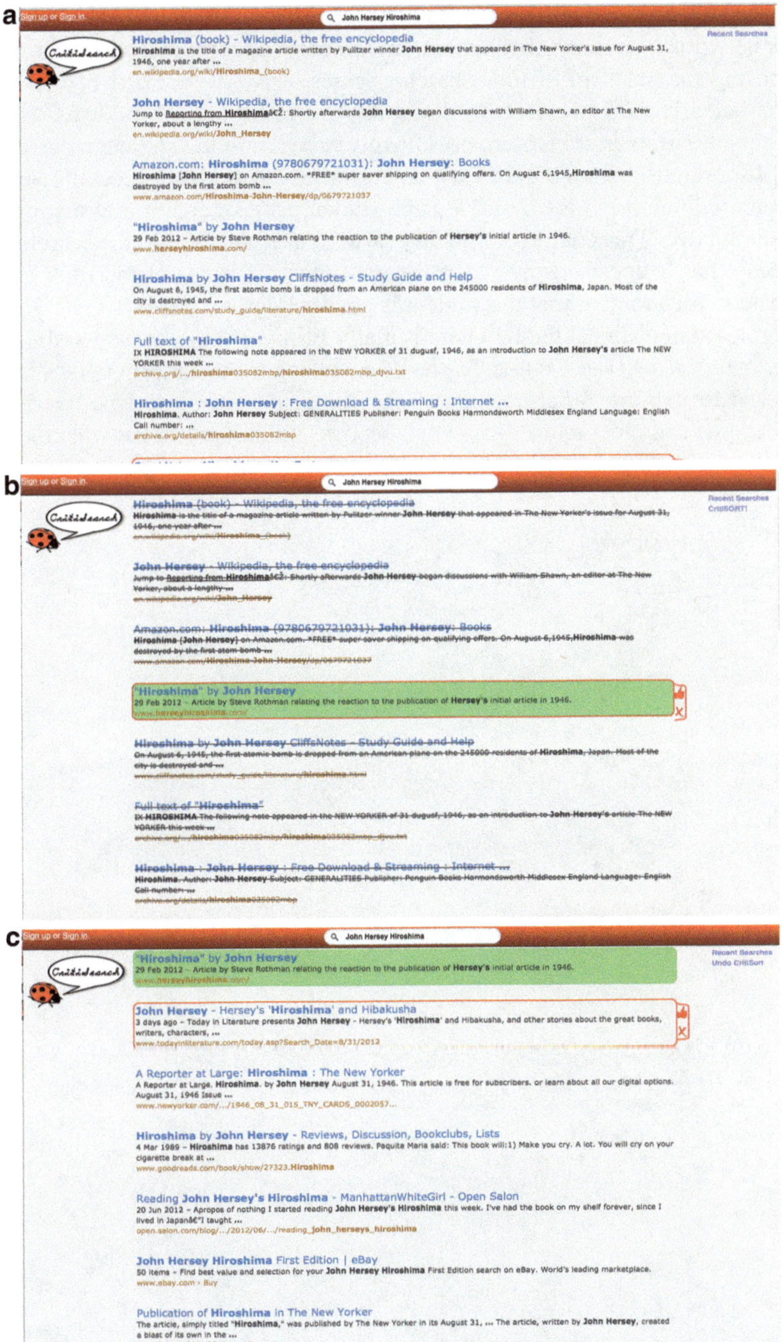

Fig. 2 The CritiSearch tool provides a simple interface for searching and reflection about the nature of search. (**a**) An initial search on a typical 8th grade book leads to many irrelevant options. (**b**) The student marks some as irrelevant, some as potentially important, and some (not shown) not at all. (**c**) Hitting "CritiSORT" rearranges the screen, demoting the irrelevant and making new options easily visible. Note the Undo and "Recent Search" options

CritiSearch does not teach students how searching works, either algorithmically or as a networked process. CritiSearch implements support for PCT because rather than posing the problem of how search engines arrive at their list of hits for the student—clearly a CT problem—it stops short. It instead draws students' attention to the hits themselves, which are presumably relevant to the student's current purposes. It implicitly raises a contrast between what the student is seeking and what the search engine provides by asking the student to take action that distinguishes between the two. This contrast implicitly raises a question of *why* the search engine provides what it does; however, CritiSearch does not demand that this question dominate in the moment that the student is conducting the research.

A proto-computational thought here is that it is important to convey to the student that *searching is a process*. Figure 3a shows a drawing from a student in the class who was asked to illustrate what happens to the computer when you type words into a search engine and press return—not what happens on the screen, but what the search

Fig. 3 Even after 2 weeks of instruction from the librarian, student understanding of search as computer process differs. (**a**) One 8th grade student's drawing of what happens to the computer when we type words into a search engine and press return. (**b**) Another student's drawing, from the same class

engine *does*. In fact, the student has not drawn the computer's process of searching at all. This student has illustrated how a person may get a recipe by searching for how to bake a cake. With the recipe, the person may bake the cake. This is the *person's* process. However, Fig. 3b shows another more sophisticated response to the same prompt from the same class. This student has labeled the drawing "Google searches the Internet" and shows a large stick figure labeled "Google" calling out "Let's go!" to three smaller stick figures labeled "English language," "language arts", and "England" from one house to another. The prompt itself was clear to someone for whom the question of process was already well understood, but others may have no clear idea that computers are governed by processes that are decided by people, and that could operate differently.

Another implicit property of the design of CritiSearch is to support the more general notion that representations produced by a search engine need not be taken at face value but can be evaluated and rearranged, quietly encouraging the discovery of human agency as consumers.

CritiSearch permits the student to get distractions out of the way. It allows them to promote promising material right away. By itself, this action may lay the groundwork for critical thinking. It puts the computer in the position of responded to the human need rather than enforcing the human's adaptation to the computer. However, it also creates the possibility of a more pointed opportunity for CT itself—later. The items that the student marks as irrelevant are not deleted, but demoted. After the student has conducted their research, he/she can, by himself or herself or in a class, consider the category of demoted items and the category of promoted items as wholes, thinking about how to construct better search terms in the future. The design of search terms is an example of language use, which is of interest both in the study of English and CT.

The initial response of students in the class suggested that they liked using it. Furthermore, once given the URL, several students reported using it, unprompted, in research for other classes and even showing it to other students. There were even hints of a "meme-like" spread of the idea. Furthermore, the teacher was enthusiastic. We have since redesigned it and are currently studying the new design.

The point of this account is to draw attention to the way this simple proto-computational design can introduce important questions that lay the groundwork for inquiry about what how computational systems work and how we interact with them.

The Sound of Fractions

CritiSearch is a simple technology that is meant to adjust the user's point of view about searching slightly. The Sound of Fractions (SoF) is more complex as an idea, a technology, and a curricular focus. As mentioned earlier, we conducted observations in a 6th grade arithmetic class in a school designated as "failing" by the state. Almost all children were eligible for free and reduced price lunch. The school was 96% African-American. These particular children had failed their 5th grade high-stakes mathematics test that largely featured fractions. One of the university students observed that all the students in this class were drumming with their fingers. Another observable element was that students were slumped over, inactive, and slow to respond even by the second week of classes. The university students conjectured that this was because the 6th graders were bored. Elements of the situation included that, having publicly failed the high-stakes test and being put in a special class, they were asked to have double periods of mathematics every school day. This mathematics largely replicated the curricula and approaches that they had seen earlier. The curriculum was reinforced through the use of an online mathematics learning system that one of the university students described in his reflection as "miserable drill and practice."

"Bored" is an everyday word describing an everyday feeling for some teenagers. And as mentioned earlier, the study participants' in this study were often observed to be tapping their fingers. Sometimes this kind of tapping and other fidgeting is seen as learned behavior to be extinguished either because it is seen as distracting by teachers or because it is indicative of lack of self-monitoring (Szwed & Bouck, 2013) and/or effortful control (Valiente, Lemery-Chalfant, Swanson, & Reiser, 2008). However, we viewed this behavior as constituting a potential starting point for engagement because it acknowledged the students' position. On inquiry we also found out that, as it happened, all the children in the class were in the school band; they were also aware of and attached to hip-hop music and familiar with percussive polyrhythms. Thus, the idea arose of teaching them fractions through percussion.

The Sound of Fractions started from the idea that there are many parallels between percussive rhythm and fractions. Both are systems that require attention to units at different scales at the same time. In music, we might point to the experience of "beats" and "measures." Indeed, the term "beat" may be used to describe elements at different levels of abstraction—including both a demarcation of time and a rhythmic pattern. The fact that the word has dual meanings suggests that it captures an embodied and felt experience of a tie between the larger units of the music and the individual beats. This is important because it relates to a crucial concept in the psychology of fraction learning: that we must "require students to mentally iterate a unit-fractional part of a whole, establishing a multiplicative relationship between part and whole" (p. 5, Norton & Wilkens, 2013).

Furthermore, many people are able to interact with complexity in musical patterns not only through pleasure in listening but also through embodied experiences such as dancing and drumming. Our curricular and representational intention was to work backward, as it were, from an experience of complex phenomena (the simultaneous experience of larger and smaller patterns within the percussive pattern) experienced through drumming on tables, alone and together, and making predictions about that drumming (such as "which beat will come first, your third one or his?") to the creation of similar visual and auditory patterns using technology and from there to more standard mathematical representations.

Figure 4 shows the first implementation of "the Sound of Fractions." Hitting the play button caused the four different instruments (snare, high hat, kick drum, and synthesizer) to play in tandem. Students could change the number of beats per measure by clicking on an instrument area (in the figure, the snare is selected) and then using the slider to change the beats per measure. Clicking on the rectangle that represented the beat toggled between turning that beat on and off. Long rectangles were chosen to represent the measures and subdivided to represent the beats because that is a representation that the teacher used to teach fractions.

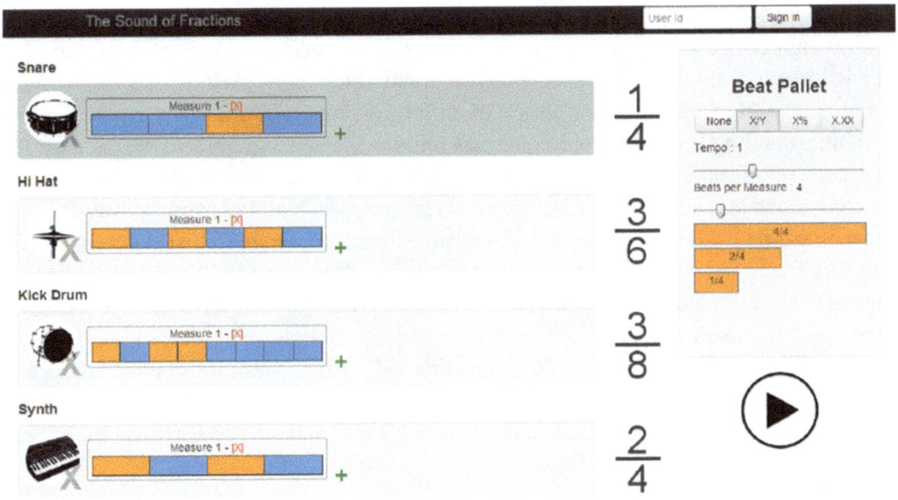

Fig. 4 Initial implementation of the Sound of Fractions

The theory of improvement in PCT lay in the focus on the relationships between different representations. Students could easily see, hear, and feel the relationship between different patterns. The teacher could pose questions about the relationships between modalities, about which rhythmic element would be played before others in relationship to how many parts there were in the measure, about equivalence between different portions of the representations, and about the naming of particular beats. These are fractional questions. They are also questions that expose properties of representations. CT involves choosing amount different representations because of particular properties. PCT simply involves noticing that representations have properties.

On the initial trial, the students loved first drumming on the table and then using the Sound of Fractions to create rhythms. This was encouraging and very gratifying for the university student teams, although they noted that the students probably would have appreciated any novelty. We had developed a curricular approach and lesson plan; however, the classroom implementation proved only a partial success mathematically because the students could answer questions by visual inspection without actually manipulating and exploring the important interface elements. That is, although we were on the track of PCT, the representations did not sufficiently support exploration. By analogy, it operated more like a calculator than an abacus. Additionally, although the interface showed that a person could make sums that constituted equivalent fractions—that is, one fourth could be made by playing the first of four beats, the second of four, the third of four, the fourth of four, the first two of eight, the second and third of eight, and so forth—the students had seen many prior illustrations of equivalence. The representation did not seem to raise questions. We also came to see that by reproducing the rectangular representation that the teacher was already working with, we had also reproduced the limitations of that particular representation. We needed to create a situation that contrasted different visual representations but tied those representations together through reproducing auditory and embodied similarity. Following on Bransford and Schwartz' (1999) notion of contrasting cases, we also needed to turn standard mathematical fractional statements such as one half from a foregone conclusion, into the solution of an interesting problem.

Understanding fractions means understanding that, even though 16 is bigger than 15, that same representation written as one and then six denotes a smaller thing than one five when that one and six is below the line in a denominator. Numbers are symbols that are given meaning by the system in which they are embedded, whether that is through place value, in fractional notation, or on a number line. A full notion of CT involves representing models of situations with objects whose properties must be aligned with relevant processes that use them. The curriculum and redesigned system need to end up with such an alignment; however, the PCT idea that we gleaned from the classroom experience was that we had to reintroduce the students to the idea of a system and that we could do so through an embodied physical analogy that makes it easier to see the importance of experiencing both parts and wholes as mutually defining.

Discussion

We started with the call for CT and suggested why an integrated approach might be important. We examined one mechanism, a class, for achieving such integration. The idea of *PCT* emerged as a result of our program of interaction with classrooms and teachers, especially in low-SES schools. Although we had the chance to investigate and implement curricula and technology that might have looked more like standard CT on the surface, our diagnosis of the situations at hand emphasized the importance of broad thinking that focused on elements both difficult for students to master and that arguably undergird a mastery relationship toward technology.

The strengths in the overall approach are that we addressed issues that at least one teacher saw as being on his/her critical subject area teaching path, that our approach supports equity though integration in classes that all students take, and that our designs respond directly to the situation as we found it. One limitation is that, because the project was primarily concerned with whether we could work with undergraduate and graduate teams to create novel tasks and ideas, we did not take the projects all the way to demonstration of efficacy at scale.

However, we think it is important to write about this approach and our directions. Part of the rationale for integrated CT has to do with issues of equity in schools. We entitled it "PCT: *the Uncomfortable Underpinnings*." PCT activities are by definition underpinnings. They are *uncomfortable* when we are drawn to them because we perceive deficits in schooling. The students in the failing 6th grade that we observed could and perhaps ought to have been learning about representational fluency earlier in their school experience. Some students in the more affluent 8th grade English class already knew about the workings of the search engines; but others had no inkling that there was anything that required explanation.

A question raised by this work about the future is what it means to teach CT without addressing PCT. We know that we can teach students as young as 8 to program and, arguably, you cannot program without some notion of CT. But limitations similar to those we observed in this district might stop students from reaching the full prospects of CT, even when using curricula and materials that are highly successful in other contexts. The science of education has not yet provided a fully accepted explanation why school performance is so highly correlated with socioeconomic standing, but we do know that there is a history of so-called lethal mutations (Brown & Campione, 1996, p. 291) by which innovations are implemented in ways that lose their pedagogical point. Furthermore, the poorest children are the least likely to have opportunities to interact with technology in an engaging way that propels their thinking toward future use (Dolan, 2016; Becker, 2000). Just as "16" has a different meaning when under the line of a fraction than it does when above, our curricula may have different significance under conditions of school poverty. PCT is not in competition with CT. But it is also not just a primitive kind of CT. It is a cultural phenomenon. The definition of CT, the goals of ICT, and the acknowledgment or failure to acknowledge the importance of PCT are political as well as epistemological acts and hence important because our well-meant interventions in the area of CT may reinforce existing social inequities.

Acknowledgments We would like to thank and acknowledge the contributions of the district administration and teachers we worked with as well as colleagues and especially students at VT, especially Taylor O'Connor, Siroberto Scerbo, Dennis Kafura, and Stephanie Rivale. Thanks to Whitney Wall Bortz. We would also like to thank the NSF, which awarded us planning Grant No. CNS-1132227. NSF is not responsible for findings of the work reported.

References

Becker, H. J. (2000). Who's wired and who's not: Children's access to and use of computer technology. *The Future of Children, 10*(2), 44–75.

Bransford, J., & Schwartz, D. (1999). Rethinking transfer: A simple proposal with multiple implications. *RRE, 24*(1), 64–100.

Brown, A., & Campione, J. (1996). Psychological theory and the design of innovative learning environments. In *On procedures, principles and systems*. Mahwah, NJ: Lawrence Erlbaum.

Burns, R., Pollock, L., & Harvey, T. (2012). Integrating hard and soft skills: Software engineers serving middle school teachers, *ACM SIGCSE Computer Science Education (SIGCSE)*.

Cobb, P., Confrey, J., Lehrer, R., & Schauble, L. (2003). Design experiments in educational research. *Educational Researcher, 32*(1), 9–13.

Cohen, D. K., Raudenbush, S. W., & Ball, D. L. (2003). Resources, instruction, and research. *Educational Evaluation and Policy Analysis, 25*(2), 119–142.

Computer Science and Telecommunications Board. (2010). *Report of a workshop on the scope and nature of computational thinking*. Washington, DC: National Academy.

Dolan, J. (2016). Splicing the divide: A review of research on the evolving digital divide among K–12 students. *Journal of Research on Technology in Education, 48*(1), 16–37.

Ehn, P. (1989). *Work-oriented design of computer artifacts* (2nd ed.). Stockholm: Arbetslivscentrum.

Empson, S. B. (1999). Equal sharing and shared meaning: The development of fraction concepts in a first-grade classroom. *Cognition and Instruction, 17*(3), 283–342.

Empson, S. B., & Levi, L. (2011). *Extending children's mathematics: fractions and decimals: innovations in cognitively guided instruction* (p. 272). Portsmouth, NH: Heinemann.

Grover, S., & Pea, R. (2013). Computational thinking in K–12: A review of the state of the field. *Educational Researcher, 42*(1), 38–43.

Kafura, D., & Tatar, D. (2011). Initial experience with a computational thinking course for computer science students. In *Proceedings of the 42nd ACM technical symposium on computer science education (sigCSE'11)* (pp. 251–257).

Kensing, F., & Blomberg, J. (1998). Participatory design: Issues and concerns. *Computer-Supported Cooperative Work, 7*(3–4), 167–185.

Maloney, J., Burd, L., Kafai, Y., Rusk, N., Silverman, B., & Resnick, M. (2004). Scratch: A sneak preview [education]. In *Proceedings of the second international conference on creating, connecting and collaborating through computing* (pp. 104–109). IEEE.

Mouza, C., Marzocchi, A., Pan, Y.-C., & Pollock, L. (2016a). Development, implementation and outcomes of an equitable computer science after-school program: Findings from middle-school students. *Journal of Research on Technology in Education (JRTE), 48*, 84.

Mouza, C., Marzocchi, A., Pan, Y.-C., & Pollock, L. (2016b). Equitable computer science teaching: Implementation and outcomes from middle school students. In *American Educational Research Annual Meeting*.

National Research Council. (1999). *How people learn: brain, mind, experience, and school.* Washington, DC: National Academy.

Norton, A., & Wilkens, J. (2013). Supporting students' constructions of the splitting operation. *Cognition and Instruction, 31*(1), 2–28.

Pollock, L. & Harvey, T. (2011). Combining multiple pedagogies to boost learning and enthusiasm. *ITiCSE'11*, pp. 258–262.

Pollock, L., McCoy, K., Carberry, S., Hundigopal, A., & You, X. (2004). Increasing high school girls' self confidence and awareness of cs through a positive summer experience. In *ACM SIGCSE Technical Symposium on Computer Science Education*, pp. 185–189.

Reardon, S. F. (2011). The widening academic achievement gap between the rich and the poor: New evidence and possible explanations. *Whither Opportunity, 2011*, 91–116.

Repenning, A., Webb, D., & Ioannidou, A. (2010). Scalable game design and the development of a checklist for getting computational thinking into public schools. In *Proceedings of sigCSE '10, the 41st conference on computer science education*.

Resnick, M., & Wilensky, U. (1998). Diving into complexity: Developing probabilistic decentralized activities through role-playing activities. *Journal of the Learning Sciences., 7*(2), 153–172.

Resnick, M., Maloney, J., Monroy-Hernández, A., Rusk, H., Eastmond, E., Brennan, K., Millner, A., Rosenbaum, E., Silver, J., Silverman, B., & Kafai, Y. (2009). Scratch: Programming for all. *Communications of the ACM, 52*(11), 60–67.

Spradley, J. P. (1980). *Participant observation*. New York, NY: Holt, Rhinehart and Winston.

Steffe, L. P. (2010). The partitioning and fraction schemes. In L. P. Steffe & J. Olive (Eds.), *Children's fractional knowledge* (pp. 315–340). New York, NY: Springer.

Szwed, K., & Bouck, E. C. (2013). Clicking away: Repurposing student response systems to lessen off-task behavior. *Journal of Special Education Technology, 28*(2), 1–12.

Valiente, C., Lemery-Chalfant, K., Swanson, J., & Reiser, M. (2008). Prediction of children's academic competence from their effortful control, relationships, and classroom participation. *Journal of Educational Psychology, 100*, 67–77.

Weintrop, D., Beheshti, E., Horn, M., Orton, K., Jona, K., Trouille, L., & Wilensky, U. (2016). Defining computational thinking for mathematics and science classrooms. *Journal of Science Education and Technology, 25*(1), 127–147.

Wilensky, U. (2002). *Modeling nature's emergent patterns with multi-agent languages*. Evanston, IL: Northwestern University.

Wilensky, U., & Stroup, W. (1999). Learning through participatory simulations: Network-based design for systems learning in classrooms. In *Proceedings of the conference on computer supported collaborative learning*.

Wilensky, U., & Stroup, W. (2000). Networked gridlock: Students enacting complex dynamic phenomena with the hubnet architecture. In *The fourth international conference of the learning sciences* (June 14–June 17, 2000), pp. 282–289.

Wing, J. (2006). Computational thinking. *Communications of the ACM, 49*(3), 33–36.

Wolz, U., Stone, M., Pullmood, S. M., & Pearson, K. (2010). Computational thinking via interactive journalism in middle school. In *Proceedings of sigCSE '10, the conference on computer science education*, pp. 239–243.

Zimmerman, J., Forlizzi, J., & Evenson, S. (2007). Research through design as a method for interaction design research in HCI. In *Proceedings of the SIGCHI conference on human factors in computing systems* (pp. 493–502). New York, NY: ACM.

Part II
Higher Education

Medical Computational Thinking: Computer Scientific Reasoning in the Medical Curriculum

Peter Musaeus, Deborah Tatar, and Michael Rosen

Abstract Computational thinking (CT) in medicine means deliberating when to pursue computer-mediated solutions to medical problems and evaluating when such solutions are worth pursuing in order to assist in medical decision making. Teaching computational thinking (CT) at medical school should be aligned with learning objectives, teaching and assessment methods, and overall pedagogical mission of the individual medical school in relation to society. Medical CT as part of the medical curriculum could help educate novices (medical students and physicians in training) in the analysis and design of complex healthcare organizations, which increasingly rely on computer technology. Such teaching should engage novices in information practices where they learn to perceive practices of computer technology as directly involved in the provision of patient care. However, medical CT as a teaching and research field is only beginning to be established in bioinformatics and has not yet made headway into the medical curriculum. Research is needed to answer questions relating to how, when, and why medical students should learn to engage in CT, e.g., to design technology to solve problems in systemic healthcare and individual patient care. In conclusion, the medical curriculum provides a meaningful problem space in which medical computational thinking ought to be developed. We argue not for the introduction of a stand-alone subject of medical CT, but as researchers, teachers, clinicians, or curriculum administrators, we should strive to develop theoretical arguments and empirical cases about how to integrate the demand for medical CT into the medical curriculum of the future.

P. Musaeus (✉)
Centre for Health Sciences Education, Aarhus University, Aarhus, Denmark
e-mail: peter@cesu.au.dk

D. Tatar
Department of Computer Science, Virginia Tech, Blacksburg, VA 24061, USA
e-mail: tatar@cs.vt.edu

M. Rosen
Department of Anesthesiology and Critical Care Medicine, Johns Hopkins University, Baltimore, MD 21218, USA
e-mail: mrosen44@jhmi.edu

P.J. Rich, C.B. Hodges (eds.), *Emerging Research, Practice, and Policy on Computational Thinking*, Educational Communications and Technology: Issues and Innovations, DOI 10.1007/978-3-319-52691-1_6

Keywords Clinical reasoning • Curriculum reform • Medical school • Medical diagnosis

Introduction

Medicine is undergoing a computational revolution that has yet to lead to curriculum reform. This essay argues that the medical curriculum provides a meaningful problem space in which medical computational thinking (CT) ought to be developed. The medical curriculum is a meaningful context for CT because medicine and CT share a focus on relevance and problem-solving or decision making leading to change or design of solutions. We conceive of medical CT as medical students' (and physicians') ability to know when a computer-mediated solution to a medical problem is worth pursuing. It includes processes often associated with CT such as using heuristics of reduction, transformation, simulation, and abstraction (Wing, 2008). Medical CT is about formulating problems and their solutions (Wing, 2006) in the context of medicine and computer-mediated tools for facilitating diagnosis, treatment planning, and monitoring of health. Our use of the notion of computational thinking (CT) follows Ado's classical definition:

> We consider computational thinking to be the thought processes involved in formulating problems so their solutions can be represented as computational steps and algorithms. An important part of this process is finding appropriate models of computation with which to formulate the problem and derive its solutions (Aho, 2012, p. 833).

Wing credits the following formulation to Aho:

> Computational thinking is the thought processes involved in formulating problems and their solutions so that the solutions are represented in a form that can be effectively carried out by an information-processing agent (Cuny, Snyder, Wing cited in Wing, 2010).

In summary, medical CT highlights the importance of how medical novices learn to think through the strengths and limitations of computational designs as they apply to modern complex healthcare systems.

Chapter Overview

In this chapter we draw broadly from the research fields of medical education, medical informatics, and medical decision making. We will argue that medical CT could bridge these research fields in focusing on computer-mediated medical reasoning and problem-solving as a design process. Thus, educational researchers, clinicians, and medical school administrators can gain inspiration from the computational revolution in the biosciences and medicine in order to help reform the medical curriculum toward encompassing medical CT. In short, medical CT might be a necessary infusion of new ideas into the established medical curriculum, but currently there is no basis for recommending it as a stand-alone subject with easily integrated sets of skills. Medical CT is a way of reasoning that must be integrated at different levels (subject, year, difficulty, etc.) of the medical curriculum.

A Plea for Medical CT

There are three reasons why medical CT is pertinent in the medical curriculum. First, computer technology and computational biosciences are rapidly transforming medicine. Computer decision support is increasingly implemented at hospitals to improve clinical workflows (Kaushal, Shojania, & Bates, 2003), online consultations, electronic health records practice (Audet et al., 2004), individualized health monitoring and algorithms for treatment (Steinhubl, Torkamani, & Topol, 2015), and in robotic surgery (Diana & Marescaux, 2015). Yet computer science is not taught at most medical schools apart from as an implicit part of a (graduate) course on biostatistics.

Second, CT in the sense defined in the introduction has not been given explicit educational political attention by leading educational institutions in medicine such as the Institute of Medicine in the United States or the Graduate Medical Council (GMC) in Britain. The Dutch Federation of University Medical Centres recommends that medical students as future doctors learn about computer technology and electronic resources for computation, but as the following chapter will elaborate, medical CT is much more than merely learning about computer technology.

Third, concrete initiatives have been made to introduce computational subjects in curricula similar to medicine. Thus, proponents of genomics, i.e., the science of studying the genome through computational means, make perhaps the strongest plea for a new computational subject that should be taught at medical school. Notably, Nelson and Mcguire (2010) argue that genomics should be taught at medical school. We believe that their rationale for introducing genomics could be extended to apply to medical computational thinking (CT):

> The time has come to make changes not in the factual content of medical education but in the thinking process that physicians in this century will need to manage the unique challenges of the information explosion (Nelson & McGuire, 2010, p. 2).

The plea for genomics indicates a need for medical curriculum reform toward integrating courses with emphasis on CT where medical students learn to use computing activities to learn to regulate their thinking as medical decision makers and navigators in the expanding (exploding) universe of information.

In summary, computational tools are pervasive in biomedicine, but not yet in the medical curriculum or in medical educational research. As research is rapidly emerging on computational bioscience and more slowly on teaching of computational bioscience, we lack directions on the relevance for medical education. We lack didactic queries into computational thinking as an important competence in medical education.

It is likely that the medical curriculum will increasingly start drawing from computational biosciences. However, several questions need to be investigated in terms of what medical CT is and how it should be integrated into medical school.

Curricula Issues

In this section we will discuss nine issues we take to be important for medical CT to be integrated in the medical curriculum. The issues raise questions first about the content or subject matter of medical CT, i.e., clarifying the role of computer literacy, assessment, abstraction, and diagnosis. Second, the principal issues raise challenges relating to the practicalities of introducing CT into the medical school relating to new subjects.

Delineating Medical CT

As our definition in the introduction made clear, we follow those who argue that CT is much more than computer fluency and computer literacy. Other subjects and concerns compete at the curricula level with CT in terms of what medical students are supposed to learn. In this section we will first delineate medical CT from various levels of computer literacy/fluency/proficiency. Second, we will delineate medical CT from computer programming.

The first question is whether medical students should become computer literate. Computer literacy can briefly be defined as the act of knowing about computers or knowing how to use relevant computer software for medical problem-solving. It would be too easy to claim that computer proficiency is not at some level a pre-requirement for medical CT because computers have been ubiquitous in medical education for several years (Ellaway & Masters, 2008; McAuley, 1998). Simpson et al. (2002) argue in the context of Scottish undergraduate medical education that as the practice of medicine is becoming more complex in terms of knowledge and use of technology, medical students must learn about computer technical skills:

> [Being competent] in basic information-handling skills ranging from simple record keeping to accessing and using computer-based data. As well as having the technical skills to undertake such tasks it is important that graduates appreciate the role of informatics in the day-to-day care of patients and the advancement of medical science in genera (Simpson et al., 2002, p. 140).

According to Simpson's list, required skills include being able to use common software such as e-mail and word processing, using statistical packages and medical databases. This list might strike the computer scientist as very low in ambition: What about using computational techniques to derive at higher-order thinking, computer-mediated problem-solving, understanding dynamic systems, or whatever we might think CT is given that it goes beyond computer literacy? Physicians strive to restore health not devise and manage whole system hospital care. Furthermore, medical students are educated as decision makers rather than experts in computational bioinformatics or computer science.

The second question is whether medical students should learn computer programming. Pioneering attempts by Denning (2010) have been made to teach computing to noncomputer science majors including liberal arts students. Being able to program is a more advanced skill than computer literacy. One argument for medical students to learn programming is that they need computing skills before they can learn medical CT. This is the argument for proponents of teaching CT in bioinformatics that without a certain prerequisite in programming CT is not achievable.

> [A] single one-semester course, which does not assume a basic programming course as a prerequisite, is likely to miss the goal of teaching computational thinking and computational concepts to life science students. If basic programming is taught from scratch, not enough time will be left for the higher level computational concepts and their relations to biology, so the depth of coverage of computational thinking will be smaller (Rubinstein & Chor, 2014, p. 3).

Thus, Rubinstein and Chor (2014) argue that life science students need a basic course on programming and software tool handling before being given a course on computational thinking. For instance, a procedural course on how to use a particular tool (R, Python, etc.) might mask the underlying or more abstract computational ideas, but without recourse to basic programming skills, the bioscience, and probably also by implication the medical, student cannot comprehend the underlying computational scientific ideas that lie behind CT. If life science and bioinformatics students have a hard time building computational models, how should medical students who are not trained in bioinformatics fare when given the task of building computer models of healthcare systems? The answer is that we do not know, but probably medical students should be first given introductory programming and second asked to build simple models before they can acquire deeper level CT. Rubinstein and Chor (2014) suggest that a technical courses on concrete bioinformatics tools does not teach deep-level thinking about computation.

This begs the related question whether programming skills should be entry-level requirements to medical school? In the USA, students entering medical school are currently under no obligation to take computational coursework (Nelson & McGuire, 2010). The situation is similar in Europe and Asia where students enter medical school at university right after high school: Computer skills are not an entry requirement for medical students, and computational thinking (CT) is to our knowledge neither taught systematically nor on the grand scale at any medical school in the world. Empathy and scientific reasoning are more closely aligned with the traditional role of doctoring and hence deemed as more important entry-level requirements compared with computer programming skills. In summary, research is lacking on the role of computer science, programming, not to say CT in the (undergraduate and graduate) medical curriculum: What should medical students learn, how and when?

Third, there is the question about whether medical students should learn anything remotely resembling computer science. We agree with Wing's various (2006, 2008) assertion that CT is more than computer literacy and basic programming skills. Medical students should develop the ability to know when a computer-mediated solution to a medical problem is worth pursuing. This has been pointed out by Wing (2006, 2008) and Denning (2010) who argue that teaching CT to noncomputer majors should teach competences such as using heuristics of reduction, transformation, simulation, and abstraction (Wing, 2008). Clearly this goes far beyond computer literacy, but it is arguably unrealistic to expect a medical student or physician in training who has no programming skills to write and apply code to medical tasks such as designing health systems of diagnosis and care. It is hardly the best use of resources to design a curriculum where students or physicians in training spend too much time coding the information systems for health systems. However, it could be a learning objective that they learn to be on the teams that are developing such information systems. To be effective members of a health transdisciplinary team, some knowledge of the domain expertise of others is required; hence a curriculum incorporating medical CT must reflect this.

In summary, given the pervasiveness of computers in healthcare, we might demand some level of computer proficiency in medical students. While computational biology students clearly need programming skills, this is hardly yet a realistic demand to make on medical students. But acquaintance with programming could make medical students progress toward higher-order CT, and hence it could be beneficial for the medical curriculum administrators aiming to strike a balance between computer literacy and full-fledged computer science competences. Without getting stuck in the nitty-gritty, but important questions about subject matter, the aim should be clear: Educating medical students to be able to move on to explore advanced areas of computing and design of computer-mediated healthcare.

Medical CT Could Facilitate Students' Learning to Diagnose

In the following we will investigate whether integrating medical CT into the medical curriculum could help medical students learn critical diagnostic reasoning. Our argument is that CT might teach medical students to (1) diagnose as a string of actions, (2) avoid fixation errors, (3) avoid pseudodiagnosticity, and (4) perceive abstractions in diagnosis. The underlying argument is that medical CT could teach students to qualify their diagnostic choices.

First, CT could be introduced in subjects emphasizing diagnosis. Diagnosis can be conceived as an instrument of thinking for the doctor because the diagnosis helps the doctor perceive a problem and cascade a string of actions with various effects on the patient's and doctor's further actions (Pauli, White, & McWhinney, 2000). Thus a central tenet of medicine is that the physician acts as decision maker and that medical student must learn to think critically about complex situations involving diagnosis. It is becoming commonplace that the physician's acts of diagnosis rely on computer tools developed in bioinformatics and computer science. Interdisciplinary research in cognitive informatics is casting light on how physicians think, diagnose, and problem solve as mediated by computer technologies (Patel et al., 2009; Patel, Kaufman, & Cohen, 2014; Patel, Kaufman, & Kannampallil, 2013). For instance, attending physicians routinely use laboratory tests to diagnose patients, and these tests derive increasingly from computational bioscience, most notably from computational genomics (Dhar, Alford, Nelson, & Potocki, 2012; Nelson & McGuire, 2010). In spite of this seminal work on medical reasoning within cognitive informatics, the field of medical education knows preciously little about how to teach medical reasoning such as diagnosis. Needless to say, we know even less about how CT can be integrated into the teaching of diagnosis.

But, one lesson about how to teach medical diagnosis through computational means would be to delineate rather than decompose diagnosis: CT could support the teaching of diagnosis as a string of actions. Shortliffe and Blois (2006) point out that diagnosis should not be decomposed and that diagnosis should not be conceived or indeed taught as a modular activity. The point is that diagnosis is not an activity decomposed into fragmented and isolated acts where one or more acts delimit what might be called the diagnosis (Elstein, 2009). The problem is when medical students are led to view diagnosis as a process that physicians carry out in isolation before choosing therapy for a patient or proceeding to other modular tasks rather than viewing diagnosis as an ongoing process. A number of classical studies have shown that this model is oversimplified and that such a decomposition of cognitive tasks may be quite misleading (Elstein, Kagan, Shulman, Jason, & Loupe, 1972). This research suggests that by learning to engage in CT as an iterative process, students' diagnostic skills might improve.

Second, CT could teach students about fixation errors. Shortliffe and Blois (2006) argue that a physician must be flexible and open-minded in order to continuously update and possibly alter the original diagnosis. CT might help the clinician avoid the diagnosis fixation problem where the clinician too early fixes on one set of alternative diagnoses and thus become biased toward other evidence. Teaching computational diagnosis should remind the student that patient treatment and assessment involves an ongoing or iterative process of analysis of data and treatment results, monitoring of progression of disease (Leblanc, Brooks, & Norman, 2002; Shortliffe & Blois, 2006). CT might remind the student to keep a scientific and open mind about alternative hypotheses. Teaching CT could help medical students identify when categorization into classes of diseases, for instance, is possible and when the ambiguity and messiness of diagnostic reasoning make this impossible because of multiple and mutually overlapping or embedded explanations and diagnoses (Monteiro & Norman, 2013). Although basic CT might involve basic categorization tasks, higher-level medical CT should engage students to identify features of the patients' diseases that do not call for separable options, but nested paths (ibid).

Third, medical CT might be integrated in the medical curriculum in order to teach students about pseudodiagnosticity. Working with computer-mediated diagnostic tools might help medical students understand Bayesian reasoning and avoid what by Doherty, Mynatt, Tweney, and Schiavo (1979) was labeled pseudodiagnosticity referring to failure to correctly identify and select relevant information for diagnosis. This reasoning draws from Bayesian reasoning, where Bayes' theorem can be used to evaluate the probability of event A in relation to event B in which the dispersion of the disease in the population is known (Kern & Doherty, 1982). Pseudodiagnosticity then is the effect of selecting irrelevant information in diagnostic tasks. Medical students need to learn to make balanced judgment of single symptoms in relation to a single diagnosis (Kern & Doherty, 1982). The point is that it could be relevant to teach medical students in Bayesian reasoning in order to increase medical students' ability to choose appropriate symptom information and thus perform differential diagnosis.

Fourth, medical CT might be aligned with the purpose of teaching students about abstraction. Abstraction in medicine can mean using algorithms that are guidelines in some often abbreviated, yet useful format that have been developed in virtually any clinical medical specialty (Elstein, 2009; Kassirer, 2010). It would be a worthy learning objective if medical CT could help the medical student see the limitations of these algorithms or of diagnostic heuristics because computer science had a tradition for abstraction and evaluation superior to other scientific fields, but we sincerely doubt it. In particular how abstraction can serve medical diagnosis and help the student understand the essence of a subject matter or in the clinical situation use models to ameliorate a risk for information overload and high degree of contingency (Patel et al., 2009). Computer models might possibly reduce a complex clinical situation to one that is more manageable with reduced redundancy. While this is practical, it also raises the risk of simplification and various errors including flawed inductive reasoning and the simplistic idea that abstraction in computer science can somehow help transcend the physical dimension of time and space, the contingencies and plethora of clinical cases demanding a clear diagnosis.

In summary, diagnosis is arguably among the most important activities about which medical students need to develop critical assessment and reasoning. Since computer technology in modern healthcare is a central aid to physicians' diagnosis, medical students should learn to use and design improvements in such diagnostic tools. Hence the benefits of teaching medical students about the strengths and limitations of computational diagnosis tools might be considerable.

Medical CT Could Teach Medical Students to Analyze Data

This section deals with the question whether medical students should learn to engage in CT in order to become better data analysts. This concern is pertinent since, according to the American Association of Medical Colleges, a third of the students entering medical school have non-science and non-mathematics backgrounds as evident in the following quotation:

> Toward this aim, physicians with integrity and sophistication should partner closely with computer and data scientists to reimagine clinical medicine and to anticipate its ethical implications. It is important to systematically validate data from mobile health and consumer-facing technologies, particularly for cases in which dynamic intervention is provided (Darcy, Louie, & Roberts, 2016, p. 552).

Given the transformation of medicine into a data science (Steinhubl, Torkamani, & Topol, 2015), there might both be a concern that doctors become data centric and lose touch with patients or equally that they become illiterate in using computational thinking. In other words there is a need for assessing what it could mean to educate physicians to become competent data analysts by learning CT.

Aligned subjects with CT such as statistical computation and bioinformatics are taught in computational medicine that exists as a research field e.g., Johns Hopkins University. But medical CT, or something like computational medicine, is generally not taught or systematically built in to the medical curriculum at any medical school anywhere in the world. What we know is that medical students are taught medical statistics either as a stand-alone course or in subjects like social medicine or epidemiology. Thus medical students learn to formulate statistical/mathematical models of medically relevant phenomena (Freeman, Collier, Staniforth, & Smith, 2008). This focus on statistics in medical school goes back at least to the 1993 General Medical Council report Tomorrow's Doctors which recommended that medical education be required to promote the critical evaluation of evidence. Here they are likely to learn to use computer programs or statistical packages.

But the concern is that medical students might not necessarily learn to abstract representations from complex data or to computationally represent complex medical phenomena. Nelson and McGuire (2010, p. 2) write in their plea for genomics teaching in medical school and CME: "The growing field of genomics provides the most visible example of the explosion of medical data, but it is still only one component of the rapidly changing face of modern health care." In the face of an explosion in medical data and in the opportunities for extracting such data, computational methods such as machine learning are needed to help physicians make sense of this data.

We can summarize and say that evidence is mounting that medical students will need to develop skills in manipulating computational data mining tools such as machine learning and evaluate how such tools can be used in delivering integrated, person-centered healthcare.

Discussion: Integrating Medical CT into the Curriculum

Introducing computational thinking as a new subject into the medical curriculum introduces three challenges:

1. *New subjects in the medical curricula need a research (and/or political) base.* The first challenge is that a new subject needs to be well founded in some sort of justification such as research based, needs assessment, a political agenda, patient

perspective, etc. New subjects in the medical curricula such as the clinical subjects of patient safety, quality insurance, and team training or the more fundamental subjects such as mathematics arguably have stronger justifications (more educational research, for instance) than say a new subject called medical CT. In other words there are also good arguments why say patient safety should be taught at (any) medical school in the world, as we hope to have provided good reasons why medical CT should be introduced.

Perhaps medical CT does not stand first in line for being elected as a new subject at medical school. Research is lacking on what medical CT could mean and we need to show how medical CT can be aligned with existing subjects and curricula goals. For instance, given that there is irrefutable evidence that large numbers of patients are harmed by healthcare delivery systems, it could be argued that patient safety should be a priority in the healthcare curricula at all levels. The need medical CT is addressing is a bit more general, but cuts deep into many subjects in a similar fashion as patient safety does; it is not restricted to a 1-week course, but about creating a whole curriculum. In other words, the new field of medical CT might stand side by side with other worthy subjects not readily introduced into the medical curriculum. This speaks to the need to integrate medical CT into existing subjects rather than attempt designing a standalone (say 1-week summer) course as argued in the following.

2. *CT must be integrated into other subjects rather than compete with them.* Our argument is that CT must be integrated into the medical curriculum, i.e., become part of several relevant subjects ranging from statistics, biochemistry, to clinical medicine that could be argued briefly in terms of five overlapping lines of evidence:

   First, following the integrated science introductory curriculum developed at Princeton University (by David Botstein and William Bialek) and elaborated by others to show that CT should not be a stand-alone course (Qualls & Sherrell, 2010). If this argument holds for medical education, and we believe it does since medicine is a bioscience and a clinical science, CT needs to be integrated into the curriculum in order to be effectively learned.

   Second, with reference to the earlier mentioned point that medical CT should not be introduced as a mere instrumental course, as if CT was merely a procedural skill. CT should not be reduced to course in how to use bioinformatics tools, but the underlying computational ideas and principles should be explained (Pevzner & Shamir, 2009).

   Third, CT should be introduced early in the medical curricula as part of clinical as well as bioscience learning in order for medical students to see their profession at a holistic level rather than individual subjects by making connections among different subjects say genetics and pharmacology and pathology by giving students a sense of the conceptual base of the computer models they can learn about to model these subjects.

   Fourth, CT should be aligned with the idea of encapsulating concepts in the medical curriculum. It should not be left to the medical student to bridge CT with other medical subjects. When working with basic biosciences and patients early in the curriculum, medical CT should be integrated into these subjects.

Fifth, it has repeatedly been found that medical students are burdened with a big working load (Bordage, 1987). Thus it could be questioned whether CT can seamlessly be added to the medical curricula; it is not clear whether there is room for CT in medical education as a stand-alone course or even if it is expected that medical students learn CT on top of what other requirements they have. A strong case must be made how CT can aid the medical student to use other subjects (statistics, clinical medicine, etc.) and not just be an added burden.

3. *CT should avoid making false promises.* Ambitious, high-flung promises seem to follow new subjects in order to make a political strong case for being implemented. Examples of problems include when proponents promise that this or that subject can teach thinking or critical reasoning. Care must be taken with medical CT not to repeat potential pitfalls as when other subjects were introduced (such as "humanities in medicine," "writing medical science," or "critical thinking"). Perhaps in order to gain acceptance, some subject might end up making unwarranted or hard to defend claims about their effectiveness in producing valued goods such as (humanities in medicine) producing empathy or (writing courses) producing scientific thinking. So proponents of CT should be careful not to make such promises.

   To be clear, the issue here is not with any particular subject such as "humanities in medicine," which is a subject with well-documented rationale and positive effects on student professionalism. The point is not to compete with the humanities and social sciences subjects in medicine, but seek to integrate itself into these and in fact most biological and medical subjects. For instance, a subject such as "medical ethics" could be a course that could integrate CT and pose two critical questions: What are the alienating effects of computer technology on patient-physician relations? What are the possible moral dimensions of computational thinking on the practice of medicine?

   A related problem is that it remains to be explained how medical students can learn critical or computational thinking—or any other thinking—in the abstract, i.e., without attending to the subject or material that the student is acquiring. Such generic thinking subjects risk becoming detached from the immediate concerns of medical students which are to pass the next difficult exam or engage in clinical duties immediately seen as relevant to being a physician unless they are taught by physicians or experts who know medicine. Medical CT should not run into the same risk of being perceived as detached from the main concerns of being a physician.

   In summary, it could be argued that the rapidly expanding biosciences stand next in line to be adopted together with computer science into medical curriculum. However, that would be to underestimate how much resistance medical curricula reforms can encounter.

Concluding Discussion

Medical computational thinking should not be introduced hastily as the next subject in vogue in the medical curriculum. As we have argued, medical CT should be carefully integrated into the clinical and social and bioscientific subjects. This way student will have a basis when they learn at the bedside and laying the foundations for their clinical practice. Becoming a clinician who can use computational tools to solve clinical problems starts with teaching integrated CT in other subjects in the medical curricula. But it also requires medical teachers who are steeped in computer scientific reasoning and can demonstrate how this produces clinical improvements and help treat patients.

Future work must investigate how the medical curriculum can integrate computational bioinformatics while at the same time keeping a focus on students' early patient contact and the lesson that complex health solutions are value driven and constrained in terms of cost and capability. We need research to develop blueprints for how computing skills can be integrated seamlessly into the curriculum and whether it should replace other subjects. Furthermore, future studies must elucidate how the medical curriculum can teach medical students and novice physicians to become competent members of multidisciplinary health teams that design medical computational solutions. Medical students need to know enough about other ways of thinking and skill sets to interact effectively without necessarily spending time on large-scale computer coding.

Medical CT, as an educational task, could be about reasoning, exploring, trying things out virtually, and perhaps designing and evaluating, and given this content it might help develop an attitude of inquisitiveness in the students. Medical CT might specifically develop a theoretical attitude toward health and medicine around the notion of uncertainty and risk in decision making. Such uncertainty is amenable to be modeled in computational models and in models involving risk

If medical CT were taught internationally, resource sharing could occur across medical schools. Medical CT can become a welcomed addition to the medical curricula if a research based can be build. Medical CT calls for research investigating and initiatives supporting how healthcare is in the midst of a computational transformation. We need to address a vision for the future of how the medical curriculum, from the pregraduate, graduate, to postgraduate level, can support the teaching, utilization, and design of computational medical science and healthcare.

References

Aho, A. V. (2012). Computation and computational thinking. *Computer Journal, 55*(7), 833–835. doi:10.1093/comjnl/bxs074.

Audet, A.-M., Doty, M. M., Peugh, J., Shamasdin, J., Zapert, K., & Schoenbaum, S. (2004). Information technologies: When will they make it into physicians' black bags? *MedGenMed: Medscape General Medicine, 6*(4), 2.

Bordage, G. (1987). The curriculum: Overloaded and too general? *Medical Education, 21*(3), 183–188. doi:10.1111/j.1365-2923.1987.tb00689.x.

Darcy, A. M., Louie, A. K., & Roberts, L. W. (2016). Machine learning and the profession of medicine. *Jama, 315*(6), 551–552. doi:10.1001/jama.2015.18421.

Denning, P. J. (2010). The great principles of computing. *American Scientist, 98*(5), 369–372. doi:10.1145/948383.948400.

Dhar, S. U., Alford, R. L., Nelson, E. a., & Potocki, L. (2012). Enhancing exposure to genetics and genomics through an innovative medical school curriculum. *Genetics in Medicine, 14*(1), 163–167. doi:10.1038/gim.0b013e31822dd7d4.

Diana, M., & Marescaux, J. (2015). Robotic surgery. *British Journal of Surgery, 102*(2), 15–28. doi:10.1002/bjs.9711.

Doherty, M. E., Mynatt, C. R., Tweney, R. D., & Schiavo, M. D. (1979). Pseudodiagnosticity. *Acta Psychologica, 43*(2), 111–121.

Ellaway, R., & Masters, K. (2008). AMEE Guide 32: e-learning in medical education Part 1: Learning, teaching and assessment. *Medical Teacher, 30*(5), 455–473. doi:10.1080/01421590802108331.

Elstein, A. S. (2009). Thinking about diagnostic thinking: A 30-year perspective. *Advances in Health Sciences Education, 14*(Suppl. 1), 7–18. doi:10.1007/s10459-009-9184-0.

Elstein, A. S., Kagan, N., Shulman, L. S., Jason, H., & Loupe, M. J. (1972). Methods and theory in the study of medical inquiry. *Journal of Medical Education, 47*, 85–92.

Freeman, J. V., Collier, S., Staniforth, D., & Smith, K. J. (2008). Innovations in curriculum design: a multi-disciplinary approach to teaching statistics to undergraduate medical students. *BMC Medical Education, 8*, 28. doi:10.1186/1472-6920-8-28.

Kassirer, J. P. (2010). Teaching clinical reasoning: Case-based and coached. *Academic Medicine: Journal of the Association of American Medical Colleges, 85*(7), 1118–1124. doi:10.1097/ACM.0b013e3181d5dd0d.

Kaushal, R., Shojania, K. G., & Bates, D. W. (2003). Effects of computerized physician order entry and clinical decision support systems on medication safety: A systematic review. *Archives of Internal Medicine, 163*(12), 1409–1416. doi:10.1001/archinte.163.12.1409.

Kern, L., & Doherty, M. E. (1982). "Pseudodiagnosticity" in an idealized medical problem-solving environment. *Journal of Medical Education, 57*, 100–104.

Leblanc, V. R., Brooks, L. R., & Norman, G. R. (2002). Believing is seeing: the influence of a diagnostic hypothesis on the interpretation of clinical features. *Academic Medicine: Journal of the Association of American Medical Colleges, 77*(Suppl. 10), S67–S69.

McAuley, R. J. (1998). Requiring students to have computers: Questions for consideration. *Academic Medicine, 73*(6), 669–673.

Monteiro, S. M., & Norman, G. (2013). Diagnostic reasoning: Where we've been, where we're going. *Teaching and Learning in Medicine, 25*(Suppl. 1), S26–S32.

Nelson, E. A., & McGuire, A. L. (2010). The need for medical education reform: genomics and the changing nature of health information. *Genome Medicine, 2*(3), 18. doi:10.1186/gm139.

Patel, V. L., Kaufman, D. R., & Cohen, T. (2014). In V. L. Patel, D. R. Kaufman, & T. Cohen (Eds.), *Cognitive informatics in health and biomedicine. Case studies on critical care complexity and errors*. London: Springer. doi:10.1007/978-1-4471-5490-7.

Patel, V. L., Kaufman, D. R., & Kannampallil, T. G. (2013). Diagnostic reasoning and decision making in the context of health information technology. *Reviews of Human Factors and Ergono, 8*, 149–190. doi:10.1177/1557234X13492978.

Patel, V. L., Shortliffe, E. H., Stefanelli, M., Szolovits, P., Berthold, M. R., Bellazzi, R., & Abu-Hanna, A. (2009). The coming of age of artificial intelligence in medicine. *Artificial Intelligence in Medicine, 46*(1), 5–17. doi:10.1016/j.artmed.2008.07.017.

Pauli, H. G., White, K. L., & McWhinney, I. R. (2000). Medical education, research, and scientific thinking in the 21st century (part three of three). *Education for Health (Abingdon, England), 13*(2), 173–186. doi:10.1080/13576280050074435.

Pevzner, P., & Shamir, R. (2009). Computing has changed biology–biology education must catch up. *Science (New York, N.Y.), 325*(5940), 541–542. doi:10.1126/science.1173876.

Qualls, J. A., & Sherrell, L. B. (2010). Integrated into the curriculum. *JCSC, 25*(5), 66–71.

Rubinstein, A., & Chor, B. (2014). Computational thinking in life science education. *PLoS Computational Biology, 10*(11), e1003897. doi:10.1371/journal.pcbi.1003897.

Shortliffe, E., & Blois, M. (2006). The computer meets medicine and biology: emergence of a discipline. *Biomedical Informatics*, 3–45. doi:10.1007/0-387-36278-9_1.

Simpson, J. G., Furnace, J., Crosby, J., Cumming, A. D., Evans, P. A., Friedman Ben David, M., et al. (2002). The Scottish doctor–learning outcomes for the medical undergraduate in Scotland: A foundation for competent and reflective practitioners. *Medical Teacher, 24*(2), 136–143. doi:10.1080/01421590220120713.

Steinhubl, S. R., Torkamani, A., & Topol, E. J. (2015). Digital medical tools and sensors. *The Journal of the American Medical Association, 313*(4), 353–354. doi:10.1001/jama.2014.17125.

Wing, J. M. (2006). Wing06-ct. *Communications of the ACM, 49*(3), 33–35. doi:10.1145/1118178.1118215.

Wing, J. M. (2008). Computational thinking and thinking about computing. *Philosophical Transactions: Mathematical, Physical and Engineering Sciences, 366*(1881), 3717–3725. doi:10.1109/IPDPS.2008.4536091.

Wing, J. M. (2010). Research notebook: Computational thinking–what and why?. The magazine of the Carnegie Mellon University School of Computer Science. Retrieved from http://www.cs.cmu.edu/link/research-notebook-computational-thinking-what-and-why.

Integrating Computational Thinking in Discrete Structures

Gerard Rambally

Abstract Computational thinking (CT) is broadly defined as the thought processes involved in formulating problems and their solutions so that the solutions can be automated. In this twenty-first century, computation is fundamental, and often unavoidable, in most endeavors, thus computing educators have the responsibility to instill in future generations of scientists, mathematicians, and engineers key computational thinking skills. There is a compelling case to be made for the infusion of CT skills into the K-16 education of everyone, given the pervasiveness of computers in all aspects of our lives. This poses the following critical educational challenge: how and when should students learn CT and how and when should it be taught? While discussions, deliberations, and debates will likely continue, the tightly knitted relationship between computational thinking and mathematical thinking suggests that one avenue to acquire CT skills is to integrate CT in the K-16 mathematics curriculum. This chapter describes a study that uses a problem-driven learning pedagogical strategy and the APOS theoretical framework to integrate computational thinking in CSCE 2100, a sophomore level discrete structures course which is a required course for all Information Technology majors. Results demonstrate that integrating computational thinking in a discrete structures course can effectively and significantly influence students' understanding of a range of CT concepts.

Keywords Abstraction • Algorithmic thinking • Computational thinking • Heuristic reasoning • Problem reduction • Problem transformation

Introduction

There is no universally agreed upon definition of computational thinking (CT). However, Wing (2006) demonstrated through a wide range of examples that CT involves the thought processes in formulating problems and their solutions so that

G. Rambally (✉)
Department of Mathematics and Information Sciences, University of North Texas at Dallas, Dallas, TX 75241, USA
e-mail: Gerard.Rambally@untdallas.edu

P.J. Rich, C.B. Hodges (eds.), *Emerging Research, Practice, and Policy on Computational Thinking*, Educational Communications and Technology: Issues and Innovations, DOI 10.1007/978-3-319-52691-1_7

the solutions are represented in a form that can be effectively carried out by an information-processing agent. Computational thinking centers on principles and practices that are fundamental to the computational sciences. It includes epistemic and representational practices, such as problem reduction, transformation, and modularization; recursion and iteration; parallel processing; constructing multiple layers of abstraction; problem decomposition; modeling and simulation; creating representations; testing, verification, and error correction; and heuristic reasoning. These practices are also central to reasoning and problem-solving in mathematics.

There is ample evidence that mathematical thinking (MT) is central to CT. For example, Computing Curriculum 2001 (Roberts, 2002) included discrete structures in the undergraduate CS core curriculum, and most undergraduate CS curricula normally require discrete structures, calculus, linear algebra, and probability (Henderson, Baldwin, et al., 2001). Rich, Leatham, and Wright (2013) illustrated the cross-domain influence on learning mathematics and computer programming. Their analysis of two convergent principles, namely, *core attributes* and *duality*, revealed important causal, correlational, and anecdotal relationships when learning complementary subjects as mathematics and computer programming. The pedagogical implication is profound: mathematics, when taught and applied effectively, provides a set of powerful intellectual tools that leads to strong analytical skills. Mathematics is an indispensable tool for problem-solving and conceptual understanding in computing. MT directly translates into thinking recursively, iteratively, abstractly, logically, precisely, and procedurally. Through these experiences students explicitly learn a number of critical CT principles and more importantly, develop a cognitive model for computational phenomena. Knuth (1985) observed that MT and CT share several modes of thought, particularly in representation of reality, reduction to simpler problems, abstract reasoning, information structures, and algorithms.

Many researchers have put forward convincing arguments that mathematical thinking plays a crucial role in CT (Henderson et al., 2001; Larson, Fitzgerald, & Brooks, 1996; Sobel, 2000). It is the purpose of this research to capitalize on the synergistic relationship between CT and MT to instill in students key computational thinking skills. This study reports on the results of our experimentation that assesses the impact of teaching discrete structures via a computational thinking approach. In one section of a sophomore level discrete structures course, concepts in discrete structures were taught using the traditional problem-driven approach without the integration of CT concepts. In another section, concepts in discrete structures were taught using a problem-driven approach that infused CT concepts. Using a problem-driven learning pedagogical strategy and the APOS theoretical framework to teach concepts in discrete structures, students were exposed to a range of key CT skills. The study demonstrates a minds-on, seamless (i.e., no new content), problem-driven integration of CT in discrete structures which expose students to crafting solutions for problems in a representation that can be executed by an information-processing agent, thereby fostering key computational thinking skills without computer programming.

Theoretical Basis

The APOS theoretical analysis proposes a model of cognition. A model of cognition is a description of specific mental constructions that a learner might make in order to develop an understanding of mathematical concepts. These mental constructions are called ***A** ctions*, ***P** rocesses*, and ***O** bjects*, which an individual organizes into ***S** chemas*; resulting in the theoretical framework being referred to as the APOS Theory (Asiala et al., 1996). The APOS Theory, a constructivist theory of learning, is an extension of Piaget's (1970) theory of reflective abstraction (Dubinsky, 1991) applied to the cognitive development of mathematical concepts. An individual may use several types of reflective abstraction, such as *interiorization*, *coordination*, *encapsulation*, *de-encapsulation*, *reversal*, and *generalization* to construct the mental structures: *actions*, *processes*, *objects*, and *schemas*.

In developing a theoretical description of a learner's thinking about a concept and designing pedagogy to help the learner develop the mental constructions (action, process, object, and schema) related to the concept, a three-component framework is used. First, a preliminary genetic decomposition is devised, which is a model of cognition. This model of cognition is a detailed description of the mental constructions (actions, processes, objects, and schemas) that a learner might make in order to develop an understanding of the concept.

Secondly, based on this theoretical analysis, instructional materials are developed and implemented. It is in this second component of the framework that the instructional materials include pedagogical strategies integrated with CT principles. Pedagogical strategies considered in this component include cooperative/collaborative learning, inquiry-based learning, direct instruction, problem-based learning, quest-based learning, visualization, drill-and-practice, and project-based learning. In this second phase, an empirical assessment of the preliminary genetic decomposition is conducted by having learners complete the instructional treatment that echoes the preliminary genetic decomposition. In this second component of the APOS-CT framework, the instructional treatment always includes a CT component, which is necessary to stimulate cognitive processes that resulted in the assimilation of investigated concepts.

Thirdly, observations of the learner's thinking provide an opportunity to collect and analyze data. Analysis of the data is used to determine whether the preliminary genetic decomposition closely approximates the learner's thinking or whether revision is necessary. The revised genetic decomposition is accompanied by revision of the instructional materials. Implementation of this revised instruction allows for further data collection and analysis, which may result in additional revisions of the genetic decomposition. The cycle is repeated until the epistemology of the concept is understood and an effective pedagogical approach has materialized.

Related Work

The Alabama Math, Science, and Technology Initiative (AMSTI) implemented an instructional treatment involving the immersion of computational thinking into the high school mathematics curriculum. The instructional treatment introduced students in high schools math classes to CT skills such as abstraction and generalization via computer programming (Jenkins, Jerkins, & Stenger, 2012). Participants in this study were first introduced to a problem, and then they were guided through the process of developing mini-programs for each mathematical concept needed and to write a general expression for each mathematical concept. The participants then created a Python program that solved the initial problem for specific cases. Finally, the participants wrote a convincing argument that their solution was true in general. The primary outcome of this study showed that participants in this instructional treatment made significant improvement in their ability to abstract, generalize, and write a convincing argument. A major difference between the AMSTI study and the study reported in this chapter is no computer programming was utilized in this study to teach CT concepts.

McMaster (2008) characterized two frameworks for mathematics, one based on proving theorems and the other based on solving problems. By examining word frequencies in various traditional, applied, and computational mathematics books, they developed two scales for measuring the theorem-proving gestalt or problem-solving gestalt exhibited in these textbooks. A Logical Math scale measures theorem-proving gestalt and a Computational Math scale measures problem-solving gestalt. Their research concluded that the word frequencies suggest that Mathematical, Abstract, and Computational (MAC) thinking framework integrate a broad array of topics relevant to computing. They showed that the word groups "model/modeling" and "algorithm/method" describe the main approach utilized in MT and CT to solving problems.

A number of computing organizations and researchers have identified areas of focus regarding MT in computer science education and have proposed undergraduate computing curricula that integrate appropriate mathematics throughout the curricula (Henderson et al., 2001; Roberts, 2002). Such curricula promote the connections between logic and programming (Henderson, 2003), reinforce the view of algorithms as constructive proofs (Lu & Fletcher, 2009), apply mathematical concepts such as relations to relational database systems (Gorman, Gsell, & Mayfield, 2014), Boolean algebra to computer architecture (Baldwin, Walker, & Henderson, 2013), and grammars to compilers (Henderson, 2003).

At the K-12 level, the CSTA and ISTE working group identified five dispositions that reflect values, motivations, feelings, and attitudes applicable to CT (Barr & Stephenson, 2011). Kmoch (2013) demonstrated the strong synergism of MT and CT by exploring the correlations between these CT dispositions and the eight learning outcomes from the Standards for Mathematical Practice (SMP) that are included in the Common Core State Standards in Mathematics.

CT Skills Integrated in Discrete Structures Concepts

Algorithmic Thinking

Using heuristic reasoning and algorithmic thinking to develop efficient solutions is a critical computational thinking skill. Exposing students to algorithmic thinking can be accomplished while discussing concepts such as the greatest common divisor. Recall that the greatest common divisor of two nonnegative integers p and q, denoted GCD (p, q), is the largest integer that divides both p and q evenly.

Euclid's algorithm (Cormen, Leiserson, Rivest, & Stein, 2001) which uses the modulus (mod) operator is an elegant solution for finding the GCD (p, q). Euclid's algorithm is based on repeated applications of the equality GCD (p, q) = GCD (q, p mod q) until p mod q is equal to 0. Since GCD (p, 0) = p, the last value of p is also the greatest common divisor of the initial p and q. For example, GCD (75, 30) = GCD (30, 15) = GCD (15, 0) = 15.

Students can then be exposed to the following more structured English-description of Euclid's algorithm to compute the GCD (p, q):

Step 1: If q = 0, return the value of p as the GCD and stop; else, go to Step 2.

Step 2: Divide p by q and assign the value of the remainder to r.

Step 3: Assign the value of q to p and the value of r to q. Go to Step 1.

Step 2 provides an excellent opportunity for instructors to expose students to the modulus operator, which is explicitly used in the pseudocode below. Instructors may now convert this structured English version of the algorithm into the following pseudocode:

```
GCD (p, q)
while (q ≠ 0) do
  r ← p mod q;
  p ← q;
  q ← r;
return p;
```

The algorithm accepts, as input, two parameters p and q which are nonnegative integers. The output, namely, the GCD, is contained in the returned value, p.

Instructors may now compare the efficiency of Euclid's algorithm with the efficiency of the exhaustive linear search algorithm for computing the GCD. This comparison provides the opportunity to discuss yet another key computational thinking skill—that of choosing an appropriate representation for a problem. It also emphasizes the core CT concept of a function, which is indispensable in modularizing solutions to complex problems.

Exposing students to algorithmic thinking can also be accomplished while discussing concepts in combinatorics such as the permutations, combinations, and subsets. Consider the problem of generating all the permutations of the elements of a set. For simplicity, assume that the elements of the set are the integers from 1 to n. Recall that the set {1, ..., n} has n! permutations.

One algorithm for generating all permutations in non-lexicographical order is the Johnson-Trotter algorithm (Johnson, 1963; Trotter, 1962). In this algorithm, a direction is associated with each component k in a permutation. The direction is indicated by an arrow above the component in question,

$$\text{e.g., } \overrightarrow{2}\ \overrightarrow{3}\ \overleftarrow{4}\ \overleftarrow{1}.$$

Using this notation, the component k is said to be *mobile* if its arrow points to a smaller number adjacent to it. Thus, in the example immediately above, only 4 is mobile, while 3, 2, and 1 are not. Note that if an integer is on the rightmost column pointing to the right, it is not mobile. Similarly, if an integer is on the leftmost column pointing to the left, it is not mobile. The Johnson-Trotter permutation algorithm may be stated as follows:

```
PERMUTATIONS (n)                                          ← ←   ←
Initialize and display the first permutation as 1 2  … n ;
while (a mobile integer k still exists) do
{
  Identify the largest mobile integer k;
  Swap k and the adjacent integer to which its arrow points;
  Invert the direction of all integers that are larger than k;
  Display the permutation;
}
```

The algorithm accepts, as input, a positive integer n. The output is a list of all permutations of {1, …, n}. Tracing the PERMUTATIONS algorithm for n = 3 produces the following output with the largest mobile integer shown in bold:

$$\overleftarrow{1}\overleftarrow{2}\overleftarrow{\mathbf{3}}\quad \overleftarrow{1}\overleftarrow{\mathbf{3}}\overleftarrow{2}\quad \overleftarrow{3}\overleftarrow{1}\overleftarrow{\mathbf{2}}\quad \overrightarrow{\mathbf{3}}\overleftarrow{2}\overleftarrow{1}\quad \overleftarrow{2}\overrightarrow{\mathbf{3}}\overleftarrow{1}\quad \overleftarrow{2}\overleftarrow{1}\overrightarrow{3}$$

Exposing students to tracing Euclid's algorithm to calculate the greatest common divisor of two integers and the Johnson-Trotter algorithm to generate permutations is precisely the type of minds-on activity that will strengthen their algorithmic thinking skills.

Problem Transformation

Another key skill of computational thinking is reformulating a difficult problem into one whose solution is familiar, using techniques such as reduction, transformation, modularization, or simulation. This subsection will address the technique of transformation, while the next subsection will focus on the technique of reduction.

Table 1 Mapping the 1-1 correspondence between the 2^3 subsets of the set A = {a_1, a_2, a_3} and the 2^3 bit strings

Decimals	0	1	2	3	4	5	6	7
Bit strings	000	001	010	011	100	101	110	111
Subsets	∅	{a_3}	{a_2}	{a_2, a_3}	{a_1}	{a_1, a_3}	{a_1,a_2}	{a_1, a_2, a_3}

Consider the problem of generating all the subsets of a given set A = {a_1, a_2, …, a_n}. Recall that the set of all subsets of a set is called its *power set* and the number of elements in the power set is 2^n.

The problem of generating the power set can be used to illustrate the technique of *transforming* a problem into one that is computationally tractable and efficient. This transformation is based on the one-to-one correspondence between all 2^n subsets of an n element set and all 2^n bit strings of length n.

Consider the case of n = 3. The problem now reduces to finding all the subsets of A = {a_1, a_2, a_3}. Since all bit strings of length 3 are 000, 001, 010, 011, 100, 101, 110, and 111, the one-to-one correspondence between the subsets and the bit strings easily yields the power set, as illustrated in (Table 1).

As illustrated in (Table 1), there is a one-to-one correspondence between all 2^n bit strings b_1, …, b_n of length n and all 2^n subsets of an n element set A = {a_1, a_2, …, a_n}. The simplest way to establish such a correspondence is to assign a_i as an element of the subset if b_i = 1in the corresponding bit string and if b_i = 0 then a_i is not an element of the subset. With this correspondence established, we can generate all the bit strings of length n by generating successive binary numbers from 0 to $2^n - 1$, padded, when necessary, with an appropriate number of leading 0s.

The technique of *transformation* can also be illustrated by solving the problem of computing x^n. The transformation technique utilized to compute x^n is based on the representation change idea. Specifically, represent n as a binary string, i.e., let n = $b_Q \ldots b_q \ldots b_0$. This implies that the value of n can be computed by evaluating the polynomial $p(2) = b_Q 2^Q + \ldots + b_q 2^q + \ldots + b_0$. For example, if n = 23, its binary representation is 10111 and $23 = 1{*}2^4 + 0{*}2^3 + 1{*}2^2 + 1{*}2^1 + 1{*}2^0$. Thus, $x^n = x^{p(2)} = x^b Q^{2^Q} + \cdots + b_q 2^q + \cdots + b_0$.

Consider the problem of computing 3^9. Since $9 = 1001_2$, then $3^9 = 3^{1001}$. (The notation 1001_2 simply means that the number 1001 is being represented in the base 2 or binary number system.) A simple technique for computing binary exponentiation is as follows: Since the leading digit in the bit string representing the exponent is always 1, set the initial value of the accumulator to the base (in this case 3) then continue scanning the bit string and square the last value of the accumulator for each bit. If the current bit is 1, also multiply the value in the accumulator by the base (i.e., 3 in this example). So 3^9 can be computed as follows:

Binary digits of the exponent:	1	0	0	1
Product accumulator:	3	$3^2 = 9$	$9^2 = 81$	$(81)^2{*}3 = 19{,}683$

This technique can be formally described using the following algorithm:

```
BinaryExponentiation (x, bQ ... b0)
power ← x;
for i ← Q - 1 downto 0 do
  power ← power * power;
  if bi = 1 then power ← power * x;
return power;
```

Thus the problem of computing decimal exponentiation was transformed into the simpler problem of computing binary exponentiation. The BinaryExponentiation algorithm accepts as input a number x and a binary string $b_Q \ldots b_0$ representing n. It computes x^n by scanning the binary string from left to right. The BinaryExponentiation algorithm is significantly more efficient than the brute-force algorithm for computing x^n.

Problem Reduction

The problem-solving strategy of *problem reduction* can be summarized as follows: in order to solve a problem, reduce it to another problem that you know how to solve.

Recall that Euclid's algorithm was used above to calculate the *greatest common divisor* of two nonnegative integers p and q, denoted GCD (p, q). Now consider the problem of finding the *least common multiple* of two positive integers, p and q, denoted LCM (p, q). Recall that the LCM (p, q) is defined as the smallest integer that is divisible by both p and q. For example, LCM (18, 60) = 180. A middle-school algorithm for computing the LCM is to compute the product of all the common prime factors of p and q times the product of p's prime factors that are not in q times the product of q's prime factors that are not in p. For example,

18 = 2 * 3 * 3

60 = 2 * 2 * 3 * 5

LCM (18, 60) = (2 * 3) * 3 * 2 * 5 = 180.

A far more efficient algorithm for computing the least common multiple can be designed by using *problem reduction*. Notice that the product of LCM (p, q) and GCD (p, q) includes every prime factor of p and q exactly once and therefore is the product of p and q. This generates the formula

LCM (p, q) * GCD (p, q) = p * q → LCM (p, q) = (p * q) /GCD (p, q)

where GCD (p, q) can be computed using the efficient Euclid's algorithm. For example:

LCM (18, 60) = (18 * 60) /GCD (18, 60) = 1080/6 = 180.

So we have reduced the problem of finding the least common multiple to the problem of finding the greatest common divisor.

Heuristic Reasoning with Backtracking

Utilizing heuristic reasoning to develop efficient solutions is yet another key CT skill. As an application of the power set (discussed above), consider the **subset-sum problem** which involves finding the subsets of a set $S = \{s_1, \ldots, s_n\}$ of n positive integers whose sum is equal to z. For example, for $S = \{1, 3, 4, 7, 11\}$ and $z = 8$, there are two solutions: $\{1, 7\}$ and $\{1, 3, 4\}$. Instructors can demonstrate the inefficiency of using exhaustive search to solve the subset-sum problem and then use heuristic reasoning with backtracking to generate a more efficient solution.

An exhaustive search algorithm for the subset-sum problem is as follows:

Step 1: Determine all the subsets of the set of n items given.

Step 2: Compute the sum of the elements of each subset.

Step 3: Identify the subsets whose sum is equal to z.

As a specific example, consider finding the subsets of the set $S = \{1, 3, 4, 7, 11\}$ whose sum is equal to 8, i.e., $z = 8$. Table 2 shows an implementation of the exhaustive search algorithm.

Recall that the number of subsets of an n-element set is 2^n. Thus, an exhaustive search algorithm for the subset-sum problem is extremely inefficient. With a 20-element set, there will be 1,048,576 subsets to evaluate, and with a 30-element set, there will be 1,073,741,824 subsets to evaluate. Instructors can use such data as an obvious gateway into developing a more efficient solution for the subset-sum problem and discuss other CT concepts such as heuristic reasoning, search space, state-space trees, branch-and-bound and backtracking. One heuristic that can be utilized is to sort the set's elements in increasing order. Thus, $s_1 \leq s_2 \leq \ldots \leq s_n$. The state-space tree can be constructed as a binary tree as shown in Fig. 1 for $S = \{1, 3, 4, 7, 11\}$ and $z = 8$. The number inside a node is the sum of the elements already included in subsets represented by the node. The inequality below a leaf indicates the reason for its termination. Note that every subtree of the tree represents a subset of the given set.

The root of the tree represents the starting point. At this point, no decisions have been made about any of the elements of the set. The left child of the root represents *inclusion* of s_1 in a subset being sought. The right child of the root represents *exclusion* of s1 in a subset being sought. Similarly, the left children of all nodes of the first level of the tree correspond to inclusion of s_2, while the right children of all nodes of the first level of the tree correspond to exclusion of s_2, and so on. Therefore, a path from the root to a node on the ith level of the tree dictates which of the first i members of the set have been included in the subset represented by that node. The sum, s', of these elements is recorded inside the node. If $s' = z$, then one solution has been found. To find other possible solutions, continue by backtracking to the node's parent. If $s' \neq z$, two heuristics dealing with inequalities can be utilized, namely, the node can be terminated as non-promising if either of the following inequalities is true:

$s' + s_{i+1} > z$ (i.e., the sum s' is too large)

Table 2 Implementation of the exhaustive search algorithm for the subset-sum problem

Subset	Sum	Sum = 8
∅	0	No
{1}	1	No
{3}	3	No
{4}	4	No
{7}	7	No
{11}	11	No
{1, 3}	4	No
{1, 4}	5	No
{1, 7}	**8**	**Yes**
{1, 11}	12	No
{3, 4}	7	No
{3, 7}	10	No
{3, 11}	14	No
{4, 7}	11	No
{4, 11}	15	No
{7, 11}	18	No
{1, 3, 4}	**8**	**Yes**
{1, 3, 7}	11	No
{1, 3, 11}	15	No
{1, 4, 7}	12	No
{1, 4, 11}	16	No
{1, 7, 11}	19	No
{3, 4, 7}	14	No
{3, 4, 11}	18	No
{3, 7, 11}	21	No
{4, 7, 11}	22	No
{1, 3, 4, 7}	15	No
{1, 3, 4, 11}	19	No
{1, 4, 7, 11}	23	No
{1, 3, 7, 11}	22	No
{3, 4, 7, 11}	25	No
{1, 3, 4, 7, 11}	26	No

$$s' + \sum_{n}^{j=i+1} (s_j) < z \qquad \text{(i.e., the sum } s' \text{ is too small)}$$

If a node is non-promising, continue by recursively backtracking to the node's parent as illustrated in Fig. 1. This heuristic state-space backtracking algorithm also finds the solution subsets {1, 3, 4} and {1, 7}. However, in the exhaustive search algorithm, all 32 subsets had to be evaluated, while only 18 subsets had to be evaluated in the heuristic state-space backtracking algorithm.

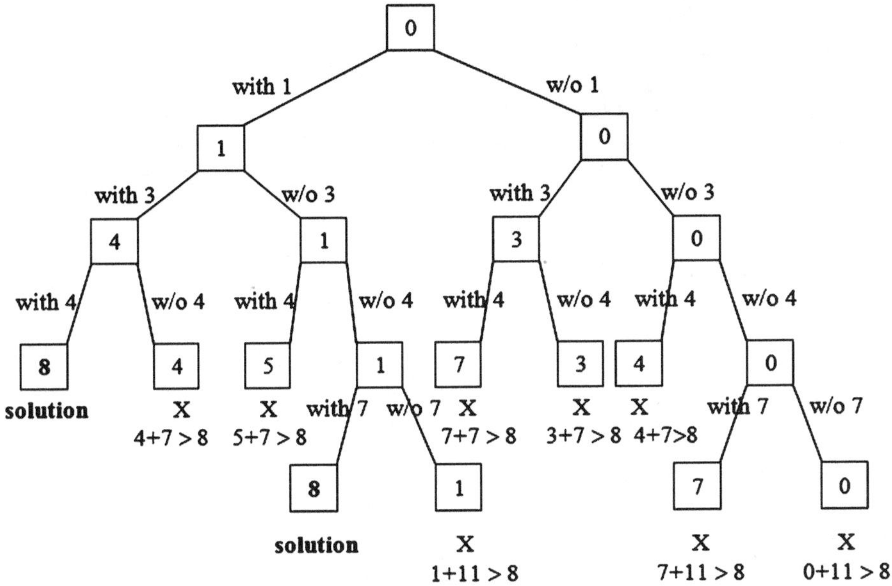

Fig. 1 State-space tree of the backtracking algorithm for the subset-sum problem with S = {1, 3, 4, 7, 11}, z = 8

Problem Representation

Another critical computational thinking skill involves choosing an appropriate representation for a problem or modeling the relevant aspects of a problem to make it tractable.

To illustrate the technique of choosing an appropriate representation, consider the problem of computing the value of a polynomial.

$$p(x) = a_n x^n + a_{n-1} x^{n-1} + \ldots + a_1 x + a_0 \quad (1)$$

at a given point x. For example, evaluate $p(x) = 3x^4 - x^3 + 2x^2 + x - 5$ at x = 3.

Horner's rule (Cormen et al., 2001) is a very elegant and efficient algorithm for evaluating a polynomial. Horner's rule illustrates clearly the value in choosing an appropriate representation for a problem and is based on representing p(x) by a formula different from (1) above. The new representation is obtained from (1) by successively taking x as a common factor in the remaining polynomials of decreasing degree:

$$p(x) = (\ldots(a_n x + a_{n-1})x + \ldots)x + a_0 \quad (2)$$

For example, transforming the representation of the polynomial $p(x) = 3x^4 - x^3 + 2x^2 + x - 5$ using Horner's algorithm, we get.

Table 3 Evaluating $p(x) = 3x^4 - x^3 + 2x^2 + x - 5$ at $x = 3$ using Horner's representation

Coefficients	3	−1	2	1	−5
x = 3	3	3*3 + (−1) = 8	3*8 + 2 = 26	3*26 + 1 = 79	3*79 + (−5) = 232
Components of formula (3)		Value of 3x − 1	Value of x(3x − 1) + 2	Value of x(x(3x − 1) + 2) + 1	Value of x(x(x(3x − 1) + 2) + 1) − 5

$$\begin{aligned} p(x) &= 3x^4 - x^3 + 2x^2 + x - 5 \\ &= x(3x^3 - x^2 + 2x + 1) - 5 \\ &= x(x(3x^2 - x + 2) + 1) - 5 \\ &= x(x(x(3x - 1) + 2) + 1) - 5 \end{aligned} \tag{3}$$

Using the representation in formula (2), we can now substitute a value for x at which the polynomial needs to be evaluated. This is far more efficient than using formula (1). The calculation can be structured with a three-row table, as illustrated in (Table 3). The first row contains the polynomial's coefficients listed from the highest a_n to the lowest a_0. Include all coefficients equal to zero, if any. The first entry in the second row contains a_n. The remaining entries in the second row are used to store intermediate results. Thus, the next entry is computed as the x's value times the last entry in the second row plus the next coefficient from the first row. The final entry computed is the answer, i.e., p(3) = 232. The third row is used simply to show the relationship to formula (3).

Evaluating a polynomial using the transformed Horner's representation can also be accomplished using an algorithmic representation. This provides yet another opportunity to reinforce algorithmic thinking in the mathematics curriculum. Horner's algorithm may be written as follows:

```
Horner(P[0..n], x)
v ← P[n];
for i ← n -1 downto 0 do
    v ← x * v + P[i];
return v;
```

Horner's algorithm accepts as input an array P[0…n] of coefficients of a polynomial of degree n stored from the lowest to the highest and a number x. The value of the polynomial at x is returned in the variable v.

Horner's algorithm could also provide an excellent gateway into another key computational thinking skill, that of using heuristic reasoning and algorithmic thinking to develop efficient solutions. The time efficiency for evaluating a polynomial in standard form, i.e., Eq. (1), is exponential, while the time efficiency for Horner's algorithm is linear. The number of multiplications, M(n), and the number of additions, A(n), are given by the same sum:

$$M(n) = A(n) = \sum_{i=0}^{n-1} 1 = n \in \Theta(n)$$

Recursion

Another key skill of computational thinking involves mastering the concepts of recursion and iteration. After all, the computing constructs, sequencing, selection, iteration, and recursion, are the building blocks of algorithms. The concept of recursion can be illustrated by solving the problem of multiplying large integers. Many cryptographic algorithms require multiplication of integers that are over 100 digits in length. Such integers are obviously too large to fit in a single memory word of current computers and therefore require special treatment.

Consider the problem of multiplying two n-digit integers x and y where n is a positive even number. One approach to solving this problem uses the divide-and-conquer technique recursively. Specifically, both numbers are divided in the middle. Denote the first half of x by x_1 and the second half by x_0, and the first half of y by y_1 and the second half by y_0. Using this notation, $x = x_1x_0$ implies that $x = x_1 10^{n/2} + x_0$ and $y = y_1y_0$ implies that $y = y_1 10^{n/2} + y_0$. Thus:

$z = x * y = (x_1 10^{n/2} + x_0) * (y_1 10^{n/2} + y_0)$

$= (x_1 * y_1)10^n + (x_1 * y_0 + x_0 * y_1)10^{n/2} + (x_0 * y_0)$

Now apply the same divide-and-conquer technique recursively to compute $(x_1 * y_1)$, $(x_1 * y_0)$, $(x_0 * y_1)$, and $(x_0 * y_0)$. The recursion is stopped when n = 1.

Consider the case of n = 4 and the specific problem of computing 1928 * 3746. Let x = 1928 and y = 3746. Dividing both numbers in the middle yields $x_1 = 19$, $x_0 = 28$, $y_1 = 37$, and $y_0 = 46$. Therefore, $x = 19 * 10^2 + 28$, and $y = 37 * 10^2 + 46$. Thus, $z = x * y = (19 * 10^2 + 28) * (37 * 10^2 + 46)$

$$= (19 * 37)10^4 + (19 * 46 + 28 * 37)10^2 + (28 * 46) \quad (4)$$

Now apply the divide-and-conquer technique recursively to compute (19 * 37).

$19 * 37 = (1 * 10^1 + 9) * (3 * 10^1 + 7)$

$= (1 * 3)10^2 + (1 * 7 + 9 * 3)\, 10^1 + (9 * 7)$

Note that now n = 1, i.e., all multiplications involve one-digit numbers and so the multiplications can be performed, yielding

$19 * 37 = (3)10^2 + (7 + 27)10^1 + 63 = 300 + 340 + 63 = 703.$

Similarly, apply the divide-and-conquer technique recursively to compute (19 * 46), (28 * 37), and (28 * 46) which will produce 874, 1036, and 1288. Finally, unwind the recursion using backward substitutions in Eq. (4) above to generate the answer of 7,222,288.

Abstraction

One school of thought claims that computing is all about constructing, manipulating, and reasoning about abstractions. Thus, having the ability to use multiple layers of abstraction to understand and solve problems in an efficient manner is a critical CT skill.

The concept of abstraction can be illustrated by solving the *prerequisite-course problem* (Cormen et al., 2001) which involves sequencing a set of courses so that a student takes the prerequisite course first. Consider the following specific example: A student must take a set of five required courses {C1, C2, C3, C4, C5} to fulfill the requirements for some degree program. The courses can be taken in any order as long as the following course prerequisites are met:

C1 and C2 have no prerequisites,
C3 requires C1,
C4 requires C2, C3, and C5
C5 requires C2.

What is the most efficient order in which the student should take the courses to ensure that all course prerequisites are met?

Let's illustrate how abstractions such as **directed graphs (digraphs)** can be used to solve this problem. This problem can be modeled by a digraph, as shown in Fig. 2, in which vertices represent courses and directed edges illustrate prerequisite requirements.

Using this abstraction, the problem becomes as follows: can the vertices in the digraph be listed in such an order that, for every edge in the digraph, the vertex where the edge starts is listed before the vertex where the edge ends? Finding such an ordering is referred to as *topological sorting*. A necessary and sufficient condition for topological sorting to be possible is that the digraph has no cycles. The topological sorting algorithm is based on a *decrease and conquer* technique and can be stated as follows:

- Repeat
- Identify in a remaining digraph a *source*, which is a vertex with no incoming edges, and delete it along with all the edges outgoing from it.
- If there are several sources, break the tie arbitrarily.

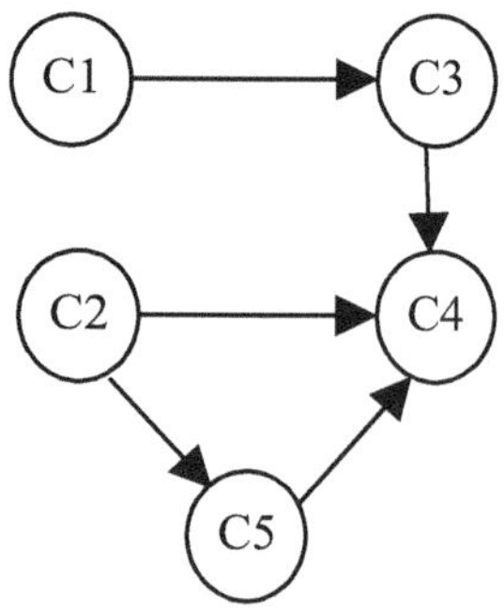

Fig. 2. The prerequisite structure of the courses represented as a digraph

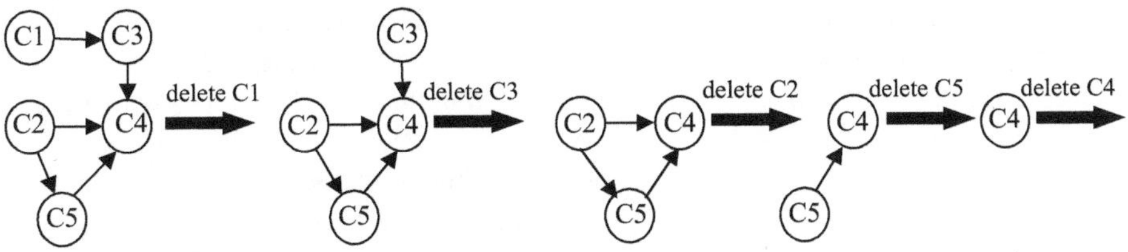

Fig. 3 Illustration of topological sorting for the five-course prerequisite problem

- If there is no source and vertices still exist, stop because the problem cannot be solved.
- Until (all vertices have been deleted).
- The order in which the vertices are deleted yields a solution to the topological sorting problem.

Figure 3 illustrates an execution of the topological sorting algorithm and generates the solution: C1, C3, C2, C5, and C4. Note that the topological sorting algorithm may generate several alternative solutions.

Controlled Experiment

The purpose of this study was to discover whether, by infusing CT concepts in discrete structures, students are better able to formulate solutions to problems so that the solutions are represented in a form that can be effectively automated.

To determine the impact of this APOS-CT approach on students' acquisition of CT skills, a quasi-experimental study was conducted in two sections of CSCE 2100, a sophomore level discrete structures course at a midsize south-western state university. Each course met over a 15-week semester in two 75-min sessions each week. The same instructor taught both sections, using the same example problems, the same homework problems, and the same content material. In Sect. 1, the control group, concepts in discrete structures were taught using the traditional problem-driven approach and the APOS framework *without* the integration of CT concepts. In Sect. 2, the treatment group, concepts in discrete structures were taught using a problem-driven approach and the APOS framework that infused the CT concepts discussed in the previous section.

Participants

The control group had 12 students, 10 of whom were males and 2 females. Eight of these students were IT majors, while the other four were mathematics majors. All of the students had taken one computer science course, namely, Computer Science I, which is a computer programming course in Java. All of the students had also taken Calculus I, which was the highest level of mathematics course taken. Both Computer Science I and Calculus I are prerequisites for the Discrete Structures course. The treatment group had 11 students, 9 of whom were males and 2 females. Eight of these students were IT majors, while the other three were math majors. All of these students had also taken Computer Science I and Calculus I.

Instructional Treatment

In the instructional treatment of the treatment group, instruction proceeded under the assumption that participants were familiar with the three basic programming constructs, namely, sequence, decision, and repetition. The APOS theory of concept acquisition augmented with CT concepts was applied with the treatment group. This constructivist approach implemented the following archetype: First, a problem was selected whose solution required utilizing one or more of the key CT skills discussed above. The second step focused on students' understanding of the problem (decontextualize), such as identifying the range and type of input, identifying the output, thinking about special cases, etc. The third step focused on designing an algorithm to solve the problem. Various algorithm design techniques were discussed. Students designed their algorithms using pseudocode, a natural language high-level description of an algorithm that uses the structural conventions of programming languages, but is intended for human reading rather than machine reading. In the fourth step, students had to prove that their algorithm yields the required result for every legitimate input using techniques such as mathematical induction. Finally, students analyzed their algorithm to determine the time efficiency using the big theta notation (Θ).

Data Collection and Analysis

At the end of the semester, students from both groups participated in a number of graded activities designed to test their CT abilities. These activities involved tracing algorithmic solutions to problems; designing algorithmic solutions; detecting errors in algorithmic solutions; applying abstractions and heuristics to solve problems; reformulating problems using transformation, reduction and modularization; and choosing appropriate representations for problems. The results are summarized in Table 4. We used a statistical difference of means test to analyze the two groups, in which a student's t-statistic of at least 1.33 (representing 90% confidence) was required to demonstrate significance.

Table 4 Summary of the skills test results for the two groups

Skills test activity	Treatment group	Control group	t
Tracing algorithms	42.1/50	41.4/50	0.93
Designing algorithmic solutions	35.2/40	27.3/40	1.36
Detecting algorithmic errors	44.0/50	33.8/50	1.39
Applying abstractions and heuristics	23.5/25	19.7/25	1.35
Reformulating problems	22.7/25	17.6/25	1.38
Choosing appropriate representations	12.6/15	10.2/15	1.37

Results and Discussion

All 12 students from the control group and all 11 students from the treatment group completed the course. All students in both groups participated in all the skills test activities. As the results in Table 4 show, there was no significant difference between the two groups' algorithm tracing skills. This could be explained by the fact that both groups had a course in computer programming. However, the treatment group had made significant improvement in their ability to design algorithmic solutions; to detect errors in algorithmic solutions; to utilize abstractions and heuristic reasoning; to reformulate problems using techniques such as reduction, transformation, and modularization; and to choose appropriate representations for problems.

Tracing algorithms. Students from the control group and the treatment group were given 30 min in a classroom setting to trace three algorithms of varying difficulty. For example, the intermediate level question was to trace the following algorithm for the array [W, I, M, B, L, E, D, O, N] and generate the contents of the array after two iterations of the outer for loop:

```
SelectionSort(A[0..n - 1])
        for i ← 0 to n - 2 do
                min ← i;
                for j ← i + 1 to n - 1 do
                        if (A[j] < A[min])min ← j;
                swap A[i] and A[min];
```

There was no statistically significant difference in the scores between the two groups. This could be explained by the fact that both groups had successfully completed a course in Java programming and were familiar with tracing computer programs and algorithms.

Designing algorithmic solutions. Students from the control group and the treatment group were given 45 min in a classroom setting to design three algorithms to solve three different problems of varying difficulty. For example, the intermediate level question was to design a presorting-based algorithm for finding the median of a list of n numbers which are stored in an array, A. The algorithm must have a maximum computing time of $\Theta(n \log n)$.

The treatment group outscored the control group on this activity to a degree exceeding statistical significance (90% confidence). In the control group, raw scores ranged from a low of 11 to a high of 31 out of 40, with an average score of 27.3. In the treatment group, raw scores ranged from a low of 26 to a high of 38 out of 40, with an average score of 35.2.

Detecting algorithmic errors. Students from the control group and the treatment group were given 45 min in a classroom setting to identify and correct logic errors in three algorithms to solve three different problems of varying difficulty. For example, the intermediate level question was to identify and correct the errors in the following algorithm so that the algorithm evaluates a polynomial at a given point, x:

```
EvalPoly(P[0..n], x)
        p ← P[0];
        for i ← n downto 0 do
                p ← x * p + P[i];
        return p;
```

The treatment group outscored the control group on this activity to a degree exceeding statistical significance (90% confidence). In the control group, raw scores ranged from a low of 21 to a high of 38 out of 50, with an average score of 33.8. In the treatment group, raw scores ranged from a low of 32 to a high of 50 out of 50, with an average score of 44.

Applying abstractions and heuristics. Students from the control group and the treatment group were given 45 min in a classroom setting to apply abstractions and heuristics to solve three different problems of varying difficulty. For example, the intermediate level question was to draw the binary tree representing the following infix expression: $9/(6-3)+5*(3+1)$. Using the binary tree, convert the expression to postfix notation and then evaluate the postfix expression using a stack.

The treatment group outscored the control group on this activity to a degree exceeding statistical significance (90% confidence). In the control group, raw scores ranged from a low of 9 to a high of 22 out of 25, with an average score of 19.7. In the treatment group, raw scores ranged from a low of 18 to a high of 25 out of 25, with an average score of 23.5.

Reformulating problems. Students from the control group and the treatment group were given 45 min in a classroom setting to reformulate three problems of varying difficulty using the techniques of transformation and/or reduction. For example, in the intermediate level question, students were given the following algorithm which determines whether all the elements in a given array are distinct:

```
ElementUniqueness(A[0..n - 1])
        for i ← 0 to n - 2 do
           for j ← i + 1 to n - 1 do
              if A[i] = A[j] return false;
        return true;
```

They were then asked to write a transform-and-conquer version of this algorithm by first sorting the elements of the array.

The treatment group outscored the control group on this activity to a degree exceeding statistical significance (90% confidence). In the control group, raw scores ranged from a low of 7 to a high of 20 out of 25, with an average score of 17.6. In the treatment group, raw scores ranged from a low of 17 to a high of 25 out of 25, with an average score of 22.7.

Choosing appropriate representations. Students from the control group and the treatment group were given 45 min in a classroom setting to choose and apply various representations to solve three different problems of varying difficulty. For example, the intermediate level question was to represent a given digraph as an adjacency matrix and then solve the topological sorting problem for the digraph using the adjacency matrix.

The treatment group outscored the control group on this activity to a degree exceeding statistical significance (90% confidence). In the control group, raw scores ranged from a low of 5 to a high of 12 out of 15, with an average score of 10.2. In the treatment group, raw scores ranged from a low of 10 to a high of 14 out of 15, with an average score of 12.6.

In summary, solutions proposed by the treatment group in all of the test activities were more sophisticated, elegant, and robust than solutions proposed by the control group. Furthermore, based on the results of several other studies (Kynigos, 2007; Sherin, 2001), it is safe to extrapolate and conclude that integrating CT in mathematics courses, in general, can serve as an effective vehicle for learning a wide range of CT and MT concepts more robustly than with the traditional APOS method.

Conclusions

Statistical analysis of our results give promising indications that infusing CT in a discrete structures course does, in fact, positively and significantly impact the acquisition of CT skills of students that participate. We found it possible to provide practical, concrete, learning experiences about a variety of CT concepts using a problem-driven approach rather than programming. Our experience suggests that students developed firm mental models of various elements of CT and were able to apply such cognition to solve a range of discrete structures problems so that the solutions are represented in a form that can be effectively automated.

This study attempted to provide concrete experimental evidence of the synergistic relationship between CT and MT. Motivated by this relationship, this study demonstrated that CT as an important tool for problem-solving and an effective aid to the conceptual understanding of mathematics. The central hypothesis of this study is that the development of MT in the K-16 curricula can be synergistically supported by a mathematics curriculum that integrates CT.

While this study was conducted at the post-secondary level, it is more important to introduce CT concepts much earlier, specifically, in the K-12 mathematics curricula. It is important to emphasize that integrating CT in the mathematics curriculum is just one of many possible avenues to expose K-16 students to CT, which in turn can improve their MT. Future work should involve collaborative efforts of educators and computer scientists to develop concrete examples of how computational thinking could be embedded in the core content areas, from literacy and the arts to mathematics and science.

References

Asiala, M., Brown, A., DeVries, D. J., Dubinsky, E., Mathews, D., & Thomas, K. (1996). A framework for research and curriculum development in undergraduate mathematics education. *Research in Collegiate Mathematics Education, 2*, 1–32.

Baldwin, D., Walker, H., & Henderson, P. (2013). The roles of mathematics in computer science. *ACM Inroads, 4*(4), 74–80.

Barr, V., & Stephenson, C. (2011). Bringing computational thinking to K-12: What is involved and what is the role of the computer science education community? *ACM Inroads, 2*(1), 48–54.

Cormen, T., Leiserson, C., Rivest, R., & Stein, C. (2001). *Introduction to algorithms*. Cambridge, MA: MIT.

Dubinsky, E. (1991). Reflective abstraction in advanced mathematical thinking. In D. Tall (Ed.), *Advanced mathematical thinking* (pp. 231–250). Dordrecht: Kluwer.

Gorman, J., Gsell, S. & Mayfield, C. (2014). Learning relational algebra by snapping blocks. In *Proceedings of the 45th SIGCSE technical symposium on computer science education* (pp. 73–78).

Henderson, P. B. (2003). Mathematical reasoning in software engineering education. *Communications of the ACM, 46*(9), 45–50.

Henderson, P. B., Baldwin, D., et al. (2001). Striving for mathematical thinking, ITiCSE 2000 working group report. *SIGCSE Bulletin–Inroads, 33*(4), 114–124.

Jenkins, J. T., Jerkins, J. A., & Stenger, C. L. (2012). A plan for immediate immersion of computational thinking into the high school math classroom through a partnership with AMSTI. In *Proceedings of the 50th annual ACM southeast regional conference* (pp. 148–152).

Johnson, S. M. (1963). Generation of permutations by adjacent transposition. *Mathematics of Computation, 17*, 282–285.

Kmoch, J. (2013). Computational thinking dispositions and the common core math standards. *CSTA Voice, 9*(4), 3–5.

Knuth, D. (1985). Algorithmic thinking and mathematical thinking. *The American Mathematical Monthly, 92*(3), 170–181.

Kynigos, C. (2007). Using half-baked microworlds to challenge teacher educators knowing. *Journal of Computers for Math Learning, 12*(2), 87–111.

Larson, P., Fitzgerald, J., & Brooks, T. (1996). Applying formal specification in industry. *IEEE Software, 13*(3), 48–56.

Lu, J. & Fletcher, G. (2009). Thinking about computational thinking. In *Proceedings of the 40th SIGCSE technical symposium on computer science education* (pp. 260–264).

McMaster, K. (2008). Two gestalts for mathematics: Logical vs. computational. *Information Systems Education Journal, 6*(20), 1–13.

Piaget, J. (1970). *Genetic epistemology*. New York, NY: Columbia University Press.

Rich, P., Leatham, K., & Wright, G. (2013). Convergent cognition. *Instructional Science, 41*(2), 431–453.

Roberts, E. (Ed.). (2002). *Computing curricula 2001: Computer science final report*. New York, NY: IEEE Computer Society.

Sherin, B. (2001). A comparison of programming languages and algebraic notation as expressive languages for physics. *International Journal of Computers for Mathematics Learning, 6*(1), 1–61.

Sobel, A. (2000). Empirical results of a software engineering curriculum incorporating forma methods. *SIGCSE Bulletin, 32*(1), 157–161.
Trotter, H. F. (1962). Algorithm 115: Perm. *Communications of the ACM, 5*(8), 434–435.
Wing, J. M. (2006). Computational thinking. *Communications of the ACM, 49*(3), 33–35.

A Computational Approach to Learning Programming Using Visual Programming in a Developing Country University

Ago MacGranaky Quaye and Salihu Ibrahim Dasuki

Abstract The paper outlines how computer science students in developing countries can acquire computational skills using visual game programming environments aimed at motivating them to learning programming. The study shows how visual game programming using Alice supports various concepts of computational thinking and also how these concepts enhance the learning of introductory computer programming. We based our analysis on 15 first-year computer science students of the American University of Nigeria who used Alice in their introduction to computer science course. The results of the study show that Alice motivates students to learn programming and also enhances the successful use of computational thinking skills such as problem solving, debugging, simulation, algorithm building, and collaboration. The study concludes with some implications for theory and practice.

Keywords Computational thinking • Programming • Alice 3D

Introduction

Efforts are being made by universities in developing countries to ensure that their graduates are not left behind in the competitive global information society; thus, these universities have adopted computing degree programs in almost all their universities (Dasuki, Ogedebe, Kanya, Ndume, & Makinde, 2015). Many of these universities have adopted the IEEE/ACM simulated computing curricular (Bass & Heeks, 2008). Computing programming courses using various programming languages dominate these curricular depending on the length of the program whether it's 4 years or 3 years. Sarpong, Authur, and Owusu (2013) explain computer programming to be an art that involves a person's ability to deduce problems into solutions. Computer programming is a crucial skill that must be grasped by any individual interested in pursuing a career in the computing sciences. Despite the reforms by universities of developing countries and the strong and growing need for

A.M. Quaye • S.I. Dasuki (✉)
American University of Nigeria, Yola, Nigeria
e-mail: aquaye@aun.edu.ng; salihu.dasuki@aun.edu.ng

P.J. Rich, C.B. Hodges (eds.), *Emerging Research, Practice, and Policy on Computational Thinking*, Educational Communications and Technology: Issues and Innovations, DOI 10.1007/978-3-319-52691-1_8

computer scientists to stimulate economic growth, students' interest in computer science degrees have continued to plunge globally (Kelleher & Pausch, 2007).

Various factors contribute to the loss of student interest in degrees in computer science. One major factor is the perceived difficulty in any degree course that involves programming (Bergin & Reilly, 2005; Kelleher & Pausch, 2007). This difficulty has, therefore, resulted in the high failure and dropout rates in introductory programming courses at the university level. Furthermore, students' lack of computing skills has further hindered their learning and understanding of programming. As such, there have been calls for the integration of computing skills into the tools and teaching concepts in computer science education (Wing, 2008; Armoni, Meerbaum-Salant, & Ben-Ari, 2015). In computer science education, these skills have been referred to as computational thinking. Within the computer science domain, there has been wide debate on the definition of computational thinking (CT). However, the most referred definition in the literature is that of Jeannette Wing (2006) who defines computational thinking as a problem-solving approach concerned with conceptualizing, developing abstractions, and designing systems which overlap with logical thinking and require concepts fundamental to computing.

Various studies have argued that it is essential for students to develop skills in CT before being introduced to introductory programming courses (Qualls & Sherrell, 2010; Kazimoglu, Kiernan, Bacon, & MacKinnon, 2012; Lee et al., 2011; Han, Kim, & Wohn, 2015). As such, researchers in the domain of computer science education have conducted various studies to understand the different skills and approaches that constitute CT and which methods and tools can be used to teach and support students enrolled for computer science majors (Kazimoglu et al., 2012; Moreno, 2012; Katai & Toth, 2010). The use of visual programming using game-plays has been proposed as a pedagogical framework for learning computational skills on the one hand and motivating students to learn programming on the other hand (Lee et al., 2011; Han et al., 2015). In the current literature, studies that explored computational thinking through programming for university students taking computer science courses have been done in developed countries (Moreno, 2012; Katai & Toth, 2010). There has been little or no research in the context of developing countries.

Thus, in this paper, we examine how visual programming using Alice can support tertiary-level students in developing countries with computational skills and motivate them to learn introductory programming language. The next section reviews the relevant literature on computational thinking. The research method, the research setting, and the analysis of the case are then presented. The final section concludes the study and provides some practical and theoretical implications.

Computational Thinking

It is widely accepted in the literature that students perceive the learning of programming difficult and boring, thus resulting in a high failure rate in introductory programming courses. According to Moreno (2012), it is significant for students to focus not only on semantics and syntax of programming languages, but also demonstrate an understanding of patterns evident in programming. To accomplish this, the notion of computational thinking has been a trending research area particularly within the computer science domain with the aim of incorporating computational thinking into all levels of the computing education curriculum (Qualls & Sherrell, 2010; Wing, 2006). According to Wing (2006), CT involves five key elements, namely, conditional logic, distributed processing, debugging, simulation, and algorithm building. Wing noted that CT combines all the vital skills that are involved in solving problems with logical and systematic thinking and also engineering and mathematical thinking.

Berland and Lee (2011) go further to classify CT into five categories and two stages. The five categories include conditional logic, algorithm building, debugging, simulation, and distributed computation. The two stages are local logic and global logic. Dierbach et al. (2011) on the other hand identify the critical set of CT as identifying and applying problem decomposition, evaluating, building algorithms, and developing computational models to problems. Ater-Kranov, Bryant, Orr, Wallace, and Zhang (2010) noted that the two common computational skills that are dominant in the literature are problem solving and critical thinking. Kazimoglu et al. (2012) noted that there is a lack of precise categories of CT skills, thus making it difficult to teaching CT across various disciplines outside computer science (Ater-Kranov et al., 2010). To this end, digital game design and visual programming tools have been proposed as frameworks to teach both CT and introductory programming concepts at the same time because games are motivational and attractive in nature.

Werner, Campe, and Denner (2012) outline an innovative game model for learning computational thinking (CT) skills through digital game-play. They analyze how this game supports various CT concepts and how these concepts can be mapped to programming constructs to facilitate learning introductory computer programming. Han et al. (2015) on the other hand introduce Entry, a visual programming application which is developed to facilitate student's computational thinking. As an HTML5-based visual programming platform, Entry provides students with little or no programming background with an integrated environment in which they not only learn programming in an easy and fun way but also create, post, and share their own programs. Werner et al. (2012) examine students learning of computer science concepts via Alice game programming. They noted that Alice game design demonstrates a successful use of high-level computer science concepts such as student-created abstractions, concurrent execution, and event handlers. Other tools that have been discussed to support computational skills and motivate students into learning introductory concepts of programming include strategic board games (Berland & Lee, 2011) and mobile game development (Grover & Pea, 2013). Despite these efforts, there are still calls for more studies to show how game design can be associated with CT and how the teaching and learning of introductory programming can be supported by game design (Ibrahim, Yusoff, Omar, & Jaafar, 2011; Sung et al., 2011). Werner et al. (2012) go further to state that there is paucity of empirical evidence in developing CT for the purpose of learning programming through playing digital games. Thus, there is a pressing need to have a better understanding of the impact of gaming in the teaching and learning of introductory programming courses and the development of CT skills through visual game programming.

To address this issue, this study explores Alice visual game programming and its benefits in motivating students in a developing country to learn introductory programming concepts and acquiring CT skills at the same time. We demonstrate how Alice visual game programming motivates students to learn programming and also how it supports students' computation thinking skills which are integral elements of learning programming. The following section discusses the philosophical assumptions underpinning this study. It also introduces the research strategy and the methods used for conducting the research. Both the methodology and its associated methods were chosen with the aim of having a 'valid' research approach commensurate with the limited resources available for this study.

Methodology

Research Design

The research is based on a case study method because it enables multiple methods of data collection to gather information from one or a few entities such as people, groups, or organizations (Benbasat, Goldstein, & Mead, 1987). The research was carried out at the American University of Nigeria (AUN) in North East Nigeria. Our choice of AUN was a selection of convenience: the authors are faculty members in the computing department and were involved in the teaching of programming courses. The study was explanatory in nature (Yin, 2003) with the aim of understanding how Alice 3D animated programming language motivates students to learn programming using concepts of computation thinking. Fifteen first-year computer sciences students enrolled in the introduction to computer science course taught by one of the authors. Participation in all parts of the study was voluntary, and we are reporting on all the 15 students who indicated interest to participate in the study (see Table 1 for participant information).

Table 1 Participant information

Demographic description		Frequency
Age	18–20	12
	21–25	3
Gender	Male	7
	Female	8
Major	Computer science Software engineering	10 5
Status	1st year	15

Game Activity

The students were asked to create an animated boat racing game using Alice 3D visual programing, a free and innovative 3D programming environment that is designed to introduce students to object-oriented programming. Some of the students have never programmed before nor had any related experience with using Alice, although there were four of them who had little experience of Ruby programming language due to their participation in the university's computer science club. The students were encouraged to feel free to discuss during the course of the game design. One major goal of the course was to provide an opportunity for students to learn the fundamental concepts of introductory programming language and problem solving. Qualitative data collection methods consisting of observations and interview with students working with Alice are the basis of viewpoints presented in this paper. The qualitative methodology was chosen over the quantitative methodology due to its ability to show how the students learn programming using computational skills via Alice over time and to provide an account of the context within which the learning process is taking place.

Each interview lasted between 30 min and 1 h and was conducted during the two-day workshop of teaching Alice during the research fieldwork. Interviewees were asked probing follow-up questions on new and emerging topics as well as given opportunities to raise any other issues they considered relevant. Overall, a total of about 17 h from the interviews were compiled, organized, and analyzed. One of the authors acted as a practitioner researcher who Oates (2006) described as someone who already has a job and decides to put on a researcher's "hat" to investigate their own work organization.

In this study, observation was very important as the authors could observe the difficulties faced by the students while learning programming in various programming classes. A total of approximately 2 h of observation was conducted, and two pages of observation notes were compiled. Data collected from interviews and observations were analyzed using thematic analysis, a process of encoding qualitative information (see Table 2). The themes and key concepts that were identified were related to concepts of computational thinking (see Table 2). Five themes related to computational thinking were identified, namely, problem solving, debugging, simulation, developing algorithm, and collaboration. The data collected formed the basis of analysis presented in the next section (Table 3).

Case Narrative

The students were presented with lab workshop to design a motorboat racing game. In the racing game, the player is required to steer a boat with the arrow keys through various rings trying to beat the clock to the finish line. The player must maneuver through each ring before getting to the finish line, and a score will keep track of how

Table 2 Sample of themes and transcript excerpts used in thematic coding

Themes	Meaning and sources	Sample-coded excerpts from transcripts/ field notes
Problem solving	CT has been defined as a problem-solving approach (Wing, 2006)	"I was so confused but after brain storming with my friends, we designed a plan and we decided we will create a timer object and link it to the motorboat because when the boat starts moving, the timer should start and then when we solve that problem we will move to the next"
Debugging	Debugging is a vital element of both programming and CT (Wing, 2006)	"Me and my friends are going the instructor tomorrow during his office hours in order to debug this game. I don't feel comfortable that my animation is not working. I thought I could show my friends what I have developed but it doesn't seem so"
Simulation	Simulation is modeling or testing of algorithms or logic (Wing, 2006)	"My friends' boat was flying rather than moving on the waters. Apparently he forgot to link the move method within the water object to the move method within boat object"
Developing algorithm	It is the planning of actions for events that are taking place; in its complex form, it is planning for unknown events (Wing, 2006)	"I am so happy I can see the way the animate boat moves immediately after running the program. Immediately I saw that the motorboat object was too big, I immediately started looking for the command method for resizing object because I remember we used the move command for installing motion into boat"
Collaboration	Computational thinking as distributed computing in which different pieces of information or logic are contributed by different players during the process of debugging, simulation, or algorithm building (Berland & Lee, 2011)	"I was so confused but after brain storming with my friends, we designed a plan and we decided we will create a timer object and link it to the motorboat because when the boat starts moving, the timer should start and then when we solve that problem we will move to the next"

many rings the player has driven through. The students already had Alice installed on their laptops a week before this lab session and had already sketched the various scenes of their game; thus, once they arrived in the classroom, they immediately started the lab tutorials to design the game world using the water template and two objects which are the motorboat and the torus. Many of the students did not have any difficulties carrying out this task as they had already created rough sketches of how they wanted the virtual world to look like and also had gone through the Alice user interface before coming into the workshop. Alice already has built-in action commands; hence, the students immediately added the action "move" for the boat.

Table 3 Summary of findings and their relationship with CT concepts

Game task	Related CT concepts	Theoretical justification for CT concepts
The students had to brainstorm and strategize a solution on how they could create a boat where a player could navigate through various rings to get scores within a period of time. Many of them designed a sketch of their world and how they wanted the movement of the boat. The students implemented this sketch on Alice using the various objects available on Alice and tested it to check if it helped solved the problem of creating the racing scenario	Problem solving	Computation thinking has been described as a problem-solving approach in various literatures (Wing, 2008; Berland & Lee, 2011; Kazimoglu et al., 2012)
Students debugged their game scoring method to check for errors and then simulated their scoring method to see if the method was working accurately. The students' continuous debugging and simulations of their methods and functions helped them in developing their abstraction as well as good programming practices	Debugging and simulation	Wing (2006, 2008) describe debugging and simulation as core significant elements of programming and computation thinking
The students developed a visual storyboard to show the various scenes and transitions in the game design	Developing algorithm	Dierbach et al. (2011) identifies computational thinking skills constitute building an algorithm that passes through a series of development life cycle
To discuss and interact freely with fellow students in order to compare solutions and find answers to problems during the design and development of the game	Collaboration	Berland and Lee (2011) discusses about the social element of computation thinking that involves players coming together to contribute different logics during the process of algorithm building, simulation or debugging

The various commands that were added were drawn upon from the textual storyboard the students created. The students then simulated the behavior of the objects. The students got immediate feedback regarding the correctness of their program by simply looking at the behavior of the objects. After this first simulation step, many started facing some challenges as their objects were too big and therefore needed to be resized. Several students started playing around with action commands and were able to add the "resize" action command to change the physical nature of the motorboat and torus.

"Starting off with Alice has completely eased the way for me to understand Ruby programming language...Now I understand the whole idea of objects in programming...the motorboat is the object and the blue color are the attributes..."

"A lot of other students say programming is difficult but when the instructor showed us how Alice works, I felt this was fun and pleasurable... It has lots of different characters and animations."

"I am so happy I can see the way the animated boat moves immediately after running the program. Immediately I saw that the motorboat object was too big, I immediately started looking for the command method for resizing object because I remember we used the move command for installing motion into boat."

Once the scene was ready, the students were tasked to plan and write a program for animating interactions between the objects and also between the objects and the virtual world in which they reside. Many students were confused on what step to take next.

"I don't know if I should start creating the timer for the boat racing, the instructor is not giving us any tips, he said we are programmers and we should think properly on how these objects will work and that's what we are doing I guess."

"I was so confused but after brainstorming with my friends, we devised a plan and we decided we will create a timer object and link it to the motorboat because when the boat starts moving, the timer should start and then when we solve that problem we will move to the next."

It was unanimously agreed during the lab session that the timer method be created first, and the instructor gave the students a hint of how to go about it. All students decided to create an object called time, create variable "value" to store the time, and then set the time object to the motor boat. Next, the students created the method for time countdown. Here, the students were introduced to conditions such as the while loop and if-else. After running this task, the students started encountering various problems.

Some of the students realized that they were using the wrong condition and some did not properly link the timer object to the motorboat object. At this stage, there was a lot of debugging and brainstorming taking place between students. On many occasions, the students laughed at each other when their colleagues' game was encountering execution errors as shown in the quote below:

"My friend's boat was flying rather than moving on the waters. Apparently he forgot to link the move method within the water object to the move method within boat object."

Students also shared their difficulties with the instructor so that they could observe together and at the same time find out what was wrong and then follow the teacher's instructions. In this way, students could correct the code and continue working.

"The instructor was so nice and funny that he made the lab session so enjoyable and he never got angry despite all our numerous mistakes and always answered all our silly questions."

The lab session ended and many were so excited that they did not want to leave for their next class.

"I didn't want to go for my next class because I wanted to find out what was the problem and solve it right then and there. But immediately I am done with classes today I am going straight away to work on my game design using Alice."

"My friends and I are going to meet the instructor tomorrow during his office hours in order to debug this game..I don't feel comfortable that my animation is not working. I thought I could show my friends what I have developed but it doesn't seem so."

"The instructor was so interesting. He knew the subject so well and motivated us to learn."

By the time the students resumed their next lab section, many of them had already implemented the timing for the game and were ready for their next task which was implementing the scoring system for the game. The students further created two methods that will increase the score when the player successfully steers the boat through the ring. Thus, as students participated in more sessions, they became more familiar with programming concepts:

"I thought the course would be very difficult because it is programming but after engaging the game tutorial, the class became easier and fun."

Thus, by the end of the second lab session, students had already implemented an instruction method so that players know the rules of the game when they start the game. The students concluded the tutorials by taking home an assignment of creating methods for win and lose when the games ends. After completing the tutorials, the students went ahead on their own to make their games harder by reducing the amount of time in the game and also modifying the virtual world by adding various colors and objects. The instructor also asked the students to present a report on their experience with Alice, the problems they encountered, and the algorithms they applied to solve the problems. In the following lab sessions, the students and instructor examined several problems and their solutions presented by the students, exposing both their weaknesses and strengths during the discussion phase. This brainstorming phase enabled students to gain a deeper and in-depth understanding of the problems and their algorithmic solution.

Furthermore, the instructor challenged students to shed light on their own ideas, thus motivating them to discuss the subject matter more and critique their solutions and look for alternatives. By doing so, the students were able to organize their own thoughts and understand areas they found difficult.

"For my game, I didn't use a function when ending the game, and I learnt that was an easy way out, however other students did use a function and maybe that's the reason their timing worked properly and mine didn't but I was able to resolve it."

In summary, the introduction to programming concepts using Alice has taught the students the use of sequence and logic skills through game development which has really encouraged and helped the students to learn programming concepts such as functions, loops, condition, sequence, and methods which they can use in more advanced programming languages. However, some of the students who have experienced some Ruby programming language in the university computer science club workshop noted that:

"In Alice too much of the work is done for you with the whole idea of drag and drop unlike the traditional languages like Ruby and Java where you need to do a lot of coding with both logic and syntax errors."

Furthermore, students complained of the continuous crashing of Alice and their inability to save their codes. According to one student:

"In the middle of your work, Alice just crashes and when it does crash, it requires you to recreate your method again because it doesn't allow us to save our code."

Case Analysis

Problem Solving

In the game activity, the students were tasked with the activity to create a boat racing game. Thus, the students had to brainstorm and strategize a solution on how they could create a boat where a player could navigate through various rings to get scores within a period of time. For example, many of them designed a sketch of their world and how they wanted the movement of the boat. The students implemented this sketch on Alice using the various objects available on Alice and tested it to check if it helped solved the problem of creating the racing scenario. As described in the case narratives, many of them faced difficulties with sizing the objects and had to work out a way of resizing them to fit the screen. Some students kept trying various ways of mapping out their ideas of boat racing game into Alice until they were satisfied with their outputs. Overall, students refused to be discouraged with the various problems and were even excited trying to solve more complex problems as they learned this was part of the learning process of programming.

Throughout the course of the tutorial, students learned the problem-solving approach of mapping out their ideas and trying them out through an iterative cycle until they solved the particular problem. With Alice when solving a problem, one gets an immediate feedback on how the animated program runs. This highly visual feedback of problem solving allowed the students to map their algorithms to the animated actions. The immediate feedback to problem solving resulted in an understanding of the various concepts of object-oriented programming languages.

Debugging and Simulation

Many of the students found the testing and debugging mechanism of Alice very important. It allowed them to test their ideas to the animated actions. Majority of the debugging the students carried out focused mainly on their methods and functions. For example, students debugged their scoring method to see if the method was working accurately. The students' continuous debugging of their methods and functions helped them in developing their abstraction as well as good programming practices. It also enabled students to critically think about their solutions, i.e., to ask themselves if there was a better alternative to the solution they had implemented. Furthermore, the case study showed that students used Alice to program simple simulations. In this case, the goal of the simulation the students designed is to move a motorboat through various rings in order to beat a clock. Thus, the students created various scenes and events and further tested them to see how the game simulation works.

Developing Algorithm

The students developed a visual storyboard to show the various scenes and transitions of the game. They used a blue pencil color to paint and illustrate the water and the blue skies. They then drew a boat on top of the water and then added some rings on the pathway of the boat. The students used Alice's scene editor to add objects to the virtual world and then meticulously organized the objects into various positions. As each successive scene is created, a screen capture is made and copied to a document. The students also developed a textual storyboard containing the list of actions the boat should perform; thus, the actions in the textual storyboard can also be referred to as pseudo code. The textual storyboard allowed the students to prepare a planned structure of the programming codes to be implemented for the game animation.

Collaboration

The findings of the study showed that students continuously interacted with each other when attempting to design and implement their game designs. When trying to debug an error or making a motion appear more realistic, the students usually shared ideas with each other. A lot of the students laughed at each other when their animations looked funny; as such, the students found Alice extremely fun to use. Also the game design using Alice brought about interactions between members of the class, many of whom usually do not talk to each, hence leading to team building skills among the students. Many students took pride in their work by playing their games and showing it off to their friends.

The Proposed Model

After analyzing the qualitative data, a model as shown in Fig. 1 was developed to understand the computational approach to learning programming using Alice visual game programming. The model suggests that computational thinking influences the use of Alice 3D visual programming tool which in turn also influences computational thinking. Moreover, Alice 3D visual programming tool motivates students to learning programming. The ability to learn and understand programming concepts with the help of Alice 3D visual programming also influences computational thinking skills.

Discussion and Conclusion

The purpose of this research was to examine a computational approach to learning introductory programming course using visual game programming in developing countries using a case study of the American University of Nigeria. The importance

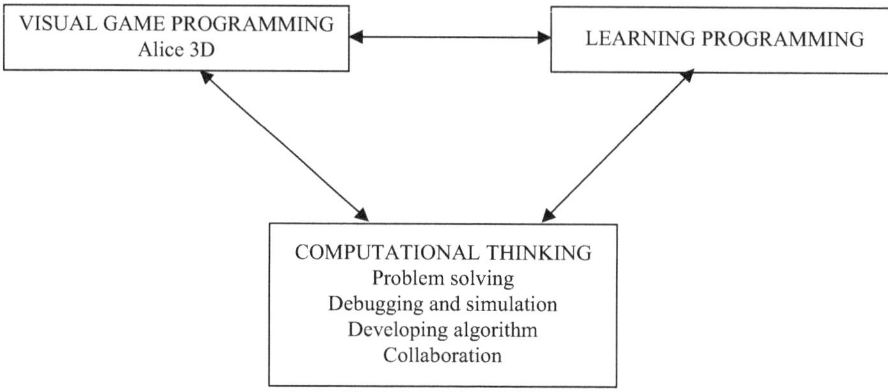

Fig. 1 Proposed Conceptual Model for Understanding the Learning of Programming at the Computational Thinking Level using Visual game programming

of this study stems from the paucity of research on how the teaching and learning of programming could be further enhanced in universities in developing countries. The study further contributes to the research on computer education in developing countries by proposing a model to understand computational thinking process when undertaking introductory programming courses using visual game programming.

The findings of the study showed the use of visual game programming as a promising strategy to introduce computer programming concepts to students. The findings show that students demonstrated an understanding of a range of computational thinking skills such as problem solving, debugging, simulation, building algorithms, and collaboration while using Alice to make games. The use of Alice to program was also fun, thus motivating students to learning common programming constructs such as method, functions, and events. Our results build on prior studies to show that Alice 3D does induce computational thinking into students and also motivates them towards the learning of programming (Kazimoglu et al., 2012; Kelleher & Pausch, 2007).

The higher levels of motivation reported by the students to learn programming should enhance retention, because many students drop out due to the lack of motivation and the difficulty to understand programming concepts (Moreno, 2012). However, Alice does not teach them how to perform advance programming. Armoni et al. (2015) found similar results when they investigated the use of the Scratch environment for teaching computational thinking concepts to middle school students. They found out that students who had learned programming concepts using Scratch struggled with advanced concepts in Java such as typecasting and dynamic programming, which are not shared in Scratch. Also our studies found that as a result of students' discussion and participation in the class activities, they were able to solve programs they encountered in the design of the game. This is significant because it shows that pair programming was an effective method to use for engaging students in CT (Berland & Lee, 2011).

The model proposed in this paper is based on data grounded in the experiences of IS students in a programming course at a Nigerian university and has not been tested. It is important to consider the context of the study. First, the course was hands-on; as such, the paper is focused on technical IS courses. The model in this paper may not be relevant to lecture-based courses such as business information systems. This idea and validation of the model could be examined in future research. The study was limited in that only a single focused case study was undertaken under severe time limitations; however, there is scope for undertaking a longitudinal study on the basis of current results to further provide an insight into how computational thinking can be taught to students as they continue to enroll in computer degree programs in universities across the country. The findings of this study cannot be generalized; the students who enroll at the university may be different from other students who enrolled at other universities. The results may not hold for students in public or bigger universities; however, other concepts can be developed and explored further in similar research settings.

References

Armoni, M., Meerbaum-Salant, O., & Ben-Ari, M. (2015). From scratch to "real" programming. *ACM Transactions on Computing Education, 14*, 4.

Ater-Kranov, A., Bryant, R., Orr, G., Wallace, S., & Zhang, M. (2010). Developing a community definition and teaching modules for computational thinking: accomplishments and challenges. In *Proceedings of the 2010 ACM conference on information technology education (SIGITE '10)* (pp. 143–148). New York, NY: ACM.

Bass, M. J., & Heeks, R. (2008). Changing computing curricula in Africa Universities: Evaluating progress and challenges via design-reality gap analysis. *Electronic Journal of Information Systems in Developing Countries, 48*(5), 1.

Benbasat, I., Goldstein, D. K., & Mead, M. (1987). The case research strategy in studies of information systems. *MIS Quarterly, 11*(3), 369–386.

Bergin, S., & Reilly, R. (2005). The influence of motivation and comfort-level on learning to program. In *Proceedings of the 17th annual workshop on the psychology of programming interest group* (pp. 293–304). Brighton: University of Sussex.

Berland, M., & Lee, V. R. (2011). Collaborative strategic board games as a site for distributed computational thinking. *International Journal of Game-Based Learning (IJGBL), 1*(2), 65–81.

Dasuki, I., Ogedebe, P., Kanya, R. A., Ndume, H., & Makinde, J. (2015). Evaluating the implementation of international computing curricular in African universities: A design-reality gap approach. *International Journal of Education and Development using Information and Communication Technology (IJEDICT), 11*(1), 17–35.

Dierbach, C., Hochheiser, H., Collins, S., Jerome, G., Ariza, C., Kelleher, T., Kleinsasser, W., Dehlinger, J., & Kaza, S. (2011). A model for piloting pathways for computational thinking in a general education curriculum. In *Proceedings of the 42nd ACM technical symposium on computer science education (SIGCSE '11)* (pp. 257–262). New York, NY: ACM.

Grover, S., & Pea, R. (2013). Using a discourse-intensive pedagogy and android's app inventor for introducing computational concepts to middle school students. In *Proceeding of the 44th ACM technical symposium on computer science education (SIGCSE '13)* (pp. 723–728). New York, NY: ACM.

Han, A., Kim, J., & Wohn, K. (2015). Entry: Visual programming to enhance children's computational thinking. In *Adjunct Proceedings of the 2015 ACM International Joint Conference on Pervasive and Ubiquitous Computing and Proceedings of the 2015 ACM International Symposium on Wearable Computers*.

Ibrahim, R., Yusoff, R., Omar, H. M., & Jaafar, A. (2011). Students perceptions of using educational games to learn introductory programming. *Computer and Information Science, 4*(1), 205–216.

Katai, Z., & Toth, L. (2010). Technologically and artistically enhanced multi-sensory computer-programming education. *Teaching and Teacher Education, 26*(2), 244–251.

Kazimoglu, C., Kiernan, M., Bacon, L., & MacKinnon, L. (2012). Learning programming at the computational thinking level via digital game-play. *Procedia Computer Science, 9*(2012), 522–531.

Kelleher, C., & Pausch, R. (2007). Using story telling to motivate programming. *Communications of the ACM, 50*, 7.

Lee, I., Martin, F., Denner, J., Coulter, B., Allan, W., Erickson, J., Malyn-Smith, J., & Werner, L. (2011). Computational thinking for youth in practice. *ACM Inroads, 2*(1), 32–37.

Moreno, J. (2012). Digital competition game to improve programming skills. *Educational Technology and Society, 15*(3), 288–297.

Oates, B. (2006). *Researching information systems and computing*. London: Sage.

Qualls, J. A., Sherrell, L., B. (2010) Why computational thinking should be integrated into the curriculum, Journal of Computing Sciences in Colleges, 25, 5, 66–71.

Sarpong, K. A., Authur, J. K., & Owusu, P. Y. (2013). Causes of failure of students in computer programming courses: The teacher—learner perspective. *International Journal of Computer Applications, 77*, 12.

Sung, K., Hillyard, C., Angotti, R. L., Panitz, M. W., Goldstein, D. S., & Nordlinger, J. (2011). Game-themed programming assignment modules: A pathway for gradual integration of gaming context into existing introductory programming courses. *IEEE Transactions on Education, 54*(3), 416–427.

Werner, L., Campe, S., & Denner, J. (2012). Children learning computer science concepts via Alice game-programming. In *Proceedings of the 43rd ACM technical symposium on computer science education (SIGCSE '12)* (pp. 427–432). New York, NY: ACM.

Wing, J. M. (2006). Computational thinking. *Communications of the ACM, 49*(2), 33–35.

Wing, J. M. (2008). Computational thinking and thinking about computing. *Philosophical Transactions of the Royal Society A: Mathematical, Physical and Engineering Sciences, 366*, 3717–3725.

Yin, R. (2003). *Case study research: Design and methods*. London: Sage.

Creating and Evaluating a Visual Programming Course Based on Student Experience

Kadir Yucel Kaya and Kursat Cagiltay

Abstract The purpose of this study was to deduct guidelines from an introductory programming course to understand the critical points based on the opinions of the students. These critical points could be a guide for future course designs. An introductory visual programming course was designed for novice learners during 2014, fall term at Middle East Technical University, Turkey. Qualitative data were collected with interviews and observations. From the interviews, five themes emerged: communication, computational thinking, environment, motivation, and course recommendations. Results of the study revealed what motivates students, what parts of the course students found useful, and what parts should be replaced. An environment which is easy, visual, and communicative through an informal interface could be useful, especially in terms of motivation. Additionally, examples with useful products rather than meaningless algorithm examples could motivate students better. Interviews also revealed topics students found to be difficult. Results of this study could be a guide for future visual programming course designs.

Keywords Novice programmers • Visual programming • App Inventor

Introduction

Computing technology influences everyone's life, thinking, and behaviors, and it is getting more popular day by day (Kwon, Yoon, & Lee, 2011; Kazimoglu, Kiernan, Bacon, & MacKinnon, 2011). From the last years of the twentieth century to recent years, computer and mobile software technologies have become more popular. Despite its growing popularity, technology is only a product for many people. Many who claim to be experienced with technology (and so-called digital natives) are more like consumers rather than producers (Smutny, 2011). There is a growing interest in helping others to become creators of technology rather than just

K.Y. Kaya (✉) • K. Cagiltay
Middle East Technical University, Çankaya, Ankara, Turkey
e-mail: kykaya@metu.edu.tr; kursat@metu.edu.tr

P.J. Rich, C.B. Hodges (eds.), *Emerging Research, Practice, and Policy on Computational Thinking*, Educational Communications and Technology: Issues and Innovations, DOI 10.1007/978-3-319-52691-1_9

consumer. This has been promoted through computational thinking and programming. However, programming is a very complex task to teach and learn, and it requires special attention (Kwon et al., 2011). When it comes to inexperienced learners, programming language education is one of the most serious issues in teaching computational thinking (Saito & Yamauara, 2013).

Since the 1970s, a variety of solutions have been offered to solve this problem (Sorva, Karavirta, & Malmi, 2013) such as microworlds, visualization software, and visual programming languages (Malliarakis, Satratzemi, & Xinogalos, 2013; Rolandsson, 2013). One powerful solution is visual programming languages. Visual programming language is described by Smutny (2011) as "a programming language that lets users to create programs by manipulating program elements graphically rather than specifying them textually" (p. 358). The earliest and best known visual programming language is Logo (Papert, 1980 as cited in Sengupta, Kinnebrew, Basu, Biswas, & Clark, 2013). Many visual programming languages have since been developed to help people learn programming. In recent years, Alice, Scratch, BlueJ, and App Inventor (AI) are some of the more popular visual programming languages. Especially, AI provides an easy way to create their own mobile software programs that could help adult novice programmers, while others are mainly for K-12 level and educational purposes only. "MIT App Inventor is a drag-and-drop visual programming tool for designing and building fully functional mobile apps for Android" (Pokress & Veiga, 2013, p.1). Google App Inventor for Android was created for users without coding experience to make simple apps for mobile phone released in 2010 (Bertea, 2011).

There are lots of empirical studies about learning programming. However, they mostly focus on learning outcomes, during or after the course (Bennedsen & Caspersen, 2012). This study sought to design a course by reshaping it based on the data collected from students through observation, interviews, and literature. The purpose of this study was to provide guidelines for an introductory collegiate-level visual programming course design for non-programming majors.

Method

The overarching research questions for this study was: What are the guidelines for an effective, efficient and motivating introductory visual programming course regarding higher education level?

To answer this question, interviews were conducted with students, and progress of the students was observed throughout the course, following students' discussions from the course Facebook group. Under the main research question, researchers also aim to discover: How could a visual programming course improve computational thinking skills of higher education students?

The study aimed to design an effective course for novice/non-programmers. There were two criteria to select participants: (1) they should have basic computer skills; (2) they should be a novice or non-programmer. The course started with 12 participants, but one student dropped out at the beginning. There were five participants from the Department of Elementary Mathematics, three from Computer Education and Instructional Technology, two from Elementary Science Education, and one from the Department of Mathematics. Most of the participants came from the faculty of education since the course opened in a department under the faculty of education. The course was 10 weeks long. Instead of a final exam, all of the participants were required to create their own application by using App Inventor and present it at the final week.

A course is given at the Department of Computer Education and Instructional Technology in a University in Turkey. The AI environment was used in the course. A qualitative methodology was used to collect and analyze data. Data were collected through interviews, observations, and documents. The course's success was assessed based on the data collected during and after the course from students. Creswell's (2012) steps were used to analyze qualitative data. Steps include (1) reading the data initially, (2) dividing the text into segments of information, (3) labeling the segments of information with codes, (4) reducing overlap and redundancy, and (5) collapsing codes into themes.

Results of this study aim to develop effective, efficient, and motivating introductory programming course guidelines which could lead to an advanced level programming education and help novice programmers to grasp computational thinking.

Findings

Five themes emerged from the interviews, namely, computational thinking, environment, motivation, course recommendations, and communication. Interviews were coded as S1 to S11, which stands for student with a random number after it to distinguish participants. We discuss each of these themes in greater detail in the following sections.

Computational Thinking and Programming Concepts

Computational thinking is defined as an analytic approach to problem solving, understanding human behavior by drawing on the concepts fundamental to computer science (Wing 2006). Some of the basic concepts like what is an algorithm and converting daily routines into algorithmic expression were taught, in addition to lab courses with step-by-step tutorials from the Massachusetts Institute of Technology (MIT). After the third week, an algorithmic question was posed to students each week. In the first week, students were having a hard time solving the question since they were still waiting for a step-by-step tutorial, which revealed that, in a visual programming course, a tutorial-only approach could lead students to simply copy what they see. The instructor guided them to think like the algorithmic problems that were mentioned at the lecture hours. Students learned to put a complex daily life routine (e.g., brewing tea, getting on the bus) into simple steps. It helped students to solve the problem.

Several students commented that after taking this course, they started to break a complex problem or a daily routine to basic steps. They started to think differently, especially dividing a problem to smaller steps.

> After the first week, my perspective changed towards daily life. I began to think that types of things like the brewing tea example (implying the algorithm example). Like how can this also be like that (implying dividing into steps). (S2)
>
> At least, I can say that it helped us to think differently. The course showed us a way like "to reach the end, you have to follow these steps" You have to break it down to pieces and then reach to the whole. (S11)

A student with previous programming experience stated that he not only learned the concepts better with the help of a visual programming environment, but the course also helped to choose the shorter route the solve the problem. Having multiple solutions to a problem and choosing the appropriate or easier one are also related to computational thinking (namely, they are a form of efficiency, which is an important aspect of computational thinking):

> I understand variables better. And one other thing is, say you will develop a program. There are two ways of doing it, one is long one is short. This course taught me to choose the short one. (S8)

At the end of the course, some students thought that they understood algorithmic thinking or programming logic. One student related the programming logic in the course with the logical reasoning in mathematics, which was her major:

> You know, there is a thing called logical reasoning. We are using that in this course. And the source of it actually is mathematics. (S11)
>
> Since the codes are hidden in the blocks that are ready to use, the environment was more appealing for the first time learning. I learned the logic behind the programming now. In my opinion, it helps us so much to understand the programming logic. (S2)
>
> We have been doing some stuff related to algorithms without knowing it. We were hearing from (students in) computer engineering like "this is my algorithm", now we also know it. (S3)

Environment

The programming environment was one of the most critical elements of this study. While some of App Inventor's properties directly affected the other findings, in this part specifically positive and negative sides of the environment were examined. Curiously, few of them were controllable by the researcher. Nevertheless, these findings could be helpful for programming environment designers. Additionally, it could be helpful for the instructors to see the pros and cons of AI.

Some statements of the students are summarized in the table above about positive and negative sides of the AI environment. Regarding the positive sides, one of the most popular answers is that AI is easy. Students found the environment easy to learn, easy

Table 1 Positive and negative sides of App Inventor Environment based on the student interviews

Positive	Negative
Easier to understand	Slow
Easier to use	UI arrangement and design issues
Visual, drag and drop, syntax alternative	Companion app errors (reset button)
Simultaneous testing/publishing	Restrictions/not flexible enough
Do not let syntax mistakes/instant feedback	Undo button does not exist
Let you being creative	Save issues
Separate design and block interface	Do not let offline and group work
Interesting	
Colored blocks	

to understand, and easy to create in comparison to other programming environments. First time learners made similar comments. The main reason behind this was the visual nature of the environment. Being syntax-free also related to the easiness of the environment, which also reduced the mistakes novice programmers might commit.

Students were also in favor of simultaneous testing. With the help of the companion app or emulator, the programmer could see every change she/he made instantly. There were many positives that students mentioned (see Table 1) that can be examined by future instructors.

There were also numerous negative sides to using the AI environment. The most frequent comment was that AI is slow. As the application is getting more complex, it is getting harder to work on the environment. In addition to its speed, students with previous programming experience complained about the environment's inflexibility. They thought that if the programmer wanted to create a more complex program, the environment would limit them. While we agree with this opinion, the purpose of AI is not for creating the most complex applications, but rather for helping novice programmers to learn programming and rapidly develop a working product. In this aspect, AI appeared to be a good choice.

Motivation

Espinar Redondo and Ortega Martín (2015) defined motivation as "what encourages students to freely devote their time to a specific activity" (p. 127). As the activities become more difficult and complex like programming, motivation becomes a bigger problem. Keller's (1987) ARCS model, which is a method for improving motivation in education, was used as a framework to motivate and evaluate the motivation of students based on the interviews and the observations. The nature of AI helped to apply some motivation strategies into the course, such as (attention) active participation, use of humor, and real-world examples, (relevance) link to previous experience, perceived present worth, and perceived future usefulness (confidence) facilitating self-growth, providing feedback, giving learners control (satisfaction) presenting rewards, and immediate application of the knowledge. Since the main reason for using ARCS was to evaluate the course itself, the strategies that were mentioned above were not evaluated by the students. However, some of the opinions about the course overlapped with the strategies.

All of the students (N = 11) stated that they enjoyed the course. All of the students except one stated that they will take a follow-up course if it's offered. The exception student was thinking she learned sufficient about AI so she didn't need it. Since motivation is having the desire to keep doing something, even at the end of the course, nearly all of the students demonstrated motivation towards learning programming. Unrelated with the environment and programming, students also found that the instructor's being communicative, humorous, and sincere was another motivator.

According to students, the most important motivator was developing a working product, not just meaningless examples but an application that worked on their phones. Every week students created a hands-on working product rather than offering them just theoretical information. All of the students were very happy to create a product in lab hours. They found it interesting and enjoyable, as illustrated through their comments below:

> Developing an application in course hour was very nice, not boring at all. (S1)
>
> If I need any application why won't I develop. I don't want to be a leech now. I want to try by myself now. (S2)

AI also provided users an easier environment to create a product. Several students stated that the easy-to-create nature of AI was another source of motivation for them.

> I, for example, had no knowledge of programming. This course gave me the knowledge of programming. What part is used for what (in traditional programming languages) was very complicated for me. I became familiar with it. (S7)
>
> It seems simple. Being simple makes me think like I will drag this and this will happen. Actually it motivates people more to create. (S11)

One student who had taken a mandatory C programming course for her major stated that AI's visual environment made it more motivating.

> (Implying C language) It was a little theoretic, we couldn't see what we were doing. We could only see it when we printed it (implies compiling). But AI was very enjoyable, we can see it directly as an application. We can see it right on the phone. (S10)

Observations of the researcher throughout the course also support this finding. Some students tested the applications with enjoyment and curiosity. In week 2, one student stated, "I will show this to my roommate and tell him, 'look I developed an application!'" One student said the course was fun because she created applications during lab hours.

> I mean the course was fun in general, especially compared to the other (courses). Lab hours were focused solely on creating something, so it was very nice. We were the ones who created them, that was also nice. In the end, developing a product was very good as the result. (S6)

Even the students with programming experience were very satisfied about taking the course. One student stated that "every student in our department (computer education and instructional technology) should take this course" Another student with previous programming knowledge was more confident now than before, expressing:

> With AI I know that I can develop applications now, even if they are simple ones… I was thinking of learning Java for programming. This (mentioning AI) could be a substructure for it. (S5)

In conclusion, according to the interviews, communication with instructor, creating useful products, learning a new skill, and the easiness of the environment were the main motivators for the students.

Recommendations for the Course

Students' opinions and recommendations were taken for the future implementation and reshaping the course into a more effective one. The survey asked about what are the parts that should be changed, removed from, or added to the course. The parts they did not like, parts they found boring, and parts that they were having difficulty to learn were also asked to see what parts are not working for them. Variables, the clock component, and database blocks were the popular answers regarding the difficult topics. Students wanted more attention to these topics, especially more hands-on simple examples.

The most popular answer when it comes to having difficulty in the course was variables. After the week that variables were used, some of the students referred to them as "orange things" since the color of the variable blocks was orange.

> I didn't understand the variables at first (S1).
>
> Actually at the very beginning, orange things… Now I know what they are: "variables." It was kind of difficult but I understood the logic behind it now. (S2)
>
> As I have said before, orange things were our scary dream. (S9)
>
> Orange things… Variables. After defining the variables… I mean ok we define it but how to use it (was the problem). (S11)

At first, some students tried to solve the problems without the use of variables. However, use of variables in some examples was a must. It was obvious that most students did not understand variables with the tutorials taken from MIT. Even with repeated practice, they had a hard time understanding the concepts. One possible reason could be that they confounded variables in programming with the concept of variables in mathematics. Some students stated that defining variables was the confusing part, because they do not do such a process in mathematics.

> Because in mathematics, we use variables but when we came here, we assigned it a value. That's why it is different. (S3)
>
> I was having difficulty defining variables. But in the last application I have developed, I defined 2 and it worked without any problem. (S9)

Another part that was found difficult by students was the clock component. The clock component is a timer, which is widely used in AI examples. T clock is like a loop with a changeable interval and can be turned on or off with functions. This concept was foreign to the students. They stated they were having difficulty understanding it.

> For example, I had a hard time understanding the logic of the clock component but I understood after. What is an interval, what is enabled (the properties)? After using it for some time, I was like "is that it?" (S2)
>
> Using the double clock was a little confusing. I guess that is also understood now. (S9)

As a solution to this, one student recommended providing a basic example that focused solely on the properties of the clock component.

> There could be something like a counter example like this increase and that decrease. (S2)

Students wanted to learn some confusing components in detail with basic examples rather than MIT's tutorials. Another difficult concept was that of database. The database component was used to carry information between multiple screens in one example. Some students tried using it for more complex tasks in their own projects. They requested more use of databases at the end of the course.

> We only had a quick look at database. We could have spent more time on it (S5).
>
> Variables and Database. When I was adding it (database) to the project, I realized that I had to look it again. (S9)
>
> Database topic was really confusing. (S4)

One of the unexpected recommendations that some of the students suggested was providing more homework for them. This could also be a part of motivation because students demanded to have more homework, which means devoting more of their free time for the course.

> There could be more like homework. We create one in course, we could have make one more at home for each week. (S1)
>
> I mean one or two homework assignments would not get us tired. It could have been good. (S2)
>
> You could have assigned short homework related with the topic of the week that could have helped us. (S11)

One student (S10) wanted the instructor to teach the programming concepts during lecture hours theoretically and create the application during lab hours. Another student found theoretical instruction helpful because it helped her to understand the part she did not.

> If it could go together like learning in theoretical course and creating it at the following course hour, it could be more effective. (S1)

Lecture hours for this course were used for an introduction to algorithms and let the students create algorithms of their own. But according to the students, additional theoretical hours should serve as supplementary instruction.

Communication

We asked students how they would most prefer to communicate throughout the course. Among options like e-mail, LMS messaging of the university, and Facebook, Facebook was chosen as the main communication tool. A group was created for the course, which was used for communication, resource, and homework sharing. Every participant already used Facebook. Furthermore, all participants reported they were very happy to use it. According to the expectancy of the instructor, students were to post their homework, ask their questions when they had a problem with their homework or project. Interviews pointed out three subcategories regarding the use of Facebook group: better communication, Facebook group as resource, and using direct messaging. While the first two were positive sides of the Facebook group, using direct messaging proved negative.

The main positive side effect of Facebook group according to students was providing a better communication than e-mail and LMS messaging, stating that communication among them was very good because of the Facebook group. This was evident in their comments, some of which we outline below:

> In my opinion, it was good. We could have had a hard time without it. E-mail is a little more formal. (S2)
>
> It was good, I mean better communication… was established. Because we definitely were logging in to Facebook. (S6)
>
> We were always in contact since it is the Facebook environment. (S10)

Two of the features that students found useful about Facebook were its widespread use of instant notifications. Students were able to see the posts instantly.

> Nearly everyone uses Facebook and uses it a lot. Even if they are not using (at that time), their phone sent a notification when something posted. (S1)
>
> Most of us log in to Facebook 5–6 h a day. We know already what is in there and there was a warmer environment. (S2)
>
> In my opinion, the Facebook group was good, it was nice. I don't always log in to METU online (university's LMS) but Facebook is always open, I can see it right away. (S7)

Open communication also helped student to use the Facebook group as a resource by learning from each other's mistakes. Students were encouraged to ask questions through the wall, which was open to all members. Sometimes they answered each other's questions by commenting on the post. The Facebook group was not only a communication medium for the students but also a resource and guide. Communication between instructor-student and student-student could be seen by everyone. Students found it very helpful, as evidenced by the following quotes;

> Everyone's asking questions to each other or sharing something in Facebook was nice because in a point where my friend knows better than me, it can help me. I mean we are not solely dependent on you. We can get new information from the other classmates, I mean sharing on Facebook is very nice. (S5)
>
> Using Facebook seriously provides easiness and it was very nice. Because we learned from mistakes and questions of our classmates in there. But in the other courses, our friends contact for their project via e-mail and learned just for himself. I mean we had a little chance to learn it. Or didn't even hear about it. (S8)

Some students stated that they prefer Facebook group over e-mail communication which they found more "formal." The Facebook environment provided them a friendlier medium since all of them use it for fun and communicating with their friends.

Another part of the Facebook group was an additional source of knowledge and using it as a resource by the students. Other than the instructor's informative posts, students were also encouraged to post into the wall of the Facebook group. Students were directed to regularly post their progress and encountered problems about their project with screenshots. If possible, other students would help if they could. In some cases, the instructor assigned students to solve each other's problems. Since the problems and the solutions were openly exposed, other students also learned the problem and its solution.

> We can see the posts of others. We can use it also as a resource when we stuck in anywhere. When I was doing the project, I looked it like what my friends have done and how did they do it. (S1)
>
> I posted (on Facebook) but not much. I mostly answer your questions. But when I saw comments of my classmates, I learned the things I need to ask. (S7)
>
> I mean seeing what everyone else is doing was nice of course. So group was good and you (instructor) said that do not message your questions, post them on the wall, that was really good. Because we could see what our classmates having problem with. (S10)

One common problem among students about the use of the Facebook group was direct messaging. Even though the instructor encouraged students to use the page's wall to ask questions, nearly all of them used the direct messaging for some type of questions. Messaging's direction was sometimes student to instructor and sometimes student to student. The main reason behind that was fear of shame because they were thinking that their question was too easy to ask. They thought that if they asked the question openly to everyone, their classmates would think they were stupid. One student answered the question of if he used the messaging instead of posting the wall as follows:

> S5: It happened a couple of times actually, I messaged to my friends directly rather than posting on the wall.
>
> Instructor: I mean that's one of the things I realized, there was always a direct messaging going on. Why was that?
>
> S5: I mean… Sometimes I've had a very easy question in mind, and I think like 'is it appropriate to ask' and then asked with direct messaging.
>
> If the thing I did not understand is too simple, it is like fear of being ashamed in front of the class. It is a psychological situation actually. (S11)

The main point of using the wall instead of messaging was to provide a bridge between students who knew the solution and who were having difficulty. However, sometimes students kept their questions private or to themselves. This was the only problem that was faced while using Facebook group. Both students and instructor found use of Facebook as a communication medium more successful than their experiences with other mediums they had used in other courses, such as e-mail groups or LMS messaging.

Discussion

The main research question of this study was, "What are the guidelines for an effective, efficient and motivating introductory visual programming course in higher education?" Most of the studies in the area are based on expert opinion about how to design a programming course. According to Samurçay (1989), it is important to collect information about students' conceptions and their learning process through the course. Their opinions about the course can be a guide for the instructor and the future design of such courses.

First of all, there are no ideal programming environments for all levels of learners or purposes. Instructors should review all of the relevant environments based on the target audience's needs and characteristics. Participants of this study are university students with low or no programming experience. While visual programming could be a good choice for novice learners, not all of the visual programming environments are relevant. For example, an environment like Scratch is very similar to AI but may be more suitable for younger learners.

Based on the findings, five themes emerged: communication, computational thinking, environment, motivation, and recommendations for the course. From these themes, important parts that could help to reshape the course into a more efficient, effective, and motivating one were extracted.

A visual representation of the themes that emerged is presented in Fig. 1. The model does not include all of the findings, but it could act as a guide for future courses that promote computational thinking among novice programmers. Each of these is discussed in greater detail in the following section.

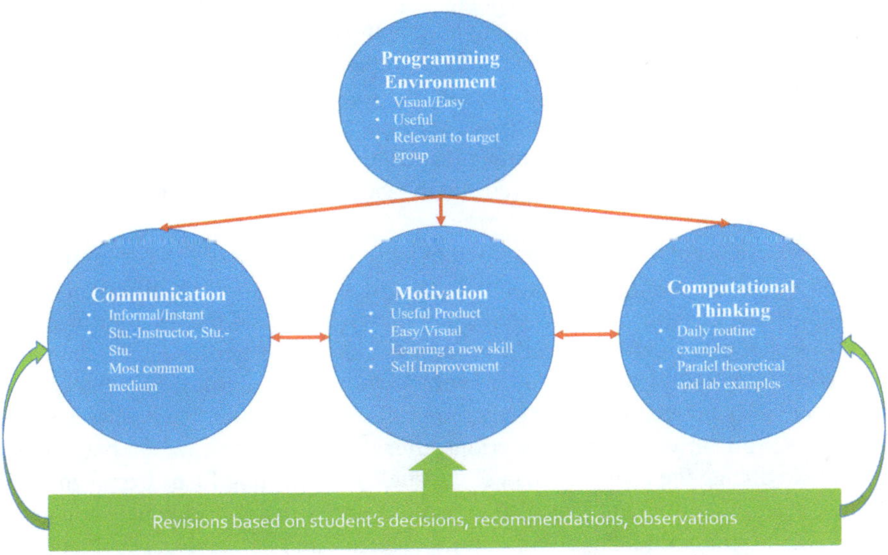

Fig. 1 Representation of findings based on students' experiences

Computational Thinking

Because the main purpose of the course was to learn programming, students were not previously aware of what computational thinking consisted of. Through course exercises, they learned the basics, such as what is algorithm and how to break a complex problem into pieces. Even the most basic algorithm examples helped students to change their perspectives about their daily routines.

Kafai and Burke (2013) stated that while teaching computational thinking, programming language (syntax, properties of the language) should not be the focus of teaching. Even three decades ago, it was very similar to today's thoughts. Soloway and Spoher (1989) proposed that learning programming can help students to develop "good habits of mind" which will make them more creative and effective problem solvers. Computational thinking comes with programming education as a good side effect.

Computational thinking can be used while solving a complex task or designing a complex system by reformulating it into little pieces that we know how to solve (Wing, 2006). For computational thinking, regardless of the environment, real-life algorithmic examples should be given to establish the connection between daily routines and computational thinking. In addition to tutorials, problems should be presented at the lab hours that are solvable with basic steps. Computational thinking can be understood better with a combination of non-computer-related problems such as daily routines and basic programming problems that can be solved with little steps. According to the US National Research Council's (2010) report "computers can facilitate this process by guiding students as they explore complex problems, use scientific visualization, and collaborate with peers" (p. 62).

An easy-to-learn programming environment could help students to focus on computational thinking and problem solving rather than focusing on syntax (semicolons, parentheses, debugging). It is essential for a teacher, especially in an introductory programming course, to provide students a programming-centered learning environment rather than a programming language-centered environment. As a visual programming environment, AI proved suitable because of its focus on programming rather than syntax.

This course is not a "computational thinking" course. However, basic algorithms and the visual nature of the environment helped students to think differently than before the course. Some students stated that they see things different now, meaning they saw that every problem could be divided into little steps. One of the most important outcomes is that one student with previous programming experience said that he not only understood some programming concepts better, but he also learned to solve a problem with shorter solutions after this course. The reason behind this could be reducing the cognitive load of the student by shifting focus from syntax to think through the problem. It is also essential to construct a bridge between algorithm and programming. Even with minimum effort and no emphasis on computational thinking, students started to discover a new way of thinking with the help of the visual programming course.

Environment

The programming environment was one of the most important parts of this study. Opinions of the students about the environment were also taken. Based on the answers and characteristics of the students, the most important feature of the environment is being visual and easy as expected. Cunniff, Taylor, and Black (1989) also state that visual programming languages can help novice programming learners. The environment is like the hub of this study. Nearly all of the findings were related with the environment. Since those features have investigated at the other parts, positive and negative sides of the environment were mentioned by the student. It is not at the control of the instructor, but findings regarding the positive and negative sides could help the design team of AI and future instructors that will think to choose AI as their course's environment. If they are planning to design a course for advance programming, it is obvious that AI is not the best environment for them.

Motivation

Motivation is one of the critical components not only for learning programming but also any kind of learning. Lai (2011) defines motivation as "reasons that underlie behavior that is characterized by willingness and volition" (p. 2). Some strategies adapted to the environment based on Keller's (1987) ARCS model were used to motivate students. According to the Wolber, Abelson, Spertus, and Looney (2011), visual programming environments could be an essential motivator for the programming classes (cited in Mihci & Ozdener, 2014). However, there was a lack of information about what parts were more motivating based on the students' opinions. According to the students, they were mostly motivated by (1) creating useful products, (2) the easiness of the programming environment, (3) learning a new skill, and (4) good communication with instructor. The first three will be investigated further since they are directly related to computer programming.

Creating Useful Products. Based on the findings, one of the most powerful motivators was developing an actual, working product. Most of the examples in introductory programming courses that teachers want students to produce are pointless and boring. They mostly consist of examples like computing the sum of squares of first twenty odd numbers (Papert & Solomon 1989). Instructors should use examples that are useful rather than examples just focus on teaching the basic concepts.

Ease of Use. The easiness of the environment also motivated and encouraged students to learn and keep learning computer programming. Most students stated that they might develop their own application even after the course ended, because they thought that they could easily create what they needed. Boulay, O'Shea, and Monk (1989) stated that it is better to use a simple and visible first language for the novice learner. That appears to have been the case in this study, which motivated novice learners to extend their knowledge beyond the classroom.

Learning a New Skill. Some students stated that learning a skill that they had never studied before made the course more interesting for them. This finding could be seen as inconsistent with the high dropout rate (up to 50%) of computer programming courses for the new comers (Ma, Ferguson, Roper, & Wood, 2011; Porter, Guzdial, McDowell, & Simon, 2013). It is likely that the formerly mentioned finding of programming environment easiness mitigated dropout. Instead, students turned their focus away from programming complexity and were able to seem to focus on the fundamentals with the help of visual programming environment.

Recommendations for the course

Students suggested some changes for the course, highlighting some topics they had some problems understanding or using. The most common topics they struggled to understand were variables, clock, and database. Soloway and Spoher (1989) have previously outlined difficult concepts for novice programmers, such as variables, loops, and arrays (as cited in Robins, Rountree, & Rountree, 2003). Students' answers regarding the difficult topics were consistent with the literature. They also offered solutions about how to overcome these difficulties. Variable was the most popular answer by far when it comes to having difficulties. Some students noted that they did not understand the concept very well. They explained that the concept did not fit to their knowledge of variables in mathematics. Samurçay (1989) also emphasized that the concept of variable in computer programming is different than the concept in mathematics and therefore a new concept for new learners. Instructors should be aware of this discrepancy and inform the learners about the differences to remove the interference; to overcome this problem, students also offered a strategy: teach variables with basic examples separated from the normal tutorials.

Since the course did not have enough time to go deeper into databases, students recommended reserving more time for that specific topic. Clock was another topic that some students did not understand easily. Clock is very similar to loops with an interval. Students also suggested that clock should be taught with some basic examples, removed from the tutorials, and that every property of it should be tested by itself.

Finally, 3 weeks of theoretical lectures were also presented to the class to teach basic algorithm concepts. However, students recommended that there should be more theoretical hours, and those hours should act as recitation for the lab examples. In addition to this suggestion, some students indicated that they should have more homework. In sum, students felt that they could have better understood the topics they struggled with if more time were given to those topics individually rather than in the midst of more complete projects.

Communication

Although the goal of this course was to cultivate computational thinking among non-CS majors, one of the most important elements to facilitate successful interactions occurred through our chosen method of communication. A Facebook group was created for communication and resource sharing. Mori (2007) reported that over 95% of undergraduate students regularly use Facebook (cited in Menzies, Petrie, & Zarb, 2015). All of the participants in this study were already using Facebook and favored Facebook group use. Based on the findings, students wanted to communicate in a more informal and faster way than e-mail or LMS communication systems. Madge et al. (2009) states that Facebook is already used as a learning medium among students for informal learning or academic discussions among friends, but not for formal teaching from instructor to students (as cited in Sterling, 2016). In this study, students showed that their communication with the instructor or other students was better than the other courses because of the informal environment facilitated through Facebook. In this theme, some overlapping answers revealed the critical points of communication medium of the course, namely, (1) better communication because of always online status, (2) the instant course notifications, (3) using it as a resource by looking at other students' projects and mistakes, and (4) being ashamed of asking easy question directed some students to direct messaging. Only the fourth critical point was negative, because it prevented conversion of some knowledge from tacit to explicit. This phenomenon did not occur consistently. It occurred only for the so-called "easy" questions for the students. However, it leads to asking very similar questions with messages. Verbal encouragement could be helpful but it is not enough for some students. As a solution to this, in addition to verbal encouragement, the instructor could ask students to post their questions to the Facebook wall for each week and give extra credit to the questions, no matter how easy they were.

All in all, the Facebook group was successful based on opinions of the students and observations of the instructor. However, creating a Facebook group might not be the universal answer for all of the courses or audiences. We recommend picking the communication medium by asking the target students and analyzing the course's structure, since the popularity of the different mediums vary among people and some topics may not be suitable with specific medium. For example, e-mail could be a better choice for older adult learners who do not use social media as regularly.

Conclusion

Even though computational thinking is not limited to computer programming, this introductory programming course demonstrated the potential for teaching computational thinking to non-CS majors. Results of this study show that choosing a relevant environment to students is important since potential of the course is shaped around the environment. It can be said that an environment that supports learners and offers useful products as the end products is essential for novice programmers. Even though students had difficulties in understanding some concepts, they understood those concepts with the help of a scaffolded environment and effective communication among students. Students were motivated to complete the course since they believe that it is useful and changed their perspectives on things as quotidian as their daily routines. This finding also shows the implication for the computational thinking potential of a well-designed introductory programming course. More research studies that include opinions and student feedback may provide guidance for instructors from a different perspective. In short, in our case, the use of visual programming language, paired with tasks that sought to demonstrate computational concepts in everyday lives and facilitated through a well-used communication medium, proved to be an effective method for teaching computational thinking to non-CS majors.

Acknowledgments Authors would like to thank TUBITAK, the scientific and technological research council of turkey, for their financial support including this research study and visiting scholarship grant.

References

Bennedsen, J., & Caspersen, M. E. (2012). Persistence of elementary programming skills. *Computer Science Education, 22*(2), 81–107.

Bertea, A. F. (2011). *Mobile Learning Applications Using Google App Inventor for Android.* Bucharest: The International Scientific Conference eLearning and Software for Education.

Boulay, B. D., O'Shea, T., & Monk, J. (1989). The black box inside the glass box: presenting computing concepts to novices. In E. Soloway & J. C. Spoher (Eds.), *Studying the Novice Programmer* (pp. 431–446). NJ: Lawrence Erlbaum Associates.

Creswell, J. W. (2012). *Educational Research: Planning, Conducting, and Evaluating Quantitaive and Qualitative Research.* Boston, MA: Pearson.

Cunniff, N., Taylor, R. P., & Black, J. B. (1989). Does programming language affect the type of conceptual bugs in beginners' programs? A comparison of FPL and Pascal. In E. Soloway & J. C. Spoher (Eds.), *Studying the Novice Programmer* (pp. 419–429). NJ: Lawrence Erlbaum Associates.

Espinar Redondo, R., & Ortega Martín, J. L. (2015). Motivation: the road to successful learning. *Profile: Issues in Teachers' Professional Development, 17*(2), 125–136. http://doi.org/10.15446/profile.v17n2.50563.

Kafai, Y. B., & Burke, Q. (2013). Computer Programming Goes back to School. *Phi Delta Kappan, 95*(1), 61–65.

Kazimoglu, C., Kiernan, M., Bacon, L., & MacKinnon, L. (2011). Understanding computational thinking before programming: developing guidelines for the design of games to learn introductory programming through game-play. *International Journal of Game-Based Learning, 1*(3), 30–52.

Keller, J. M. (1987). Development and use of the ARCS model of motivational design. *Journal of Instructional Development, 10*(1932), 2–10. http://doi.org/10.1002/pfi.4160260802.

Kwon, D., Yoon, I., & Lee, W. (2011). Design of programming learning process using hybrid programming environment for computing education. *KSII Transactions on Internet and Information Systems, 5*(10), 1799–1812.

Lai, E. R. (2011). Motivation: A Literature Review. Retrieved from http://images.pearsonassessments.com/images/tmrs/CriticalThinkingReviewFINAL.pdf

Ma, L., Ferguson, J., Roper, M., & Wood, M. (2011). Investigating and improving the models of programming concepts held by the novice programmers. *Computer Science Education, 21*(1), 57–80.

Madge, C., Meek, J., Wellens, J., & Hooley, T. (2009). Facebook, social integration and informal learning at University: 'It is more for socialising and talking to friends about work than for actually doing work'. *Learning, Media and Technology, 34*(2), 141–155. doi:10.1080/17439880902923606.

Malliarakis, C., Satratzemi, M., & Xinogalos, S. (2013). A holistic framework for the development of an educational game aiming to teach computer programming. In *Proceedings of the European Conference on Games Based Learning* (pp. 359–368).

Menzies, R., Petrie, K., & Zarb, M. (2015). A case study of Facebook use: Outlining a multi-layer strategy for higher education. *Education and Information Technologies, 22*(1), 39–53. http://doi.org/10.1007/s10639-015-9436-y.

Mihci, C., & Ozdener, N. (2014). Programming education with a blocks-based visual language for mobile application. In *10th International Conference Mobile Learning* (pp. 149–156).

Mori, I. (2007). *Student expectations survey*. Coventry: Joint Information Systems Committee.

National Research Council, (U.S.). (2010). *Report of a Workshop on the Scope and Nature of Computational Thinking*. Washington, D.C.: National Academies Press.

Papert, S. & Solomon, C. (1989). Twenty Things to do With a Computer. Studying the novice programmer. In E. Soloway & J. C. Spoher (Eds.), *Studying the Novice Programmer* (pp. 3–28). NJ: Lawrence Erlbaum Associates.

Pokress, S. C., & Veiga, J. D. (2013). *MIT App Inventor: Enabling Personal Mobile Computing*. New York: ACM.

Porter, L., Guzdial, M., McDowell, C., & Simon, B. (2013). Success in introductory programming: what works. *Communications of the ACM, 56*(8), 34–36.

Robins, A., Rountree, J., & Rountree, N. (2003). Learning and teachin programming: a review and discussion. *Computer Science Education, 13*(2), 137–172.

Rolandsson, L. (2013). Changing computer programming education; the dinosaur that survived in school: an explorative study of educational issues based on teachers' beliefs and curriculum development in secondary school. In *2013 Learning and Teaching in Computing and Engineering* (pp. 220–223).

Saito, D., & Yamauara, T. (2013). A new approach to programming language education for beginners with top-down learning. *International Journal of Engineering Pedagogy, 3*, 16–23.

Samurçay, R. (1989). The concept of variable in programming: its meaning and use in problem-solving by novice programmers. In E. Soloway & J. C. Spoher (Eds.), *Studying the Novice Programmer* (pp. 161–178). NJ: Lawrence Erlbaum Associates.

Sengupta, P., Kinnebrew, J. S., Basu, S., Biswas, G., & Clark, D. (2013). Integrating computational thinking with K-12 science education using agent-based computation: a theoretical framework. *Education and Information Technologies, 18*(2), 351–380.

Smutny, P. (2011). Visual programming for smartphones. In *International Carpathian Control Conference* (pp. 358–361.) Velke Karlovice.

Sorva, J., Karavirta, V., & Malmi, L. (2013). A review of generic program visualization systems for introductory programming education. *ACM Transactions on Computing Education, 13*(4), 15:1–15:64.

Soloway, E., & Spoher, J. C. (Eds.). (1989). *Studying the Novice Programmer*. NJ: Lawrence Erlbaum Associates.

Sterling, E. (2016). Technology, time and transition in higher education – two different realities of everyday *Facebook* use in the first year of university in the UK. *Learning, Media and Technology, 41*(1), 100–118. http://doi.org/10.1080/17439884.2015.1102744.

Wing, J. M. (2006). Computational Thinking. *Communications of the ACM, 49*(3), 33–35.

Wolber, D., Abelson, H., Spertus, E., & Looney, L. (2011). *App inventor: Create your own android apps*. Sebastapool, CN: O'Reilly Media.

Using Model-Based Learning to Promote Computational Thinking Education

Hong P. Liu, Sirani M. Perera, and Jerry W. Klein

Abstract Digital technology in the twenty-first century is characterized by omnipresent smart devices and ubiquitous computing that enable computation to occur almost anytime and anywhere. This contributes to increased complexity, rapidly changing technologies, and big data challenges to professionals in most every disciplinary field. In this environment, computational thinking (CT) becomes a fundamental skill to empower our next generation of the American workforce. Consequently, CT education across all disciplines and grade levels is being advocated by academic institutions, governmental agencies, and private industrial corporations. However, existing academic programs in K-12 schools and small teaching universities are inadequately structured to prepare students with the needed computational thinking skills and knowledge. In addition, there is a scarcity in research on learning CT to guide development of CT curriculum and instructional practices across all grade levels. To mitigate this problem, we propose several model-based learning programs that the authors have been exploring since 2012 to promote active learning of CT for students of different age groups. Most of the programs were designed to exploit out-of-school time education and hands-on team research projects to advance CT education from K6 to K16 students. Under the CT context, the proposed and existing programs emphasize cultivating student problem solving ability through problem-based learning (PBL) in which students learn computational thinking by completing team projects. We also illustrate how small universities and K-12 schools can cost-effectively offer CT education by forming coalitions, leveraging emerging cyberlearning technology, and sharing educational resources.

Keywords Computational thinking • Model-based learning • Informal learning • Learning-on-demand • Problem-based learning

H.P. Liu (✉) • S.M. Perera
Embry-Riddle Aeronautical University, Daytona Beach, FL 32114, USA
e-mail: hong.liu14@gmail.com; pereras2@erau.edu

J.W. Klein
Syracuse University, Syracuse, NY 13244, USA
e-mail: jwklein@syr.edu

P.J. Rich, C.B. Hodges (eds.), *Emerging Research, Practice, and Policy on Computational Thinking*, Educational Communications and Technology: Issues and Innovations, DOI 10.1007/978-3-319-52691-1_10

Introduction

Four years after Wing's influential short paper about computational thinking (CT), Cuny, Snyder, and Wing (2010) offered the following definition of CT:

> "Computational thinking is the thought processes involved in formulating problems and expressing its solution as transformations to information that an agent can effectively carry out."

By its definition, computational thinking involves multiple disciplinary fields including computer science, mathematics, and various application disciplines. Currently, relatively few K-12 teachers have such multidisciplinary knowledge, which seriously delays the spread of CT education. However, it is not only secondary schools that lack the resources and qualified teachers to provide CT learning opportunities, most small teaching universities are also inadequately structured to prepare students with the needed computational thinking skills and knowledge. This chapter illustrates how small universities and K-12 schools can cost-effectively offer CT education by forming coalitions and leveraging emerging cyberlearning technology (Borgman et al. 2008). Reforming in-school K-12 CT education takes too long to effectuate, and consequently, we argue that first implementing CT in out-of-school time education can provide an efficient path for implementing CT K-12 education (Liu & Klein, 2013). The K-12 programs we explore in this chapter are designed to exploit out-of-school settings. This strategy is similar to corporations that have research and development organizations creating next-generation products; after-school programs can be used to develop and refine CT programs and then migrate them into the in-school curriculum as either new courses, or by integrating lessons and learning activities into the existing mathematics and science courses such as algebra and chemistry courses.

To promote active learning of CT for students of different age groups and diversified academic backgrounds such as different majors and experiences, we propose several model-based learning programs that emphasize cultivating student problem solving ability through problem-based learning (PBL). Mathematical modeling plays the central role in helping students abstract and formulate complex real-world problems. In our programs, an R&D process was used to provide a coherent framework for designing instruction and assessing learning in which the instructional and assessment methods were aligned with a common idea: model-based learning and reasoning. To be more specific, we use the term model-based learning to refer to learning from models, learning with models, and learning by modeling (Spector, 2009). On the other hand, model-based reasoning is associated with the mental models that constitute the fundamental basis for qualitative reasoning (Johnson-Laird, 1983). Seel and Blumschein (2009) note that model-based reasoning occurs when an individual mentally manipulates an environment in order to simulate (in the sense of a thought experiment) specific transformations of the system which may occur in real-life situations. In our model-based learning programs, conceptual modeling is emphasized to precede mathematical modeling because it provides the traceability of the underlying assumptions of the mathematics models and hence facilitates model validation (Liu & Raghavan, 2009). In addition, conceptual modeling is essential for model-based learning assessment because it helps the observer know how learners approach a problem and provides external representations of their mental models (Seel & Blumschein, 2009).

Besides this introduction, the rest of the chapter is organized as follows: The next section discusses what to teach and how to teach in order to facilitate CT learning. The section also surveys prior funded CT programs for secondary and postsecondary schools. Section "Promoting Computational Thinking at ERAU" describes two projects to promote CT for undergraduates. Section "Middle School Computational Thinking" discusses methods for developing CT in middle schools within the context of programing and creating simulations. Section "Future Work" presents future work in providing CT programs in local secondary schools as well as colleges. In section "Conclusion," we conclude the chapter with our vision of the next steps for implementing CT education by employing emerging educational technologies.

What to Teach, How to Teach, and Relevant CT Programs

The report by the President's Council of Advisors on Science and Technology, *Prepare and Inspire: K-12 Science, Technology, Engineering, and Math (STEM) Education for America's Future* (2010, p. 46), proposed a definition of K-12 STEM education that includes computer science and states that students need

> "a deeper understanding of the essential concepts, methods and wide-ranging applications of computer science, students should gain hands-on exposure to the process of algorithmic thinking and its realization in the form of a computer program, to the use of computational techniques for real-world problem solving, and to such pervasive computational themes as modelling and abstraction, modularity and reusability, computational efficiency, testing and debugging, and the management of complexity. Where feasible, active learning, higher-level thinking, and creative design should be encouraged by situating new concepts and techniques within the context of applications of particular interest to a given student or project team."

Critical thinking, analytical thinking, and problem solving are consistently ranked in the top list of the twenty-first-century cognitive skills needed to tackle the challenges of increasing complex technology and big data (Finegold & Notabartolo, 2011; Zorn et al. 2014; Liu, Ludu, & Holton, 2015a). As the crucial problem solving skills for the next generation of work force, students need to learn how to leverage computing resources, how to abstract the relevant problems in mathematics formalism, and how to make sense of data. Wing (2006) summarized that the two cornerstones of CT abilities are abstraction and automation. Abstraction depends on the mathematical modeling ability to conceptualize a problem and reduce its complexity by vetting the nonessential factors and breaking it down into manageable smaller problems. Automation depends on the engineering ability to formulate tasks that the computer or smart devices can execute.

It is beyond the scope of this chapter to discuss computational skills for specific STEM domains such as computational biology, physics, etc., and we limit our discussion to generic skills such as mathematical modeling for problem abstraction and the engineering principles for task automation. In order to address "how to teach," we focus on out-school-time learning and project-based learning. Our literature review and survey of prior funded CT projects will be limited to the most relevant programs from a computational mathematics perspective and their corresponding learning platforms.

What Can We Teach to Enhance Computational Thinking Abilities of Students?

The Society for Industrial and Applied Mathematics (SIAM) workshop on modeling across the curriculum II made the following two recommendations to math teachers and STEM education policy makers (Turner, Levy, & Fowler, 2015): build a pipeline for K-16 education in mathematical modeling (Andrew, 1998) and connect math to reality (Barr & Stephenson, 2011). Levy (Joint Mathematical Meetings 2015) summarized one of the three major SIAM educational initiatives as:

> "The Modeling Across the Curriculum, was built around the idea that modeling can build many job skills students need and can be an important educational tool at not only the secondary and undergraduate levels, but throughout the educational experience."

The Applied Mathematics Education Activity Group of SIAM is the task force advocating computational science and engineering (CSE) education which is an emerging multidisciplinary field of study that focuses on the integration of knowledge and methodologies from computer science, applied mathematics, engineering, and science to solve real-world problems (Society of Industrial and Applied Mathematics 2015). CSE provides the critical mathematical modeling skills and data analytical skills that apply to all STEM fields. Therefore, Turner and Petzold (2011) advocate that CSE courses and curricula should be a viable option for every undergraduate STEM major. A careful inspection of the definitions of CT and CSE shows that CSE contains the essential knowledge and skills for helping learners develop CT thought process and problem solving abilities (e.g., abstraction and automation) and that the essential difference between CT and CSE is one of perspective: CT looks at the overarching thought process and problem solving ability, while CSE focuses on computational methods and relevant domain-specific knowledge. Our goal is to equip students with the CSE skills that will enable them to solve open-ended science, engineering, and technical problems which in turn enhances their CT ability.

How to Teach Computational Thinking

CT programs have mushroomed since Wing promoted the concept of computational thinking in 2006 (NRC, 2010). However, according to a report by the National Research Council (NRC, 2011, p. 4), there is a scarcity of research informing how to teach computational thinking in the early grades, and computer science is often taught without consideration of age-appropriate learning. Consequently, we will rely on generalizing from successful instructional programs and learning activities from closely related and similar subjects such as Algebra and Calculus. We briefly review the history of mathematical education reform which provides insights to teaching methods for developing CT (Chai et al. 2014).

Edmund F. Robertson (1968) quoted the following message from the biography of Richard Hamming:

> "We live in an age of exponential growth in knowledge, and it is increasingly futile to teach only polished theorems and proofs. We must abandon the guided tour through the art gallery of mathematics, and instead teach how to create the mathematics we need. In my opinion, there is no long-term practical alternative.
>
> The way mathematics is currently taught it is exceedingly dull. In the calculus book we are currently using on my campus, I found no single problem whose answer I felt the student would care about! The problems in the text have the dignity of solving a crossword puzzle – hard to be sure, but the result is of no significance in life."

The essential problem is that our mathematics curricula condense too many assumed indispensable concepts, which were developed over three centuries, into a course of three semesters. However, 30 years of college mathematical education reform has resulted in new instructional practices such as project-based learning (PBL); rule of three which includes graphs, analysis, and numerical representation (Schoenfeld, 1995); inquiry-based interactive teaching (Eseryel & Law, 2012); and learning management practices such as the flipped class (McGivney-Burelle & Xue, 2015) which have become popular in research and development grants. In practice, however, most mathematics teachers still use the least common denominator approach defined by Schoenfeld (1995): lecturing and assigning homework which results in dull and meaningless instruction. However, the approach is still popular because it is the most efficient way to cover the information and easiest way to manage learning (Schoenfeld, 1995). We are not suggesting that this method should be replaced. But it needs to and can be improved. For example, we can use query-based teaching to enhance interactive learning within the context of the traditional setting (Eseryel & Law, 2012, and Kirschner, Sweller, & Clark, 2006). Generally, PBL and other instructional schemes are being employed within the context of the traditional classroom and are slowly but steadily gaining ground in mathematics education. However, given the slow pace of reform, we are convinced that the best way to improve K-12 CT instruction is through out-of-school time education (Liu & Klein, 2013). At the college level, CT can be improved by (a) forming coalitions such as networked improvement communities (Carnegie Foundation, 2016) and coalitions for undergraduate CSE education and (b) providing research and development projects. These two approaches for creating and deploying CT instruction are exemplified in the next two sections.

Promoting Computational Thinking at ERAU

Embry-Riddle Aeronautical University (ERAU) has been offering a BS in computational mathematics since 2008, and in order to provide CSE courses and learning experiences for students pursuing various majors (e.g., engineering, meteorology), the mathematics department initiated two projects: the Coalition for Undergraduate CSE Education and the Eco-Dolphin Project.

Coalition for Undergraduate CSE Education

Because of low enrollment, most small universities cannot cost-justify providing undergraduate CSE courses. Consequently, in order to offer CSE courses within the justifiable costs, ERAU initiated an NSF-sponsored project in 2013 to create a cluster of collaborating institutions that combined students into common classes and used cyberlearning technologies to deliver and manage instruction.

The project resulted in the establishment of a coalition among ERAU's Daytona Beach and Prescott Arizona Campuses and Adams State University (ASU) in Colorado. A faculty member from each of the colleges took turns developing, reviewing, and teaching courses. Two courses in *Mathematical Modeling and Simulation* and a course in *Data Mining and Visualization* were developed and offered twice. More than a hundred students completed the CSE courses which were otherwise unavailable at any of the campuses. The courses were taught by a professor in the classroom at one location, and students in the other two universities attended class in a classroom using live two-way communications. In addition, the professor at the distant campus sat in on the class which greatly reduced student anxiety of taking a course from an unknown teacher. The project also conducted three summer research workshops for 18 students from 2013 to 2015. The project also created massive open online courses (MOOCs) and multimedia course materials for all three courses which are available at www.gps2dreamcollege.com.

The R&D process employed in this project provides a coherent framework for designing instruction and assessing learning in which all the processes and methods are aligned with a common idea: model-based learning and reasoning. The learning goals are aligned with the three CSE learning goals set by the SIAM Working Group for CSE Undergraduate Education. These goals essentially advocate reasoning from first principles and learning to generate mathematical models. This alignment is consistent with recommendations by Sabelli (2008) that STEM education should focus on a small set of models and avoid the "inch deep, mile wide" problem in designing instructional programs. For example, in order to help students gain deep understanding of the critical concept of eigenvalue and eigenvector, the concept is taught in three modules spirally with increasing depths and complex contexts. In the first module, the concept occurs in a very intuitive and natural way as the stable long-term population of the Leslie population model. In the second module, it is defined formally using matrix algebra and the concept is applied in solving the Google Page Ranking problem (Bryan & Leise, 2006). In the third module, the same concept is taught to solve linear ordinary differential equation systems and to visually explain the stability of the system of equations.

In order to further reinforce deep learning and facilitate learning assessment, research experiences were integrated within the three courses using a process called ACE (analysis, computation, and experimentation). This research and development process was used to provide a coherent framework for designing instruction and assessing learning. Course design centered on model-based learning which proposes that students learn complex content by elaborating on their mental model and class projects required students to develop a conceptual model, generate a mathematical model, and conduct experiments to validate and revise their conceptual and mathematical models. All courses included a mandatory team research projects and the students had the option to participate in a 2-week summer research workshop. Student projects in the Mathematical Modeling and Simulation course focused on mathematical models and computer-aided simulation. Data Mining and Visualization course projects focused on applying data mining to analyze large data sets and render prediction models. The summer projects extended the projects conducted during courses and produced peer-reviewed publications. For example, five students at ASU completed a team project using Stella to model and simulate a landing system of small spacecraft when they took the Mathematical Modeling and Simulation course. They then constructed a payload gear for a weather balloon and tested it at the Wave Motion Lab of Daytona Beach Campus. The team successfully used their experimental data to validate their computational models. Based on the course projects and the summer research project, four articles coauthored by students were published and five students coauthored papers were presented at technical conferences.

A software tool called HIMATT was used for deep learning assessment by evaluating how students think through and model complex, ill-defined, and ill-structured realistic problems (Pirnay-Dummer, Ifenthaler, & Spector, 2010). Traditional learning assessments (e.g., rubrics and quizzes) and student feedback demonstrated that all three cyberlearning courses achieved the project's major goal: fostering student computational skills and developing computational thinking ability. In the Mathematical Modeling and Simulation I course, students learned how to use the system engineering modeling methodology and procedures to translate real-world problems into mathematical models. Students also gained hands-on experience in using software tools such as MATLAB and STELLA to model and simulate real-world projects with team members. In the Data Mining and Visualization course, students learned how to use data mining techniques and software tools such as R, Weka, and MATLAB to conduct research to solve real-world applications. Research projects included using data mining to predict student retention based on the records of a cohort of 973

Table 1 Modular structure of course content for Mathematical Modeling and Simulation

Content	Module 1 matrix algebra	Module 2 matrix calculus	Module 3 methodology	Module N dynamic system
Topic objective	Linear Transform. Eigenvectors, Singular Value Decomposition	Jacobian and Hessian Matrices, Multivariate Approximation, Regression, Least Squares	Model Classifications, Modeling Process and Methodology, Conceptual Models	Linear and Nonlinear ODE Systems, Eigen values to Solve Linear System ODE, Vector Field and Phase
Prototype problems	Population Geometry, GPS Coordinate Transform, Google Page Ranking	Curve Fitting, Linear and Nonlinear Optimization, Simplex Method, Kalman Filter for GPS Computation	State Diagram of Traffic Light, State Model of Cruise Control, Matrix Repres. of State Transitions	Dynamic System of Interactive, Population Models, Disease Spread Model, Robotic Navigation Control Dynamics
Tools	MATLAB	MATLAB	OPCAT, STELLA	STELLA

students, classify seagrass and macroalgae based on satellite image data, and adjust real-estate book values based on GIS data and official appraisal data. Results of the project indicated that the courses were effective and appealed to students majoring in math, computer science, physics, engineering, and meteorology.

Built on the success of the prior project, we are scaling up the project by adding two more universities to the coalition and adding four new CSE courses. These courses are a database course and three domain-specific courses: problems in atmosphere and hydrosphere, computational biology, and genomics and bioinformatics. For all courses, we will use a similar framework for deriving and organizing content. This framework is illustrated in Table 1 for the Mathematical Modeling and Simulation I.

Eco-Dolphin Project

The mathematics department of ERAU hosts two hands-on research labs, the Wave Motion Lab and Leverage Robotics Lab. The Wave Motion Lab has a 32 ft. long, four feet wide, and six feet tall wave tanks and computer-controlled wave generators. These two labs facilitate experimentation component of our ACE Research Experiences for Undergraduate (REU) program (Liu & Ludu 2012). Hosted in the Leverage lab and supported by the Wave Lab, the Eco-Dolphin project was cosponsored by internal REU grants and industry donations during the past 4 years as well as a research grant from an Air Force Research Lab (AFRL). The project is building, maintaining, and using a fleet of autonomous underwater vehicles (AUV) called

Eco-Dolphins to collect coastal environmental data (Liu & Shi et al. 2015b). This project serves as a platform to support hands-on REU for the SIAM Student Chapter. The various projects will be used to compete for additional external grants to support the REU program and environmental research.

Since the Eco-Dolphin started in 2012, graduate assistants and undergraduate students from several academic departments (e.g., engineering, physics) have been involved in conducting research in the Leverage lab. The graduate students and faculty from the mathematics department serve as mentors. As a robotics research project per se, there are numerous challenging problems across a range of STEM domains including mechanical engineering problems; electronic, computer, and software engineering problems; and computational mathematics problems. There are no reference textbooks or courses for students and mentors to use in designing and constructing such a complex system. However, there are open-source tutorials, how-to videos, and instructions scattered across the web, and the mentors and students use these resources to learn as needed (i.e., learning-on-demand) in conducting their projects. We observed that this learning method is most effective and time efficient compared to traditional course-based instruction which results in "just-in-case" learning and consequently students do not know where and when the knowledge will be used.

Another benefit of the Eco-Dolphin project is that it provides a platform for solving computational mathematics problems spanning undergraduate research to a PhD thesis. For example, since a submerged AUV cannot receive GPS signals, the Eco-Dolphin project uses different positioning methods from simple triangulation based on acoustic sonars to sophisticated photogrammetric computation based on dynamical video images. Other computation-intensive research problems include navigation control problems, which can be as simple as 2D linear control using only trigonometry to the complex 3D rigid body dynamic control using nonlinear ordinary differential equation systems. In addition, the project involves image processing and data mining problems such as classifying seagrass and macroalgae from satellite images and identifying marine animals such as sea turtles, dolphins, and manatees. The Eco-Dolphin project is not only a platform to facilitate REU programs but also the fuel to drive computational mathematics research.

Middle School Computational Thinking

Middle school students are at the age where they make up their minds on what they can or cannot do, and our primary intention in our projects is to develop CT abilities and STEM professional identity which can be described as students seeing themselves as an engineer, mathematician, or some other STEM professional. As discussed in section "Introduction," CT involves applying computer science and mathematics in various application disciplines, and there are multiple application domains that can be used to develop CT at the middle school level including robotics and computer games which are currently very popular. However, our project has selected modeling and simulation as the target application. We will develop CT within the context of modeling and simulating environmental science phenomena because it appeals to both male and female students, and environmental science encapsulates most traditional STEM domains including biology and robotics (students build an underwater robot with sensors to collect environmental science research data).

Specifically, the authors proposed to create a community-based CT network designed to develop computational thinking skills, STEM professional identity, persistence, and proportional reasoning by adapting existing instructional materials. The project will focus on after-school and out-of-school time middle school programs such as local environmental science centers.

Introducing Programming

Creating computer programs is one of the most effective ways to develop computational thinking, and one effective tool for introducing students to programming is Data Harvest's ACE system (ACE, 2016) which develops the notion of algorithms by enabling students to create flowcharts to control physical devices and observing program execution. An example of a program to control a traffic light is shown in Fig. 1.

The student creates the flowchart by dragging and dropping two predefined elements in the flowchart: outputs and processes. When students execute the program, each step in the process is highlighted. *ACE* also provides a text view of the program and a database view of light changing states. *ACE* also provides graphical animation showing the traffic light switching between red, green, and yellow. The student can also attach a small physical traffic light which is controlled by their computer.

In addition to constructing simple flowcharts, students learn programming concepts of encapsulation and decomposition by creating procedures composed of

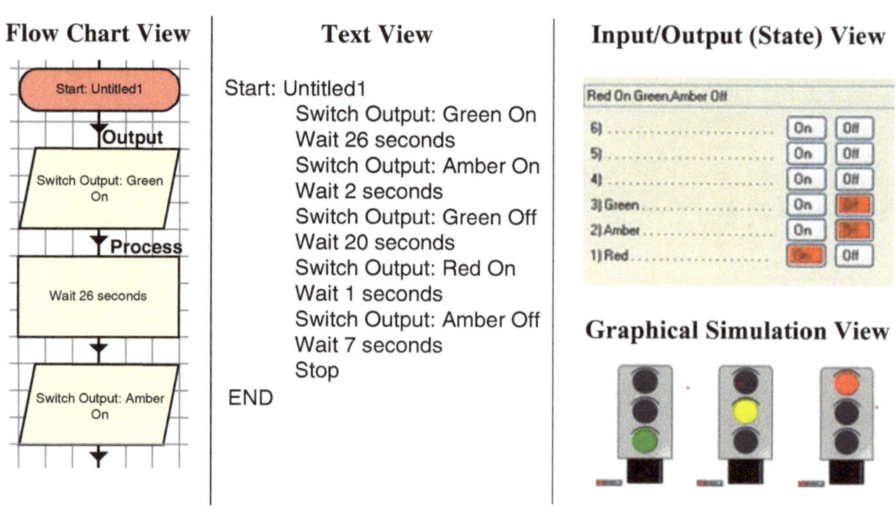

Fig. 1 Programming in the ACE system

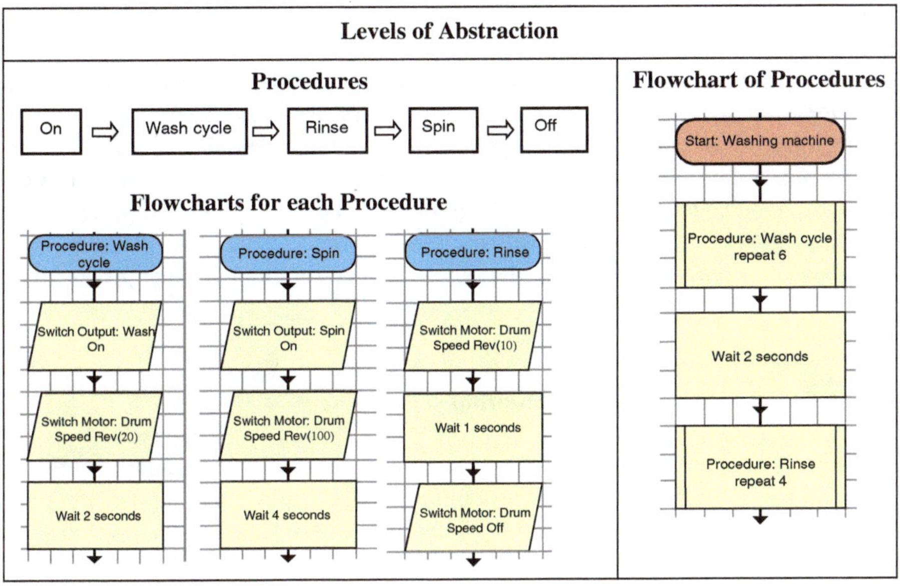

Fig. 2 Learning encapsulation & decomposition

multiple flowcharts. This is illustrated in Fig. 2 for another *ACE* project in which students create a simulation of a washing machine. In this project, students create *procedures* which encapsulate multiple sequences of processes and outputs specified in a flowchart. Students first create a flowchart for each procedure and then construct a higher-level flowchart of procedures executed by the computer. In the example shown below, students create a procedure for the wash cycle, spin cycle, and rinse cycle and then create a flowchart of procedures.

By employing this software, middle school students learn how to construct algorithms in the form of a flowchart and develop the concept of a database, the notion of loops, and the concepts of decomposition and encapsulation all of which are core concepts in computational thinking.

Modeling and Simulation

Creating simulations is an effective way to develop mental models and deep learning across the range of STEM domains (Eseryel & Law, 2012; Furhmann, Salehi, & Blikstein 2013). In addition to developing deep learning of STEM content, modeling is a *core practice* in science and is included in the Next Generation Science Standards (NGSS). The intention of the project is to develop and implement a curriculum that addresses this standard. More specifically, our primary learning objective is that students will be able to build causal loop diagrams, agent-based simulations, and bifocal models of environmental phenomenon.

Causal Loop Diagrams

Causal loop diagrams solicit and capture mental models of individuals about a complex system. They can be used as preliminary sketches of causal hypothesis during model development of a complex system and provide a simple illustration to communicate cause-effect relationships and feedback loops responsible for complex system behavior. A causal loop diagram consists of arrows denoting the causal links among system components with each link assigned as having a positive (+) or a negative (−) symbol to indicate the type of effect: direct or inverse proportional relationship as shown in the Fig. 3.

Agent-Based Modeling and Simulation

StarLogo is another programming system used in developing computational thinking in middle school instructional curriculum, and a complete instructional program is available from the Girls Growing Up Scientifically (GUTS) project developed by the Santa Fe Institute (GUTS, 2016).

StarLogo is an agent-based modeling approach in which the student identifies entities called *agents* (people, molecules, trees, etc.), defines their behavior (e.g., reactions), establishes connections, and runs simulation. Next, the global behavior emerges as a result of interactions of many individual behaviors. For instance, to study the behavior of a chemical reaction, a student would define the behavior of individual molecules, assign rules to agents, and then set them into motion (Blikstein,

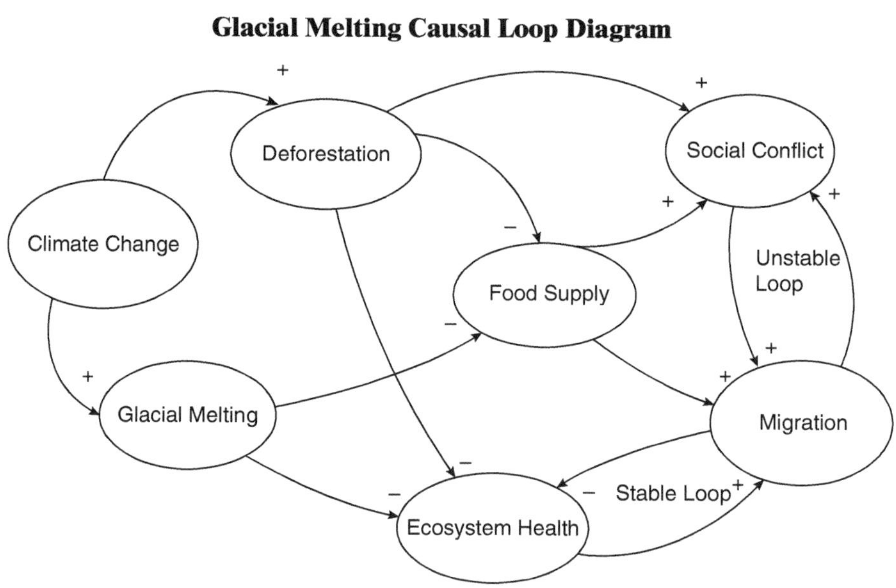

Fig. 3 Glacial melting causal loop diagram

Fuhrmann, Greene, & Salehi, 2012). Wilensky and colleagues associated with the *ModelSim* project have produced a large body of research showing the power of this technology for learning and view agent-based modeling as a fundamental new way of thinking. The agent-based approach is successful in promoting deep learning because it taps into student intuitions in subject areas which are traditionally experienced as nonintuitive. Once learners can identify and computationally interact with entities at the agent level, they can use their intuitions to reason about properties of the larger system (ModelSim Project, 2016).

Creating agent-based simulations using visual programming languages such as *StarLogo* makes learning programming concepts more intuitive and visual by dragging and dropping graphical objects which reduces programming complexity and consequently makes programming accessible to middle school students.

Bifocal Modeling

While agent-based modeling develops deep learning of science phenomenon, they develop an incomplete picture of the phenomenon under study: making the connection between the simulation and the physical world. Bifocal modeling addresses this issue by having students conduct research and collect data (Blikstein & Wilensky, 2007):

> In bifocal modeling, students connect computational behavior in virtual simulations with phenomena detected by physical sensors or produced in the physical world by motors or other output devices. The similarities and contrasts between virtual and physical systems stimulate conceptual reflection and "debugging" processes through which student adjust their physical and virtual models simultaneously. Bifocal modeling activities thus provide a critical "missing link" between laboratory experiences and the construction of explanatory models and theories. (ModelSim Project, 2016)

Students can make the connection between their simulations and the physical world by collecting data from research projects. They discover discrepancies between their simulation and their research results, explain why a mismatch between their model and their data exists, and, if appropriate, revise their simulation accordingly.

Proportional Reasoning and Multivariate Models of Causality

Proportional reasoning is essential in modeling and simulation tasks and is considered as one of the most important skills that middle school students develop. In addition, it is deemed as the turning point in K-12 mathematics curriculum in which students move from elementary mathematics to higher mathematics (Lesh, Post, & Behr, 1988). In order to provide the context for developing proportional reasoning, schools and out-of-school programs have been using project-based learning. Building robotics in particular have become a popular project across the education landscape, and a number of educators and researchers have highlighted the potential use of robotics project to reinforce students' mathematical understanding (Alfieri et al. 2015; Benitti, 2012; Vollstedt, Robinson, & Wang, 2007). However, staff at the Carnegie Mellon Robotics Academy (2016) have noted while many teachers say they were using robotics to teach mathematics, they found that few actually taught robot math in ways that were effective and many teachers avoided talking about mathematics at all. The Academy also observed that when teachers tried to teach robot math and robot programming, at the same time, many students were confused and the Academy staff were not able to measure significant learning gains. In addition, they concluded that teachers should teach math before they begin teaching students how to program their robots. Consequently, the Carnegie Mellon Robotics Academy developed *Expedition Atlantis* in order to motivate students to use math rather than "guess and check" as their way through robot programming. *Expedition Atlantis* is an underwater robotics game that develops both proportional thinking and proportional methods and provides tutorials and contextualized practice. It also includes a teacher guide. It currently is in beta testing, but the program is available now at http://www.education.rec.ri.cmu.edu/atlantis/why-use-it/.

Scale City is an interactive game-oriented set of instructional materials designed to develop proportional reasoning that focuses on scale and scaling. Its development was initiated by the Kentucky Educational Television (KET) and developed in collaboration with three other state public television networks and a task force of teachers, university professors, and Kentucky Department of Education staff. *Scale City* is organized around a road trip in which students explore roadside attractions and learn about the mathematics of scale. At each stop, a short video field trip, an interactive simulation, and a set of instructional materials are provided to help students learn proportional reasoning. For example, students explore what happens to the area of a two-dimensional figure like a mural and what happens to the surface area and volume of three-dimensional scale models when different scale factors are used. All of these are done in a hands-on manner, manipulating concrete objects to develop a deeper understanding of these concepts. The materials can be downloaded from the *Scale City* website: https://www.ket.org/scalecity/

An important attribute of the program is that it focuses on using tables and graphs rather than the standard "cross-multiplication" method for understanding proportional relationships. This teaching philosophy is aligned with the NCTM standards:

> Instruction in solving proportions should include methods that have a strong intuitive basis. The so-called cross-multiplication method can be developed meaningfully if it arises naturally in students' work, but it can also have unfortunate side effects when students do not adequately understand when the method is appropriate to use. Other approaches to solving proportions are often more intuitive and also quite powerful (NCTM, 2000, p. 220).

Multivariate Mental Models of Causality: Conducting research projects on complex systems can be very challenging for middle school students due to the multivariate causal analysis required in understanding the relationship between several factors. Our instructional methods are similar to the *Food Chain* program which effectively develops multivariate mental models (Eseryel & Law, 2012). *Food Chain* is an interactive simulation program which develops deep learning by scaffolding each step in the inquiry process by providing relevant information as needed and prompting students. For example, in the develop hypothesis step, it provides relevant content, and at the end of the test hypothesis step, it provides charts and graphs depicting the states of different variables which are intended to help students discover the interrelationships among the variables. Our project will use similar instructional methods except that students select an ecosystem problem of local interest, implement scaffolding by providing instruction as needed, and employing college students as mentors who provide question prompts to guide reflection. In addition, students will (a) collect real data, (b) use *InspireData* to record the data in tables, (c) graph the relationship of each variable to the factor under study, and then (d) graph the relationship of pairs of variables. This method is based on instructional strategies developed by Ramsey and Kuhn (2012) which are aimed directly at helping students progress from univariate to multivariate mental models of causality.

In summary, the project will develop computational thinking within the context of modeling and simulating environmental phenomenon which provides students the opportunity to engage in meaningful projects. Students will develop causal loop diagrams, agent-based simulations, bifocal models, proportional reasoning skills, and multivariate causal models. They will also develop professional identity and persistence by conducting small team projects and having access to college students who will mentor and tutor them. In addition, staff from local corporations and government agencies will meet and discuss their work with students, and students will conduct research projects at local environmental centers or preserves.

Future Work

Section "Promoting Computational Thinking at ERAU" discussed a prior CT project as well as ongoing CT education projects for college students. Section "Middle School Computational Thinking" presented the ideas on how to use agent-based modeling and bifocal modeling to scaffold CT education for middle school students. In order to further investigate how to teach CT in age-appropriate pedagogy and application contexts, the authors proposed two projects including more diverse applications and age groups. One is the SeaEdger project designed to support a REU program and a middle school summer camp in computational math with environmental science applications. The other is the MAKE-MS-EC program that provides research experiences in computational mathematics with diverse application contexts for local high school students.

SEAEDGER Project

SEAEGDER stands for Surveillance of an Estuary Area for Environmental Data Gathering, Education, and Research. The goals of the SEAEDGER project are to use a buoy-based sensor network system to gather data in the Indian River Lagoon and provide data-enabled environmental research experiences for undergraduates as well as an environmental education summer workshop for local middle school students. There are four project objectives:

1. Extend and test a smart data acquisition network (SDAN) system including a ground station, three Eco-Dolphins, and nine sensor buoys. The major tasks are to design, purchase, assemble, and program microcontrollers to control hydrophones and GoPro cameras. The SDAN system will have three clusters of buoys, each consisting of three sensor buoys. Each cluster will be anchored at three vertices of an equilateral triangle in one site. Altogether, nine buoys will make three clusters and will be deployed to three sites. The sensor buoy clusters will collect images for 1 to 2 weeks each season.
2. Train ten undergraduates to collect imagery data using the SDAN system in 12 sites in the Indian River Lagoon and use machine learning algorithms to identify seagrass, dolphins, manatee, and sea turtles. After the volume of the image data is reduced to a manageable size, we can label the verified data and use them to train a machine learning tool, which can then be used to efficiently classify the targets.
3. Once images are processed, we can distinguish (a) manatees, sea turtles, and dolphins from other marine animals and (b) seagrasses from macroalgae. We can also collect benthic vegetation data.
4. Conduct a 1-week (6-day) summer workshop on SeaPerch Robots and environmental science education for middle school students. During the workshop, we will demonstrate fun and inspiring environmental science projects in the morning and tutor students in constructing their own SeaPerch robot as a team project in the afternoon. Each team will have three to four students. To encourage the participation of parents, we will use Saturday to host a SeaPerch Robotic competition and an environmental science poster competition.

MAKE-MS-EC Program for Local High School Students

Over a 2-year period, the Mathematical Application Knowledge Enhancement of Marginal Students to Empower Community (MAKE-MS-EC) is proposed to enhance learning of mathematical knowledge using hands-on research, exploratory studies, and guided discovery. MAKE-MS-EC includes activities that enrich high school students' learning, especially females who are discouraged by the gender bias of our culture for their mathematics ability, through trifocal mathematical modeling (tm^2) while ensuring cognitive skills have been internalized. Trifocal mathematical modeling focuses on the derivation of mathematical models using real-world experiments, verification, and validation of models with computer tools and peer competitions in a virtual environment. MAKE-MS-EC will enhance and foster a kinesthetic learning environment by utilizing the Wave Laboratory and Leverage Robotics Laboratory at ERAU.

Through the MAKE-MS-EC program, students will explore real-world research problems in mathematics via novel mathematical models: the traffic monitoring interpolate model, carry-on Aero capacity model, fashion mannequin model, population model for sea turtles, payload carrying capacity of autonomous underwater vehicles, and the water wave model for low and high tide seasons in connection to the science, engineering, technology, and arts pipeline. There will be two tiers of student involvement within the MAKE-MS-EC program: the first tier consists of students, with a focus on females, actively participating within the research of applied mathematics problems based on Wave and Leverage Robotics Labs and other activities taking place through a tm^2 website. The second tier will consist of students observing ongoing research activities conducted at ERAU that are intended to inspire the students to enter the STEM pipeline. The goals of MAKE-MS-EC are to:

- Explore mathematical concepts in connections to the real-life problem solving via data analysis, experiments, computational tools, and open virtual environment.
- Enrich critical, analytical, and logical thinking in mathematics through guided mentoring.
- Foster student conceptual mathematical knowledge in a creative and original manner.

The overall intention of MAKE-MS-EC program is to develop analytical, critical, and logical thinking skills and cultivate problem solving capabilities enabling the community to:

- Bring novel pedagogy to mathematics education in the science, engineering, technology, and arts pipeline.
- Educate, advise, and stimulate high school female students to pursue a STEM career.
- Develop mathematical concepts within the context of solving real-world problems in STEM.
- Build a virtual tm^2 learning environment.
- Enhance SIAM, KME (Kappa Mu Epsilon), and ERAU collaborations.

Conclusion

This chapter presented a brief literature review and case studies of CT education programs. We propose that CSE provides the educational content to enhance the CT ability of learners. We believe a pragmatic approach to promote and improve K-12 CT education is through out-of-school time programs and improving college level CT education by forming coalitions and providing research projects. Out-of-school time, project-based, and inquiry-based programs engage students and promotes learning-on-demand as students take responsibility for their own learning. Literature consistently shows that innovative education practices such as model-based REU programs and robotics research problems have advantages in motivating student learning and facilitating deep learning. However, in its current stage, these methods are still perceived as more expensive than the conventional lecturing method. We presented a cost-effective CSE program that uses cyberlearning, crowdsourcing, and codeveloped courses to reduce costs without compromising quality.

In the 10 years since Wing promoted the notion of computational thinking, CT education programs have flourished with support from government and private foundations. These projects have often resulted in "best practices." The task before us now is to move these "best practices" to "common practices" in both K-12 schools and colleges which will require a substantial investment in teacher training and the development of instructional resources.

Acknowledgments The cyberlearning project for CSE and summer REU workshops described in section "Coalition for Undergraduate CSE Education" was sponsored by the NSF TUES grant (1244967), and the Eco-Dolphin project described in "Eco-Dolphin Project" was partially sponsored by the Air Force Research Lab under award FA8750-15-1-0143.

References

ACE. (2016). Instructional Software and Materials. Retrieved from: http://www.data-harvest.co.uk/catalogue/technology/primary/software/primary-software.

Alfieri, L., Higashi, R., Shoop, R., & Schunn, C. D. (2015). Case Study of a robot-based game to shape interests and home proportional reasoning skills. *International Journal of STEM Education, 2*(4). doi:10.1186/s40594-015-0017-9.

Andrew, V. (1998). The purpose of mathematical models is insight, not numbers. *Decision Line, 29*(1), 20–21.

Barr, V., & Stephenson, C. (2011). Bringing computational thinking to K-12: what is involved and what is the role of the computer science education community? *ACM Inroads, 2*(1), 48–54.

Benitti, F. B. V. (2012). Exploring the educational potential of robotics in schools: a systematic review. *Computers & Education, 58*(3), 978–988.

Blikstein, P., & Wilensky, U. (2007). Bifocal modeling: a framework for combining computer modeling, robotics and real-world sensing. In *Paper presented at the annual meeting of the American Educational Research Association (AERA 2007), Chicago, USA*.

Blikstein, P., Fuhrmann, T., Greene, D., & Salehi, S. (2012). Bifocal modeling: mixing real and virtual labs for advanced science learning. *In Proceedings of the 11th International Conference on Interaction Design and Children (IDC '12)* (pp. 296–299). ACM: New York.

Borgman, C. L., Abelson, H., Drinks, L., Johnson, R., Koedinger, K. R., Linn, M. C., & Szalay, A. (2008). Fostering Learning in the Networked World: The Cyberlearning Opportunity and Challenge. Retrieved from: http://www.nsf.gov/pubs/2008/nsf08204/nsf08204.pdf

Bryan, K., & Leise, T. (2006). The $25,000,000,000 eigenvector: the linear algebra behind google. *SIAM Review, 48*(3), 569–581.

Carnegie Foundation. (2016). Using improvement science to accelerate learning and address problems of practice. Downloaded 04/14/2016 from http://www.carnegiefoundation.org/our-ideas/.

Carnegie Mellon Robotics Academy. (2016). http://education.rec.ri.cmu.edu/roboticscurriculum/.

Chai, J., Friedler, L. M., Wolff, E. F., Li, J., & Rhea, K. (2014). A cross-national study of calculus. *International Journal of Mathematical Education in Science and Technology, 46*(4), 481–494. doi:10.1080/0020739X.2014.990531.

Cuny, J., Snyder, L., & Wing, J.M. (2010). Demystifying Computational Thinking for Noncomputer Scientists. Unpublished manuscript in progress. Retrieved from: http://www.cs.cmu.edu/~CompThink/resources/TheLinkWing.pdf
Eseryel, D., & Law, V. (2012). Effect of cognitive regulation in understanding complex science systems during simulation-based inquiry learning. *Technology, Instruction, Cognition and Learning, 9*, 111–132.
Finegold, D., & Notabartolo, A. S. (2011). 21st Competencies and Impact. Retrieved from http://www.hewlett.org/uploads/21st_Century_Competencies_Impact.pdf.
Fuhrmann, T., Salehi, S., & Blikstein, P. (2013). Meta-modeling knowledge: Comparing model construction and model interaction in bifocal modeling. *In Proceedings of the 12th International Conference on Interaction Design and Children (IDC '13)* (pp. 483–486). New York: ACM. doi: 10.1145/2485760.2485810
GUTS. (2016). Computer Science in Science. Retrieved from: http://www.projectguts.org/.
Johnson-Laird, P. N. (1983). *Mental Models: Towards a Cognitive Science of Language, Inference, and Consciousness*. Cambridge: Cambridge University Press.
Joint Mathematical Meetings. (2015). Transforming Post-Secondary Education in Mathematics., San Antonio, TX.
Kirschner, P. A., Sweller, J., & Clark, R. E. (2006). Why minimal guidance during instruction does not work: an analysis of the failure of constructivist, discovery, problem-based, experiential, and inquiry-based teaching. *Educational Psychologist, 41*, 75–86. doi:10.1207/s15326985ep4102_1.
Lesh, R., Post, T., & Behr, M. (1988). Proportional reasoning. In J. Hiebert & M. Behr (Eds.), *Number Concepts and Operations in the Middle Grades* (pp. 93–118). National Council of Teachers of Mathematics: Reston, VA.
Liu, L., & Ludu, A. (2012). ACE – a model centered reu program standing on the three legs of cse: analysis, computation and experiment. In H. Ali, Y. Shi, D. Khazanchi, M. Lee, G. D. van Albada, J. Dongarra, et al. (Eds.), *Proceeding of the ICCS 2012, Omaha, NE. Procedia Computer Science* (Vol. 9, pp. 1773–1782).
Liu, H., & Klein, J. (2013). Using REU project and crowdsourcing to facilitate learning on demand. In *Proceedings of the IADIS International Conference on Cognition and Explorative Learning at Digit Ages* (pp. 251–258). Fort Worth, TX: International Assn for Development of the Information Society.
Liu, H., Ludu, M., & Holton, D. (2015a). Can K-12 math teachers train students to make sound logic reasoning? – A question affecting 21st century skills. In X. Ge, M. Spector, & D. Ifenthaler (Eds.), *Emerging Technologies for STEAM Education* (pp. 331–353). Switzerland: Springers.
Liu, H., & Raghavan, J. (2009). A mathematical modeling module with system engineering approach for teaching undergraduate students to conquer complexity. In *The Proceedings of the Conference ICCS 09, Baton Rouge, LA, USA, Part II, LNCS5545* (pp. 93–102).
Liu, H., Shi, X., Shao, J., Zhou, Q., Joseph-Ellison, S., Jaworski, J., & Wen, C. (2015b). The mechatronic system of eco-dolphin – a fleet of autonomous underwater vehicles. In *Proceeding of the International Conference of Advanced Mechatronics System 2015* (pp. 108–113). Beijing, China: IEEE. doi:10.1109/ICAMechS.2015.7287138.
McGivney-Burelle, J., & Xue, F. (2015). Flipping Calculus. *PRIMUS, Problems, Resources, and Issues in Mathematics Undergraduate Studies, 23*(5), 477–486. doi:10.1080/10511970.2012.757571.
ModelSim Project. (2016). Enabling Modeling and Simulation-Based Science in the Classroom. Retrieved from: http://modelsim.tech.northwestern.edu/info/
National Council of Teachers of Mathematics (NCTM). (2000). *Principles and Standards for School Mathematics*. Reston, VA: NCTM.
National Research Council. (2010). *Report of a Workshop on the Scope and Nature of Computational Thinking*. Washington, DC: The National Academies Press. doi:10.17226/12840.
National Research Council (NRC). (2011). *Report of a Workshop of Pedagogical Aspects of Computational Thinking*. Washington, DC: National Academy Press. http://www.nap.edu/catalog.php?record_id=13170.
Pirnay-Dummer, P., Ifenthaler, D., & Spector, J. M. (2010). Highly integrated model assessment technology and tools. *Educational Technology Research & Development, 58*(1), 3–18.

Ramsey, S., & Kuhn, D. (2012). Developing multivariable. *Cognitive Development, 35*, 92–110.
Robertson, E. F. (1968). Short Biograph of Richard W. Hamming, For His Work on Numerical Methods, Automatic Coding Systems, and Error-detecting and Error-correcting Codes. Retrieved from: http://amturing.acm.org/award_winners/hamming_1000652.cfm
Sabelli, N. (2008). *Applying What We Know to Improve Teaching and Learning, the Carnegie/IAS Commission on Math Science Education*. Menlo Park, CA: SRI International.
Schoenfeld, A. H. S. (1995). A brief biography of calculus reform. *UME Trends: News and Reports on Undergraduate Mathematics Education, 6*(6), 3–5.
Seel, N. M., & Blumschein, P. (2009). Modeling and Simulation in Learning and Instruction: A Theoretical Perspective, "Model-based Approaches to Learning: Using Systems Models and Simulations to Improve Understanding and Problem Solving in Complex Domains". In P. Blumschein, W. Hung, D. Jonassen, & J. Strobel (Eds.), *Modeling and Simulations for Learning and Instruction, 4*. Dordrecht, Netherlands: Sense Publishers.
Society for Industrial and Applied Mathematics. (2015). *Modeling across the curriculum II*. Philadelphia, PA: 2nd SIAM-NSF Workshop. Retrieved from: https://www.siam.org/reports/ModelingAcross%20Curr_2014.pdf.
Spector, M. (2009). Foreword, "Model-based approaches to learning: using systems models and simulations to improve understanding and problem solving in complex domains". In P. Blumschein, W. Hung, D. Jonassen, & J. Strobel (Eds.), *Modeling and Simulations for Learning and Instruction, 4*. Dordrecht, Netherlands: Sense Publishers.
Turner, P., & Petzold, L. (2011). Undergraduate computational science and engineering education. *SIAM Review, 53*(3), 561–574.
Turner, P., Levy, R., & Fowler, K. (2015). Collaboration in the Mathematical Sciences Community on Mathematical Modeling Across the Curriculum, Chance, Using Data to Advance Science, Education, and Society. Retrieved from: http://chance.amstat.org/2015/11/math-modeling.
Vollstedt, A. M., Robinson, M., & Wang, E. (2007). Using robotics to enhance science, technology, engineering, and mathematics curricula. In Proceedings of the American Society for Engineering Education Pacific Southwest Annual Conference, Honolulu, HI
Wing, J. M. (2006). A vision for the 21st century: computational thinking. *Communication of ACM, 49*(3), 33–35.
Zorn, P., Bailer, J., Braddy, L., Carpenter, J., Jaco, W., & Turner, P. (2014). *The INGenIOuS project-mathematics, statistics, and preparing the 21st century workforce*. Washington, DC: Mathematical Association of America. Paper presented at the 7th World Conference on Educational Sciences, (WCES-2015), 05–07 February 2015, Novotel Athens Convention Center, Athens, Greece.

Part III
Teacher Development

Teaching Computational Thinking Patterns in Rural Communities

Carla Hester Croff

Abstract In this chapter you will learn how a community college in rural Wyoming is implementing professional development resources in Computer Science and computational thinking skills for middle and high school teachers in their communities. The objective of the community college was to build relationships with schools to teach Computer Science concepts and computational thinking skills in the classroom. In this day and age, many people young and old are spending time on playing games or simulations. Why not teach Computer Science concepts and computational thinking skills through gaming and simulations? The project included teaching teachers about computational thinking patterns when teaching their students computer gaming and simulation creations. The creation of computer games and simulations requires algorithmic, critical thinking, problem-solving, and computational thinking skills. Teachers were taught what computational thinking patterns are, how to teach their students about computational thinking patterns, and how to create computer games and simulations stressing computational thinking skills. The teacher progress is measured by recorded observations, completed student projects, and surveys.

Keywords Teaching computational skills • Computational problem-solving • Computer thinking • Professional development

Community College Initiative

Teaching Computational Thinking Skills in Rural Communities

Wyoming is vastly open plains with most towns being at least an hour and a half from each other. In addition, the weather can be unpredictable, causing travel delays. The region that the Western Wyoming Community College (WWCC) serves is the southwest region of the state. The counties included in this region are

C.H. Croff (✉)
Western Wyoming Community College, 2500 College Dr, Rock Springs, WY 82901, USA
e-mail: chester@westernwyoming.edu

P.J. Rich, C.B. Hodges (eds.), *Emerging Research, Practice, and Policy on Computational Thinking*, Educational Communications and Technology: Issues and Innovations, DOI 10.1007/978-3-319-52691-1_11

Sublette, Lincoln, Uinta, Sweetwater, and Carbon counties. The college campus is located in Rock Springs, Wyoming, which is in Sweetwater County. There are a total of seven community colleges in the state of Wyoming that split regions within the state. This does not mean a community college cannot reach out to other counties. Each community college is a 2-year institution that provides vocational and educational services to their region. WWCC works closely on initiatives with the K-12 district schools including hosting the science fair, Engineering week, spelling bee, Computer Science teacher workshops, and college credit courses for high school students to name a few. The University of Wyoming is the only state provider of advanced education, and their outreach locations tend to be located at the community colleges.

In order for community colleges to play a role in delivering Computer Science and computational thinking skills with teachers in middle and high school, they must build relationships through networking. In Western Wyoming, to build these types of relationships, it is done more on a one-to-one connection bases. When promoting initiatives, the preferred method of communication is through face-to-face interaction and phone conversations. The technology through online environments is catching on as well. The main factor with online environments is there has to be a skilled instructor as the facilitator. This eliminates any distractions from the online meeting or lesson. Many teachers in these rural communities interact with different counties by seeing each other at conferences, science fairs, and community events. To get teachers involved in implementing computational thinking projects into their classrooms, it is important to have workshops at regional conferences and events. The preferred conferences and events would be Science, Technology, Engineering, and Mathematics (STEM) related. Participants at these events are very eager to learn and share information with their classrooms. One of the main reasons of attending these types of sessions is the networking opportunities.

Understanding Computational Thinking Skills

In addition to building relationships, the community college faculty must completely understand computational patterns and the skills required to master these proficiencies. Understanding computational skills before implementing initiatives with the middle and high school teachers is imperative. Many individuals relate the field of Computer Science to computational thinking. The awareness that computational thinking patterns can be found in various disciplines other than Computer Science (CS) is catching on. The community college is aware that computational skills are part of their offered computer programming courses. However, the focus has not been on what computational skills are being covered in the assignments for college students. The focus in these courses has primarily been on if students know how to program in various computer languages. Even though exploring the process of algorithms is presented in CS classes, there is no assessment of computational thinking skills per se.

To assist in the implementation of teaching middle and high school teachers and students computational thinking patterns, exercises in this subject for college students were initiated. These exercises included the use of computer gaming, simulations, virtual mapping, virtual environments, data compression, pattern recognition, and algorithms. All these are considered computational thinking skills. In order to meet the student needs in WWCC's region, CS courses are offered online. The challenge of teaching these skills over an online environment can be somewhat problematic. The resource found to be effective is the use of clear instructions, examples, videos on computational concepts being covered, and immediate instructor feedback. With resources being limited for community college faculty to work on a one-to-one basis with each student, pairing students was beneficial. However, additional assignments needed to be geared on an individual basis to verify understanding of knowledge gained. When creating exercises, technology needs to be tested to make sure students were able to complete these exercises virtually. Students were given instructions on what software was needed on their computer systems at home, and they were required to provide a screenshot of applications working on their end. This helped the instructor determine which students were having technology trouble, if any. Furthermore, college students were able to evaluate and provide feedback on computational thinking skill activities that would be given to middle and high school students.

Teacher Training in Computational Thinking Skills

Community college faculty teamed up with the University of Colorado Boulder on the Scalable Game Design (SGD) project and the University of Wyoming on the ITEST uGame-iCompute project. Both initiatives included the use of computer gaming and simulations to teach Computer Science concepts and computational thinking skills. The projects were geared toward middle and high school teachers and students. Community college faculty played a supportive role by recruiting and providing training, tutorials, and one-on-one support. To start the recruiting process as community college faculty, workshops and presentations were presented at conferences where middle and high school teachers participated. The sessions provided hands-on exercises that middle and high school instructors could take back to their classrooms. In addition, teachers received resources such as support, tutorials, and cheat sheets to effectively get started.

Faculty relied on word of mouth through colleagues and community connections. Once the connections were made, faculty contacted teachers at the schools that were interested in the Scalable Game Design and ITEST initiatives. The recruited teachers attended a 3–4-day summer training or participated in a 4-week online computer gaming course. The community college faculty were part of the training process for teachers. Teachers received stipends for attending these trainings. The training provided exercises to teach Computer Science concepts and computational skills in the classroom. The online tutorials provided by the community college included game overview, examples, preparing class, computational thinking lesson plans, rubrics, and cheat sheets. Below is an illustration of an online training tutorial:

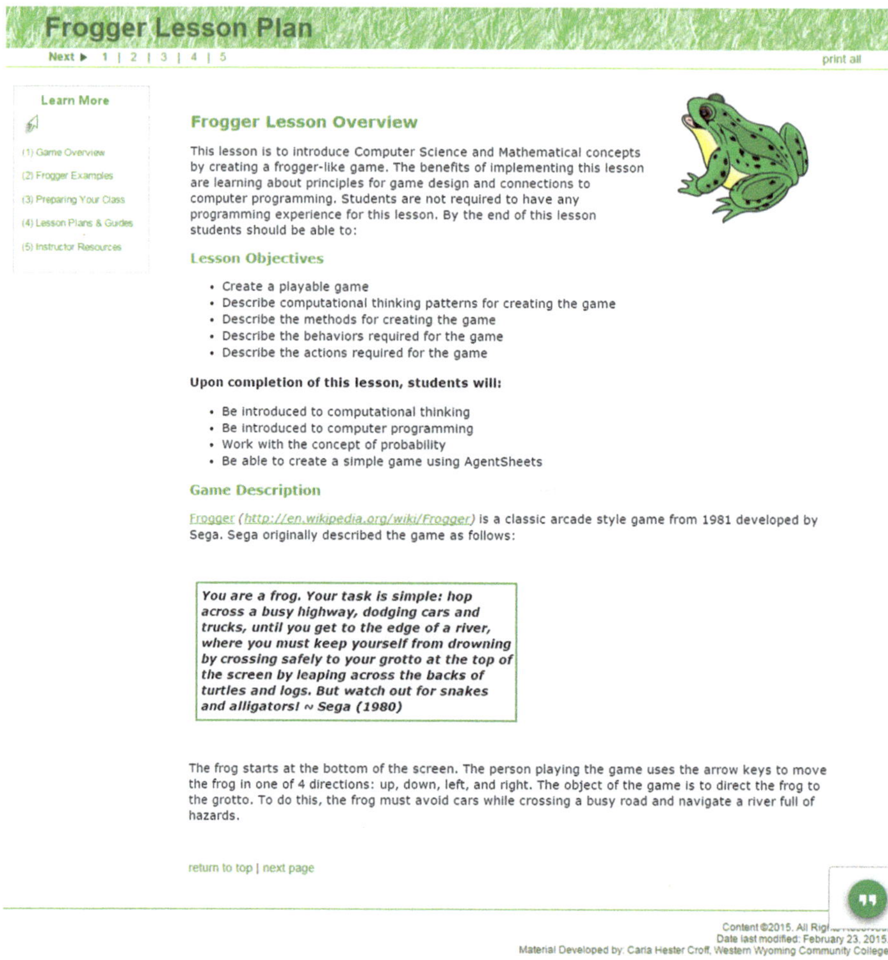

Frogger Lesson Plan

Next ▶ 1 | 2 | 3 | 4 | 5 print all

Learn More

(1) Game Overview
(2) Frogger Examples
(3) Preparing Your Class
(4) Lesson Plans & Guides
(5) Instructor Resources

Frogger Lesson Overview

This lesson is to introduce Computer Science and Mathematical concepts by creating a frogger-like game. The benefits of implementing this lesson are learning about principles for game design and connections to computer programming. Students are not required to have any programming experience for this lesson. By the end of this lesson students should be able to:

Lesson Objectives

- Create a playable game
- Describe computational thinking patterns for creating the game
- Describe the methods for creating the game
- Describe the behaviors required for the game
- Describe the actions required for the game

Upon completion of this lesson, students will:

- Be introduced to computational thinking
- Be introduced to computer programming
- Work with the concept of probability
- Be able to create a simple game using AgentSheets

Game Description

Frogger *(http://en.wikipedia.org/wiki/Frogger)* is a classic arcade style game from 1981 developed by Sega. Sega originally described the game as follows:

> ***You are a frog. Your task is simple: hop across a busy highway, dodging cars and trucks, until you get to the edge of a river, where you must keep yourself from drowning by crossing safely to your grotto at the top of the screen by leaping across the backs of turtles and logs. But watch out for snakes and alligators! ~ Sega (1980)***

The frog starts at the bottom of the screen. The person playing the game uses the arrow keys to move the frog in one of 4 directions: up, down, left, and right. The object of the game is to direct the frog to the grotto. To do this, the frog must avoid cars while crossing a busy road and navigate a river full of hazards.

return to top | next page

Content ©2015. All Rig
Date last modified: February 23, 2015.
Material Developed by: Carla Hester Croff, Western Wyoming Community College

In addition to the workshops, summer training, and online course for middle and high school teachers, the Google Computational Thinking for Educators self-paced online course was recommended by the community college faculty. This was a method that instructors could use in their own time. The course focused on integrating computational thinking into course curriculum. The course was directed toward Humanities, Math, Science, and Computing educators; however, any educator could be part of the course. The Google Computational Thinking for Educators course content consisted of the Introduction to Computational Thinking,

Exploring Algorithms, Finding Patterns, Developing Algorithms, and Applying Computational Thinking. Upon completion, each participant received a certificate of completion from Google indicating the understanding of computational thinking. The problem with the self-study method was there was no accountability of completion. Verbal connections were made with teachers, and many indicated that they did not have a chance to complete the online course.

Assistance to Teachers

Due to limited community college faculty resources, Computer Science (CS) interns were recruited to schools within the district. These CS interns were trained on the implementation of computational skills through computer gaming and simulations. These were the same games being created in the middle and high school sessions. The computational thinking patterns were implemented in the Computer Science intern projects. Each CS intern received credit for successfully completing their computer game and simulations. In addition, the students received credit for working with a middle or high school teacher. The CS interns were provided as a resource to the teachers, to help with the delivery of the computational thinking concepts. Rubrics were used to determine the completion of each student's projects and their understanding of the computational skills. At the middle and high school level, students were given grades and points on their projects. The limitation to using Computer Science interns is the availability outside of the campus county.

In addition to the CS interns being trained on computational thinking skills, other CS students were introduced during the Introduction to Computer Science course. Typically, basic programming is taught, and gaming and simulation projects were embedded as midterm and final projects. In the more advanced Computer Science I course, college students were introduced to computer simulations. These simulations challenged students to think more critically. Computational thinking directives were indicated and graded based on project completion. College-level students felt that including these types of projects was an invaluable way to break up the class. The college instructor felt that students being part of such a project increased their knowledge and collaboration skills.

As faculty that provided support to teachers, email communications and phone conversations performed an important role in the dialog. Teachers who worked in the community college district felt more comfortable about contacting the community college for assistance. A majority of Wyoming teachers were recruited by the community college faculty. In rural communities, previously knowing individuals and the one-to-one connection are important. The assistance from the community college would include what necessary paperwork needs to be completed, license numbers for software, how to communicate effectively with their Information Technology department, tutorials that were available, and any issues they may have in implementing computational thinking skills in the classroom to name a few. The responses from community college faculty needed to be timely and helpful.

Observations

The community college faculty played an active role in conducting observations of school sessions. On many occasions, the community college faculty would travel to locations to help teachers get their projects started. It was important to have community college administration on board with travel, to approve absences from campus. The benefits to the college and college students were enhancing teaching skills, building relationships, and learning new skills. These skills were very beneficial to college faculty in teaching college classes. The knowledge gained by observations kept faculty up-to-date on the latest technologies to use in teaching college students, which in turn engaged student learning.

As the initiative progressed and the community college teamed up with universities, which is covered in more detail later in the chapter, there was more travel funding. In order to assess how well teachers were conducting their computational thinking sessions, the community college became certified as a Dimensions of Success (DoS) observer, which is an observation tool for STEM programming. According to the DoS certification, when certified you are aware of the procedures for using DoS appropriately to assess STEM program quality. The DoS process verifies that teachers have paid attention to organization, materials, space utilization, participation, purposeful activities, engagement with STEM, STEM content learning, inquiry, reflection, relationships, relevance, and youth voice. Each category is rated with a scale from 1 to 4, and comments are provided from the observer on what took place during observations.

In most sessions, sessions were conducted in a classroom setting with students working at either desktop or laptop computers. Students tended to work in groups of two. Part of the process of observing computational thinking skills was to make sure teachers provided relative activities and student self-reflections on activities. It was important to have students actively reflecting on the STEM content, as well as computational thinking skills, in meaningful ways. Interactions among students and between facilitators and students were consistently positive, creating a warm and friendly learning environment.

Community College Projects

Scalable Game Design (SGD)

During the early implementation of working with schools in their district, WWCC was asked to work on the Scalable Game Design project with East Junior High School. In an effort to make the implementation of STEM criteria in the classroom easier for teachers, the University of Colorado Boulder has developed two computer programs AgentSheets and AgentCubes as part of their Scalable Game Design (SGD) research project. This project introduced students to Computer Science concepts and computational thinking skills through computer games and simulations.

During this beginning phase of working with middle and high school teachers within WWCC's region, the faculty worked with only the East Junior High School. This was feasible since the school was located in the same district. Students were introduced to simple 2D games using AgentSheets like Frogger and Mazes. AgentSheets provided an easy method for adding characters to the game, creating worksheets, and a drag and drop method for adding behaviors to characters. The educational goal was to learn and apply computational thinking skills in the context of a familiar game or simulation. WWCC Faculty would assist the teacher during the classroom session and provide training resources at the junior high. The session was conducted during regular class time, and many students were interested in taking the course. The feedback from students was excitement and motivation for learning more about computational thinking patterns. After learning a simple game, students were encouraged to create their own games and simulations using computational patterns.

In addition, college faculty attended the summer institute provided by the SGD research project. This gave invaluable training on implementing computational thinking skills in the classroom, as well as understanding of computational patterns. This opportunity provided collaboration with other teachers, resources, and motivation to begin working with other schools in the college's region.

uGame-iCompute Project Using LMS

As a result of working with the University of Colorado Boulder on the SGD project, WWCC faculty was asked to work with the University of Wyoming on the uGame-iCompute project. This 3-year project included the use of AgentSheets and AgentCubes as well. As previously mentioned, AgentSheets and AgentCubes are computer gaming and simulation programs, which assist in teaching computational thinking skills. During the first year, the community college played an active role in recruiting, training, and providing resources and one-on-one support to teachers. In this study, middle and high school teachers participated in an online course to learn about creating computer games and simulations. The course consisted of an online learning management system (LMS) with conference capabilities to demonstrate the games and simulations The training materials used for instruction were online tutorials that provided information on how the game is played, lesson plans, step-by step cheat sheets, an example of the game, related computational skills, and various other resources. The rationale used for most of the instruction was that the teacher needed to create the game or simulation themselves before teaching their students. The process of creating their projects before teaching their students was vital. In the case of simulations, teachers were encouraged to do some research with their students first. For example, before doing a forest fire simulation, students would research information about how forest fires are started, how they work, who is involved in putting out the fire, and how much damage they can cause. This gives the students a "real-world" example. The community college faculty provided an online tutorial for the forest fire, to help teachers implement this project in their classroom.

After training, teachers introduced their students to Computer Science and Mathematics concepts by creating computer games and simulations. Students learned about principles for game design and connections to computer programming. With the forest fire pre-exercise of researching forest fires and the creation of the forest fire simulation, students learned the concept of probability, the use of graphs to graph their understanding, and the use of mean and variance in analyzing the simulation. In addition, these playable games and interactive simulations used computational thinking patterns, methods, behaviors, and actions. The sessions were interactive, completely hands-on and required no prior computer programming experience.

uGame-iCompute Project Using Adobe Connect

During the second and third year, the Western Wyoming Community College (WWCC) continued to work on the uGame-iCompute project, which continued to incorporate computer gaming into middle and high school classrooms in their region. Again, this project included the NASC 5770-60 Visualization Basics teachers' course that explored how game programming and robotics can be used effectively in the middle and high school curriculum. The course syllabus included the common threads that would be covered: (a) the computational thinking skills that are required to build computer games and program robots and (b) how these relate to the appropriate teaching standards. The course is split into two 8-week parts. During the first part, participants learn about game programming using AgentSheets and AgentCubes. The second part consisted of putting together and programming EV3 robots. The community college faculty's primary role in the course was delivering some of the computer gaming course content and teacher support, which included providing assistance, resources, and materials for them to complete their game programming projects. In addition, an online learning environment and online collaborative meetings were used to work one-on-one with teachers on their projects. The gaming exercises included computational skills such as algorithmic thinking, critical thinking, efficient solutions, innovative thinking, problem-solving skills, and scientific thinking. To verify that students understood the computational thinking involved in their games, they were instructed on where these skills took place in their projects. For example, when creating a virtual bouncing ball, think about how to simulate the ball bouncing virtually and implement it.

At this time, the course used Adobe Connect to deliver the online course. Adobe Connect is a web conferencing, online training, and desktop sharing environment. The method of instruction for the gaming programming piece was a "flipped classroom" arrangement. Teachers were given short videos and game programming assignments to complete before and during the online class session. The instructor covered game programming concepts and allowed teachers time to complete their projects with teacher support being available. In addition, the class gave an opportunity to discuss the materials that are being covered and to collaborate on ideas related to integrating computer gaming in the classroom.

Google Initiative (CS4HS)

Recently, WWCC was asked to take part in a project with Google and the University of Colorado Boulder entitled Google CS4HS (Computer Science for High School). This project aims is to teach principles in Computer Science, again through the use of AgentSheets and AgentCubes. The objective of the initiative was to bring middle and high school teachers together to learn and teach Computer Science concepts and computational thinking skills specifically for high school students. The implementation for this initiative was to conduct a summer session for teachers. The summer session would be specifically for Wyoming teachers. The community college played an active role on setting up the Wyoming summer institute with teachers. The University of Colorado Boulder provided training materials that were given to each teacher, which included explanations of computational thinking exercises and student training materials for their classrooms. In addition, the community college provided additional training materials. There were 15 teachers in the summer session that worked on computer games and simulations to learn about computational thinking patterns. This event proved to be an effective way of networking teachers. And once teachers and students created their games in the 2D AgentSheets format, it was easier to move into the 3D AgentCubes version of the games and simulations.

Initially, teachers were given a survey about when and where they would implement their lessons on computational thinking. Teachers were primarily from the Computer Technology, Science, and Math fields. Many instructors indicated having their sessions during school hours, and a few decided to have after-school programs. Teachers sent flyers home with students, and the students choose whether to be part of the sessions. The average size of the computer sessions is 10–15 students, meeting once or twice a week. Many of them will work on creating a simple computer game like Frogger. The grade levels for these students can range from 4th to 9th grade. Even though the focus is for high school students, there is room for younger students to take part in order to increase the knowledge in computational thinking skills as students' progress through school.

Teacher Feedback

Many teachers were recruited for a combination of initiatives. Consequently, some teachers worked on a couple initiatives at a time. Being in rural communities, the same teachers are interested in computational thinking projects, and it is not uncommon to have them working on the same projects. The Google CS4HS teachers were surveyed, after completing one semester of implementing computational thinking skills in their classroom. Teachers were asked if they created their own computer games and simulations before teaching their students. More than half indicated that they did create their own before teaching the concepts. We found that it was important to have teachers go through the exercises on their own, in order to have a successful session with students. Even though cheat sheets were provided to teachers, it was strongly recommended not to use these as a teaching method, but more as a resource. The training methods that were used for these teachers ranged anywhere from an online course to self-study, face-to-face training session, and videos. The instructors indicated that they had taken part in several of the training methods. All teachers concluded that the training was beneficial, which indicated that it was effective. The majority of teachers felt they were ready to teach their students after training.

During their sessions, a lot of the teachers felt they would prefer to work in groups with other teachers. This can be difficult in rural communities. One way to rectify this is by recruiting a couple of teachers from each county and teaming them up in the same districts. There were several teachers that did work together on after-school programs, which teachers indicated was a good way to implement these programs. When asked about what computational thinking skills their students learned, more than half indicated that the students learned algorithmic thinking, critical thinking skills, innovative thinking, problem-solving, and scientific thinking. Below is a comment from Adrienne Unertl from the Clark Elementary in Evanston, Wyoming:

> "I have enjoyed implementing game design because it has benefited my students to solve their own problems. They have begun talking in conversational programming when describing what they would like to happen in their game. They have become content creators instead of just consumers. They have also learned to debug their program and pinpoint which agent has the issue that needs resolved. They collaborate with their peers and challenge each other to create better games and point out flaws with constructive comments."

In addition, teachers used other computational thinning activities in their classroom. These included Math critical thinking problems, getting students to work backward from a solution, critical thinking, and investigative research. The challenges they felt they encountered were having students at different levels of understanding, having glitches in the program being used, large class sizes, out-of-date computers, not enough storage space, too many students per computer, and time.

WWCC has found that the challenges in teaching computational thinking skills to middle and high school teachers can be numerous. Instructional concerns are pacing, fitting it in with existing curriculum and support. There may be a learning curve for some teachers. One of the implementation concerns is deciding when to implement. Working with the Information Technology department at each school is another concern. When working with Information Technology departments, it is imperative to provide software requirements, any installation issues that may occur, additional plug-ins that may be needed, as well as licensing information. These instructions will prevent technology difficulties in implementing projects in the middle and high school classroom. Another roadblock to implementing these initiatives in the classroom is administrative buy-in. This is where the community college faculty can play an important role. In each district, it is encouraged for schools to work with the community college on initiatives; therefore, having a community college faculty collaboration is imperative. This collaboration should bring about administrative support from school administrators.

Teaching Computational Thinking Through Gaming

Educators are finding game makers an important asset in creating games and simulations relative to their subject area. There are communities such as teachers that are capable of recognizing what sorts of things are worth checking out, discussing them, and championing them (Steinkuehler, Squire, & Barab, 2012). These individuals are forming communities to collaborate on what is the best way to use games and simulations in the classroom and which applications to use. Educators are provided with various resources, which include gaming groups, tutorials, and actual games that are already produced for learning. For example, if a teacher wants to cover computational concepts in their classroom, they can have students create a simple game that includes programming steps such as how the frog moves in the game Frogger or what happens when the frog jumps into traffic. Educators can also simulate real-world events like a mud slide, by having their student's research mud slides and then actually having students create a simulation or game. Since playing games in our society has increased, this seems to be an effective way to teach computational thinking concepts in education.

Another important factor to consider is how to teach skills through gaming. Where do you start? The first item is to have the technologies to implement the gaming in the first place, i.e., required hardware and software. Halverson and Smith (2010) describe two different use patterns for technologies in learning environments: technologies for learning and technologies for learners (Steinkuehler et al., 2012). These technologies are important to effectively teach through gaming. Once you have the technologies to support games for learners, the teacher can concentrate on the delivery of the teaching in the learning environment. Designing learning environments is not merely a matter of getting the curricular material right but is crucially also a matter of getting the situated, emergent community structures and practices right (Steinkuehler et al., 2012). After an educator has the learner requirements to create the game and the structure of how to teach the learner concepts through gaming structure, then the teacher can focus on the delivery of the content. In the twenty-first century, games play an important social connection among people who play them and in the learning process regarding various subjects.

Community College Perspective

This section is focused on the challenges that community college faculty have in implementing such projects in their workload. Typically, community college faculty have a class load of 28–32 credit hours an academic year, which averages about five classes a semester. The workload includes classroom instruction, face-to-face interaction, serving on several college communities, implementing community events and showcases, maintaining courses in their subject area, maintaining program system portfolios, attending subject area conferences, as well as working with community businesses to enhance employee skills. In addition, there are no teaching assistants, so grading becomes another time-consuming task. There is little time for extra projects or research in a particular area. The focus at the community college is more on teaching then research. There are numerous ways to implement research in an area at the community college level. First, alternate classes during a semester, and provide 16-, 12-, and 10-week classes. Team teach courses. Provide an internship course in the content area, which allows interns to work on research projects. This prevents overloading. Team up with other like-minded colleagues to implement a research symposium. Include students in active research in partial methods. For example, allow college-level students to evaluate computational skills exercise that will be used in middle and high schools. Feedback from college-level students is beneficial in the successful implementation of projects. Provide networking opportunities for interns and K-12 teachers. Team up with universities that are doing research in the area that is being taught. Currently, there are more opportunities for undergraduate research at community college than ever. Team up with community college research initiatives and become members of their committees.

The process of implementing computational thinking skills in the classroom is relatively easy. Teachers should be provided with program installation instructions, training, instructional tutorials, and cheat sheets. In addition, educators should be provided with continual support in delivering activities in the classroom. Instructors can be teamed up with other educators who have already implemented these activities. Teachers are encouraged to share ideas and gather new ideas for computer gaming and simulation activities.

In Western Wyoming, where there are more antelope then people, it is important to collaborate with other teachers at the community college level or the K-12 sector. Starting out with a few K-12 teachers to work with on research initiatives is recommended. Another effective method of sharing ideas and implementing computational thinking projects in rural communities is to have online meetings. Having experience with web conferencing, designing online training tutorials, and providing workshops or classes online are ideal. Documenting the progress of projects through school videos and pictures is helpful. Videos and pictures can provide administrative support for projects. There are many online training websites that can enhance skills in virtual technologies.

Building relationships is the most effective way to implement projects across the board. Another key factor is communication. The initiatives benefited the college by enhancing collaboration with schools in the region, along with building relationships with the University of Wyoming and the University of Colorado Boulder. Furthermore, the enhanced and updated knowledge in education and computational thinking skills were gained.

Conclusion

By providing teachers with a real-world example, they can motivate their students to engage in the learning process and possibly have a renewed interest in STEM occupations. STEM occupations are projected to grow by 17.0 percent from 2008 to 2018, compared to 9.8 percent growth for non-STEM occupations, and STEM workers experience higher wages and less joblessness in today's economy. Preparing US students from diverse backgrounds to fill these jobs is a national priority (NSF, 2010). The field of Computer Science is a portion of the STEM occupations that is rapidly growing. As part of the initiative to recruit the younger generation into Computer Science occupations, it is imperative that they are introduced to Computer Science and computational thinking patterns at an early age. "Exposing middle school students to computer science through game design appears to be a promising means to mitigate the computer science pipeline challenge" (Koh, Repenning, Nickerson, Endo, & Motter, 2013). The execution of computer gaming and simulations can be integrated into already existing courses, an after-school program, or a separate assignment during an academic year. Creating a computer game does not have to be conducted in a technology course; it can be included in any course. "Research suggests that exposure to short game design activities is effective in motivating large percentage of students in a wide variety of demographic groups" (Koh et al., 2013).

A successful education programming environment would include accessibility, making a working game in a short amount of time, and understanding the concepts of computational thinking. According to the National Center for Women and Information Technology (NCWIT) (2016), developing relevant and interesting assignments that appear to a broader audience is recommended for fostering a climate where the non-predisposed can belong both academically and socially, recruiting students who are not predisposed to pursuing computing, and exposing fundamental computing concepts to inexperienced learners.

Computer games along with simulations can be a good way to learn and teach computational thinking, critical thinking, and problem-solving skills. When a learner can learn the concepts on how a virus spreads and then create a computer simulation on how this happens, the learner can connect the concepts of the subject. This enhances the learning experience. In turn, learning these concepts through actual hands-on activities does bring it into the real world. In our society, the use of games, simulations, and even mobile apps is becoming common place. If there are avenues that can be taken to easily present a subject or skill through games and simulations, why not go for it.

Acknowledgments I would like to thank the University of Colorado Boulder, Scalable Game Design (SGD) project team, for including WWCC on their projects; it has been an invaluable experience. To the University of Wyoming, ITEST team, on letting me take part in their initiative, especially with the Wyoming schools. To my colleagues who have supported me along the way, Kim Farley, Paul Johnson, Craig Thompson, and Susan Heyborne. To Bernadine Craft at Sweetwater BOCES for continued project support. To all the Wyoming K-12 teachers I have worked with over the years on teaching Computer Science concepts and computational thinking skills. To the teachers that provided invaluable feedback for this book chapter: Adrienne Unertl, Clark Elementary; Kait Quinton, Rock Springs Junior High; Ken Aragon, Twin Spruce Junior High; Sharon Seaton, Black Butte High School; Shonie Mitchelson, Lincoln Middle School; and Tracy Clement, Monroe Intermediate. And last but not least to my family, my husband Mark, and my kiddos Evan and Eva for putting up with my time away from home.

References

Halverson, R., & Smith, A. (2010). How new technologies have (and have not) changed teaching and learning in Schools. *Journal of Computing in Teacher Education, 26*(2), 49–54.

Koh, K. H., Repenning, A., Nickerson, H., Endo, Y., & Motter, P. (2013). Will it stick? Exploring the sustainability of computational thinking education through game design. In *ACM Special Interest Group on Computer Science Education Conference, (SIGCSE 2013), March 6–9, 2013, Denver, Colorado, USA* (Vol. 1). doi:10.1145/2445196.2445372.

National Center for Women & Information Technology (2016). How Do You Introduce Computing in an Engaging Way?. Retrieved from https://www.ncwit.org/resources/how-do-you-introduce-computing-engaging-way/how-do-you-introduce-computing-engaging-way.

National Science Foundation (2010). Preparing the Next Generation of STEM Innovators: Identifying and Developing our Nation's Human Capital. Retrieved from http://www.nsf.gov/nsb/publications/2010/nsb1033.pdf.

Steinkuehler, C., Squire, K., & Barab, S. (2012). *Games, Learning, and Society: Learning and Meaning in the Digital Age*. New York: Cambridge University Press.

Teacher Transformations in Developing Computational Thinking: Gaming and Robotics Use in After-School Settings

Alan Buss and Ruben Gamboa

Abstract The challenges of addressing increasing calls for the inclusion of computational thinking skills in K-12 education in the midst of crowded school curricula can be mitigated, in part, by promoting STEM learning in after-school settings. The *Visualization Basics: Using Gaming to Improve Computational Thinking* project provided opportunities for middle school students to participate in after-school clubs focused on game development and LEGO robotics in an effort to increase computational thinking skills. Club leaders and teachers, however, first needed to develop proficiency with the computational tools and their understanding of computational thinking. To achieve these goals, teachers participated in two online professional development courses. After participating in the courses, teachers' understanding of and attitudes toward computational thinking skills were mostly positive. Observations of club sessions revealed that teachers provided a mix of structured and open-ended instruction. Guided instruction, such as using detailed tutorials for initial exposure to a concept or process, was most commonly observed. One area identified for improvement was the duration of the courses, which provided limited time for teachers to develop deep and robust computational thinking skills. Despite this limitation, the data collected thus far suggest that teachers' understanding of and attitudes toward computational thinking skills improved.

Keywords Game development • Robotics • Teacher professional development • Computational thinking

---

A. Buss (✉) • R. Gamboa
University of Wyoming, 1000 E. University Ave, Laramie, WY 82071, USA
e-mail: abuss@uwyo.edu; ruben@uwyo.edu

P.J. Rich, C.B. Hodges (eds.), *Emerging Research, Practice, and Policy on Computational Thinking*, Educational Communications and Technology: Issues and Innovations, DOI 10.1007/978-3-319-52691-1_12

Introduction

The history of US public schools is replete with calls for increased skills for dealing with current and future challenges. These calls include improvements in problem-solving and critical thinking skills (Educational Policies Commission, 1961), twenty-first-century skills (Uchida, Cetron, & McKenzie, 1996), and, more recently, computational thinking skills (Barr, Harrison, & Conery, 2011; Wing, 2006). Responding to these calls is a significant challenge on multiple fronts, including curriculum constraints and professional development. Demands on teachers' time to address existing curriculum requirements are high, leaving little or no room for new content, such as with computational thinking (Grover & Pea, 2013; National Research Council, 2011). Out-of-school activities, including after-school programs, however, provide greater opportunities to address computational thinking (CT) due to greater flexibility with curriculum and widely available web-based resources (National Research Council, 2011).

In 2013 the University of Wyoming received NSF Innovative Technology Experiences for Students and Teachers (ITEST) funding to implement a three-year program focused on developing middle school students' computational and spatial visual thinking skills in after-school settings. The resulting program, *Visualization Basics: Using Gaming to Improve Computational Thinking (UGICT)*, helped public school teachers and community members form after-school game development and robotics clubs. As most club teachers did not have experience with programming or robotics, professional development (PD) was provided in the form of two synchronous web-based courses. Data were gathered on teachers' understanding of CT and instructional practices through the use of pre-post surveys and club observations. This chapter focuses on results from years 1 and 2 of the grant project, in which 28 teachers in grades 4–8 from 18 schools in Wyoming participated.

Theoretical Framework

While there is a definite "cool" factor for selecting game development and robotics as tools for improving computational thinking skills, the use of such technology tools for learning is rooted in the ideas of constructionism. The key to learning is activity and experience (Dewey, 1916, 1958), whether through social interaction (Lave & Wenger, 1991; Salomon & Perkins, 1998; Vygotskiĭ & Cole, 1978), play (Honeyford & Boyd, 2015; Piaget & Inhelder, 1969), experimentation, or creation and construction (Burke, O'Byrne, & Kafai, 2016; Kafai, 1995, 2006; Kafai & Burke, 2013; Papert & Harel, 1991). Using programming to create new artifacts such as games and robotic controls is an effective tool for learning computer science concepts, mathematics, and problem-solving (Akcaoglu, 2016; Ardito, Mosley, & Scollins, 2014; Denner, Werner, & Ortiz, 2012; Kafai, 1996; Li, 2010; Papert, 1980). Furthermore, the use of game design and robotics promotes a specific type of thinking skills known as computational thinking (Atmatzidou & Demetriadis, 2016; Bers, Flannery, Kazakoff, & Sullivan, 2014; Nickerson, Brand, & Repenning, 2015; Repenning et al., 2015).

Computational Thinking in K-12 Education

Capturing the essence of CT, particularly in the context of K-12 education, in a simple definition is a vexing problem (Atmatzidou & Demetriadis, 2016; Barr & Stephenson, 2011; Grover & Pea, 2013; NRC, 2011). The definitions of CT that have been offered differ in some details, but they are largely consistent with one another. One of the earliest and most widely accepted definitions is from Jeannette Wing (2006), who emphasized that CT is a general attitude and broad skill set, as opposed to an explicit and narrow list of facts.

Wing's seminal ideas on CT had broad influence, and have been largely incorporated into the definition of CT from the *International Society for Technology and Education (ISTE)* and the *Computer Science Teachers Association (CSTA)*. These groups are two of the main voices in the establishment of K-12 computing education, and proposed an authoritative definition of CT comprised of two parts (Barr et al., 2011). The first involves *characteristics* of the CT *process*, which include the ability to:

Formulate problems in a way that enables the use of computers
Logically organize and analyze data
Represent data through abstractions such as models and simulations
Automate solutions through algorithmic thinking
Identify, analyze, and implement different possible solutions with efficiency in mind
Generalize this problem-solving approach to a wide variety of problems

Technical computing skills are not sufficient by themselves to solve problems via the use of computing power. Problem-solving with computers is a difficult and often lengthy process, so success also requires a set of attitudes that allow students to persevere in the face of adversity. These attitudes include:

Confidence in dealing with complexity
Persistence in working with difficult problems
Tolerance for ambiguity
The ability to deal with open-ended problems
The ability to communicate and work with others

There is a rich and growing research base on the use of gaming and robotics to address specific CT skills in students (Atmatzidou & Demetriadis, 2016), providing evidence of increased communication and collaboration skills (Ardito et al., 2014; Khanlari, 2013; Yuen et al., 2014), motivation (Webb, Repenning, & Koh, 2012), complex problem-solving skills (Akcaoglu, 2016; Akcaoglu & Koehler, 2014), abstraction (Nickerson et al., 2015), and transfer (Repenning et al., 2015).

Another important issue is how much CT skills the teachers themselves need (Repenning et al., 2015; Yadav, Mayfield, Zhou, Hambrusch, & Korb, 2014). Additionally, simply having the CT skills may not be enough; self-awareness of these skills may be necessary. While it is convenient to believe that teachers with general skills and expertise in non-computing subjects can learn just enough computing through professional development to introduce CT in their classrooms, we believe that it is crucial that teachers have first-hand experience with the affective challenges that face anyone who is learning CT.

Professional Development of CT

Rather than attempting to address all of the elements of CT in the UGICT project, an operational definition was developed based on the following precepts:

- Modeling is at the heart of CT.
- CT is not just about programming skills.
- Solutions can be generalized and transferred to other situations.
- CT is about persistence and dealing with failure.

To help teachers achieve these understandings and skills, the UGICT professional development focused around a set of modeling challenges involving both game programming and robotics, such as writing a simple version of *Pac-Man* and making a robot move in a circle with a 1 m diameter. From the computing perspective, these challenges may only be moderately difficult, requiring only sequential thinking and the basic principles of variables, alternation, and loops. However, for teachers who had little or no prior training in computing, these were daunting challenges. Additionally, teachers of different backgrounds found the challenges to be easier or more difficult, depending on those backgrounds. It was also natural for participants to find themselves working at different rates. This meant that the PD had to be very flexible.

Class Descriptions

In the first 2 years of the UGICT project, 28 participating teachers enrolled in short courses to prepare them for working with the target gaming and robotics technologies. These courses focused on software functionality and an exploration of how gaming and robotics can be used effectively to develop computational thinking skills, both in the participating teachers and in their students.

In the first year of the project, a single 8-week course was delivered, with 4 weeks dedicated to gaming and 4 weeks to robotics. In the second year, additional time allowed for the delivery of two 8-week courses, one for each technology. Due to the low population density of Wyoming, it was infeasible to have classes meet face-to-face every week. Class sessions were held synchronously online to allow for screen and file sharing, chatting, and display of instructor webcam video. Class sessions were held once a week in 2-hour blocks and were recorded.

During the gaming segment participants learned about programming using AgentSheets, AgentCubes (Repenning, 2012), Scratch, and Bootstrap authoring systems. The second segment introduced participants to building and programming with the LEGO EV3 system. Common threads of the courses included (1) modeling (meaning, data, and knowledge representation) as the heart of programming, (2) the computational thinking skills that are required to build computer games and solutions to robotics challenges, and (3) how these relate to appropriate STEM content standards.

AgentSheets is a visual programming environment that can be used to create 2D games and simulations. The playing field, called a *worksheet*, is comprised of a 2D array of cells, each of the same size, e.g., 32 × 32 pixels. Each cell can house one or more *agents*, which may be stacked on top of each other. Agents make up all of the visual elements in the game, including the background, stationary objects like rocks, an avatar for the player to control, the antagonists, and any other game components such as robots and chairs. Programming in AgentSheets consists of choosing which agents to place in a worksheet and providing behavior via custom rules.

Computational thinking is explicit in the AgentSheets and AgentCubes programming environments through the idea of *Scalable Game Design (SGD)* (Repenning et al, 2015). An important aspect of SGD is the psychological principle of *flow*, which seeks to strike a middle ground between boredom and anxiety for students at different stages in computational thinking. This is accomplished, in part, via a sequenced curriculum with a progression of games that are increasingly difficult to build and with different computational thinking patterns (see Fig. 1). Consequently, as students progress in their technical skills, they are exposed to more challenging

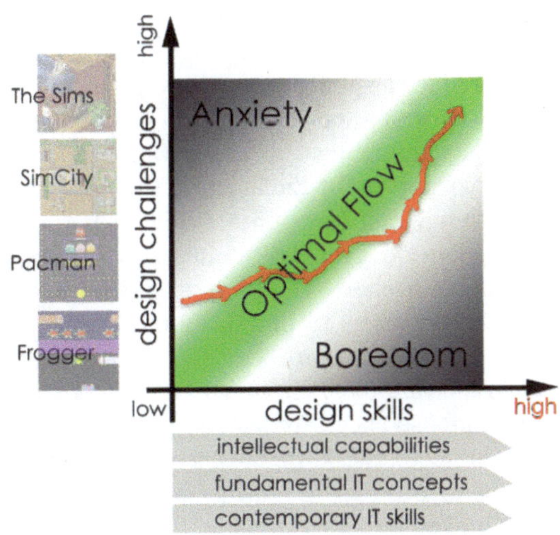

Fig. 1 Interrelationship of design challenges and anxiety in determining optimal flow (*Source*: http://www.agentsheets.com/education/scalable-game-design/index.html)

problems. In turn, as they work on more challenging problems, they learn more computational thinking patterns, helping their skills develop further. In the end, students are working on simulations, as opposed to games, but they learn that concepts such as diffusion or hill climbing that they learned in the context of computer games transfer very naturally to the context of simulations in science, public policy, or any number of different fields.

The notion of computational thinking patterns is also pedagogically important in SGD. The idea is that games and simulations are constructed using a relatively small set of patterns, such as diffusion and hill climbing which are central to the game of *Pac-Man*. In fact, programs in AgentSheets and AgentCubes can be inspected mechanically for evidence that they use these patterns, which provides an easy, automated way of measuring growth in computational thinking patterns, if not the totality of computational thinking as defined by ISTE and CSTA.

Our PD program was designed to help teachers understand how to use AgentSheets and AgentCubes and how these programs foster computational thinking. We proceeded by leading teachers through a sequence of activities that they could use directly in their after-school program, and as we did so, we discussed the CT skills and attitudes that were involved.

The very first task was to create one or more agents. In AgentSheets, the agents are 2D image files, and as mentioned previously, are of a fixed size, e.g., 32 × 32 pixels. Similarly, agents in AgentCubes are 3D models that live inside a volume of fixed size, e.g., 32 × 32 × 32 voxels. This activity was open-ended, and both instructors and participants had the opportunity to be as creative as they wished. Some chose to use minimal artwork, creating nothing more than stick figures, or to find suitable images on the Internet. Others, however, seized the opportunity to exercise their creative talents and produce, for example, magnificent 3D plants and animals. We encouraged this artistic exploration, because it gave teachers and students a chance to make their creations uniquely theirs. An important aspect of this exploration is that it gave participants the opportunity to bring in their sense of culture into their project. There is great value in having each participant produce a different game, one that is uniquely meaningful to him or her, as opposed to having all students produce an almost identical version of *Pac-Man*.

The 2D image or 3D model is only a portion of the agent. Agents can have more than one image, or *depiction*, which they can change programmatically. The other portion of the agent is the programmatic part, which is encoded as a list of behaviors. An agent's behavior is grouped into methods, which are activated upon a trigger. For example, a method may be active when the agent is asked to "move left," or it may simply be active whenever the agent "is running." A method consists of one or more rules of the form *IF some-condition-is-true THEN do-some-action*. The conditions can check the value of program variables and agent variables, check which agents are in the agent's cell or neighboring cells, and also check for user actions, such as pressing the space bar or an arrow key. The second task, then, was to add behavior to the agents, so that they would respond to arrow keys. For instance, when the user pressed the left arrow key, the agent moved left.

These first activities addressed many of the aspects of CT. In particular, participants could readily appreciate the power of abstraction. For example, agents appear to follow a corridor, but the program is simply checking that the image in the cell next to the agent is a depiction of a floor which can be transversed. Additionally, participants were able to automate solutions through algorithmic thinking, such as creating rules for controlling the movement of agents. In this case, the basics may seem obvious: If the user presses the left arrow key, then the agent moves to the adjacent left cell. However, even this simple rule is riddled with complexities, such as "What if the agent is in the leftmost cell?" or "What if the cell to the left is already occupied?" As this illustrates, before attempting the task participants needed to clearly organize their thoughts, an act which is the essence of computational thinking. Through these activities, participants also learned to appreciate the attitudes necessary for success in these activities, such as the ability to work on open-ended problems and persistence.

Persistence is probably the most important quality one needs to have when dealing with computers. Computing professionals spend more time correcting their programs than writing them. Some errors are caused by nothing more than carelessness. For example, once the rule for moving left is complete, it is easy to modify it to create a rule for moving right. In doing so, however, it is possible, and even likely, that the new rule is slightly wrong, perhaps by still moving the agent left instead of right. These errors can be painful, and almost all participants experienced the frustration of not being able to spot these trivialities immediately.

More subtle problems arose because of misunderstandings. The simplicity of AgentSheets belies a very complex execution model. For example, consider two agents close to each other. The one to the left moves right whenever the cell to the right is unoccupied, and the one to the right does the same, but moving left. Is it possible for both agents to move to an unoccupied cell at the same time? This depends, of course, on the order in which the tests and movement of the agents take place. In other words, this depends on the way that AgentSheets implements the agent behavior, and these details are deliberately hidden from the programmer. It is, after all, what makes AgentSheets simple.

Normally, this does not present a problem, because however AgentSheets chooses to implement the agents' behavior will not materially affect the outcome of the game. In those cases where it does make a difference however, it is important to determine exactly what will happen, and the only way to know is through experimentation. The designing of good experiments, which is to say small programs, requires more aspects of computational thinking. In particular, it requires participants to formulate problems in ways that enable the use of computers, and logically organize and analyze data.

Once the participants understood the basics of AgentSheets, they could begin to create playable games. So for the next activity, we asked the participants to consider what makes an arcade-style game. The main components were quickly identified, such as an avatar, one or more dangers, one or more goals, and one or more antagonists. The first project was the game of *Frogger*, with the frog as the protagonist, trucks and water as antagonists, and the grotto across the river as the goal.

To ease into this complex game, the participants first developed a simple game in which a protagonist moved according to user inputs, and one or more antagonists moved at random. Participants were given no further instructions, so had to be creative in choosing the game's setting, characters and rules.

There was no single right solution to this activity, and many participants found this freedom of choice unsettling. They received more detailed instructions for the next activity, however, which was to recreate a small version of *Frogger*. Participants were surprised to discover that no new skills were required to build *Frogger*. The only differences were in scale and complexity, in that there were many more agents in the game of *Frogger*.

The final project that participants were asked to build was a small version of *Pac-Man*. The primary difference between *Pac-Man* and the first activity they engaged in is the behavior of the ghosts. Whereas in the first activity the antagonists moved at random, in *Pac-Man* the ghosts *appear* to follow the avatar. We emphasize the word "appear," because the ghosts are actually following a much simpler rule. Again, this was used to build another connection to computational thinking, namely, formulating problems in a way that enables the use of computers and representing data through abstractions.

The way in which the ghosts appear to chase *Pac-Man* is quite clever, and we openly shared this solution with the participants. The protagonist, *Pac-Man*, is a source of "heat," so the cell in which *Pac-Man* resides is very hot. Heat flows from hotter cells to the neighboring cells in a process called *diffusion*, which SGD counts as one of the basic computational thinking patterns. The ghosts can sense the temperature of their cell and the surrounding cells, and they move toward the hottest neighboring cell, breaking ties at random. This process is called *hill climbing*, and it is another of the basic computational thinking patterns.

The combination of diffusion and hill climbing creates the illusion that the ghosts are chasing *Pac-Man*, but in reality each process is a simple mathematical rule that looks only at the value of "temperature" in neighboring cells. This last example emphasizes the importance of abstraction in computational thinking. The entire concept of "temperature" flowing from *Pac-Man* to its surroundings is a fable born of abstraction. The more mundane reality is strictly about cell values and averages. However, it is the essence of computation that seemingly complex behaviors – such as ghosts chasing *Pac-Man* – are the product of simple rules. This is the last lesson that participants gained from game programming, and it is an important one.

After learning how to build games with AgentSheets and AgentCubes, participants switched to robotics with the LEGO EV3 system. Programming the EV3 is quite different than game programming with the SGD platform. EV3 programs are constructed by dragging and connecting LEGO-style bricks on the screen. Each brick corresponds to a programming concept, such as an IF-statement or a loop, and the connections between the blocks specify the order in which blocks are executed. Blocks can have different parameters, such as the amount of power for a specific motor, and parameters may be filled in directly (e.g., 50%) or taken from another block by connecting the two with a wire. Despite the LEGO-style interface, programming the EV3 is a lot closer to traditional programming than the SGD platform, because the blocks and wires correspond very naturally to programming language constructs, such as control statements and variables. Moreover, the execution of an EV3 program is mostly sequential, so that students can think of "which block is currently executing," much as programmers in Python or another traditional language think of "which line is currently executing." This stands in contrast to AgentSheets and AgentCubes, where each agent is executing its own program at the same time as all other agents, and as mentioned previously, this can lead to subtle timing interactions between agents.

There is, of course, another fundamental difference between game programming with SGD and robotics programming with the EV3. Robotics programming includes a physical component, which is the EV3 robot, its sensors, and the motors that communicate with the outside world. This creates an opportunity to emphasize a computational thinking principle, namely, that programs are *models* of certain aspects of a world. The world could be completely virtual, as in a game, where the laws of physics may be substantially different than in our own. Or it may be our world, in which case the model needs to capture enough of the real world to be useful. For instance, in robotics, the model may need to take into account the friction between the robot's wheels and the ground.

The first robotics activity was intended to familiarize the participants with the EV3 "brick" robot, its motors, and sensors. Participants started with the most common sensors, including the color and ultrasound sensors, which can be used to follow a road and stop when approaching an obstacle. They also learned about the touch sensor, which is commonly used as a button or to confirm contact with a fixed object. Participants also learned about the buttons on the EV3 brick and how it can be connected with a computer running the EV3 software, so they could download simple programs to the robot. They were then given a simple task to build a robot with a single motor and a rotation indicator. Building the robot was the focus of this task, which was intended to help participants become comfortable with the physical materials.

Once this first task was complete, participants were asked to become familiar with the EV3 programming environment. In particular, they learned about the different (virtual) blocks in the environment and how they interact with the input (sensors) and output (motors) of the EV3 brick. They also learned the more abstract blocks that correspond to programming concepts, such as wait, loops, conditionals, and variables. The activities then turned to debugging programs. This process is complicated in robotics, because the programming takes place on the EV3 environment, but the program is run in the actual EV3 brick. So when participants wrote a program (by placing and connecting virtual LEGO blocks on the screen), they had to imagine what the robot would do. Later, when they ran the program, they observed what the robot actually did, and from those observations had to infer what went wrong and make adjustments to the program.

Next, we gave the participants a program that drives the robot around a square. However, the program intentionally contained four bugs, which the participants were asked to find. Some of these bugs were subtle, and participants were unlikely to find them without actually running the program and observing what the robot did. For example, one of the bugs was that the robot turned right but said "left" as it did so. The purpose of this exercise was twofold. First, it exposed participants to the unique challenges of debugging programs that run on a real-world robot. Second, it reinforced the idea that debugging is a natural part of the programming process and one that should not make them feel embarrassed or inadequate.

When participants engaged in a brute-force approach to the program/observe/modify cycle, they learned very little computational thinking. For example, suppose there is a goal to move the robot by 20 cm, and the programmer commands the motors to turn for 10 seconds. When the program is run the robot moves 21 cm, so the programmer changes the time to 9 s, which is not quite enough. By repeating this process, the programmer can eventually find the time required to move 20 cm, but with no full understanding of how the motor run time is related to the distance the robot travels.

A more nuanced approach is steeped in computational thinking. Instead of running the program once and seeing how far the robot moves, participants were encouraged to run the program multiple times with the same settings and record their observations. Surprisingly, the robot did not move the exact same distance each time. What participants then recognized is that the real world includes some variability; for example, as the robot moved along a carpet, it experienced different drag due to loose strands in the material. By taking multiple observations, they could find the average distance traveled for a given time, and from this table of facts, they could infer the exact time required to move exactly 20 cm. All of this reinforced the idea that the program is really modeling an aspect of the real world. Moreover, the simplistic model that is suggested by measuring the circumference of the wheels ignores the interaction between the wheels and the ground, so only works in ideal circumstances – what physicists refer to as "rolling without slipping."

Assessment of Teacher CT Attitudes and Practices

A pre-post survey of attitudes toward CT, modified from Yadav, Zhou, Mayfield, Hambrusch, and Korb (2011), was administered to each cohort of participating teachers. Twenty-one items presented statements about CT and CS in five key areas, to which participants responded on a four-point strongly agree/disagree Likert scale with no neutral option (see Fig. 2). These areas include understanding CT, self-efficacy, intrinsic motivation, integration of CT in classroom practice, and career relevance of CT.

Statement	**SA**	**Agree**	**Disagree**	**SD**
Computational thinking involves using computers to solve problems.				
Computational thinking can be incorporated in the classroom by allowing students to problem solve.				

Fig. 2 Sample CT/CS survey items

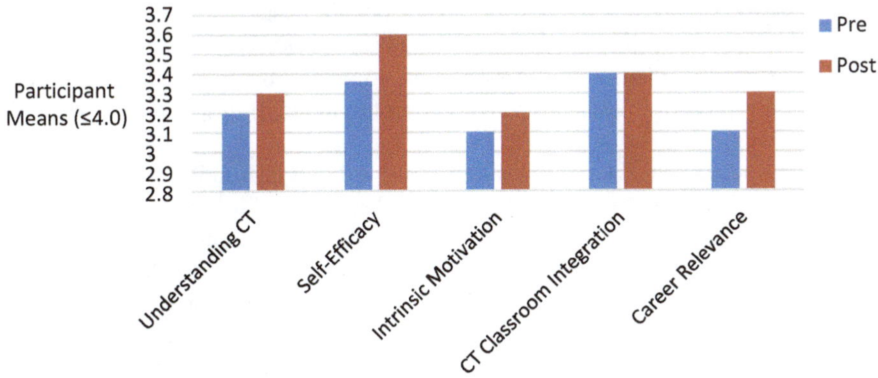

Fig. 3 Changes in teacher CT understanding and attitudes

The first year cohort consisted of twelve teachers, so analyses of survey results were not conducted for statistical significance. Descriptive data from the first cohort of twelve teacher participants revealed that attitudes and dispositions toward CT were positive and remained relatively stable in all five areas (see Fig. 3).

While participating in the PD classes, teachers demonstrated evidence of their own computational thinking. For instance, one challenge the participants faced was that of programming a robot to drive in the shape of an equilateral triangle, stopping as close as possible to the start point. The robot construction guide was simplified for quick assembly, using as few pieces as possible, including the use of a non-turning rear wheel. The participants soon discovered that the robot design was not adequate for what they needed to accomplish, both in terms of robot stability and maneuverability. One teacher noted, "The drag on the back of the robot would cause the robot to go off track and course. The attachments to the wheels are not tight so that impacted it as well." To solve this, some of the participants replaced the wheel with a ball bearing. Another suggested, "You could also make a swivel wheel with the NXT kit that doesn't have the ball."

Site visits were also made to conduct observations of teacher practices during club sessions. From these observations, patterns of teacher behaviors emerged that appeared to either facilitate or inhibit student success and CT development. Some teachers, out of a desire to let students have maximum freedom to create and explore, provided little direct instruction and left learning activities unstructured. These teachers were mostly confronted with frustrated and unsuccessful students. One middle school teacher, for instance, allowed students to work individually or in groups on their unique robotics projects. No instruction on the use of programming solutions or strategies was provided. As a result, students primarily used trial and error to address problems. A student working by himself had built a robot that was meant to drive forward and knock objects out of the way with a rotating arm. The student repeatedly set the robot on the floor aimed at a specific object and activated the program. Most of the tests resulted in the robot missing the object, as the rotating arm would randomly change the robot's path. The student's solution was to move the object closer to maximize the likelihood of contact. The student persevered for the entire session, but was frustrated with his lack of success. It was later learned that he had not considered the use of sensors to detect the object and had limited programming expertise. Thus, his robot was programmed to simply drive forward in a straight line.

The most successful teachers provided a mix of direct instruction and open-ended exploration. These successful teachers were observed scaffolding student knowledge of computational thinking through the use of specific tutorial lessons. This often took the form of teaching a specific skill or concept at the beginning of a session. All of the teams would then be asked to create a simple program that would then incorporate the skill or concept and then create a larger project. Students in one club learned how to use a sound block to create a single tone on the music scale and then string together four or five tones to play the beginning of a familiar tune. Teams were then challenged to program their robots to move rhythmically or "dance" while playing a full tune of their choice. One team successfully tackled the challenge of programming the entire melody of "The Star-Spangled Banner."

For gaming, many successful teachers used *Frogger* tutorials as a starting point for their students. This allowed students to learn the functions of the software and game design processes, including debugging, in a structured setting, with increasing level of difficulty. Some teachers then asked students to use the *Pac-Man* tutorials, while others asked students to create original maze games based on the same premise.

Regardless of the teaching approach, most of the teachers were observed providing encouragement and problem-solving hints and tips, while asking probing questions to develop and extend computational thinking skills. These typically took the form of "what if you were to," "how would you," and "have you considered" probes. To develop problem-solving skills, teachers stated that they also promote the use of other strategies, including drawing solutions, discussing alternative solutions as teams, and relating challenges to more familiar circumstances. One teacher said that she tells her students, "Failure is a learning opportunity, not an end." Another told her students to "work backward when you encounter a roadblock – see where the problem is." Through this, she was trying to teach her students the concept of "resilience."

Conclusion

We learned much from our observations. Probably the most important and hopeful realization we made is that promoting computational thinking requires many skills and that teachers already have most of them. Dealing with complexity, having perseverance, and accepting open-ended problems are important skills in the computational thinking context, but this is not the only context in which these attitudes are useful. Teachers are already consciously helping these students to develop these skills, and where they need help is in placing these skills in the context of computational thinking.

Another observation we made regards the difference between computational and technology skills. As a general rule, both students and teachers tended to be well versed in technology. At the risk of overgeneralizing, we can also add that most students tend to be more comfortable with technology than most teachers. This can create an obstacle, as some teachers question whether they can teach their students about computing at all. This fear, however, may stem from confusion between computational thinking and knowing about technology. As we have seen, computational thinking is a rich mixture of cognitive skills and attitudes, whereas knowing about technology simply entails extensive time with the latest devices. What many students and teachers fail to realize is that becoming an expert in playing video games does not translate into expertise in programming, whether game programming, robotics programming, or any other form. Familiarity with technology is helpful, for example, in understanding about files, printers, or creating images, but it does not lead directly into computational thinking.

We also found that classrooms that were focused on questions, as opposed to answers, were more effective in fostering computational thinking. For instance, when a student is failing at solving a problem, such as having a robot move in a straight line for a specific distance, the teacher can respond either by suggesting a solution or by asking an appropriate question. In this particular case, a teacher may respond by showing the student how to change the block that controls the motors, or she may ask the student how far he thinks the robot will go if the wheels turn ten times. This type of inquiry leads to deeper insights and to the discipline at the heart of computational thinking. Providing teachers with good questions to ask will better prepare them to help their students to learn computational thinking, not just to solve the computing problem at hand.

We also identified some deficiencies of the program, which should lead to changes in future iterations. The PD class we offered teachers was only 8 weeks. This was barely enough time to familiarize the teachers with the projects and activities that they could share with their students in their after-school programs. Teachers were asked to perform significant computing tasks, and not all could afford the commitment of time required to finish these tasks. Consequently, many teachers were still uncertain about their own abilities in computational thinking, and that led to significant stress as they engaged with their own students. Moreover, the short time did not allow the teachers to delve deeply into the question of methods for imparting computational thinking to their own students. Both of these issues can be addressed by lengthening the PD.

Despite these limitations, the data already collected suggests that these after-school programs do work in enhancing students' computational thinking skills. Moreover, teachers who are sufficiently confident in their own skills to let students work independently – as opposed to blindly following instructions – are the most effective. Further support to increase teachers' comfort with computing and the pedagogy of computational thinking will lead to improved success.

Acknowledgments This material is based upon work supported by the National Science Foundation (DRL #1311810). Any opinions, findings, conclusions, or recommendations expressed in this material are those of the authors and do not necessarily reflect the views of the National Science Foundation.

References

Akcaoglu, M. (2016). Design and implementation of the Game-Design and Learning program. *TechTrends, 60*(2), 114–123. doi:10.1007/s11528-016-0022-y.

Akcaoglu, M., & Koehler, M. J. (2014). Cognitive outcomes from the Game-Design and Learning (GDL) after-school program. *Computers & Education, 75*, 72–81. doi:10.1016/j.compedu.2014.02.003.

Ardito, G., Mosley, P., & Scollins, L. (2014). WE, ROBOT: Using robotics to promote collaborative and mathematics learning in a middle school classroom. *Middle Grades Research Journal, 9*(3), 73–88.

Atmatzidou, S., & Demetriadis, S. (2016). Advancing students' computational thinking skills through educational robotics: A study on age and gender relevant differences. *Robotics and Autonomous Systems, 75*(Part B), 661–670. doi:10.1016/j.robot.2015.10.008.

Barr, D., Harrison, J., & Conery, L. (2011). Computational thinking: a digital age skill for everyone: the National Science Foundation has assembled a group of thought leaders to bring the concepts of computational thinking to the K-12 classroom. *Learning & Leading with Technology, 38*(6), 20.

Barr, V., & Stephenson, C. (2011). Bringing computational thinking to K-12: what is Involved and what is the role of the computer science education community? *ACM Inroads, 2*(1), 48. doi:10.1145/1929887.1929905.

Bers, M. U., Flannery, L., Kazakoff, E. R., & Sullivan, A. (2014). Computational thinking and tinkering: Exploration of an early childhood robotics curriculum. *Computers & Education, 72*, 145–157. doi:10.1016/j.compedu.2013.10.020.

Burke, Q., O'Byrne, W. I., & Kafai, Y. B. (2016). Computational Participation. *Journal of Adolescent & Adult Literacy, 59*(4), 371–375. doi:10.1002/jaal.496.

Denner, J., Werner, L., & Ortiz, E. (2012). Computer games created by middle school girls: Can they be used to measure understanding of computer science concepts? *Computers & Education, 58*(1), 240–249. doi:10.1016/j.compedu.2011.08.006.

Dewey, J. (1916). *Democracy and education: an introduction to the philosophy of education*. New York: Macmillan.

Dewey, J. (1958). *Experience and Nature* (Vol. 1st ser, 2nd ed.). La Salle, IL: Open Court Publishing Company.

Educational Policies Commission. (1961). *The Central Purpose of American Education* (p. 27). Washington, D.C: National Education Association. Retrieved from http://eric.ed.gov/?id=ED029836.

Grover, S., & Pea, R. (2013). Computational thinking in K-12: A Review of the state of the field. *Educational Researcher, 42*(1), 38–43. doi:10.3102/0013189X12463051.

Honeyford, M. A., & Boyd, K. (2015). Learning through play: portraits, photoshop, and visual literacy practices. *Journal of Adolescent & Adult Literacy, 59*(1), 63–73. doi:10.1002/jaal.428.

Kafai, Y. (1995). *Minds in Play: Computer Game Design As a Context for Children's Learning*. Hillsdale, NJ: L. Erlbaum Associates Inc..

Kafai, Y. (1996). Software by kids for kids. *Communications of the ACM, 39*(4), 38.

Kafai, Y. (2006). Playing and making games for learning: instructionist and constructionist perspectives for game studies. *Games and Culture, 1*(1), 36–40. doi:10.1177/1555412005281767.

Kafai, Y., & Burke, Q. (2013). Computer programming goes back to school: Learning programming introduces students to solving problems, designing applications, and making connections online. *Phi Delta Kappan, 95*(1), 61–65.

Khanlari, A. (2013). Effects of robotics on 21st Century Skills. *European Scientific Journal, 9*(27.) Retrieved from http://search.proquest.com.libproxy.uwyo.edu/docview/1524821792/abstract/E91502C4C03E4CCEPQ/1.

Lave, J., & Wenger, E. (1991). *Situated Learning: Legitimate Peripheral Participation (Learning in Doing: Social, Cognitive and Computational Perspectives)*. Cambridge, UK: Cambridge University Press.

Li, Q. (2010). Digital game building: learning in a participatory culture. *Educational Research, 52*(4), 427–443. doi:10.1080/00131881.2010.524752.

National Research Council. (2011). *Committee for the Workshops on Computational Thinking: Report of a Workshop on the Pedagogical Aspects of Computational Thinking*. Washington, DC: National Academies Press.

Nickerson, H., Brand, C., & Repenning, A. (2015). *Grounding Computational Thinking Skill Acquisition Through Contextualized Instruction* (pp. 207–216). Proceedings of the eleventh annual *International Conference on International Computing Education Research*. Omaha, NE: ACM Press. doi:10.1145/2787622.2787720.

Papert, S. (1980). *Mindstorms: Children, Computers, and Powerful Ideas*. New York: Basic Books.

Papert, S., & Harel, I. (1991). Situating Constructionism. In *Constructionism* (pp. 1–11). Norwood, NJ: Ablex Publishing Corporation. Retrieved from http://www.papert.org/articles/SituatingConstructionism.html.

Piaget, J., & Inhelder, B. (1969). *The Psychology of the Child*. New York: Basic Books.

Repenning, A. (2012). Programming goes back to school. *Communications of the ACM, 55*(5), 38. doi:10.1145/2160718.2160729.

Repenning, A., Webb, D. C., Koh, K. H., Nickerson, H., Miller, S. B., Brand, C., et al. (2015). Scalable game design: a strategy to bring systemic computer science education to schools through game design and simulation creation. *ACM Transactions on Computing Education (TOCE), 15*(2), 1–31. doi:10.1145/2700517.

Salomon, G., & Perkins, D. N. (1998). Individual and social aspects of learning. *Review of Research in Education, 23*, 1–24. doi:10.2307/1167286.

Uchida, D., Cetron, M., & McKenzie, F. (1996). *Preparing-Students-for-the-21st-Century*. Lanham, MD: Rowman & Littlefield Education. Retrieved from https://rowman.com/ISBN/9781578860470/Preparing-Students-for-the-21st-Century.

Vygotskiĭ, L. S., & Cole, M. (1978). *Mind in Society: the Development of Higher Psychological Processes*. Cambridge: Harvard University Press.

Webb, D. C., Repenning, A., & Koh, K. H. (2012). Toward an emergent theory of broadening participation in computer science education. In *Proceedings of the 43rd ACM technical symposium on Computer Science Education* (pp. 173–178). ACM. Retrieved from http://dl.acm.org.libproxy.uwyo.edu/citation.cfm?id=2157191.

Wing, J. (2006). Computational thinking. *Communications of the ACM, 49*(3), 33–35.

Yadav, A., Mayfield, C., Zhou, N., Hambrusch, S., & Korb, J. T. (2014). Computational thinking in elementary and secondary teacher education. *Transactions on Computing Education, 14*(1), 5:1–5:16. doi:10.1145/2576872.

Yadav, A., Zhou, N., Mayfield, C., Hambrusch, S., & Korb, J. T. (2011). Introducing computational thinking in education courses. In *Proceedings of the 42Nd ACM Technical Symposium on Computer Science Education* (pp. 465–470). New York, NY, USA: ACM. doi:10.1145/1953163.1953297.

Yuen, T. T., Boecking, M., Stone, J., Tiger, E. P., Gomez, A., Guillen, A., & Arreguin, A. (2014). Group tasks, activities, dynamics, and interactions in collaborative robotics projects with elementary and middle school children. *Journal of STEM Education: Innovations and Research, 15*(1), 39.

Computational Thinking in Teacher Education

Aman Yadav, Sarah Gretter, Jon Good, and Tamika McLean

Abstract Computational thinking (CT) has been offered as a cross-disciplinary set of mental skills that are drawn from the discipline of computer science. Existing literature supports the inclusion of CT within the K-12 curriculum, within multiple subjects, and from primary grades upward. The use of computers as a context for CT skills is often possible, yet care must be taken to ensure that CT is not conflated with programming or instructional technology, in general. Research had suggested that instructing preservice teachers in the use of CT can help them develop a more accurate and nuanced understandings of how it can be applied to the classroom. This chapter reports results from a study about preservice teachers' conceptions of CT and how it can be implemented within their classrooms. Results suggested that preservice teachers with no previous exposure to CT have a surface level understanding of computational thinking. Participants largely defined CT in terms of problem-solving, logical thinking, and other types of thinking and often requiring the use of computers. The chapter offers implications for teacher educators to embed computational thinking in preservice education courses through educational technology as well as content specific methods courses.

Keywords Computational thinking • Preservice teachers • Teacher education

Introduction

Recently, computational thinking (CT) has been advocated as a twenty-first-century skill that students should possess in order to develop problem-solving skills using principles from computer science (Selby, 2015). Wing (2006) described computational thinking as "solving problems, designing systems, and understanding human behavior, by drawing on the concepts fundamental to computer science" (p. 33).

A. Yadav (✉) • S. Gretter • J. Good • T. McLean
Michigan State University, East Lansing, MI 48824, USA
e-mail: ayadav@msu.edu; sgretter@msu.edu; goodjona@msu.edu; mcleant2@msu.edu

P.J. Rich, C.B. Hodges (eds.), *Emerging Research, Practice, and Policy on Computational Thinking*, Educational Communications and Technology: Issues and Innovations, DOI 10.1007/978-3-319-52691-1_13

Since then researchers have suggested that computational thinking involves a number of subskills, including breaking down complex problems into familiar ones (problem decomposition), developing algorithmic solutions to the problems (algorithms), and capturing the fundamental simplicity of a problem to develop quick heuristics that might lead to a solution (abstraction) (Barr & Stephenson, 2011; Grover & Pea, 2013; Wing, 2008; Yadav et al., 2014). Furthermore, given that computation is a crucial driver of innovation and productivity in today's technology-rich society (Selby, 2015), it is imperative that students engage in computing ideas at the K-12 level (CSTA & ISTE, 2011). In order for computational thinking to become part of K-12 curriculum, there is a critical need to prepare teachers who are well trained to integrate computational thinking in their everyday pedagogical activities (Lye & Koh, 2014). This chapter discusses computational thinking, its implementation in K-12 classrooms, and the role of CT in teacher education. We present results from a study that surveyed 134 preservice teachers about their views of computational thinking and their role in teaching computational thinking in K-12 classrooms. The purpose of the survey was to understand preservice teachers' perceptions of computational thinking in their specific subject areas and assess how they would implement it in their future classroom. In light of the computational thinking competencies put forth by the Computer Science Teachers Association (CSTA) and the International Society for Technology Education (ISTE), we discuss the need for training preservice teachers and provide recommendations for integrating computational thinking into teacher preparation programs.

Computational Thinking in K-12

Wing (2006) discussed that while computing ideas have traditionally been a subject of interest in computer science for decades, advances in computing technology have changed the landscape of the skills needed for a twenty-first-century economy. Wing (2008) envisioned that computational thinking would play an instrumental role in virtually every field and profession in the near future and should therefore become an integral part of children's education. It is important to note that computational thinking does not exclusively equate with computer science or with programming, but that rather, it represents key computer science practices that can be applied to a variety of problem-solving tasks. Denning (2009) argued that computational thinking has a venerable history in not only computer science but all sciences. He discussed how computational thinking has been around since the 1950s as algorithmic thinking, which means "a mental orientation to formulating problems as conversions of some input to an output and looking for algorithms to perform the conversions" (Denning, p.28). Thus, computational thinking can be considered a problem-solving toolset that goes beyond information technology (IT) fluency to apply computing principles such as abstraction, decomposition, generalization, pattern recognition, and algorithmic and parallel thinking (Astrachan, Hambrusch, Peckham, & Settle, 2009; Selby, 2015).

The Computer Science Teachers Association (CSTA) and the International Society for Technology in Education (ISTE) (2011) suggested that computational thinking offers students an opportunity to develop problem-solving and critical thinking skills by harnessing the power of computing. Developing a computational thinking mindset would allow students to create, design, and develop technologies, tools, or systems that will be instrumental in advancing any field in the future. While computational thinking does not equate to programming, becoming a computational thinker does mean understanding today's digital tools in order to solve challenges from sciences to the humanities (Bundy, 2007). Not only can computational thinking prepare students for computing jobs, it also prepares them to think outside the box and use problem-solving skills with or without the support of computers in different areas of their personal, academic, and professional lives (CSTA & ISTE, 2011; Selby, 2015). Recently, a variety of computational thinking initiatives are being implemented in K-12 classrooms to expose students to CT concepts and practices. These initiatives range from single exposure to CT through hour of code type activities to the design of whole curriculum, such as the College Board's Advanced Placement (AP) computer science principles course.

Additionally, current educational reforms and standards reflect the relevance of computational thinking for K-12 students (Gretter & Yadav, 2016). For example, the Next Generation Science Standards (NGSS) includes using computational thinking as one of the key scientific and engineering practices that students should be exposed to in K-12 science classrooms. Practices such as the use of computational tools to model complex systems through simulations and visualizing data to examine patterns provide an opportunity to introduce K-12 students to computational thinking ideas in science classrooms. While these examples showcase how to integrate computational thinking in a content area, the College Board is launching an AP CS Principles course in Fall 2016 based on six computational thinking practices (see College Board (2014) for a detailed discussion of the practices). Some organizations have also promoted computational thinking material and curricula for educational institutions. For example, Google developed a curriculum, CS First, to engage students in computer science and computational thinking concepts in after-school theme-based clubs across the country. Similarly, Code.org offers a K-12 curriculum to expose students to the world of computing and computational thinking. Lastly, many organizations have focused on introducing CT to traditionally underrepresented groups in computer science. For example, Girls Who Code, Black Girls Code, and La TechLa have created programs to reach girls and minorities and encourage them to take part in CT and CS activities.

While computational thinking has been suggested as a problem-solving approach using principles from computer science, many of the existing efforts use programming tools and environments to expose students to computational thinking. Fletcher and Lu (2009) argued that this approach might continue the misconceptions about computer science as being equivalent to "programming." Instead, they suggested, "just as proficiency in basic language arts helps us to effectively communicate and proficiency in basic math helps us to successfully quantitate, proficiency in computational thinking helps us systematically and efficiently process information and tasks"

(Fletcher & Lu, p. 23). This effort to lay foundations of CT needs to start early on in students' K-12 experience before they learn programming languages (Fletcher & Lu). Hence, we need to develop ways to embed computational thinking concepts and practices across disciplines both with and without the programming context to benefit students with varied interests.

Barr and Stephenson (2011) proposed nine core computational thinking concepts and abilities to integrate CT concepts in K-12 classrooms across core content areas. These core computational thinking ideas include data collection, data analysis, data representation, problem decomposition, abstraction, algorithms and procedures, automation, parallelization, and simulation. These computational thinking concepts can be implemented in K-12 classrooms through digital storytelling, data collection and analysis, and scientific investigations (Lee, Martin & Apone, 2014), creating games (Howland & Good, 2015; Lee et al., 2014; Nickerson, Brand, & Repenning, 2015), educational robotics (Atmatzidou & Demetriadis, 2014), physics (Dwyer, Boe, Hill, Franklin, & Harlow, 2013), visual programming languages like Scratch or other interactive media (Brennan & Resnick, 2012; Calao, Moreno-Leon, Correa, & Robles, 2015), and even through maker movements (Rode et al., 2015). While computational thinking is relatively is a new concept, Mannila et al. (2014) found that a majority of K-9 teachers from various disciplines were already practicing and implementing CT concepts and practices in their own teaching. These implementations ranged from using of data collection, analysis, and representation to algorithm design and writing (i.e., programming).

Additionally, in a review of 27 empirical studies about programming in K-12 and higher education settings, Lye & Koh (2014) reported that visual programming languages were most often used in K-12 to create digital stories and games. They found that constructionism was a common instructional strategy used by teachers, involving students to create artifacts displaying their understanding of CT concepts. Moreover, research has also exhibited that exposing students to computational thinking ideas also improves their problem-solving abilities and critical thinking skills (Akcaoglu & Koehler, 2014; Calao et al., 2015; Lishinski, Yadav, Enbody, & Good, 2016). For example, Akcaoglu & Koehler (2014) used a Scratch-based curriculum to examine the influence of CT on middle school students' problem-solving skills as measured by a PISA problem-solving test. When compared to the control group, the results suggested that students who participated in Scratch activities significantly increased their problem-solving skills, including system analysis and design, decision-making, and troubleshooting skills. In another study, Calao et al. (2015) embedded computational thinking in a sixth grade mathematics classroom. Their results suggested that the intervention significantly improved students' understanding of mathematical processes when compared to a control group that did not learn about computational thinking ideas in their math class.

Taken together, these policy-related and practical initiatives strongly highlight the significance of introducing students to computational thinking in K-12 classrooms. However, preparing teachers to embed these concepts in their teaching or in their specific subject areas can be a daunting task. Barr and Stephenson (2011) highlighted that a systematic change regarding CT implementation in school could not be accomplished without educational policies that include teacher preparation to help educators understand and implement CT in their teaching. Even though most of the computational thinking initiatives we describe in this chapter underline the necessity to train teachers in all subject areas to embed CT, little has been done to examine the instructional, curricular, and pedagogical implications for teacher preparation, particularly for preservice teachers (Lye & Koh, 2014).

Preparing Teachers for Computational Thinking Instruction

There is an increasing need for teachers to be prepared to integrate CT into their classroom practices (Prieto-Rodriguez & Berretta, 2014). Recent efforts to expose teachers to computational thinking have focused on both preservice teachers through modules in existing teacher education courses (Yadav et al., 2014) as well as in-service teachers through professional development (Prieto-Rodriguez & Berretta, 2014). At the in-service level, a majority of the work has involved working with teachers through short professional development opportunities to embed computational thinking. Blum and Cortina (2007) examined how a weekend-long workshop to introduce teachers to computational thinking and the role of computer science in relation to other disciplines influenced their perceptions of computer science (CS). Results from the study suggested that teachers' perceptions of computer science significantly changed from being focused on CS as programming to viewing CS as being applicable to other disciplines. Teachers reported that they not only changed their ideas about computer science but the workshop also allowed them to present CS in a way that would make it relevant to their students' day-to-day lives. Similarly, in another study Prieto-Rodriguez and Berretta (2014) focused on in-service teachers' thinking about the nature of computer science and whether teachers' perceptions about computer science change after a workshop. Findings suggested that connecting teachers to the skills and resources needed to teach computer science and computational thinking concepts can have a positive impact on their perceptions of computer science.

While there has been a considerable focus on professional development for in-service teachers, there is limited work on how to prepare preservice teachers to embed computational thinking in their future classrooms. In one study, Yadav et al. (2014) introduced preservice teachers to computational thinking and how to embed computational thinking in the K-12 classroom through a one-week module in an introductory educational psychology course. The authors used a quasi-experimental design to examine the effectiveness of the module on preservice teacher's definition of computational thinking and their ability to embed CT in their future classrooms. Results from the study suggested that preservice teachers who were exposed to the modules were significantly more likely to accurately define computational thinking and were also more likely to agree that computational thinking could be implemented in the classroom by allowing students to problem-solve (and not just by using computers). The results from this study are promising; however, while a one-week module might be enough to develop preservice teachers' understanding of computational thinking, it might not provide them with enough knowledge to embed computational thinking in meaningful ways. We need to consider how to expose preservice teachers to computational thinking constructs within the context of the subject area they will teach in their future classrooms. Barr & Stephenson (2011) recommended that in order for computational thinking to be part of every student's education, all preservice teacher preparation programs need to include a class on computational thinking across the disciplines. We would argue that teacher preparation programs should go beyond one class and teach computational thinking in subject matter context of methods courses. The majority of teacher education programs offer an introductory educational technology course, which could serve as a core class to introduce preservice teachers to CT ideas. The teaching methods courses could then be used to expand on preservice teachers' understanding of computational thinking within the context of their subject area and build upon that knowledge to embed CT in their future classes.

Given the calls to expand the pool of teachers who "teach" computational thinking (Cuny, 2012; Yadav et al., 2014; Yadav, Hong, & Stephenson, 2016; Gretter & Yadav, 2016), teacher preparation programs are critical and provide an opportune setting to introduce future teachers to CT. However, before being able to guide preservice teachers' implementation of CT in their future classrooms, we need to better understand how these student teachers think about CT. Specifically, we need to examine how teachers view computational thinking and its role in their classrooms given that teachers' conceptions can significantly influence and even stereotype students' views about what computer scientists do. Guzdial (2008) explained how the field of computing education research can start looking at what non-computing students—here, the training of future teachers—understand about computing in order for formal education to enhance their knowledge of computing. This study, therefore, addressed the following research questions:

1. How do preservice teachers define CT?
2. How do preservice teachers perceive the implementation of CT in their classroom?

Method

Participants

One hundred and thirty-four preservice teachers enrolled in a teacher education program at a large Midwestern university participated in the study. The majority of the participants (N = 95) were female, which is not surprising given the traditional demographics in teacher preparation programs are overwhelmingly female (Ingersoll, Merrill, & Stuckey, 2014). Participants included 41 sophomores, 55 juniors, and 29 seniors (nine participants did not report their year of schooling). The average age of participants was 20.70 years old and the average GPA was 3.34.

Measures

In order to examine preservice teachers' conceptions of computational thinking and how they would embed computational thinking in their future classrooms, we utilized an open-ended questionnaire that had previously been used by Yadav et al. (2014). The questionnaire also included demographic question that asked participants to identify gender, year in school, age, and GPA of the participants. There were two open-ended questions that asked preservice teachers to explain computational thinking based on their prior knowledge of the concept and to share how they would implement computational thinking in the content area that they planned to teach in their future classrooms.

Procedure and Data Analysis

Two hundred and three preservice teachers enrolled in a teacher education course were invited to complete the questionnaire through a web-based survey. One hundred and thirty-four preservice teachers completed the survey, resulting in a response rate of 66%, which is deemed good (Creswell, 2002). Content analysis processes were used to code the open-ended responses. The open-ended responses were imported into a qualitative analysis software (NVivo) and jointly coded by two coders. An emergent coding scheme was used to generate codes and develop an understanding of preservice teachers' conceptions of computational thinking. For example, when defining computational thinking, one preservice teacher responded, "I would have to guess that you take what you know about computers and thinking and use that knowledge on a computer." This response was coded as "using a computer." Another preservice teacher replied with "[Computational thinking means] you break down a problem and solve it in some logical way," which was coded as "problem decomposition" and "logical thinking." When a disagreement occurred about the appropriate code, the coders discussed until a consensus was reached. The initial list of codes were then collapsed into overarching themes that represented their overall understanding of computational thinking and approaches to embedding it in their classroom. Frequencies were calculated to reflect the number of participants whose responses were categorized under a particular code.

Results

The qualitative analysis of open-ended survey responses initially resulted in 51 codes, which were collapsed into two overarching themes with three sub-themes each, namely, (i) preservice teachers' definitions of computational thinking and (ii) how they would implement computational thinking in their future classrooms. The following sections discuss these broad themes in relation to our research questions.

Defining Computational Thinking

When asked to define the concept, preservice teachers in our study discussed computational thinking along a number of dimensions, such as defining it as problem-solving, logical or mathematical thinking, and using computers. We discuss these sub-themes in detail below.

Computational Thinking Involves Problem-Solving and Logical Thinking

The most prominent theme (N = 61) that emerged from preservice teachers' definition of CT was that it was problem-solving approach. For example, one participant reported that "computational thinking is a way of thinking to problem-solve." Another preservice teacher elaborated that CT was "how you can solve problems in a logical and certain way like in steps to break the problem down." Preservice teachers also described that computational thinking was problem-solving based on prior knowledge, as highlighted by one participant who stated that "computational thinking is using what you already know to logically solve problems."

Closely related to the problem-solving approach was the concept of logical thinking. A number of preservice teachers (N = 36) also brought up the idea that CT involved using logical thinking to solve problems. For example, one participant stated that CT was "thinking logically to solve problems, using step by step problem-solving, and applying skills to other situations." In a similar fashion, another participant highlighted that "It is a way of thinking very logically, like a computer, in a very systematic way."

While problem-solving and logical thinking were two types of thinking that preservice teachers most associated with computational thinking, participants also connected CT with a variety of other categories of thinking processes.

Computational Thinking Includes Various Types of Thinking

Participants in the study (N = 49) reported that computational thinking included additional ways of thinking, including mathematical thinking (N = 9), algorithmic thinking (N = 24), and computer-like thinking (N = 9). The idea of mathematical thinking was brought up as preservice teachers described that CT required "thinking about numbers and equations," "doing numerical work," and "using formulas." Preservice teachers also stated that computational thinking involved using step-by-step or systematic (i.e., algorithmic thinking) approach, which was closely related to problem-solving and logical thinking approaches discussed above. The idea of using algorithms was highlighted by the following quote from one preservice teacher: "CT is going through certain steps to arrive at a logical answer." Within this theme, participants also discussed that computational thinking involved "breaking down a problem into smaller sections and solving each in succession in a way/order that makes sense to solve the whole problem." Moreover, participants linked CT with the idea of "thinking like a computer." In some instances, preservice teachers said that CT was "a way of thinking that uses your mind like a computer," "speaking/ thinking in a computer-like way," or thinking about "how computers think." Interestingly, preservice teachers related CT not only to "thinking like a computer" but also to using a computer as a tool.

Computational Thinking Implies Using a Computer

Emerging from preservice teachers' definitions of computational thinking was the use of computers as a tool to solve problems or complete tasks (N = 24). Along these lines, participants considered computers to be an integral part of CT. For instance, they remarked that "CT is thinking in ways that require computing" or "using a computer to help you solve a problem you otherwise could not." Overall, these participants expressed that "there are many problems that are easier to solve with computers." In addition, preservice teachers believed that CT involved using computers as an instrumental tool. For example, participants agreed that computational thinking involved "knowing how to use a computer to get a task done." Similarly, one participant stated that she associated CT with "using technology to make tasks simpler," while another described that "CT entails using a computer to look up information to help you best complete your task." In general, preservice teachers who integrated computers in their definitions of CT saw computers as a resource or "a means of research and data collection, a means of interpretation, a means of convenience and ease."

In the next section, we move from theoretical conceptions of CT to practical applications, as we look at how preservice teachers envisioned implementing CT in their future classrooms.

Implementing Computational Thinking in the Classroom

Preservice teachers reported that computational thinking could be implemented in a number of ways, such as using technology in the classroom, embedding CT in core content areas or implementing CT ideas through problem-solving. The present section discusses preservice teachers' conceptions of how they would incorporate CT in their future K-12 classrooms.

Computational Thinking Can Be Embedded Through Technology

One of the prominent themes that preservice teachers brought up (N = 40) was that they would use technology to embed their conception of computational thinking in the classroom. These ideas were generic uses of technology to implement CT in the classroom, as highlighted by this comment: "I would use CT to help students have more interaction. No longer would students read a book, but they could use computers to watch video, play games and perform activities," or, as another preservice teacher stated, "I would use computer programs to help kids understand concepts better." Other general uses of technology to embed CT in the classroom included "a smartboard in my classroom," "online games," "digital media," "computer programs," "calculators," or "software," for instance. Participants added that as teachers, they would also use computers to provide students easy access to information. For example, one participant stated that "I will start a class website where students can review notes/class lectures, take practice test, and have a class message board for homework help." In practical terms, participants saw the use of technology as a way for students to practice CT concepts. This could also be achieved, according to preservice teachers, through the use of technology in a variety of classroom activities. For example, participants proposed to embed CT by having students "work on computers for some lessons that can go at their speed and hit the area they need"; "use keyboards to type words and use online sources to read, online media"; and "use the computer for many projects, papers, and assignments." Although many preservice teachers saw CT being integrated in the classroom through technology, others viewed problem-solving as a central aspect of such integration.

Computational Thinking Can Be Taught Through Problem-Solving

A number of preservice teachers (N = 45) in the study discussed that computational thinking could be embedded in the classroom by teaching students how to use steps to solve problems and that they would use problem-solving approaches to teach CT in their future classrooms. One preservice teacher stated that she would embed CT by having "students learn to problem-solve in the classroom." Another participant agreed that he would facilitate CT and "present students with problems and use them to solve them with CT" in the classroom. Participants envisioned problem-solving activities in different ways. One preservice teacher said: "I can implement computational thinking by giving students problems to solve that can be solved in multiple ways, and asking that they solve the problem is the least complicated manner." Another explained that he would "show students why working through a problem a certain way is logical, or try to explain what needs to happen in order to solve problems." Other ideas included "doing real world problems," "giving students problems to solve that can be solved in multiple ways," "assign things that can be solved by thinking in a systematic way," or "work problems that can be difficult overall but can be broken down into easier steps." Furthermore, the idea of problem-solving was also discussed alongside the use of algorithms, or step-by-step instructions. For example, one of the participants stated that she would implement computational thinking by having students "solving problems step by step, solving a problem and asking questions in sequential parts." Other participants reflected similar thoughts, describing that CT involved helping students "figure out the steps of getting the answer," teach them "what steps to go through to solve a problem," or have them "show their work and steps of how they got to the answer." Although problem-solving was perceived by preservice teachers as a general concept through which to infuse CT, they also reflected on how CT implementation would look like in their core content area.

Computational Thinking Can Be Applied in Core Content Areas

Another theme that emerged when preservice teachers were asked about computational thinking was its implementation through core content areas, such as mathematics, language arts, social studies, and science. Embedding CT through mathematics was one of the main themes that emerged in this category ($N = 24$). Specifically, preservice teachers explained that computational thinking fits with mathematics because of its problem-solving aspect. Along these lines, one participant stated, "I think CT fits well into math as they are heavily related. I would try to show students why working through a problem a certain way is logical, or try to explain what needs to happen in order to solve problems (that way they can use their own logic to solve it orderly)." Another participant expressed the same sentiment stating, "computational thinking can be implemented by having the students work together on a math problem. This will allow the students to solve the problem in a systematic and logical way." Beyond mathematics, preservice teachers also discussed ways to embed computational thinking in science as well as non-STEM disciplines, such as language arts, social studies, or arts. In these subjects, preservice teachers' conceptions of computational thinking centered around using problem decomposition, algorithms, or patterns. This view is reflected by one preservice teacher who suggested that in an English language arts classroom, students could break down stories (i.e., problem decomposition) to identify patterns (i.e., pattern recognition), in order to help them "solve crime mysteries." Similarly, another preservice teacher suggested that identifying patterns and logical thinking were very useful "especially in Spanish grammar" to understand the structure of the language. Overall, preservice teachers varied in their views of CT implementation in their future classrooms. While some saw technology as central to CT implementation, others believed that problem-solving was a key concept, or that CT was subject dependent.

Discussion

The results from the study suggest that preservice teachers' views about computational thinking encompass a broad spectrum of concepts, from simply using computers to using computational tools to solve problems. Their views also reflected the idea of computational thinking being connected to other types of thinking, such as mathematical or logical thinking. Furthermore, preservice teachers also discussed a number of ways they would implement computational thinking in their future classrooms, which aligned closely with their views of what computational thinking was. Preservice teachers commented that computational thinking could be embedded in a K-12 classroom through technology integration as well as through exercises to solve problems. When mentioned in the core content areas, mathematics was the most mentioned subject where preservice teachers saw computational thinking more easily apply.

In order to integrate computational thinking at the K-12 level, we need a multidimensional approach for a systematic change to prepare teachers to embed computational thinking. This includes preparing teachers for computational thinking competencies. Starting with preservice teachers during their teacher education program years provides the right time frame to develop their understanding of computational thinking in the context of the subject matter they will teach (Yadav et al., 2014). The results from this study suggest that preservice teachers' views about computational thinking cover a wide range of ideas and often do not align with current thinking and CT standards being proposed by national organizations such as the CSTA and ISTE. Even when preservice teachers might have an understanding about what computational thinking involves, it is important that they are provided with sufficient opportunities and time to engage in CT constructs within the context of their grade level and subject area. As the results from this study suggest, it seems that preservice teachers have grasped computational thinking ideas as being related to problem-solving and logical thinking. Participants in our study expanded on the idea of problem-solving by including sequential, step-by-step, or computer-like ways to solve problems (i.e., algorithms). While some of these ideas were consistent with computational thinking concepts, they were limited to simplified conceptions of the idea and did not showcase an in-depth understanding of what computational thinking involves.

Preservice teachers' views on approaches to embedding computational thinking in K-12 further reflected a shallow comprehension of computational thinking. The majority of participants mentioned that mathematics was a natural fit to expose students to computational thinking. Their oversimplified views of computational thinking as a problem-solving approach might have inclined them to see mathematics as a natural fit to incorporate CT in the classroom.

Preservice teachers also talked about using computers or technology to introduce computational thinking to their students. These results are consistent with the literature on this subject, which suggests that teachers' conceptions about computational thinking are not always accurate and they typically value one CT concept more than others (Good, Yadav, & Lishinski, 2016; Yadav et al., 2014). These initial conceptions about computational thinking could serve as a starting point upon which we could build and connect CT concepts to what teachers do in the classroom. For example, Mannila et al. (2014) examined how teachers perceived their own classroom activities in relation to computational thinking. The results from the survey found that teachers reported concepts related to data collection, data analysis, and data representation as the most common computational thinking idea. The teachers also reported that the use of web resources, social media, and office productivity suites as technology tools could be used to promote computational thinking in their classrooms. Similarly, preservice teachers in our study focused on problem-solving aspects of computational thinking and reported that they would use computers to embed CT in their classrooms. Given the recent conversations around computing, in general, and computational thinking as a twenty-first-century problem-solving approach (Wing, 2006; Yadav et al., 2014), it is possible that preservice teachers have encountered the idea that CT is related to computing; however, they have not formed a comprehensive understanding of computational thinking.

Implications for Educators and Researchers

Our findings that preservice teachers possess oversimplified views of computational thinking have important implications for teacher educators and provide directions for future research. With the increased focus on computer science education and efforts to introduce elementary and secondary students to computing ideas (ISTE, 2011), preparing teachers in this area has become vital. The current efforts to train teachers in computing education have mainly focused on in-service teacher professional development at the national level, such as Exploring Computer Science (ECS), Project Lead the Way (PLTW), and Code.org. However, training in-service teachers is only a temporary solution to the long-term problem of developing a pipeline of future teachers who are prepared to embed computational thinking in their classrooms. The teacher training needs to begin early on in the teacher preparation programs to allow preservice teachers to understand how computational thinking ideas are related to their content areas. Preservice teacher education can play a critical role in addressing this issue and continuously train new teachers who are ready to teach computational thinking to their students. One of the first steps in promoting computational thinking is to address the underlying misconceptions that teachers have about it (Qualls & Sherrell, 2010). Teacher educators and computer science educators need to collaborate to develop means to introduce computational thinking ideas both by establishing new pathways in computer science education and by expanding CT within current teacher preparation coursework. Introducing computational thinking through existing coursework is a promising approach, as many of the computational thinking ideas may be naturally fit into what is already covered in the courses. For example, many introductory educational psychology courses cover heuristic reasoning and algorithms as problem-solving approaches, which might be ideally suited as CT topics. Yadav et al. (2011, 2014) did exactly that as they implemented a one-week module in their required introductory educational psychology course for all preservice teachers. Another opportunity to introduce computational thinking to preservice teachers is through educational technology courses, which are offered in majority of teacher education programs (Polly, Mims, Shepherd, & Inan, 2010). In the early 2000s the US Department of Education funded teacher education programs to prepare tomorrow's teachers to use technology through its PT3 grants program. The program funded 441 projects for over 300 million dollars and resulted in many teacher education programs restructuring or developing new educational technology courses for preservice teachers, along with faculty professional development for teaching these courses (http://www2.ed.gov/programs/teachtech/). The focus of educational technology coursework has evolved from using office suites to Web 2.0 technologies over the last decade (Polly et al., 2010).

It is time for teacher educators to transform educational technology toward computing education and to structure courses to engage preservice teachers in computational thinking tools and ideas. Beyond these opportunities, teacher education faculty involved in teaching content-specific methods courses could also tie computational thinking constructs and vocabulary to teachers' day-to-day classroom activities. For example, preservice teachers could help their students acquire the skills to think about abstraction within language arts classes by using similes (i.e., showing similarities between two related things) and metaphors (i.e., implicit comparisons between unrelated things) (Barr & Stephenson, 2011). Similarly, preservice teachers in science could learn to use pattern recognition and idea formation from computational thinking when discussing data collection, analysis, and representation aspects of scientific experiments. Modeling and simulation in science classrooms provide other ways to discuss abstraction where students can choose "a way to represent an artifact, to allow it to be manipulated in useful ways" (Csizmadia et al., 2015, p. 15). In summary, it is important that teacher educators work to introduce preservice teachers to computational thinking skills where appropriate and add its vocabulary where they can (ISTE, 2011). Computational thinking concepts and capabilities developed by the Computer Science Teachers Association (CSTA) and the International Society for Technology in Education (ISTE) in their documentation provide a starting point for introducing these terms, as their documents include definitions, shared vocabulary, and examples of CT applications for each grade level (Barr, Conery, & Harrison, 2011).

Our findings have important implications for researchers and for future research. The current study used open-ended questions to examine preservice teachers' conceptions of computational thinking, and the results suggested that their understanding of CT is limited in scope. Future research should conduct an in-depth examination of how preservice teachers think of computational thinking through interviews. This would allow researchers to further probe what preservice teachers view as CT, or explore how problem-solving relates to computational thinking, for instance. Research could also examine preservice teachers' understanding of CT through vignettes that provide preservice teachers with hypothetical teaching scenarios of computational thinking in a classroom context. Vignettes provide a good context validity to measure preservice teachers' competencies in a given domain (Brovelli, Bölsterli, Rehm, & Wilhelm, 2014). In summary, in order for computational thinking ideas to be successfully implemented in classrooms across the globe, preservice teacher education has to be the focus of researchers, teacher educators, and policy makers.

Acknowledgment We would like to thank all the teachers who participated in this study. This work is supported by the National Science Foundation under grant numbers CNS-0938999 and 1502462. Any opinions, findings, and conclusions or recommendations expressed in this material are those of the author(s) and do not necessarily reflect the views of the National Science Foundation.

References

Akcaoglu, M., & Koehler, M. J. (2014). Cognitive outcomes from the Game-Design and Learning (GDL) after-school program. *Computers & Education, 75*, 72–81.

Astrachan, O., Hambrusch, S., Peckham, J., & Settle, A. (2009). The present and future of computational thinking. *ACM SIGCSE Bulletin, 41*(1), 549–550.

Atmatzidou, S., & Demetriadis, S. (2014). How to support students' computational thinking skills in educational robotics activities. In *Proceedings of 4th International Workshop Teaching Robotics, Teaching with Robotics & 5th International Conference Robotics in Education* (pp. 43–50).

Barr, D., Conery, L., & Harrison, J. (2011). Computational thinking: A digital age skill for everyone. *Learning & Leading with Technology, 38*(6), 20–23.

Barr, V., & Stephenson, C. (2011). Bringing computational thinking to K-12: What is involved and what is the role of the computer science education community? *ACM Inroads, 2*(1), 48–54.

Blum, L., & Cortina, T. J. (2007). CS4HS: An outreach program for high school CS teachers. *ACM SIGCSE Bulletin, 39*(1), 19–23.

Brennan, K., & Resnick, M. (2012). New frameworks for studying and assessing the development of computational thinking. In *Proceedings of the 2012 annual meeting of the American Educational Research Association, Vancouver, Canada.*

Brovelli, D., Bölsterli, K., Rehm, M., & Wilhelm, M. (2014). Using vignette testing to measure student science teachers' professional competencies. *American Journal of Educational Research, 2*(7), 555–558.

Bundy, A. (2007). Computational thinking is pervasive. *Journal of Scientific and Practical Computing, 1*(2), 67–69.

Calao, L. A., Moreno-León, J., Correa, H. E., & Robles, G. (2015). Developing mathematical thinking with scratch. In *Design for Teaching and Learning in a Networked World* (pp. 17–27). Cham: Springer.

College Board. (2014). AP Computer Science Principles Draft Curriculum Framework. Retrieved 26 June 2015 https://advancesinap.collegeboard.org/stem/computer-science-principles

Computer Science Teachers Association, & International Society for Technology in Education. (2011). *Computational Thinking: Leadership Toolkit* (1st ed..) Retrieved from http://www.csta.acm.org/Curriculum/sub/CurrFiles/471.11CTLeadershiptToolkit-SP-vF.pdf.

Creswell, J. W. (2002). *Educational Research: Planning, Conducting, and Evaluating Quantitative*. New Jersey, Upper Saddle River: Pearson.

Csizmadia, A., Curzon, P., Dorling, M., Humphreys, S., Ng, T., Selby, C., & Woollard, J. (2015). Computational Thinking A Guide for Teachers.

Cuny, J. (2012). Transforming high school computing: A call to action. *ACM Inroads, 3*(2), 32–36.

Denning, P. (2009). The profession of IT Beyond computational thinking. *Communications of the ACM, 52*, 28–30.

Dwyer, H., Boe, B., Hill, C., Franklin, D., & Harlow, D. (2013). Computational Thinking for Physics: Programming Models of Physics Phenomenon in Elementary School.

Fletcher, G. H., & Lu, J. J. (2009). Education human computing skills: rethinking the K-12 experience. *Communications of the ACM, 52*(2), 23–25.

Good, J., Yadav, A., & Lishinski, A. (2016). Measuring computational thinking preconceptions: analysis of a survey for pre-service teacher's' conceptions of computational thinking. In *Paper presented at Society for Information Technology and Teacher Education, Savannah, GA.*

Gretter, S., & Yadav, A. (2016). Computational thinking and media & information literacy: An integrated approach to teaching twenty-first century skills. *TechTrends, 60*, 510–516. doi:10.1007/s11528-016-0098-4.

Grover, S., & Pea, R. (2013). Computational thinking in K–12: A review of the state of the field. *Educational Researcher, 42*(1), 38–43. doi: 10.3102/0013189X12463051.

Guzdial, M. (2008). Education paving the way for computational thinking. *Communications of the ACM, 51*(8), 25–27.

Howland, K., & Good, J. (2015). Learning to communicate computationally with Flip: A bi-modal programming language for game creation. *Computers & Education, 80*, 224–240.

Ingersoll, R., Merrill, L., & Stuckey, D. (2014). Seven Trends: The Transformation of the Teaching Force. Retrieved from: http://cpre.org/sites/default/files/workingpapers/1506_7trendsapril2014.pdf

ISTE. (2011). Teacher Resources. Retrieved from https://www.iste.org/explore/articledetail?articleid=152

Lee, I., Martin, F., & Apone, K. (2014). Integrating computational thinking across the K-8 curriculum. *ACM Inroads, 5*(4), 64–71.

Lishinski, A., Yadav, A., Enbody, R., & Good, J. (2016). The influence of problem solving abilities on students' Performance on Different Assessment Tasks in CS1. In *Proceedings of the 47th ACM Technical Symposium on Computing Science Education* (pp. 329–334). New York: ACM.

Lye, S. Y., & Koh, J. H. L. (2014). Review on teaching and learning of computational thinking through programming: What is next for K-12? *Computers in Human Behavior, 41*, 51–61.

Mannila, L., Dagiene, V., Demo, B., Grgurina, N., Mirolo, C., Rolandsson, L., & Settle, A. (2014). Computational thinking in k-9 education. In *Proceedings of the Working Group Reports of the 2014 on Innovation & Technology in Computer Science Education Conference* (pp. 1–29). New York: ACM.

Nickerson, H., Brand, C., & Repenning, A. (2015). Grounding computational thinking skill acquisition through contextualized instruction. In *Proceedings of the Eleventh Annual International Conference on International Computing Education Research* (pp. 207–216). New York.

Polly, D., Mims, C., Shepherd, C. E., & Inan, F. (2010). Evidence of impact: transforming teacher education with preparing tomorrow's teachers to teach with technology (PT3) grants. *Teaching and Teacher Education, 26*(4), 863–870.

Prieto-rodriguez, E., & Berretta, R. (2014). Digital technology teachers' perceptions of computer science: It is not all about programming. In *IEEE Frontiers in Education Conference*. doi:10.1109/FIE.2014.7044134.

Qualls, J. A., & Sherrell, L. B. (2010). Why computational thinking should be integrated into the curriculum. *Journal of Computing Sciences in Colleges, 25*(5), 66–71.

Rode, J. A., Weibert, A., Marshall, A., Aal, K., von Rekowski, T., el Mimoni, H., & Booker, J. (2015). From computational thinking to computational making. In *Proceedings of the 2015 ACM International Joint Conference on Pervasive and Ubiquitous Computing* (pp. 239–250). New York: ACM.

Selby, C. C. (2015). Relationships: computational thinking, pedagogy of programming, and bloom's taxonomy. In *Proceedings of the Workshop in Primary and Secondary Computing Education on ZZZ* (pp. 80–87). New York: ACM.

Wing, J. M. (2006). Computational thinking. *Communications of the ACM, 49*(3), 33–35.

Wing, J. M. (2008). Computational thinking and thinking about computing. *Philosophical Transactions of the Royal Society of London A: Mathematical, Physical and Engineering Sciences, 366*(1881), 3717–3725.

Yadav, A., Hong, H., & Stephenson, C. (2016). Computational thinking for all: Pedagogical approaches to embedding a 21st century problem solving in K-12 classrooms. *TechTrends, 60*, 565–568. doi:10.1007/s11528-016-0087-7.

Yadav, A., Mayfield, C., Zhou, N., Hambrusch, S., & Korb, J. T. (2014). Computational thinking in elementary and secondary teacher education. *ACM Transactions on Computing Education, 14*(1), 1–16.

Yadav, A., Zhou, N., Mayfield, C., Hambrusch, S., & Korb, J. T. (2011). *Introducing Computational Thinking in Education Courses, Proceedings of ACM Special Interest Group on Computer Science Education (pp. 465–470). Dallas, TX.* doi:10.1145/1953163.1953297.

Computational Thinking Conceptions and Misconceptions: Progression of Preservice Teacher Thinking During Computer Science Lesson Planning

Olgun Sadik, Anne-Ottenbreit Leftwich, and Hamid Nadiruzzaman

Abstract This study examined 12 preservice teachers' understanding of computational thinking while planning and implementing a computational thinking activity for fifth grade students. The preservice teachers were enrolled in an add-on computer education license that would certify them to teach computer courses in addition to their primary major area (11 elementary education majors, 1 secondary social studies education major). The preservice teachers were asked to develop a 2 h instructional project for fifth grade students to build on the computational thinking concepts learned during the "Hour of Code" activity. Data was collected from preservice teachers' initial proposals, two blog posts, video recordings of in-class discussions, instructional materials, final papers, and a long-term blog post 3 months after the intervention. Results showcased that the process of developing and implementing computational thinking instruction influenced preservice teachers' understanding of computational thinking. The preservice teachers were able to provide basic definitions of computational thinking as a problem-solving strategy and emphasized that learning computational thinking does not require a computer. On the other hand, some preservice teachers had misconceptions about computational thinking, such as defining computational thinking as equal to algorithm design and suggesting trial and error as an approach to computational problem solving. We provide recommendations for teacher educators to use more directed activities to counteract potential misconceptions about computational thinking.

Keywords Algorithms • Computational thinking • Computer science education • Misconception • Problem solving

O. Sadik (✉) • A.-O. Leftwich • H. Nadiruzzaman
Indiana University, Bloomington, IN 47405, USA
e-mail: olsadik@indiana.edu; left@indiana.edu; hnadiruz@indiana.edu

P.J. Rich, C.B. Hodges (eds.), *Emerging Research, Practice, and Policy on Computational Thinking*, Educational Communications and Technology: Issues and Innovations, DOI 10.1007/978-3-319-52691-1_14

Introduction

Computers are a ubiquitous part of our society. To further the use and innovation surrounding computer science as it is used in our society, we need to prepare more computer scientists (Emmott & Rison, 2005). In fact, studies have shown that 50% of the jobs needed in the future are computer science related (Code.org, 2016). In President Obama's 2016 State of the Union Address, he placed emphasis on the importance of computer science education when he proposed a new initiative, "Computer Science for All," which focuses on providing students of all ages with access to quality CS education to improve their computational thinking skills for our increasingly computer-focused society (Smith, 2016). Many have acknowledged that this initiative is a milestone for computer science education and computational thinking movement in US K-12 education (Department of Education, 2016).

The Computer Science for All initiative emphasizes the need for more research on defining what computational thinking is, curriculum needs, how it could be integrated into the current education system, and how to prepare teachers for these major changes at the preservice and in-service levels (Smith, 2016). Our research study focuses on the teacher side of those needs and examines how a group of preservice teachers' understanding of computational thinking evolved after developing and implementing a computational thinking instructional project in an elementary school.

Computational Thinking

Papert and Harel (1991) were the first who coined the term "computational thinking" in their 1991 paper on constructionism. They proposed that computational thinking was a shift on students' thinking by contributing to their mental growth and become producers of knowledge using computing. Computational thinking received broader recognition from Wing (2006) who suggested that computational thinking was a critical twenty-first-century skill comparable to reading or math. Wing described computational thinking as "the thought processes involved in formulating a problem and expressing its solution in a way that a computer—human or machine—can effectively carry out" (p. 33). In other words, computational thinking can prompt critical thinking and problem-solving skills (DeSchryver & Yadav, 2015). Computational thinking can be applied to solve problems that extend beyond computer science (Li & Wang, 2012). Since 2006, the professional and academic computer science communities have attempted to define computational thinking, as well as detail where and how it could be applied. Two organizations involved in supporting computer science education are the Computer Science Teachers Association (CSTA) and International Society for Technology in Education (ISTE). In collaboration with educators and scholars, ISTE and CSTA (Computer Science Teachers Association CSTA, 2011) together provided an operational definition of computational thinking and emphasized computational thinking as a process of formulating and solving problems. Both organizations highlighted the importance of computational thinking as a skill necessary for all students, highlighting that computational thinking was "a problem-solving tool for every classroom" (Phillips, 2009, p. 1). We have summarized computational thinking key tenets as described from a wide range of scholars into six categories: problem solving, decomposition, pattern recognition, abstraction, algorithms, and evaluation.

In most of these aforementioned studies, the researchers have suggested these as potential, but not necessarily required, characteristics to understand and achieve computational thinking skills. Voogt, Fisser, Good, Mishra, and Yadav (2015) suggested that although these characteristics are helpful, they are by no means definitive in defining computational thinking:

> Understanding a concept does not require developing a series of necessary and sufficient conditions that need to be met. In contrast we seek to develop a more graded notion of categories with an emphasis on the possible rather than the necessary. (p. 719)

Therefore, in our study, we do not limit our own definition of computational thinking to these six characteristics as definitive conditions. However, they helped us conceptualize and identify examples of computational thinking in our participants' statements and artifacts.

Computational Thinking in K12

According to Jonassen (2000), problem solving is the most important cognitive activity that we perform in everyday and professional contexts. He suggested that problem solving could be as simple as how to tie a shoelace or as complex as how to extract protein without lipid contamination. In both situations, we follow a set of specific guidelines, which lead to desirable outcomes. Students in various settings encounter experiences that require problem-solving skills (Hmelo-Silver, 2004). One example of a more specific approach to problem solving can be computational thinking. Many scholars have argued for the inclusion of computational thinking in the K-12 curriculum (Barr & Stephenson, 2011; Lee et al., 2011; Lu & Fletcher, 2009; Sanford & Naidu, 2016; Wing, 2006; Yadav et al., 2014;). For example, Lu and Fletcher (2009) proposed that "teaching students computational thinking early and often..." (p. 261) should be consistently embedded in K-12 teaching activities in order to develop critical thinking and problem-solving skills. Other researchers and educators (Barr & Stephenson, 2011; Lee et al., 2011; Qualls & Sherrell, 2010; Sanford & Naidu, 2016; Yadav et al., 2014) have also provided similar recommendations.

There have been numerous studies at the postsecondary level to examine the affordances of teaching computational thinking in a variety of contexts (Chao, 2016; Cortina, 2007; Li & Wang, 2012; Qin, 2009). For example, in an undergraduate information communication program, 158 students from three classes were introduced to computational thinking during a C++ programming course (Chao, 2016).

In this study, Chao found out that programming could prompt students' problem solving "by iteratively formulating diverse programming strategies in a visualized and constructive way" (p. 212). In a different study, Qin (2009) found that 39 students in an undergraduate bioinformatics class were able to use computational thinking abstraction and pattern recognition strategies to solve problems and improve their conceptual understanding of a biology topic. In both of these studies, it is evident that computational thinking could be embedded as part of multiple postsecondary education courses to help future professionals advance their problem-solving skills.

Scholars have suggested that computational thinking can play an important role in the K-12 curriculum (Barr & Stephenson, 2011), suggesting that computational thinking be integrated into other core areas like reading, writing, and mathematics (Sanford & Naidu, 2016). Studies have shown that when computational thinking is integrated into K-12 classrooms, students tend to become motivated from being passive consumers of technology to active contributors, thereby fostering creativity (Voogt et al., 2015). For example, for a high school history class, a student can create an infographic timeline to portray the cause and effect of the Civil War utilizing decomposition and pattern recognition. The infographic creation process itself is an example of an algorithm progression.

Bers, Flannery, Kazakoff, and Sullivan (2014) conducted a study on 53 kindergarten students employing the "TangibleK" curriculum. TangibleK is a developmentally appropriate technology education curriculum focusing on early childhood robotics and a "learn by doing" approach to programming (Bers et al., 2014). Bers and colleagues found that these young children were intrigued by each other's work, negotiated their ideas to work collaboratively, and were engaged in problem-solving activities. They found that the young children learned computer science, robotics, and computational thinking skills from the TangibleK curriculum. In another study, Lee et al. (2012) used a game play concept to teach 10–15-year-old children computational thinking skills without introducing traditional programming. They designed a system, CTArchade, based on tic-tac-toe and assessed 18 children's conceptual understanding of computational thinking as measured by decomposition, pattern recognition, abstraction, and problem solving or algorithms. The results implied that children were able to articulate more about algorithmic thinking and showed interest in game play after being introduced to the CTArchade system. Both of these studies suggested that benefits of integrating computational thinking into K-12 settings might include dissecting tasks, looking at general patterns, solving problems, and above all fostering critical thinking. However, in an analysis of peer-reviewed empirical 27 articles between 2009 and 2013, Lye and Koh (2014) found that "these studies might not be representative of typical classrooms and these results show that students' learning from computational thinking in naturalistic classroom settings are still not well understood" (p. 57). Currently, teaching computational thinking is typically focused on high school computer science classrooms and some out-of-school environments (Lee et al., 2011). One reason for this may be due, in part, to a lack of teacher knowledge and experience on computational thinking (Kordaki, 2013).

Preparing Teachers for Computational Thinking

To integrate computational thinking in the K-12 setting, Stephenson, Gal-Ezer, Haberman, and Verno (2005) suggested that teachers need to be included in the process. As with any innovation, teachers have been identified as one of the primary factors that make significant impacts on the successful implementation of innovations. For example, in a study with 25 in-service computer science teachers, Kordaki (2013) found that teachers were critical to the successful implementation of high school computing courses. Therefore, it seems plausible that teachers would also need to be involved in planning for computational thinking in K-12 classrooms. National organizations have recognized that teachers have strong potential influence in the implementation of computational thinking in the classroom (CSTA, 2015). In addition, those same national organizations have provided guidance and resources to teachers in order to embed computational thinking into their curriculum. For example, CSTA and ISTE provide resources on their websites to support the integration of computational thinking into their teaching and learning activities. CSTA has also provided computational thinking standards for kindergarten to twelfth grade. In another example, Google (2015) developed a website that includes lesson plans, videos, and other resources on computational thinking for teachers and administrators in an effort to encourage the integration of computational thinking into all subject areas. Google even started an online certification program for teachers that guide them step by step through the application of computational thinking skills in different subjects, including, but not limited to, math, science, and geography. Other organizations such as Code.org and CS Unplugged have created curriculum focusing on teaching K-12 computational thinking and computer science.

Because scholars have recognized the importance of preparing future teachers to integrate computational thinking into the K-12 classroom, more are conducting studies with preservice teachers to examine their current knowledge and how to best prepare them. For example, Yadav et al. (2014) incorporated one week of computational thinking instruction during an educational psychology course. The 200 preservice teachers had no prior experience with computer science. The instruction focused on how computational thinking ideas could be incorporated into the classroom. The results revealed that the preservice teachers were able to improve their understanding after completing the training module on computational thinking. Yadav et al. (2014) suggested the next step would be to study whether preservice teachers could learn computational thinking by observing teachers as they model related thinking strategies and guide students to use these strategies independently. As suggested by Yadav and colleagues, introducing computational thinking to preservice teachers in their teacher education program may improve their understanding and allow them to see the possible benefits of computational thinking for K-12 students. Furthermore, Yadav et al. stated that "there is very little research on how teachers could be prepared to incorporate [computational thinking] ideas in their own teaching" (p. 13). Therefore, our research question investigated: How do preservice teachers' concepts of computational thinking evolve while planning and implementing a computational thinking activity for fifth grade students?

Method

This study used a single-case research design to examine preservice teachers' understanding of computational thinking while planning and implementing a computational thinking activity for fifth grade students (Yin, 2013).

Setting

This case focused on a group of 12 preservice teachers enrolled in an advanced computer education course in a teacher education program at a Midwestern University. All preservice teachers had primary majors in education (11 elementary education majors, 1 secondary social studies education major). The preservice teachers were enrolled in the course to pursue an add-on computer education license, which would certify them to also teach computer applications and computer science, in addition to their primary major area. This course focused on the following concepts: HTML, CSS, algorithms, introductory programming with robotics kits (LEGO Mindstorm, DashDot, Littlebit, Ozobot, Kibo, Sphero), and K-12 programming environments (Scratch, Scratch jr, Code.org). Instruction on computational thinking was embedded within the introductory programming robotics kits and the K-12 programming environments. Preservice teachers were asked to create a video development project to define and describe algorithms. The instruction on computational thinking was covered in the last 6 weeks of the course in the fall of 2015. In addition to this instruction, all 12 preservice teachers read the definitions on the Google (2015) Computational Thinking Certification program online. For the final course project, the preservice teachers developed a 2 h instructional project for fifth grade students to build on the computational thinking concepts learned in the "Hour of Code" activity. The preservice teachers titled this instructional project "Two Hours of Code" and delivered the instruction to a group of 120 students in a public elementary school. The entire project was worth 20% of their final grade in the course. For the "Two Hours of Code" project, the preservice teachers were challenged to meet at least one of the Computer Science Teacher Association (CSTA) standards on computational thinking for grades 3–6. There were three steps to this project: (1) initial proposal development in small group, (2) fifth grade teacher proposal feedback and selection, (3) final proposal revised and developed with all the preservice teachers' collaboration in the class, and (4) implementation of the selected proposal.

Initial Proposal

Preservice teachers were initially grouped into four groups of three people. Each group had one week to work on a proposal for teaching computational thinking to the fifth grade students. The proposal described an instructional activity that would teach computational thinking. In addition, the proposal needed to explain how the activity would address the CSTA computational thinking standard(s). Each group recorded a video presenting their proposal to the fifth grade teachers.

Fifth Grade Teacher Proposal Selection

One of the fifth grade teachers, who had several years of experience with teaching the "Hour of Code," reviewed all four groups' proposals and selected the best option(s). He selected one activity (Teacherbot) from Group 1 and one activity (Scratch Maze) from Group 2 and suggested combining these two proposals. He provided feedback on instructional ideas and conceptual understanding of computational thinking.

Fully Developed Instructional Plan

Next, all the preservice teachers as a class proceeded to develop the computational thinking activity, including manipulatives and resources. The preservice teachers received 3 weeks (six 90 min class sessions) to complete the fully developed proposal. The fully developed proposal included two activities: TeacherBot and Scratch Maze activity. In TeacherBot, students wrote down instructions to navigate their teachers from one spot in the room to another, working around obstacles. In the Scratch Maze activity, students were tasked with creating their own maze in Scratch. After students had created their maze, students created code to navigate their sprite through their maze.

Implementation of Selected Proposal

All preservice teachers were paired up and implemented the two activities into a different fifth grade classroom. Each fifth grade classroom had approximately 20 students. Two preservice teachers taught each group of 20 students.

Data Collection

Seven data sources were used to document the computational thinking skills of the preservice teachers. The data sources are discussed in chronological order.

The Initial Group Proposal

There were four groups that submitted initial group proposals. In these proposals, groups described their suggested potential activities in great detail. They mentioned concepts of computational thinking and pedagogical approaches. They videotaped a presentation of their proposal and sent it to a fifth grade teacher:

- Group 1 (Preservice Teacher A, B, C)
- Group 2 (Preservice Teacher D, E, F)
- Group 3 (Preservice Teacher G, H, I)
- Group 4 (Preservice Teacher J, K, L)

Pre-blog Reflection Post

Preservice teachers created a pre-blog reflection post on their proposals. The blog posts ranged from 200 to 500 words. They were asked to reflect on "where is computational thinking in this proposal?," "how would you consider the needs of the teacher and the students in your proposal?," and "how do you find resources and start planning?"

Video Feedback

One of the fifth grade teachers provided feedback on the video proposals. The teacher briefly talked about each proposal (strengths and weaknesses). He described the rationale behind the two activities he selected.

Video Discussion

After the two activities were selected, the preservice teachers worked together to develop instruction. This collaborative worktime was done during class. This discussion and worktime was videotaped. The worktime lasted 60 min and 75 min in two sessions.

Post-blog Reflection Post

Preservice teachers were asked to reflect on their proposal. They were charged with answering questions on their understanding of computational thinking such as "where is computational thinking in the selected proposal?"

Final Paper

Preservice teachers were required to complete a final paper. The final paper asked preservice teachers to reflect on their and students' experience on implementing the computational thinking project and answer questions such as "how was the students' experience with computational thinking based on your observations?"

Long-Term Reflection

Three months after the class ended, preservice teachers enrolled in a follow-up course (n = 10) were asked to complete a follow-up blog post reflecting on their long-term working memory of computational thinking. Preservice teachers were asked to answer questions about computational thinking such as "how would you explain the concept of computational thinking?"

Data Analysis

To analyze the data, we utilized the six characteristics of the framework described in Table 1. After reviewing all the data, two of the researchers went through the first chronological data source (initial group proposal) together. While reviewing this data source, the researchers discussed all codes and found that two additional categories emerged during analysis (definition, misunderstanding): every proposal showed evidence of these additional categories. After the researchers had established a general agreement on the additional categories and practiced coding the first data source together, they divided and coded the remaining data sources separately. Finally, they came together to discuss each coded data. When the researchers' codes disagreed, researchers discussed those instances until agreement was reached (Carey, Morgan, & Oxtoby, 1996). Based on the coded data, the research team reviewed the coded data to establish themes within each code. These are described in the results.

Results

Computational Thinking

In this study, preservice teachers conveyed accurate knowledge of computational thinking: computational thinking does not require a computer, and computational thinking includes elements of problem solving and scaffolding. Although computational thinking emerged from the computer science field, it does not necessarily need

Table 1 Six categories of computational thinking tenets

Characteristic	Definitions (Google, 2015)	Studies that emphasized this characteristic
Problem solving	Formulating a problem and designing a solution based on the principles of computing	Lu and Fletcher (2009), Wing (2008), Yadav, Mayfield, Zhou, Hambrusch, and Korb (2014)
Decomposition	Breaking down data, processes, or problems into smaller, manageable parts	Atmatzidou and Demetriadis (2016), Barr, Harrison, and Conery (2011), Mannila et al. (2014), Qin (2009), Weintrop et al. (2016)
Pattern recognition	Observing patterns, trends, and regularities in data	Deschryver and Yadav (2015), Grover and Pea (2013), Peters-Burton, Cleary, and Kitsantas (2015)
Abstraction	Identifying the general principles that generate these patterns	Deschryver and Yadav (2015), Grover and Pea (2013), Kramer (2007), Qin (2009), Sanford and Naidu 2016, Wing (2008)
Algorithms	Developing the step-by-step instructions for solving this and similar problems	Mannila et al. (2014), Peters-Burton et al. (2015), Wing (2008), Yadav et al. (2014)
Evaluation	Testing and verifying the solution	Atmatzidou and Demetriadis, (2016), Grover and Pea (2013), Peters-Burton et al. (2015), Weintrop et al. (2016)

to be learned and practiced using a computer (Barr et al., 2011). Preservice teachers were able to represent this knowledge claim. They expressed that computational thinking could exist outside computers and computer science in their initial proposals and maintained this idea through their final papers and 3 months after the course. In all the initial group proposals (which were completed at the beginning of the instructional project), the preservice teachers included instructional activities that did not require a computer to develop fifth grade students' computational thinking skills. One of the groups suggested using pieces of paper to simulate algorithms: "The intro activity [is] an algorithm using computer free-exercises because it only requires the students to move the pieces of paper around to understand the concept" (Group 3, proposal). Another group shared a similar idea where a computer was not necessary: "The snowman activity is computer-free but still shows how algorithms work" (Group 4, proposal). Preservice teachers also expressed the idea of not using computers to teach computational thinking in their pre-blog reflections: "In the warm up, the students have to think about exactly how the teacher can get to the door" (Preservice Teacher B). After the implementation with fifth grade students, the preservice teachers' observations were also aligned with what they planned and then expressed in the final paper:

> During the teacherbot activity, most students physically got up and tried their algorithms out instead of just guessing from their seats. This shows how the students knew how they learned and that acting it out would be more beneficial for them. (Preservice Teacher D)

When asked to define computational thinking in a blog post 3 months after the class, some of the preservice teachers sustained that learning computational thinking can be learned without a computer. For example, one preservice teacher explained how she conducted a computational thinking activity without using computers in a different school environment with third grade students:

> The stop motion dry erase board project I worked on with my 3rd grade class is a really good example. Students look at the problem, think about how they would solve it on paper, write out a plan with a max of 6 slides they draw out to help explain it, think about the way they will word it, and then explain it in a simple yet efficient way to someone who's thinking may not be the same as their [thinking]. (Preservice Teacher G)

Computational Thinking and Problem Solving

When asked to define computational thinking, all preservice teachers associated the term with problem solving. For example, in the initial group proposals, one group suggested that students could build a Scratch Maze. When describing their rationale for including this activity, the group stated that "[the students] will also be able to demonstrate their understanding of how the maze and coding can be used to solve a problem" (Group 1), illustrating that they viewed the maze activity as a problem that could be solved using computational thinking skills. Re-blog reflections, which were written after the initial group proposals, also showed the alignment of problem solving and computational thinking: "the concept of computationally thinking has to do with the idea of finding solutions to general, open-ended problems" (Preservice Teacher A). The same theme was observed in the post-blog reflections (e.g., "CT is thinking about how to solve a problem that does not exactly have one answer," Preservice Teacher B) and the final papers (e.g., "Without telling [the 5th graders] how, I guided them in the right direction, and when I came back later they had figured it out and expended upon what I showed them," Preservice Teacher E). These examples highlight the preservice teachers' conceptual understanding of how computational thinking encompasses problem-solving skills. In fact, when asked to define computational thinking 3 months after, all the preservice teachers still expressed problem solving as the purpose of computational thinking. Preservice Teacher I defined it as formulating a problem and solving it: "Computational thinking is the process of thinking and finding solutions to problems." Preservice Teacher G also emphasized problem-solving characteristics of computational thinking: "Computational thinking is the process of thinking and finding solutions to problems." Both these examples show that the preservice teachers sustained the idea that the purpose of computational thinking is problem solving.

Efficiency in Computational Thinking

Efficiency also emerged from preservice teachers' descriptions. The preservice teachers emphasized that one problem may have multiple solutions and computational thinking could encourage people to find the most efficient solution. This theme was expressed primarily in the initial proposals and post reflections. In the proposals, one group explicitly described efficiency as a requirement in computational thinking: "Each group will be asked to write an algorithm for the teacherbot to use to move through the classroom; however, they are asked to create this using the 'least amount of commands'" (Initial Group Proposal 2). In one preservice teacher's pre-blog reflections, she explicitly shared the requirement for the most efficient solution:

> On a simpler level, when the students create and direct the teacherbot, they have to consider how many times they need the teacherbot to follow the [instructions]. If there is a way to *simplify it* (loop), they need to solve it by fixing the [instructions]. (Preservice Teacher G)

Although efficiency was only mentioned by seven preservice teachers in the first six data sources, nine preservice teachers mentioned this concept after three months, emphasizing the possibility of multiple solutions and the importance of finding the most efficient one. For example, Preservice Teacher A expressed the possibility of finding multiple solutions in computational thinking: "Sometimes we can have similar but different step by steps to get the same outcome."

Characteristics of Computational Thinking

Preservice Teachers' Conceptions of Algorithms

The preservice teachers seemed to present a valid understanding of an algorithm as a set of instructions to complete a task and shared relevant definitions and examples of algorithms throughout the process. For example, groups defined algorithms in their initial proposal as a "set of specific instructions that explains how to complete a task" (Group 4) and provided algorithm examples such as "making a peanut butter and jelly sandwich" (Group 2). In the Initial Group Proposal 4, preservice teachers created an activity that required writing instructions to draw a snowman: "The snowman activity is an algorithm design. Students have to see that they are following a specific set of instructions that gets them to an end of activity." In the Initial Group Proposal 3, preservice teachers designed a robotics activity to teach students algorithms: "Students will be practicing algorithms as well as basic robotics through the cup stacking warm-up activity." These are both relevant examples of algorithms because they focus on step-by-step instructions to complete activities. In the post-blog reflections, preservice teachers placed similar focus on step-by-step instructions in both their definitions and examples. One of the preservice teachers explained how the Teacherbot activity should allow the fifth grade students to create and test their algorithm: "Students have to give the teacher explicit instructions and the teacher has to follow those exact instructions even if they are not correct" (Preservice Teacher D, post-blog reflection).

Even though the preservice teachers had a good understanding of algorithms, they demonstrated a misconception that algorithm design was equivalent to computational thinking. For example, in the initial proposals, Group 2 stated "students will have to use computational thinking to write an algorithm to move their teacherbot around the room." This example shows a misunderstanding that computational thinking is a method for creating an algorithm. Another preservice teacher expressed a similar misconception, equating computational thinking with an algorithm: "Both activities use the idea of creating an algorithm which reflects the idea of computational thinking"

(Preservice Teacher F, pre-blog reflection). The algorithm misconception was still prevalent 3 months after the class. Preservice Teacher H related computational thinking to algorithms in his description of computational thinking: "Computational thinking is thinking and working using the same methods that a computer would. For example, solving problems using algorithms, step by step mathematical tools that can lead a computer or an individual to a solution." Although this is not necessarily a comprehensive example, it shows that the preservice teacher may be starting to conceptualize computational thinking as a new type of thinking strategy that could guide them and their students to problem solution and product development.

Preservice Teachers' Understanding of Pattern Recognition and Abstraction

After discussing computational thinking with their classmates and implementing the activity in the elementary school, several of the preservice teachers started using other key components of computational thinking, although they did not use the correct vocabulary and explicitly identify those key components (e.g., observing patterns, trends, and regularities and identifying the general principles that generate these patterns). When the preservice teachers were asked to define and connect pattern recognition and abstraction concepts to activities in their assignments, they were not able to identify those and define them explicitly. However, they included examples in the activities. For example, later on in one of the video recordings, they provided an example of abstraction: "We are not going to show them how to make the maze but give them the main components they are going to need to make a maze" (Video Recording 1). Since abstraction is reducing complexity and creating a model of a product, this example shows the preservice teachers' understanding of abstraction because they were recognizing the different components necessary to build the maze. In another preservice teacher's post-blog reflections, she described pattern recognition in the Teacherbot activity: "The robot is recognizing a pattern laid out for them and reads the design code sheet to know what movements to make" (Preservice Teacher D). Although some additional characteristics of computational thinking were briefly described by some later in the process, these characteristics were weakly defined.

Evolution of Trial and Error Approach to Evaluation

At the beginning strategies of proposal development and the first reflections, the preservice teachers defined a trial and error approach as a strategy to design and test solutions using computational thinking. For example, in the initial proposals, one group suggested using a trial and error approach to test their activities: "trial and error [can] identify what works and does not work in both the Scratch and intro activities" (Group 1). Another group stated using trial and error as a strategy to be used in their activity and real life: "Not only in reference to a corn maze, but students can use this concept to apply the strategy of trial and error in real life situations" (Group 2). These examples show that preservice teachers' focused on using a trial and error approach, which is inconsistent with computational thinking because it suggested formulation of a problem and a solution. However, as they progressed in the activity design and after implementing it, they had a clearer purpose focusing on an evaluative approach instead, testing the accuracy of their solutions. For example, in the final papers, preservice teachers shared that the students observed each other's mazes to evaluate their own designs: "[The students] also got to play each other's mazes and see what different techniques they used" (Preservice Teacher G). After the implementation of the activity, the preservice teachers confirmed that working in groups and evaluating each other's mazes were important parts of the activity. One preservice teacher elaborated on the importance of evaluation and how the benefits transferred to product design:

> Another thing that went well was that not all of the teacherbots were perfect algorithms, which allowed for the students to discuss why their algorithms might be off a little. This helped students see how sometimes an algorithm may not work and therefore must be manipulated to work. This was a great way to lead in to Scratch because we let the students know that sometimes their algorithm may not work for scratch and therefore they must change their codes to fix this problem. (Preservice Teacher D, Final Paper)

This example shows that preservice teacher viewed evaluation as an important characteristic of computational thinking process for validating and increasing the efficiency of the students' solutions.

Discussion

We conducted a case study in order to understand how preservice teachers' concept of computational thinking evolved while designing and implementing a computational thinking instructional project. Twelve preservice teachers developed and implemented a 2 h computational thinking instructional project for fifth grade students (n $\approx$ 125). Results showed that the process of developing and implementing computational thinking instruction seemed to improve preservice teachers' understanding of computational thinking. However, there were still misconceptions of preservice teachers' expressions of computational thinking at the end of the course.

Wing (2006) stated that computational thinking was a necessary skill for K-12 students, similar to reading, writing, and algebra. Computational thinking has been described in a myriad of ways ranging from "an approach to problem solving" (Barr et al., 2011, p. 115) to "an expertise that children are expected to develop" (Grover & Pea, 2013, p. 40). There is not one commonly agreed definition and structure in the literature (Barr & Stephenson, 2011). Our results reaffirm the need for a clearer and consistent definition of computational thinking (Voogt et al., 2015). This lack of consistent definition and understanding creates difficulty when measuring computational thinking (Rich & Langton, 2016). Furthermore, teachers will likely not be able to embed computational thinking in their instruction due to their lack of understanding of the concept (Bower & Falkner, 2015).

In this study, the preservice teachers were able to provide basic definitions of computational thinking as a problem-solving strategy. Efficiency, which was mentioned by some preservice teachers, is commonly presented as one of the criteria for better solutions in problem solving using computational thinking (Weintrop et al., 2016). The preservice teachers also emphasized that learning computational thinking does not require a computer (CSTA, 2011). Computers and programming can make computational thinking stronger conceptually; however, computational thinking without computers is an important unplugged understanding to have as a basic concept before introducing the computer (Lu & Fletcher, 2009). Although the preservice teachers were not able to clearly define or exemplify pattern recognition, decomposition, and abstraction components in their instructional project designs, they were able to successfully define and/or exemplify algorithms and evaluation in the computational thinking process. This understanding of algorithms might be due to their instructor's emphasis on algorithm design in the course and assigning the preservice teachers to create an instructional video about what an algorithm is as a requirement before this project. However, too much emphasis on algorithms seemed to have caused a misconception, causing them to think that algorithms and computational thinking were equivalent. Similar misconceptions about computational thinking have occurred in other studies. In one study, 32 preservice teachers had a misconception that computational thinking was using technology to solve problems (Bower & Falkner, 2015) such as using an office application to complete a task. In another survey study of 200 preservice teachers, Yadav et al. (2014) found that they equated computational thinking with programming. In our study, the preservice teachers interchangeably used algorithms to refer to computational thinking. Even though algorithms are an inevitable part of computational thinking, they are not equivalent to computational thinking (Guzdial, 2010). Algorithms are step-by-step instructions that can help guide us while solving problems; however, computational thinking is more than just algorithm design.

Even though evaluation in computational thinking was not explicitly covered in the course content, the preservice teacher's emphasis on the importance of evaluation in the computational thinking process emerged in their discussions and observations of the fifth grade students' interactions (testing and validating their solutions with other students in the Teacherbot and Scratch Maze activity). The preservice teachers mentioned trial and error in their initial proposals. However, as they progressed in the process and implemented their instructional project with the fifth grade students, the term trial and error evolved to a planned evaluation strategy as part of the computational thinking learning goal (Yadav et al., 2014). In real life, people in science fields do not make decision based on a trial and error approach, instead most "analyze a design by creating a model or prototype and collect extensive data on how it performs, including under extreme conditions" ("NSTA," 2013, p. 9). Hence, we can conclude that developing and implementing an instructional project may have prompted preservice teachers to think more about the process and helped them understand evaluation as a critical characteristic of computational thinking.

Limitations

The sample size was one limitation of this study as we only focused on 12 preservice teachers from one university. The results would likely change by increasing the sample size or conducting the same research at a different university or classroom context. Furthermore, we did not account for the preservice teachers' background with computers and assumed all to be similar. Their backgrounds may have made a difference on their conceptions of computational thinking.

The preservice teachers were asked to complete the Google Education's Computational Thinking Certification (2015) before starting the design and implementation of the instructional project. However, the training website was unavailable for some of the course, and none of the students were able to complete the training. We believe that if they had enrolled and completed the certification, their understanding of computational thinking may have been more defined and comprehensive.

Conclusion

With its growing importance in K-12 education, it becomes crucial to prepare both preservice and in-service teachers for embedding and implementing computational thinking in their curriculum (Schweingruber, Keller, & Quinn, 2012). This study provided one instance of how computational thinking can progress with preservice teachers as they design computational thinking instruction. In addition, it also helped illuminate where possible misconceptions could exist and what preservice teachers might struggle with in terms of computational thinking. In summary, future work in this area is needed and should include more directed activities to counteract potential misconceptions about computational thinking. Specifically, we suggest that teacher educators work with preservice teachers to help identify the key characteristics such as pattern recognition and abstraction. In our future classes, we intend to use Code.org and CS Unplugged to help further these ideas for our own preservice teachers. Furthermore, we suggest to include computational thinking activities in the current K-12 curricula and prepare preservice teachers from all core subject areas to plan and implement computational thinking as a problem-solving skill in their own classroom (Sengupta, Kinnebrew, Basu, Biswas, & Clark, 2013).

References

Atmatzidou, S., & Demetriadis, S. (2016). Advancing students' computational thinking skills through educational robotics: A study on age and gender relevant differences. *Robotics and Autonomous Systems, 75*, 661–670.

Barr, D., Harrison, J., & Conery, L. (2011). Computational thinking: A digital age skill for everyone. *Learning & Leading with Technology, 38*(6), 20–23.

Barr, V., & Stephenson, C. (2011). Bringing computational thinking to K-12: What is involved and what is the role of the computer science education community? *ACM Inroads, 2*(1), 48–54.

Bers, M. U., Flannery, L., Kazakoff, E. R., & Sullivan, A. (2014). Computational thinking and tinkering: Exploration of an early childhood robotics curriculum. *Computers & Education, 72*, 145–157.

Bower, M., & Falkner, K. (2015). Computational thinking, the notional machine, pre-service teachers, and research opportunities. In *Proceedings of the 17th Australasian Computing Education Conference, Sydney, Australia.*

Carey, J. W., Morgan, M., & Oxtoby, M. J. (1996). Intercoder agreement in analysis of responses to open-ended interview questions: Examples from tuberculosis research. *Cultural Anthropology Methods, 8*(3), 1–5.

Chao, P. Y. (2016). Exploring students' computational practice, design and performance of problem-solving through a visual programming environment. *Computers & Education, 95*, 202–215.

Code.org. (2016). Promote Computer Science. Retrieved from https://code.org/promote.

Cortina, T. J. (2007). An introduction to computer science for non-majors using principles of computation. *ACM SIGCSE Bulletin, 39*, 218–222.

Computer Science Teachers Association. (2015). CSTA National Secondary School Computer Science Survey. Retrieved from http://www.csta.acm.org/Research/sub/Projects/ResearchFiles/CSTA_NATIONAL_SECONDARY_SCHOOL_CS_SURVEY_2015.pdf.

Computer Science Teachers Association (CSTA). (2011). Operational Definition of Computational Thinking for K–12 Education. Retrieved from https://csta.acm.org/Curriculum/sub/CurrFiles/CompThinkingFlyer.pdf.

Department of Education. (2016). Computer Science for All. Retrieved from http://innovation.ed.gov/what-we-do/stem/computer-science-for-all/.

DeSchryver, M. D., & Yadav, A. (2015). Creative and computational thinking in the context of new literacies: Working with teachers to scaffold complex technology-mediated approaches to teaching and learning. *Journal of Technology and Teacher Education, 23*(3), 411–431.

Emmott, S. & Rison, S. (2005). Towards 2020 Science. Retrieved from http://research.microsoft.com/en-us/um/cambridge/projects/towards2020science/

Google. (2015). Computational Thinking for Educators. Retrieved from https://computationalthinkingcourse.withgoogle.com/unit?lesson=8&unit=1.

Grover, S., & Pea, R. (2013). Computational thinking in K–12: A review of the state of the field. *Educational Researcher, 42*(1), 38–43.

Guzdial, M. (2010). Does contextualized computing education help? *ACM Inroads, 1*(4), 4–6.

Hmelo-Silver, C. E. (2004). Problem-based learning: What and how do students learn? *Educational Psychology Review, 16*(3), 235–266.

Jonassen, D. H. (2000). Toward a design theory of problem solving. *Educational Technology Research and Development, 48*(4), 63–85.

Kordaki, M. (2013). High school computing teachers' beliefs and practices: A case study. *Computers & Education, 68*, 141–152.

Kramer, J. (2007). Is abstraction the key to computing? *Communications of the ACM, 50*(4), 36–42.

Lee, I., Martin, F., Denner, J., Coulter, B., Allan, W., Erickson, J., & Werner, L. (2011). Computational thinking for youth in practice. *ACM Inroads, 2*(1), 32–37.

Lee, T. Y., Mauriello, M. L., Ingraham, J., Sopan, A., Ahn, J., & Bederson, B. B. (2012). CTArcade: Learning computational thinking while training virtual characters through game play. In *Proceedings of the Human Factors in Computing Systems Conference, China.*

Li, T., & Wang, T. (2012). A Unified approach to teach computational thinking for first year non–CS majors in an introductory course. *IERI Procedia, 2*, 498–503.

Lu, J. J., & Fletcher, G. H. (2009). Thinking about computational thinking. *ACM SIGCSE Bulletin, 41*, 260–264.

Lye, S. Y., & Koh, J. H. L. (2014). Review on teaching and learning of computational thinking through programming: What is next for K-12? *Computers in Human Behavior, 41*, 51–61.

Mannila, L., Dagiene, V., Demo, B., Grgurina, N., Mirolo, C., Rolandsson, L., & Settle, A. (2014). Computational thinking in k-9 education. In *Proceedings of the Working Group Reports of the 2014 on Innovation & Technology in Computer Science Education Conference* (pp. 1–29). New York, NY: ACM.

NSTA. (2013). Next Generation Science Standards. Retrieved from http://www.nextgenscience.org.

Papert, S., & Harel, I. (1991). Situating constructionism. *Constructionism, 36*, 1–11.

Peters-Burton, E. E., Cleary, T. J., & Kitsantas, A. (2015). The development of computational thinking in the context of science and engineering practices: A self-regulated learning approach. In *Proceedings of the Cognition and Exploratory Learning in the Digital Age Conference, Maynooth, Greater Dublin, Ireland.*

Phillips, P. (2009). Computational Thinking: a problem-solving tool for every classroom. *Communications of the CSTA, 3*(6), 12–16.

Rich, P. J., & Langton, M. B. (2016). Computational Thinking: Toward a unifying definition. In J. M. Spector, D. Ifenthaler, D. G. Sampson, & P. Isaias (Eds.), *Competencies in teaching, Learning, and Educational Leadership in the Digital Age: Papers from CELDA 2014*. Switzerland: Springer.

Qin, H. (2009). Teaching computational thinking through bioinformatics to biology students. *ACM SIGCSE Bulletin, 41*(1), 188–191.

Qualls, J. A., & Sherrell, L. B. (2010). Why computational thinking should be integrated into the curriculum? *Journal of Computing Sciences in Colleges, 25*(5), 66–71.

Sanford, J. F., & Naidu, J. T. (2016). Computational thinking concepts for grade school. *Contemporary Issues in Education Research, 9*(1), 23.

Schweingruber, H., Keller, T., & Quinn, H. (2012). *A Framework for K-12 Science Education: Practices, Crosscutting Concepts, and Core Ideas*. Washington, DC: National Academies Press.

Sengupta, P., Kinnebrew, J. S., Basu, S., Biswas, G., & Clark, D. (2013). Integrating computational thinking with K-12 science education using agent-based computation: A theoretical framework. *Education and Information Technologies, 18*(2), 351–380.

Smith, M. (2016. Computer Science For All. Retrieved from https://www.whitehouse.gov/blog/2016/01/30/computer-science-all.

Stephenson, C., Gal-Ezer, J., Haberman, B., & Verno, A. (2005). The new educational imperative: Improving high school computer science education. In *Final Report of the CSTA Curriculum Improvement Task Force*.

Voogt, J., Fisser, P., Good, J., Mishra, P., & Yadav, A. (2015). Computational thinking in compulsory education: Towards an agenda for research and practice. *Education and Information Technologies, 20*(4), 715–728.

Weintrop, D., Beheshti, E., Horn, M., Orton, K., Jona, K., Trouille, L., & Wilensky, U. (2016). Defining computational thinking for mathematics and science classrooms. *Journal of Science Education and Technology, 25*(1), 127–147.

Wing, J. M. (2006). Computational thinking. *Communications of the ACM, 49*(3), 33–35.

Wing, J. M. (2008). Computational thinking and thinking about computing. *Philosophical Transactions of the Royal Society of London A: Mathematical, Physical and Engineering Sciences, 366*(1881), 3717–3725.

Yadav, A., Mayfield, C., Zhou, N., Hambrusch, S., & Korb, J. T. (2014). Computational thinking in elementary and secondary teacher education. *ACM Transactions on Computing Education, 14*(1), 5.

Yin, R. K. (2013). *Case study research: Design and methods*. Thousand Oaks, CA: Sage Publications, Inc.

The Code ABC MOOC: Experiences from a Coding and Computational Thinking MOOC for Finnish Primary School Teachers

Tarmo Toikkanen and Teemu Leinonen

Abstract The Finnish primary school curriculum will feature programming and computational thinking as mandatory cross-curricular elements in all teaching starting from the first grade. Many teachers are quite concerned about this and feel ill-prepared. A group of volunteers created a MOOC for teachers and, with no budget, trained over 500 primary school teachers to be competent teachers of programming (38% of the participants). The results from a study conducted within the course indicate that Finnish teachers seem to think that coding is an important addition to the school curriculum and they exhibit low levels of anxiety over it. The MOOC design focused on connectivist design principles (cMOOC) and was considered extremely successful by the participants. The MOOC participants seemed confident that the MOOC would equip them to face the new challenge, and indeed, the feedback from the MOOC and its results support this.

Keywords MOOC • Core curriculum • cMOOC • Scratch • ScratchJr • Racket

Introduction

This chapter describes a massive open online course (MOOC) that was developed and implemented by a group of volunteer teachers and academics during the autumn of 2015 in Finland. The MOOC was called "Koodiaapinen MOOC," which can be translated loosely to "Code ABC MOOC." Programming in schools is a timely topic in Finland, since the upcoming core curriculum for the autumn of 2016 includes programming and computational thinking as new cross-curricular elements starting in the first grade of primary education. The issue has been broadly discussed in the media, and many teachers are understandably concerned as they feel ill-prepared.

T. Toikkanen (✉) • T. Leinonen
Aalto University, 02150 Espoo, Finland
e-mail: tarmo.toikkanen@iki.fi; teemu.leinonen@aalto.fi

P.J. Rich, C.B. Hodges (eds.), *Emerging Research, Practice, and Policy on Computational Thinking*, Educational Communications and Technology: Issues and Innovations, DOI 10.1007/978-3-319-52691-1_15

This chapter begins by explaining the curricular reform going on in Finland. We continue by describing the design principles of the MOOC, followed by the impact and results of the MOOC. We will finish by outlining some of the ideas and creations shared by the teachers who participated in the MOOC and their views on how computational thinking and various tools might find a role in Finnish schools.

Coding in the Finnish curriculum

We will begin by describing the Finnish primary school system and how its curriculum works. We will then discuss how coding and computational thinking are presented in the new core curriculum and what their goals are. Finally we will compare the Finnish approach to other European approaches.

The Finnish Curriculum

The highly trained, trusted, and autonomous teachers are a distinguishing feature of Finnish primary education. To be a proficient teacher in Finland, one needs a master's degree in education, with extensive minor studies in the subjects one expects to teach. As a result of the high level of professionalism, teachers are given significant freedom in how they practically execute their teaching.

Teachers' autonomy also shows in the Finnish national curriculum, which is a core curriculum that describes in general the skills and knowledge that pupils in various subject areas and grade levels are expected to attain. The national framework is renewed about every 10 years. The 313 municipalities of the country are responsible for running the schools. Each municipality works through the framework and produces its own refined version. After this, each school, led by its rector, will produce their own curriculum based on the municipal frame. And finally, each teacher is free to organize their teaching in whatever way they chose within the school's curriculum framework. There is no top-down control on the implementation of the national framework as the rectors and heads of education in the municipalities lead the process.

From the governance point of view, teachers' autonomy is sometimes seen as a double-edged sword. On the one hand, it allows individual teachers to engage in experiments and the piloting of new methods of teaching quite freely—producing outstanding individual teachers who often make headlines in national and even international media. On the other hand, it may make centrally governed reforms difficult to achieve. It can be hard to get any new views on pedagogical approaches or didactic practices widely adopted in schools as individual teachers are accustomed to their autonomy and some of them may not be willing to change their ingrained ways of working.

Coding and computational thinking in Finland

The national core curriculum (http://www.oph.fi/english/curricula_and_qualifications/basic_education)—which was completed in 2014 and comes into force in the autumn of 2016—has several new features compared to the previous one, including seven wide areas of competence: (1) thinking and learning to learn; (2) cultural competence, interaction, and self-expression; (3) self-efficacy and everyday skills; (4) polyliteracy; (5) information and communications technology (ICT); (6) working life and entrepreneurship; and (7) participating in society and building a sustainable future. These competences should be fostered in all educational activities. Programming and computational thinking are part of competence 5, ICT competences.

While almost everyone in school talks about *coding*, the terms used in the core curriculum are *computational thinking* and *programming*. Computational thinking is seen as a goal and programming or coding as a means to reach that goal. Here are some relevant passages from the national core curriculum, freely translated from the National Board of Education (2014):

- Grades 1–2: "Pupils receive and share experiences of working with digital media and age-appropriate programming" (p. 101).
- Grades 3–6: "While programming, pupils experience how technology is dependent on decisions made by humans" (p. 157). "Motivate pupils to create functional instructions as computer programs in a visual programming environment" (p. 235).
- A requirement for a good grade in maths at grade 6: "The pupil can program a functional application in a visual programming environment" (p. 239).
- Grades 7–9: "Programming is practiced as part of different subject areas" (p. 284).
- A requirement for a good grade in maths at grade 9: "The pupil can apply the principles of computational thinking and program simple applications" (p. 379).

Coding in Finnish Schools and Elsewhere in Europe

Our summary of how computational thinking or programming is incorporated in other European countries' primary education curricula is based on the report "Computing our Future" by European Schoolnet (Balanskat & Engelhardt, 2014). This report was published while the Finnish curriculum was still being developed, so it only mentions Finland as "having plans."

Of the 20 countries surveyed, seven include coding at the primary school level, another five in the lower secondary school level, and another four in the upper secondary school level. In many European schools, coding only seems to appear in the secondary level of education. Most European countries either have coding as a specific subject or part of ICT courses. Only Italy has positioned coding as a cross-curricular element in primary education, like Finland. However, in Italy, regional and school decisions can affect whether coding is a mandatory part of education. In Finland, the municipalities and schools may only decide how they will teach or organize their education so that the pupils will reach the competencies mentioned in the national curriculum framework.

In summary, only Finland has positioned coding as a mandatory, cross-curricular element in education, starting from the first grade of primary school. Although it is mandatory to make sure that all the students will achieve the defined competences, there are very few guidelines on how the actual teaching should be conducted. Therefore, the MOOC described in this chapter was not only a training program but also a development effort to activate teachers to plan their teaching so that their students will meet the requirements of the national curriculum and for teachers to use programming in a meaningful way—to increase motivation, creativity, and self-expression—and not just use it as a technological way of doing math exercises.

The Design Principles of the MOOC

The Code ABC MOOC for Finnish school teachers was in all measures a success, as detailed in the next section. In this section, we will discuss the background work and design principles that we consider to have contributed to the success.

The objectives for the MOOC participants were:

- To learn computational thinking and basic programming concepts (such as commands, loops, and conditional statements)
- To get hands-on experience of the programming tools that are considered to be suitable for pupils
- To study how computational thinking could be brought to students in a meaningful way so that the learning objectives of the curriculum are met
- To study how the teacher's role and classroom practices are changing
- To study how coding could be used in all school activities, from sports to music and art and from cooking and crafts to academic subjects and STEM (science, technology, engineering, and mathematics)

These objectives reflect the Finnish way of organizing teachers' professional development. When there is a new concept in the curriculum, such as computational thinking, teachers are expected to define it and to find out how it could be brought to their classroom practice and their students. The idea is to involve teachers in the development rather than tell them what to do. Teachers' participation in the planning and ownership of their work is an important cornerstone of the system.

The MOOC consisted of three tracks, each targeted at teachers of different grade levels and using different programming environments. For grades K–2 we used ScratchJr, for grades 3–6 we used Scratch, and for grades 7–9 we used Racket.

Each track was headed by one teacher who currently teaches the same grade levels. They built the course materials themselves, produced introductory and feedback videos, and helped the participants during the MOOC. We consider these peer teachers as a crucial feature of the MOOC as they ensured the materials and support really took into account the context of the participants. Our track leaders also recorded feedback videos after each week, where they reflected on the work the participants had undertaken the previous week. This created authentic feedback from participants, even though we did not have the resources to give individual feedback to everyone.

In general, our MOOC is closer to a connectivist style cMOOC than an automatically graded, professor-centric xMOOC, which are common in computer science. We felt it is important to respect our participants and their time. Our MOOC did not have any multiple-choice quizzes, and we tried to remove any artificial hoops the participants would have to jump through. We provided them with succinct textual instructions and background information, as well as a short introductory video, during each segment of the MOOC. Each exercise was designed and chosen because it helped participants to understand some concept of computational thinking.

Another key feature was the combination of practical experience and pedagogical thinking. We knew from experience that the reservations of many teachers toward coding stem from fear of the unknown, and this would be dispelled simply by allowing them to try out age-appropriate programming tools and realize how simple and engaging they are. The idea was that teachers will try out the programming tools but are not in any way forced to bring them into their classrooms. Another prong of the MOOC was to engage teachers in thinking about pedagogy and how they could incorporate programming activities into their teaching and lesson plans.

Achieving trust between us and our participants played a big role. By design we did not follow how studiously participants followed our instructions. We trusted them to know what they were doing. The only activity we actually assessed was the final exercise, which consisted of a programming exercise and a pedagogical outcome (such as a lesson plan).

To enhance the feeling of working with other people, we emphasized sharing during the MOOC. During each segment, participants shared short pedagogical ideas, which everyone had access to. Having hundreds of shared ideas just two days after each segment began had an awe-inspiring effect on everyone.

Technically speaking, we used a weblike approach in building the platform: "small parts loosely joined." Our learning management system (LMS) was a Finnish course platform Eliademy (based on Moodle), but we used Google Forms for feedback, Padlet for sharing, and YouTube for videos. While this required our participants to understand that they were jumping from one service to another (and we were a bit wary of this), this setup seemed to be easy enough for teachers to understand.

The Impact on and Experiences of Teachers

Based on the feedback we received from the MOOC participants, here we outline the impact that the MOOC had on them and describe the experiences teachers had during and after the MOOC. There are a number of master's theses in the works that will analyze the collected data in more detail, but here we provide an overview.

The total number of teaching staff in Finnish primary and lower secondary schools is about 40,000. The Code ABC MOOC was developed by four people in their own time, without funding. There was no marketing budget. Simply through social media channels and using free traditional media visibility, over 2700 people enrolled to the course. As the course content was not visible without registering, many of them were only visiting to see what the course looked like and did not start the course by engaging with the exercises.

During the initial days of the course, 1301 people started actually going through the weekly exercises. Of these, 501 completed the course, resulting in a completion rate of 38.5% of the people who started the course, which for a MOOC can be considered quite high, as the average completion rate of MOOCs in recent years has been 6.5% (Hattie, 2013).

Of the feedback we gathered, about 5–10% contained criticism or development suggestions, while 70–90% contained positive praise, and the rest contained a mix of both or were neutral in tone. Most criticism concerned the technical operation of the MOOC platform. On answering the question "Would you recommend this course to a colleague?," on a scale of 1–10, the average response was 9.1 and the Net Promoter Score was 88, which is exceedingly high.

The three tracks of the MOOC employed different pedagogical approaches, and we could see that no single solution would suit everyone. Teachers, like any learners, are individuals. A particular issue was that in the Scratch and ScratchJr tracks, no model answers were provided. Each programming exercise had a clear description of the final outcome, but no concrete model solution code was given. Some teachers (a minority but still worth noting) had issues with this and wished for exact model answers so they could see whether they understood the assignment or not. This is a marked difference from pupils in primary school, who are quite happy to attempt to explore and solve the assignments, and when they feel they have accomplished the task, they move on to the next assignment.

A subset of participants responded to voluntary questionnaires before and after the course. When asked about when they could imagine being ready to teach programming, the median answer was "three months from now" as the course was starting and "one month from now" after the course. As the course lasted about two months, the teachers seemed optimistic that the MOOC would prepare them adequately, and indeed, after the course, this was reflected in their answers.

The preconceptions of participants before the course started were collected using a localized version of UTAUT (the unified theory of acceptance and use of technology) (Venkatesh, Morris, Davis, & Davis, 2003). The answers were analyzed in a master's thesis by student teachers who concluded that "the general attitude and lack of anxiety among the respondents denotes that Finnish teachers are open-mindedly welcoming programming into primary school's curriculum" (Karvonen & Laukka, 2016). Indeed, 74.1% partially agreed or strongly agreed with the statement that "the teaching of programming is needed in primary school" (Karvonen & Laukka, 2016).

Pedagogical Ideas Shared by Participants

During the MOOC, thousands of pedagogical ideas were shared by teachers. Here we present the main categories of ideas and a few representative examples.

We used Padlet, an online tool for collaborative note-taking, as the platform for collecting pedagogical ideas. The ideas presented in Padlet were produced collaboratively by the participants and categorized by track leaders. Therefore, they do not represent the researchers' interpretation but a consensus gained by the participants and track leaders. They are published as open data and can be used in further studies. As an example, during week 2 in the Scratch track, when the concept of a "loop" was being discussed, the prompt for Padlet sharing came through devising an assignment for pupils where loops are used, both with Scratch and without technology. The participants came up with 382 ideas, including these detailed below:

- Physical education: aerobic exercises or dance movements and sequences of moves and loops over them
- Maths: turning a sequence of additions into a loop and hence multiplication
- Arts: using paper to draw, rotate, and repeat and following up by doing the same in Scratch
- Music: rhythms built into loops and into a composition

In the ScratchJr track, during week 5 participants were asked to share ideas on how programming can support pupils' learning and ownership of the learning process (as required by the new core curriculum) and what connections can be found to link programming to other wide competence areas. The participants came up with 228 ideas, including these detailed below:

- When coding, goals can be reached through multiple ways, which increases pupils' ownership and understanding of their own learning process.
- When coding, pupils are creating something of their own, which challenges them in a different way than when completing predetermined exercises; there are no correct answers, and both pupils and teachers are in a new situation.
- Spontaneous discussions among pupils naturally lead to improved discussion and collaboration skills.
- At its best, coding leads to a flow state and amply rewards the efforts put into it.
- Coding develops polyliteracy as pupils work with many formats and forms of media.
- Coding is an exciting way of working that also motivates the "back row pupils" who are usually not interested in anything at school.
- Coding is actually a familiar way of working for many teachers; they have not used programming, but the similar affordances that programming brings have been utilized by many classroom teachers for years, and this revelation also shows that coding is something that fits into a pedagogically sound classroom without problems.
- Coding teaches persistence, exploration, trying out various solutions, and learning from mistakes.

Many teachers expressed their awe at all the brilliant ideas others had shared. The sharing of ideas was possibly the most valuable aspect of the whole MOOC, at least based on participant feedback. Sharing created a sense of working together and was also immensely useful for participants when they start planning their upcoming teaching activities.

The pedagogical ideas are published as an open resource bank for all teachers on the Finnish Wikiversity. The questionnaire data is published as open data on Github for anyone to use.

Teachers' Views on Programming Tools

The MOOC introduced teachers to ScratchJr, Scratch, or Racket. We describe how teachers see these and other programming tools as part of their future teaching activities.

As expected, many preconceptions and reservations disappeared completely once the teachers tried out a programming tool in practice. The ease of use was a surprise to those who had perhaps studied a bit of computer science during their university studies.

Another key insight many had was what these tools allowed; they meshed really well with an ideal pedagogical approach. Some special education teachers noted that they had been doing "coding" for years, but just using colored paper and other craft materials, and had not realized they could call it programming. While of course some teachers struggled to learn computational concepts, the vast majority had no trouble with the tools and seeing their immediate benefits in their classrooms.

The three tools used in the MOOC were not portrayed as the only choices, but simply as selected tools that are commonly used with good results. Several participants already had experiences of various robotics kits and other programming environments. But one of the goals of the MOOC was to ensure all participants get practical hands-on experiences with at least one age-appropriate programming tool.

Looking at the various programming tools out there, it seems that the ideas behind the programming environment LOGO (Papert, 1973) still hold true. LOGO was the tool that allowed users to draw line graphics by controlling a turtle with simple commands. What makes Racket immediately useful and usable by students is the LOGO-like turtle function for drawing graphics. Even in Scratch, which facilitates the creation of games and animations, when kids realize there's a "pen.down" function, they start drawing these LOGO-like figures. There is something mesmerizing about turning abstract movements and geometry into beautiful images that captures the imagination and motivates children to no end.

In Fig. 1 there are some drawings that the MOOC participants made at the beginning of the course. The assignment was to draw a national flag using Racket code, but after someone drew a Moominhouse, the bar was raised and everything from molecules, logos, faces, and animals were created. And yes, both Angry Birds and a Minecraft Creeper face were produced by these teachers.

Fig. 1 A sampling of the LOGO-like drawings teachers made with Racket during the first segment of the MOOC

Discussion and Conclusions

Based on the participant completion rate and the feedback they provided, the Code ABC MOOC has been a resounding success and will be reimplemented during the spring of 2016 and twice during the academic year 2016–2017. How Finnish teachers eventually adopt programming into their teaching activities will become apparent during that academic year. We hope that our MOOC equips teachers to meet the objectives set in the national curriculum by using programming as a creative learning tool in all their teaching activities. We also sincerely hope that Finnish textbook publishers take heed and aim for an equally valuable presentation of programming and computational thinking in their upcoming textbooks.

This experimental MOOC and the studies of it have limitations too. To truly understand the real impact, we should conduct a longitudinal study that examines how the participants eventually implemented computational thinking and coding in their classroom practices. The MOOC project, however, was able to provide one possible design to advance the idea of computational thinking in schools.

Acknowledgments We thank the invaluable individuals who volunteered to be teachers in the MOOC—to prepare the weekly schedules and materials, to give feedback and support, and to do all of these in their free time: Tero Toivanen, special needs teacher and teacher trainer; Vuokko Kangas, lower primary school class teacher; and Tiina Partanen, upper primary school mathematics teacher.

References

Balanskat, A., & Engelhardt, K. (2014). *Computing our future: Computer programming and coding – Priorities, school curricula and initiatives across Europe*. Brussels, Belgium: European Schoolnet.

Hattie, J. (2013). *Visible learning: A synthesis of over 800 meta-analyses relating to achievement*. New York, NY: Routledge.

Karvonen, V., & Laukka, P. (2016). Suomalaisten Opettajien Asenteita ja Valmiuksia Ohjelmoinnin Opetukseen (Master's Thesis).

The National Board of Education. (2014). *Perusopetuksen opetussuunnitelman perusteet 2014 (No. 2014:96)*. Tampere, Finland: Opetushallitus.

Papert, S. (1973). Uses of Technology to Enhance Education (No. AIM-298).

Venkatesh, V., Morris, M. G., Davis, G. B., & Davis, F. D. (2003). User acceptance of information technology: Toward a unified view on JSTOR. *MIS Quarterly, 27*(3), 425–478.

Part IV
Assessing Computational Thinking

Assessing Computational Thinking Across the Curriculum

Julie Mueller, Danielle Beckett, Eden Hennessey, and Hasan Shodiev

Abstract Computational thinking (CT) refers to a set of processes through which people arrive at solutions to problems using principles based in computer science. A CT approach to problem-solving is increasingly valuable in education and workplace settings as the economy grows more dependent on digital literacy. Given the importance of CT, it is essential to assess these skills. However, a reliable assessment tool is absent from the current literature. This chapter, therefore, defines CT across the Ontario (Canada) Elementary School curriculum in elementary classrooms and addresses the need for effective instructional strategies and assessment of CT-related problem-solving abilities. Finally, we establish where CT concepts and skills already exist or are missing from the curriculum and suggest a workable tool to assess CT based on existing literature.

Keywords Assessment of problem-solving • Computational thinking (CT) • Curriculum expectations • Elementary education

Introduction

A growing digital economy and the need for an ever increasing percentage of the population to work with twenty-first century skills (e.g., problem-solving, creating, collaborating, communicating, critical thinking) demand that these skills be addressed and supported starting from an early age and that they remain a focus as students develop (Dede, 2010). Learning theory for a digital age emphasizes authenticity, audience, and authorship—children are creating, sharing, and learning with purpose (Bellanca & Brandt, 2010). The Computer Science Teachers Association (CSTA) and the International Society for Technology in Education (ISTE) (2011)

J. Mueller (✉) • E. Hennessey • H. Shodiev
Wilfrid Laurier University, 75 University Ave W, Waterloo, ON N2L 3C5, Canada
e-mail: jmueller@wlu.ca; henn8280@mylaurier.ca; hshodiev@wlu.ca

D. Beckett
Brock University, 1812 Sir Isaac Brock Way, St. Catharines, ON L2S 3A1, Canada
e-mail: daniellebeckett@gmail.com

P.J. Rich, C.B. Hodges (eds.), *Emerging Research, Practice, and Policy on Computational Thinking*, Educational Communications and Technology: Issues and Innovations, DOI 10.1007/978-3-319-52691-1_16

suggest that the following dispositions or attitudes accompany these skills: "confidence in dealing with complexity, persistence in working with difficult problems, tolerance for ambiguity, the ability to deal with open-ended problems, and the ability to communicate and work with others to achieve a common goal or solution" (p. 7). Although these skills and dispositions do not require technology, they are supported by and encouraged in a digital environment. Computational thinking and problem-solving are related to higher-order thinking skills that are recognized as fundamental to success in a digital age.

Computational thinking can be considered a specific type of problem-solving (i.e., approaching a problem with a particular mind-set utilizing computer technology). Computer programming involves the identification of a problem and the creation of a solution using a language and logic that directs a computer to perform actions leading to that solution. Computational thinking (CT) takes computer science outside of the computer lab and makes it accessible to everyone, rather than computer programming, often seen as a narrow and "tedious, specialized activity, accessible only to those with advanced technical training" (http://scratch.edu, 2016).

Considering and using computational thinking across disciplines to solve problems places computer programming within the reach of students at any age. A change in emphasis in learning, from knowledge acquisition to higher-order knowledge construction, makes it important for teachers to transform practice to approach computational thinking for students in all disciplines and not solely in computer science. Introducing creative and critical thinking is not a brand new endeavor for teachers (Griffin, 2014), but it can be more deliberate, specifically recognizing when a computer can help us to gather, analyze and manipulate data, create simulations, and persist with complex and difficult problems (Barr & Stephenson, 2011; CSTA & ISTE, 2011; Voskoglou & Buckley, 2012; Wing, 2006).

What is missing from the literature, and most learning frameworks, however, is a valid and reliable assessment of computational thinking skills. Some research recommends using multiple assessments in a "systems of assessments" approach to assessing computational thinking (Grover, 2015). However, employing many assessment tools can be costly and onerous. We, therefore, propose a more comprehensive assessment of computational thinking skills to provide an understanding of how such skills may be applied across disciplines.

Computational thinking is not, and should not be, an additional area of curriculum content, but rather an integrated component of already existing curricula. Teachers may not be prepared to include more content in what many describe as an "overcrowded" curriculum. One school principal, Brian Nichols, summarized an online "#edchat" (i.e., a weekly Twitter discussion of educators; 2010) on "how to manage standards and an overloaded curriculum," using three key themes: preparedness, essentiality, and integration. He suggests that in "covering the curriculum," teachers need to choose content and skills that prepare students for a workforce dependent on "the ability to create new ideas, synthesize information, and problem solve with people all over the globe." Further, teachers must identify what is "essential" and integrate such skill sets across disciplines rather than addressing problem-solving strategies in isolation.

This chapter identifies a working definition of computational thinking across the curriculum in Ontario's elementary classrooms and addresses the need for effective instructional strategies and assessment of problem-solving abilities. Further, we analyze where CT concepts and skills already exist or are missing from the Ontario Elementary School curriculum (Ministry of Education, Ontario, Canada). Finally, we suggest a workable CT assessment tool based on existing literature and current findings (Brennan & Resnick, 2012; Hesse, Care, Buder, Sassenberg, & Griffin, 2015; Voogt, Fisser, Good, Mishra, & Yadav, 2015; Wilson, Scalise, & Gochyyev, 2015).

What and Where Is Computational Thinking?

A Working Definition

Before a construct can be discussed, debated, and analyzed, an agreed-upon definition is generally a starting point. Wing's (2006) definition of computational thinking is considered to be that starting point although many researchers and educators have reviewed the definition, massaged its components, and set it in context since (e.g., Barr & Stephenson, 2011; National Research Council, 2010; Shelby & Woollard, 2013). In a recently published examination of computational thinking in compulsory education, Voogt, Fisser, Good, Mishra, and Yadav (2016) spoke to the need for a definition of computational thinking that includes "peripheral skills" important to CT but not "necessary and sufficient" if CT is to be implemented in the practice of teachers across disciplines.

Researchers have identified seven core *concepts* that are useful in programming, including sequences, loops, parallelism, events, conditionals, operators, and data. Computational *practices* consist of eight terms and refer to how one is learning: experimenting and iterating, testing and debugging, reusing and remixing, and abstracting and modularizing. Computational *perspectives* capture how programmers' perspectives are impacted during CT in three ways: expressing, connecting, and questioning.

The purpose of this chapter is not to review the historical development of the definition of the term, but rather to set a working definition in context for assessing CT across the curriculum in an elementary school setting using coding as a tool to teach this approach to problem-solving. The challenge is to identify where and when the concepts, practices, and perspectives that define computational thinking are, can, and should be introduced to learners.

Given the importance of computational thinking in the future, it is of related interest where and how much the present elementary curriculum addresses CT and associated processes. Indeed, an understanding of how the existing curriculum already addresses CT can (1) establish a starting place for educators who wish to expand the curriculum to incorporate or expand CT resources and (2) provide educators with evidence of where they already address CT. In effect, we suggest that adapting current teaching materials should not be intimidating. This could increase openness to dialogue around where CT may be "hiding in plain sight" within the current elementary school curriculum.

As an example, we conducted a systematic content analysis of the Ontario Elementary School curriculum (grades 1 through 8) for 38 terms (see Table 1) associated with computational thinking (Brennan & Resnick, 2012; Grover & Pea, 2013; Scratch Ed, 2016; Yadav et al., 2011). Content analysis refers to a research technique for making inferences from data to their context (Krippendorff, 2012). The goal of a content analysis is to systematically review and extract text into meaningful categories, which can then be used to draw conclusions.

Our primary research questions in this content analysis included:

1. *Frequenciesacross subject areas*: How often do the specific phrases "computational thinking" and "problem-solving" appear in the Ontario Elementary School curricula and across which subject areas? How often do CT-related terms (and their iterations) appear in the Ontario Elementary School curricula and across which subject areas?
2. *Grade level*: In which grade levels are students introduced to CT-related terms (and their iterations) across the Ontario Elementary School curricula?
3. *Context/location*: In which sections of the Ontario Elementary School curricula do CT-related terms (and their iterations) appear?

Method

Ontario curriculum documents are accessible to the public in multiple formats. We specifically analyzed the text files versus the print or PDF files given the large volume of data. In total, the Ontario curriculum documents total 1496 pages. Subject areas include kindergarten, mathematics, arts, sciences, language, health and physical education, social studies, French as a second language, and Native language studies (average page count was 187 pages). The Ministry of Education mandates that each year a number of subject areas enter the review process, so they remain relevant and age appropriate. Thus, educators, parents, and students at least once between 2005 and 2015 have reviewed subjects comprehensively.

In the current study in particular, we reviewed kindergarten, mathematics, arts, science and technology, health and physical education, social studies, French as a second language, and Native language studies for frequencies of terms. Then, we narrowed our search to a subset of terms and disciplines (i.e., mathematics, science and technology, language, and arts), focusing on areas relevant to our future applied research in classrooms. We reviewed each subject area for frequency of terms as well as context and location (i.e., curriculum expectations, front matter). Two trained researchers (i.e., graduate students in social psychology and business/computer science) conducted analyses, and any discrepancies were resolved through discussion. As well, we conducted an in-depth content analysis of the context,

Table 1 Computational thinking key terms searched in content analysis

Key term	Derivatives
1. Abstract	Abstracting[a]; abstraction
2. Algorithm	Algorithmic
3. Analyse	Analysis; analyze; analyzes; analyzed
4. Apply	Application; applied; applying
5. Automate	Automated; automatically; automation
6. Code	Coder; coding; coded; codes
7. Collection	
8. Computational thinking	Computational
9. Compute	Computed; computes; computer; computing
10. Conditionals[a]	
11. Connecting	
12. Data	Data analysis; data collection; data representation
13. Debugging[a]	
14. Decompose	Decomposed; decomposing; decomposition
15. Events[a]	
16. Experimenting[a]	
17. Expressing[a]	
18. Generalize	Generalization; generalized; generalizing
19. Identification	
20. Iterating[a]	
21. Logic	Logical
22. Loops[a]	
23. Management	
24. Model	Modeling; modeling
25. Modularizing[a]	
26. Operators	
27. Parallel	Parallelization
28. Problem	
29. Problem-solve	Problem-solves; problem-solvers; problem-solving
30. Questioning[a]	
31. Recursive	
32. Remixing[a]	
33. Representation	
34. Reusing[a]	
35. Sequence[a]	
36. Simulate	Simulated; simulation
37. Technology	Technological
38. Testing[a]	

[a]Terms from Brennan and Resnick (2012) used in specific search.

grade, and location of the terms within the curriculum document (i.e., curriculum expectations or front matter) using only the concepts, processes, and perspectives identified by Brennan and Resnick (2012). Preliminary results of the more specific content analysis of the disciplines are presented here (See Table 2). A more detailed examination of the results within context will be included in a forthcoming article by Hennessey, Mueller, Beckett, and Fisher (Unpublished manuscript).

To first determine frequencies of our terms across the various curricula, we wrote a script using Python (the programming language) to search for each word using regular expression pattern matching (see Goyvaerts, 2016). The script was designed to find all terms associated with CT processes. Included in this larger search were the focal CT definition terms delineated in Brennan and Resnick (2012). The script was designed to match all variations of each word stem in our search list [e.g., we searched for all variations of "code" such as "coding," "coded," "coder," and "codes" with the pattern cod(e|ing|ed|er|es)] while excluding words that were nested within other words which were not of interest (e.g., variations of "sequence" were found; however, variations of "consequence" were excluded). The most up-to-date version of each curriculum was searched with the script. Wherever possible, the plaintext version of the curriculum was searched. However, not all of the most up-to-date curricula have a plaintext version made publicly available. In these cases, the PDF version was first converted to a text file in order to be searched. This conversion process is inherently imperfect, and as such, the final frequency count for these curricula is expected to be a slight underestimation, as the converted text may have been broken up in the conversion process such that the regular expression would no longer match.

Results and Discussion

Frequencies of CT-related terms appear in Table 1. Our analyses showed that while the exact phrase "computational thinking" does not appear in the Ontario Elementary School curricula, the term "computational" alone appears sparsely and only in the mathematics curriculum (15 instances), mostly in a title describing "computational strategies." Iterations of the term "compute" appear more frequently in the mathematics curriculum (30 instances), but are less frequently cited in arts (10 instances), language (11 instances), or the science and technology (3 instances) curricula. The phrase "problem-solve" and its iterations appear with more frequency than "computational thinking" in the mathematics (459 instances) and science and technology (134 instances) curricula; however, "problem-solving" is sparsely mentioned in the arts (76 instances) and language (38 instances) curricula.

Although CT itself is not found explicitly in the current elementary curriculum, there are related terms present across disciplines. Initial frequency analyses indicated that terms associated with CT mostly appeared in the mathematics (1,259 instances) and arts (935 instances) curricula. These terms were also fairly commonly used in science and technology (886 instances). Terms associated with CT appeared somewhat often in the language (522 instances), kindergarten (447 instances), and health and physical education (276 instances) curricula and less frequently in the Native languages (53 instances) document.

A more specific analysis of the mathematics, science and technology, arts, and language documents using the computational *concepts*, *practices*, and *perspectives* from Brennan and Resnick's (2012) definition suggests that the frequencies of terms differ across disciplines and grades and that *concepts* are addressed more often than *practices* or *perspectives*. See Table 2 for frequencies of each term across different subject areas.

All four of the disciplines we examined include the terms "data" and "events." The mathematics curriculum, not surprisingly, uses the term "data" much more frequently than the other three disciplines. Both arts and language, however, also include the term "sequences," while mathematics and science, interestingly, do not. The only other specific CT *concept* that was found in the documents was "operators" (3 instances) in the science and technology curriculum. Any specific CT *practices* were referred to only in the science and technology curriculum—"testing" (19 instances) and "reusing" (3 instances). Only 1 instance of "abstracting" was found in the arts. Frequencies of terms defined as CT *perspectives* (i.e., "expressing," "connecting," and "questioning") were spread more evenly across the documents—

Table 2 Frequency of CT concepts, practices, and perspectives in mathematics, science and technology, language, and arts curricula

Subject area	Mathematics	Science and technology	Language	Arts
Key term concepts				
Data	253	28	5	3
Events	21	12	33	36
Operators	0	3	0	0
Sequences	0	0	3	8
Loops	0	0	0	0
Parallelism	0	0	0	0
Conditionals	0	0	0	0
Practices				
Testing	0	19	0	0
Reusing	0	3	0	0
Abstracting	0	0	0	1
Incremental	0	0	0	0
Iterative	0	0	0	0
Debugging	0	0	0	0
Remixing	0	0	0	0
Modularizing	0	0	0	0
Perspectives				
Connecting	23	2	17	7
Expressing	2	1	4	2
Questioning	1	1	9	4

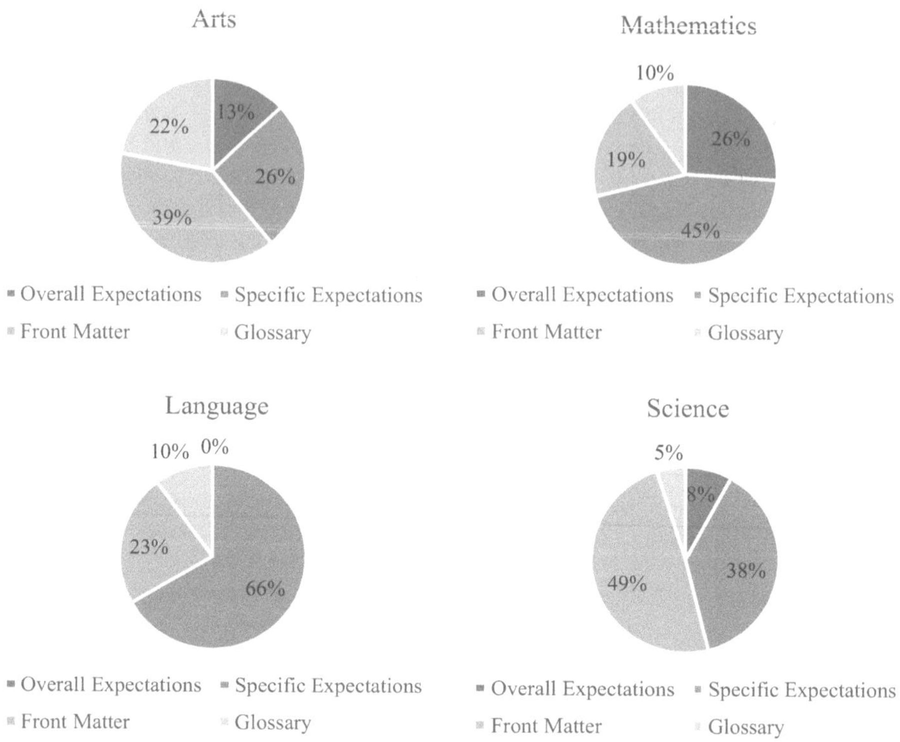

Fig. 1 Percentage of CT terms by location in curriculum documents

all had at least 1 instance of each term, but not in large numbers. The perspective of "connecting" was used most frequently in mathematics, followed by language, while language and arts included "questioning" more often than mathematics or science, each with just a single instance.

This initial analysis of instances of computational thinking terminology within the curriculum across disciplines suggests that terms related to the concepts of computational thinking can be found within the current curriculum, but specific terms unique to computer programming are not. It appears that a questioning and connecting perspective is a part of the current content in the elementary curriculum in the language and arts disciplines, suggesting that students may be learning the *concepts* and *perspectives* that form a foundation for computational thinking. What may be missing are the actual *practices* involved in computational thinking.

Examining "where" instances of CT-related terms are found within the curriculum may shed additional light on the meaning of the analysis. See Fig. 1 for a breakdown of percentages in location within the curriculum document.

The largest percentage of CT-related terms in the language and mathematics curricula is found in specific expectations—the "what" or content that is to be taught—while analysis of both the science and arts curricula indicates that CT-related terms

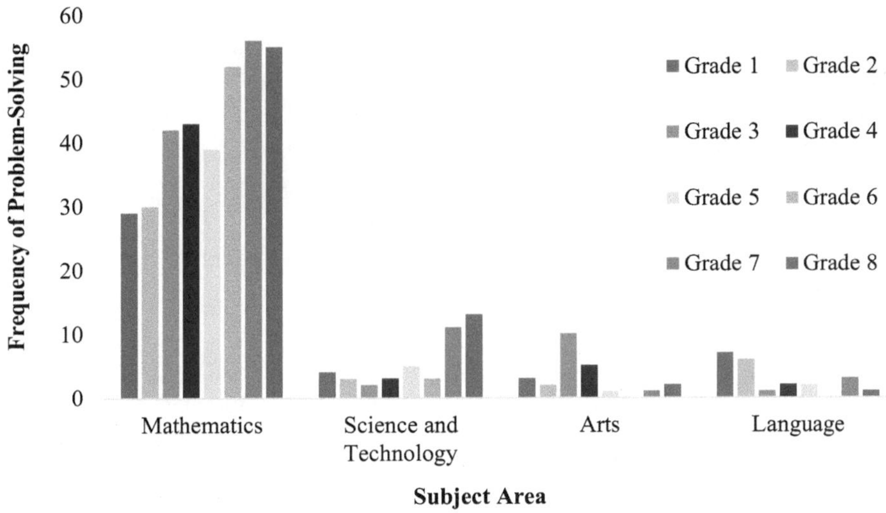

Fig. 2 Frequency of problem-solving in subject areas across grade levels

are most frequently found in the front matter of those documents, the "how" the subject is to be taught, the program planning, assessment and evaluation, and general overview of the discipline.

Aside from the frequency of computational thinking-related terms across disciplines, the developmental sequence across grades is also of interest. "Computational thinking" specifically is not a term used in any of the curriculum documents at any grade, but "solving problems" and "problem-solving" are terms used in increasing quantity within the documents. See Fig. 2 for the progression across grades in each of the four discipline areas examined in more detail.

Politicians, industry leaders (e.g., Google; Wing, 2014; Code.org), parents, and the computer science community are encouraging educators, beginning at the elementary level, to "transform" their teaching practices so that CT is added to current curriculum (Barr & Stephenson, 2011; Repenning, Webb, & Ioannidou, 2010). These types of sweeping changes and calls for transformation in educational practice and content rarely see immediate or substantial change. Identifying what currently "works" and sharing with educators where this way of thinking can be found in their curriculum and what these concepts, practices, and perspectives look like across grades and disciplines serves as a first step in making the necessary adjustments to twenty-first century education. Jun, Han, Kim, and Lee (2014) examined the computational literacy of Korean elementary students using information and communications technology (ICT) literacy as a broader issue, suggesting that the curriculum needs to be revised to include computational problem-solving skills and that teaching methods need to be more accessible and effective for teachers. Preliminary review of the Ontario Ministry of Education Curriculum for elementary students indicates that specific skills and practices used in computer programming may need to be included in revised and updated curriculum, but CT perspectives and ways of questioning may already be present in the curriculum—hiding in plain sight. A key question then is how educators teach these skills, practices, and perspectives to develop computational thinking across the disciplines and grades and how those concepts and skills are measured and assessed.

Teaching Computational Thinking and Problem-Solving Through Coding Across Disciplines

Developments and advancement in programming languages and digital technology have made coding and computer programming more accessible and user friendly, and Dr. Wing's (2006) vision possible. More recently, a debate (see Charlton & Luckin, 2012; Barr & Stephenson, 2011; Naughton, 2012) has emerged suggesting that not everyone can, or should, be a computer scientist, with arguments analogous to those suggesting that you do not need to be a mechanic to drive a car. However, twenty-first century global problems—social, economic, and environmental—demand that our educational institutions develop citizens who are able to approach these problems in creative and innovative ways, refining problems, developing solutions, and evaluating outcomes virtually and in real life (Barr & Stephenson, 2011). The sheer volume of information available and the data involved in solving these problems require computer-supported approaches .

Computational thinking enables the scaling of problem-solving. According to Constable (2005),

> "...Computers change the scale at which resources can be examined, and they already provide sufficient discriminatory powers that scale and speed compensate for their currently limited intelligence as they draw conclusions, make predictions, and participate in discoveries...The challenge for society is to assimilate digital knowledge and to improve the human condition by its application." (p. 1)

Coding has been introduced and perhaps even "hailed" as a panacea to ensure that learners are indeed introduced to, and develop, the ability to solve complex twenty-first century problems using computer programming. US President Obama's 2017 budget, in fact, includes four billion dollars to support computer science in schools, identifying computer science as a "basic skill" in his Computer Science for All initiative (Shear, 2016).

Computational thinking can be made accessible to students and teachers through concrete approaches to computer coding. Utilizing the potential and benefits of computer coding to develop skills and strategies across disciplines and across developmental levels will begin to provide a foundation for the development of computational thinking for everyone. Activities to learn and improve specific skills can be used across grade levels from kindergarten to grade 12, e.g., abstraction, algorithms and procedures, automation, simulation, and parallelization (CSTA & ISTE, 2011). In order to measure the effectiveness of the activities and the impact on problem-solving beyond those activities, tools measuring these twenty-first century skills must be developed, validated, and utilized. Problem-solving can be measured using complex, authentic examples in context or using a confined approach with one or two solution problems within limitations (Voskoglou & Buckley, 2012; Voskoglou & Perdikaris, 1993). Further evidence can then be collected through the use of verbal protocol, interviews, and naturalistic observation, and one can use computers to track strategies and approaches to problems within Web or applications.

Resources have been developed and utilized to support teachers in the kindergarten to grade 12 environment using computer coding to represent problems and collect data (e.g., CSTA & ISTE, 2011). Advances in computer technology have created applications and programs that allow the user to build and create without knowing a complex computer language. One such application was developed at MIT and is available to users online: Scratch (http://scratch.mit.edu). The platform was designed for students from ages 8 to 16 but is used by people of all ages across learning contexts and disciplines. Using "drag, drop, and click" blocks of code, users can build projects to animate, simulate, tell stories, and make music. Utilizing a software application such as Scratch, measuring problem-solving ability before and after its use across curriculum areas (disciplines) and age levels, will allow us to assess the impact of instruction related to computational thinking on problem-solving ability and introduce CT to teachers and students (see Koehler & Ackaolgu, 2014).

The key question is whether learning to code is an effective method for developing problem-solving that transfers across disciplines and contexts. An examination of the curriculum and how CT is addressed, or not, at the elementary level serves as a starting point for measuring computational thinking using a systematic approach.

Measuring Computational Thinking and Problem-Solving

Even when using the most effective teaching methods, teachers cannot assume that learning occurs. It is well documented that students develop and learn at different rates (Angelo & Cross, 1993; Cashin, 1990; Drake, Reid, & Kolohan, 2014; Sternberg, 1986, 2009) and teaching quality varies from classroom to classroom; therefore, teachers should not assume all students have grasped what has been taught (Western and Northern Protocol for Collaboration in Education, [WNPC], 2006). As a result, classroom assessment and evaluation are essential to measure what students have learned. To date, extensive research exists on traditional classroom assessment strategies that promote effective instruction and student learning (Andrade, 2009; Brookhart, 2009; Black, Harrison, Lee, Marshall, & Wiliam, 2003; Black & Wiliam, 2009; Dann, 2014; Earl, 2003; Hattie, 2012).

What's lacking presently in classroom assessment research is the twenty-first century context of classroom assessment. Specifically, with the influx of new skills deemed necessary for the twenty-first century (e.g., computational thinking skills), teachers are at a loss of how to teach and assess such skills (Griffin & Care, 2015; DiCerbo, 2014). In fact, the Association for Computing Machinery (ACM) and the Computer Science Teacher Association (CSTA) stress the major factor that limits computational thinking into schools is the lack of assessments available to teachers.

Computational thinking has a wide application beyond computing itself. It is the process of recognizing aspects of computation in the world and applying tools and techniques from computing to understand and reason about natural, social, and artificial systems and processes (Csizmadia et al., 2015). It allows students to tackle problems, to break them down into solvable chunks, and to devise algorithms to solve them. Therefore, computational thinking concentrates on students performing a thought process, not on the production of artifacts or evidence. This in itself can be problematic for assessment because it is difficult to measure actual thought processes.

Although we advocate for a systems of assessment approach whereby "assessment as, of, and for learning" are used purposely, we recognize that "assessment as learning" plays a large role in effective "assessment of" students' computational thinking. That is, in order for teachers to truly know what and how students are thinking, students are required to demonstrate their thought processes in some way. One of most effective methods for assessing student thinking is the think-aloud method (Ahonen & KanKaanranta, 2015). Two methods are available for collecting student think-aloud data: concurrent and retrospective think-alouds (Ericsson & Simon, 1993). During a concurrent think-aloud, students think aloud as they complete a task with the intent of unveiling the cognitive processes they engage in and the information they attend to while they are solving a problem (Leighton & Gierl, 2007). In contrast, retrospective think-alouds are conducted after students have solved the problem, providing students an opportunity to describe any metacognitive processes in which they engaged while solving the problem (Ericsson & Simon, 1993). Although both methods can provide rich accounts of students' computational thinking, concurrent think-alouds collect data from short-term memory which is preferable when assessing computational thinking skills because they are not tainted by perception, providing the most accurate representation of knowledge and ability. And yet, this method can be costly in terms of time and scale. It is unreasonable to expect teachers to be able to use it writ large. Recently, however, easier accessibility to new and older technologies in schools, such as audio and video recordings and screencasting with student narration, mitigates some of the caveats of the think-aloud method.

Metacognition is often tied with think-alouds as it requires students to think about their own thinking (Flavell, 1979). Think-alouds and metacognitive processes are at the crux of deep, purposefully "assessment as learning." Computational thinking is a systematic thinking process, and for this reason the think-aloud is a valuable method for properly understanding how computational thinking happens at the cognitive level. That is, this method provides teachers with rich student data about how the student is thinking through a problem, consequently allowing the teacher to provide deliberate, personalized instruction to further student learning. However, one of the drawbacks of this method is that younger children are not always aware of their own cognition, and therefore thinking aloud could distract them from the task. This brings to light that metacognition is not an innate ability; it must be taught. Volante and Beckett (2011) suggested a "lockstep process" to teaching AaL; that is, teachers provide guidance to students when cultivating evaluative knowledge and expertise and reflecting on what they have learned. It is beneficial for teachers to provide students with a pool of appropriate strategies to bring their own performance closer to the desired goal (Sadler, 1989). This argument is strongly aligned with Earl's (2003) conceptual framework of the three purposes of assessment in that she believes teachers should establish an environment in which AaL is central to student learning and that all other assessments are rooted in such practices.

The bidirectional transmission between teacher assessment (i.e., AaL and AfL) and student self-assessment (i.e., AaL) is a vital factor for optimal assessment of computational thinking. What remains to be created in the area of computational thinking though is an assessment tool that will allow teachers to evaluate CT and scaffold additional teaching and learning. Before an assessment tool can be developed, a clear description of what is being assessed is required.

We provide a set of teacher verbal protocols to aid in the evaluation of students' computational thinking processes. By asking these types of questions, teachers will be able to gain a deep understanding of students' computational thinking ability and how it relates to problem-solving outside of coding. Specifically, the questions are broken down by processes so that teachers can pinpoint which are areas of strength and areas of needed improvement.

The questions are categorized based on skills and processes that are inherent to computational thinking and as such would be useful skills to transfer across disciplines to solve problems. For instance, in order to evaluate students' algorithmic thinking across disciplines, teachers can ask "Can the student create a set of steps to solve a problem" and "Can the student solve similar problems with the same set of steps or principles?" See Table 3 for a possible list of questions. By using this set of questions, teachers may gain a more comprehensive understanding of students' ability to transfer computational skills and processes into other disciplines and guide further instruction.

This set of questions can also be used as a communication tool between teachers and students. Evaluation as communication can promote student learning and development of computational thinking and problem-solving skills. Specifically, a discussion (with these questions as a guide) can confirm with students the quality of their performance and provide insight on how they can improve and further develop their computational thinking skills. The questioning in and of itself encourages and scaffolds metacognition and computational thinking. With that said, our intention is not to reduce or oversimply the evaluation of computational thinking only to these sets of skills. We recognize this as a starting place and a means to support discussion and provoke thought around how to assess computational thinking skills. Ultimately, computational thinking is a process and therefore should not be evaluated as an end product. It is an ongoing learning progression through grade levels and across subject areas to eventually produce effective and productive twenty-first century thinkers. Future research will examine the "think-alouds" of children as they participate in tasks intended to develop computational thinking to further inform the types of questions to be used in assessment of CT and provide criteria and examples of development across grades and disciplines.

Table 3 Assessment tool for concepts, processes, and perspectives in problem-solving and computational thinking

Skill (source)	Questions
Algorithmic thinking	Can the student create a set of steps to solve a problem? Can the student solve similar problems with the same set of steps or principles?
Decomposition	Can the student break down the problem into smaller, more manageable parts?
Generalization/inferencing	Can the student transfer prior knowledge and skills? Can the student identify patterns, similarities, and connections between prior and current problems? Can the student make inferences?
Abstraction	Can the student evaluate what is valuable information and what is not? Can the student remove unnecessary information? Can the student add or remove details to clarify a problem?
Evaluation	Can the student evaluate if the solution is a good one?
Incremental/iterative thinking	Can the student identify a concept for the project? Can the student develop a design plan? Can the student implement the design plan? Is the student comfortable adapting the plan in response to new or different information?
Testing and debugging	Can the student develop strategies for dealing with problems? Can the student anticipate and plan for problems? Is the student comfortable using a trial and error method?
Reusing and remixing	Is the student efficient in researching relevant information? Can they use research to their advantage while maintaining authenticity? Can the student embed others' work into their own in a meaningful way? Does the student have critical code reading ability?
Modularizing	Can the student put together smaller parts to make something larger? Can the student piece together parts of a solution to solve a problem?

Note: Categories of skills were informed by Brennan and Resnick (2012) and Csizmadia et al. (2015)

Conclusion

The demand for CT to be integrated into elementary education is clear. What that looks like in terms of curriculum, practice, and assessment is not well defined. The data analysis process itself that was used in this research was an example of utilizing computational thinking and coding processes to analyze an expansive set of information such as the Ontario Curriculum documents. This chapter provides a preliminary analysis of one provincial-level elementary curriculum and recognizes the existence of computational thinking and related terms across disciplines. For example, there is an emphasis on CT-related concepts and perspectives in seemingly unrelated disciplines of language and the arts, with fewer instances of specific practices necessary for computer programming as evidenced by the low prevalence of key terms. Computational thinking is present in a variety of forms and contexts in the existing curriculum as both content (i.e., curriculum expectations) and pedagogical approaches (in planning, teaching strategies, and assessment). Educators therefore need to build on current expectations in each discipline to further develop CT as a way of thinking from elementary education onward. This chapter acknowledges the importance of identifying and defining CT as a metacognitive thinking process that teachers assess in collaboration with students. A set of questions is proposed to allow teachers and students to communicate the development of problem-solving skills across disciplines and developmental stages, serving as a foundational assessment tool for measuring CT in instruction and research.

Acknowledgments The research discussed in this chapter is supported by a Social Science and Humanities Research Council Insight Development Grant.

References

Ahonen, A. K. & Kankaanranta, M. (2015). Introducing assessment tools for 21st century skills in Finland. In P. Griffin & E. Care (Eds.), *Assessment and teaching of 21st century skills* (pp. 213–225). Springer.

Andrade, H. L. (2009). Students as the definitive source of formative assessment: Academic self-assessment and the self-regulation of learning. In H. L. Andrade & G. J. Cizek (Eds.), *Handbook of formative assessment* (pp. 90–105). New York, NY: Taylor & Francis.

Angelo, T. A., & Cross, P. (1993). *Classroom assessment techniques: A handbook for college teachers* (2nd ed.). San Francisco, CA: Jossey-Bass.

Barr, V., & Stephenson, C. (2011). Bring computational thinking to K-12: What is involved and what is the role of the computer science education community? *ACM Transaction on Computational Logic, 2*(1), 48–54.

Bellanca, J., & Brandt, R. (Eds.). (2010). *21st century skills. Rethinking how students learn.* Bloomington, IN: Solution Tree Press.

Brennan, K., & Resnick, M. (2012). New frameworks for studying and assessing the development of computational thinking. In *Proceedings of the 2012 annual meeting of the American Educational Research Association, Vancouver, Canada.*

Black, P., Harrison, C., Lee, C., Marshall, B., & Wiliam, D. (2003). *Assessment for learning: Putting it into practice*. New York, NY: Open University Press.

Black, P., & Wiliam, D. (2009). Developing the theory of formative assessment. *Educational Assessment, Evaluation and Accountability, 21*, 5–31. doi:10.1007/s11092-008-9068-5.

Brookhart, S. M. (2009). Mixing it up: Combining sources of classroom achievement information for formative and summative purposes. In H. L. Andrade & G. J. Cizek (Eds.), *Handbook of formative assessment* (pp. 279–296). New York, NY: Taylor & Francis.

Cashin, W. E. (1990). Students do rate different academic fields differently. *New Directions for Teaching and Learning, 43*, 113–121. doi:10.1002/tl.37219904310.

Charlton, P., & Luckin, R. (2012). Computational thinking and computer science in schools. In *'What The Research Says' Briefing 2*. The London Knowledge Lab, Institute of Education: United Kingdom.

Computer Science Teachers Association (CSTA), & The International Society for Technology in Education (ISTE). (2011). *Computational Thinking. Teacher Resources* (2nd ed.). USA: National Science Foundation. Grant No. CNS-1030054.

Constable, R. L. (2005). *Transforming the academy: Knowledge formation in the age of digital information*. New York, NY: Cornell University Publishing.

Csizmadia, A., Curzon, P., Dorling, M., Humphreys, S., Ng, T., Selby, C., & Woollard, J. (2015). *Computing at School*. Retrieved from http://www.computingatschool.org.uk

Dann, R. (2014). Assessment as learning: Blurring the boundaries of assessment and learning for theory, policy, and practice. *Assessment in Education, 21*(2), 149–166. doi:10.1080/0969594X.2014.898128.

Dede, C. (2010). Comparing frameworks for 21st century skills. In J. Bellanca & R. Brandt (Eds.), *21st century skills: Rethinking how students learn*. Bloomington, IN: Solution Tree Press.

DiCerbo, K. (2014). Review of the book chapter Assessment and teaching of 21st century skills, by P. Griffin, E. Care, & B. McGaw, Eds. *Assessment in education: Principles, policies, and practices, 21l*(4), 502-505. doi:10.1080/0969594X.2014.931836

Drake, S. M., Reid, J. L., & Kolohan, W. (2014). Interweaving curriculum and assessment in the 21st century: Engaging students in 21st century leanring. Toronto, ON: Oxford University Press.

Earl, L. (2003). *Assessment as learning*. Thousand Oaks, CA: Corwin Press.

Ericsson, K. A., & Simon, H. A. (1993). *Protocol analysis: Verbal reports as data*. Cambridge, MA: MIT Press.

Flavell, J. H. (1979). Metacognition and cognitive monitoring: A new area of cognitive-developmental inquiry. *American Psychologist, 34*(10), 906–911. doi:10.1037/0003-066X.34.10.906.

Goyvaerts, J. (2016). *Regular-expressions*. Retrieved from: http://www.regular-expressions.info/index.html

Griffin, P. (2014). Performance assessment of higher order thinking. *Journal of Applied Measurement, 15*(1), 1–16.

Griffin, P., & Care, E. (Eds.). (2015). *Assessment and Teaching of 21st Century Skills: Methods and Approach*. Dordrecht: Springer.

Grover, S. (2015). *"Systems of Assessments" for deeper learning of computational thinking in K-12*. Draft paper presented at the Annual Meeting of the American Educational Research Association, Chicago, April 15–20, 2015.

Grover, S., & Pea, R. (2013). Computational thinking in K–12: A review of the state of the field. *Educational Researcher, 42*(1), 38–43.

Hattie, J. (2012). *Visible learning for teachers*. New York, NY: Routledge.

Hennessey, E., Mueller, J., Beckett, D., & Fisher, P. *Hiding in plain sight: Assessing how much and where computational thinking is represented with the ontario elementary school curriculum*. Unpublished manuscript.

Hesse, F., Care, E., Buder, J., Sassenberg, K., & Griffin, P. (2015). A framework for teachable collaborative problem solving skills. In *Assessment and teaching of 21st century skills* (pp. 37–56). Dordrecht: Springer.

Jun, S. J., Han, S. G., Kim, H. C., & Lee, W. G. (2014). Assessing the computational literacy of elementary students on a national level in Korea. *Educational Assessment, Evaluation and Accountability, 26*, 319–332. doi:10.1007/s11092-013-9185-7.

International Society for Technology in Education (ISTE). (2011). Retrieved from www.iste.org/computational-thinking

Leighton, J. P., & Gierl, M. J. (Eds.). (2007). *Cognitive diagnostic assessment for education: Theory and applications*. Cambridge, MA: Cambridge University Press.

National Research Council. (2010). *Report of a Workshop on the Scope and Nature of Computational Thinking*. Washington, DC: The National Academies Press. doi:10.17226/12840.

Naughton, J. (2012). Why all our kids should be taught how to code. *Observer New Review, 31*(3), 12.

Repenning, A., Webb, D., & Ioannidou, A. (2010). Scalable game design and the development of a checklist for getting computational thinking into public schools. In *Proceedings of the 41st ACM technical symposium on Computer science education: ACM, 265-269.*

Scratch Ed (2016). *Computational thinking with scratch.* Retrieved February 12, 2016, from http://scratched.gse.harvard.edu/ct/defining.html

Sadler, D. R. (1989). Formative assessment and the design of instructional systems. *Instructional Science, 18*(2), 119–144.

Shear, M. D. (2016). *Obama's budget urges a deeper commitment to computer education. New York Times.* Retrieved from http://www.nytimes.com/2016/01/31/us/politics/obamas-budget-urges-a-deeper-commitment-to-computer-education.html?_r=0

Shelby, C. & Woollard, J. (2013). Computational thinking: The developing definition. Available: http://eprints.soton.ac.uk/356481

Sternberg, R. J. (1986). *Intelligence applied.* New York, NY: Harcourt Brace Jovanovich.

Sternberg, R. J. (2009). Foreword. In D. J. Hacker, J. Dunlosky, & A. C. Graesser (Eds.), *Handbook on metacognition in education* (pp. viii–viix). New York, NY: Routledge.

Volante, L., & Beckett, D. (2011). Formative assessment and the contemporary classroom: Synergies and tensions between research and practice. *Canadian Journal in Education, 34*(2), 239–255.

Voogt, J., Fisser, P., Good, J., Mishra, P., & Yadav, A. (2015). Computational thinking in compulsory education: Towards an agenda for research and practice. *Education and Information Technologies, 20*, 715–728.

Voskoglou, M. G., & Buckley, S. (2012). Problem solving and computers in a learning environment. *Egyptian Computer Science Journal, ECS, 36*(4), 28–46.

Voskoglou, M. G., & Perdikaris, S. C. (1993). Measuring problem-solving skills. *International Journal of Mathematical Education in Science and Technology, 24*(3), 443–447.

Western and Northern Protocol for Collaboration in Education. (2006). *Rethinking classroom assessment with a purpose in mind.* Retrieved from http://www.wncp.ca/media/40539/rethink.pdf

Wilson, M., Scaliseb, K., & Gochyyev, P. (2015). Rethinking ICT literacy: From computer skills to social network settings. *Thinking Skills and Creativity, 18*(1), 65–80.

Wing, J. M. (2006). Computational thinking. *Communications of the ACM, 49*(3), 33–35.

Wing, J. (2014). Computational thinking benefits society. *Social Issues in Computing Blog.* Retrieved from: http://socialissues.cs.toronto.edu/2014/01/computational-thinking/

Assessing Algorithmic and Computational Thinking in K-12: Lessons from a Middle School Classroom

Shuchi Grover

Abstract As educators move to introduce computing in K-12 classrooms, the issue of assessing student learning of computational concepts, especially in the context of introductory programming, remains a challenge. Assessments are central if the goal is to help students develop deeper, transferable computational thinking (CT) skills that prepare them for success in future computing experiences. This chapter argues for the need for multiple measures or "systems of assessments" that are complementary, attend to cognitive and noncognitive aspects of learning CT, and contribute to a comprehensive picture of student learning. It describes the multiple forms of assessments designed and empirically studied in *Foundations for Advancing Computational Thinking*, a middle school introductory computing curriculum. These include directed and open-ended programming assignments in Scratch, multiple-choice formative assessments, artifact-based interviews, and summative assessments to measure student learning of algorithmic constructs. The design of unique "preparation for future learning" assessments to measure transfer of CT from block-based to text-based code snippets is also described.

Keywords Computational thinking • Middle school computer science • K-12 computer science education • Deeper learning • Systems of assessments • Algorithmic thinking

> "*...assessment provides a powerful lever. Assessments shape the public mind, and everything else flows from that*"—Schwartz and Arena (2013)

S. Grover (✉)
SRI International, Menlo Park, CA 94025, USA
e-mail: shuchi.grover@sri.com

P.J. Rich, C.B. Hodges (eds.), *Emerging Research, Practice, and Policy on Computational Thinking*, Educational Communications and Technology: Issues and Innovations, DOI 10.1007/978-3-319-52691-1_17

Making the Case for Assessments of Computational Thinking

With the bold call for "Computer Science For All" in January 2016, the President of the United States echoed the beliefs of many—that all children from "kindergarten through high school need to learn computer science and be equipped with the computational thinking skills they need to be creators in the digital economy, not just consumers, and to be active citizens in our technology-driven world" (Whitehouse.gov, 2016). This announcement came on the heels of a decade of efforts among researchers, educators, and advocacy groups nationwide working in concert with organizations such as the NSF, ACM CSTA, and Code.org that involved building a shared understanding around what it means for children to learn computational thinking (CT) and computer science (CS) in formal K-12 educational settings (Grover & Pea, 2013; Wing, 2006). There is now consensus in the national education discourse that computational problem-solving, logical and algorithmic thinking, abstraction, and modeling of real-world phenomena—all undisputed aspects of CT—should be taught not only in CS classrooms but also in the context of STEM and other subjects.

Many of the introductory CT experiences for K-12 settings are being designed around programming using block-based programming environments such as Scratch, Alice, Blockly, MIT App Inventor, and Snap!, among others. These have focused on providing kids with an engaging exposure to the creation of computational artifacts and largely ignored issues of assessment. Consequently, assessments of CT remain underdeveloped and under-researched (Yadav et al., 2015) and this issue has been called out as a key future CS education research imperative (Cooper, Grover, Guzdial, & Simon, 2014). They are conspicuously missing from the early introductory programming curricular offerings rolled out online by entities such as Code.org and Khan Academy. Without sufficient attention to thoughtful assessment, CT can have little hope of scaling in K-12 education (Grover & Pea, 2013). While the goal of assessments is mostly to measure student learning, it need not necessarily result in awarding student grades, but rather, in providing a useful means to highlight gaps in student understanding that can in turn inform refinements in curriculum and/or pedagogy. Measures that enable educators to assess student learning, both formatively and summatively, need to be created, tested, and validated in various settings with diverse learners.

Furthermore, few efforts, if any, have looked at the issue of transfer of CT skills beyond the immediate curriculum. Transfer of learning is an aspect of assessment that deserves attention since computational experiences at various levels of K-12 aim to serve as bridges to future computational work. New approaches to transfer such as *Preparation for Future Learning* (PFL; Bransford & Schwartz, 1999; Schwartz, Bransford, & Sears, 2005) have shown promise in the context of science and mathematics learning at the secondary level (Chin et al., 2010; Dede, 2009; Schwartz & Martin, 2004). Interventions in CS education could similarly benefit from these emergent ideas in the learning sciences.

This chapter describes the design, use, and study of a comprehensive suite of assessments created for an introductory CS and programming curriculum for middle school, *Foundations for Advancing Computational Thinking*, or FACT. The goals of the assessments were to assess student learning of algorithmic thinking (mainly) in introductory programming and to evaluate the curriculum that was also designed as part of this research effort. The assessment design and use were influenced and informed by prior research on assessments described in the literature review below.

(Lack of) Assessments of CT in K-12: A Literature Review

Some progress has been made in creating assessments for established high school curricula such as Exploring Computer Science (ECS; Goode, Chapman, & Margolis, 2012) and AP CS Principles (Astrachan et al., 2011) being used nationally. SRI International (2013)'s Principled Assessments of Computational Thinking use evidence-centered design (ECD; Mislevy, Steinberg, & Almond, 2003) to create assessments that support valid inferences about CT practices (Bienkowski, Snow, Rutstein, & Grover, 2015) for the ECS curriculum. Learning in the AP CS Principles course is assessed using through-course assessments involving "performance tasks" in addition to the end-of-course AP Exam comprising multiple-choice questions (College Board, 2014).

The few research efforts that have specifically targeted tackling the issue of CT assessment especially in the context of activities involving programming (e.g., Fields, Searle, Kafai, & Min, 2012; Koh, Nickerson, Basawapatna, & Repenning, 2014; Meerbaum-Salant, Armoni, & Ben-Ari, 2010; Werner, Denner, Campe, & Kawamoto, 2012; Werner, Denner, & Campe, 2015) suggest that assessing the learning of computational concepts and constructs in popular programming environments is a challenge.

Manually checking students' completed projects is a customary form of assessment. However, it is subjective and time-consuming, especially with large student populations, an issue that is being addressed to some extent through tools such as *Dr. Scratch*, a Scratch-specific tool for assessing the complexity of a program (Moreno-León, Robles, & Román-González, 2015). However the existence of computational constructs in the code may not always provide an accurate sense of students' computational competencies (Brennan & Resnick, 2012). Kurland and Pea (1985) reported that students aged 11 and 12 years who had logged more than 50 h of LOGO programming experienced under "discovery learning" conditions were able to write and interpret short, simple programs but had much difficulty on programs involving fundamental programming concepts. In interviews, students revealed many incorrect conceptions about how programs work. These findings clearly point to problems inherent in completed student programs alone as a measure of their understanding of CT concepts. Artifact-based interviews can help provide a more accurate picture of student understanding of their programming projects as shown by Barron, Martin, Roberts, Osipovich, and Ross (2002). Such procedures, while valuable for research and for providing a holistic view of student learning, may not be practical to scale, especially in curricula used in regular school classrooms.

Werner et al. (2012) assessed student learning through a specially designed *Fairy Assessment* created in Alice that required middle school students to code parts of a predesigned program to accomplish specific tasks to demonstrate understanding of algorithmic thinking, abstraction, and code. They found student performance to be the highest on the simplest task which measured comprehension and lowest on the task which measured complex problem-solving skills using debugging. The task, however, was specific to Alice, and rubric-based scoring of student projects was reported to be cumbersome.[1]

There is thus a need for assessment instruments that will illuminate student understanding of specific computing concepts and other CT skills such as debugging, code tracing, problem decomposition, and pattern generalization. Black & Wiliam (1998), Glass & Sinha (2013) contend that well-designed multiple-choice assessments can be used to further learners' understanding and provide learners with feedback and explanations in addition to simply testing student understanding. Cooper created a multiple-choice instrument for measuring learning of Alice programming concepts (Moskal, Lurie, & Cooper, 2004), but it has not been used to measure student learning in K-12 education. Lewis et al. (2013) used simple quizzes that get at students' understanding of Scratch blocks. Meerbaum-Salant et al. (2010) used assessments designed to measure understanding of programming concepts in Scratch before, during, and after the intervention.

Other innovative forms of assessment involve the design of gaming environments that teach and assess aspects of CT (e.g., Lee, Ko, & Kwan, 2013) or the design of simulations that assess CT in the context of Science classrooms (e.g., Weintrop et al., 2014). Some limited progress has been made in the development and use of automated tools to assess evidence of CT in programs created in block-based languages such as Scratch, Blockly, and Alice (e.g., Fields, Quirke, Amely, & Maughan, 2016; Grover, et al., 2016; Werner, McDowell, & Denner, 2013). Many of these "learning analytics" efforts are still nascent. Other efforts to assess CT have included studying growth and use of the CS vocabulary and "CT language" (Fletcher & Lu, 2009) to measure CT as children engage in computationally rich activities (Grover, 2011).

Large-scale efforts to roll out introductory computing curricula at the middle school level such as the UK national effort and the Israel Ministry of Education's Science and Technology Excellence Program that includes a national CS curriculum and exam (Zur Bargury, 2012) provide ideas for how CT is being assessed in introductory CS settings internationally. The UK curriculum includes formative assessments, Scratch programming assignments, and a final project of the student's choosing (Scott, 2013). The use of multiple-choice assessments and attendant rubrics to measure learning at scale in the Israeli effort (Zur Bargury, Pârv, &

[1] In an ongoing NSF-funded collaborative research effort, SRI International and Carnegie Mellon University are examining ways of automating assessment using log data from the Fairy Assessment in Alice captured by Denner and Werner. We are employing a combination of computational learning analytics/educational data mining techniques and the ECD framework to study students' programming *process* and automate the assessment of programming tasks such as the Fairy Assessment. Grover, Basu, & Bienkowski (2017) & Grover et al. (2017) provide a glimpse of our work in progress using this computational psychometrics approach.

Lanzberg, 2013) is particularly pertinent to the work described in this chapter. Their nationwide exam in 2012 comprised nine questions (with roughly 30 sub-questions). Arguably such multiple-choice measures are easier to implement on a large scale than open-ended student projects. They use Bloom's taxonomy to classify the questions and inferences that can be drawn about the appropriate learning level of the associated computing concepts. The research and design on CT assessments in FACT described in this chapter builds on many of these prior efforts.

Research Framework and Methodology

Foundations for Advancing Computational Thinking: Curriculum and Assessment Design

The introductory programming units of FACT, the middle school curriculum at the center of this research, were designed as a structured in-classroom learning experience that leveraged pedagogical ideas for deeper understanding and transfer, and also included various forms of formative and summative assessments. FACT included elements designed to build awareness of computing as a discipline while promoting engagement with foundational computing concepts in introductory programming, mainly, elements of algorithmic flow of control, and CT practices such as code reading, writing pseudo-code, and debugging. The various units in FACT focused on computing in our world, the basics of computational problem-solving, algorithmic thinking, and programming in Scratch (Table 1). The curricular units were deployed as a course on Stanford University's OpenEdX platform to facilitate a 7-week blended in-class learning experience. The online materials comprised short Khan Academy-style videos ranging between 1 and 5 min in length that led learners through the thinking involved in the construction of computational solutions using the Scratch programming environment. This was inspired by the use of worked examples that have been found to reduce cognitive load initially for novices encountering conceptually challenging tasks in programming (Morrison, Margulieux, & Guzdial, 2015). The videos were interspersed with directed as well as open-ended programming activities to be completed individually or in pairs, peer

Table 1 FACT curriculum unit-level breakdown

Unit 1	Computing is everywhere!/What is CS?
Unit 2	What are algorithms and programs? Precise sequence of instructions in programming
Unit 3	Iterative/repetitive flow of control in a program: loops and iteration
Unit 4	Representation of information (data and variables)
Unit 5	Boolean logic and advanced loops
Unit 6	Selective flow of control in a program: conditional thinking
	Final project (student's own choice; could be done individually or in pairs)

discussions, and online "quizzes" that used automated grading with feedback, and explanations of solutions. The course ended with an open-ended game design project of choice.

Transfer and PFL for text-based computing contexts (from the block-based Scratch environment) was mediated through expansive framing (Engle et al., (2012) and providing learners opportunities to work with analogous representations (Gentner et al., 2003) of the computational solutions—plain English, pseudo-code, in addition to programs coded in Scratch. Details of the curriculum design and pedagogical underpinnings of FACT are described in Grover, Pea, and Cooper (2015). The curriculum and assessments were refined over two iterations of design-based research (DBR) with students in middle school classrooms (N = 26 in Study#1; N = 28 in Study#2). Student's learning outcomes, classroom experiences, and feedback on the curriculum and assessments were used to inform revisions. Grover and Pea (2016) detail the DBR process that influenced design decisions. This chapter focuses specifically on the refined assessments used in the second iteration (Study#2) of teaching FACT in a middle school classroom setting.

The "Deeper Learning" Lens

"Deeper learning" (Pellegrino & Hilton, 2013) is increasingly seen as an imperative for helping students develop robust, transferable knowledge and skills for the twenty-first century. The phrase acknowledges the cognitive, intrapersonal, and interpersonal dimensions of learning while also underscoring the need for learners to be able to transfer learning to future contexts. Ideas of deeper learning find resonance in *How People Learn* (Bransford, Brown, & Cocking, 2000)—the seminal treatise that explicated the need for learning environments to be assessment-centered in addition to learner-, knowledge-, and community-centered.

Assessments are designed artifacts of the learning environment aimed at providing feedback to the learner and to the teacher about student understanding. FACT's assessment design was guided by Barron and Daring-Hammond's (2008) assertion that robust assessments for meaningful learning must include (1) intellectually ambitious performance assessments that require application of desired concepts and skills in disciplined ways, (2) rubrics that define what constitutes good work, and (3) frequent formative assessments to guide feedback to students and teachers' instructional decisions. Furthermore, Conley and Darling-Hammond (2013) assert that in addition to assessments that measure key subject matter concepts, assessments for *deeper learning* must measure (1) higher-order cognitive skills as well as skills that support transferable learning and (2) abilities such as collaboration, complex problem-solving, planning, reflection, and communication of these ideas through the use of appropriate vocabulary of the domain in addition to presentation of artifacts to a broader audience.

These assertions point to the need for different measures of learning or "systems of assessments" that arc complementary, encourage and reflect deeper learning, and contribute to a comprehensive picture of student learning. *In light of these recommendations for assessments of deeper learning, multiple and innovative measures of assessment were used in FACT to help create a multifaceted picture of student learning as described in the sections below.* The following research questions were probed through empirical inquiry: (1) What is the variation across learners in learning of algorithmic flow of control (serial execution, looping constructs, and conditional logic) through the FACT curriculum? (2) Does FACT promote an understanding of algorithmic concepts that goes deeper than tool-related syntax details as measured by "preparation for future learning" (PFL) transfer assessments? (3) What is the change in the perception of the discipline of CS among learners as a result of the FACT curriculum? This chapter describes FACT's "systems of assessments" that measured growth of algorithmic thinking skills, transfer of these skills, as well as noncognitive aspects such as beliefs and perceptions of computing. It also briefly describes the results of empirical research involving their use.

FACT's Systems of Assessments

FACT's multifaceted assessments included the following types of measures. They are described in more detail below:

1. Open-ended and directed programming assignments with attendant rubrics that built on the concepts taught
2. Innovative programming exercises inspired by Parson's puzzles (Parsons and Haden, 2006)
3. Low-stakes high-frequency quizzes[2] with open-ended, multiple-choice items that were interspersed throughout the course for formative feedback to the learner though feedback and explanations, and to the teacher. These were aimed at assessing understanding of individual concepts and constructs just taught.
4. A summative assessment with multiple-choice items (most of which were reused from the 2012 Israel National Exam)
5. Final project of students' choosing (to be done in pairs)
6. Final project presentation to the whole class along with individual written student reflections and a "studio" of students' final projects on Scratch website
7. Student artifact-based interviews around their final projects
8. Block-to-text-based programming PFL assessment
9. Open-ended responses to questions such as "What do computer scientists do?" and "Computing is ____________________________."
10. Pre-post surveys on student interest and attitudes toward CS and programming
11. A pretest to allow for assessing pre-to-post-FACT learning gains on questions based on Scratch code (inspired by Ericson & McKlin, 2012)

In keeping with its learner-centered philosophy, FACT placed a heavy emphasis on "learning by doing" in the Scratch programming environment. In addition to open-ended time to dabble with programming following example videos (that modeled algorithmic thinking and computational problem-solving in Scratch through worked examples), there were specific assignments with attendant rubrics that built

[2] FACT's quizzes and summative assessment have been shared on the assessment platform, Edfinity. http://edfinity.com/join/9EQE9DT8.

Table 2 FACT's structured and open-ended Scratch programming assignments

Programming assignments (Scratch/ pseudocode)	Algorithmic/CT concepts/constructs
Share a recipe	Serial execution; repetition; selection
(Scratch) Make a life cycle of choice	Serial execution
(Scratch) Draw a spirograph with any polygon	Simple nested loop + creative computing
(Scratch) Create a simple animation	*Forever loop*
(Scratch) Generic polygon maker	Variables; user input
Look inside Scratch code and explain the text version of code	Algorithms in different forms (analogous representations for deeper learning)
(Scratch) Draw a "Squiral"	Loops, variables, creative computing
Open-ended project (in pairs): Create a game using "repeat until"	*Loops ending with Boolean condition*
(Scratch) Maze game	Conditionals; event handlers
(Scratch) Guess my number game	Loops, variables, conditionals, Boolean logic
(Scratch) Final, open-ended project of choice	*All CT topics taught in FACT*

on the concepts taught in the videos (Table 2). *Rubrics included items for creativity to encourage student self-expression through programming.*

Some programming exercises inspired by Parson's puzzles (Denny, Luxton-Reilly, & Simon, 2008; Parsons & Haden, 2006) involved presenting all the Scratch blocks (in jumbled sequence) required for a program that students needed to snap in correct order.

Low-stakes, high-frequency auto-graded quizzes throughout FACT tested students' understanding of specific CS concepts and constructs, and included explanations, to give learners immediate feedback on their response (examples shown in Figs. 1 and 2). Following these quizzes, some learners would re-watch the video lecture, or try things out in Scratch, thus taking more control of their learning. Many quiz questions were based on small snippets of Scratch or pseudo-code; these were designed to help learners develop familiarity with code tracing—the ability to read/understand code has been found to be positively correlated with code writing (Bornat, 1987; Lopez et al., 2008).

Summative assessments included a posttest conducted online that included multiple-choice and open-ended response items. These items were aimed at assessing learners' CT ability through questions that required code tracing and/or debugging (Figs. 3 and 4). It included six out of nine questions from the 2012 Israel National Exam that are described in Zur Bargury et al. (2013). A final project of learners' choosing to be done with a partner or individually was also part of the summative assessments. Aligning with the social and participatory aspects of learner-centered environments, each student pair also presented the final projects to the whole class on a special "Expo" day and showcased their projects in an online Scratch studio of games, so peers could play (and test) the games and provide peer feedback. Students also individually wrote reflections on their final projects using a

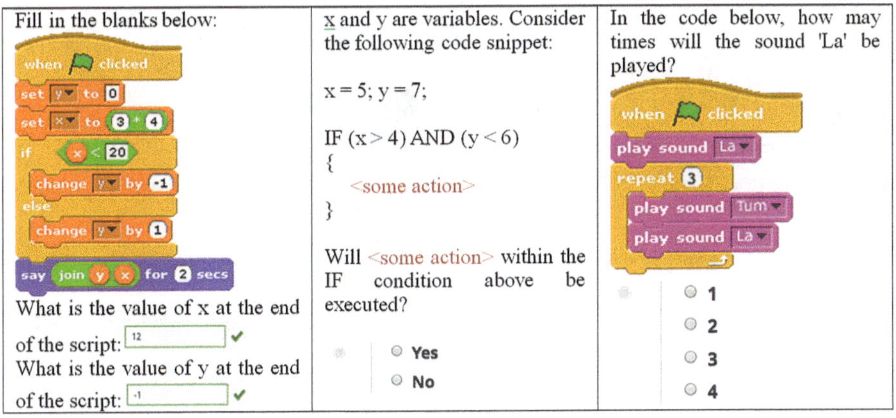

Fig. 1 Sample quiz questions used in formative assessments

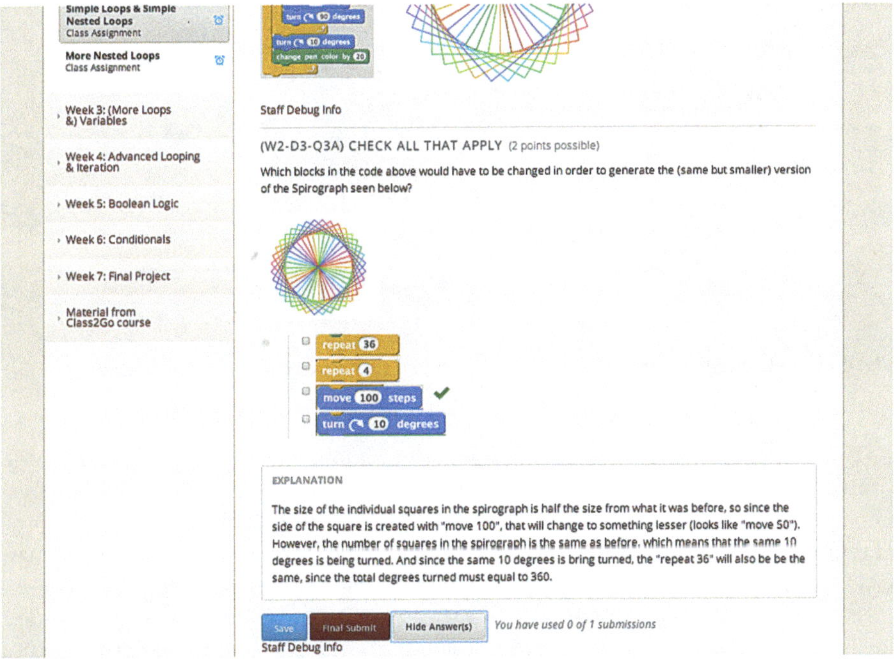

Fig. 2 Auto-graded quiz question with explanation on OpenEdX

document adapted from Scott (2013). The final project thus afforded learners the opportunity to problem-solve, code, debug, collaborate, plan, communicate, present, and reflect on their work. Inspired by past research (Barron et al., 2002), "artifact-based interviews" around the final Scratch projects were also conducted individually with each student.

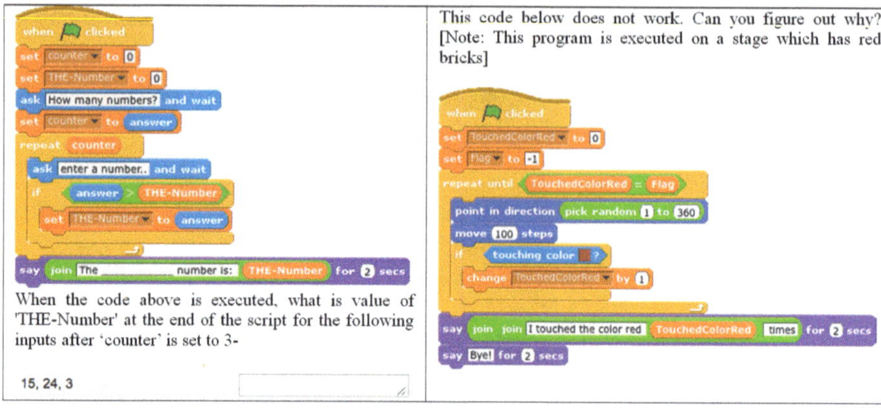

Fig. 3 Sample questions in the CT summative test

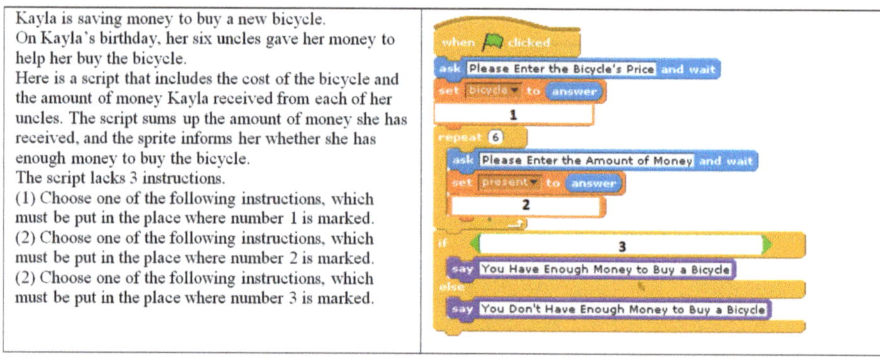

Fig. 4 Sample question from the 2012 Israel National Exam in the CT summative test

FACT's unique PFL test was designed and administered after the end of the course to specifically assess how well students were able to transfer their computational understanding built in FACT in the context of the block-based Scratch programming environment (and through extensive use of pseudo-code throughout FACT) to the context of a text-based (Java-like) programming language. PFL assessments evaluate how well students learn with new resources or scaffolding that are included as part of the assessment (Schwartz & Martin, 2004; Schwartz et al., 2005). The PFL assessment items were preceded by "new learning" in the form of syntax in a text-based language for constructs that students had encountered in the context of Scratch in FACT. To help learners make connections back to the past learning context (Pea, 1987) and see "the old in new" (Schwartz, Chase, & Bransford, 2012), references are made to the equivalent constructs in Scratch, for example, *PRINT displays things specified in parenthesis to the computer screen one line at a time (like SAY in Scratch)* (Fig. 5). Two different types of syntax were explained, one of a Pascal-like, and the other of a Java-like, language. These were followed by

'<–' (left arrow) is used to assign values to variables. *For example:* n <–5 assigns the value 5 to the variable n
If there are blocks of compound statements (or steps), then the **BEGIN..END** construct is used to delimit (or hold together) those statement blocks (like the yellow blocks for REPEAT and IF blocks in Scratch).
FOR and **WHILE** are loop constructs like REPEAT & REPEAT UNTIL in Scratch

```
WHILE (some condition is true)
BEGIN
... (Execute some commands) .....
END
```

PRINT displays things specified in parenthesis to the computer screen <u>one line at a time</u> (like SAY in Scratch).
Commas are used inside the PRINT command like JOIN in Scratch to combine a text message with a variable

==

Question #1: *When the code below is executed, what is displayed on the computer screen?*

```
PRINT("before loop starts");
num <–0;
WHILE (num < 6) DO
BEGIN
        num <–num + 1;
        PRINT("Loop counter number ", num);
END
PRINT("after loop ends");
```

Fig. 5 Sample PFL question following new syntax specification

questions involving simple code snippets that used the text-based syntax in order to measure students' ability to read and understand the text-based code snippets.

Lastly, since perspectives and practices of the discipline are key ingredients of modern STEM learning, affective aspects such as students' growth in their beliefs and understanding of computing as a discipline and changes in their attendant attitudes toward CS were also assessed through pre-post attitude surveys and responses to the free-response question—"*What, in your view, do computer scientists do?*"

Participants, Procedures, and Data Measures

In its second iteration, FACT was taught over a seven week period in a public middle school classroom in Northern California. The student sample comprised 28 children from 7th and 8th grade (20 boys and 8 girls; mean age, ~12.3 years) enrolled in a semester-long "Computers" elective class. The class met for 55 min, four times per week. The classroom teacher and researcher were present in the classroom at all times. IRB permission was sought from parents and students prior to the start of the study. An independent researcher assisted with grading. The following data measures were used in the research:

- *Prior experience survey*: This gathered information about students' prior experiences in computational activities (adapted from Barron, 2004).
- *Pre-post CS perceptions survey*: This included the free-response question "*What do computer scientists do?*"
- *Pre-post CT assessments*: This measured pre- and post-FACT CT skills.

- *Formative quizzes*: These captured student progress and targets of difficulty throughout the course.
- *Scratch projects:* About ten directed and open-ended programming projects through the course (along with rubrics).
- *Final Scratch projects, presentations, and artifact-based student interviews on the final project.*
- "*Preparation of future learning*" (PFL) assessment designed to assess transfer of learning from block-based to a text-based programming language.

Since the current focus is on assessments rather than a description of the curriculum and study procedures (described in detail in Grover et al., 2015), the remainder of the chapter includes results and a brief discussion.

Results

Due to space constraints, qualitative grading of Scratch projects is not discussed here. This section chapter focuses on quantitative scoring of students' performance on the designed summative and PFL tests, and touches briefly on qualitative analysis of artifact-based interviews after the final project.

The pretest-to-summative test effect size (Cohen's *d*) was ~2.4, and all learners showed statistically significant learning gains (Tables 3 and 4). Students found 'serial execution' or the concept of sequence to be the easiest, followed by conditionals; and loops were the hardest for students to grasp. This was perhaps because most of the questions on loops also involved variable manipulation—a concept that novice learners often struggle with.

Details in Zur Bargury et al. (2013) on scoring and student performance in the student sample of ~4000 middle school students in Israel allowed us to conduct a comparative analysis between our results and those reported in Israel. This analysis revealed comparable performances by our students on the six questions we used

Table 3 Within-student comparison of pretest and summative test scores (Cohen's $d = 2.4$)

	Pretest score		Summative score			
N	Mean	SD	Mean	SD	t-stat	p-value
28	28.1	21.2	81.6	21.0	-15.5	<0.001

The t-stat and its following p-value come from a t-test to test whether the pre- and post-means are the same

Table 4 Summative test scores breakdown by CS topics

	Mean	Std. dev.
Overall score	81.6	21.2
By CS topic		
Serial execution	91.1	20.7
Conditionals	84.9	20.5
Loops	77.2	26.3
Vocabulary	77.4	22.2

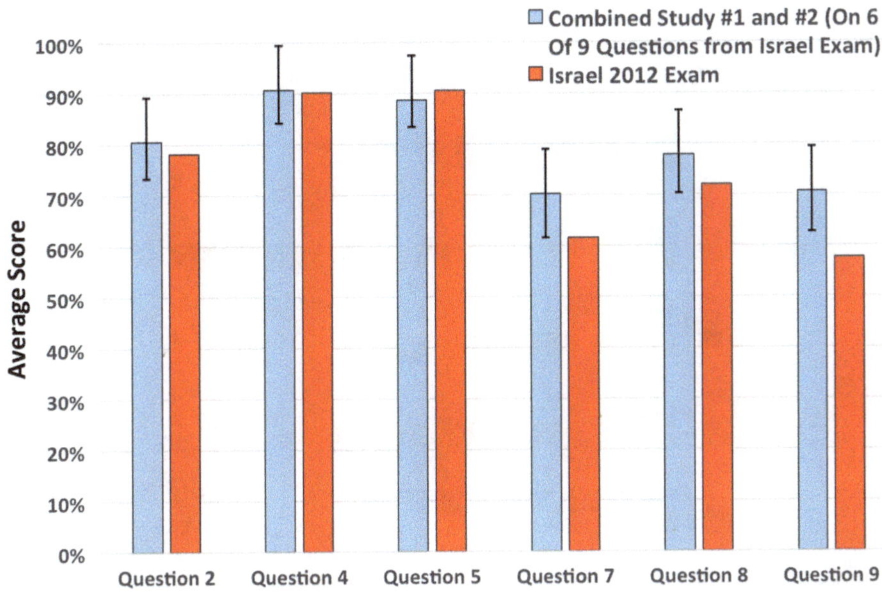

Fig. 6 Student performance post-FACT vs. 2012 Israel National Exam results (N = 4082). **Note:** *Error bars represent the margin of error* (half-width of a 95% confidence interval)

from the Israel exam (Fig. 6). Interviews around a difficult summative test question (from the Israel National Exam) suggested that those items needed to be refined to improve their validity.

On the PFL test, there was evidence of understanding of algorithmic flow of control in code written in a text-based programming language. Grover, Pea, and Cooper (2014a) provide more details on the PFL questions and their scoring. Regression analyses revealed that ELL students had trouble with the text-heavy PFL test (Grover, Pea, & Cooper, 2016a, b), which may explain the mean score of 65%.

Students' pre-post responses to the question "What do computer scientists do?" revealed a significant shift from naive "computer-centric" beliefs of computer scientists as people who engage mostly in fixing, making, studying, or "experimenting" with computers to embrace a view of CS as a creative problem-solving discipline with diverse real-world applications (Fig. 7). More details on this aspect of the research are detailed in Grover, Pea, & Cooper, 2014b.

Final projects were graded based on a rubric inspired by Martin, Walter, and Barron (2009) who used it for grading game projects in AgentSheets. The difference in programming contexts necessitated modifications to make it work for Scratch projects. As in the original rubric, grading criteria were separated into "game design" and "programming" items. It should be noted that the rubric was designed less as a tool for giving the student a grade than to understand students' application of CT concepts learned. Additionally, individual "artifact-based interviews" were conducted around students' final projects and guided by questions such as:

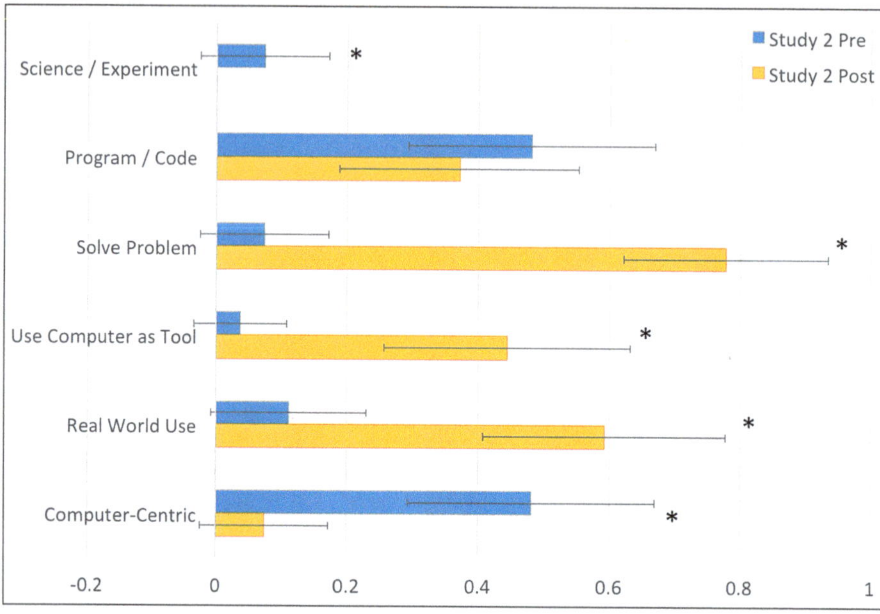

Fig. 7 Pre-post FACT responses to "What do computer scientists do?"

- How did you decide on your project?
- What does it do? How did you do it? (*Student controls the mouse to points things on the screen while talking*)
- What was it like working on this project? [*Fun/challenging/difficult/creative/boring?]*

The qualitative rubric-based grading of the final projects (Fig. 8) and student interviews both revealed that even the students who had low English proficiency and had performed poorly in the summative CT and PFL tests were able to demonstrate high levels of engagement in the final project as well as a reasonable understanding of algorithmic constructs. Two such students were Kevin and Isaac (pseudonyms) who worked together to build a Halloween-themed three-level *Scary Maze* game. The game was not complex, although three levels of increasing difficulty were cleverly incorporated with increasingly narrow passageways. The challenge was to navigate the maze without touching the walls (that narrowed in width from level 1 to level 3). The game elements and visual execution were bare bones, but the students had added interesting effects such as background music during navigation, and a scary scream accompanying a scary face to end the game. Though simple, the game implemented a coherent theme and had an intuitive game play which was very engaging. The programming was not very complex; no variables were used (although they mentioned in the interview that they wanted to add a timer). They implemented different levels by having the scene change when the sprite touched a red door. The game had a bug related to where to position the sprite

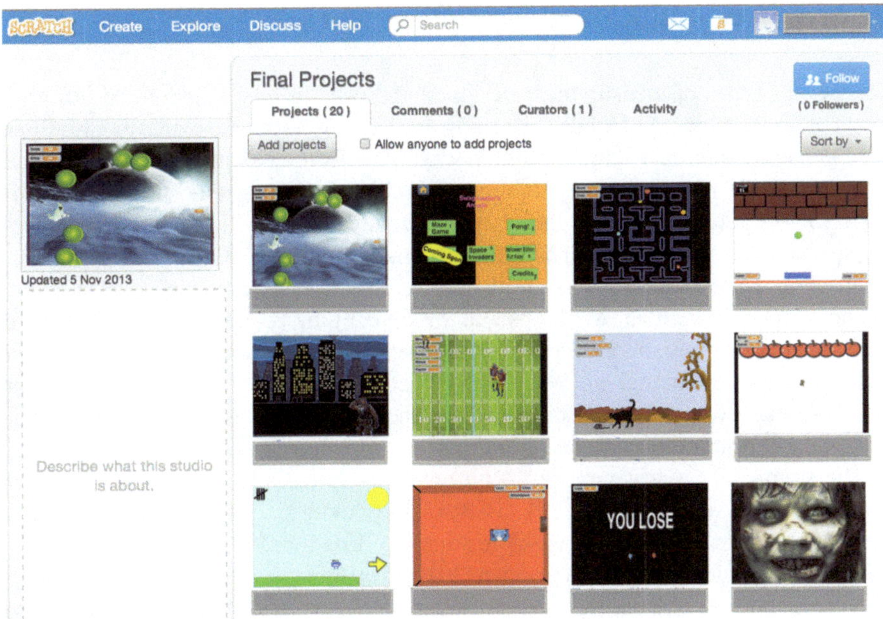

Fig. 8 Studio of students' final projects on Scratch website

Table 5 Highlights of "artifact-based" interview with Kevin (pseudonym)

Observation/interpretation	*Student quote(s) or exchanges with interviewer*
Connected "scary" final project idea with event in personal life	*"we watched* ***Insidious*** *the day before… and then we got this project assigned and we just decided to do something scary. coz we were traumatized coz of the movie"*
Decision to do Maze game, (but with conscious effort to make enhancements)	*"We decided to do a maze because, uhm, well, we had an assignment where we were supposed to do a maze… before… We also added like uhm, like levels and stuff like that"*
Able to describe what the code did, referred to specific code elements while talking	e.g. *"we have in forever our up and arrow keys..." "And each level has a different color red, so when you touch it it'll take you to the next level"*
Was aware of a bug in the code and showed it	*Here you see when you touch the black, it'll start you down here, instead of up there… and w-we don't know why. We tried to fix it but… we couldn't fix it, I don't know what was going on…*

In talking through problem causing the bug, he managed to figure that an IF-ELSE would be needed to know which level they were on and reset the position accordingly

at the start of each level. The artifact-based interview with Kevin (excerpts in Table 5) revealed that he was aware of the bug. In the process of talking through the problem during the interview, he was also able to figure how to fix the bug (with the use of a 'level' variable and a conditional to test which level the user was on).

Discussion & Implications for Future Work

The various types of measurement designed and used in FACT addressed different facets of understanding of student learning and provided students with opportunities to demonstrate their learning in multiple ways. The formative quizzes were a unique feature of FACT not routinely seen in middle school curricula. They provided useful feedback to students on their learning and understanding as well as to the researchers on aspects of curriculum design based on student performance. Given their formative nature, they were used to inform midcourse curriculum adjustments. For example, students' performance on the 'loops and variables' quiz prompted more time to be dedicated to that topic. In post-course student surveys, while some students indicated that there were "too many" online quizzes, other students found them to be useful for their learning. Some students specifically acknowledged the usefulness of the feedback and explanations they received in response to incorrect answers in quizzes.

The summative assessment test with multiple-choice and open-ended Scratch-based questions as well as the PFL assessment pointed to difficulties that students had with loops with changing variable values. While those topics are traditionally difficult for novices to grasp (Cooper, 2010; du Boulay, 1986; Ebrahimi, 1994); Robins, Rountree, & Rountree, 2003; Spohrer & Soloway, 1986), the results also suggested that other pedagogies may be more productive in introducing children to those CT concepts.[3] Results on the PFL test also suggest that they would benefit from redesign. For a balanced set of questions with robust construct validity, the PFL test should assess learners on transfer of individual concepts taught—serial execution, variables, conditionals, and loops—in addition to some questions that involve multiple concepts. Additionally, assessments need to be designed such that they do not disadvantage learners who have difficulty with the English language. The multiple-choice questions in the formative quizzes demonstrated face validity but would benefit from additional reliability studies.

It was apparent that learners benefited from being given opportunities to demonstrate their understanding in multiple ways. This was true for all students regardless of their performance on the formative quizzes and summative CT test. In their artifact-based interviews, each student expressed how much they enjoyed the final project and indicated a personal connection to the final project. In contrast to the decontextualized summative test with questions that involved making sense of Scratch code and answering questions based on them, the final project was a more meaningful form of performance assessment for which Barron and Darring-Hammond (2008) argue. It embodied learner agency and instilled a sense of personal accomplishment in every student as they presented their projects to their peers. Most importantly, it worked well for all students, even those who performed poorly on the summative test. That said, the value of tests that can be graded easily and objectively to assess understanding of specific CT constructs, however, should not be underemphasized. This is especially pertinent considering the challenges of grading open-ended projects.

[3]This question is at the heart of my ongoing NSF-funded research project (#1543062) at SRI International being conducted in partnership with San Francisco Unified School District (https://www.sri.com/work/projects/middle-school-computer-science).

No single type of assessment alone would have captured the cognitive, affective, and transfer aspects of deeper learning described earlier in this chapter. Each type of assessment served a purpose, and together, they provided a comprehensive view of student learning. Additionally, as this research experience has shown, not all assessments work equally well for all students to demonstrate their learning. This appears to be especially true for those students who are otherwise disadvantaged and/or have poor academic preparation and/or out-of-school experiences that are not intellectually enriching. It is important to keep this in mind as "CS For All" aims to broaden participation and level the playing field in CS for all, with special attention to those groups that have historically been marginalized. This research therefore argues for "systems of assessments" for algorithmic thinking aspects of CT and also presents empirically tested examples for an introductory computing course.

This article addresses a critical gap in the prevalent thinking about the design of introductory computing experiences in formal K-12 CS education. It presents results from the second iteration of a DBR effort. Follow-up work currently underway includes validating an assessment of introductory programming and algorithmic concepts informed by this research. Results from its pilot use in diverse middle school CS classrooms in Northern California have revealed new insights into student misconceptions about loops, variables and expressions (Grover & Basu, 2017). It is hoped that educators and curriculum designers will also be able use the ideas presented in this chapter to inform the design of introductory CS learning experiences at various levels of K-12 education, especially aspects related to assessment of deeper CS learning.

Acknowledgments The research described in this chapter was part of my Ph.D. dissertation at Stanford University. This effort benefited immensely from the support and guidance from my advisors and members of my doctoral committee. I am very grateful for the intellectual contributions of Dr. Roy Pea, Dr. Daniel Schwartz, and Dr. Brigid Barron at the Stanford Graduate School of Education, and Dr. Stephen Cooper at the Department of Computer Science, Stanford University. I would also like to acknowledge the support of the school district, principal, classroom teacher, and students who participated in this research. This project was funded by a grant from the National Science Foundation (#1343227).

References

Astrachan, O., Barnes, T., Garcia, D. D., Paul, J., Simon, B., & Snyder, L. (2011). CS principles: piloting a new course at national scale. In *Proceedings of the 42nd ACM technical symposium on computer science education* (pp. 397–398). ACM.

Barron, B. (2004). Learning ecologies for technological fluency: Gender and experience differences. *Journal of Educational Computing Research, 31*(1), 1–36.

Barron, B., & Daring-Hammond, L. (2008). How can we teach for meaningful learning? In L. Daring-Hammond, B. Barron, P. D. Pearson, A. H. Schoenfeld, E. K. Stage, T. D. Zimmerman, G. N. Cervetti, & J. L. Tilson (Eds.), *Powerful learning: What we know about teaching for understanding*. San Francisco, CA: Jossey-Bass.

Barron, B., Martin, C., Roberts, E., Osipovich, A., & Ross, M. (2002). Assisting and assessing the development of technological fluencies: Insights from a project-based approach to teaching computer science. In *Proceedings of the conference on computer support for collaborative learning: Foundations for a CSCL community* (pp. 668–669). International Society of the Learning Sciences.

Bienkowski, M., Snow, E., Rutstein, D. W., & Grover, S. (2015). *Assessment design patterns for computational thinking practices in secondary computer science: A First Look* (SRI Technical Report) Menlo Park, CA: SRI International. Retrieved from http://pact.sri.com/resources.html

Black, P., & Wiliam, D. (1998). *Inside the black box: Raising standards through classroom assessment*. Granada Learning.

Bornat, R. (1987). *Programming from first principles*. Englewood Cliffs, NJ: Prentice Hall International.

Bransford, J. D., & Schwartz, D. L. (1999). Rethinking transfer: A simple proposal with multiple implications. In A. Iran-Nejad & P. D. Pearson (Eds.), *Review of research in education* (Vol. 24, pp. 61–101). Washington, DC: American Educational Research Association.

Bransford, J. D., Brown, A., & Cocking, R. (2000). *How people learn: Mind, brain, experience and school* (Expanded ed.). Washington, DC: National Academy.

Brennan, K., & Resnick, M. (2012). New frameworks for studying and assessing the development of computational thinking. In *Proceedings of the 2012 annual meeting of the American Educational Research Association*. Vancouver, Canada.

Chin, D. B., Dohmen, I. M., Cheng, B. H., Oppezzo, M. A., Chase, C. C., & Schwartz, D. L. (2010). Preparing students for future learning with Teachable Agents. *Educational Technology Research and Development, 58*(6), 649–669.

College Board. (2014). *AP computer science principles: Performance assessment*. Retrieved from https://advancesinap.collegeboard.org/stem/computer-science-principles/course-details.

Conley, D. T., & Darling-Hammond, L. (2013). *Creating systems of assessment for deeper learning*. Stanford, CA: Stanford Center for Opportunity Policy in Education.

Cooper, S. (2010). The design of Alice. *ACM Transactions on Computing Education (TOCE), 10*(4), 15.

Cooper, S., Grover, S., Guzdial, M., & Simon, B. (2014). A future for computing education research. *Communications of the ACM, 57*(11), 34–36.

Dede, C. (2009). Immersive interfaces for engagement and learning. *Science, 323*(5910), 66–69.

Denny, P., Luxton-Reilly, A., & Simon, B. (2008). Evaluating a new exam question: Parsons problems. In *Proceedings of the fourth international workshop on computing education research* (pp. 113–124). ACM.

du Boulay, B. (1986). Some difficulties of learning to program. *Journal of Educational Computing Research, 2*(1), 57–73.

Engle, R. A., Lam, D. P., Meyer, X. S., & Nix, S. E. (2012). How does expansive framing promote transfer? Several proposed explanations and a research agenda for investigating them. *Educational Psychologist, 47*(3), 215–231.

Ebrahimi, A. (1994). Novice programmer errors: Language constructs and plan composition. *International Journal of Human-Computer Studies, 41*(4), 457–480.

Ericson, B., & McKlin, T. (2012). Effective and sustainable computing summer camps. In *Proceedings of the 43rd ACM technical symposium on computer science education* (pp. 289–294). ACM.

Fields, D. A., Quirke, L., Amely, J., & Maughan, J. (2016). Combining big data and thick data analyses for understanding youth learning trajectories in a summer coding camp. In *Proceedings of the 47th ACM technical symposium on computing science education* (pp. 150–155). ACM.

Fields, D. A., Searle, K. A., Kafai, Y. B., & Min, H. S. (2012). Debuggems to assess student learning in e-textiles. In *Proceedings of the 43rd SIGCSE technical symposium on computer science education*. New York, NY: ACM.

Fletcher, G. H., & Lu, J. J. (2009). Human computing skills: Rethinking the K-12 experience. *Communications of the ACM, 52*(2), 23–25.

Gentner, D., Loewenstein, J., & Thompson, L. (2003). Learning and transfer: A general role for analogical encoding. *Journal of Educational Psychology, 95*(2), 393–408.

Glass, A. L., & Sinha, N. (2013). Providing the answers does not improve performance on a college final exam. *Educational Psychology, 33*(1), 87–118.

Goode, J., Chapman, G., & Margolis, J. (2012). Beyond curriculum: The exploring computer science program. *ACM Inroads, 3*(2), 47–53.

Grover, S. (2011). *Robotics and engineering for Middle and High School students to develop computational thinking*. Paper presented at the annual meeting of the American Educational Research Association. New Orleans, LA.

Grover, S., & Pea, R. (2013). Computational thinking in K–12: A review of the state of the field. *Educational Researcher, 42*(1), 38–43.

Grover, S. & Pea, R. (2016). Designing for deeper learning in a blended computer science course for Middle School: A design-based research approach. In *Proceedings of the 12th international conference of the learning sciences*, Singapore.

Grover, S. & Basu, S. (2017). Measuring student learning in introductory block-based programming: Examining misconceptions of loops, variables, and boolean logic. In: *Proceedings of the 48th ACM Technical Symposium on Computer Science Education* (SIGCSE '17). Seattle, WA. ACM.

Grover, S., Bienkowski, M., Basu, S., Eagle, M., Diana, N. & Stamper, J. (2017). A framework for hypothesis-driven approaches to support data-driven learning analytics In measuring computational thinking in block-based programming. In: *Proceedings of the 7th International Learning Analytics & Knowledge Conference (2017)*. Vancouver, CA. ACM.

Grover, S. Basu, S., & Bienkowski, M. (2017). Designing programming tasks for measuring computational thinking. In: *Proceedings of the Annual Meeting of the American Educational Research Association*. San Antonio, TX.

Grover, S., Pea, R., & Cooper, S. (2014b). Remedying misperceptions of computer science among Middle School students. In *Proceedings of the 45th ACM technical symposium on computer science education* (pp. 343–348). ACM.

Grover, S., Pea, R., & Cooper, S. (2015). Designing for deeper learning in a blended computer science course for Middle School students. *Computer Science Education, 25*(2), 199–237.

Grover, S., Pea, R., & Cooper, S. (2016a). Factors influencing computer science learning in Middle School. In *Proceedings of the 47th ACM technical symposium on computing science education* (pp. 552–557). ACM.

Koh, K. H., Nickerson, H., Basawapatna, A., & Repenning, A. (2014). Early validation of computational thinking pattern analysis. In *Proceedings of the 2014 conference on innovation and technology in computer science education* (pp. 213–218). ACM.

Kurland, D. M., & Pea, R. D. (1985). Children's mental models of recursive LOGO programs. *Journal of Educational Computing Research, 1*(2), 235–243.

Lee, M. J., Ko, A. J., & Kwan, I. (2013). In-game assessments increase novice programmers' engagement and level completion speed. In *Proceedings of the ninth annual international ACM conference on international computing education research* (pp. 153–160). ACM.

Lewis, C. M., et al. (2013). *Online curriculum*. Retrieved from http://colleenmlewis.com/scratch.

Lopez, M., Whalley, J., Robbins, P., & Lister, R. (2008). Relationships between reading, tracing and writing skills in introductory programming. In: *Proceedings of the Fourth international Workshop on Computing Education Research* (pp. 101–112). ACM.

Martin, C. K., Walter, S., & Barron, B. (2009). Looking at learning through student designed computer games: A rubric approach with novice programming projects. *Unpublished paper, Stanford University.*

Meerbaum-Salant, O., Armoni, M., & Ben-Ari, M. (2010). Learning computer science concepts with scratch. In *Proceedings of the sixth international workshop on computing education research (ICER '10)* (pp. 69–76). New York, NY: ACM.

Mislevy, R. J., Steinberg, L. S., & Almond, R. G. (2003). Focus article: On the structure of educational assessments. *Measurement: Interdisciplinary research and perspectives, 1*(1), 3–62.

Moreno-León, J., Robles, G., & Román-González, M. (2015). Dr. Scratch: Automatic analysis of scratch projects to assess and foster computational thinking. *Revista de Educación a Distancia, 46*. doi:10.6018/red/4.

Morrison, B. B., Margulieux, L. E., & Guzdial, M. (2015). Subgoals, context, and worked examples in learning computing problem solving. In *Proceedings of the eleventh annual international conference on international computing education research* (pp. 21–29). ACM.

Moskal, B., Lurie, D., & Cooper, S. (2004). Evaluating the effectiveness of a new instructional approach. *ACM SIGCSE Bulletin, 36*(1), 75–79.

Parsons, D., & Haden, P. (2006). Parson's programming puzzles: A fun and effective learning tool for first programming courses. In *Proceedings of the 8th Australasian conference on computing education* (Vol. 52, pp. 157–163). Australian Computer Society.

Pea, R. D. (1987). Socializing the knowledge transfer problem. *International Journal of Educational Research, 11*(6), 639–663.

Pellegrino, J. W., & Hilton, M. L. (Eds.). (2013). *Education for life and work: Developing transferable knowledge and skills in the 21st century*. Washington, DC: National Academies.

Robins, A., Rountree, J., & Rountree, N. (2003). Learning and teaching programming: A review and discussion. *Computer Science Education, 13*(2), 137–172.

Schwartz, D. L., & Arena, D. (2013). *Measuring what matters most: Choice-based assessments for the digital age*. Cambridge, MA: MIT.

Schwartz, D. L., & Martin, T. (2004). Inventing to prepare for future learning: The hidden efficiency of encouraging original student production in statistics instruction. *Cognition and Instruction, 22*(2), 129–184.

Schwartz, D. L., Bransford, J. D., & Sears, D. (2005). Efficiency and innovation in transfer. In J. Mestre (Ed.), *Transfer of learning from a modern multidisciplinary perspective* (pp. 1–51). Greenwich, CT: Information Age.

Schwartz, D. L., Chase, C. C., & Bransford, J. D. (2012). Resisting overzealous transfer: Coordinating previously successful routines with needs for new learning. *Educational Psychologist, 47*(3), 204–214.

Scott, J. (2013). The royal society of Edinburgh/British computer society computer science exemplification project. In *Proceedings of ITiCSE'13* (pp. 313–315).

Spohrer, J. C., & Soloway, E. (1986). Novice mistakes: Are the folk wisdoms correct? *Communications of the ACM, 29*(7), 624–632.

SRI International (2013). Exploring CS curricular mapping. Retrieved from http://pact.sri.com.

Weintrop, D., Beheshti, E., Horn, M. S., Orton, K., Trouille, L., Jona, K., & Wilensky, U. (2014). Interactive assessment tools for computational thinking in High School STEM classrooms. In *Intelligent Technologies for Interactive Entertainment* (pp. 22–25). Springer International Publishing.

Werner, L., Denner, J., & Campe, S. (2015). Children programming games: a strategy for measuring computational learning. *ACM Transactions on Computing Education (TOCE), 14*(4), 24.

Werner, L., Denner, J., Campe, S., & Kawamoto, D. C. (2012). The fairy performance assessment: Measuring computational thinking in Middle School. In *Proceedings of the 43rd ACM technical symposium on computer science education (SIGCSE '12)* (pp. 215–220). New York, NY: ACM.

Werner, L., McDowell, C., & Denner, J. (2013). A first step in learning analytics: Pre-processing low-level Alice logging data of Middle School students. *JEDM-Journal of Educational Data Mining, 5*(2), 11–37.

Whitehouse.gov (2016). Computer science for all. Retrieved from https://www.whitehouse.gov/the-press-office/2016/01/30/weekly-address-giving-every-student-opportunity-learn-through-computer.

Wing, J. (2006). Computational thinking. *Communications of the ACM, 49*(3), 33–36.

Yadav, A., Burkhart, D., Moix, D., Snow, E., Bandaru, P., & Clayborn, L. (2015). *Sowing the seeds: A landscape study on assessment in secondary computer science education*. New York, NY: Computer Science Teacher Association.

Zur Bargury, I. (2012). A new curriculum for junior-high in computer science. In *Proceedings of the 17th ACM annual conference on innovation and technology in computer science education* (pp. 204–208). ACM.

Zur Bargury, I., Pârv, B. & Lanzberg, D. (2013). A nationwide exam as a tool for improving a new curriculum. In *Proceedings of ITiCSE'13* (pp. 267–272). Canterbury, England, UK.

Part V
Computational Thinking Tools

Principles of Computational Thinking Tools

Alexander Repenning, Ashok R. Basawapatna, and Nora A. Escherle

Abstract Computational Thinking is a fundamental skill for the twenty-first century workforce. This broad target audience, including teachers and students with no programming experience, necessitates a shift in perspective toward Computational Thinking Tools that not only provide highly accessible programming environments but explicitly support the Computational Thinking Process. This evolution is crucial if Computational Thinking Tools are to be relevant to a wide range of school disciplines including STEM, art, music, and language learning. Computational Thinking Tools must help users through three fundamental stages of Computational Thinking: problem formulation, solution expression, and execution/evaluation. This chapter outlines three principles, and employs AgentCubes online as an example, on how a Computational Thinking Tool provides support for these stages by unifying human abilities with computer affordances.

Keywords Computational Thinking Process • Three stages of the Computational Thinking Process • Computational Thinking Tools • Principles of Computational Thinking Tools

Introduction

The term Computational Thinking (CT), popularized by Jeannette M. Wing (2006), had previously been employed by Papert (1996) in the inaugural issue of Mathematics Education. Papert considered the goal of CT to *forge explicative ideas* through the use of computers. Employing computing, he argued, could result in ideas that are

A. Repenning (✉) • N.A. Escherle
School of Education, University of Applied Sciences and Arts Northwestern Switzerland FHNW, Windisch 5210, Switzerland
e-mail: alexander.repenning@fhnw.ch; nora.escherle@fhnw.ch

A.R. Basawapatna
Department of Mathematics and Computer Information Systems, SUNY Old Westbury, Old Westbury, NY 11568, USA
e-mail: basawapatnaa@oldwestbury.edu

P.J. Rich, C.B. Hodges (eds.), *Emerging Research, Practice, and Policy on Computational Thinking*, Educational Communications and Technology: Issues and Innovations, DOI 10.1007/978-3-319-52691-1_18

more accessible and powerful. Meanwhile, numerous papers, e.g., Grover and Pea (2013), and reports, e.g., National Research Council (2010), have created many different definitions of CT. Recently, Wing (2014) followed up her seminal call for action paper with a concise operational definition of CT: “Computational thinking is the thought processes involved in formulating a problem and expressing its solution(s) in such a way that a computer—human or machine—can effectively carry out.”

While the term Computational Thinking is relatively new, the process implied by Wing can be recognized as a computationally enhanced version of the well-established scientific method. Based on Wing’s definition, the Computational Thinking Process (Fig. 1) can be segmented into three stages. The example in Fig. 1 of a mudslide simulation is used to illustrate the three Computational Thinking Process stages:

(1) Problem formulation (abstraction): Problem formulation attempts to conceptualize a problem verbally, e.g., by trying to formulate a question such as “How does a mudslide work?” or through visual (Arnheim, 1969) thinking, e.g., by drawing a diagram identifying objects and relationships.
(2) Solution expression (automation): The solution needs to be expressed in a non-ambiguous way so that the computer can carry it out. Computer programming enables this expression. The rule in Fig. 1 expresses a simple model of gravity: if there is nothing below a mud particle, it will drop down.

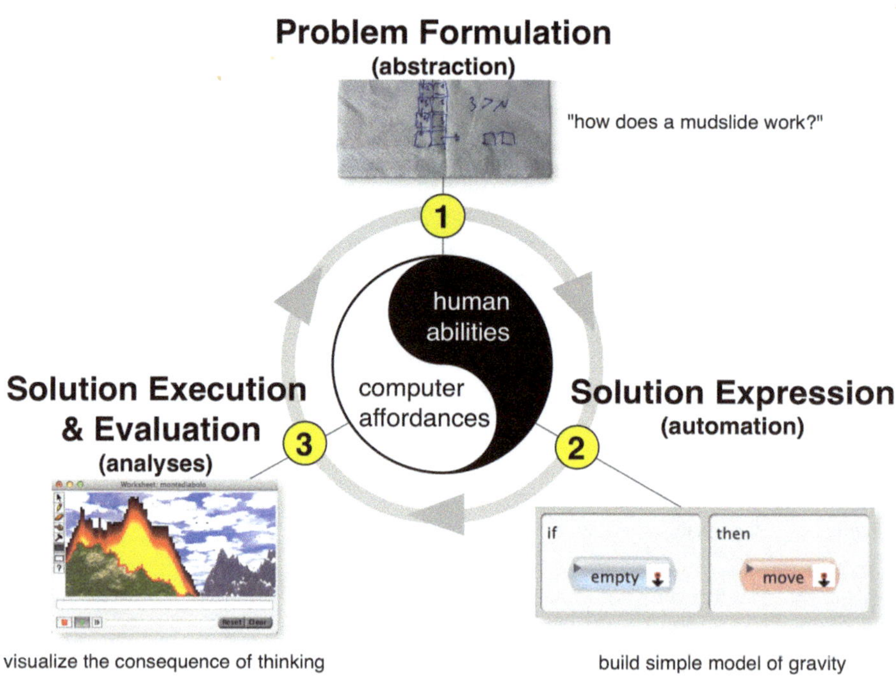

Fig. 1 Three stages of the Computational Thinking Process

(3) Execution and evaluation (analysis): The computer executes the solution in ways that show the direct consequences of one's own thinking. Visualizations—for instance, the representation of pressure values in the mudslide as colors—support the evaluation of solutions.

As shown in Fig. 1, Computational Thinking is an iterative process describing *thinking with computers* by synthesizing human abilities with computer affordances. The three stages describe different degrees of human and computer responsibilities. The solution execution appears to be largely the responsibility of the computer and the problem expression largely the responsibility of the human. Although problem formulation is typically considered the responsibility of the human, computers can help support the conceptualization process as well, for instance, through facilitating visual thinking.

Principles of Computational Thinking Tools

The fundamental goal of a Computational Thinking Tool is to support all stages of the Computational Thinking Process outlined above. Programming should be, and can be, an exciting new literacy in the sense described by diSessa (2000) enabling constructivist learning for all (see Yager, 1995). Using traditional programming languages severely limits this practice outside of computer science class contexts. For example, a student in a STEM class attempting to make a basic predator prey simulation with traditional programming languages may have to write hundreds of lines of code. Conversely, the goal of Computational Thinking Tools leads to three core principles corresponding to the three stages of the CT process. Computational Thinking Tools should support:

(1) Problem formulation: Similar to playing with numbers in a spreadsheet, using a mind map tool, or just doodling on a whiteboard, Computational Thinking Tools should empower users to explore representations without the need to code.
(2) Solution expression: Computational Thinking Tools should employ end-user programming approaches (see Lieberman, Paternò, & Wulf, 2006; Repenning, 2001), to allow computer users who may not have or may not want to gain professional programming experience and to create relevant computational artifacts such as games (Repenning et al., 2015) and simulations (Repenning, 2001).
(3) Solution execution and evaluation: Computational Thinking Tools should include accessible execution visualization mechanisms helping users to comprehend and validate computational artifacts such as simulations.

The AgentCubes online end-user programming environment (Ioannidou, Repenning, & Webb, 2009; Repenning, 2013b; Repenning & Ioannidou, 2006; Repenning et al., 2014) will be employed as an example to illustrate these principles, but these principles can be applied to any CT Tool. The AgentCubes user interface is relatively simple. The toolbar at the top of Fig. 3 provides a number of controls to start/stop a simulation, to manage worlds, and to operate the 3D camera. The panel to the left contains all the user-defined agents. The top panel is the current world. The three bottom panels contain the drag and drop programming environment with the condition palette to the left, the agent behavior in the middle, and the palette of actions to the right. The following sections discuss the three Computational Thinking Tool principles and provide concrete examples through AgentCubes.

Supporting Problem Formulation

Problem formulation is a conceptualization process (Repenning et al., 2015) dealing with abstractions often based on verbal or visual thinking, which can be supported by tools. Computational Thinking Tools can support visual thinking by offering various evocative spatial metaphors. Mind map tools capture concepts as nodes and links (Willis & Miertschin, 2005). Spreadsheets (B. A. Nardi & Miller, 1990) are two-dimensional grids containing numbers and strings. The versatile nature of grids has helped spreadsheets to become the world's most used programming tools. Tools such as Boxer (diSessa, 1991) and ToonTalk (Kahn, 1996) employ the notion of microworlds based on containers to represent relationships. In logo, Papert (1993) argues the notion of a turtle helps users comprehend difficult geometric transformations through body syntonicity, that is, the ability for people to project themselves, as turtle, into geometric microworlds. Papert (1993) and Turkle (2007) consider the use of *evocative objects to think with* as a powerful conceptualization approach. All these tools help the forging of abstractions serving as the beginning of a path from problem formulation to solution expression. Wing (2008) suggests that finding these kinds of abstractions is an essential part of Computational Thinking: "In working with rich abstractions, defining the 'right' abstraction is critical. The abstraction process—deciding what details we need to highlight and what details we can ignore—underlies computational thinking" (p. 3718).

Abstractions need to be made explicit to enable transfer. Ideally, Computational Thinking Tools should not only support users to find rich, evocative abstractions but also make these abstractions explicit in order to facilitate their transfer and application within other problem-solving contexts. For instance, the use of phenomenalistic (Michotte, 1963) abstractions describing object interactions such as *collision* and *diffusion* was found to support student formulation of STEM simulations in middle school curricula (Koh, Basawapatna, Bennett, & Repenning, 2010; Repenning et al., 2015). In our research, the patterns found to be especially helpful in allowing students to create elements of games and simulations we termed Computational Thinking Patterns (CTPs). Figure 2 lists examples of Computational Thinking Patterns. For example, the *collision* CTP describes both the interaction of a truck hitting a frog in a Frogger-like game and the interaction of molecules colliding in a STEM simulation. Similarly the *generate* CTP could describe a ship shooting lasers

Fig. 2 Examples of Computational Thinking Patterns

- **Change:** One agent changes into another agent.
- **Absorb:** One agent makes another agent disappear.
- **Transport:** One agent transports another agent.
- **Push:** One agent pushes another agent.
- **Random Movement:** An agent moves randomly.
- **Tracking:** One agent chases another agent.
- **Keyboard Movement:** keyboard button presses control an agent's movement.

in a Space Invaders-type game but also two foxes mating and creating offspring in a predator prey simulation. Learning these CTPs provides students with a useful high-level language to begin thinking about a problem before coding begins, and previous research has shown that novice users can recognize these patterns across contexts and implement them in their project creations (Basawapatna, Koh, Repenning, Webb, & Marshall, 2011).

How AgentCubes Supports Problem Formulation

AgentCubes online supports the problem formulation stage similarly to a mind map tool by enabling users to organize information visually setting the stage for coding. At the problem formulation stage, AgentCubes online can be used much like a whiteboard is used for drawing. The 2D or 3D objects, called agents, created by users are similar to Papert's objects to think with (Papert, 1993). In AgentCubes, information can be organized in 3D space to create 3D worlds. Similar to Minecraft, users create one-, two-, or three-dimensional grids and stacks by placing agents using the pen tool (Repenning et al., 2014). At this stage no coding is necessary. Users can explore their worlds by employing 3D camera tools to navigate or manipulate their worlds by adding, removing, and rearranging agents. AgentCubes allows users to select any agent and assume its perspective by switching to first-person camera mode. This ability, we speculate, may help to achieve the body syntonicity (Repenning & Ioannidou, 2006) that Papert is referring to.

Visual thinking is supported by AgentCubes online through a four-dimensional grid structure called the agent matrix (Fig. 3). The grid is based on cells organized as rows, columns, and layers. Each cell, in turn, contains a stack of agents. Agents can be simple textured shapes such as cubes, spheres, or cylinders but can also be quite sophisticated user-created 3D shapes implemented as inflatable icons (Repenning et al., 2014). Users' ability to produce their own 3D shapes has been identified as an important creativity tool to overcome affective challenges of programming, but it can also be useful to quickly sketch out 3D worlds similar to the use of a cocktail napkin in the formulation stage depicted in Fig. 1.

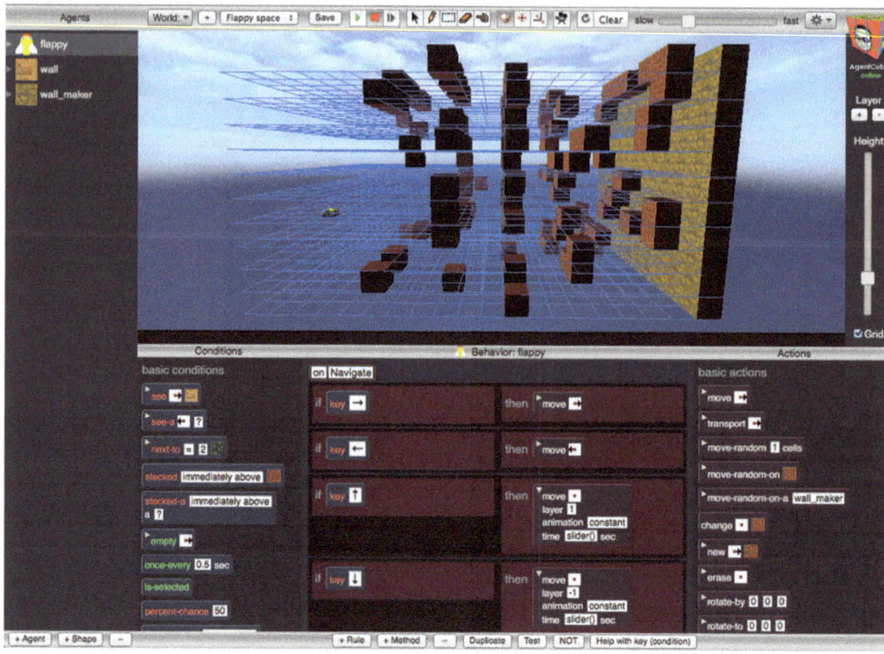

Fig. 3 AgentCubes online environment depicting a side view of an example "Flabby Bird 3D" game

As an example, an interesting problem could be how to generalize a 2D side-scrolling game into a 3D scrolling game. In Fig. 3, the grid has been enabled to show the AgentCubes cell structure of a game called "Flabby Bird 3D," which is a generalization of the popular 2D scrolling phone game "Flappy Bird." In Flabby Bird 3D, the objective is to navigate a bird called Flabby past oncoming cubes. Usually, a player would see this game from the first-person camera viewpoint of Flabby (Fig. 4). The enabled grid helps to reveal the 3D scrolling approach of the game. To the right there is a solid wall of cube maker agents creating cubes (an example of the *generate* CTP) with an increasing probability depending on the level of the game. These cubes are flying toward Flabby as depicted in Fig. 4. Playing the game, by seeing it from Flabby's point of view, the player gets the illusion of flying through a never-ending labyrinth of walls. To make the game more challenging, the approaching walls reconfigure occasionally.

Breaking down game descriptions into explicit abstractions enables students to transition from problem formulation to solution expression (Repenning et al., 2015). Computational Thinking Patterns serve as framework of useful abstractions describing the interactions between objects and the interaction of users with objects. For instance, the creation of Flabby Bird involves the implementation of various Computational Thinking Patterns such as *collision*, *generation*, *absorption*, and *keyboard control*. Part of the support structure for this activity is external. For instance, some teachers hang up posters describing the Computational Thinking

Fig. 4 First-person view perspective of the "Flabby Bird 3D" game

Patterns and make students refer to these posters when working on problem formulation tasks. However, it is essential that the Computational Thinking Tool provides for a solution expression that is an intuitive implementation of the problem formulation. It should be noted that this step can be fully integrated into the tool itself. For example, tools that allow users to program agents directly, through Computational Thinking Patterns, have successfully been piloted in the past, further bridging the act of problem formulation with solution expression (Basawapatna, Repenning, & Lewis, 2013).

Supporting Solution Expression

The goal of Computational Thinking is to be an instrument for problem solving that is not limited to computer scientists or professional programmers. For example, assuming an educational context, such as STEM classes, Computational Thinking Tools need to be viable in noncomputer science classes by avoiding the need for difficult and excessive coding. CT employing traditional programming tools is likely to introduce a significant amount of accidental complexity, as opposed to dealing with the intrinsic complexity (Dijkstra, 2001) of the problem-solving process. If the intended outcome is to become a professional programmer, then this approach may be highly effective or indeed entirely necessary.

If instead the goal is to become a Computational Thinker, then the resulting overhead and lack of support may turn into an insurmountable educational obstacle. Focusing less on the notion of essence but on understandable mappings, natural programming (Myers, Pane, & Ko, 2004) attempts to better align the expression of a solution with the problem formulation based on peoples' intuitive comprehension of semantics such as the use of Boolean operators. Rittel differentiated the notion of human computer interaction from human problem-domain interaction (Rittel & Webber, 1984) to clarify this important philosophical dichotomy. Guzdial (2015) reached a similar conclusion in the context of computing education by suggesting that "If you want students to use programming to learn something else [e.g., how to author a simulation] then limit how much programming you use" (p. 48). The limitation of accidental complexity can be supported at three different levels:

(1) Syntax: Visual programing approaches such as drag and drop programming (Conway et al., 2000; Repenning & Ambach, 1996; Resnick et al., 2009a; 2009b) can avoid frustrating syntactic challenges such as missing semicolons.
(2) Semantics: Live programming (Burckhardt et al., 2013; McDirmid, 2013; McDirmid, 2007) and similar approaches help users to understand the meaning of programs by illustrating the consequences of changes to programs.
(3) Pragmatics: Domain-oriented (Fischer, 1994) or task-specific (B. Nardi, 1993) programming languages support users in employing programming languages to achieve their goals.

How AgentCubes Supports Solution Expression

At the syntactic level, AgentCubes offers drag and drop programming, which its predecessor, AgentSheets, pioneered over 20 years ago (Repenning & Ambach, 1996). A first version of AgentSheets initially introduced the idea of agent-based graphical rewrite rules (Repenning, 1994, 1995), a programming by example (Repenning & Perrone, 2000; Repenning & Perrone-Smith, 2001) approach to define the behavior of agents by demonstrating it. However, the graphical rewrite rules were ultimately considered to be too constraining (Schneider & Repenning, 1995). Meanwhile, the benefits of drag and drop programming have become quite clear, and consequently drag and drop programming has proliferated to a very large number of programming environments for kids (Conway et al., 2000; Resnick et al., 2009a; 2009b).

Semantic support is considerably harder than syntactic support (Repenning, 2013a). At the level of semantics, AgentCubes offers not only live programming (McDirmid, 2013; McDirmid, 2007) but also a technique called Conversational Programming (Repenning, 2013a). Conversational Programming will observe the agent a user is interested in and then annotate the program behaviors of that particular agent in its particular situation by running the program one step into the future to illustrate which agent behavior rules will evaluate to true, which will evaluate to false, and which rules will not be tested. For instance, in a Frogger-like game, a user can click the frog agent and look at its behavior rules to see what will happen to the frog after it has just jumped in front of a car moving toward it. In this case, if the frog-car *collision* pattern is programmed correctly, the behavior rule wherein the frog dies and the game restarts will be annotated by Conversational Programming to appear as true.

Fig. 5 15-square puzzle

Of the three levels, pragmatics is the most challenging one to support. One might naturally want to have a simple mapping between the problem domain and the solution domain. However, the least amount of code cannot be the only objective. For example, languages such as APL are well known for their parsimonious nature but not for their general readability. Instead, programs should be short and intuitive expressions of a given idea. An example may help to illustrate this.

The 15-square puzzle, shown in Fig. 5, is a classic children's toy. The game consists of sliding 15 numbered squares into a sorted arrangement, 1–15, in a 4 × 4 grid. Many computer program implementations of the game exist. From a CT point of view, the core idea is simple: click the square you want to slide into the empty space. From a coding point of view, however, efforts can vary widely. A Python program to implement the "click to slide" functionality (see Sweigart, 2010) quickly runs into hundreds of lines of code not including the functionality to solve the puzzle. The view here is not to be negative regarding coding. If a CS class codes the 15-square puzzle to learn about arrays, loops, animations, or Python syntax, then writing the 300 lines of code could be extremely beneficial.

An AgentCubes implementation, in contrast, will include very little coding overhead. The "click to slide" functionality requires only four rules, checking if there is an empty spot adjacent to the clicked square and then moving into that spot. This is depicted in Fig. 6. Trading in clarity for brevity, one could even employ the more arcane MoveRandomOn (background) AgentCubes action to solve the 15-square puzzle benchmark in a single line of code. Comparing Python to AgentCubes seems hardly fair. In AgentCubes the notion of a grid, animations, and even numbered squares already exists. This is what domain orientation (Fischer, 1994) can do. It reduces coding overhead by providing and implementing abstractions to help users express a solution succinctly.

Of course, domain orientation introduces trade-offs. For instance, it would not be advisable to write a compiler in AgentCubes. Similar to spreadsheets—which have been used creatively to create amazing projects such as flight simulators and

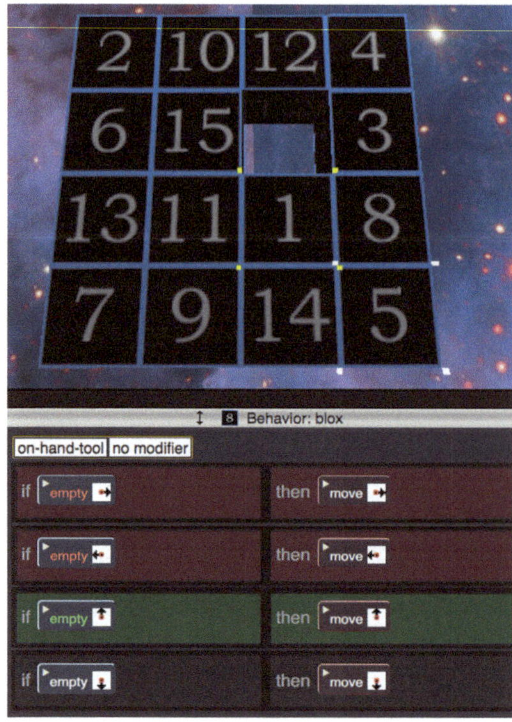

Fig. 6 AgentCubes online implementation of the 15-square puzzle with four rules

planetary models—AgentCubes' grid structure maps well onto a wide variety of projects such as 2D/3D games, simulations, and cellular automata. For instance, a simple version of the Pac-Man game can be implemented in just ten rules (if/then statements) including collaborative AI (Repenning, 2006) and win/lose detection.

Studies show that students can use such system affordances of AgentSheets and AgentCubes to successfully implement the Computational Thinking Patterns planned in the formulation step in game and simulation development (Repenning et al., 2015). Studies also show that users are highly motivated to create these artifacts, speaking to the power of reducing coding overhead (Repenning, Basawapatna, Assaf, Maiello, & Escherle, 2016). Guzdial (2008) points out the importance of avoiding coding overhead in education and refers to a number of languages explored in computer science education to establish essence by employing implicit loops and other task-specific (B. Nardi, 1993) constructs. An example of this approach in AgentCubes is the built-in management of parallelism. For instance, even a very large number of agents, looking like boxes, moving around randomly in a three-dimensional world, will automatically reshuffle and stack up correctly in parallel with very little code. Computing trajectories that can be executed in parallel, determining the order of boxes stacked up, would be complex code to write.

Supporting Execution and Evaluation

The execution and evaluation stage can be supported by helping users debug their programs as well as reveal their misconceptions. Pea (1983) describes debugging as "systematic efforts to eliminate discrepancies between the intended outcomes of a program and those brought about through the current version of the program" (p. 3). Given that the computer does not currently "understand" the problem, it will not be able to automatically compute these discrepancies, but there are still strategies for Computational Thinking Tools to aid the debugging process. One strategy is to simply reduce the gap between solution expression and solution execution and evaluation. Punch cards are the classical negative example resulting in an extremely large gap. As this gap increases, users quickly lose sight of the causal relation between changes made to a program and manifestations of different behaviors exhibited by running the modified program (Repenning, 2013a).

Live programming (McDirmid, 2013) can help by enabling users to instantly see the consequences of any change to a program. Unfortunately, there are issues such as the halting problem in computer science theory with practical consequences, suggesting that it is not actually possible to determine all consequences of arbitrary program changes. However, for a more constrained class of programs, including spreadsheets, this is not a problem. Very much in the spirit of live programming, spreadsheets will instantly update results when formulae or cell values are changed by a user.

A Computational Thinking Tool would support visualization through the inclusion of easy-to-use visualization affordances. Additionally, a Computational Thinking Tool may apply the idea of visualization to itself by annotating programs in ways to make discrepancies between the programs users have and the ones they want more understandable (Repenning, 2013a).

How AgentCubes Supports Execution and Evaluation

To support the goal of visualizing the consequences of one's own thinking, a number of visualization techniques are included in AgentCubes. In the mudslide example (Fig. 1 solution execution and evaluation), it helps considerably to understand the pressure distribution among the thousands of agents employed in the model. The simple visualization scheme mapping each pressure value into a single color helps the forging of explicative ideas by depicting pressure buildup.

Particularly useful when making simulations, AgentCubes supports the plotting of simulation properties. An example would be to plot the number of predators and prey in an ecological simulation. One can also use 3D plotting to visualize value fields in real time. For instance, in a city traffic simulation, 3D plots (Fig. 7) show the spatial distribution of wait times in the city over the world grid itself. Finally, AgentCubes online narrows the gap between solution expression and execution through Conversational Programming (introduced above in Supporting Solution Expression) (Repenning, 2013a), extending the notion of live programming (McDirmid, 2013).

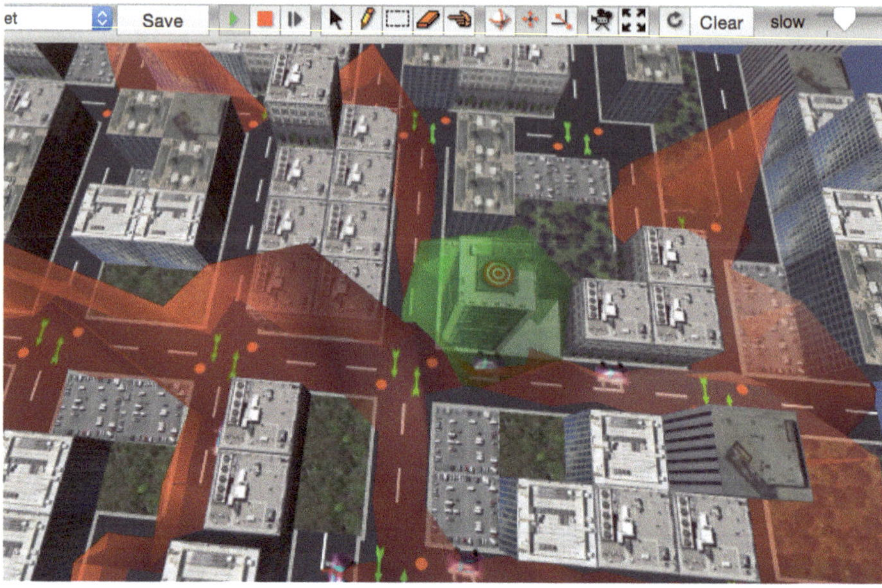

Fig. 7 Bird's eye view of a city traffic simulation in AgentCubes with an overlaid 3D plot of traffic wait times with the higher red peaks indicating a longer wait

Even when a game is not running, by selecting an agent in the world, AgentCubes will execute relevant code fragments one step into the future and annotate the code, specifying which rule will execute, in order to visualize potential discrepancies between the programs users have and the programs users want (Pea, 1983). This indicator can guide users into another iteration cycle depicted in Fig. 1 yielding more useful representations.

Conclusions

Computational Thinking Tools should support Papert's vision of enabling users to forge explicative ideas through the use computers. By minimizing coding overhead, Computational Thinking Tools can allow all users to focus on the essence of abstraction, automation, and analysis. In contrast to traditional programming environments, Computational Thinking Tools support all three stages, problem formulation, solution expression, and execution and evaluation, of the Computational Thinking Process. This support will make Computational Thinking feasible to a wide range of applications including STEM, art, music, and language.

Acknowledgments This work is supported by the Hasler Foundation and the National Science Foundation under Grant Numbers 0833612, 1345523, and 0848962. Any opinions, findings, and conclusions or recommendations expressed in this material are those of the authors and do not necessarily reflect the views of these foundations.

References

Arnheim, R. (1969). *Visual thinking*. Berkley, CA: University of California Press.

A. Basawapatna, K. H. Koh, A. Repenning, D. C. Webb, & K. S. Marshall. (2011). *Recognizing computational thinking patterns*. Paper presented at the the 42nd ACM technical symposium on computer science education (SIGCSE), Dallas, TX, USA.

Basawapatna, A. R., Repenning, A., & Lewis, C. H. (2013). *The simulation creation toolkit: An initial exploration into making programming accessible while preserving computational thinking*. Paper presented at the 44th ACM technical symposium on computer science education (SIGCSE 2013), Denver, CO, USA.

Burckhardt, S., Fahndrich, M., Halleux, P. D., McDirmid, S., Moskal, M., Tillmann, N., & Kato, J. (2013). *It's alive! continuous feedback in UI programming*. Paper presented at the proceedings of the 34th ACM SIGPLAN conference on programming language design and implementation, Seattle, WA, USA.

Conway, M., Audia, S., Burnette, T., Cosgrove, D., Christiansen, K., Deline, R., & Pausch, R. (2000). *Alice: Lessons learned from building a 3D system for novices*. Paper presented at the CHI 2000 conference on human factors in computing systems, The Hague, Netherlands.

Dijkstra, E. W. (2001). The end of computing science? *Communications of the ACM, 44*(3), 92. doi:10.1145/365181.365217.

diSessa, A. A. (1991). An overview of boxer. *Journal of Mathematical Behavior, 10*, 3–15.

diSessa, A. (2000). *Changing minds: Computers, learning, and literacy*. Cambridge, MA: MIT.

Fischer, G. (1994). Domain-oriented design environments. In *Automated software engineering* (Vol. 1, pp. 177–203). Boston, MA: Kluwer Academic.

Grover, S., & Pea, R. (2013). Computational thinking in K–12: A review of the state of the field. *Educational Researcher, 42*(1), 38–43. doi:10.3102/0013189X12463051.

Guzdial, M. (2008). Education: Paving the way for computational thinking. *Communications of the ACM, 51*, 25–27.

Guzdial, M. (2015). Learner-centered design of computing education: Research on computing for everyone. *Synthesis Lectures on Human-Centered Informatics, 8*, 1.

Ioannidou, A., Repenning, A., & Webb, D. (2009). AgentCubes: Incremental 3D end-user development. *Journal of Visual Language and Computing, 20*(4), 236–251.

Kahn, K. (1996). *Seeing systolic computations in a video game world.* Paper presented at the proceedings of the 1996 IEEE symposium of visual languages, Boulder, CO, USA.

Koh, K. H., Basawapatna, A., Bennett, V., & Repenning, A. (2010). *Towards the automatic recognition of computational thinking for adaptive visual language learning*. Paper presented at the conference on visual languages and human centric computing (VL/HCC 2010), Madrid, Spain.

Lieberman, H., Paternò, F., & Wulf, V. (Eds.). (2006). *End user development* (Vol. 9). Dordrecht: Springer.

McDirmid, S. (2007). *Living it up with a live programming language.* Paper presented at the proceedings of the 22nd annual ACM SIGPLAN conference on object-oriented programming systems and applications (OOPSLA '07).

McDirmid, S. (2013). *Usable live programming*. Paper presented at the SPLASH onward!, Indianapolis, IN, USA.

Michotte, A. (1963). The perception of causality. (T. R. Miles, Trans.). London: Methuen

Myers, B. A., Pane, J. F., & Ko, A. (2004). Natural programming languages and environments. *Communications of the ACM, 47*(9), 47–52. doi:10.1145/1015864.1015888.

Nardi, B. (1993). *A small matter of programming*. Cambridge, MA: MIT.

Nardi, B. A., & Miller, J. R. (1990). *The spreadsheet interface: A basis for end user programming*. Paper presented at the INTERACT 90–3rd IFIP international conference on human-computer interaction, Cambridge, http://www.miramontes.com/writing/spreadsheet-eup/

National Research Council, Committee for the Workshops on Computational Thinking, Computer Science and Telecommunications Board, Division on Engineering and Physical Sciences.

(2010). Report of a workshop on the scope and nature of computational thinking. Washington, DC: National Academies.
Papert, S. (1993). *The children's machine*. New York, NY: Basic Books.
Papert, S. (1996). An exploration in the space of mathematics educations. *International Journal of Computers for Mathematical Learning, 1*(1), 95–123.
Pea, R. (1983). *LOGO programming and problem solving*. Paper presented at symposium of the annual meeting of the American Educational Research Association (AERA), "Chameleon in the Classroom: Developing Roles for Computers" Montreal, Canada, April 1983.
Repenning, A. (1994). *Bending icons: Syntactic and semantic transformation of icons*. Paper presented at the proceedings of the 1994 IEEE symposium on visual languages, St. Louis, MO.
Repenning, A. (1995). *Bending the rules: Steps toward semantically enriched graphical rewrite rules*. Paper presented at the proceedings of visual languages, Darmstadt, Germany.
Repenning, A. (2001). *End-user programmable simulations in education*. Paper presented at the HCI international 2001, New Orleans.
Repenning, A. (2006). *Collaborative diffusion: Programming antiobjects*. Paper presented at the OOPSLA 2006, ACM SIGPLAN international conference on object-oriented programming systems, languages, and applications, Portland, Oregon.
Repenning, A. (2013a). *Conversational programming: Exploring interactive program analysis*. Paper presented at the 2013 ACM international symposium on new ideas, new paradigms, and reflections on programming and software (SPLASH/Onward! 13), Indianapolis, Indiana, USA.
Repenning, A. (2013b). Making programming accessible and exciting. *IEEE Computer, 18*(13), 78–81.
Repenning, A., & Ambach, J. (1996). *Tactile programming: A unified manipulation paradigm supporting program comprehension, composition and sharing*. Paper presented at the 1996 IEEE symposium of visual languages, Boulder, CO.
Repenning, A., & Ioannidou, A. (2006). *AgentCubes: Raising the ceiling of end-user development in education through incremental 3D*. Paper presented at the IEEE symposium on visual languages and human-centric computing 2006, Brighton, UK.
Repenning, A., & Perrone, C. (2000). Programming by analogous examples. *Communications of the ACM, 43*(3), 90–97.
Repenning, A., & Perrone-Smith, C. (2001). Programming by analogous examples. In H. Lieberman (Ed.), *Your wish is my command: Programming by example* (Vol. 43, pp. 90–97). San Francisco, CA: Morgan Kaufmann Publishers.
Repenning, A., Basawapatna, A., Assaf, D., Maiello, C., & Escherle, N. (2016). *Retention of flow: Evaluating a computer science education week activity*. Paper presented at the special interest group of computer science education (SIGCSE 2016), Memphis, Tennessee.
Repenning, A., Webb, D. C., Brand, C., Gluck, F., Grover, R., Miller, S., et al. (2014). Beyond minecraft: Facilitating computational thinking through modeling and programming in 3D. *IEEE Computer Graphics and Applications, 34*(3), 68–71. doi:10.1109/MCG.2014.46.
Repenning, A., Webb, D. C., Koh, K. H., Nickerson, H., Miller, S. B., Brand, C., et al. (2015). Scalable game design: A strategy to bring systemic computer science education to schools through game design and simulation creation. *Transactions on Computing Education (TOCE), 15*(2), 1–31. doi:10.1145/2700517.
Resnick, M., Maloney, J., Monroy-Hernández, A., Rusk, N., Eastmond, E., Brennan, K., & Kafai, Y. (2009a). Scratch: Programming for all. *Communincation of the ACM, 52*(11), 60–67.
Resnick, M., Maloney, J., Monroy-Hernández, A., Rusk, N., Eastmond, E., Brennan, K., Millner, A., Rosenbaum, E., Silver, J., Silverman, B., & Kafai, Y. (2009b). Scratch: Programming for all. *Communications of the ACM, 52*, 60.
Rittel, H., & Webber, M. M. (1984). Planning problems are wicked problems. In N. Cross (Ed.), *Developments in design methodology* (pp. 135–144). New York, NY: Wiley.
Schneider, K., & Repenning, A. (1995). *Deceived by ease of use: Using paradigmatic applications to build visual design*. Paper presented at the proceedings of the 1995 symposium on designing interactive systems, Ann Arbor, MI.

Sweigart, A. (2010). *Invent your own computer games with Python, A beginner's guide to computer programming in Python.*

Turkle, S. (2007). *Evocative objects: Things we think with.* Cambridge, MA: MIT.

Willis, C. L., & Miertschin, S. L. (2005). *Mind tools for enhancing thinking and learning skills.* Paper presented at the proceedings of the 6th conference on information technology education, Newark, NJ, USA.

Wing, J. M. (2006). Computational thinking. *Communications of the ACM, 49*(3), 33–35.

Wing, J. M. (2008). Computational thinking and thinking about computing. *Philosophical Transactions of the Royal Society, 2008*(366), 3717–3725.

Wing, J. M. (2014). *Computational thinking benefits society.* http://socialissues.cs.toronto.edu/index.html%3Fp=279.html

Yager, R. (Ed.). (1995). *Constructivism and learning science.* Mahway, NJ: Lawrence Erlbaum Associates.

Exploring Strengths and Weaknesses in Middle School Students' Computational Thinking in Scratch

Kevin Lawanto, Kevin Close, Clarence Ames, and Sarah Brasiel

Abstract We live in a century where technology has become part of our lives, and it is crucial that we become active creators of technology, not just passive users. Learning to program computers enables a person to create twenty-first-century solutions. Computer programming is more than just learning how to code; it also exposes students to the opportunity to develop computational thinking (CT), which involves problem-solving using computer science concepts. In this chapter, we explore strengths and weaknesses of students' CT skills and compare a group of seventh- and eighth-grade students who engaged in a Scratch programming environment. Scratch is a popular visual programming language that introduces computer programming to youth. We use Dr. Scratch, a CT assessment tool, to analyze students' Scratch projects for evidence of CT. The results of this study can show researchers and educators how they might use Dr. Scratch to analyze students' Scratch data to help improve their CT.

Keywords Computer programming • Visual data analytics • Problem-solving

Introduction

One common strategy to develop computational thinking (CT) skills is computer programing, which may be among the most important skills of the twenty-first century (Wing, 2011). While an increasing number of high school students are being exposed to computer science courses and principles, there is a growing belief that experiences with computer programming must start at an earlier age. Research has shown that when students are introduced to this kind of STEM curricula early, it can

K. Lawanto (✉) • K. Close • C. Ames • S. Brasiel
Department of Instructional Technology and Learning Sciences, Utah State University, Logan, UT 84322-2830, USA
e-mail: kevin.lawanto@aggiemail.usu.edu; kevin.j.close@gmail.com; clarence.ames@yahoo.com; sarahha2z@sbcglobal.net

P.J. Rich, C.B. Hodges (eds.), *Emerging Research, Practice, and Policy on Computational Thinking*, Educational Communications and Technology: Issues and Innovations, DOI 10.1007/978-3-319-52691-1_19

positively impact their perceptions, encouraging them to continue developing important STEM skills (DeJarnette, 2012). For computer science, middle school is a particularly important time in which quality curricula can support the development of CT skills and ultimately influence career choices (Repenning, Webb, & Ioannidou, 2010; Settle et al., 2012). Despite this, computer programing curricula are not widely implemented in the US K-12 education system, with the greatest inconsistency occurring in grades K-8 (CSTA, 2012).

Although the idea of CT is not new, until recently finding a definition of CT that everyone agrees upon had proven difficult for the CS education community (Mannila et al., 2014). There was little agreement on what CT encompasses (Allan, Barr, Brylow, & Hambrusch, 2010; Barr & Stephenson, 2011) and even less agreement around strategies to be used for assessing the development of CT in youth (Brennan & Resnick, 2012). In one of the first countrywide efforts to integrate computing into public education, England did a complete overhaul of the national curriculum which launched in September of 2014 (Department for Education, 2014). Right now, five organizations and over 100 researchers, educators, and advisors in the computer science community are working to develop one cohesive set of standards and guidelines for K-12 computer science education (K12CS.org, 2016). Though this idea is only recently gaining traction, forces are beginning to coalesce around what CT means. According to Wing (2006), CT basically means thinking like a computer scientist, using principles and concepts learned in computer science as part of our daily lives. A of couple examples of CT key concepts applicable to day-to-day life include problem decomposition, which means breaking down problems into smaller, manageable parts and algorithmic design, where one develops step-by-step instructions for solving problems.

The National Council for Research (2010) and Steve Furber (2012) from the Royal Society defined CT as using the methods of computer science to understand a wide variety of topics. They also suggest that CT is the process of recognizing aspects of computation and applying tools and techniques from computer science, representing data through abstraction, such as models and simulations, automating solutions through algorithmic thinking, and identifying, analyzing, and implementing possible solutions with the goal of achieving the most efficient and effective combination of steps and resources (Barr, Harrison, & Conery, 2011; Furber, 2012; National Council for Research, 2010). This can range from creating computational models of scientific phenomena to creating algorithms to plan one's day more efficiently. Even with these the advances being made around CT, more research is needed to understand key components of CT that can be effectively implemented and assessed in K-12 schools.

In 2006, Wing introduced five core aspects of CT, including conditional logic, distributed processing, debugging, simulation, and algorithm building. Brennan and Resnick (2012) proposed seven key concepts of CT through the programming language (Scratch) they developed, which include sequences, loops, parallelism, events, conditionals, operators, and data. In 2013, Grover and Pea further examined essential concepts of CT suitable for use in K-12 education and developed a list that is now used by the Computer Science Teacher Association (CSTA). The key components Grover and Pea (2013) suggested include abstractions and pattern generalizations; systematic processing of information; symbol systems and representations; algorithmic notions of flow of control; structured problem decompositions; iterative, recursive, and parallel thinking; conditional logic; efficiency and performance constraints; and debugging and systematic error detection.

Recently, Moreno-León and Robles (2015) created a slightly more concise list highlighting seven components of CT that included abstraction and problem decomposition, parallelism, logical thinking, synchronization, flow control, user interactivity, and data representation. This list is specifically designed to facilitate the assessment of CT. Even though CT components keep shifting as the definition of CT keeps progressing, these new components are consistent with the nine key components from Grover and Pea (2013). Since the components suggested by Moreno-León and Robles (2015) align with the components used by the CSTA and are designed to facilitate assessment of CT, they are felicitous for promoting and assessing the development of CT in K-12 environments.

Background

Despite the growing need to integrate computer science (CS) into K-12 education, many people, including teachers and their students, have inaccurate perceptions of CS, which influence their attitudes toward CS learning and careers (Israel et al., 2015). Research suggests some of the reasons for the declining enrollment in CS relate to teachers' beliefs that the only computing experiences available to students occur through learning programming languages such as Java or C++ (Goode, 2007). Many teachers find mastering these kinds of programming languages and teaching related CS concepts to be difficult, which is why they tend to select students they believe are inherently skilled at this type of thinking to participate in CS curriculum (Burke & Kafai, 2010). Because complex programming languages are chosen to provide computing experiences, students often think that CS is boring, confusing, and too difficult to master (Wilson & Moffat, 2010).

Resnick et al. (2009) mentioned the term "low floor, high ceiling," as one of the guiding principles to foster the use of CT in K-12 education. It essentially means that though it should be easy for a beginner to cross the threshold to create a working program (low floor), the tool should also be complex enough to fulfill the needs of advanced programmers (high ceiling). Visual programming languages such as Scratch, Tynker, Storytelling Alice, and Greenfoot have generated renewed interest in developing the CT skills of K-12 students through programing (Grover, Pea, & Cooper, 2014; Kafai & Burke, 2013). At least in part, this is because they are better able to adequately scaffold student learning, enable knowledge transfer, support equity, and be systemic and sustainable (Repenning, Webb, & Ioannidou, 2010).

Scratch programming has risen in prominence as one of the potential programming languages for fostering CT in K-12 computer science curricula (Resnick et al., 2009). The Scratch programming language uses a syntax-free drag and drop interface with a visual element showing the result of the student code. As a result, Scratch provides a programming experience less cognitively taxing for users with a timely and visual feedback system. We used Scratch for our study because Scratch has a large youth user community with publicly available data. Furthermore, Scratch's interface allows an easier interpretation of core CT constructs. We are not interested in simply measuring knowledge of a programming language; we are interested in strategies of thinking. These strategies of thinking computationally are less likely to be conflated with knowledge of programming language in a simple programming language like Scratch where syntax is removed from the equation and the programmer's focus rests rather on the logic of how to arrange the code to achieve a specific outcome.

Assessing CT

Despite the many efforts aimed at assessment of CT (Basawapatna, Koh, Repenning, Webb, & Marshall, 2011; Fields, Searle, Kafai, & Min, 2012; Grover, Pea, & Cooper, 2014; Meerbaum-Salant, Armoni, & Ben-Ari, 2013), assessing the learning of CT concepts and constructs in a programming environment such as Scratch remains a challenge. The use of surveys had been one of the main methods used to assess CT for the past few years (e.g., Clark, Rogers, Spardling, & Pais, 2013; Mishra, Balan, Iyer & Murthy, 2014). Though the results from surveys can be useful, they are unable to accurately assess the majority of CT components (Grover, Pea, & Cooper, 2014).

Though tools that can assess CT do exist, there is still a lack of tools that support educators in the assessment of the development of CT and the evaluation of projects programmed by students. Several researchers (e.g., Boe et al., 2013; Close, Janisiewicz, Brasiel, & Martin, 2015) have proposed different approaches for evaluating the development of CT by analyzing students' projects. Unfortunately, most tools require intermediate-level knowledge of complex programming languages, which make them less suitable for educators who are not confident with such environments.

The Scratch community includes not only users but also developers and academicians. A group of these developers created Dr. Scratch, a digital instrument which is easy to use without needing background knowledge or knowledge in programming. Dr. Scratch can automatically measure the degree of CT evidenced in a certain Scratch project (Moreno-León & Robles, 2015). Though CT has been difficult to define, much less measure, Dr. Scratch approaches the problem by focusing on the elements of CT most easily interpretable, such as logic, data representation, parallelism, synchronization, user interactivity, flow control, and abstraction (see http://drscratch.programamos.es/ for more information). For each of these measures, users can earn 0–3 points. For example, a user will get 0 points

Table 1 Scoring system measuring user interactivity

Points	Evidence	Example code
0	Uses only the most basic interactive block "when green flag is pressed" block	
1	Uses other types of interactive blocks utilizing mouse clicking, mouse positioning, question asking blocks, and sprite clicking	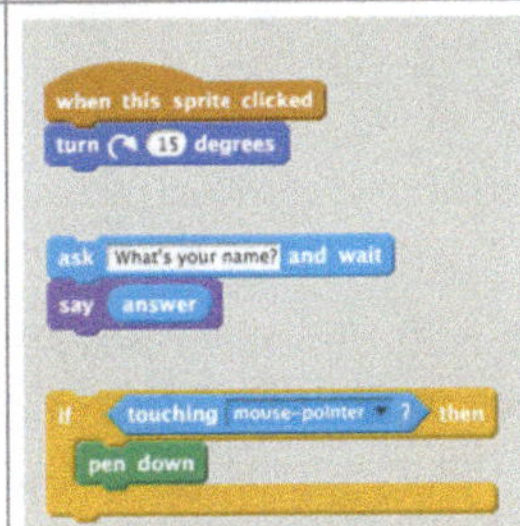
2	Uses complex interactive blocks utilizing webcam and microphone input	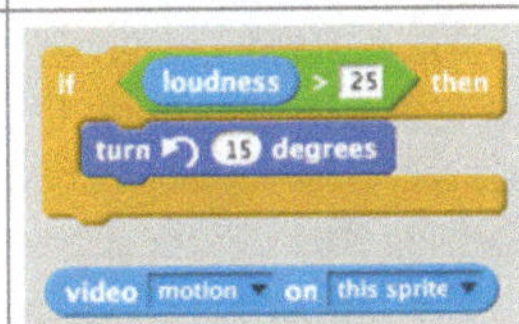
3	If all of the requirements for user interactivity according to Dr. Scratch are met, Scratch blocks are in chronological working order	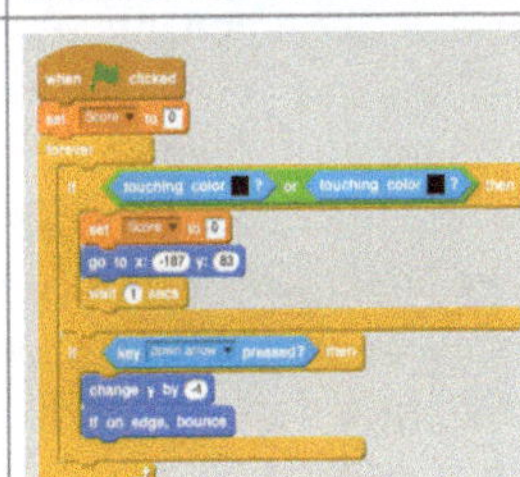

for synchronization if they only use "wait commands" to synch up two or more scripts, earn 1 point for broadcasting messages to other scripts, earn 2 points if these broadcasted messages have complex wait commands that ensure scripts run in a certain order, or earn 3 points if users fulfilled all of the criteria described by Dr. Scratch (for another example, see Table 1).

This information is then organized into user-friendly dashboards that show student progress, allowing teachers to personalize instruction and cater to individual student needs. Dr. Scratch provides scores related to each of these seven CT components (flow control, data representation, abstraction, user interactivity, synchronization, parallelism, and logic). A score of three showed proficiency in an area, and zero means that the skill was not evident. These scores are then totaled to show overall competence in CT. Depending on the overall CT score (which can range from 0 to 21), distinct data will be displayed on the dashboard page and provide users with suggestions and links to information on how to improve their programming habits.

Publicly Available Scratch Data

Teaching computational thinking (CT) has been a focus of recent efforts to broaden the reach of computer science education. Barr and Stephenson (2011) argued that today's students would live and work in a world that is heavily influenced by computing principles. A report by the National Council for Research (2010) also introduced a similar idea that CT is a cognitive skill that an average person needs. The report highlighted

> "(1) that students can learn thinking strategies such as CT as they study a discipline, (2) that teachers and curricula can model these strategies for students, and (3) that appropriate guidance can enable students to learn to use these strategies independently." (p. 62)

Thus, the term CT has quickly become a prerequisite skill for many endeavors of the twenty-first century (Wing, 2011).

In our current study, we examined the elements of CT found in the projects of seventh- and eighth-grade students. Specifically, we used Dr. Scratch to examine whether there were patterns in the students' computational thinking skills. Based on our literature review, it is clear that CT, as a construct, still needs exploration. We were primarily interested in finding clues about how CT develops. Are there similarities between CT profiles for middle school students? Are these CT profiles affected by the type of projects attempted such as coding a game versus coding a story? Is there a difference between CT components scores for seventh-grade and eighth-grade students?

In order to explore the elements of CT found in seventh- and eighth-grade students' Scratch projects, we analyzed a dataset of 183 student projects from a publicly available repository of projects online at scratch.mit.edu. Using the Dr. Scratch tool, we analyzed seventh-grade projects (n = 93) and eighth-grade projects (n = 90) produced by middle school students located in the East Coast with the same teacher who taught a computer education course. In this exploratory study, we looked for evidence of particular CT behavior. There were three specific questions that we explored in this study:

1. What are common computational thinking strengths and weaknesses?
2. What are the differences between seventh- and eighth-grade student genre of programming (e.g., stories, games, arts, music, animations)?
3. How similar or different are the CT scores for grades 7 and 8 students?

Based on prior research on Scratch programming among youth and our previous experience working with Scratch, we hypothesized that student CT profiles would have common strengths and weakness. We expected students to show higher scores in skills such as flow control and parallelism and lower scores in skills such as abstraction and data representation. This progression seems common based on the progression of help manuals on the Scratch website (see scratch.mit.edu/help) in these areas. As for differences in seventh- and eighth-grade students, our hypothesis was less clear. We expected to see higher scores in CT skills for eighth-grade students, but were not sure which skills would differentiate between the two grade levels the most. In the development of CT skills, the actual pathway of learning is understudied and therefore difficult to hypothesize.

Methods

Participants

We collected 183 middle school student projects from a publicly available and de-identified dataset available on the Scratch website. The teacher updated these projects regularly and identified the students as either seventh- or eighth-grade students from 2014 to 2015 school year. Accordingly, we analyzed 93 seventh-grade projects and 90 eighth-grade projects. Though we do not know the specific classroom practices or demographics of the participants, we controlled for some potential differences by taking projects produced for students of the same teacher. Importantly, this work can be reproduced by other researchers by taking other publicly available projects on the Scratch website, which increases the external validity of our study (see https://scratch.mit.edu/users/avstoloff/ to access the publically available projects that we analyzed).

Procedure and Design

We searched the Scratch website to find publicly available Scratch project libraries made by seventh- and eighth-grade students with the same school and the same class, as described earlier. Using Dr. Scratch, we analyzed each of these projects to see if there was any sort of a trend in students' CT scores. The total score classified student projects as basic, developing, or master. In order to analyze the data, we grouped the data by grade levels and examined descriptive statistics to look for potential strengths and weaknesses. We used line graphs to examine patterns visually as well as the Mann-Whitney U test to understand significant similarities or differences between seventh- and eighth-grade students' Scratch projects. The Mann-Whitney U test is a nonparametric method designed to detect whether two or more samples come from the same distribution or to test whether medians between underlying distributions are the same. However, if the two distributions have a different shape, we can also use this test to compare mean ranks. This study uses the Mann-Whitney U test to compare the mean rank of each of the seven CT components between the seventh- and eighth-grade students' project.

Measures

Using Dr. Scratch, we analyzed projects for evidence of seven CT components (abstraction, parallelism, logic, synchronization, flow control, user interactivity, and data representation) on a scale from 0 to 3 points. For example, in the abstraction and problem decomposition category, students who use more than one scripts or sprites earn 1 point, students who define their own blocks earn 2 points, students who use clones earn 3 points, and students without any of these coding sequences or blocks earn 0 points. Likewise, for each category, Dr. Scratch searches for particular pieces of code or certain blocks (see Table 2).

Table 2 Rubric for scoring CT components

CT component	Score 1 point	2 points	3 points
Flow control	Uses sequence of blocks	Uses *repeat* and *forever* blocks	Uses *repeat until* block
Data representation	Uses modifiers for sprite properties	Uses operations on variables	Uses operations on lists
Abstraction	Uses more than one scripts and more than one sprites	Defines own block	Uses clones
User interactivity	Uses *green Flag* block	Uses *key pressed, sprite clicked, ask and wait, mouse* blocks	Uses video and audio features
Synchronization	Uses *wait* block	Uses *broadcast, when I receive message, stop all, stop program, stop program* sprite	Uses *wait until, when backdrop change to, broadcast, and wait* blocks
Parallelism	Uses two scripts on green flag	Uses two scripts on key pressed, two scripts on sprite clicked on the same sprite	Uses two scripts on *when I receive message* block, create clone, two scripts on *backdrop change to* block
Logic	Uses *if* block	Uses *if else* block	Uses logic operations

Table 3 Summary of computational thinking average scores for each component

CT components	Computational thinking average scores (standard deviation) Grade 7 (n = 93)	Grade 8 (n = 90)	All students (n = 183)
Flow control	2.19 (0.39)	2.51 (0.52)	2.35 (0.49)
Data representation	1.27 (0.44)	1.78 (0.44)	1.52 (0.51)
Abstraction	1.02 (0.21)	1.08 (0.37)	1.05 (0.30)
User interactivity	2.00 (0)	2.00 (0.15)	2.00 (0.11)
Synchronization	2.40 (1.17)	2.93 (0.25)	2.66 (0.89)
Parallelism	2.57 (0.73)	2.82 (0.53)	2.69 (0.65)
Logic	1.67 (0.93)	2.38 (0.97)	2.01 (1.01)

Results

Research question #1: What are common computational thinking strengths and weaknesses?

Looking at the means of all student scores (n = 183) for each CT measurement, based on the scale developed by Moreno-Leon and Robles to measure CT with Dr. Scratch, the results show that our participants are, on average, best at synchronization, parallelism, and flow control. These strengths are followed by user interactivity and logic, with relative weaknesses in data representation and abstraction (see Table 3 for means and standard deviations for each CT measure). These scores match our hypothesis for this research question. As stated earlier, some of this can be attributed to features of Scratch, such as the help pages, which, for example, encourage users to learn to synchronize scripts before using more advanced data code blocks.

Of note, user interactivity has a very small standard deviation of 0.11 revealing very little variance in user scores, whereas logic scores, with a standard deviation of 1.01, varied greatly. Synchronization was also highly variable with a standard deviation of 0.89, suggesting that students show strong differentiation in synchronization skills and logic skills, but very little in user interactivity skills. These numbers show that CT skills do not develop uniformly. Students who share similar user interactivity skills may vary significantly in their use of logic or synchronization, meaning researchers, teachers, and learners should not think about CT as a monolithic skill, but, rather, a family of related skills.

Further analysis revealed common computational thinking strengths and weaknesses. If such a common pattern exists, we would expect the strengths and weaknesses of seventh- and eighth-grade students to be similar, since they are, typically, only separated in age by 1 year. Figures 1 and 2 show the mean score for each of the

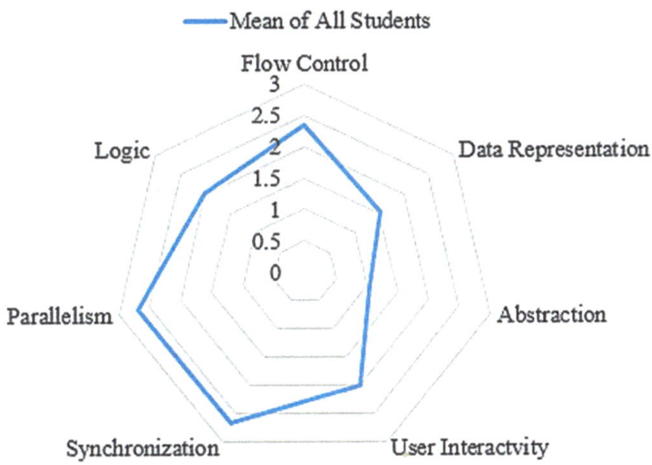

Fig. 1 CT skill development with all dataset

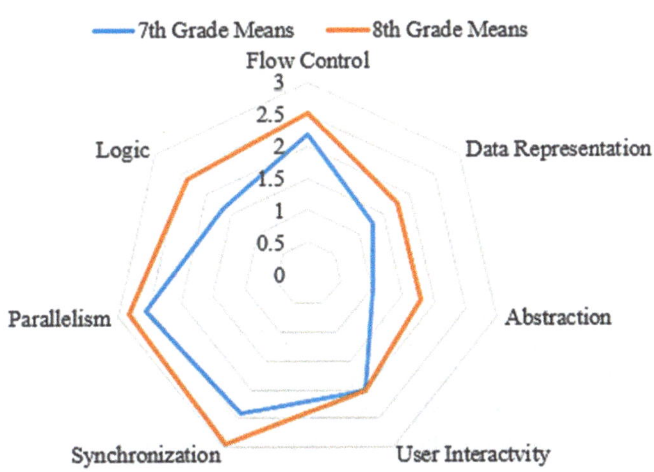

Fig. 2 CT skill development for seventh- and eighth-grade students

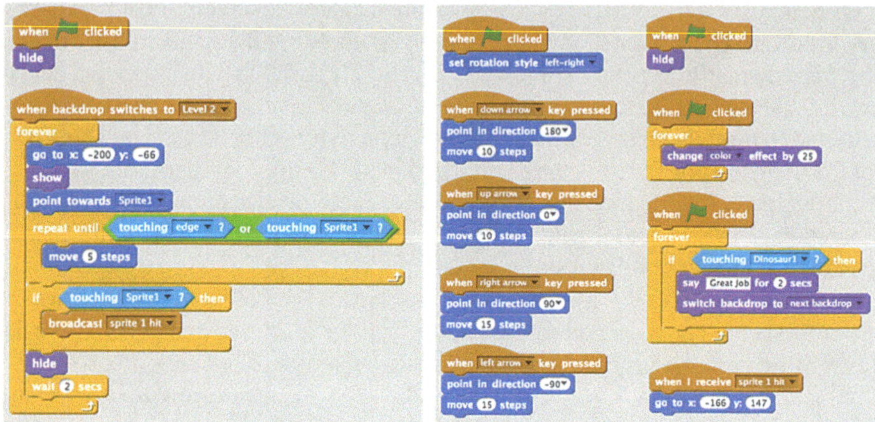

Fig. 3 Sample code from a seventh-grade project with high scores for synchronization, parallelism, and flow control, but poor scores for abstraction and data representation

CT components within the whole dataset (see Fig. 1) and with the mean scores of seventh- and eighth-grade CT components separate (see Fig. 2). On these weblike figures, CT components mean scores near the edge indicate higher levels of mastery, and mean scores near the middle of the web indicate a lower level of mastery, so, if there were a common pattern of strengths and weaknesses to detect, we would expect the webs of seventh graders and eighth graders to have a similar shape. As can be seen in Fig. 2, the shapes are similar, indicating a common pattern of strengths and weaknesses. Also, eighth-grade students show slightly higher scores in every category on average (except user interactivity).

The data seems to indicate that there are indeed common strengths and weaknesses among middle school students and, in particular, that middle school students excel at synchronization, parallelism, and flow control (i.e., using advanced wait commands, using multiple sprites and scripts, and using *repeat* blocks), but struggle with abstraction and data representation (i.e., using clones, defining blocks, using operations on variables and lists). For example, Fig. 3 shows code from a seventh-grade project showing advanced synchronization (using backdrop changes and broadcast blocks), parallelism (several scripts), and flow control (uses *repeat until* and forever blocks). However, the same project scored poorly on abstraction (no clones used or new blocks defined) and data representation (no operations on variable or lists).

Research question #2: What are the differences between seventh- and eighth-grade student genres of programming (e.g., stories, games, arts, music, animations)?

After examining the descriptive statistics of CT component scores, we looked at each specific Scratch project and coded the project for genre type. Perhaps different genres of Scratch projects account for the slight variability in CT component scores. Specifically, our exploratory analysis revealed that the seventh-grade students made a game project in class, more specifically a maze game, which means that our CT

Fig. 4 One example from a seventh-grade maze project

Table 4 Eighth-grade student project genre

	Eighth-grade project genre (n = 90)		
	Game	Story	Unknown
Number of projects	83	4	3

component scores for the seventh-grade were controlled by genre (see Fig. 4). The eighth-grade students, on the other hand, produced more project genre variations, which may be due to the teacher expectation or assignment constraints, though the majority (92%) still created a game-based project (see Table 4).

These findings do not reveal the answer to our question about how programming genres vary across grade level, but they do reveal that the CT scores that Dr. Scratch computed for each project were primarily computed for game projects. Further research, in which users have more variation by project genre and, perhaps, even differentiate types of game projects, is needed to determine the answer to our research question.

Research question #3: How similar or different are the CT scores for seventh- and eighth-grade students?

Though descriptive statistics revealed a slight difference in CT component scores from seventh- to eighth-grade students' projects, we are interested in determining the significance of that similarity or difference. We used a Mann-Whitney U test to understand significant similarities or differences between seventh- and eighth-grade students' Scratch projects. As mentioned previously, the Mann-Whitney U test is a nonparametric method designed to detect whether two or more samples come from the same distribution or to test whether medians between comparison groups are different. In Fig. 5, we provide histograms to show the distribution of CT component scores for seventh- and eighth-grade students for purpose of comparison.

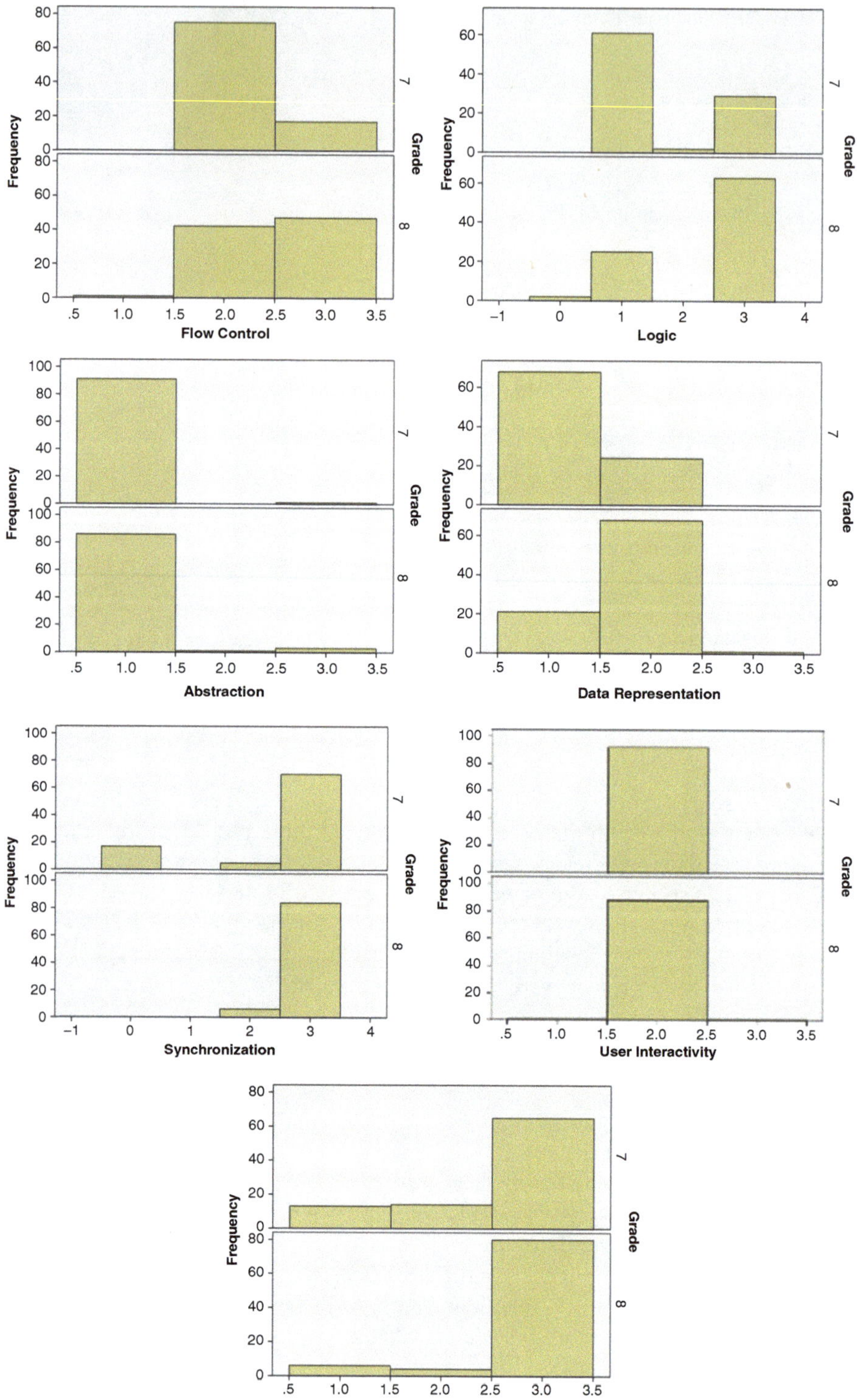

Fig. 5 Histograms comparing seventh- and eighth-grade students' CT component scores

Table 5 Mann-Whitney U score across CT components

	CT components						
	Flow control	Abstraction	User interactivity	Synchronization	Parallelism	Logic	Data representation
μ	2.35	1.05	2.00	2.66	2.69	2.01	1.52
SD	0.49	0.30	0.11	0.89	0.65	1.01	0.51
U	2780.5	4001.5	4140	3375	3401	2635	2034
p	0.000	0.169	1.000	0.001	0.003	0.000	0.000

A Mann-Whitney test indicated that five of the seven CT components (flow control, synchronization, parallelism, logic, and data representation) were greater for eighth-grade students than for seventh-grade students ($p < 0.05$; see Table 5 for results). Data representation, logic, and flow control components exhibited the lowest U scores, indicating the greatest level of variability between seventh- and eighth-grade students. In other words, eighth-grade student projects exhibit significantly better CT scores for flow control, synchronization, parallelism, logic, and data representation; the greatest difference occurred in flow control, logic, and data representation. User interactivity and abstraction mean differences were not significant.

These findings are significant because they begin to illustrate potential strengths and weaknesses in computational thinking for students in grades 7 and 8. Our findings also suggest that CT does not develop evenly, as a unified construct, but rather, certain elements of CT (e.g., data representation, logic) likely develop more quickly for some than others. The suggestion of such a finding has implications, not only for the way CT is taught but also for the direction of research regarding CT.

Examples of Students' Projects and Recommendations for Students' CT Improvement

Next, we present two examples from seventh- and eighth-grade students' projects in the developing category and seventh- and eighth-grade students' projects in the master category. The developing group consists of students who scored 8–14, and the master group is for those students who scored 15–21. No students in the seventh- or eighth-grade class scored 7 or below, which is considered the basic category. At the end we also provide limitations of our study and view suggestions that instructors can implement in their classrooms to improve students' computer programming skill.

Developing

When comparing seventh- and eighth-grade students' projects in the developing category, we noticed that there were more students in the seventh-grade group (n = 71) who are in this category, compared to students in the eighth-grade group

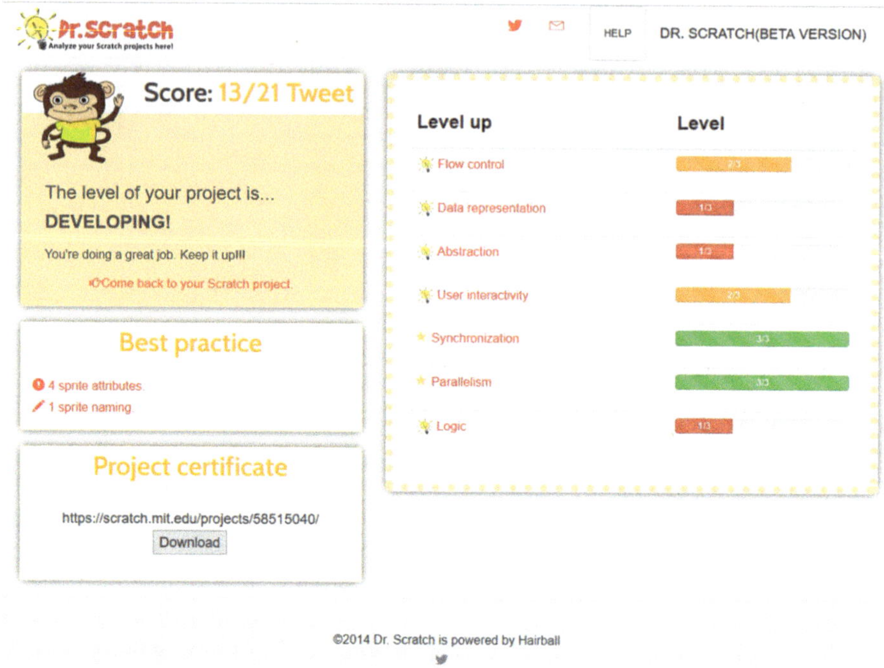

Fig. 6 Example of one seventh-grade student who is in the developing category

(n = 25) who are in the same category. The majority of the seventh-grade students in this category received a score of 13 (n = 39), while the majority of the eighth-grade students in this category received a score of 14 (n = 10). From our data analysis, we then looked at the average CT scores across seven CT components, and we noticed a similar trend where both seventh- and eighth-grade students are low in three different CT areas: data representation ($\mu = 1.14$, $\mu = 1.4$, respectively), abstraction ($\mu = 1.0$ for both grades), and logic ($\mu = 1.25$, $\mu = 1.0$, respectively). In Fig. 6, we provide an example of one of the seventh-grade students' projects in the developing category and what they see on their dashboard once their project has been assessed by Dr. Scratch.

When a student receives a score that puts them in the developing stage, Dr. Scratch will only give two types of information that students can use to improve their Scratch project: sprite naming and sprite attributes. Dr. Scratch developers, Moreno-León and Robles (2015), considered these two types of information as bad programming habits. When a student starts to program with Scratch, it is very typical for them to leave the naming of their sprite with the default name. When one has a few sprites, it is very easy to know the name of each of the characters. However, when the number of characters increases, it is more complicated. So, it is a good practice to name each individual sprite in students' projects differently, because then their programs can be read more efficiently.

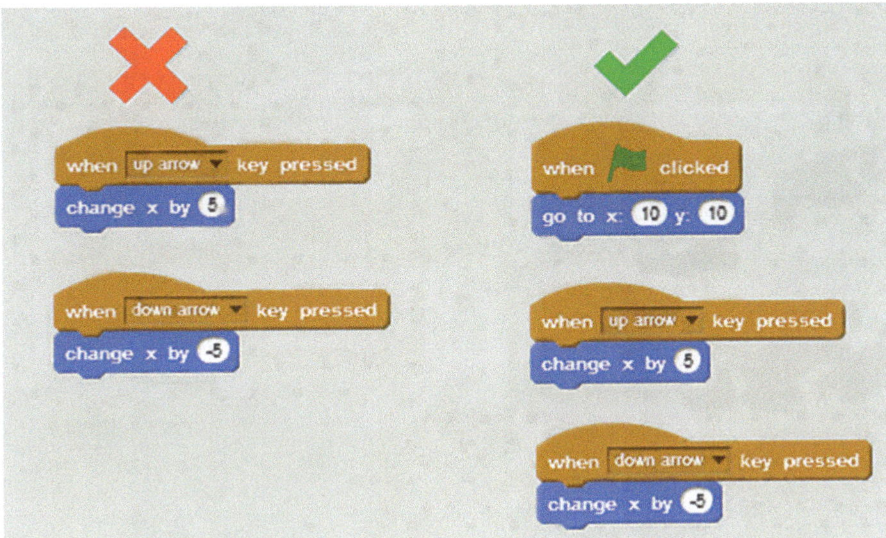

Fig. 7 Example of incorrect attribute initialization (*left*) and correct attribute initialization (*right*)

The second bad programming habit, according to Moreno-León and Robles (2015), that students tend to do is attribute initialization. One of the mistakes that many programmers repeat when they learn to program is to not initialize correctly the objects' attributes. Sprite attributes are the characters' features that can be modified in the execution of a project, like their position, their size, their color, and their orientation. When students have blocks that modify characters' features, they should always assign the value of their starting point. For example, students should have the block "go to" under the block "when green flag clicked," in order to place the character in its initial position (see Fig. 7).

Master

Unlike the results in the developing category, when comparing seventh- and eighth-grade students' projects in the master category, we noticed that there were more students in the eighth-grade group (n = 65) who are in this category, compared to students in the seventh-grade group (n = 22) who are in the same category. The majority of the eighth-grade students in this category received a score of 17 (n = 32), while the majority of the seventh-grade students in this category received a score of 16 and 17 (both n = 9). From our data analysis, we then looked at the average CT scores across seven CT components, and we noticed that seventh-grade students are low in data representation ($\mu = 1.68$) and abstraction ($\mu = 1.09$) and eighth-grade students are low in only abstraction ($\mu = 1.11$). In Fig. 8, we provide an example of one of the eighth-grade students' projects scored by Dr. Scratch as being in the master category.

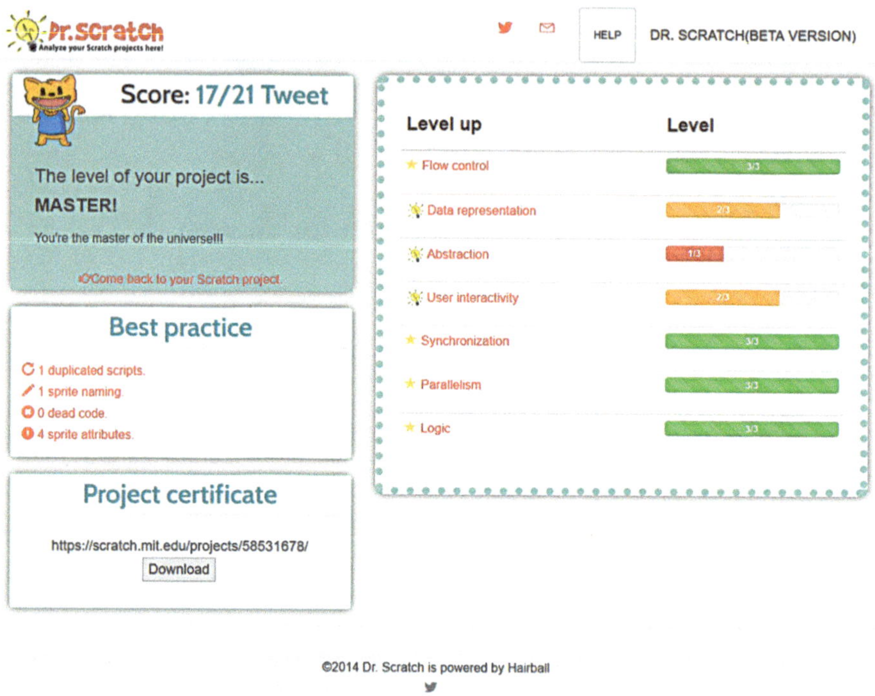

Fig. 8 Example of one eighth-grade student who is in the master category

In addition to changing the sprite names and sprite attributes, Dr. Scratch also adds two more bad programming habits for students who are placed in the master category: duplicated scripts and dead code. As a novice programmer, it is very typical for students to duplicate their Scratch scripts to do the same tasks over and over again. In this scenario, it is recommended for the students to make his/her own block that defines this behavior and use this new block in all programs where needed. Thus, if students want to change the outcome, they just have to go to the block they defined (see Fig. 9).

The fourth bad programming habit, according to Moreno-Leon and Robles (2015), that students tend to do is putting dead code in their Scratch scripts. Dead codes are parts of programs that are never executed. Typically, dead codes are formed when students forget to put an event block (e.g., "when green flag clicked" or "when this sprite clicked") or when there is a program that is waiting for a message that never is sent (see Fig. 10). The presence of dead code could cause the Scratch project to not work as expected or not run efficiently.

Recommendations and Study Limitations

Helping students reduce their bad programming habits can be the first step in helping them to become great computer programmers. With the availability of CT assessment tools such as Dr. Scratch, teachers are now able to look at their students'

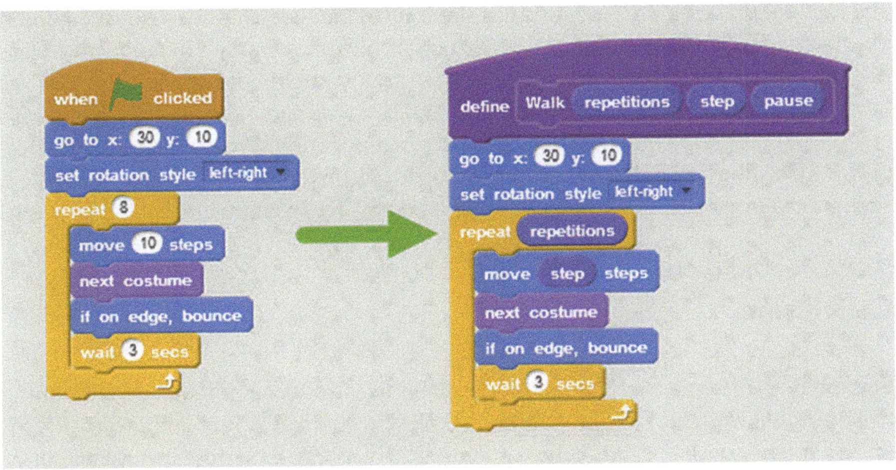

Fig. 9 Example of efficient script duplication

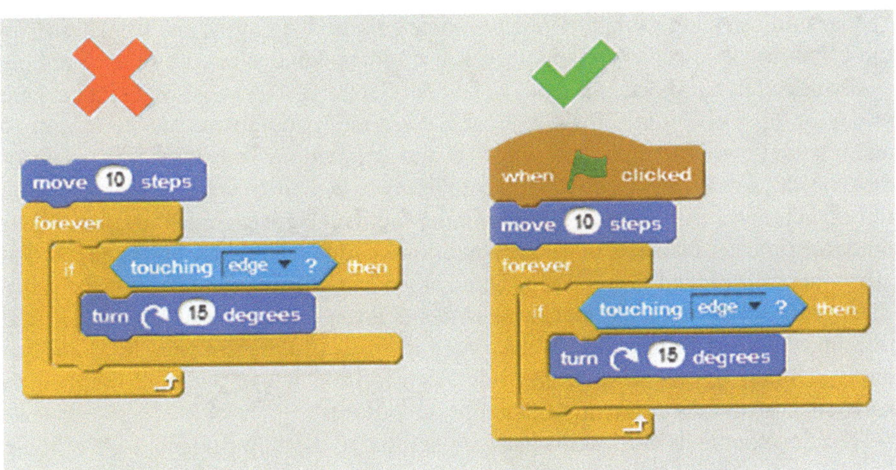

Fig. 10 Example of "dead code" (*left*), example of correct code initialization (*right*)

progress in each of the designated CT skills and also tailor instructions or activities based on individual students' scores to help them improve their computer programming skills. Based on the results of our study, we see that both seventh- and eighth-grade students generally have the most difficulty with abstraction and data representation. With Dr. Scratch, teachers are able to click on the link provided to see how they can help their students to understand more about the components with which they struggle and how they can increase the effectiveness of their instruction on these components.

This study has several limitations. All of our participants in seventh- and most of the eighth-grade level made a game for their project (i.e., maze); thus, we were not able to look at their genre differences. Moreno-Leon and Robles (2015) mentioned that the tool that they created is still in Beta; thus, they are still not sure whether the use of a particular Scratch blocks or a group of blocks is enough to confirm student fluency on certain CT concepts. Lastly, Dr. Scratch could not measure some of the key CT components that Grover and Pea (2013) described, such as debugging, efficiency and recursive thinking, and pattern generalization. We hope that with additional tools like Dr. Scratch being developed and existing tools being enhanced, such innovations will facilitate improvements in CT education and future research.

Conclusions

Scratch is a free web tool that allows teachers to introduce computer programming to K-12 students, and Dr. Scratch provides a way to analyze Scratch projects. This allows educators and researchers to automatically assign a CT score to student projects as well as detect potential bad programming habits. The aim is to help learners to develop CT skills and interest in computer science and to support educators in evaluating outcomes from their instruction.

Our findings suggest that there were some common strengths and weaknesses in the CT skills of seventh- and eighth-grade students demonstrated by their publicly available Scratch projects. Analysis of student Scratch projects showed that they are strong in three different CT skills (synchronization, parallelism, and flow control) and relatively weak in data representation and abstraction. Translated into a day-to-day context, this means these students are likely to be able to understand and reason through complex information they are presented with (synchronization), focus their thinking process in more than one direction (parallelism), and create plans that allow them to succeed in the face of both known and unknown events (flow control). These results also indicate that these students are not likely to be as proficient at filtering out what information is necessary to solve problem (abstraction) and are also less likely to demonstrate the ability to prioritize in a way that allows them to solve their problems efficiently (data representation).

The development of CT skills has the potential to develop students' self-efficacy in relation to the field of computer science and prepare them for greater success in the twenty-first-century workplace. We hope this research provides educators, students, and researchers with a better understanding of why CT skills are so important and specific things they can do to help improve computational thinking among K-12 students. We also hope that our findings can support other researchers interested in improving strategies for assessing CT in K-12 schools through the use of learning analytic tools, such as Dr. Scratch.

References

A Framework for K-12 Computer Science Education. (2016). *Computing leaders ACM, CSTA, Code.org, CIC, and NMSI launch effort to guide educators and state and district policy makers about K-12 computer science*. Retrieved from https://k12cs.org/

Allan, V., Barr, V., Brylow, D., & Hambrusch, S. (2010). Computational thinking in high school courses. In *Proceedings of the 41st ACM technical symposium on computer science education* (pp. 390–391). Milwaukee, WI: ACM.
Barr, D., Harrison, J., & Conery, L. (2011). Computational thinking: A digital age skill for everyone. *Learning and Leading with Technology, 38*(6), 20–23.
Barr, V., & Stephenson, C. (2011). Bringing computational thinking to K-12: what is involved and what is the role of the computer science education community? *ACM Inroads, 2*(1), 48–54.
Basawapatna, A., Koh, K. H., Repenning, A., Webb, D. C., & Marshall, K. S. (2011). Recognizing computational thinking patterns. In *Proceedings of the 42nd ACM technical symposium on computer science education* (pp. 245–250). New York, NY: ACM.
Boe, B., Hill, C., Len, M., Dreschler, G., Conrad, P., & Franklin, D. (2013). Hairball: Lint-inspired static analysis of scratch projects. In *Proceeding of the 44th ACM technical symposium on computer science education* (pp. 215–220). New York, NY: ACM.
Brennan, K., & Resnick, M. (2012). New frameworks for studying and assessing the development of computational thinking. In *Proceedings of the 2012 annual meeting of the American Educational Research Association.* Vancouver, Canada.
Burke, Q., & Kafai, Y. B. (2010). Programming and storytelling: Opportunities for learning about coding and composition. In *Proceedings of the 9th international conference on interaction design and children* (pp. 348–351). New York, NY: ACM.
Clark, J., Rogers, M. P., Spradling, C., & Pais, J. (2013). What, no canoes? Lessons learned while hosting a scratch summer camp. *Journal of Computing Sciences in Colleges, 28*(5), 204–210.
Close, K., Janisiewicz, P., Brasiel, S., and Martin, T. (2015). What do I do with all this data? How to use the FUN! Tool to automatically clean, analyze, and visualize your digital data. In *Proceedings of the 11th games and learning society conference.* Madison, WI, USA.
Computer Science Teacher Association. (2012). *CSTA K-12 computer science standards.* Retrieved October 8, 2015, from http://www.csta.acm.org/Curriculum/sub/K12Standards.html
DeJarnette, N. (2012). America's children: Providing early exposure to STEM (science, technology, engineering and math) initiatives. *Education, 133*(1), 77–84.
Department for Education, (2014). *National curriculum in England: Computing programmes of study.* Retrieved from: https://www.gov.uk/government/publications/national-curriculum-in-england-computing-programmes-of-study/national-curriculum-in-england-computing-programmes-of-study
Fields, D. A., Searle, K. A., Kafai, Y. B., & Min, H. S. (2012). Debuggems to assess student learning in e-textiles. In *Proceedings of the 43rd ACM technical symposium on computer science education* (pp. 699–699). New York, NY: ACM.
Furber, S. (2012). *Shutdown or restart? The way forward for computing in UK schools.* London: The Royal Society.
Goode, J. (2007). If you build teachers, will students come? The role of teachers in broadening computer science learning for urban youth. *Journal of Educational Computing Research, 36*(1), 65–88.
Grover, S., & Pea, R. (2013). Computational thinking in K–12. A review of the state of the field. *Educational Researcher, 42*(1), 38–43.
Grover, S., Pea, R., & Cooper, S. (2014). Promoting active learning and leveraging dashboards for curriculum assessment in an OpenEdX introductory CS course for middle school. In *Proceedings of the first ACM conference on Learning@ scale conference* (pp. 205–206). New York, NY: ACM.
Israel, M., Pearson, J. N., Tapia, T., Wherfel, Q. M., & Reese, G. (2015). Supporting all learners in school-wide computational thinking: A cross-case qualitative analysis. *Computers and Education, 82*, 263–279.
Kafai, Y. B., & Burke, Q. (2013). The social turn in K-12 programming: Moving from computational thinking to computational participation. In *Proceeding of the 44th ACM technical symposium on computer science education* (pp. 603–608). New York, NY: ACM.
Mannila, L., Dagiene, V., Demo, B., Grgurina, N., Mirolo, C., Rolandsson, L., & Settle, A. (2014). Computational thinking in K-9 education. In *Proceedings of the working group reports of the 2014 on innovation and technology in computer science education conference* (pp. 1–29). New York, NY: ACM.

Meerbaum-Salant, O., Armoni, M., & Ben-Ari, M. (2013). Learning computer science concepts with scratch. *Computer Science Education, 23*(3), 239–264.
Mishra, S., Balan, S., Iyer, S., & Murthy, S. (2014). Effect of a 2-week scratch intervention in CS1 on learners with varying prior knowledge. In *Proceedings of the 2014 conference on innovation and technology in computer science education* (pp. 45–50). New York, NY: ACM.
Moreno-León, J., & Robles, G. (2015). Dr. Scratch: A web tool to automatically evaluate scratch projects. In *Proceedings of the workshop in primary and secondary computing education* (pp. 132–133). New York, NY: ACM.
National Research Council. (2010). *Report of a workshop on the scope and nature of computational thinking*. Washington, DC: National Academies.
Repenning, A., Webb, D., & Ioannidou, A. (2010). Scalable game design and the development of a checklist for getting computational thinking into public schools. In *Proceedings of the 41st ACM technical symposium on computer science education* (pp. 265–269). New York, NY: ACM.
Resnick, M., Maloney, J., Monroy-Hernández, A., Rusk, N., Eastmond, E., Brennan, K., & Kafai, Y. (2009). Scratch: Programming for all. *Communications of the ACM, 52*(11), 60–67.
Settle, A., Franke, B., Hansen, R., Spaltro, F., Jurisson, C., Rennert-May, C., & Wildeman, B. (2012). Infusing computational thinking into the middle-and high-school curriculum. In *Proceedings of the 17th ACM annual conference on innovation and technology in computer science education* (pp. 22–27). New York, NY: ACM.
Wilson, A., & Moffat, D. C. (2010). Evaluating Scratch to introduce younger schoolchildren to programming. In *Proceedings of the 22nd annual psychology of programming interest group*. Leganes, Spain.
Wing, J. M. (2006). Computational thinking. *Communications of the ACM, 49*(3), 33–35.
Wing, J. M. (2011). Computational thinking. Retrieved from https://csta.acm.org/Curriculum/sub/CurrFiles/WingCTPrez.pdf

Measuring Computational Thinking Development with the FUN! Tool

Sarah Brasiel, Kevin Close, Soojeong Jeong, Kevin Lawanto, Phil Janisiewicz, and Taylor Martin

Abstract Computational thinking (CT) has been given recent attention suggesting that it be developed in children of all ages. With the creation of K-12 computer science standards by the Computer Science Teacher Association, states such as Massachusetts and Washington are leading the nation in adopting these standards into their school systems. This seems somewhat premature, when there are so few measures of computational thinking or computer programming skills that can be applied easily in a K-12 setting to assess outcomes of such state-wide initiatives. Through funding from the National Science Foundation, we developed an analysis tool to efficiently capture student learning progressions and problem-solving activities while coding in Scratch, a popular visual programming language developed by MIT Media Lab. Our analysis tool, the Functional Understanding Navigator! or FUN! tool, addresses the need to automate processes to help researchers efficiently clean, analyze, and present data. We share our experiences using the tool with Scratch data collected from three different week-long summer Scratch Camps with students in grades 5 to 8. Based on our preliminary analyses, we share important considerations for researchers interested in educational data mining and learning analytics in the area of assessing computational thinking. We also provide links to the publically available FUN! tool and encourage others to participate in a community developing new measures of computational thinking and computer programming.

Keywords Computational thinking • Educational data mining • Learning analytics

S. Brasiel (✉) • K. Close • S. Jeong • K. Lawanto
Department of Instructional Technology and Learning Sciences, Utah State University, Logan, UT 84322, USA
e-mail: sarahha2z@sbcglobal.net; kevin.j.close@gmail.com; sadsjs@gmail.com; kevin.lawanto@aggiemail.usu.edu

P. Janisiewicz
Agile Dynamics, Houston, TX 77043, USA
e-mail: pjanisiewicz@gmail.com

T. Martin
O'Reilly Media, Sebastopol, CA 95472, USA
e-mail: tmartin@oreilly.com

P.J. Rich, C.B. Hodges (eds.), *Emerging Research, Practice, and Policy on Computational Thinking*, Educational Communications and Technology: Issues and Innovations, DOI 10.1007/978-3-319-52691-1_20

Introduction

In recent years, researchers have given computational thinking (CT) considerable attention suggesting that CT be taught to all ages influencing nearly all disciplines (Wing, 2006, 2011). Though research suggests computer programming is an effective way to teach CT (Rich, Leatham, & Wright, 2013), computer programming is still not widely implemented in the United States K-12 curricula (Watters, 2011). Recently, the Computer Science Teacher Association (CSTA) created computer science standards for K-12 education, and so far only a handful of states have adopted these standards into their school systems (e.g., Massachusetts and Washington; Close, Janisiewicz, Brasiel, & Martin, 2015). However, researchers have developed very few assessments of computational thinking or computer programming that can easily be applied to large data sets such as a district or state data set.

Though it is clear that computer programming needs to be more widely integrated into K-12 student learning experiences, there is still much that we do not know about how to assess learning in this area. Therefore, we developed an analysis tool to efficiently capture student learning progressions and problem-solving activities while coding. The Functional Understanding Navigator! or FUN! tool addresses the need to automate processes to help researchers and instructors efficiently clean, analyze, and present data (Close et al., 2015). For illustrative purposes, we applied an initial version of our tool to a data set from Scratch (developed by MIT Media Lab), a popular visual programming language among novice programmers, to measure their computational thinking skills.

Background

Scratch programming has risen in prominence as one of the potential programming languages for K-12 computer science programs (Boe et al., 2013). Visual-based programming languages like Scratch are able to better facilitate K-12 students' computational thinking, because traditional programming syntax is reduced (Lye & Koh, 2014). Using Scratch, students are able to create their own interactive stories, games, and simulations and then eventually share their creations with their peers in an online community from around the world using an intuitive drag-and-drop code mechanism that helps reduce their cognitive load, making the testing and debugging process less demanding (Resnick et al., 2009). This allows students to develop computational problem-solving practices more easily and eventually allows them to focus on the logic and structures involved in programming rather than worrying about the mechanics of writing programs (Kelleher & Pausch, 2005).

Through funding from a National Science Foundation Cyberlearning grant, we have been working primarily on educational data mining as described by Bienkowski, Feng, and Means (2012) in their report *Enhancing Teaching and Learning Through Educational Data Mining and Learning Analytics: An Issue Brief*, as the focus was on the development of tools, algorithms, and/or models to detect patterns in students' Scratch data. Our preliminary work focused on measures of micro-concepts in Scratch at primarily the code block level, such as whether students use the "green flag" block to initialize a sprite or other feature of their program. This is an important initial step to set up the building blocks of the tool for the creation of more complex measures of computational thinking or other type of concept related to learning in Scratch. This tool then can be applied by learning analytics researchers to large Scratch data sets to understand learning of computational thinking and influence practice at scale across a school, district, or state.

Though automated analysis tools are already being used in the corporate sector, the FUN! tool is a tool that can be a solution for larger and more complex data sets in education (Close et al., 2015). We have been conducting machine learning and data mining techniques to take the rather unstructured data and find patterns in the data to extract meaning through the development of measures related to computational thinking using the large set of data collected from several Scratch workshops held with students in grades 5 to 7.

However, to develop measures of computational thinking, we had to reference domain knowledge in this area from prior research. Prior research has established some common components used to measure CT. We reviewed these measures and have developed measures related to some of these CT components so far in our work developing the FUN! tool. In Table 1, we show our understanding of the components discussed by three seminal papers on this topic and also note the areas where we have been developing related measures.

Table 1 Components of computational thinking referenced in prior research and this study

Components of CT	Moreno-León and Robles (2015)	Grover and Pea (2013)	Brennan and Resnick (2012)	Present study
Abstraction	✓	✓	✓	
Parallelism	✓	✓	✓	✓
Logical thinking (e.g., conditional logic, operators, events)	✓	✓	✓	✓
Synchronization	✓		✓	✓
Algorithmic notions of flow of control	✓	✓		
User interactivity	✓		✓	
Data representation	✓		✓	
Iterative and recursive thinking (e.g., loops)		✓	✓	✓
Efficiency and performance constraints		✓		
Debugging and systematic error detection		✓		
Pattern generalization		✓		✓
Systematic processing of information		✓		

Methods

Summer Scratch Workshops

Our study takes place within the context of a larger exploratory research project funded by the National Science Foundation to develop the automated assessment, the FUN! Tool, and then to apply learning analytics and ethnographic methods to examine thousands of program snapshots from 64 students (novice level in programming), ages 10–13, who participated in summer workshops ("Scratch Camps") where they engaged in Scratch programming for approximately 30 h across 5 days.

The Scratch workshops were designed by Dr. Deborah Fields from Utah State University and graduate students who worked on the project. The first week of workshops was led by Dr. Fields. Subsequent workshops were co-facilitated by Dr. Fields and graduate students working on the project. The workshops included the tasks shown in Table 2 that students were challenged to complete within Scratch following a basic introduction to Scratch. For more information about the Scratch workshop instruction, see Fields et al. (2016a, 2016b).

There were three sets of workshops conducted over the following three weeks during summer 2014: June 2–6, June 16–20, and July 14–19.

Table 2 Overview of Scratch activities for each day of Scratch Camp

Day of Scratch Camp	Activity title	Description	Examples of code blocks or programming used
Day 1	Scribble time	Students learn Scratch basics and explore and create a project of their own design	Move, turn, next costume, if on edge bounce
	Name project	Students animate the letters of their name or Scratch username	Multiple sprites, hide/show, initialization, position
Day 2	Story project	Students develop their own animated story using multiple characters and a special effect	Position, repeat/forever loops, graphical effects, broadcast/receive, green flag, synchronization, background changes
Day 3	Music video project	Students create a music video synced to provided music using a timer	Synchronization, when key is pressed, conditionals, variables, background changes, sounds
Day 4	Video game project	Students created a video game with an instruction screen on how to play the game, fully developed user controls, two or more levels, variables to track game-related outcomes (e.g., health)	User interaction, health meter or other outcome, variables, data
Day 5	Free choice	Students complete previous days' work or start a new project	Blocks of student choosing learned previously or selected based on personal choice

Table 3 Overview of data collected summer 2014

Scratch Camp Summer 2014	Number of students	Number of projects	Range of projects per student
June 2–6	24	499	6–33
June 16–20	19	508	17–42
July 14–19	22	531	16–39
Total	65	1,538	6–42

Note: The number of students with data includes students with parent consent and student assent for use of data in our research analyses

Across the 5 days of Scratch Camp, there were six main activities. Therefore, we would expect at least 390 projects (65 students with six projects each). However, we have close to four times as many projects (1,538). We believe this is mostly due to a behavior observed frequently where students would start a project and then decide they wanted to go in a different direction. Instead of modifying their existing project, they would create a new project. For this reason, we provide the range of number of projects per student in Table 3. This is important to understand the amount of data we had to include in our analyses, which ranges between six and 42 projects per student.

Scratch Data

Scratch, developed by the MIT Media Lab, allows users to drag and drop blocks (Boolean commands, loops, variables, etc.) into a script (see Fig. 1). Each programmer can run the script on a sprite (or object) to see a visual representation (such as an animation) in a window (see Fig. 2). The program is syntax-free and, therefore, more accessible and enjoyable for novice programmers. Although the environment itself is simple, the scripts can be very complex requiring advanced planning and well-developed computational thinking to design.

Scratch 2.0 makes collecting data for researchers simple. Every Scratch program saves a user's state (data about their current project code) in the form of a JSON file, or JavaScript Object Notation file, every 2 min or anytime a user causes a triggering event (such as a manual save). State data are defined as a collection of metadata (e.g., time stamp and user ID) about the targeted state, measures on that state, and data of that state. For example, with Scratch, a state is a Scratch save, which includes information such as the current background, the sprite costume, and other features such as sounds.

This finely grained data allows researchers to analyze user actions over time. While Scratch 2.0 is based online, we were able to collect data from MIT's servers, through a data-sharing agreement, by simply gaining permission from the participants then sending the participant's user ID and the research start and end date to the MIT Media Lab. The quality of data and ease of collection make Scratch 2.0 an ideal program with which to test the FUN! tool. In Table 4, we provide an overview of the range of data saves of the project states per student across the 32,465 state saves in our data set.

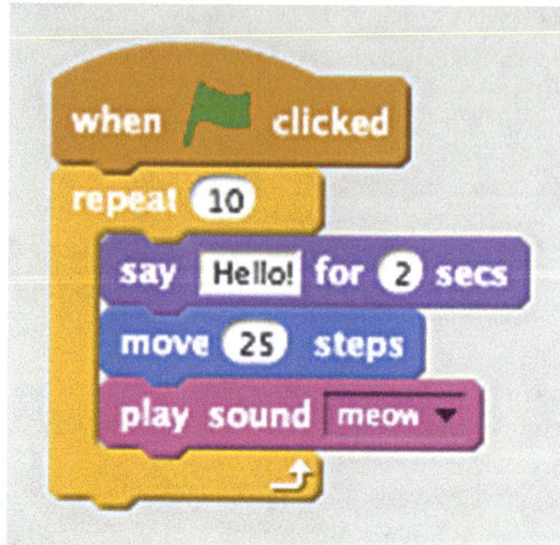

Fig. 1 Sample Scratch script using code blocks

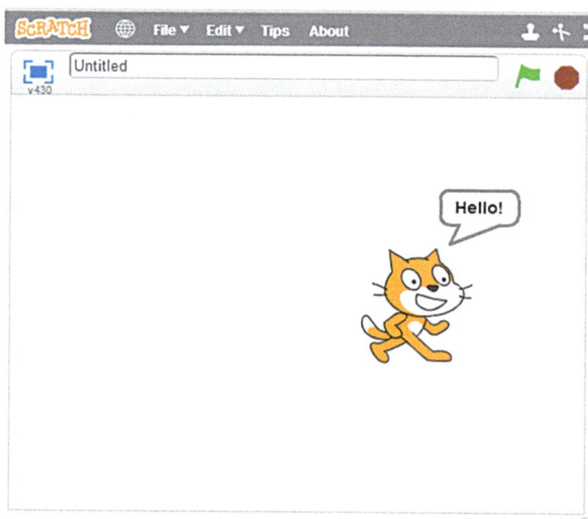

Fig. 2 Sample Scratch visual representation of code commanding a sprite

The range in saved states across projects and across students shown in Table 4 is important when it comes to considering types of analyses where we might want to look at changes over time. If a project has only one saved state, we would not be able to look at changes over time within that particular project. However, students had 99–993 saved states across projects, so we would be able to look at changes over time across all projects for a student for measures of interest.

Table 4 Overview of project state saves for summer 2014

Scratch Camp Summer 2014	Number of students	Range of projects per student	Range of project state saves per student	Number of projects	Range of project state saves per project
June 2–6	24	6–33	99–618	499	1–179
June 16–20	19	17–42	322–905	508	1–269
July 14–19	22	16–39	295–993	531	1–428
Total	65	6–42	99–993	1,538	1–428

Note: The number of students with data includes students with parent consent and student assent for use of data in our research analyses

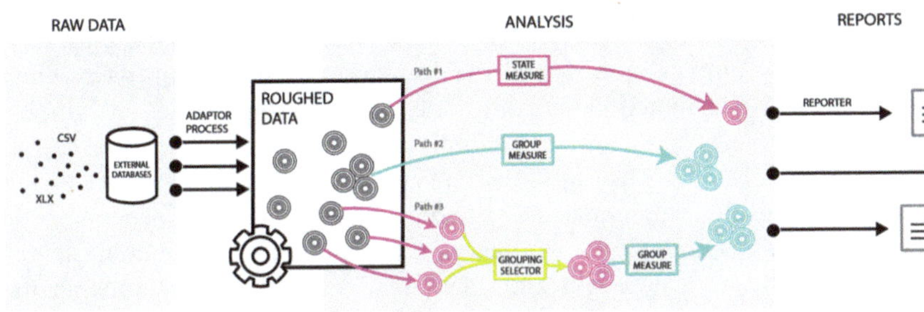

Fig. 3 Diagram showing how data ideally flows through the FUN! tool

FUN! Tool for Automated Data Analysis

As researchers we have experienced the challenge of conducting complex analyses for multiple projects in an inefficient manner repeating similar processes with each new data set for different projects. We have also suffered from the consequences of either lack of documentation or incomplete documentation of research analysis processes. The FUN! tool allows us to (1) organize our workflow process, (2) record log data from our analyses, and (3) share our work with others through GitHub, an online code-sharing repository. We have found this type of research behavior is more common among data scientists and less common among education researchers. Therefore, the FUN! tool can be helpful in requiring research team members to follow more appropriate data management and analysis processes.

The FUN! tool moves data through a workflow process that includes four parts: adaptors, selectors, measures, and reporters (as shown in Fig. 3). Data are adapted from a raw form (JSON in the case of our Scratch data) into something usable by adaptors. This data includes state data, which is a collection of metadata about the targeted state, measures on that state, and data of that state. The metadata would be the information about that save, such as the user ID and time when saved. There is also group data, which is a collection of states, such as all state data for a particular user. The researcher can program the FUN! tool to select from the data based on various measures that exist within the FUN! tool or that are created.

The analysis part of the FUN! tool involves selecting states (or group of states) and applying measures to those states or groups of states. For example, to analyze how many code blocks are in a single student's Scratch project, first the tool selects the state (in this case the code snapshot of a student's Scratch code), and then the tool applies a measure (in this case the measure would be the block count). The same process can be applied to increasingly complex measurements and include analysis over time. Instead of selecting a single state and running a single measure, the tool selects a group of states and runs a measure on that group. For example, to measure a student's average use of code blocks over the course of a Scratch summer camp, the tool selects all of the states with that particular student ID (using a grouping selector) and then measures the block count for each state and averages those counts (using a group measure).

The FUN! tool reporter essentially outputs the result of each analysis. Currently, the reporter simply outputs spreadsheet file formats such as csv and tsv, which researchers can use in conjunction with other software to produce tables and graphs. The reporter also selects and shows a randomly selected sample state in text (.txt) file format. Researchers can use this randomly selected sample state text file to double-check the result of their analysis or to debug their analysis, if necessary.

Depending on the complexity of the measure, programming the initial measures may be difficult. Though powerful and adaptable, rewriting or repurposing the adaptor and measure elements of the FUN! tool requires at least an intermediate knowledge of the Python programming language. The majority of the analysis was conducted using nothing beyond Python core libraries. The NumPy and SciPy libraries were used with pandas for cluster analysis. While it may sound as if the data move in a single path through the FUN! tool, the processes can interact with each other in a nonlinear approach depending on the complexity and stage of analysis. For example, researchers dealing with new data may begin by adapting, selecting, measuring, reselecting, and then remeasuring prior to conducting their analysis and reporting out their findings.

Additional Data Mining Approaches

Once the data is reported into a format, such as csv, additional analytic tools may be used following other educational data mining approaches. According to Baker (2011), there are five educational data mining technical methods:

- *Prediction* where the goal is to understand why a particular behavior or data element predicts another data element or outcome of interest. For example, does use of initialization blocks in Scratch predict use of more advanced programming components (e.g., loops)?
- *Clustering* where data points can be divided into categories and grouped based on patterns. For example, Scratch users or Scratch projects could be grouped based on use of particular code blocks or based on measures of computational thinking developed based on combinations of code blocks.

- *Relationship mining* where relationships between variables in a data set are encoded as a variable or rule to be used later. For example, there may be a relationship between Scratch users who do not initialize their sprites and challenges with their project design. Using association rule mining, one could create a variable to flag students with this difficulty to be used to inform future instruction for these students or inform design of a feature of the Scratch program that could provide a student with a reminder to initialize their sprite. Using sequence pattern mining is also possible with data on project saves over time as we were able to obtain from MIT.
- *Distillation for human judgment* is related to visual data analytics where data are depicted so that people can easily classify features of the data.
- *Discovery with models* is appropriate once there is knowledge in the domain in addition to relationships from other data mining techniques to establish a model of a concept that can be used to find other relationships. For example, in Scratch the concept of abstraction might be important when trying to understand the development of computational thinking. Once this measure of abstraction is created as a model, a research could consider whether projects of particular genres of programming in Scratch (animation, art, game, music, or stories) are related to use of greater levels of abstraction in student projects.

We started with a visual analysis of data across the three Scratch Camps. Then we did some exploration to determine common code blocks used versus code blocks with the most missing data. Then we applied clustering techniques to our initial set of measures, which were primarily counts of different code blocks used. Specifically, *k*-means was used to understand whether there were clusters of programming profiles across the student projects. The type of clustering approach selected is informed by the data variable scales, units of measure, and other factors. *k*-means is used to segment or cluster the data based on similar types of users and grouping them together (Schutt & O'Neil, 2013). K is the number of bins or buckets you want to put the data attributes in. One challenge of the *k*-means approach is that the researcher has to select the value of *k,* which is between one and the number of data points. The researcher has to adjust k until there are natural groupings. Another weakness of *k*-means is that the answer may not be useful or there may be challenges with interpretation. However, for exploratory data mining, it can be an easy first step to begin to look for patterns and groupings in the data. Next, we provide the results from our initial set of analyses.

Visual Analysis

To begin we considered how appropriate it would be to combine the data from all 3 weeks of Scratch Camps when they were each conducted with a different group of students. We started with a simple visual analysis of the number of code blocks and sprites in student projects over time across the 5-day period for each of the three Scratch Camps. In Fig. 4, the top line is the number of code blocks used, and the

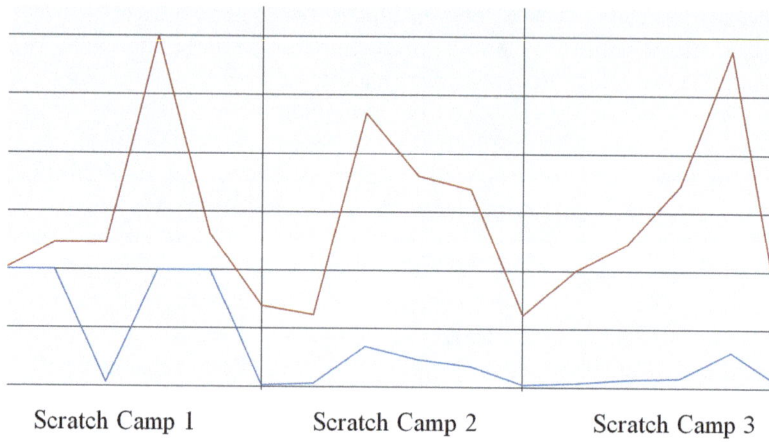

Fig. 4 Time series plot of code block and sprite use over time

bottom line is the number of sprites used. There is a definite spike in code blocks and sprites around Day 4 when students remixed one of the five programs provided.

We decided to remove the data for Day 4 from our next exploration of the data, since the students were given one of the four starter games to remix by looking at the existing code and modifying the code to create their video game. In many cases, these games included a much larger number of code blocks than the students' total Scratch Camp code blocks independently created, so it might skew our findings. For example, if we see a "broadcast" code block within a student's set of data, we might assume they know how to use "broadcast"; however, that block may have only been within the Day 4 starter game that they modified. It may not necessarily mean they know how to use this block appropriately. Therefore, we used a grouping selector to group projects from Days 1 to 3 and 5 for analysis.

Exploratory Analysis

We started with approximately 129 measures developed in the FUN! tool based on available code blocks within Scratch user data from students in the Scratch Camp. These measures are provided in Table 5. Some of these measures are counts of a particular script (code block) used by the student in their project. Other measures are used to test whether a block is present or not. Within the FUN! tool, the measures used to count particular blocks have the word "count" at the end of the measure name. For example, the "Broadcast" measure would measure whether the "Broadcast" block was ever used by a student, while the "Broadcast_Count" measure would count how many times a block was used by a student. These measures can then be used to create additional measures using mathematical functions, such as the ratio of "Broadcast_Count" scripts to "Total scripts."

Table 5 Alphabetical list of initial measures developed within the FUN! tool

Answer	Glide seconds to XY elapsed from	Set pen hue to
Append to list	Go back by layers	Set pen shade to
Background index	Go to sprite or mouse	Set rotation style
Bounce off edge	Go to the top	Set size to
Bounce up	Go to XY	Set tempo to
Broadcast	Green flag scripts	Set variable to
Call	Green flag sprites	Set video state
Change graphic effect	Hide	Set volume to
Change pen hue by	Hide list	Show
Change pen shade by	Hide variable	Show variable
Change pen size by	Instrument	Stamp costume
Change size by	Key pressed	Start scene
Change tempo by	Letter of	Start scene and wait
Change variable by	Line count of list	Stop all sounds
Change volume by	List contains	Stop scripts
Change X position by	Look like	String length
Change Y position by	Mouse pressed count	Think
Clear pen trails	Mouse X	Think duration elapsed from
Come to front	Mouse Y	Time and date
Computer function of	Next costume	Timer
Concatenate with	Next score	Timer reset
Control blocks	Not	Timestamp
Costume index	Note on duration elapsed from	Total scripts
Count 1–9	Number of scripts	Total sprites with scripts
Create clone of	Pen color	Total sprites
Delete clone	Pen size	Touching
Delete line of list	Play drum	Touching color
Distance to	Play sound	Turn left
Do ask	Point toward	Turn right
Do broadcast and wait	Procedure defined	Volume
Do forever	Put pen down	Wait elapsed from
Do if	Put pen up	When
Do if else	Random from to	When blocks
Do play sound and wait	Read variable	When clicked
Do repeat	Rest elapsed from	When cloned
Do until	Rounded	When green flag
Do wait until	Say	When I receive
Filter reset	Say duration elapsed from	When key pressed
Forward	Scale	When scene starts
Get attribute of	Scene name	When sensor greater than
Get line of list	Sense video motion	X position
Get parameter	Set graphic effect to	Y position
Get user name	Set line of list to	

Table 6 Measures with the least and most missing data from Scratch Camps

Measures with the least missing data	Measures with the most missing data
Green flag	Broadcast
Number of scripts	Change size
Total scripts	Change tempo
Total sprites	Change volume
Total sprites with scripts	Clear pen trails
	Come to front
	Costume index
	Create clone
	Broadcast and wait

After running our analysis of basic measures within the FUN! tool to count types of code blocks for projects used Days 1–3 and 5, we first looked at the measures with the least missing data (most commonly used code blocks) and the measures with the most missing data (least used blocks or blocks not used by any students), which we show in Table 6.

The measures that appear in the list of the least missing data were not a surprise, since these measures relate to blocks introduced on the first day of the camp. We were somewhat surprised to see "broadcast" in the list of measures with the most missing data, since this was covered during the camp, while "create clone" was not covered in the camp during instruction or review of student projects, so it was expected to appear in the list of measures with the most missing data. Therefore, the measures in the list with the most missing data do not necessarily relate to the complexity of programming, but rather an area that was not introduced during the camp either by the instructor or a student sharing their project with the class.

K-means Cluster Analysis

Next we used *k*-means cluster analysis to look at different "k" cluster solutions to group the student projects for Days 1–3 and 5. We clustered on attribute counts of blocks and counts of sprites. We started with a 15-cluster solution (k = 15), but did not feel that the solution was easily interpretable, because it was difficult to point to sharply different characteristics in terms of measures from one cluster to another. We reduced the amount of clusters to ten and found the maximum affinity between Clusters 2 and 3 shown in Fig. 5. Analysis using a 5-cluster solution (k = 5) was not accepted as it reduced the count of clusters to too low of a number and led to overlapping of characteristics in term of measures.

It is difficult to point too sharply to different characteristics in terms of measures from one cluster to another.

The output from the *k*-means cluster analysis provides the characteristics for each cluster based on the measures available within the FUN! tool, the values for the characteristics and the probability. Below is a comparison of the first five characteristics for each cluster as an example (Fig. 6).

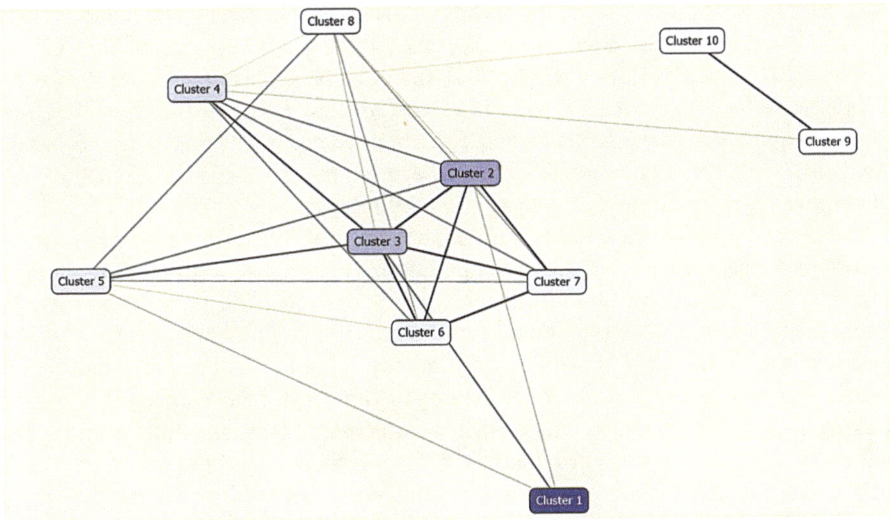

Fig. 5 Affinity diagram for 10-cluster solution

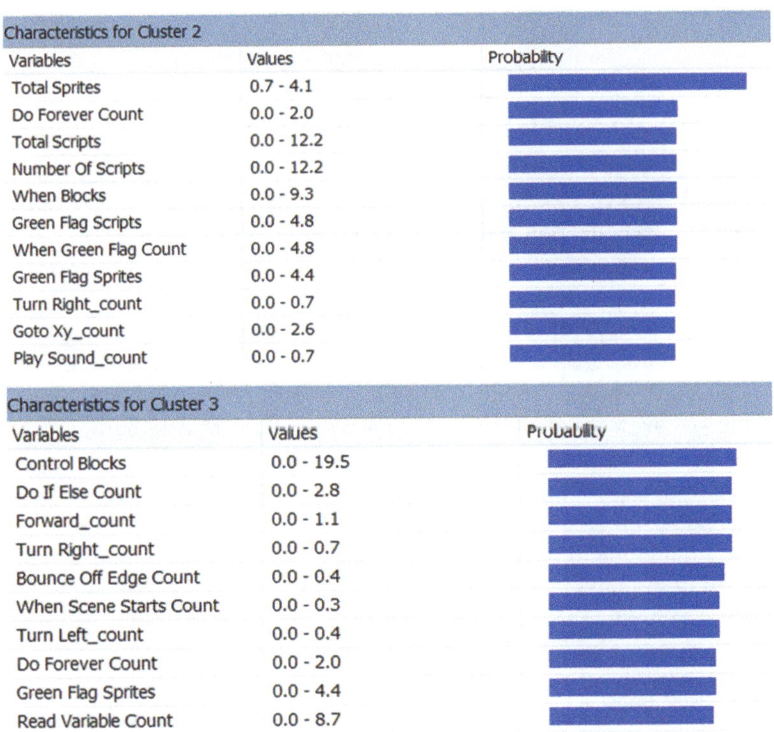

Fig. 6 Comparison of characteristics for Clusters 2 and 3

There are several characteristics where Clusters 2 and 3 have the same values: Do If Count (0.0–4.2), Green Flag Sprites (0.0–4.4), When Green Flag Count (0.0–4.8), Bounce Off Edge to Count (0.0–0.4), and Next Costume Count (0.0–0.2). While these have the exact values, the values are low. Some of the characteristics not in common between Clusters 2 and 3 had high values (e.g., "read variable count" for Cluster 3); these characteristics may be important to consider when thinking about developing measures of computational thinking.

Next, we looked at the Cluster profiles, which show the attributes and the values across the clusters as well as for the population. This seemed a little more interesting than comparing the two clusters (2 and 3) that had the greatest affinity. In Table 7, we provide a sample of these attributes with the number of projects within each cluster. Note how Cluster 5, while it only included 44 projects, had higher values than other clusters (shown by shading in Table 7) for Do Forever, Play Sound and Wait, Scripts with Green Flags, Sprites with Green Flags, and Total Scripts. The value of the cluster profiles provided by this analysis was to show which attributes might be ones that differentiate some students from others whether it be in computational thinking or other factors, such as students who spend more time on the visual or audio features of their project.

From the *k*-means cluster analysis, we learned that clustering on this many measures can be much more difficult to interpret than clustering we have done for other projects with fewer measures.

Development of Complex Measures of Computational Thinking

One unique feature of this research project was the addition of an ethnographic component of data collection and analysis conducted by Dr. Deborah Fields and her graduate research assistants. By looking at student projects, field notes collected during Scratch Camps, and the JSON data from the projects, Dr. Fields and her team (Fields et al., 2016a, 2016b) have created a set of more complex measures related to computational thinking shown in Table 8.

For additional information about Dr. Field's research on these measures, please visit http://www.workingexamples.org/uploads/File/1035. She also provides definitions of the measures and a description of why the measures are important in a document available at http://www.workingexamples.org/uploads/File/1035.

After Fields et al. (2016a, 2016b) created these labels and descriptions for measures of computational thinking that they found important from their ethnographic and data mining analyses, our next step was to create these complex measures within the FUN! tool. This task was a challenge for some measures and required a strong understanding of Python to write the code for the new measures within the FUN! tool. However, once written these measures are available to the public through GitHub to inform the work of other researchers studying the development of programming and computational thinking using Scratch.

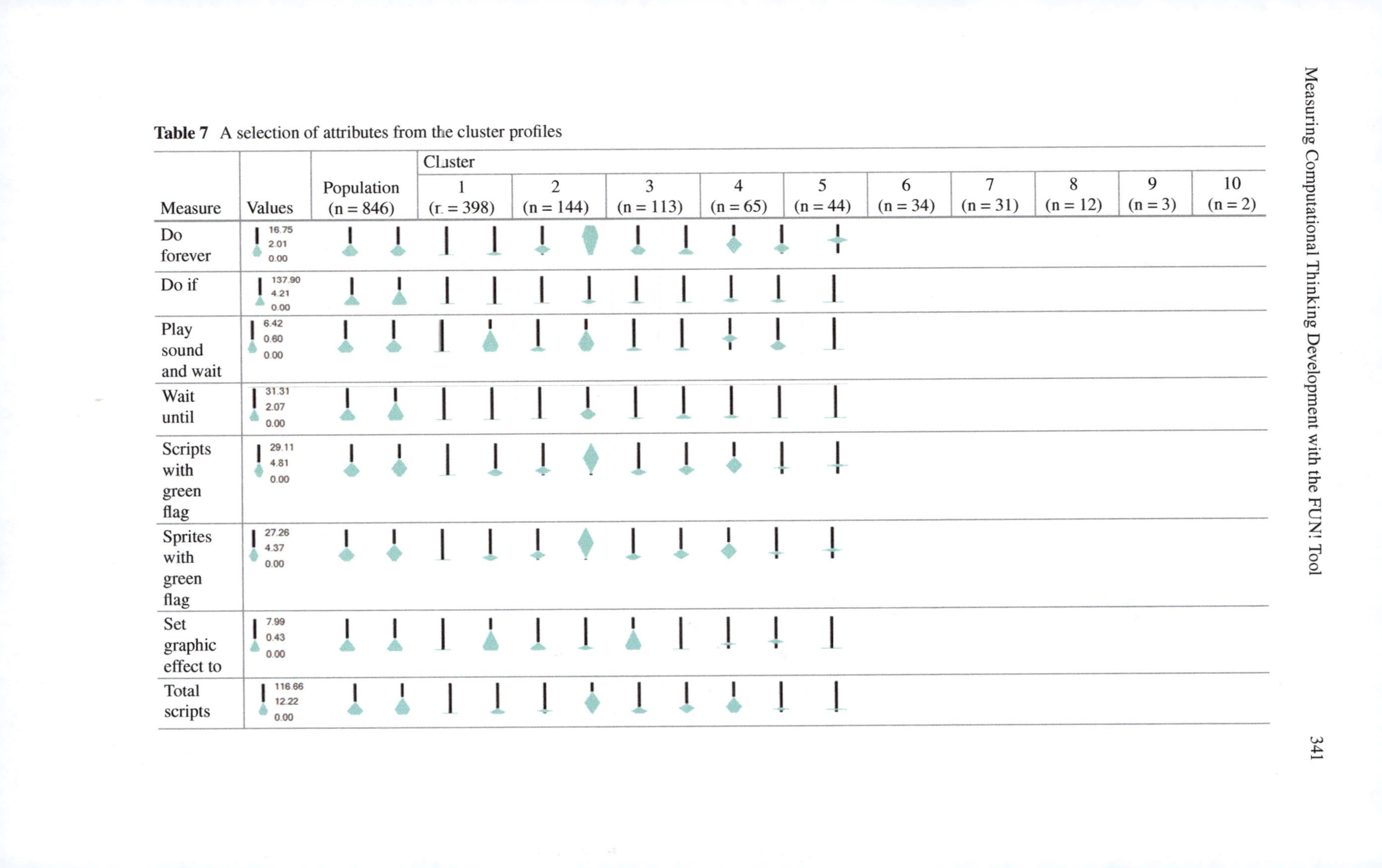

Table 7 A selection of attributes from the cluster profiles

Measure	Values	Population (n = 846)	Cluster 1 (n = 398)	2 (n = 144)	3 (n = 113)	4 (n = 65)	5 (n = 44)	6 (n = 34)	7 (n = 31)	8 (n = 12)	9 (n = 3)	10 (n = 2)
Do forever	16.75 2.01 0.00											
Do if	137.90 4.21 0.00											
Play sound and wait	6.42 0.60 0.00											
Wait until	31.31 2.07 0.00											
Scripts with green flag	29.11 4.81 0.00											
Sprites with green flag	27.26 4.37 0.00											
Set graphic effect to	7.99 0.43 0.00											
Total scripts	116.66 12.22 0.00											

Table 8 Measures of computational thinking within Scratch data

Loops	Initialization	Event-driven parallelism	Conditionals	Boolean measures	Sensing measures
Total forever loops	Initialized variables	Proportion of total sprites with a green flag	Complete conditionals	Conditionals with Booleans	User control block count
Empty forever loops	Ratio of initialized variables to total variables used	Sprites with multiple green flags	Incomplete conditionals	Conditionals with/without complete Booleans	Touching edge
Nonempty forever loops	Initialized graphic effects	Broadcasts paired with a receive	Conditionals using preexisting Scratch variables	Complete Booleans	Touching mouse
Total repeat loops	Sprites with/without initialized positions	Broadcasts with multiple receives	User-defined variables used in "if" or "until" blocks	User control block count	Touching missing argument
Repeat loops with repeat of 0 or 1	Sprites with/without an initialized direction	Sprites with multiple receives	Conditionals using sensing		Touching sprite
Empty repeat loops	Sprites with/without initialized size	Sprites with multiple identical receives	Nested conditional in conditional		Touching color
Nonempty repeat loops	Sprites with/without a tempo		Nested conditional in a loop		
Max nested loop depth	Sprites with/without a volume		Conditionals with Booleans		
Forever if	Sprites with an initialized state of "show"		Conditionals in green flag (not in a loop)		
Repeat until	Sprites with an initialized state of "hide"				
	Sprites with/without initialized layer				
	Sprites with/without an initialized pen				
	Program with/without an initialized background				
	Sprites with/without initialized costumes				
	Sprites with multiple costumes				
	Sprites with multiple costumes that are initialized				

Note: There is one additional measure developed by Fields et al. (2016a, 2016b) not shown in the table, which is a randomization measure used to count when the pick random number operator code block is used

Findings

While many data mining approaches could be used to analyze the state data, we began with traditional statistics conducting a one-way ANOVA to determine if there was a significant difference between the means for each measure for each week of Scratch Camp. We used Scheffe's post hoc to determine whether there were significant differences in pairwise comparisons of Scratch Camps. While this may not tell us much about the development of computational thinking, it is important to consider whether state data should be mined across all three Scratch Camps or whether state data should be mined separately by week of Scratch Camp. The first Scratch Camp (June 2–6) was for students in grades 5 and 6. The second Scratch Camp (June 16–20) was for students in grades 7 and 8. The final Scratch Camp (July 14–19) was a camp for girls only.

For measures of loops, all three pairwise comparisons were statistically significant ($p < .05$) for do forever empty (and not empty), do repeat, and loops with "if." When looking at measures of conditionals, the differences between camps were significant for conditionals with Scratch variables and conditionals with sensing for all three comparisons; the pairwise comparison of conditionals with user-defined variables was only significant for Camps 1–2 and 1–3 comparisons. For all Boolean measures, there were significant differences found between at least two pairs of Scratch Camps. There were three measures of sensing where there were significant differences found between all three pairwise comparisons: touching color, touching edge, and touching sprite. There were only two pairwise comparisons with significant differences for touching missing argument (Camps 1–2 and 2–3), touching mouse (Camps 1–2 and 1–3), and user control blocks (Camps 1–2 and 1–3). Finally, there were significant differences for pairwise comparisons between all three camps for total sprites, total sprites with scripts, and green flag sprites.

There are significant differences between the average scores for students in different Scratch Camps for many of the measures. For the measures of *loops*, the third Scratch Camp (girls only) was significantly lower than the first or second camp students on five of the seven measures (for all measures except "Do Repeat Empty" and "Do Repeat Not Empty"). While the students in the third camp were higher than the other camps in general on "Do Repeat Empty," this finding is not positive, since it is important to have the "Do Repeat" block not empty. However, the third camp also had the highest average for "Do Repeat Not Empty," which is an evidence that on average the students knew how to use that block. Students may momentarily add a "Do Repeat" block to their program and then decide not to use it, which is one reason it might be empty. However, if a student has measures where the "Do Repeat" block is not empty, then it at least shows they have attempted to use this type of loop.

When understanding the data that is possible using the FUN! tool, it is similar to thinking about writing an essay using a computer. There may be sections of a paper that are in one draft that are later removed from the paper. The code snapshot is one point in time where the blocks in the program are measured. Where a student had selected a "Do Repeat" block that currently is empty in the code snapshot, after time, they may either use it or remove it from their program. Our data set included 2-min snapshots over time; it is expected that at some time points there would be empty loops, where the student had used the loop code block but had not yet filled it with another block.

For the measures related to *conditionals*, the third Scratch Camp was significantly lower than the first or second camp students on two of the three measures (for all except "Conditional with Scratch Variables"). When it came to the *Boolean* measures, the third Scratch Camp was significantly lower than the first camp group on three of the four measures. For the *sensing* measure, the third Scratch Camp was significantly lower than both the first and second camp students on three of the six measures and significantly lower than one of the other camps on the other three measures. For the final set of *other* measures, the students in the third camp were significantly higher than students in the other two camps for all three areas (total sprites, total sprites with scripts, and green flag sprites). Since this area focuses on sprites, it may be that students in the third camp had more characters in their projects than the students in the first or second camp had in their projects.

What the data does not tell us is why students in the third camp performed significantly lower than students in either the first or second camp for many of the measures. We caution the reader from concluding that it had something to do with gender, when there are other factors to consider. For example, Dr. Fields was the primary facilitator of the first Scratch Camp. The second and third camp had more facilitation by Dr. Field's graduate students. While all three camps covered the same content and activities, it may be that there are some factors related to having an expert in Scratch and someone with prior experience in leading Scratch workshops facilitate the instruction. Future research could collect data on different instructional variables that may be related to improved outcomes for students. Another factor could be prior knowledge of programming skills. A short assessment could have been given at the start of the camp to collect this type of data to provide context for these differences we see between students in the three Scratch Camps. What is clear from our findings is that any additional data mining might be better conducted by Scratch Camp since we did find these significant differences between camps.

Next Steps

Our work has focused heavily on the development of the FUN! tool and preliminary measure development. However, what is needed is for the community of Scratch researchers to access the FUN! tool to develop additional measures and to provide reliable and valid interpretations of such measures. Learning analytics researchers could begin to use measures in addition to domain knowledge to begin to represent relationships and patterns using visual data analytics. For example, development of a data dashboard of computational thinking components could provide classroom teachers with data on their students that can inform their instruction. Data visualizations are also helpful at an individual student level to provide students and their parents the opportunity to monitor their learning. Having agreed on CT, component measures can provide school districts and states the opportunity to understand the impact of computer science programs introduced in K-12 to develop computational thinking.

To access the open source FUN! tool, researchers should follow these steps:

1. Download Python 3 from https://www.**python**.org/**downloads**/.
   Windows: If you have an earlier version of Python, skip this step. However, for the new Python 3.5, there is a problem that you will need to fix before downloading the FUN! tool.
2. After downloading Python 3.5, download pyyaml source from
   `http://pyyaml.org/download/pyyaml/PyYAML-3.11.zip. Run py -3 setup.py --without-libyaml install. Then follow the directions below for #3.`
   Mac: Go to step 3.
3. Download the FUN! tool.
   `Windows: Open the command prompt; run py -3 -m pip install funtool`
   `Mac: Open the terminal; run pip3 install funtool`
4. Download the FUN! tool Scratch Processes.
   `Windows: Run py -3 -m pip install funtool_scratch_processes`
   `Mac: Run pip3 install funtool_scratch_processes`
5. Download this example analysis template by navigating to https://github.com/activelearninglab/funtool-analysis and cloning the funtool-analysis to your desktop. Directions for using the FUN! tool are also available on this Github page.

Conclusions

With open education resources for teaching coding, such as resources from Code.org, coding programs are becoming part of most children's school experience, whether it be through structures like "Hour of Code," afterschool programs, or more structured school or district programs. As states add standards for computer science to their K-12 curriculum, it is important to have reliable, valid measures to understand student progress and evaluate effectiveness of education programs. In this paper, we describe an automated method of collecting and analyzing data from Scratch using the FUN! tool. Although this paper does not strictly contribute to learning theory, we hope that it will stimulate ongoing conversations about the value as well as changes of automated methods to collect and analyze data in different kinds of digital learning environments.

We were transparent about the challenges we faced with the large amount of initial measures developed based on code blocks within Scratch to inform the work of other researchers, pointing to the value gained from looking at more complex measures. The Day 4 lesson where students remixed an existing Scratch program added complexity to our exploratory analyses. All of these factors are important considerations when determining how to group data for analysis. These are also factors to consider when designing instructional programs for students where computational thinking development will be measured. Use of a pre-project and post-project design to measure changes in computational thinking may be better than the analysis of projects completed as part of an instructional program, since instructional expectations may limit or confound the data available for analysis.

Our project was limited in what we were able to learn from our use of the FUN! tool due to resource limitations for the project given the extensive costs of the development, refinement, and testing of the tool to prepare it for use by a wider audience. However, through several conference presentations and workshops on the tool, we have received positive feedback about the potential for other researchers to use the tool with their own Scratch data in addition to interest in understanding the structure of the tool to develop similar automated tools for other educational game data.

We hope this paper supports existing work in educational data mining and that the processes and measures we developed for analyses can support other researchers interested in learning analytics. We encourage researchers to download the FUN! tool and related processes and analyses from GitHub. We also recommend that researchers use GitHub to share new measures and analyses they create.

Acknowledgment This work is supported by the National Science Foundation Grant IIS-1319938. Any opinions, findings, and conclusions or recommendations expressed in this material are those of the author(s) and do not necessarily reflect the views of the National Science Foundation.

References

Baker, R. S. J. d. (2011). Data mining for education. In B. McGaw, P. Peterson, & E. Baker (Eds.), *International encyclopedia of education* (3rd ed.). Oxford: Elsevier.

Bienkowski, M., Feng, M., & Means, B. (2012). *Enhancing teaching and learning through educational data mining and learning analytics: An issue brief.* Washington, DC: Office of Educational Technology, U.S. Department of Education.

Boe, B., Hill, C., Len, M., Dreschler, G., Conrad, P., & Franklin, D. (2013). Hairball: Lint-inspired static analysis of scratch projects. In *Proceeding of the 44th ACM technical symposium on computer science education* (pp. 215–220). Denver, CO: ACM.

Brennan, K., & Resnick, M. (2012). New frameworks for studying and assessing the development of computational thinking. In *Proceedings of the 2012 annual meeting of the American Educational Research Association.* Vancouver, Canada.

Close, K., Janisiewicz, P., Brasiel, S., & Martin, T. (2015). What do I do with all this data? How to use the FUN! tool to automatically clean, analyze, and visualize your digital data. In *Proceedings from games and learning society 11 conference*. Madison, WI, USA. Retrieved from http://press.etc.cmu.edu/files/GLS11-Proceedings-2015-web.pdf

Fields, D. A., Quirk, L., Horton, T., Velasquez, X., Amely, J. & Pantic, K. (2016a). Working toward equity in a constructionist Scratch camp: Lessons learned in applying a studio design model. In *Proceedings of constructionism*. Bangkok, Thailand.

Fields, D. A., Quirk, L., Amely, J., & Maughan, J. (2016b). Combining "big data" and "thick data" analyses for understanding youth learning trajectories in a summer coding camp. In *Proceedings of the 47th ACM technical symposium on computer science education (SIGCSE '16)*. New York, NY: ACM.

Grover, S., & Pea, R. (2013). Computational thinking in K–12. A review of the state of the field. *Educational Researcher, 42*(1), 38–43.

Kelleher, C., & Pausch, R. (2005). Lowering the barriers to programming: A taxonomy of programming environments and languages for novice programmers. *ACM Computing Surveys (CSUR), 37*(2), 83–137.

Moreno-León, J., & Robles, G. (2015). Analyze your Scratch projects with Dr. Scratch and assess your computational thinking skills. In *Proceedings of the 7th international Scratch conference (Scratch2015AMS)*. Amsterdam, Netherlands.

Lye, S. Y., & Koh, J. H. L. (2014). Review on teaching and learning of computational thinking through programming: What is next for K-12? *Computers in Human Behavior, 41*, 51–61.

Resnick, M., Maloney, J., Monroy-Hernández, A., Rusk, N., Eastmond, E., Brennan, K., et al. (2009). Scratch: Programming for all. *Communications of the ACM, 52*(11), 60–67.

Rich, P. J., Leatham, K. R., & Wright, G. A. (2013). Convergent cognition. *Instructional Science, 41*(2), 431–453.

Schutt, R., & O'Neil, C. (2013). *Doing data science: Straight talk from the frontline*. Sebastopol, CA: O'Reilly Media.

Watters, A. (2011). *Should computer science be required in K-12?* Retrieved from http://ww2.kqed.org/mindshift/2011/12/15/should-computer-science-be-required-in-k-12/

Wing, J. M. (2006). Computational thinking. *Communications of the ACM, 49*(3), 33–35.

Wing, J. M. (2011). *Computational thinking*. Retrieved from https://csta.acm.org/Curriculum/sub/CurrFiles/WingCTPrez.pdf

Part VI
Policy

Reenergizing CS0 in China

Tien-Yo (Tim) Pan

Abstract As early as 1997, the Ministry of Education (MOE) of China published Document Number 155, which emphasized the importance of computing in college education regardless of discipline. As a required course for all majors, CS0 "College Computers" has been taken by around six million students each year since then. However, due to the lack of appropriate materials for the course, some professors taught students how to use computer tools, and others taught students programming skills.

This article discusses a recent CS0 reform happening in China that shifts the focus of the course from computer tools and skills to computational thinking. An MOE teaching steering committee has published *The Basic Requirements for Teaching College Computer Courses*, where 42 core concepts on computational thinking are identified as guidelines for teaching College Computers and associated entry-level computer courses. Four college-level curricula recently developed are presented in this article as case studies. They are interesting and unique in different ways: one is a CS0 course for the deaf, another is a MOOC on C Programming, the third case is a MOOC on College Computers, and the fourth is a CS0 course designed for health majors. These curricular innovations around computational thinking are reenergizing CS0 in China. In this chapter, we discuss these innovations and their implications for college study in China.

Keywords College Computers • Computational thinking • MOOC

Introduction

This chapter discusses the first (CS0) or first few college computer courses offered to non-CS-major students in China. We first describe the environment of the courses before computational thinking was adopted, point out the problems, and explain how computational thinking is reenergizing college computer education in China. Case studies will be given as examples.

T.-Y. (Tim) Pan (✉)
Microsoft Research Asia, No.5, Danling Street, Haidian District, Beijing 100080, China
e-mail: tipa@microsoft.com

P.J. Rich, C.B. Hodges (eds.), *Emerging Research, Practice, and Policy on Computational Thinking*, Educational Communications and Technology: Issues and Innovations, DOI 10.1007/978-3-319-52691-1_21

CS0 in China Before Computational Thinking

China is one of a few countries that encourage all college students to learn computing. As early as 1997, the Ministry of Education (MOE) of China published Document Number 155, which emphasized the importance of computing in college education regardless of discipline. Most universities responded to the document by offering a course called "Computer Literacy," which was later renamed "College Computers." The course has been taken by around six million students each year since then. However, the visionary policy by the MOE soon faced difficulties. First, to most college students, College Computers was literally their first computer course. Some students, as expected, knew little about computers, but many others were proficient in using computers through self-learning or extracurricular activities. Professors felt challenged to satisfy both groups of students in the same class. Second, most existing computer curricula were designed for Computer Science students. Professors could not find appropriate materials for College Computers, a two-to-three credit introductory course. Some taught students how to use computer tools such as Excel and PowerPoint. Some taught students programming skills. Third, computer technologies change so rapidly that related tools and skills became obsolete before students left campus. Hence, to many students, College Computers was not only perceived as boring but also useless.

The MOE teaching steering committee for college computer courses (the "teaching committee") supervises computer courses for non-CS-major students, which include the main CS0 and optional courses such as programming language and data structures. The teaching committee realized the necessity of reenergizing the courses, especially CS0. The new approach proposed to give students a holistic view of computing, a view which is more fundamental, structural, and stable. Members of the teaching committee visited and learned from several renowned universities in the world and concluded that College Computers should focus more on thinking and innovation, not tools and programming. Hence, a reform began, which would benefit six million college students each year.

Reenergizing CS0 with Computational Thinking

When Professor Jeannette Wing wrote "Computational Thinking" on Communications of the ACM (Wing, 2006), she might not have expected that the teaching committee in China would deeply probe into the article. In 2007, Professor Fei-Yue Wang of the Chinese Academy of Sciences translated Professor Wing's article and published it on Communications of the CCF (a Chinese equivalence of CACM). It perfectly met the needs of CS0 reform in China. The teaching committee carefully studied the article and spent huge amounts of time facilitating various computational thinking curricula that suit Chinese non-CS college students. Several MOOCs on the subject have attracted hundreds of thousands of students, and the momentum continues.

Impacts and Changes Brought by Computational Thinking

Professor Yizhi Wang from Beijing Jiaotong University has been teaching CS0 since 1997 when the MOE published Document Number 155. She and most other professors assigned to the task were enthusiastic at the beginning, but for the aforementioned reasons, they gradually felt the same frustration as students taking the course. "I believe computational thinking benefits China more than any other country," says Professor Wang. "It is a paradigm shift on how to teach College Computers. It shifts our focus from tools to thinking" (Wang 2015, personal communication). She summarizes this reform in two points:

- College Computers is not about teaching tools or skills. Instead, it teaches students a way of thinking, i.e., how to abstract a problem and solve it automatically by a system.
- College Computers is about how to think like computer scientists. However, the ideal setting to observe how computer scientists think is in the tools and skills they create.

The two seemingly paradoxical points shed light on curricular reform. We need not throw away tools and skills but use them as examples and labs for students to learn computational thinking. With a title—*National Teaching Master*, Professor Wang led the way to redesign the curriculum and asked professors in her team (i.e., 12 faculty members teaching CS0 to 3,000 students per year) to do the same. "It was magical," she says. "I haven't seen that kind of enthusiasm in years, not only for learning but for teaching!" (Wang 2015, personal communication)

Professor Lian Li—director of the teaching committee—depicts three missions to reform the CS0 collegiate course. First, investigate practices and computer knowledge relevant to the target disciplines. For example, a professor teaching College Computers in medical school needs to study how computers are used in medical environments and what kind of computer knowledge is required in the medical discipline. Second, create curricula that integrate computing and the target disciplines. This can be realized in labs and projects. Third, equip students with computational thinking for their future work and life. The third mission shifts CS0 from a technical course to a general course that introduces students to a systematic way of thinking.

CS0 reform has been ongoing for few years. More than a hundred Chinese textbooks on the subject are available, and most universities are rethinking the course. Professor Li observes the status at the beginning of 2016 in China as follows:

- The majority of the CS0 books and curricula have added a thinking segment to the original contents.
- Some pioneers have created entirely new CS0 curricula based on computational thinking.
- A few special CS0 curricula have been developed for specific disciplines (e.g., social computing and health computing).

> "It has just started," says Professor Li. "In ten years, all CS0 in China will be based on computational thinking. There is no turning back" (Li 2016, personal communication).

Basic Requirements for Teaching College Computer Courses

Professor Qinming He from Zhejiang University, a member of the teaching committee, hopes that similar to College Physics or Mathematics, College Computers and associated college computer courses should have a common framework for professors to follow. After countless meetings and workshops and many experimental courses offered and reviewed, he helped the teaching committee to draft *Basic Requirements for Teaching College Computer Courses* (the "Basic Requirements"). The 157-page document published in late 2015 roughly defines the scope of college-level computing courses for non-CS majors. The core of the courses requires computational thinking instead of tools and skills.

Why computational thinking? Professor He answered: "Knowledge around computers has been growing exponentially, but course hours are limited. We need to lay out a foundation that does not change easily. Computational thinking serves the purpose well" (He 2015, personal communication). Similar to physics and mathematics, CS0 and its associated courses are to deliver a set of core concepts shown in Table 1. There are 42 core concepts grouped in eight major categories based on Professor Peter Denning's six categories of computing principles (Denning & Martell, 2015) and Professor Jeannette Wing's observation that computing is the automation of abstractions (Wing 2012, keynote speech at Microsoft Research Asia Faculty Summit).

The core concepts summarize the way computer scientists think and computers work. However, it remains the individual professor's responsibility to convey the concepts to students in interesting ways. The teaching committee encourages CS0 professors to innovate all curricula such as programming, project-based, or explorative courses in CS-oriented or cross-disciplinary scope. There are 14 teaching templates in the Basic Requirements for various disciplines including bioinformatics,

Table 1 Core concepts in college computer courses

Categories	Core concepts in teaching
Computation (3)	Computational models—computability—complexity
Abstraction (4)	Abstraction—layers of abstraction—conceptual model—implementation model
Automation (7)	Algorithm—procedure—iteration—recursion—heuristic method—random method—intelligence
Design (6)	Decomposition—synthesis—trade-offs—reliability—reusability—security
Evaluation (5)	Evaluation criterion and benchmark—bottleneck—redundancy—fault tolerance—simulation
Communication (7)	Information and its presentation—entropy—coding and decoding—compression—cryptography—error check and correction—protocols
Coordination (5)	Synchronization—concurrence—parallelism—events—services
Recollection (5)	Data types—data structure—data organization—retrieval and indexing—locality and caching

agriculture, e-commerce, multimedia, data science, and social computing. Those templates are contributed by professors who have taught college computer courses based on core concepts to students of specific majors. Some of the courses will be introduced in the next section.

Noted in the Basic Requirements, there are three types of scientific thinking: positivism thinking that finds rules by observation and experiments, logical thinking that describes and deduces matters in a logical way, and computational thinking that designs algorithms to solve specific problems. The three are not contradictory but complementary. Students learn positivism in physics and logical thinking in mathematics at a very early stage. China is now seriously implementing the third type—computational thinking.

Role of Microsoft Research

In the summer of 2013, Professor Guoliang Chen, the director of the teaching committee, met Dr. Jeannette Wing at the Microsoft Faculty Summit. That was the first time Dr. Wing, who already joined Microsoft Research as a Corporate Vice President, learned about computational thinking activities in China. Invited by Professor Chen, Dr. Wing gave a keynote speech at the 2013 CS0 Conference and met the teaching committee in Chongqing, China—where she committed that Microsoft would join hand in hand with the Ministry of Education of China to reform CS0. Professor Lian Li who succeeded directorship of the teaching committee in late 2013 recalled, "Microsoft and Jeannette's endorsement cheered up everyone in the committee, because it greatly expanded our public appeal" (Li 2016, personal communication).

Academic collaboration is not new to Microsoft. Since a Beijing lab was set up in 1998, Microsoft Research has been working closely with the MOE and universities to improve computer science education and research in China. For example, Microsoft Research has trained more than 5,000 students through internships, offered courses at universities, and released a popular big data MOOC in China. CS0 reform that may influence several million students each year certainly interests Microsoft.

Microsoft has contributed to CS0 reform in two ways. First, Microsoft technologies help professors in teaching. For example, Office Mix, a PowerPoint plug-in, enables the making of a very low-cost MOOC. Kodu, a visual programming language, and Minecraft are easy and fun to students in schools. Videos of Microsoft projects such as *Kinect for Sign Language Translation* and *Skype Translator* have been used as examples to explain why computing is important to all disciplines, not just computer science. Second, China's Ministry of Education and Microsoft jointly announced requests for proposals (RFP) on computational thinking for College Computers (CT for CS0). Through the 2014 RFP, Microsoft funded 21 out of 99 submitted proposals. Their task was creating MOOCs as part of, or as a whole, CS0 course based on computational thinking. The first MOOC was completed in April

2015, and 11 more went online by the end of 2015. Through the 2015 RFP, Microsoft funded 26 more proposals, among which ten were MOOCs and others were plans to disseminate the computational thinking concept nationwide or to help CS0 reform in less-developed provinces.

"CT for CS0" has taken off rapidly in China. However, in a country of incredible size and diversity, change—especially in education—requires unusual patience and persistence. Microsoft will continue what has been started. In the meantime, we hope to help CS0 reform in China with expanded and additional international collaboration so that creative ideas may be exchanged worldwide.

Case Studies of CT for CS0 in China

We selected four college-level CS0 curricula that were recently developed with the concept of computational thinking. They are interesting and unique in different ways. The first case is a CS0 course for the deaf. Since sign language logic is very different from that of a spoken language, how to teach CS0 to deaf students remains a challenge. The second case is a popular MOOC on C Programming. It teaches not only programming but computational thinking behind programming. The third case is also a popular MOOC on College Computers, which can be easily converted to fit students of various disciplines and levels. Tens of thousands of students benefit from its MOOC + SPOC model. The fourth is a CS0 designed for students majoring in health and medicine.

CS0 for the Deaf

Professor Hanjing Li of Beijing Union University specializes in natural language processing (NLP). She dedicates herself to helping the deaf to communicate with others. In 2012, she collaborated with Microsoft Research on the *Kinect for Sign Language Translation* project where signs were captured by *Kinect* and translated by computers into speech. An informative video about the technology is available on the web (http://www.youtube.com/watch?v=HnkQyUo3134). Professor Li started to work on a new project at the School of Special Education in 2014. She designed a new course called "The Art of Computational Thinking" that teaches deaf students about computing and programming.

"Deaf students in China may be different from those in more developed countries, (Li 2015, personal communication)" says Professor Li. Once a child is diagnosed of a hearing impairment in an affluent and technologically advanced country, parents may work with the community to help the child develop both speaking and signing capabilities so that the child may be better integrated into society. Adversely, not all deaf children in China, especially those from rural areas, receive such help. Many deaf students in Chinese universities do not speak and perform only signs, as they may feel isolated by mainstream society.

The logic of image-based sign language is quite different from that of a spoken language. Deaf students who use sign language only may not understand a simple statement, such as "if-then-else." Hence, teaching deaf students computing is difficult, especially where most programming languages are based on a spoken language (i.e., English). Dr. Wing touches on another problem, computing is the automation of abstractions. Unfortunately, deaf students are prone to be weak in abstractions, because sign languages are based on what they "see." For example, if you ask a deaf student who packs his school bag every morning how he packs the bag, you may find him unable to describe it orderly, because he does not see the bag. Deaf students certainly own the ability of abstractions, but this ability has been limited by the language and their prior learning experiences. Professor Li taught hearing students College Computers before. She even taught literature-major students. Unfortunately, heavy frustration exists for computer science professors when teaching the deaf.

For the new course offered to deaf students, The Art of Computational Thinking, Professor Li set up a SETT (school-centered, environmentally useful, and tasks-focused tool system) framework that suits computational thinking training to the deaf. Firstly, she gathered information on the students, their studying environments, and their tasks. Secondly, she identified the problems and found traits and needs of the deaf students based on information gathered. Thirdly, she suited the traits and needs with the potential technologies. She then decided to use Scratch by MIT (http://scratch.mit.edu) as a main tool for deaf students to build computational logic, in turn bypassing their language disadvantage. With Scratch, most deaf students can comprehend core computing concepts such as iteration and procedures, which appeared more difficult to them when taught in the C language. Students learned by doing. Ninety-five percent of the deaf students never having taken any computer courses built an arithmetic calculator within ten learning hours, plus ten working hours. The calculator was the most complicated system they had ever built. Professor Li remarked, "After a few projects completed, students started to complain that Scratch is 'childish' and wanted to try C programming. I was amazed. I had never heard of my students so eager to learn C" (Li 2015, personal communication).

Professor Li also observes that although Internet and mobile technologies help the deaf to receive more information than ever before, information appears more fragmented to the deaf than to the hearing. "Computational thinking may assist the deaf to connect the fragments. That's why I started this course and feel good about it. (Li 2015, personal communication)" What we learn from this uncommon case might be picking the right scenario for your students. While it is important that all students learn to think computationally, CS0 is never a one-size-fits-all solution.

Computational Thinking in Programming

When the teaching committee started to study computational thinking years ago, there was a doubt: Does computational thinking really exist? If it does, how do we teach thinking? Some professors believe that teaching someone to think like a computer scientist should be similar to teaching a computer scientist, only that we follow what Confucius said in the Analects, "Teaching students in accordance with their aptitude." Traditional computer courses are designed for CS students who may have sufficient mathematical background and interests in technical details. Teaching non-CS or even non-STEM students, we need not dramatically change the course but change the way we teach.

Along that line of thought, some professors embed computational thinking in existing computer courses instead of creating a new course called computational thinking. A MOOC in C Programming offered by Professor Kai Weng of Zhejiang University attracts tens of thousands of students. The majority is college students of a non-CS major. Professor Weng believes that computational thinking is not just about programming, but programming remains an effective way to learn computational thinking. Weng asks, "Do we teach programming as a tool to build things or a way of thinking" (Weng 2015, personal communication)? Professor Weng recalled when he learned coding decades ago in a DOS or UNIX environment, students built working software such as a tic-tac-toe right away. Now few people do that with pure C anymore. Why do we still teach C then? There are two major reasons. For CS and some engineering students, programming lays the foundation for the next computing courses. For others, programming sharpens their thinking. Most people interested in the Hour of Code are probably doing so for the latter reason.

Thus the question remains of how to teach computational thinking in a programming course? Professor Weng gives the following code as an example:

```
Y = X × 3;    //A student defines an equation, Y equals X times 3.
X = 5;        //He assigns X as 5.
Print Y;      //Then he believes Y must be 15.
```

It seems natural that we first define an equation, give the input, and then get a correct output. However, a computer does not think that way. If X is not assigned a value before the "Y = X × 3" statement, Y is undefined. With this common mistake, Professor Weng may explain to students how a computer and its registers and arithmetic logic unit (ALU) work and why computer scientists must communicate with computers with strict procedural consistency.

Another example is that many students could not understand "Y = Y + 3," which is obviously incorrect algebraically. Students learn mathematical or logical thinking before computational thinking. Hence, concepts like assignment, recursion, and procedures are all new to most students who learn programming for the first time. If an instructor is good at giving examples and analogies, a programming course may cover most core concepts in the Basic Requirements.

Professor Weng launched his most popular programming MOOC in China in early 2015. "MOOC fits the nature of Chinese students who are often shy to ask questions in class, (Weng 2015, personal communication)" he says. Weng thus finds students posing tons of interesting questions in the discussion forums. For example, experienced programmers may use 'ø' to distinguish zero from the letter 'o'. Some professors are so used to such notation that they forget it is a CS0 class. Professor Weng did not pay attention to that for years until a student asked the question online, "What does that 'theta' mean?" Students taking the MOOC are more diversified than those in a classroom. Through thousands of discussions online, professors get feedback from students of various disciplines and backgrounds.

Learning programming itself is a journey of abstraction and automation. We abstract a real-world problem into a set of symbols and descriptions. We design algorithms so that they can be computed automatically. Programming is a straightforward way to introduce computational thinking, but how to keep the course interesting is a real challenge.

Most Popular CT for CS0

Possibly, the most popular computational thinking course in China is a MOOC by Professor Dechen Zhan of the Harbin Institute of Technology called "College Computers—An Introduction to Computational Thinking." Based on a summary at the beginning of 2016, around 180,000 students registered and 20% of them completed the course with all tests and requirements since the course was put on iCourse (i.e., the largest MOOC platform in China) 20 months ago. In the most recent term alone, it attracted 63,000 students and accumulated 610,000 entries of online discussions. Success of the course is due in part to the "MOOC + SPOC (small, private online courses)" model. Twenty-eight universities have created their SPOCs based on Professor Zhan's MOOC.

Scope of College Computers is depicted by Professor Zhan as a "tree of computing" shown in Fig. 1. His MOOC course covers the whole space in detail. Roots of the tree contain fundamental operations such as 0/1, procedures, and recursions. The trunk depicts different levels of architectures from the basic von Neumann machine to personal, distributed, and cloud computers. Branches with two colors stand for two sides of computing—algorithms and systems. Leaves represent various disci-

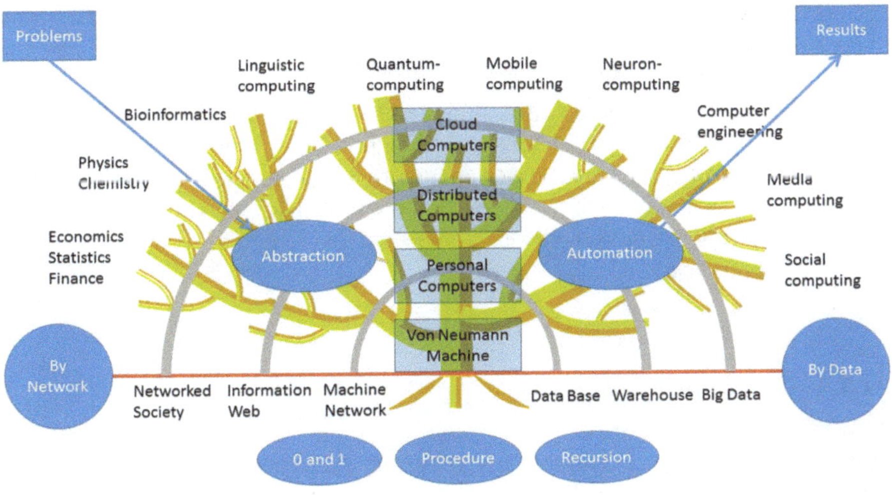

Fig. 1 Tree of computing

plines connected to computing. Problems absorbed from the leaves are "abstracted" into algorithms and "automated" by systems before results are returned. For example, we model a problem (air pollution) and then build a system (air pollution predictor) for the problem. Modeling is abstraction, and the system is automation. Layers of arcs position a topic closer to roots (more computer science) or leaves (more application). Taking the network as an example, machine network is a typical CS topic, but networked society is closer to applications. With a MOOC + SPOC model, Professor Zhan builds the MOOC as a superset of College Computers where his SPOC partners may draw materials from. Tree of computing is that superset.

"Introduction to Computational Thinking" includes four parts that coincide with the tree of computing. The first part, computing and procedures, consists of symbols, computations, structures, procedures, recursions, and systems. They are the fundamental concepts in abstraction and automation. The second part, computer systems, introduces how a computer works and how to program it. The third part, algorithmic thinking, covers the areas of modeling, algorithms, and data structure and controls. The fourth part is thinking by data and by network; by data means thinking from data acquisition and data management to data analysis and applications. "By network" means thinking from a physical network, information network, and an interactive network to a societal network. The four parts are divided into 13 chapters. More than 150 videos, around 10 minutes each, are included in the MOOC.

The course is lively with a plentitude of examples and analogies. When Professor Zhan talks about symbolization and abstraction, he uses Yin and Yang found in an ancient Chinese book, *Yi-Jing* (a.k.a., *Book of Change*), to depict 0 and 1. It is well known to Chinese students that Yin and Yang deduces Eight Diagrams (two to the third power) and further deduces 64 diagrams (two to the sixth power). 0 and 1 do the same. With binary numbers in mind, students learn Boolean algebra where symbols (Yin and Yang) are computed. Boolean can be implemented by electronic gates, from the simplest AND/OR logic to very complex integrated circuits. The lecture goes smoothly from something observable in nature like Yin and Yang, all the way to the most complicated circuitry. The digital world becomes an abstraction of the world they are familiar with.

"College Computers can be interesting to all students regardless of disciplines." As an evangelist, Professor Zhan convinces universities and professors to build SPOCs on his MOOCs. He also encourages them to share contents with more teachers. Professor Zhan says, "Six million students in China take College Computers each year. Our MOOC covers only 1%. There is a lot more to be done" (Zhan 2016, personal communication)!

COOC for Health Computing

Professor Ning An of Hefei University of Technology teaches COOCs—Collaborative Open Online Courses. He has adopted the concept to develop an online course called "Health Computing," which is a CS0 for health-related majors including the medical school.

"Health Computing" is special in many ways. First, Professor An and his collaborators study health-related cases and find out the roles computers play. He believes the purpose of College Computers is motivating students to explore the relevance between computing and their own disciplines. For example, not many people know that Florence Nightingale was not only "The Lady with the Lamp" but also a statistician. As a pioneer in the visual presentation of statistics, Nightingale is credited with developing a form of the pie chart now known as the polar area diagram, or the Nightingale rose diagram. After telling the story with a documentary video, Professor An teaches students how Nightingale turned a real-world problem into a set of numbers and symbols (abstraction) and how she presented complex statistics with pie charts (visualization). He asks, should there be a computer, what could she have done better (automation)?

Secondly, Professor An builds the MOOC collaboratively. He not only collaborates with professors of the medical school and of other universities but also collaborates with students. Those who take the class this year are asked to study more health-computing cases and hand in videos as term projects. Best videos are awarded with prizes and included in the MOOC for next terms. One of the included videos made by students this year is a study of flu trends by Internet search, a good example how computing changed healthcare. Thirdly, although case studies often interest students, it may overlook the need of some students who want to know more about computers. Hence, the MOOC provides links for those students to find more knowledge and information on the Internet.

Finally, Professor An hopes his students could soon work on medical projects collaboratively with Microsoft HoloLens. That will greatly advance the spirit of the COOC and help to show health-major students the importance of using computers.

Conclusions and Future Work

When the Ministry of Education of China was reforming collegiate computer education, the timing of computational thinking concepts was optimal. College Computers, a course taken by six million students a year, went through a paradigm shift from tool focus to thinking focus. In the past two years, the MOE teaching steering committee for College Computer Courses and Microsoft Research jointly funded professors who pioneered computational thinking curriculum and shared them online. A few hundred thousand students took the MOOC voluntarily in less than a year.

We hope to equip the whole young generation of Chinese with computational thinking. How do we move forward from here? First, pioneering college-level curriculum on computational thinking has succeeded in China for many reasons, including charismatic instructors, additional resources from the MOE and Microsoft, and the advantage of the MOOC platform. Our next step and challenge is to popularize the work. The teaching committee is holding workshops in various provinces and cities, especially in less-developed areas to promote the Basic Requirements and share best practices. Professors are encouraged to build SPOCs around MOOCs and share their materials online. It is also important in China to get support from university executives (e.g., president and provost). Such sustenance helps the morale of CS0 instructors.

Second, there are various ways to teach computational thinking in college. The existing college computer courses, including those shown in previous sections, are not as mature as General Physics or Advanced Mathematics that has undergone through decades of practices and improvements. The CACM article by Dr. Wing and the Basic Requirements by the MOE outline the core concepts of a fundamental computer course, but how to convey the concepts remains an open question. Our next step is to encourage more professors to innovate computational thinking curriculum and to share their curriculum with detailed feedback from students. It takes time to stabilize the contents of a course.

Third, learning computational thinking in college is probably too late. Just as with math and physics, computer education should start early. Although some urban K-12 schools in China offer computer courses, most teach basic computer tools such as e-mail, browser, PowerPoint, and Word. Our next step is to call the MOE's attention to computational thinking for K-12 and support teachers developing curriculum for various grades of students. Computational thinking for all is a very long journey. It will require patience and persistence. But China is invested in computational thinking, as demonstrated by the progress made in the past few years with CS0.

Acknowledgments The author wants to thank professors mentioned in this article and others for their efforts in leading CS0 reform in China and Mr. Long Zhang of Higher Education Press and Mr. Bei Li of Microsoft Research for their contribution in "CT for CS0" initiative.

References

Denning, P., & Martell, C. (2015). *Great principles of computing*. The MIT Press, US.
Wing, J. (2006). Computational thinking. *Communications of the ACM, 49*(3), 33–35.

Computational Thinking: Efforts in Korea

Miran Lee

Abstract The computer age is changing the face of education. To realize the full potential of such change, we need to move beyond a simple adoption of IT in the classroom. Students will benefit most when they learn to use computational thinking (CT) while applying the principles and best practices of computing to solve all sorts of real-world problems. This message (Wing, Communications of the ACM 49(3):33–35, 2006) was pioneered by Jeannette Wing, Corporate Vice President at Microsoft Research, which is also the main theme of the *Computational Thinking Forum* held in Seoul, South Korea.

There has been a big step forward through the collaborative efforts of many, including the Korean Information Science Education Federation, governors, policy makers, faculty members, teachers, and industry leaders such as Microsoft. The Korean government and its Ministry of Education (MoE) decided to include software education to be compulsory at K-12 schools by 2018, with the Korean MoE also having operated pilot programs at 72 schools nationwide in 2015.

This article reports the showcase projects for K-12 and higher education presented at the aforementioned forum.

Keywords Computational thinking • Computer science education • Software education

Forum Overview

It is incontrovertible that technology is reshaping the face of education. Students throughout the world today conduct research online and complete their school assignments digitally. Many students have access to laptops or tablets provided by their school. However, to truly realize the full educational power of the computer age, we need to move beyond teaching component information technologies, such as using or writing software tools, toward problem- or project-based computational

M. Lee (✉)
Microsoft Research Asia, Microsoft Research Outreach, The K-Twin Towers, Tower A 12F, 50, Jongro 1-gil, Jongro-gu, Seoul 03142, South Korea
e-mail: miranl@microsoft.com

P.J. Rich, C.B. Hodges (eds.), *Emerging Research, Practice, and Policy on Computational Thinking*, Educational Communications and Technology: Issues and Innovations, DOI 10.1007/978-3-319-52691-1_22

thinking (CT), of applying the principles and best practices of computing to solve a vast array of problems. This has been the message that Jeannette Wing, Corporate Vice President at Microsoft Research has pioneered (Wing, 2006).

This was also the message that Jeannette Wing brought to the *Computational Thinking Forum* held in Seoul, South Korea. A pioneer and tireless advocate of computational thinking, Wing maintains that CT should be taught for everyone, and not just computer scientists. CT is a concept universally applicable in designing ways to approach problems and a fundamental, basic ability that all people will be using, just as everyone learns to read, write, and multiply.

Recently, there has been remarkable progress through the collaborative efforts of many, including the Korean Information Science Education Federation, governors, policy makers, faculty members, teachers, and industry leaders such as Microsoft. The Korean government and its Ministry of Education (MoE) decided to include software education to be compulsory at K-12 schools by 2018[1]. The Korean MoE also successfully executed pilot programs at 72 schools nationwide in 2015. At the forum, showcase projects for K-12 and higher education were presented: including Yonsei University on CT curriculum development and teaching for higher education, UN's sustainable development goal with KODU—Girl's Coding for K-6, Best Middle School on CT for K-9, etc.

The article reports and showcases the projects presented at the forum.

Sessions

The first session discussed a drive from the *government's* viewpoint, which requires computer education in K-12 curriculum. Table 1 presents their guideline of new computing curriculum: Compared to the past curriculum, focused on computer literacy, such as teaching how to use software tools or programming languages, this table emphasizes on new areas of culture, data and problem modeling, and system designs. This was presented in the talk of *Computer Science Education in Korea.* Table 2 summarizes the detailed requirement of K-12 curriculum effective 2018.

The second session discussed the showcase of *university-level curriculum* being designed at Yonsei University. A critical distinction of this development is that freshmen of all majors are educated together under the universal residential college (RC) program, which is aligned with the philosophy of computational thinking for everyone. This new platform is unlike the past curriculum which was restricted to computer or related majors. This presentation discusses the first pilot offering in the fall semester of 2015 taken by nonmajor students with nine different majors. The semester consists of 16 weeks of teaching, covering ten topic areas such as computational thinking in daily life, problem solving, algorithmic thinking, modeling solution, and concurrent activity. These topics invite students to observe daily activities, such as using the ATM or using the gasoline pump, to abstract observations,

[1] http://www.koreatimes.co.kr/www/news/tech/2015/10/133_188285.html

Table 1 Detailed structure of K-12 curriculum

Area	Topics	Middle school	High school
Information culture	Information society, ethics	Privacy, copyright	Cyberethics
Information and data	Digitalization, data management	Digital representation	Data structure
Problem-solving and programming	Abstraction, algorithm, programming	Problem understanding, algorithm understanding	Problem decomposition and modeling, problem analysis
Computing systems	Operating system, physical computing	Computing devices, sensor-based programming	Networking, physical computing

Table 2 Summary of K-12 curriculum requirement effective 2018

Year	Hours
K5–6	Elective (17 credit hours/year)
K7–9	Required (34 credit hours/year)
K10–12	Elective

and find repetitive or control structure. Term projects include building conversational AI using open-source APIs. Further details can be found at http://www4.yonsei.ac.kr/fresh/ct/. Advanced courses designed for computer and related majors are under preparation.

The third session showcases the *elementary school curriculum using Microsoft Kodu*. Kodu is one of the educational programming languages, from which students can express and explore fundamental computer science concepts (Stolee et al., 2011). In this curriculum, student attentions are drawn into worldwide challenges, and they build Kodu games for attracting others' attention to the problem.

For example, this curriculum inspires students with a UN sustainable development goal, such as eliminating hunger or gender inequality. This provides a very general platform for elementary school students to come up with real-life solutions for the problems that are seemingly unrelated to computers. Once problems and solutions are identified, such as bringing awareness to widely adopted prejudices leading to gender inequalities, they are abstracted into a computer program. In this process, a complex real-life problem, such as gender inequality, is abstracted into Kodu characters and for designing the movement of characters and designing the game algorithms to decide the winner, automation approach has been used. A classroom project of an Xbox game based on Kodu (MacLaurin, 2011) was presented in this talk, where players can shoot down prejudices in the game. More examples can be found at http://elena.kr.

The fourth session shares the *proposed structure of K-12 curriculum* for middle and high schools, as summarized in Table 1. The emphasis again is not computer literacy but starting from real-life problems such as finding a desirable route from home to school, from which students identify the types of information needed and discuss how such information can be collected and digitized using computing tools. This problem is then abstracted and built into an efficient algorithm, by finding repetitive structures desirable for computers.

The last session was a *panel discussion* on the theme of *Development and Improvement of Computational Thinking for Education*. The questions raised in this session were the following:

- How is CT taught now? What are the road blocks?
- How should it change in the next 5 years? What are the steps we should take?

Regarding the first question, panelists mentioned an initial divide of interests and backgrounds. This suggests that some students are highly motivated, while some are not. Curriculum design should consider promoting the interest of all participants, especially those initially lacking the interest or backgrounds in computing. An educator from a middle school reported the increased motivation over the years of CT education, as well as the positive effect of increased parental participation in the student project showcase.

Regarding the second question and the future, educators shared the need of a sharing platform for exchanging the best practices. This article or the forum discussed can be one such venue. Our community's next steps should be to consider other forms for releasing and sharing of learning experiences. Another aspect regarding the direction of the future was the emerging interest and importance of machine learning in the area of computing and beyond. It has become (and is becoming more so) a common abstraction for solving both computing and noncomputing problems. The needs to raise the importance of abstracting problems with machine learning computing in mind were also discussed.

Conclusions

This article discusses the Korean government's academic efforts to teach CT for both computer and general education. We then presented the showcase projects ranging from K-12 education to university teaching, which were discussed at the *Computational Thinking Forum* held in Seoul, South Korea.

References

MacLaurin, M. B. (2011). The design of Kodu: A tiny visual programming language for children on the Xbox 360. *ACM SIGPLAN Notices, 46*(10), 241–246.

Stolee, K. T., et al. (2011). Expressing computer science concepts through Kodu game lab. In *ACM SIGCSE* (pp. 99–104).

Wing, J. M. (2006). Computational thinking. *Communications of the ACM, 49*(3), 33–35.

A Future-Focused Education: Designed to Create the Innovators of Tomorrow

Laurie F. Ruberg and Aileen Owens

Abstract The authors of this case study examined the transformation of a suburban Pittsburgh school district curriculum from traditional to one that includes computational thinking (CT) concepts and practices for all students. They describe the district model that guided the curricular transformation, implementation of CT lessons and processes at all grade levels, and metrics used to evaluate student performance in CT activities. Four themes emerged as critical factors for successful application of the district's STEAM Studio district-wide integration of CT:

- First, school district reform was aligned with regional efforts to improve K-12 learning through CT initiatives.
- Second, integration of CT built upon effective teaching and learning practices across all core content areas.
- Third, research partnerships helped to identify continuous improvements in CT implementation.
- Fourth, changes to existing faculty positions, student schedules, learning projects, and school spaces were necessary and were customized for this district CT implementation plan.

Keywords Computational thinking • Habits of mind • Computational practices • Computational concepts • Computational perspectives • Human-centered design • STEAM studio

---

L.F. Ruberg (✉)
West Virginia University, Morgantown, WV 26506, USA
e-mail: lfruberg@gmail.com

A. Owens
South Fayette Township School District, South Fayette Township, PA, USA
e-mail: aileen.owens@gmail.com

P.J. Rich, C.B. Hodges (eds.), *Emerging Research, Practice, and Policy on Computational Thinking*, Educational Communications and Technology: Issues and Innovations, DOI 10.1007/978-3-319-52691-1_23

Introduction

This case study examines the transformation of a suburban Pittsburgh school district curriculum from traditional to one that includes computational thinking (CT) concepts and practices for all students. While integrating CT concepts and processes across all grades and disciplines, the district that is the focus of this study has experienced a steady and positive increase in student achievement. Beginning in 2015 and continuing in 2016, this district's student reading and mathematics annual state test scores were the highest in Southwestern Pennsylvania. This interpretive study describes the district model that guided the curricular transformation, explains how this model was used to guide implementation of CT lessons and processes at various grade levels, and identifies the metrics and measures used to evaluate student performance in CT activities.

Coding as a Pathway for Building a Human-Centered Design Curriculum

Public schools around the world are adding coding to their list of primary literacies (Pretz, 2014). Students preparing for twenty-first-century high school graduation in countries like England, Estonia, Finland, Italy, and Singapore must know reading, writing, arithmetic, and coding to earn their high school graduation degree. In the USA, President Obama (The White House, Office of the Press Secretary, 2016) announced his plan for integrating computer science into K-12 school curriculum, recognizing that computer science is a basic skill students need to grasp economic opportunities and social mobility. In fact, computer science is the primary driver for job growth throughout all STEM fields (CSTA, 2013) and also an area where job openings take the longest time to fill (Kohli, 2015). A report by the Computer Science Teachers Association (CSTA & ISTE, 2011) identifies many of the reasons why most of the public schools in the USA have not previously included coding in their core curriculum. Traditionally, computer science was not identified as one of the core disciplines, which resulted in most schools marginalizing computer science curriculum.

Since computer science and systematic coding are not part of the traditional US core curriculum, on a national and local level, there is often confusion about teacher certification and licensure requirements for computer science teachers (CSTA, 2013; Guzdial, 2016). Other challenges that schools must address in order to incorporate a rigorous computer science curriculum are enlisting qualified teachers, finding room in the curriculum, funding for the technology required (Internet access, personal computer hardware and software), and recruiting students since computer science classes are often listed as electives. Another challenge that schools face is finding ways to overcome student (and to some extent parent and teacher) stereotypes about who goes into computer science fields. Women and nondominant or underrepresented youth do not often see their counterparts succeeding in computer science (Kohli, 2015).

The district investigated in this case took on the challenge of preparing all students for an innovation-driven economy by building robust career pathways and ecologies, which involve computational thinking and coding abilities across all disciplines. This study describes the district's approach to integrating K-12 CT curriculum by focusing on kindergarten through senior high's use of science, technology, engineering, art, and mathematics (STEAM) problem-solving studios and maker spaces. In this chapter, we specifically report research on the following questions:

1. What are the key features of the district model for integrating CT?
2. How are CT strategies integrated throughout the K-12 curriculum?
3. How does the district measure student achievement in CT activities?

Coding as a Pathway for Building a Human-Centered Design Curriculum

The human-centered design and problem-solving processes taught to all students in the district are an adapted version of the CT model practiced by computer scientists and engineers, which focuses on "creative solutions to problems that someone in the world has articulated" (NASEM, 2016, p. 19). In fact, one of the high school STEAM design courses emerged from a unique partnership between this district, a neighboring district, LUMA [a human-centered design training] Institute, EAFab Corporation, and All-Clad Metalcrafters. The CT processes embedded into the district curriculum are adapted from the International Society for Technology in Education (ISTE) and the Computer Science Teachers Association (CSTA) operational definition of CT. The final version of the ISTE/CSTA definition for CT listed below is the result of survey-based feedback provided by computer science teachers.

CT refers to problem-solving processes that include (but are not limited to) the following characteristics:

- Formulating problems in a way that enables us to use a computer and other tools to help solve them
- Logically organizing and analyzing data
- Representing data through abstractions such as models and simulations
- Automating solutions through algorithmic thinking (a series of ordered steps)
- Identifying, analyzing, and implementing possible solutions with the goal of achieving the most efficient and effective combination of steps and resources
- Generalizing and transferring this problem-solving process to a wide variety of problems (CSTA, 2011)

Computer science is a rigorous discipline that "teaches students to break problem-solving into small chunks" (Kohli, 2015, p. 3). Programming, according to Resnick et al. (2009) and diSessa (2000), involves the creation of external representations of problem-solving processes, and programming provides opportunities to reflect on your own thinking, even to think about thinking itself. From the MIT Media Lab perspective, digital fluency requires not just the ability to chat, browse, and interact but also the ability to design, create, and invent with new media. To do so, you need to learn some type of programming.

How are these interpretations of CT integrated into the district curriculum plan? The district curriculum incorporates the CT emphasis on problem-solving as it reflects the ability to think logically, algorithmically, abstractly, and recursively (ISTE & CSTA, 2011; NAS, 2010). CT represents the ability to take large abstract ideas and break them into smaller, easier to solve, problem sets. Jeannette Wing (2011), Corporate Vice President of Microsoft Research, suggests that CT is a problem-solving approach that works across many disciplines, noting that computer modeling, big data, and simulations are used in everything from textual analysis to medical research and environmental protection. The next section describes the shared vision guiding the district integration of CT concepts and processes.

The District STEAM Studio Model

The foundation of the district vision is based upon the integration of a science, technology, engineering, art, and mathematics (STEAM) curriculum. Since 2010, the district has executed this vision by systematically incorporating engineering and design problem-solving as an application of CT into K-12 education. The district definition of CT includes three overlapping components: (1) a specific problem-solving process, (2) characteristics of successful problem solvers or habits of mind, and (3) career vision.

Problem-Solving Process

The design problem-solving process used in this model is the process practiced by computer scientists and engineers, which is "the ability to think logically, algorithmically, abstractly, and recursively" (Gusky, 2014, p. 1) and is the foundation for the problem-solving process component of the STEAM Studio model. This process is practiced by computer scientists and engineers and is reflected in the ability to take a large abstract idea and break it into smaller, easier to solve problem sets. "We want to create students who will be successful in the world," Superintendent Dr. Bille Rondinelli explains. "It's not that we have veered away from traditional education, but we have built in a research and development space with these labs and STEAM coordinators that allows us to change and adapt as the world changes" (Berdik, 2015, p. 4).

The design problem-solving process approach is multifaceted and encompasses many different tools, such as Hummingbird Robotics, VEX IQ, 3D printing, LEGO Robotics, Raspberry Pi, Scratch, and other emerging programmable technologies.

The district model posits that the ability to program provides important benefits that greatly expand the range of what students can create and ways they can express themselves with the computer. Being able to program also expands the range of what students can learn. In particular, coding enhances CT by helping students learn important problem-solving and design strategies (such as modularization and iterative design) that carry over to nonprogramming domains.

Habits of Mind

The second aspect of CT in the STEAM Studio model includes the integration of habits of mind training as defined by Costa (2008) for both teachers and students. Key characteristics of habits of mind problem-solving include confidence dealing with complexity, persistence, a tolerance for ambiguity, and the ability to communicate and work well with others. Promoting a culture that considers habits of mind—being reflective about one's thinking and ways of approaching problem-solving—is an integral part of the district approach to teacher training and student learning of CT processes. Administrators, teachers, and students learn about and learn to be aware of and discuss which of the habits of mind characteristics are most critical to their problem-solving in different situations.

The Scratch block-based programming language was the initial coding application that kicked off the integration of CT at the K-8 level. The research and educational guidelines bundled with Scratch provided a foundation for integrating CT practices with clear educational alignments to standards and curricular goals. Guidelines for educators created by Brennan (2011) and Resnick (2007) gave a definition of CT that includes these three dimensions: *computational concepts*, the concept designers employ as they program; *computational practices*, the practice designers develop as they program; and *computational perspectives*, the perspective designers form about the world around them and about themselves. These three dimensions are useful in helping to describe how coding helps to actualize the STEAM Studio model with its focus on CT problem-solving processes and habits of mind ways of thinking. The dispositions, practices, and perspectives outlined in Scratch (Brennan, Balch, & Chung, 2014) and ScratchJr (Bers & Resnick, 2016) support materials that helped teachers promote strategies for students to think about their thinking and metacognitive processes.

Career Vision

The third component of the district STEAM Studio model is career vision, which is embedded in all STEAM initiatives to give students a sense of awareness of career contexts and understanding of how careers reflect their learning. The career vision component focuses on giving students an awareness of career contexts where problem-solving processes, dispositions, and attitudes apply. This helps students understand and envision how different careers and career pathways are related to their learning through problem-solving activities. The district integrates career vision connections for students through project-based learning as well as through simulations within the curriculum. Support for the district career contexts is provided through a partnership with the LUMA Institute whose human-centered design thinking practices promote a discipline of developing solutions in the service of people (Luma Institute, 2012).

Innovation is another feature of the district integration of a career vision as a key component of their CT alignment. The STEAM Studio model of implementing CT applies a view of innovation that goes beyond the process of just creating a creative solution to a problem. In the district model of CT, students are challenged to translate their idea or invention into a good or service that addresses a social need or proposes a marketable product. Students are then guided to make their innovation replicable, to show what specific need their solution satisfies, and to project an estimated economical cost. More information about how the district is expanding entrepreneurship education as part of its integration of CT in a later section describes how the STEAM Studio model is implemented.

Thus, the vision for the youngest to graduating senior student includes a blending of CT, the process of working effectively with others, and the ability to be innovative with computer-based technology. Achieving these three abilities is considered in the district academic plan to be as important to children's future as the more familiar basic literacies of reading, writing, and mathematics. The district method for integrating new coding-focused curriculum follows the existing interdisciplinary STEAM approach. The first step is to develop and test incubator projects and prototypes. Next, projects that are viewed successful and relevant are integrated into the curriculum alongside professional development experiences. The STEAM Studio model provides students with experiential learning activities that promote CT both within the curriculum and in after-school experiences to transform teaching and learning.

Method

This case study examines how one school district integrated CT across kindergarten through 12th grade. Analysis of this case will provide a description of the overarching model that guided this CT district-wide alignment as well as specific curriculum strategies. The results will suggest strategies that can be applied to other districts. This case analysis provides a means for understanding issues involved in implementing such a wide-ranging curriculum transformation and will suggest implications for teacher training and areas for further educational research.

The school district featured in this case study illustrates how a K-12 curriculum can successfully meet core content requirements while also integrating computer science as a rigorous discipline for the youngest through oldest students. The setting for this case-based research is a suburban, public school district located 14 miles (23 km) southwest of Pittsburgh. As of 2016, the district enrollment was 3044 students. Every student is listed as having access to high-speed broadband. This school reports a 1:1 student to device ratio (Digital Promise, n.d., b), with 66% of K-12 students having access to a personal school-provided device.

The district operates four schools: the high school (9–12th), middle school (6–8th), intermediate school (3rd–5th), and elementary school (K-2nd). All four schools sit on a single campus that was farmland in the 1970s. The intermediate school was put to use in time for the 2013–2014 school year. This is a relatively affluent district compared to others in Pennsylvania. About 12.7% of its students are eligible for free or reduced-price lunch (PSPP, 2016) compared with the state average of 40%. The median household income for families living in this district is 85% higher than the average for Pennsylvania districts statewide (U.S. Census Bureau, 2013).

Understanding the case study sample group also requires understanding the infrastructure required to support the STEAM Studio curriculum framework as of 2015. The district invested in computing devices and broadband Internet both inside of school to support its integration of CT activities and practices. In 2010–2011, a new technology infrastructure was put into place. The six campus buildings (high school, middle school, intermediate, elementary, administration, and pupil services) are each connected to the high school main data closet through a 10-gigabyte fiber connection. The broadband Internet speed for the district is 500 megabytes per second download and 500 megabytes per second upload. Each individual building has a 10-gigabyte fiber connection running to each remote data closet. All desktop computers are connected to the network with a 1-gigabyte connection. Every network port within the district is a 1-gigabyte connection. All buildings have Wireless N access with data rates as high as 600 mbps. The district is in its first year of a 4-year one-to-one laptop implementation. Every student in first and second grade receives an iPad, while students in grades 3–8 receive HP Revolve laptop tablets. High School students will start using Revolve laptops in the fall of 2016. During the past 5 years, the district has leveraged grant funding, new school construction, and creative scheduling to give nearly 3,000 students, from kindergarten through 12th grade, dedicated spaces for hands-on projects to support coding, 3D printing, computer-aided design, and robotic activities as part of the school curriculum.

Table 1 explains what data were used to address each of the three research questions. The survey and interview data about specific coding projects include student and teacher reflections. As this case study will show, many factors are involved in integration of CT. A mixed method research design was applied to study this case. Research questions guiding this case study were:

1. What are the key features of the district model for integrating CT?
2. How are CT concepts and practices integrated across the curriculum?
3. How does the district measure student achievement in CT activities?

Table 1 Alignment of research questions with data and data analysis

Research questions	Data sources	Data analysis
1. What are the key features of the district model for integrating CT?	• CSTA (2011) CT guidelines • ISTE (2011) CSE standards • Costa (2008) *Habits of Mind* • Brennan and Resnick (2012) *Frameworks for Studying and Assessing CT* • Wagner (2012) *Creating Innovators* • District website • District profile on Digital Promise	Identifies: • Guidelines for district-level decisions • Processes used to engage faculty, students, parents, and community partners • Plan that emerged for curriculum transformation
2. How are CT strategies integrated throughout the K-12 curriculum?	Description of CT implementation steps and processes w/ examples of: • Classroom-based CT activities • Tools, resources, and external partners • Resulting institutional and organizational changes	• Interpretive analysis yields a historical timeline of the sequence of curricular events at the classroom, grade, school, and district level
3. How does the district measure student achievement in CT activities?	Descriptions of: • Learning artifacts that represent CT process and project outcomes • Student accomplishments by students, teachers, and others • Results from instruments designed to assess student proficiencies with CT practices • New metrics created through partnerships and grant initiatives—i.e., to measure student design and leadership abilities • Results from student and teacher interviews and surveys about CT processes. Results from standardized tests during time of CT implementation	• Identifies what CT metrics and artifacts of learning look like across disciplines, activities, grade levels, and formal as well as informal learning contexts • Describes how metrics can be used in individual and group learning environments

Analysis and Discussion

This section applies data collected from teacher and student focus group interviews, student surveys, student assessments, and observations of implementation of CT activities in traditional classes and STEAM Studio labs to address each of the three research questions. The research questions guided our investigation of how the STEAM Studio model has been implemented and how this model has impacted K-12 curriculum and ways of documenting student achievement.

What Are the Key Features of the District Model for Integrating CT?

By following the existing interdisciplinary STEAM approach, developing and testing incubator projects or prototypes, and then integrating into the curriculum alongside professional development experiences, the STEAM Studio model is providing students with experiential learning activities that promote CT both within the curriculum and in after-school experiences to transform teaching and learning. This model is being developed to address the district STEAM Studio vision to:

1. Facilitate learning in innovative "studio" contexts to foster creativity and innovation and student development that prepares students for emerging STEM/STEAM and information and communication technology careers.
2. Promote an engaging and capacity building learning culture where teachers are prepared to utilize and integrate new technologies in ways that support their STEM/STEAM curriculum content goals and understanding of STEM/ICT careers.
3. Address the need to expand and update the K-12 curriculum to include cross curricular CT experiences and rigorous computer science course offerings within an administrative environment that includes funding shortfalls and limited teacher preparation for the workplace STEM/STEAM computational skills and abilities.
4. Support the existing school goals for academic, artistic, and individual student development.

Using tools like Scratch with students in elementary through high school gives young learners the ability to design their own interactive media. Brennan and Resnick (2012) also propose that teaching computer science processes and practices with tools like Scratch fulfills the constructivist approach to learning that calls for engaging students in learning through design activities (Kafai & Resnick, 1996).

The online community includes numerous social networking components supporting these opportunities:

- Interacting with and providing feedback to others.
- Members can examine a project's source code to study how it was created.
- Looking at how the sprites and blocks have been connected.

This case study examines the STEAM Studio model implementation of CT as it applies essential components of the constructivist view of learning to district-wide integration of a CT approach to teaching and learning. In this context, students are given tasks as problem solvers to apply their coding skills as authors, designers, and constructors of knowledge. As explained by Jonassen and Reeves (1996), "Learners must function as designers using technologies as tools for analyzing the world, accessing information, interpreting and organizing their personal knowledge, and representing what they know to others" (p. 694).

The process of embedding CT in the curriculum has evolved to encompass:

1. The teacher vision of meaningful integration of learners as problem solvers and knowledge creators
2. Strategically planned incubator projects
3. Project-based educational research studies funded by collaborative grant initiatives that measure how STEAM Studio projects and classroom-based CT lessons impact student learning
4. Curriculum mapping processes that ensure vertical and horizontal alignment of the K-12 curriculum

Moving from Practice to Policy

CT started as an organic grassroots program and then became a full-scale movement. As this happened, the district moved from practice to policy and created an environment to accelerate and sustain innovation. To do this, they made the following organizational changes by hiring a director of technology and innovation as well as STEAM teachers to support interdisciplinary, hands-on activities for grades K-2, 3–5, and 6–8. At the same time, traditional teaching positions were modified or new positions added to create more depth and vertical alignment so that every student received CT learning experiences and learned about engineering and human-centered design.

For the last 6 years, the district has been implementing a K-12 vertically aligned CT initiative. As the program matures, the process of vertical alignment creates considerable movement and requires the STEAM team to stay connected and communicating, because lessons formerly taught in grades 3–5 are now being introduced in grades K-2, creating an opportunity to develop deeper critical thinking experiences for grades 3–6 and beyond. Below are a few examples to show how incubator and pilot activities have moved from practice contexts to fully integrated curriculum and policies. Figure 1 shown below provides a visualization of the flexible tension and ongoing movement that is needed to match STEAM Studio activities with student CT abilities and ever-changing programmable technology tools.

The Role of Partnerships in Supporting the STEAM Studio Model

The district has engaged many partners to expand and support CT. The success of this initiative can be credited in a large part to the generous support from local foundations and the network of innovators and organizations, which have come together to accelerate and sustain innovation in the Pittsburgh region. This unique and innovative approach to education, leveraging the expertise and resources from one district to help another, enhances learning for all students.

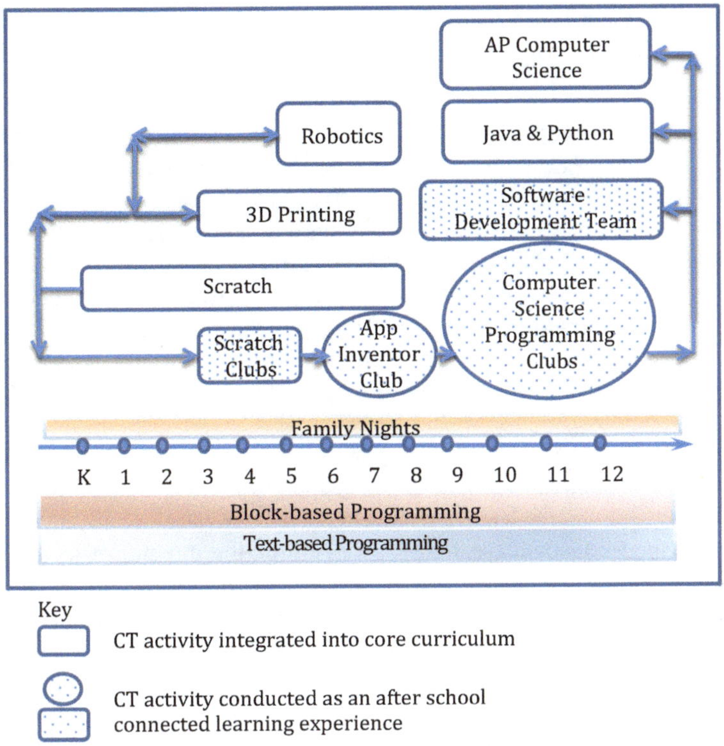

Fig. 1 A graphical depiction of the district coding progression from early learner exposure to Scratch to high school student college-equivalent CS courses

The district has been an active member of the Remake Learning Network and has benefitted by the many opportunities it provides. The Pittsburgh Remake Learning Network is a consortium of innovators and organizations that includes more than 200 organizations, empowering children and youth by creating relevant learning opportunities through the compelling use of technology, media, and the arts. One key feature of the network is that it brings thought leaders together in affinity groups and in think tanks, which meet monthly to help brainstorm new directions for Pittsburgh and to generate and launch new ideas which keep the district future focused. A summary of the city's innovation and performance committees is made public for stakeholder participation (Peduto & Lam, 2014).

The district STEAM Studio model has gained support and advice from key leaders in CT curriculum initiative inspired by the International Society for Technology in Education (ISTE), the Computer Science Teachers Association (CSTA), and supported by the National Science Foundation (NSF, 2011). This unique and innovative approach to education, leveraging the expertise and resources from one district to help another, enhances learning for all students and has the potential to transform public education in the media used to teach concepts and in the way students demonstrate their understanding of key processing and skill development.

How Are CT Concepts and Practices Implemented Across the Curriculum?

The district transformed a traditional education model to one that nurtures and develops students to be creative innovative thought leaders capable of leading an innovation-driven society (Wagner, 2012). To do this, the district created a system or ongoing process, which has become a mechanism for delivering and sustaining innovation called the STEAM Studio Model for Innovation. This system evolved over a 6-year period and consists of strategic policies and practices that, when implemented successfully, changed the district culture in terms of faculty assignments, teacher professional development processes, and administrative services.

Identifying Lead Teachers

In 2010, the superintendent created a new position, the director of technology and innovation, to develop a plan to accelerate and sustain innovation. With support from the board of education, the superintendent, school principals, and administrative staff, the director developed a K-12 vertically aligned articulated vision for building CT as a new literacy, and the team began to enact the vision incrementally. The movement to embed CT into the curriculum started as an organic grassroots program, involving a pilot program in specific classes and after-school programs. After 6 years, CT has become a school-wide practice and is a key driver of sustained innovations in teaching and learning practices at every grade level.

Initially, the district embedded CT in the elementary and middle school curriculum by identifying lead teachers with an interest in exploring the use of Scratch block-based programming language in their lessons. The director of technology and innovation and her technology assistant worked alongside teachers, employing different instructional strategies based on the teacher's vision, such as designing and co-teaching lessons, modeling classroom management, and providing training and support in the classroom. Through this method, CT using Scratch block-based code spread from middle school to elementary school in art, English, and math classrooms where its use is still growing (Owens, Unger, & Wachter, 2014).

It soon became apparent that the amount of professional development required to train teachers on CT practices to a level of confidence and mastery on an individual basis was unrealistic. Especially since the most important aspect of developing a new model of education was to create a mechanism to connect education to the rapidly changing innovation-driven economy and allow these changes to be reflected directly in a dynamic curriculum model. The curriculum model had to reflect a learning environment that nurtured innovation which was flexible, organic, nimble, and resourceful. Expecting teachers to learn and experiment with new curriculum while trying to fulfill teaching obligations, with limited access to professional development time, became a barrier to scalability. The static traditional education model needed to be displaced. The STEAM Studio model offered a dynamic approach to school-based learning where innovation could thrive.

To further support implementation and sustainability of the STEAM Studio innovative learning experiences, the district hired *STEAM teachers* for three of the four schools, K-2, 3–5, and 6–8, and created or changed existing positions such as creating the STEAM literacy teacher in grades 3–5. The grades 6–8 technology education curriculum and teacher position were redefined to reflect the updated vertical alignment of CT. Now every student in grades K-8 is engaged in CT, engineering and human-centered design instruction and problem-solving practices. STEAM Studio labs are installed in each building to support CT instruction and related hands-on lab activities. The district has applied the STEAM Studio model to guide the development of interdisciplinary learning labs for all students. In the STEAM Studio labs, authentic problem-solving activities are presented in a constructivist pedagogical context to engage students in using what they have learned about CT and habits of mind to work in collaborative teams to solve problems including coding activities.

Tables 2 and 3 provide a timeline and detailed summary of the K-12 curriculum transformation described in this section.

STEAM Teacher/Class Grades K-2

A K-2 STEAM teacher works with teachers in these three grades to develop curriculum activities that support and enhance traditional learning with CT, problem-solving activities, and reflection on relevant habits of mind that students will apply in their STEAM Studio tasks. These activities take place in a makerspace, a physical location where people gather to share resources and knowledge, work on projects, network, and build (DeLuca, Owens, & Unger, 2016). Every K-2 student has STEAM class on a rotating schedule: 3 days on for 45 min, then 6 days off. Students meet 46 days annually.

There are three STEAM Studios in the intermediate school, one of each floor for third, fourth, and fifth graders. The studios are in the center of each floor, with core classrooms on either side, a layout that reflects a philosophy transforming the entire district. In the past 5 years, the district has leveraged grant funding, new school construction, and creative scheduling to give nearly 3000 students, from kindergarten through 12th grade, dedicated spaces for hands-on projects like coding, 3-D printing, computer-aided design, and robotics, as part of their learning experiences. The STEAM labs, STEAM coordinators, and technology education teachers are part of a district-wide embrace of CT. The STEAM classes are scheduled on an 80-day rotation: 4 days on and 4 days off. Students meet 90 times during the year, combining two classes at a time. Two core curriculum teachers join the STEAM teacher for each session with over 60 participating in each STEAM session.

Table 2 Timeline of block-based CT/programming integration into classes

2011–2012	2012–2013	2013–2014	2014–2015	2015–2016
		(K-2nd): Scratch & Kodable [STEAM]	(K-2nd): Scratch, Makey Makey, littleBits, Kodable, Squishy Circuits, LEGO Robotics [STEAM]	(K-2nd): Scratch, Makey Makey, littleBits, Kodable, Squishy Circuits, LEGO Robotics, Kano [STEAM]
	(3rd–4th): Pilot: Scratch [Language Arts]	(3–5th): Scratch [STEAM]	(3rd–5th): Scratch and LEGO Robotics [STEAM and Tech Lit Class]	
		(4th): eTextile Design [STEAM]	(4–6th): VEX IQ Robotics [STEAM, Tech Lit, and Tech Ed]	(4–6th): VEX IQ Robotics, Hummingbird Robotics, Arduino [STEAM, Tech Lit, and Tech Ed]
(5–7th): Scratch [Art]	(5–7th): Scratch [Art]			(5): BlocksCAD, 3D Printing, and CAD [Tech Lit]
		(6–7th): Scratch [Art]	(6–7): Scratch [Art]	
		(7th): App Inventor [Tech Ed]	(7th): App Inventor [Tech Ed]	(7th): App Inventor [Tech Ed]
	(8th): Hummingbird Robotics [Art]	(8th): Hummingbird Robotics [Art]	(6–8): 3D Printing [Tech Ed]	(6–8th): 3D Printing and CAD [Tech Ed] (6–8th): Scratch & Hummingbird Robotics [Art] (8th): Creative entrepreneurship, 3D printing, prototype design [Tech Ed]

[ ] = Class context for CT/programming problem-solving activities

Organizational Changes

The STEAM literacy teacher position was created to further support CT integration into the curriculum. This position is responsible for teaching computer programming, design, and other tech literacy skills such as keyboarding. The instructor sees every class two times consecutively in an 8-day rotation and sees the same students 45 times during the year. The STEAM literacy class is designed to run as an additional "specials" class, which is integrated into these existing special classes: art, arts alive, orchestra, band, gym, and now also, technology literacy.

For sixth to eighth grades, the STEAM teacher coordinates with all core teachers to weave the technologies into their lesson plans. Sixth grade STEAM classes meet during a 30-day trimester on alternating (A/B) days.

Table 3 Timeline of block-based CT/programming extracurricular activities

Learning context	2010–2011	2012–2013	2013–2014	2014–2015	2015–2016
After-school connected learning experiences	(7–8th): Girls STEAM Team: Scratch	(3rd–4th): Scratch Clubs: cartooning, video, games, music	(K-2nd): MakeShop Mondays (3rd–5th): Scratch Clubs (6–8th): Girls STEAM Team (7–8th) App Inventor Club	(K-2nd): MakeShop Mondays (2nd–5th): STEAM Ambassadors (3rd–5th): Scratch Clubs (6–8th): Girls STEAM Team (7–8th) Invention Time w/ 3D printing	(2–5th): STEAM Ambassadors (3rd–5th): Scratch Clubs (6–8th): Girls STEAM Team (6–8th): Python Course (7–8th) Invention Time w/ 3D printing
Teachers	(6–8th): Teachers view Scratch at open house			(K-12): STEAM Innovation Summer Institute	(K-12): STEAM Innovation Summer Institute
Family	(6–8th): Girls STEAM Team Community Night with Scratch		(K-12): Family Inspire Series (3rd–5th): Family Programming Night	(K-12): Family Inspire Series (3rd–5th): Family Programming Night	(K-12): Family Inspire Series (3–5th): Family Programming Night
Extracurricular Partnerships and Emerging Innovation Leaders Program	(7–8th): Girls STEAM Team: Teaches Scratch {TRETC Conf}	(3rd–4th): Scratch: Video Game Design {Mexican Schools} (7–8th): Girls STEAM Team: Teaches Scratch {TRETC Conf}	(3rd–4th): Scratch: Video Game Design {Mexican Schools} (5–6th): Scratch and eTextiles {MACS & Fort Cherry}		(3): Kodu Research Pilot {CMU}

{ } = Community partner for CT/programming problem-solving activities

Every sixth and seventh grader has an A/B day for 30 days in a trimester. Eighth grade meets 45 days in a semester in an optional course. Students now learn problem-solving through computer programming, 3D design, and VEX IQ robotics. The rotation for STEAM in sixth grade allows every student to take technology education and art once each trimester. The rotation for seventh grade is technology education, family consumer science, and public speaking. The rotation for eighth grade students allows each student to choose their track rotation.

The STEAM teachers and restructured support positions act as the mechanism for embedding innovation into education. These teachers serve every student in their building. Core classroom teachers are required to come with the students to STEAM class and gain embedded professional development as they learn the activities alongside their students. In time, teachers assist their students and take STEAM lessons back to their classrooms in new ways to enhance their core curriculum. Incubator projects have become standard practice. Before going full-scale, pilot projects for innovative lessons are designed to measure student achievement and engagement at the younger grade levels before offering a full-scale rollout in the future.

Curriculum Mapping

To be certain that CT concepts including coding are vertically and horizontally aligned in core content areas, the district leadership uses Atlas Rubicon as a curriculum mapping online tool. The teaching pedagogy, academic standards, and unique curricular needs are documented through the mapping process, which helps track gaps and repetition in instruction. Each curriculum unit is mapped according to the following criteria:

Stage 1. Identifies the desired results through academic standards including Habits of Mind and MIT Media Lab's CT concepts, practices, and perspectives. The curriculum map for each grade level includes essential questions, content, major concepts, essential skills, learning objectives, and essential vocabulary.

Stage 2. Specifies what assessment will be used to provide evidence of learning.

Stage 3. Presents a learning plan including learning activities, guidelines for differentiated instruction, and resources available.

Along with following the CSTA (2013) CT guidelines, the district has incorporated the computational concepts, practices, and perspectives outlined in the Scratch Creative Computing Curriculum Guide created by the MIT Media Lab (Brennan et al., 2014) into its STEAM Studio model. The Scratch curriculum guide includes an outline for (1) computational practices, concepts, and perspectives, (2) an instrument for assessing student proficiency with computational practices, and (3) a self-reflection instrument to help teachers assess how they support CT practices in the classroom. Scratch block-based code is the foundation of the course, and the curriculum guide has been adopted and is mapped and aligned to the following standards: Pennsylvania STEM, English language arts and literacy, and computer science. The Scratch programming activities also connect to the habits of mind cognitive processes through guided activities that teachers initiate before, during, and following the Scratch programming events. Through the mapping process, the district identifies how many core concepts and standards overlap with CT and coding. Some standards are being touched on while others mastered. The standards are all intertwined, and CT is now included throughout the curriculum.

In the process of building CT as the new literacy, the district focused on redesigning the curriculum but also on connected learning activities. After-school connected learning activities serve as effective feeder programs for courses in the curriculum or vice versa. If a student discovers a passion for coding through a school course, then it becomes easier to pursue that passion through well-aligned connected learning activities. Connected learning activities become carefully orchestrated incubator projects that enable the district to implement, evaluate, and refine a pilot before placing it directly into the curriculum. These abilities are demonstrated through student-design applications, which emerge from within the curriculum. These programs become the catalysts for innovation. The district provides examples of the different types of CT learning experiences offered by the STEAM Studio model below to expand on the outline of activities provided in Tables 2 and 3.

Breakdown of CT Activities by Grade Band

Learning to code begins in kindergarten, when students learn to program robotic devices called *Bee-Bots*. Students use a keypad to move their Bot and to learn skills in directional language and programming through sequences of forwards, backwards, and left and right 90° turns. Students also use code to program other students through a physical maze and then move from the physical world to the virtual world using the app *Kodable*. First and second graders are introduced to concepts and vocabulary of CT such as sequence, loops, parallelism, and events as well as computational practices such as testing and debugging, reusing, and remixing. Concepts are introduced by making video games and interactive stories using *ScratchJr* and by using sensors and motors to program LEGO robots to move.

In elementary school, students learn the foundations of CT practices, such as collaborative problem-solving and trial and error. For example, second grade teachers ensure their students have tested every circuit they make for their math game before moving on to the next one. If one circuit does not work, students need to stop, figure out what the problem is, and fix it. This requires and reinforces persistence and good communication with fellow students, two of the "habits of mind" prominently displayed and reinforced in all classrooms as critical supports for successful computational problem-solving.

Language arts is integrated in STEAM learning. After listening to *The Hungry Caterpillar* (Carle, 1969) story, students use squishy circuits with conductible and insulated Play-Doh® to create a colorful lighted caterpillar and then design their own unique lighted animal after listening to *The Mixed Up Chameleon* (Carle, 1988). Students in K-2 also explore electrical circuitry as they build unique designs using *littleBits* electronics to make flashlights, buzzers, and other devices.

Students in K-2 have learned two block-based codes in depth, *ScratchJr* and *WeDo Lego Robotics*. Elementary students transfer their knowledge from one block-based code to another by comparing and contrasting how codes are alike and different and then building a sequence of block-based code, while others take turns interpreting and writing the code. Students make a cardboard piano keyboard and combine their knowledge of electrical circuitry and computer programming using *Makey Makey* circuitry and Scratch block-based code to program their keyboard to play music. In a second grade pilot, students built their first computer using *Kano*

Raspberry Pi kits, and next year all second to eighth graders will experience text-based code alongside block-based experiences.

In grades 3–5, students delve deeper into coding with Scratch. In Technology Literacy class, students design interactive games and stories using Scratch, based on the Creative Computing Curriculum Guide. For the last 4 years, students in fifth grade have been collaborating with four schools in Mexico to make games on being good global citizens, Internet safety, and making tutorials in Scratch for the first grade students. In grades 3–5 STEAM classes, students apply their knowledge of Scratch block-based programming to program LEGO Robotics, inventing machines that produce useful functions such as spin art machines, clocks, and robotic creatures. Students also expand on their knowledge of electrical circuits and computer programming as they use Hummingbird Robotic kits to program Arduino boards to automate three-dimensional product designs. Fourth and fifth grade students hone their problem-solving skills as they program VEX IQ robotics to run obstacle course challenges.

Scratch Clubs Third Through Fifth Grades

During 2011–2012, after-school Scratch Clubs were introduced to students in grades 3–5. The district set its sights for 15–20 students but was overwhelmed when 64 students registered, so they had to limit the number of activities each student could participate in. Since that time Scratch Clubs have been offered each year. This year, running on its third year, there are 115 students enrolled in the clubs. In addition, the district has added more after-school computer programming courses such as BlocksCAD, an incubator program that allows us to test student ability to build 3D printed prototypes using an interface similar to Scratch.

By middle school, all sixth graders program VEX IQ robotics to complete challenges, and all seventh graders use App Inventor to make an app for their mobile device. In addition, middle school students in technology education class begin using Autodesk Inventor to create product prototypes and move into CAD drawing as they gain skills. In eighth grade technology education, through a grant funded by Digital Promise and the Gates Foundation (Product Efficacy Loop, 2015), students use INVENTORcloud to create a product prototype and print the prototype using a 3D printer. Students learn as young entrepreneurs how to create a business plan, product brand, and a marketing campaign to pitch their product.

Ninth through twelfth grade students may select from an array of electives courses that embed CT, such as Java I, Java II, AP Computer Science, AP Physics C, and engineering. In addition, the high school recently created two new courses that embed human-centered design problem-solving and CT: Innovation Studio and Game Design. Local industries provide real-world problems to student teams. Students research the issues, create a solution, and then present their solution to the directors of the company. An example can be seen through the project with All-Clad Metalcrafters, a manufacturer of cookware that markets its cookware to department stores and specialty stores in the USA and overseas. *All-Clad* project leaders asked students to design a pot that an elderly person suffering from arthritis could handle comfortably. The students designed and beta tested 3D printed prototype designs for new pot handles based on anthropometric techniques. These design projects have been moved into a course called Innovation Studio where a variety of companies pose problems for students to solve. A Game Design course, written by *Zulama*, is a blended learning platform created by educators at the Entertainment Technology Center at Carnegie Mellon University. The course is taught through the high school English teacher and helps students apply the fundamental skills and techniques of game design. The course merges CT into the English classroom as students learn to develop and refine a game prototype using an iterative process.

How Does the District Measure Student Achievement in CT Activities?

As Repenning et al. (2015) explain, the integration of a systemic CT curriculum can be a good approach for many schools because it aligns well with existing standards. The CT framework supports the use and creation of models and simulations while strengthening math and literacy skills. The goal of introducing CT to schools, therefore, is not to replace existing subjects but to think of CT as a new literacy that is useful for a wide array of subjects. Our experience to date suggests that, with appropriate scaffolding, diverse groups of students not only become interested in computer science but also can transfer CT strategies to a wide variety of disciplines including STEAM. Students who use programming to create a scientific model transform their computers into highly creative instruments that support scientific processes comparable to the way actual scientists engage in research. For example, high school students can take one semester of Game Design as part of their English language arts program. "Gaming" does not only mean video games. This course breaks down the game design process step by step. Students learn the fundamentals through hands-on modding, prototyping, and iteration of a variety of games. Students' final project will include building, playtesting, and revising their own original game that can be played with family and friends and added to their game portfolio.

Standard Measures of Student Achievement

An analysis of student achievement in the South Fayette Township School District reveals a steady and positive trend of increased achievement over the last 5 years. The metrics that have been utilized to determine this trend include the annual state assessment (PSSA, 2016), which is administered to students annually in grades 3–9. This assessment is designed to measure student academic growth based on the Pennsylvania academic standards. The PSSA specifically measures student progress in mathematics, English language arts, and science. Historical data from this assessment indicates increased levels of proficiency on an annual basis over a 5-year period. In addition, on the new version of the PSSA that is aligned to the rigorous

PA Core Standards, students performed well above the state and regional average. This distinction is based on an analysis by this independent organization of multiple years of PSSA achievement data. At the high school level, performance on the required state Keystone Exams continues to indicate academic growth well above the state and regional average. These exams are administered in the areas of biology, literacy, and algebra.

The district student achievement scores have increased over the past 10-year period, achieving the distinction that both in math and reading more than 90% of the district all 11th graders are in the proficient or advanced categories. It is also worth noting that the historically underperforming category of 11th graders shows nearly double the state average percentile in proficient to advanced scores in math (79%) and science (66%) in 2015 Pennsylvania state assessments (PIMS, 2015).

One possible explanation of the district's 95.5% student achievement of proficient or advanced level in the PSSA (2015) mathematics assessment involves looking more deeply at the district's use of robotics programming and problem-solving with all middle school students (Tekkumru-Kisa, Stein, & Schunn, 2015). The robotics programming included an embedded intelligent tutoring system that gave student programmers adaptive hints to guide learners without directing them toward specific solutions. Students were able to use guessing and checking strategies and eventually realize plausible solutions. This whole learning environment was created to support young learners' development of proportional reasoning: how to recognize it, how to build upon it, and eventually to make intelligent reasoning and be able to detect possible mistakes. In the context of this robotics programming, being able to reason mathematically was closely connected to being able to reason mechanistically (C. Schunn, personal communications, February 21, 2016). Programming the robots movements facilitated proportional thinking. Learning of proportional reasoning skills, the foundation of algebraic thinking, was greatly enhanced or speeded up through the online robotics programming and simulation tools (Alfieri1, Higashi1, Shoop, & Schunn, 2015; Liu, Schunn, Flot, & Shoop, 2013). Mathematical gains for all the district's middle school students who used this program were very high (C. Schunn, personal communications, February 21, 2016).

Thus, although math achievement in the district was already high, the most recent math scores show a 14% increase in overall average student scores in the last 10 years, whereas reading scores in the district improved by 2% in that same time period.

Applying CT Processes and Practices as Additional Metrics of Student Achievement

Student capabilities for leadership and innovation are not measured on standardized tests. These abilities are demonstrated through student-design applications, which emerge from new learning opportunities built into the STEAM Studio curriculum model. An important measure of district's success is the pathway that has emerged for developing innovative leadership capabilities in students. A focus on innovative pathways has led students to shift from the role of student to teaching assistant, to curriculum developer, and to teacher. As a result of the integration of CT processes and practices, new pathways for recognizing student achievement have emerged. One of these pathways is called the Emerging Innovation Leaders Program. As students discover their passion for computer programming, engineering, human-centered design, and innovation, their interests are leading to higher-level thinking and the desire to explore and invent beyond the curriculum. Students reach out to find new ways to explore their interests, while students with similar interests are put together in teams to begin product design and development. Table 4 provides a summary showing how advanced student programming activities are enabled through formal and informal school-initiated activities, like the Innovation Leaders Program. Below are examples of catalysts and resulting Emerging Innovation Leaders Programs.

Table 4 Timeline of text-based CT/programming integration

Learning context	2010–2011	2012–2013	2013–2014	2014–2015	2015–2016
After-school connected learning experiences	(7–8th): Girls STEAM Team: Scratch	(3rd–4th): Scratch Clubs: cartooning, video, games, music	(K-2nd): MakeShop Mondays	(K-2nd): MakeShop Mondays	(2nd–5th): STEAM Ambassadors
			(3rd–5th): Scratch Clubs	(2nd–5th): STEAM Ambassadors	(3nd–5th): Scratch Clubs
			(6–8th): Girls STEAM Team	(3rd–5th): Scratch Clubs	(6–8th): Girls STEAM Team
			(7–8th) App Inventor Club	(6–8th): Girls STEAM Team	(6–8th): Python Course
				(7–8th) Invention Time w/ 3D printing	(7–8th) Invention Time w/3D printing
Teachers	(6–8th): Teachers view Scratch at Open House			(K-12): STEAM Innovation Summer Institute	(K-12): STEAM Innovation Summer Institute
Family	(6–8th): Girls STEAM Team Community Night with Scratch		(K-12): Family Inspire Series	(K-12): Family Inspire Series	(K-12): Family Inspire Series
			(3rd–5th): Family Programming Night	(3rd–5th): Family Programming Night	(3rd–5th): Family Programming Night
Extracurricular Partnerships and Emerging Innovation Leaders Program	(7–8th): Girls STEAM Team: Teaches Scratch {TRETC Conf}	(3rd–4th): Scratch: Video Game Design {Mexican Schools}	(3rd–4th): Scratch: Video Game Design {Mexican Schools}		(3): Kodu Research Pilot {CMU}
		(7–8th): Girls STEAM Team: Teaches Scratch {TRETC Conf}	(5–6th): Scratch & eTextiles {MACS & Fort Cherry}		

{} = Community partner for CT/programming problem-solving activities

The *BusBudE* app team has created and beta tested an app to help keep young students safe while traveling to and from school on the bus. Children scan their tag when entering the bus and an alert is sent to their parents letting them know the time and place their children enter and leave the bus. The BusBudE student design team traveled to Boston to present their app and discuss their work as guest bloggers for the MIT Media Lab App Inventor group. This student design team, which consists of students from multiple grade levels and backgrounds, recently won the National InfyMakers Award for their design and received a $10,000 grant to create a makerspace for their high school.

The *MyEduDecks* Team is in their fourth year of designing and beta testing a pen-based software flashcard application to be used for personalized learning and assessments. Students, from multiple grade levels and backgrounds, are conducting educational research and taking their product to maturity. Their work has been published in the book *The Impact of Pen and Touch Technology on Education* (Kothuri et al., 2015), and they have presented their work at several national conferences with assistance of their computer science department mentors at Carnegie Mellon University at the annual WIPTTE conference (Kothuri, Varun, & Kenawell, 2013).

The integration of CT processes and practices has resulted in changes to the school culture on several levels. Increased female involvement in CT activities in and outside the classroom is helping young women and girls become actively involved in computer science activities. Here is an example of how gender issues in this area are being resolved. For 3 years, teams of students have been designing and teaching after-school Python programming courses to students in the district and to neighboring districts. This year a young woman in 11th grade led the course; two of her teaching assistants were women as well. The first cohort of 25 middle school students included 11 girls.

Based on its goal of creating leaders for a technology-rich future that relies on CT and innovative problem-solving skills, the district looks for ways to measure student growth and awareness of their ability to apply the dispositions and practices of CT as well as the habits of mind skills. Our analysis of student self-report survey data shows that students increased their selection of the following skills during their App Inventor programming activities: reading, decision-making, planning tasks and schedules, organizing, and always learning. Student identification of skills that were important in their App Inventor programming activities helps us measure how students applying their CT and habits of mind training as metacognitive processes. This is an area that will be further explored as part of the district's plan for expanding and refining CT integration.

The District Takes on a Regional Leadership Role Mentoring Other Schools

The district shares their practices regionally and nationally. The district is a member of the League of Innovative Schools, a network of superintendents and district leaders designed to be a test-bed for new approaches to teaching and learning to accelerate innovation in education. League members represent more than 3.2 million students in 73 districts and 33 states. Their experiences reflect the diversity and shared challenges of public education in the USA. The district shares practices with League members and gains insight into new practices during League meetings by being actively engaged in affinity groups. In October 2015, approximately 170 superintendents and administrators visited the district for a 2-day briefing. Since that time, school districts from South Carolina, Alabama, and Vancouver have returned with their staff to go more in depth as they begin to implement similar initiatives. At the end of the 2016 school year, the district had hosted over 500 visitors seeking to vertically align CT initiatives in their districts. The district continues to be open to school partnerships and sharing what it has learned. Districts interested in more information are encouraged to contact Aileen Owens for further information.

Conclusions

This case study explored implementation of the STEAM Studio model as a district-wide constructivist approach to transform the curriculum to incorporate hands-on activities and coding projects that required students and teachers to engage in CT practices. The case study described the school district vision, strategies for integrating new CT resources, and provided evidence of success as demonstrated by a variety of standard and new student achievement measures.

Several themes emerged as important factors for successful application of the STEAM Studio district-wide integration of CT. *First*, the district was both a contributor to and recipient of regional efforts to improve K-12 learning environments through CT initiatives. Through regional collaborations with other districts, higher education teams, and local corporations, the district established learning opportunities for early exposure to CT as well as advanced, elective computer programming classes. *Second*, we note that the district was already academically strong in core content areas so that the integration of CT was built upon well-established teaching and learning practices. *Third*, as the district responded to requests to share its CT practices with other school districts, the STEAM Studio model benefitted from extended research regarding ways to improve and innovate teacher, community, and student involvement in CT implementation. *Finally*, the new positions created changes to existing faculty positions, modifications to student schedules, development of incubator projects, organization of after-school connected learning experiences, embedded opportunities for teacher professional development, and construction of new learning spaces occurred gradually over a 6-year period. District transformations will continue to explore how CT can improve student learning opportunities.

Acknowledgment We wish to thank Superintendent Dr. Bille Rondinelli and the Board of Education for removing barriers to make all things possible and to the visionary teachers and administration for remaking teaching and learning. We also acknowledge the Pittsburgh Remake Learning Network and Digital Promise: League of Innovative Schools for their outstanding partnership and support.

References

Alfieri1, L., Higashi1, R., Shoop, R., & Schunn, C. D. (2015). Case studies of a robot-based game to shape interests and hone proportional reasoning skills. *International Journal of STEM Education, 2*(1) 1–13.

Berdik, C. (2015). *Can coding make the classroom better? How "computational thinking" and collaborative problem solving is transforming some classrooms*. SLATE. Downloaded from: http://www.slate.com/articles/technology/future_tense/2015/11/computational_thinking_teaches_kids_coding_collaboration_and_problem_solving.2.html

Bers, M. U., & Resnick, M. (2016). *The official ScratchJr book: Help your kids learn to code*. San Francisco: No Starch Press.

Brennan, K. (2011). *Creative computing: A design-based introduction to computational thinking*. Downloaded from: http://scratched.media.mit.edu/sites/default/files/CurriculumGuide-v20110923.pdf

Brennan, K., Balch, C., Chung, M. (2014). *Scratch curriculum guide*. ScratchEd Team: http://scratched.gse.harvard.edu/resources/scratch-curriculum-guide

Brennan, K., & Resnick, M. (2012). *New frameworks for studying and assessing the development of computational thinking*. American educational research association annual meeting, Vancouver, BC. Downloaded from: http://web.media.mit.edu/~kbrennan/files/Brennan_Resnick_AERA2012_CT.pdf

Computer Science Teachers Association (CSTA) and the International Society for Technology in Education (ISTE) (2011) Computational thinking: Leadership toolkit. (1st ed.). This material is based on work supported by the National Science Foundation under Grant No. CNS-1030054. Downloaded from: http://www.csta.acm.org/Curriculum/sub/CompThinking.html

Carle, E. (1988). *The mixed-up chameleon*. New York: HarperCollins Publisher.

Carle, E. (1969). The very hungry caterpillar. Philomel Books, 1987, Penguin Young Readers Group. Read aloud by author at: https://www.youtube.com/watch?v=vkYmvxP0AJI

Committee on Continuing Innovation in Information Technology; Computer Science and Telecommunications Board; Division on Engineering and Physical Sciences; National Academies of Sciences, Engineering, and Medicine (NASEM) (2016). *Continuing innovation in information technology: Workshop report*. Washington, DC: National Academy of Sciences, Downloaded from: http://www.nap.edu/23393

Computer Science Teachers Association (CSTA) and The Association for Computing Machinery (ACM). (2013). *Bugs in the system: Computer science teacher certification in the U.S.* Downloaded from: http://csta.acm.org

Costa, A. L. (2008). Describing the habits of mind. In A. L. Costa & B. Kallick (Eds.), *Learning and leading with habits of mind*. Alexandria, VA: ASCD.

DeLuca, S., Owens, A. M., & Unger, M. (2016). *Explore and create workshop: How to build a makerspace for elementary innovation*. International Society for Technology in Education (ISTE): Differentiate your learning. Learn differently. Think creatively. 2016. Denver, CO. Downloaded from: https://conference.iste.org/2016/?id=100432364

Digital Promise. (n.d.a). *Competency-based recognition for professional learning*. Retrieved from: http://digitalpromise.org

Digital Promise (n.d.b). *League of innovative schools*. Retrieved from: http://digitalpromise.org/district/south-fayette-township-school-district/

diSessa, A. (2000). *Changing minds: Computers, learning, and literacy*. Cambridge, MA: MIT Press.

Gusky, N. (2014). *A reflection on South Fayette's game jam: design and the problem-solving process*. Downloaded from: http://zulama.com/tag/problem-solving/

Guzdial, M. (2016). *State of the States: Progress toward CS for all.* Blog at CACM. Commun. ACM Downloaded from: http://cacm.acm.org/blogs/blog-cacm/198790-state-of-the-states--progress-toward-cs-for-all/fulltext

Jonassen, D. H., & Reeves, T. C. (1996). Learning with technology: Using computers as cognitive tools. In D. H. Jonassen (Ed.), *Handbook of research for educational communications and technology* (pp. 693–719). New York: Macmillan.

Kafai, Y., & Resnick, M. (1996). *Constructionism in practice: Designing, thinking, and learning in a digital world.* Mahwah, NJ: Lawrence Erlbaum Associates. Retrieved from: https://llk.media.mit.edu/papers/construct-practice.html

Kohli, S. (2015). *America is failing its children by not teaching code in every high school. Quartz.* Downloadedfrom:http://qz.com/340551/america-is-failing-its-children-by-not-teaching-code-in-every-high-school/

Kothuri, R. Varun, T., & Kenawell, B. (2013). *Integrating pen based flashcards application into classrooms. Workshop on the Impact of Pen and Touch Technologies on Education (WIPTTE).* Pepperdine University. Downloaded from: http://teacherscreate.org/wiptte/AbstractsAllSessions.pdf

Kothuri, R., Kenawell, B., Hertzler, S., Babatunde, M., Wilke, N., & Cohen, S. (2015). Analyzing trends in pen computing among K-2 students through flashcards application. In T. Hammond, S. Valentine, A. Adler, & M. Payton (Eds.), *The impact of pen and touch technology on education* (pp. 259–265). Switzerland: Springer International Publishing.

Liu, A. S., Schunn, C. D., Flot, J., & Shoop, R. (2013). The role of physicality in rich programming environments. *Computer Science Education.* doi:10.1080/08993408.2013.847165.

Luma Institute. (2012). *Innovating for people handbook of human-centered design methods.* Pittsburgh, PA: Luma Institute, LLC..

National Academies of Science (NAS). (2010). *Report of a workshop on the scope and nature of computational thinking.* Washington DC: National Academies Press.

Owens, A. M., Unger, M., & Wachter, R. (2014). Interactive presentation: Let the magic begin—transform your world. Scratch@MIT 2014. Cambridge, Massachusetts. Downloaded from: http://scratchweb.nl/sites/default/files/bijlage/joek/Scratch%20at%20MIT%202014%20Conference%20Schedule.pdf

Peduto, W., & Lam, D. (2014). Mayor's make movement round table summary report. Pittsburgh: Innovation & Performance. Downloaded from: http://apps.pittsburghpa.gov/cis/Maker_Roundtable_Summary_Report.pdf

Pennsylvania School Performance Profile (PSPP) (Pennsylvania Department of Education) (2016). *Academic Performance Data (2015–2016).* Retrieved from http://paschoolperformance.org

Pennsylvania School System Assessment (PSSA). (2016). *Results: 2005–2015.* Retrieved from http://www.education.pa.gov/K-12/Assessment%20and%20Accountability/PSSA/Pages/default.aspx#.V0RpIWbvkgU

Pretz, K. (2014). *Computer science classes for kids becoming mandatory: Countries are requiring coding to be taught in primary schools.* The Institute: The IEEE News Source. Downloaded from: http://theinstitute.ieee.org/career-and-education/preuniversity-education/computer-science-classes-for-kids-becoming-mandatory

Product Efficacy Loop. (2015). Funded by digital promise and the bill and melinda gates foundation. Downloaded from: http://southfayette.org

Repenning, A., Webb, D. C., Koh, K. H., Nickerson, H., Miller, S. B., Brand, C., et al. (2015). Scalable game design: A strategy to bring systemic computer science education to schools through game design and simulation creation. *ACM Transactions on Computing Education, 15*(2), 1–31.

Resnick, M., Maloney, J., Monroy-Hernández, A., Rusk, N., Eastmond, E., Brennan, K., Miller, A. Rosenbaum, E., Silverman, J., and Kafa, Y. (2009). *Communications of the ACM 52, 11, 60–67.* Downloaded from: http://web.media.mit.edu/~mres/papers/Scratch-CACM-final.pdf

Resnick, M. (2007). Sowing the seeds for a more creative society. *Learning and Leading with Technology, 35*, 18–22.

Tekkumru-Kisa, M., Stein, M. K., & Schunn, C. (2015). A framework for analyzing cognitive demand and content-practices integration: Task analysis guide in science. *Journal of Research in Science Teaching, 52*(5), 659–685.

U.S. Census Bureau. (2013). *18th Census of the United States*. Retrieved from http://www.census.gov/

Wagner, T. (2012). *Creating Innovators: The making of young people who will change the world*. Simon and Shuster: http://creatinginnovators.com/the-book/

The White House, Office of the Press Secretary, 2016). *President obama announces computer science for All Initiative*. Downloaded from: https://www.whitehouse.gov/sites/whitehouse.gov/files/images/FACT%20SHEET%2BPresident%20Obama%20Announces%20Computer%20Science%20For%20All%20Initiative_0.pdf

Wing, J. M. (2011). *Our CS Workshop. Computer science department*. Pittsburgh, PA: Carnegie Mellon University.

Computational Participation: Teaching Kids to Create and Connect Through Code

Yasmin B. Kafai and Quinn Burke

Abstract We are proposing to reframe computational *thinking* as computational *participation* by moving from a predominantly individualistic view of programming to one that includes a greater focus on the underlying social and creative dimensions in learning to code. This reframing as computational participation consists of three dimensions: functional, political, and personal. Functional pertains to the basic programming skills and concepts that someone needs to learn in order to participate in society. Political purposes capture why understanding programming skills and concepts is relevant in society. Last, personal purposes describe the role that these skills and concepts play in personal expression for building and maintaining relationships. We discuss three focal dimensions—creating applications, facilitating communities, and composing by remixing the work of others—in support of this move to computational participation by drawing from examples of past and current research, both inside and outside of school with children programming applications such as games, stories, or animations to design artifacts of genuine significance for others. Programming in a community suggests that such significance ultimately lies in the fact that we design to share with others. Programming as remixing code makes clear that we build on the work of others and need to better understand the ramifications of this approach. We situate these developments in the context of current discussions regarding broadening access, content, and activities and deepening participation in computing, which have become a driving force in revitalizing the introduction of computing in K-12 schools.

Keyword Computational participation

Y.B. Kafai (✉)
University of Pennsylvania, Philadelphia, PA 19104, USA
e-mail: kafai@upenn.edu

Q. Burke
College of Charleston, Charleston, SC 29424, USA
e-mail: burkeqq@cofc.edu

P.J. Rich, C.B. Hodges (eds.), *Emerging Research, Practice, and Policy on Computational Thinking*, Educational Communications and Technology: Issues and Innovations, DOI 10.1007/978-3-319-52691-1_24

Introduction

In the last few years, we have witnessed a renewed interest in learning programming in K-12, propelled by several developments, including the educational initiative to promote computational thinking (Wing, 2006; Grover & Pea, 2013), a need to broaden participation in the technology culture at large (Margolis, Estrella, Goode, Holme, & Nao, 2008; McGrath-Cohoon & Asprey, 2006), and, perhaps most significantly, the wider "do-it-yourself" (DIY) ethos characteristic of digitally based youth cultures (Kanter & Kanter, 2013; Peppler, Halverson, & Kafai, 2016). Computers indeed now seem to be accessible everywhere, particularly outside of school. But with few students digitally fluent and persistent disparities in participation, it is crucial that efforts in providing computer science for all recognize the importance of what students are interested in programming, the contexts in which they do it, and how they do it. Broadly speaking, we view attention to the what, who, and how of programming as key in moving from a predominantly individualistic view of programming to one that includes a greater focus on its underlying social and creative dimensions, reframing computational thinking as *computational participation*.

To realize computational participation, we need to focus on the emergence of programming shareable artifacts (e.g., digital stories, games, art) as the focal point of learning, moving from code to applications (Kafai & Burke, 2013). Learning programming was once a practice that largely prized coding accuracy and efficiency as the signifiers of success. Today, however, rather than programming for the sake of programming, students can create authentic applications such as games and stories as part of a larger learning community. It is the quality of these shareable artifacts—a highly playable game, a sophisticated animation, or a particularly nuanced digital story—that offers entry to such coding communities and fosters camaraderie. Second, we need to see coding as no longer performed as an isolated endeavor but within a shared social context, utilizing open software environments and mutual enthusiasm to spur participation, moving our attention from programming tools to communities of learners. Finally, we need to adopt new cultural practices such as remixing, the hallmark activity of new networked communities, moving programming from scratch to remixing projects that already exist. Whereas programs once had to be created "from scratch" to demonstrate competency, today, seamless integration via remixing is the new social norm for writing programs. While this certainly presents particularly ethical challenges, remixing also offers newfound networks for participation.

The goal of this chapter is to outline how we can support this move toward computational participation based on outcomes from the research literature of educational programming. We argue that understanding applications, contexts, and practices in learning and teaching programming can help us to generate better ways of how to think differently about K-12 computing and support the pivotal roles of context and community in learning (Cole, 2005). While much attention has focused on different concepts, practices, and perspectives of computational thinking (Brennan

& Resnick, 2012; Wing, 2006), our goal is to connect to a broader conceptualization of computational participation that encompasses its functional, political, and personal purposes (Kafai & Burke, 2014). In the context of computational participation, functional purposes describe the basic skills and concepts that someone needs to learn in order to participate in society, whereas political purposes capture why understanding these skills and concepts is relevant in society. Last, personal purposes describe the role that these skills and concepts play in personal expression for building and maintaining relationships. These purposes describe the fundamental aspects of any literacy, whether it is reading and writing printed texts, engaging in mathematical or science inquiry, or using and programming digital media. The learning and teaching of concepts and skills of any literacy need to be situated within their larger social, personal, and cultural contexts. Computing is no exception. We contend that those who participate computationally not only better understand the digital publics they live in but also are able to better navigate them, critically examining their underpinnings and ultimately even contributing to their ever-shifting designs.

Framing Computational Participation for K-12 Education

The following three dimensions highlight how learning programming has shifted with the wider cultural perceptions and practices of what it is to socialize and produce in the twenty-first century and how this relates to computational thinking, resulting as we argue in better learning opportunities and, by extension, better teaching opportunities.

Designing Applications for Learning Coding

By designing a program or any application (or, on a more granular level, its procedures, algorithms, and data structures), ideas about computing become public and can then be shared with others (Harel & Papert, 1990). Learning to program is about writing code and developing algorithms, data, and control structures that result in functional—and ideally efficient—software applications. We have numerous studies of what students learn about syntax, control structures, conditionals, and recursion as well as data structures and variables while writing code, just as we have documentation on the connected challenges of learning to do so (Soloway & Spohrer, 1990). While much planning and problem-solving went into these programs, there was also prompt criticism (Noss & Hoyles, 1996) that the empirical evidence was slim in demonstrating exactly what students were learning and how such learning transferred to other subjects. Others also noticed a lack of integration with the rest of the school curriculum (Palumbo, 1990). In its initial foray into K-12 schools, programming largely existed as a stand-alone activity in which students would participate in once or twice a week for an hour at a time. Typically, these isolated moments of coding existed apart from classrooms within the computer lab after which the students were return to their "normal" classes back down the hallway.

On the tail end of this development, a new pedagogical approach to programming emerged, called instructional software design (Harel, 1991). Rather than simply composing code, students designed full-fledged software applications. This approach was inspired by writings that portrayed design practices as contexts that could promote open-ended forms of problem-solving and situated learners in the application of academic content in the design of meaningful, authentic applications. Harel's seminal study not only illustrated that treating students as designers of instructional mathematic software could make them manifestly more invested in their learning but also helped the students learn programming and mathematics significantly better than students in control classes. The instructional software design approach has since then successfully applied to other contexts such as game design (Kafai, 1995) and integrated with other school subjects such as language arts (Burke & Kafai, 2012), science (Ching & Kafai, 2008), as well as music and art (Gargarian, 1996). By leading with a project within a particular subject matter, be it digital stories in an English class or fraction games in a math course, programming pedagogy engages children with the potential to create "real-world" applications. It also builds on successful instructional practices in which educators can leverage content-based subject matter to informally design software that is meaningful and authentic beyond the classroom (Bransford, Brown, & Cocking, 2000).

Today, the surge of "app" design courses (Wolber, Abelson, Spertus, & Looney, 2011) is a testament to the recruiting pull of such applied programs and ought to be leveraged more intently for broadening participation. It widens the walls (Resnick & Silverman, 2005) in suggesting applicability of programming to a range of activities rather than just narrowing technical ones. More broadly speaking, designing applications can also be considered a direct and, more importantly, an accessible application of Wing's computational thinking (2006). It captures key aspects of designing systems, solving problems, and understanding human behaviors because designing an application like a game or simulation involves the creation of a system, albeit on a smaller scale, that requires the designers to think carefully about how users will interface with the applications they design as well as solve problems of how to implement features according to their intentions. On a personal level, the idea of designing applications has most likely generated the broadest interest and success rate in getting youth actually involved in computer programming.

Perhaps this is why making games for learning has received such widespread attention with so many programs, for profit and nonprofit alike, vying for children's attention (Kafai & Burke, 2016). Nowhere is this more evident than in the proliferation of video game-making competitions such as the National STEM Video Game Design Challenge sponsored by the White House itself and others such as Globaloria's "Globey Awards," Advanced Micro Devices' (AMD) "Changing the Game" contest, and the "Games for Change" awards. All of these competitions instill a sense of empowerment, both personal and political, that one can make what one uses. It is characteristic of the self-reliance and drive of the wider DIY movement that has grown since the advent of Web. 2.0.

Learning Programming with and from Others

Many efforts have focused on helping novice programmers to become more fluent and expressive by developing programming tools that simplify syntax by reducing the amount of typing or arranging control structures (Kelleher & Pausch, 2005). Particularly popular have been programming tools such as Scratch (Resnick et al., 2009) that facilitates the programming of different multimedia applications or Alice (Kelleher & Pausch, 2007) that engages in storytelling or AgentSheets (Repenning & Ioannidou, 2008) that facilitates the creation of simulations. Both inside and outside of schools, tools like these have been successful in lowering the floors of entering into programming. The design of computational construction kits has generated rich insights into how to make programming accessible for beginners and simultaneously support many styles and interests.

One of the primary attractions for youth in creating applications rather than simply generating code is the capacity to share such applications with others and gain status by these shared creations. For instance, early use of the Scratch tool in a Computer Clubhouse illustrated how a vibrant game design community emerged over the course of two years with hundreds of different games developed (Kafai, Peppler, & Chapman, 2009). The recent creation of Internet-based sharing sites has expanded the tool users into communities of designers (Benkler, 2006). The most prominent example is the Scratch site, one of the largest youth programming communities that was inspired in part by Seymour Papert's samba schools (Papert, 1980). It is an online community for youth to create and share stories, games, and animation with over one million registered users, primarily between the ages of 8 and 16. Scratch collaborative activities typically revolve around the production of particular types of projects in which dozens of members can participate bringing different skills such as music, graphics, or editing to the group (Aragon, Poon, & Monroy-Hernandez, 2009). More importantly, it builds on essential insights from educational research that fruitful learning is not done in isolation but in conjunction with others. While some early work by Webb et al. (1986) examined some of the challenges, as well as opportunities, in having students program in small teams, programming in K-12 contexts is still mostly an individual activity. One of the perhaps most successful collaborative designs has been the introduction of pair programming that is now widely practiced on grade levels K-16 because it has shown to be effective in helping and motivating beginning programmers (Denner & Werner, 2007).

Today, programming and design tools such as Scratch, Alice, Gamestar Mechanic, Kodu, and many others all include communities, creating open-source sites in the style of communities like Linux for youth to share, comment on, and contribute to their coded creations. While such communities have always existed—the pre-Internet Logo community is testament to that—with access to sharing programs online and finding like-minded peers and others, even novice programmers now have an audience that values their artifacts and thus provides a community or affinity group. However, designing tools that facilitate particular mechanics of programming is not enough. Rather, providing a social context in which these programming tools are used and where programming artifacts are shared is equally important. It suggests that how we engage beginners in programming can be a collaborative activity. Learning how to program collaboratively brings other elements of computational thinking into the foreground, such as decomposing a complex task and coordinating control flow between different components. In addition, we can also use computational thinking as a way for participants to parse the networked commons itself. Many data mining tools rely on algorithms to search for and extract patterns from interactions and behaviors in massive communities. Likewise, tools like crowdsourcing not only leverage feedback from others but also need to be understood in terms of how others' direct feedback can be utilized to make one's code (and the project itself) more efficient.

Learning Programming by Remixing Code

In the past, not only did most programs have to be created on a blank page—"from scratch"—to illustrate programming competencies, but the expectation was that code was very much a proprietary commodity, to be built and ever refined but certainly not freely shared. This mind-set very much sets the tone for early computing coursework as students were introduced to the potential of programming in terms of text-based functionality, yet this is not the most effective approach. To a certain degree, it is akin to learning about fiction in a language arts course by being taught the meaning of nouns, verbs, and modifiers. The idea, however, to design programs on existing building blocks is by no means a new concept. Traditionally, as part of instruction, beginning programmers are given pieces of code to modify for their own programs, and this allows novices to build far more complex designs than they could do their own. But the concept of repurposing code has taken on a new life through the Internet, mirroring prominent remix practices in digital media culture.

Today, the repurposing and remixing of code have become standard practice. It has been argued that remixing is a key practice in today's networked culture in support of our knowledge production (Jenkins, Clinton, Purushotma, Robison, & Weigel, 2006). Crediting ownership consists of referencing the intellectual origins of "text" used in media productions, be it graphics, animations, or music. Remixing is also a particular form of participation within the Scratch community, taking existing Scratch projects and changing them before uploading them back to the website. With nearly 25% of the 3 million project posted at the Scratch site as remixes, members use this practice as means to familiarize oneself with the software as well as to socialize and collaborate with others via their creations (Monroy-Hernández & Resnick, 2008). This number has been steadily increasing since its launch in 2002. In some instances, authors design programs and explicitly invite others to remix their code, thus using programs as design starters. In other cases, remixes can range from direct copying to small tweaks of code or simply serve as inspiration for new, very different programs.

Indeed, the culture of remixing in Scratch itself is not without friction as positive and negative comments are prevalent as evident in previous attempts to introduce the practice within school-based environments. In an after-school club, Scratch programmers ages 10–12 years were adamant that their fellow programmers credited the origins of programs that they had remixed and posted online. Scratch programmers initially were concerned about others taking their programs, but they soon came to understand the remixes as a form of recognition that represented attention they received from others (Kafai, Fields, & Burke, 2010). The issue of intellectual ownership looms largely in discussions, even among youth Scratch members, from feeling complimented for the attention to feeling distraught at the lack of full acknowledgment.

It is perhaps the aspect of computational thinking that raises the most interesting intersection of technical and social issues. This could be because what's prevalent in amateur creator cultures such as Scratch might not be considered appropriate in school contexts that value individual authorship and would explicitly consider remixing as a violation of their policies. A growing number of media theorists and educators posit remixing as very much a new literacy that schools need to address (Perkel, 2008). In fact, school's traditional conception of "copying" sits directly at odds with the wider culture of remix that prevails in children's interactions outside of school.

While remixing on the most basic level requires just a few mouse clicks to copy programs, making it a hard sell for any consideration of computational thinking, we do know that selective remixing can actually require a far greater degree of sophistication. Considering what to modify in selected code segments versus what to keep and where to add or delete procedures or variables within a program are examples of remixing activity that very much requires a deeper, functional understanding of the code. In some instances, remixing may very well be more complex than starting with a blank slate. On a political level, the issues of copyright in the digital domain (which extends to code and interfaces) present a highly complicated matter that is only in the process of being defined in light of new cultural practices (Lessig, 2008). Personally, for many youth, this is a complex issue to deal with. The remixing dilemma—the difficulty to promote both originality and generativity in projects—suggests that remixing can serve as an opportune case for critically understanding copyright issues and thus address the wider social implications of computational thinking, which too often get neglected in the overt focus on technical prowess.

Discussion

We outlined several directions that the K-12 educational community should emphasize in learning and teaching programming. Our key contention is that engaging with computational thinking at large, and with programming in particular, should be thought of as a social practice, hence the focus on computational participation. Programming applications are increasingly being developed in order to design artifacts of genuine significance for others. Programming in a community suggests that such significance ultimately lies in the fact that we design to share with others. Programming as remixing code makes clear that we build on the work of others and need to better understand the ramifications of this approach. Most importantly, in the context of computational thinking, this means that we need to move beyond seeing programming as an individualistic act, but rather begin to understand it as a communal practice that is steeply grounded in how we think about what students today should learn in order to become full participants in networked communities.

Computational thinking should really be thought of as computational participation to emphasize that "objects to think with"—to use one of Papert's core ideas (Papert, 1980)—are indeed "objects to share with" others (Kafai & Burke, 2014). To expand on Wing's definition of computational thinking (Wing, 2006), computational participation is then defined as the ability to solve problems, design systems, and understand human behavior in the context of computing not as an individualistic act but as a communal practice that allows for participation in networked communities. Of course, just by having kids program applications, placing them in groups, and encouraging them to remix code hardly address all of the problems associated with broadening and deepening participation in computing. In fact, a renewed focus on computational participation likely will present a whole new set of challenges when it comes to bringing programming activities back into schools. The ideas outlined in this chapter represent a modest start in beginning to address some of the challenges around facilitating such broader and deeper participation in the very design of the programming activities, tools, and practices.

Broadening Computational Participation

If computational thinking is indeed a social practice, then broadening access to participation and collaboration in communities of programming becomes a focal issue. We know from preliminary research in the Scratch community that this move toward membership in a large-scale community is a complex interplay between how young software designers develop personal agency through programming and how they gain status as "experts" among their peers (Kafai et al., 2010). Despite the myth that children are "digital natives" who naturally migrate online, observations indicated that some students initially resisted going online and uploading their program to the Scratch website, uncomfortable with sharing their own work with more experienced members online. This suggests that establishing membership in a larger programming community is not as easily achieved as one may think. Rather, navigating online communities requires an array of participation strategies that directly address this sense of vulnerability associated with sharing one's work for others to comment on and even remix for their own purposes.

Beyond broadening access to participation, we also need to broaden content of computing activities. A recent study (Lachney, Babbitt, & Ron Eglash, 2016) looked at the content of the Scratch programming site and found it heavily leaning toward commercial content from popular video games, television series, and toys but less so in terms of culturally relevant content that would appeal to other constituents. For instance, a simple search of the Scratch archive for the popular video game "Doom" will find hundreds, if not thousands, of different programs created and posted by Scratch members. Any search for other content, for example, on American Indians, will find only a handful of projects at most. The predominance of Doom and other first person shooter games does tacitly establish the boundaries of what qualifies as a game and what is valued as an upload in the Scratch community. Affinity groups that coalesce around like-minded interests are powerful learning cultures, but this also makes them exclusive cultures, perhaps not intentionally so. Here the content, and by extension the designers, signals to others joining the community what should be of interest. It is here where we see the intricate intersections of interests and values in gaming and computing and how they can invite or exclude participation in these communities in much less obvious ways (Richard & Kafai, 2016).

Beyond broadening access and content, we also need to widen our type of computing activities, moving beyond the screen. While the shift toward designing authentic applications is an important step in the right direction, we also need to realize that designing games is not the only acceptable method to achieve this goal. Game design definitely leverages the interest and informal experience of many children and youth, but it also happens to cater to a community that is still predominantly male. There are many other types of software applications that can be designed to fulfill the premise of an authentic context. For this reason, we have argued that joining the "existing" clubhouse like you would find in the Scratch community still leaves many on the outside. Rather than just focusing primarily on games and animations, we also need to further encourage story design and perhaps even introduce different materials and contexts. For instance, the design of tangibles like the electronic textile construction kits LilyPad Arduino suggests, new clubhouses can be built that serve other members rather than simply joining existing ones such as electronic textiles (Buechley, Peppler, Eisenberg, & Kafai, 2013).

Deepening Computational Participation

If broadening activities, content, and tools gets beginning programmers into the clubhouses of computing, the next challenge is about deepening their computational participation and helping them to develop fluency with various activities. This is where the real challenge lies. Getting more kids into the clubhouses of computing and opening them up to more diverse groups of players and makers is important. But once they are there, we also need to be concerned about how we can engage them more deeply so that their participation can become the meaningful and enriching learning experience it is meant to be. A series of recent data mining studies from a random sample of 5,000 users out of 20,000 who logged into Scratch from January to March 2012 examined to what extent these features promote "computing for all" (Fields, Giang, & Kafai, 2014). They found that while 45% of Scratch members posted content on the site, few leveled up to the most extensive forms of social networking and complex programming concepts in their projects. Girls who were equally active in the community were significantly underrepresented among the more advanced and experienced coding groups. Particularly relevant to deepening computational participation is the observation that posting content was a baseline for all visible participation, followed by downloading and only then by commenting. The fuller forms of computational participation only emerge once projects are also discussed, critiqued, and exchanged. Learning to code involves not just learning the technicalities of programming language and common algorithms, but also draws learning the social practices within programming communities. In other words, coding not only encompasses acquisition of technical skills but also includes engagement with social practices.

Likewise, seeing programming as a collaborative, distributed effort requires new types of agency that are usually found in assigned group work in many classrooms. For instance, in the Scratch online community, collaborative activities typically revolve around the production of particular types of Scratch projects by a small group of individuals that have commonly met one another in the online environment (Kafai & Burke, 2014). In our recent research to engineer such forms of collaborative efforts with online and offline groups, we found that many students had difficulties in participating in this type of self-organized collaborative activities (Kafai et al., 2012). Educators and researchers who design and study K-12 programming communities need to focus not only on the technical skills but also on the social skills—on how novice programmers get to participate. This issue of equity in participation is, of course, not a new one. On a basic level, the classrooms that build around design activities always formed communities where students engaged in forms of peer pedagogy (Ching & Kafai, 2008) often observed in large online networks (Benkler, 2006). But what's different now are the large-scale communities that connect hundreds, if not thousands, of young programmers and provide different contexts and opportunities for exchange. How we design communities around tools such as Scratch, Alice, or Kodu can and needs to be done both online and offline, in the local classrooms and clubs in which youth participate, as well as the online spaces that youth populate to share their designs and comment on others.

Conclusions

From our vantage point, reframing computational thinking into computational participation provides new and important directions for the design of programming activities, communities, and practices in K-12 educational computing efforts. We argue here that such reframing is an imperative if we expect to broaden and deepen participation in and perceptions of computing on a considerably larger scale than previous attempts of integration. We are not arguing that all the standard staples of previous computing courses and designs should be dismissed. The merits of writing code to learn about the nature of algorithms and developing data structures, compilers, and general architecture remain crucially important. But we want to make the case that educational computing can take the road that mathematics and science education efforts have taken long ago, leveraging the insights gained from youth digital media and networked culture in conjunction with the learning scientists' initial conception that children can, in fact, learn to program at a young age.

Acknowledgments This chapter is based on a 2013 SIGCSE conference publication. The views expressed are those of the authors and do not necessarily represent the views of the Foundation, University of Pennsylvania, or College of Charleston.

References

Aragon, C., Poon, S., & Monroy-Hernandez, A. (2009). A tale of two communities: Fostering collaboration and creativity in scientists and children. In *Proceedings of the 7th ACM Conference on Creativity and Cognition* (pp. 9–18). New York, NY: ACM.

Benkler, Y. (2006). *The wealth of networks: How social production transforms markets and freedom*. New Haven, CT: Yale University Press.

Bransford, J., Brown, A., & Cocking, R. (2000). *How people learn*. Washington, DC: National Academy Press.

Brennan, K., & Resnick, M. (2012, April). *New frameworks for studying and assessing the development of computational thinking*. Paper Presented at the 2012 Annual Meeting of the American Educational Research Association, Vancouver, Canada.

Buechley, L., Peppler, K. A., Eisenberg, M., & Kafai, Y. B. (Eds.). (2013). *Textile messages: Dispatches from the word of electronic textiles and education*. New York: Peter Lang Publishers.

Burke, Q., & Kafai, Y. B. (2012). The writers' workshop for youth programmers. In *Proceedings of the 43rd SIGCSE Technical Symposium on Computer Science Education* (pp. 433–438). New York, NY: ACM.

Ching, C., & Kafai, Y. B. (2008). Peer pedagogy: Student collaboration and reflection in learning through design. *Teachers College Record, 110*(12), 2601–2632.

Cole, M. (2005). Cross-cultural and historical perspectives on the developmental consequences of education. *Human Development, 48*(4), 195–216.

Denner, J., & Werner, L. (2007). Computer programming in middle school: How pairs respond to challenges. *Journal of Educational Computing Research, 37*(2), 131–150.

Fields, D. A., Giang, M., & Kafai, Y. B. (2014). November. Programming in the wild: trends in youth computational participation in the online scratch community. In *Proceedings of the 9th Workshop in Primary and Secondary Computing Education* (pp. 2–11). New York, NY: ACM.

Gargarian, G. (1996). The art of design. In Y. B. Kafai & M. Resnick (Eds.), *Constructionism in Practice: Designing Thinking, and Learning in a Digital World* (pp. 125–160). Mahwah, NJ: Lawrence Erlbaum.

Grover, S., & Pea, R. (2013). Computational thinking in K–12: A review of the state of the field. *Educational Researcher, 42*(2), 59–69.

Harel, I. (1991). *Children Designers: Interdisciplinary Constructions for Learning and Knowing Mathematics in a Computer-rich School*. Norwood NJ: Ablex Publishing.

Harel, I., & Papert, S. (1990). Software design as a learning environment. *Interactive Learning Environments, 1*(1), 1–32.

Jenkins, H., Clinton, K., Purushotma, R., Robison, A., & Weigel, M. (2006). Confronting the challenges of participation culture: Media education for the 21st century. In *White Paper*. Chicago, IL: The John D. & Catherine T. MacArthur Foundation.

Kafai, Y. B. (1995). *Minds in play: Computer game design as a context for children's learning*. Mahwah, NJ: Lawrence Erlbaum.

Kafai, Y. B., Fields, D. A., Roque, R., Burke, W. Q., & Monroy-Hernandez, A. (2012). Collaborative agency in youth online and offline creative production in Scratch. *Research and Practice in Technology Enhanced Learning, 7*(2), 63–87.

Kafai, Y. B., & Burke, Q. (2016). *Connected gaming: What video game making can teach about learning and literacy*. Cambridge, MA: MIT Press.

Kafai, Y. B., & Burke, Q. (2014). *Connected code: Why children need to learn programming*. Cambridge, MA: MIT Press.

Kafai, Y. B., & Burke, Q. (2013). The social turn in K-12 programming: Moving from computational thinking to computational participation. In *SIGSCE'13 Proceeding of the 44th ACM Technical Symposium on Computer Science Education* (pp. 603–608). New York, NY: ACM.

Kafai, Y., Fields, D., & Burke, W. (2010). Entering the clubhouse: Case studies of young programmers joining the online Scratch communities. *Journal of Organizational and End User Computing, 22*(1), 21–35.

Kafai, Y., Peppler, K. A., & Chapman, R. (Eds.). (2009). *The computer clubhouse: creativity and constructionism in youth communities*. New York, NY: Teachers College Press.

Kanter, M., & Kanter, D. E. (2013). *Design, make, play: Growing the next generation of STEM innovators*. New York: Routledge.

Kelleher, C., & Pausch, R. (2005). Lowering the barriers to programming: A taxonomy of programming environments and languages for novice programmers. *ACM Computing Surveys, 37*(2), 83–137.

Kelleher, C., & Pausch, R. (2007). Using storytelling to motivate programming. *Communications of the ACM, 50*(7), 58–64.

Lachney, M., Babbitt, W. & Ron Eglash, R. (2016). Software design in the 'construction genre' of learning technology: Content aware versus content agonistic. *Computational Culture: A Journal of Software Studies*. Available at http://computationalculture.net/issue-five

Lessig, L. (2008). *Remix: making art and commerce thrive in a hybrid economy*. New York: Penguin Press.

Margolis, J., Estrella, E., Goode, G., Holme, J. J., & Nao, K. (2008). *Stuck in the shallow end: Race, education, and computing*. Cambridge, MA: MIT Press.

McGrath-Cohoon, J., & Asprey, W. (Eds.). (2006). *Women and information technology: Research on underrepresentation*. Cambridge, MA: MIT Press.

Monroy-Hernández, A., & Resnick, M. (2008). Empowering kids to create and share programmable media. *Interactions, 15*(2), 50–53.

Noss, R., & Hoyles, C. (1996). *Windows on Mathematical Meanings: Learning Cultures and Computers*. Norwell, MA: Kluwer Academic Publishers.

Palumbo, D. B. (1990). Programming language/problem- solving research: A review of relevant issues. *Review of Educational Research, 60*(1), 65–89.

Papert, S. (1980). *Mindstorms: Children, computers, and powerful ideas*. New York, NY: Basic Books.

Peppler, K., Halverson, E., & Kafai, Y. B. (2016). In K. Peppler, E. Halverson, & Y. Kafai (Eds.), *Makeology: Makerspaces as learning environments* (Vol. Volume 1). New York: Routledge.

Perkel, D. (2008). "No I don't feel complimented". *Digital Youth Research*, (February 6). Available at http://digitalyouth.ischool.berekley.edu/node/105

Repenning, A., & Ioannidou, A. (2008). Broadening participation through scalable game design. In *Proceedings of the 39th SIGCSE Technical Symposium on Computer Science Education* (pp. 305–309). New York, NY: ACM.

Resnick, M., & Silverman, B. (2005). Some reflections on designing construction kits for kids. In *Proceedings of the 2005 Conference on Interaction Design and Children* (pp. 117–122). New York, NY: ACM.

Resnick, M., Maloney, J., Hernández, A. M., Rusk, N., Eastmond, E., Brennan, K., Millner, A. D., Rosenbaum, E., Silver, J., Silverman, B., & Kafai, Y. B. (2009). Scratch: Programming for everyone. *Communications of the ACM, 52*(11), 60–67.

Richard, G., & Kafai, Y. B. (2016). Blind spots in youth DIY programming: Examining diversity in creators, content, and comments within the scratch online community. In *Proceedings of the ACMSIGCHIConferenceonHumanFactorsinComputingSystems*.doi:10.1145/2858036.2858590.

Soloway, E., & Spohrer, J. (Eds.). (1990). *Empirical studies of novice programmers*. Norwood, NJ: Ablex Publishing.

Webb, N., Ender, P., & Lewis, S. (1986). Problem-solving strategies and group processes in small groups learning computer programming. *American Educational Research Journal, 23*(2), 243–261.

Wing, J. M. (2006). Computational thinking. *Communications of the ACM, 49*(3), 33–35.

Wolber, D., Abelson, H., Spertus, E., & Looney, L. (2011). *App inventor: Create your own android apps*. Sebastopol, CA: O'Reilly Media.

Index

P.J. Rich, C.B. Hodges (eds.), *Emerging Research, Practice, and Policy on Computational Thinking*, Educational Communications and Technology: Issues and Innovations, DOI 10.1007/978-3-319-52691-1

C

FSC
www.fsc.org
MIX
Papier | Fördert
gute Waldnutzung
FSC® C083411

Kolibri 360 GmbH
Ferdinand-Jühlke-Straße 7
99095 Erfurt, Deutschland
produktsicherheit@kolibri360.de